HYDROLOGY AND WATER RESOURCES EDUCATION, TRAINING AND MANAGEMENT

HYDROLOGY AND WATER RESOURCES EDUCATION, TRAINING AND MANAGEMENT

Proceedings of the International Symposium on Hydrology and Water Resources Education and Training: The Challenges to Meet at the Turn of the XXI Century

APRIL 15-19, 1991

and

Second North American Water Management Seminar

APRIL 17, 1991

Chihuahua, Chih., MEXICO
Organized by Universidad Autonoma de Chihuahua

Edited by

Jose A. Raynal
Universidad Autonoma de Chihuahua

Water Resources Publications

For Information and Correspondence:

Water Resources Publications
P. O. Box 2841, Littleton, Colorado 80161, USA

HYDROLOGY AND WATER RESOURCES EDUCATION, TRAINING AND MANAGEMENT

Proceedings of the International Symposium on Hydrology and Water Resources Education and Training: The Challenges to meet at the Turn of the XXI Century

APRIL 15-19, 1991

Edited by

Jose A. Raynal, Ph.D.
Universidad Autonoma de Chihuahua

ISBN Number 0-918334-73-X

U.S. Library of Congress Catalog Card Number: 92-80722

Copyright © 1992 Revised Edition by *Water Resources Publications*. All rights reserved. Printed and bound in the United States of America. No part of this publication may be reproduced, copied, transmitted, transcribed or stored in any form or by any means such as mechanical, electronic, magnetic, optical, chemical, manual or otherwise, without prior written permission from the publisher, Water Resources Publications, P. O. Box 2841, Littleton, Colorado 80161-2841, U.S.A.

This publication is printed and bound by BookCrafters, Inc., Chelsea, Michigan, U.S.A.

PREFACE

Water, one of the most important elements for the very survival of human beings, is the subject matter in the study of hydrology and water resources engineering. The processes of education and training play a key role in the transfer and improvement of water knowledge from one generation to another. At the current time, there exist a movement within the academic media which are questioning the effectiveness of such processes.

The International Symposium on Hydrology and Water Resources Education and Training: The Challenges to Meet at the Turn of the XXl Century, was organized to provide a forum for the interdisciplinary exchange of views on all aspects of education and training in hydrology and water resources.

The Second North American Water Management Seminar was organized to be the channel of exchange of experiences, problems and their feasible solutions to water management problems in North America. The seminar was the mechanism that promoted the acquaintance between scientists, practicing engineers and government officials from the three involved countries: Canada, Mexico and the United States of America.

The symposium was attended by seventy-eight experts from twelve countries from Africa, America and Europe. Four symposium keynote lectures were delivered by Professor Nathan Buras, University of Arizona, Mr. G.W. Gilbrich, UNESCO, Professor James E. Nash, National University of Ireland and Professor Vujica Yevjevich, Colorado State University. A special seminar keynote lecture was jointly delivered by the Honorables Dr. Narendra Gunaji and Eng. Jose A. Herrera-Solis, USA and Mexico Commissioners, respectively, of the International Boundary and Water Commission. The 1991 AWRA Outstanding Water Resources Achievement Award was presented during the seminar to the International Boundary and Water Commission.

The presentation of the thirty-four papers of the symposium was organized in eight technical sessions and two panel discussions: a) On the Role of Professional Organizations as a Conduit for International Technical Information Exchange and b) symposium and seminar conclusions. The fifteen seminar papers were organized in seven technical sessions.

I wish to thank the sponsors of the symposium and seminar, international technical committee, organizing committee, keynote speakers and members of panels, session chairmen and specially to all participants. The success of the meeting would not be possible without their valuable help. The careful and professional work of WRP staff is deeply appreciated, in particular that of Mrs. Branka McLaughlin. Her patience and continuous support were very important in the production of this book.

Jose A. Raynal
Universidad Autonoma de Chihuahua
Chihuahua, Chih., Mexico

TABLE OF CONTENTS

PREFACE
Jose A. Raynal v

PART A

1 KEYNOTE LECTURES 1

GLOBAL CHANGE AND WATER RESOURCES ISSUES
Nathan Buras 3

SOME REMARKS ON UNESCO'S PROGRAM IN
HYDROLOGICAL EDUCATION UNDER IHD / IHP
Wilfried H. Gilbrich 11

SOME MUSINGS ON HYDROLOGICAL EDUCATION
J.E. Nash 27

EDUCATION IN WATER RESOURCES UNDER CONTINUAL
EVOLUTION IN THEIR PROBLEMS AND IN SOCIETY'S
ATTITUDES AND DEMANDS
Vujica Yevjevich 35

2 PERSONAL COMPUTING IN EDUCATION AND TRAINING 57

TRANSFERRING PERSONAL COMPUTER MODELS TO
POTENTIAL USERS
Thomas N. Debo 59

CASCADE ELEMENT NUMBERING FOR GIS-BASED DISTRIBUTED
PARAMETER HYDROLOGIC MODELING: Processing Raster
Digital Elevation Models to Derive a Hydrologically Ordered
Computational Sequence for Overland Flow Modeling
Michael B. Smith and Mitja Brilly 67

AN INFORMATION SYSTEM ON WATER RESOURCES
M.L. Mercader and J.A. Salas Plata 81

FLODRO: A User-Friendly Personal Computer Package for Flood and
Drought Frequency Analyses for Education and Training
Jose A. Raynal-Villaseñor and Carlos A. Escalante-Sandoval 87

SHIFT: A PC-ORIENTED DISTRIBUTED HYDROLOGIC MODEL
BASED ON IRREGULAR TRIANGULAR FACETS
O.L. Palacios-Vélez and B. Cuevas-Renaud 95

3 TECHNOLOGY TRANSFER 105

THE TRANSFER OF TECHNICAL INFORMATION IN THE WATER
RESOURCES ARENA: TRUST AMONG COMPETING SOURCES
Dennis L. Soden, Janet S. Conary and Jerry L. Simich 107

INTERNATIONAL TECHNICAL INFORMATION EXCHANGE
AND TRAINING - SOME EXPERIENCES OF THE SWISS
NATIONAL HYDROLOGICAL AND GEOLOGICAL SURVEY
M. Spreafico and R. Grabs 115

SPECIAL WATER RESOURCES OUTREACH PROGRAMS
M.H. Watt and J.H. Hannaham 127

4 RESEARCH and EDUCATION and TRAINING 139

SEASONAL VARIATION OF RAINFALL WATER IN SOIL
R. D. Valdez-Cepeda, M. R. Almeida-Martínez and S. Rubio-Díaz 141

TIME-SERIES MODELLING AS A TOOL FOR EVALUATING AN IRRIGATION DECISION IN ADVANCE
C. Hernández-Yáñez 147

SUPPORT OF AGROMETEOROLOGY TO MANAGEMENT OF WATER RESOURCES
D.F. Campos-Aranda 157

FORECASTING METHODS APPLIED TO ESTIMATION OF WATER STORAGE IN THE LÁZARO CÁRDENAS RESERVOIR IN THE LA LAGUNA REGION, MEXICO
Rafael Figueroa-Viramontes, Leopoldo Moreno-Díaz and Ricardo Almeida-Martínez 163

EDUCATION, TRAINING AND RESEARCH AT THE HYDRO-SCIENCE CENTER OF THE COLEGIO DE POSTGRADUADOS
L. Rendon-Pimentel and R. Fernández-González 169

ROLE OF RESEARCH IN WATER SCIENCES AS A CATALYZER OF EDUCATION AND TRAINING IN SOME DEVELOPING COUNTRIES
M. Abu-Zeid, A. Hamdy and C. Lacirignola 175

THE INTEGRATED SOIL AND WATER IMPROVEMENT PROJECT TRAINING PROGRAM
M. Abu El-Magd, F. El-Nagar, J.S.A. Brichieri-Colombi and M.A. Makhlouf 183

MATHEMATICAL MODEL FOR MANEUVERING SINGULARITIES IN AN IRRIGATION CANAL NETWORK
Benjamin de Leon Mojarro 193

5 NATIONAL WATER PLANS 201

PARTICIPATION IN STATE AND LOCAL GROUND-WATER ORGANIZATIONS - A PROGRAM OF MUTUAL BENEFIT TO PUBLIC AGENCIES AND THEIR PROFESSIONAL EMPLOYEES: A Case History of the Colorado Ground-Water Association
Judith L. Hamilton 203

WATER CONSERVATION EDUCATION AND OUTREACH IN THE U. S.
Cynthia Dyballa 207

NATIONAL URBAN DRAINAGE PLAN MANAGEMENT
Levent Yilmaz 217

SPILLS ON OPEN WATERS, A CAUSE FOR CONCERN-THE NEED FOR ACTION TO PREVENT THEM
Walter A. Lyon 223

6 PROGRAMS FOR EDUCATION AND TRAINING 227

TOWARDS ESTABLISHING "WATER RESOURCES ENGINEERING" AS AN UNDERGRADUATE ENGINEERING-DEGREE PROGRAM
Ünal Öziş 229

WATER RESOURCES MANAGEMENT: A CHALLENGE FOR EDUCATORS
N. S. Grigg 237

UNIVERSITIES, INTERNATIONAL AGENCIES AND WATER
RESOURCES EDUCATION
Ronald M. North 245

INTERDISCIPLINARY EDUCATION IN WATERSHED SCIENCE:
A NATURAL RESOURCE PERSPECTIVE
C. Hawkins, J. Dobrowolski, J. McDonnell and M. O'Neill 249

EDUCATION AND TRAINING IN HYDROLOGY - SOME
PROBLEMS FROM A WMO PERSPECTIVE
John C. Rodda 255

A QUARTER OF A CENTURY: THE INTERNATIONAL COURSE
FOR HYDROLOGISTS, DELFT, THE NETHERLANDS
Mamdouh Shahin 267

HYDROLOGY AND WATER RESOURCES EDUCATION AND
TRAINING: THE CUIDES RESPONSE
John S. Miller 277

THE VADOSE ZONE: AN EDUCATIONAL FRONTIER IN
HYDROLOGY
J.M.H. Hendrickx, F.M. Phillips, J.L. Wilson, and R.S. Bowman 285

ON THE STATUS OF EDUCATION AND TRAINING IN THE
HYDROLOGIC SCIENCES, JAMAICA, WEST INDIES
J.R. Nuckols 295

HYDROLOGICAL EDUCATION IN A DEVELOPING SOCIETY:
PERSPECTIVES FROM AN AFRICAN UNIVERSITY
Brian K. Rawlins 303

NATIONAL AND INTERNATIONAL TRAINING INSTITUTES
AND THEIR ROLE IN IMPROVING WATER RESOURCES
DEVELOPMENT AND MANAGEMENT IN DEVELOPING
COUNTRIES
M. Abu-Zeid, A. Hamdy and C. Lacirignola 311

A HYDROGEOLOGICAL SURVEY IN MEXICO
J. Joel Carrillo R. and Oscar A. Escolero F. 319

EFFICIENCY OF PRACTICAL SHORT TIME TRAINING
COURSES IN HYDROCHEMISTRY-HYDROGEOLOGY AT
UNIVERSITIES OF DEVELOPING COUNTRIES
J. Bundschuh 325

HYDROLOGY AND WATER MANAGEMENT IN THE CONTEXT
OF THE CHIHUAHUA STATE PROGRAM OF SCIENCE AND
TECHNOLOGY
Adolfo Chavez and Alberto Ramirez 335

PART B

1 KEYNOTE LECTURES 339

DEVELOPMENT OF THE INTERNATIONAL BOUNDARY AND
WATER COMMISSION: INTERNATIONAL WASTEWATER
TREATMENT PLANT
Narendra N. Gunaji 341

DEVELOPMENT OF IBWC INTERNATIONAL WASTE WATER
TREATMENT PLANT
Arturo Herrera Solis 343

2 WATER QUANTITY MANAGEMENT IN NORTH AMERICA ... 347

RUNOFF PREDICTION MODEL FOR TEPETATE RECLAMATION
Héctor Manuel Arias Rojo ... 349

COMMENTS ON NORMS FOR DESIGN FLOODS OF MEXICAN DAMS
D. F. Campos-Aranda ... 355

THERMOELECTRIC WATER NEEDS FOR POWER PLANTS
Gustavo A. Paz Soldán C. ... 363

CHARACTERIZATION OF WATERSHEDS BY INTEGRATION OF REMOTE SENSING AND CARTOGRAPHIC DIGITAL DATA
Jose Luis Oropeza Mota ... 369

FACTIBILITY OF A DEEP KARSTIC LIMESTONE AQUIFER UNDER THE CITY OF CHIHUAHUA: A PROGRESS REPORT
Ignacio Alfonso Reyes Cortes ... 375

GROUNDWATER STUDIES AT THE FEDERAL ELECTRIC POWER COMMISSION OF MEXICO
Sergio A. Flores and José A. Maza ... 387

GROUNDWATER ADMINISTRATION IN MEXICO
Ruben Chavez Guillen and Pedro Martiniez Leyva ... 395

GROUNDWATER STUDIES IN SEMI-ARID AREAS OF MEXICO, A CHANGE IN PERSPECTIVE
J. Joel Carrillo R. ... 403

3 WATER QUALITY MANAGEMENT IN NORTH AMERICA ... 409

WATER, GROWTH AND THE FUTURE OF A BOOMING U.S./MEXICO BORDER COMMUNITY
Hector R. Fuentes ... 411

UNIVERSITY OF GUELPH RESPONSE TO EMERGING SOCIO-ENVIRONMENTAL ISSUES
H.R. Whiteley, R.L. Corsi, W. James and D. Joy ... 425

PROGRESS OF THE GREAT LAKES CLEANUP
William A. Steggles ... 433

INTERACTION OF POULTRY WASTE AND LIMESTONE TERRAIN ON WATER QUALITY: PROFESSIONAL AND PUBLIC INFORMATION DISSEMINATION
K.F. Steele, T.C. Daniel and D.R. Edwards ... 441

WATER QUALITY ISSUES: UNITED STATES NEW MANAGEMENT AND POLICY DIRECTIONS
Jonathan W. Bulkley ... 449

THE GREEN BAY, WISCONSIN REMEDIAL ACTION PLAN PROGRESS AND PROBLEMS
Harold J. Day ... 457

DELINEATION OF MUNICIPAL WATER SUPPLY AQUIFER PROTECTION AREAS: INSIGHT FROM SOME MIDWESTERN EXPERIENCES
Robert J. Montgomery ... 467

SYMPOSIUM AND SEMINAR LIST OF PARTICIPANTS ... 475

PART A

1 KEYNOTE LECTURES

GLOBAL CHANGE AND WATER RESOURCES ISSUES

Nathan Buras
Department of Hydrology and Water Resources
University of Arizona
Tucson, Arizona 85721, U.S.A.

ABSTRACT

Global climatic changes will probably influence significantly the operation and utilization of regional water resources. Although estimates of climatic change are rife with uncertainties, it is quite plausible that substantial changes in precipitation and temperature will affect annual runoff, yearly and seasonal runoff variability, and seasonal runoff. From the point of view of water supply, climatic change will affect regional water resources systems in three major directions: available quantity, water quality and regional water balances on a seasonal basis. From the point of view of demand for water, the relative importance of different water users may change, thus influencing policy decisions regarding allocation of scarce water resources and management of regional systems.

INTRODUCTION

Planning water resources systems involves making design decisions facing uncertainty. Similarly, management decisions anticipating an uncertain future are made continuously while operating a water resources system. Conventionally, we handle uncertainty by constructing stochastic hydrologic models based on the assumption of stationary distribution of flows. This assumption is extended also to the distribution of economic outcomes generated by a water resources system - benefits as well as costs. On both counts, the assumption of stationarity may be questioned in terms of climatic change (Matalas and Fiering, 1977). Climatic change would be reflected in the parameters of the distribution functions of major variables, such as precipitation and temperature.

Water resources systems, including their component hydraulic structures, are sensitive to climatic fluctuations. Variations in climate affect not only the quantity of the end product (water, energy, crops), but also the size of the storage facilities (Nemec and Schaake, 1982). The very detection of climatic variability is a non-trivial problem. For example, if one has a fairly extended hydrological trace - say, fifty years - and climatological data (precipitation, evapotranspiration) covering the same period, how reliable is the separation of noise from the signal proper? Until recently, relatively scant attention was paid to questions of this kind. Lately, however, with the rising concentration of CO_2 in the atmosphere, a number of scenarios, some of them extreme, were formulated.

CLIMATIC VARIATION

The earth's climate is dynamic and its variability, expressed as the amplitude of fluctuations of its two major descriptors - seasonal precipitation and temperature - differs from one part of the globe to another. The mechanisms responsible for this variability are poorly understood, yet empirical evidence indicates that globally the atmospheric content of carbon dioxide is increasing. There seems to be a general consensus that a doubling of the atmospheric CO_2 will lead to a rise in air temperature close to the land surface of about $2°C$. There is also a broad agreement that such a dramatic increase in CO_2 concentration in the atmosphere may result in a 10% drop in precipitation. What is perhaps more important from a water resources point of view is the effect that such climatic variation will have on streamflow. Here the uncertainty and the disagreement are significant. For example, in a study of the Upper Colorado River Basin in the Western United States, Revelle and Waggoner (1983) estimated that annual flows would be reduced about 40 percent if climate will change due to a doubling of atmospheric CO_2. Idso and Brazel (1984), on the other hand, considered in greater detail the effect of atmospheric CO_2 enrichment that would accompany a CO_2-induced climatic change. Accordingly, increased CO_2 content of the air tends to induce partial stomatal closure, thus reducing plant transpiration and thereby conserving soil moisture and increasing runoff to streams. Inclusion of this effect in a simple model of watershed runoff applied to twelve drainage basins in Arizona indicated that 40-60% increases in streamflow may be a likely consequence of doubling atmospheric CO_2.

WATER QUANTITY ISSUES

One of the most important influences on society of climatic changes will be the resulting changes in availability of regional water resources, especially the timing and magnitude of surface runoff and soil moisture fluctuations. Our ability to evaluate these influences is seriously hampered by the difficulty in forecasting future climatic conditions and by the uncertainty inherent in the assessment of regional effects of global changes. Methods for credible evaluation of regional hydrologic changes need to be developed so as to predict with a high degree of confidence their outcomes and thus help formulate specific policies to reduce their severity. Current evaluations are based almost entirely on general circulation models (GCM's), which solve prognostic equations representing physical and dynamic climatic processes in three dimensions (Gleick, 1986). Unfortunately, most GCM's (and especially the earlier formulations) used parameterizations of surface hydrologic processes that are greatly simplified compared to actual hydrologic phenomena observed in the field.

Early results of analyses based on GCM's, performed in the early eighties, show a wide range of potential changes in total surface annual runoff. To begin with, the scale at which most of these models were formulated was very small - their grid cells covered an area of about 10^5 km^2 (a territory of roughly 300 x 300 km). Assuming a climatic change represented by an average increase of earth's temperature by 2°C and a 10% decrease in annual precipitation, GCM's predict that surface runoff may be reduced by anything between 17 and 76 %. The decrease in the quantity of water available for use may be even greater, depending on the storage facilities in the region.

Of greater interest is the evaluation of stream flows and runoff on a reduced time-step: from annual to seasonal or monthly values. Very often, a marginal change in mean annual runoff could hide major changes in monthly distribution of stream flows, as illustrated in Figure 1.

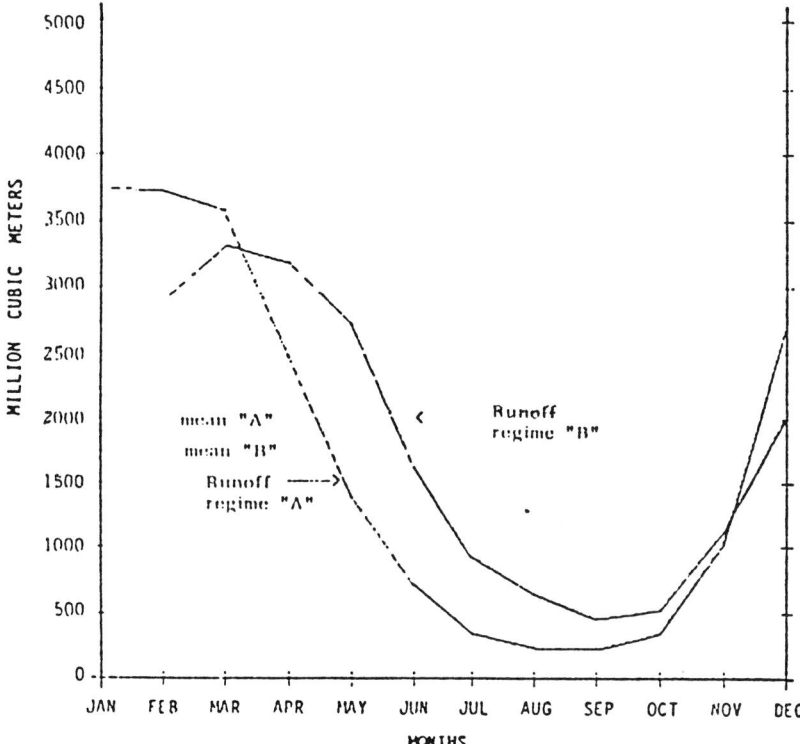

Figure 1. Monthly streamflow for two different regions. Source: Gleick, 1986.

The shift in monthly flows can have a significant influence on the seasonal yield of a reservoir (with constant active storage), thus affecting the regional availability of surface waters.

The assumption that climate will change in the direction of decreased precipitation and higher average annual temperature needs to be examined. Indeed, Flaschka et al. (1987) studied the possible changes in runoff as a function of climatic changes when precipitation and mean annual temperatures would shift either positively or negatively, using a rather simple water balance model. The study covered four watersheds in the Great Basin, an arid closed hydrological region in the Western United States, located between Sierra Nevada and the Rocky Mountains. The results, illustrated in Figure 2, were similar in all four watersheds.

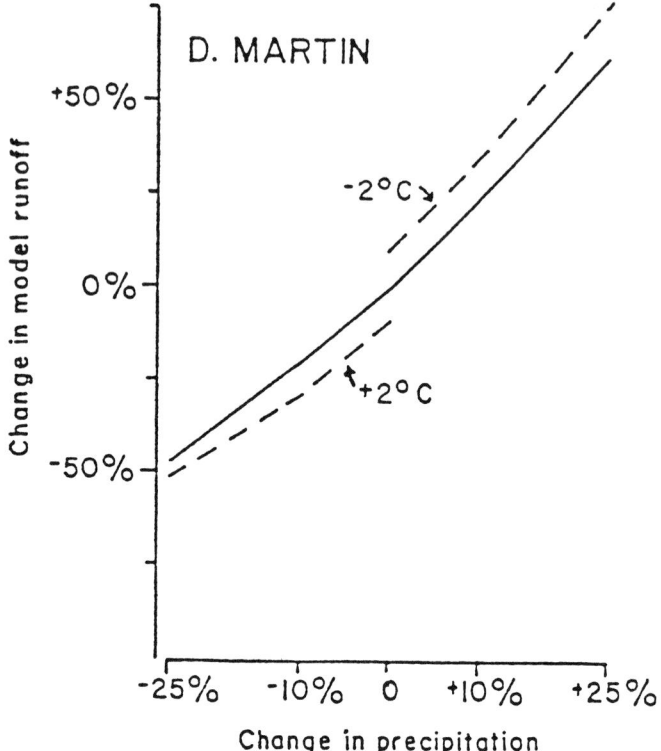

Figure 2. Change in model runoff in the Martin Creek (Nevada) as a function of climatic change. Source: Flaschka et al., 1987.

In this graph, the solid line indicates results of scenarios in which only precipitation was changed. The addition of temperature changes, + 2°C or - 2°C, is shown by the broken lines.

WATER QUALITY PROBLEMS

There is no doubt that water quality is sensitive to climatic events, whether considered on a seasonal basis, annually, on a multi-year basis, or for longer periods of time (Gleick, 1989). In particular, if climatic changes will result in a reduction of freshwater available in a region, there would be reduced availability for diluting wastewater or for repelling salinity intrusion in estuaries.

Many estimates of climatic change point in the direction of increased aridity: lower precipitation and higher mean annual temperature. Under these conditions, the capillary movement of moisture in soils will tend to increase the salt concentration in the vadose zone, leading to the salinization of lands and groundwaters. Finally, it is estimated that increased aridity will also increase sediment production in streams. The increased turbidity of surface waters and the aggradation of streams in their lower reaches will have a profound effect on the biota of rivers, lakes, and estuaries. Perennial streams may change to intermittent or ephemeral.

A REGIONAL WATER BALANCE MODEL

The quantification of the relationship between climate and hydrologic events is a task of considerable complexity. The various methods used in studying this relationship - analytical, numerical, statistical - emphasize different aspects of the problem, and their relevance is tied to the issue at hand. For example, if one is interested in the effect of climatic change during the period of economic life of a structure (which is about 30 years), the assumption of randomness of the historical hydrologic record - which is about 30 years long - is approximately correct. However, most major water resources structures, although amortized over a period of 25-50 years, are expected to function considerably longer. Then, the evaluation of chances in precipitation variability and its effect on flow frequency analysis will vary from basin to basin. As an example, the Lower Colorado River Basin is presented below.

In estimating the effects of climatic change scenarios or the mean annual runoff, a number of assumptions are made (Stockton et al., 1989), such as the following:

1. The variation in annual runoff is mostly influenced by climate, although other factors such as geology, topography, vegetation, and other may also play a role.

2. Annual runoff is not greatly affected by large scale groundwater

3. Evapotranspiration is controlled only by temperature.

4. The postulated climatic change scenarios do not modify current monthly distributions of temperature and precipitation, only their amplitudes are increased or decreased.The lower Colorado River Basin (see Fig. 3) covers an area of 400,930 sq. km., most of it in Arizona 73 percent), with smaller portions in California, Nevada, Utah, and New Mexico. The Colorado River system is unique in the sense that in spite of its relatively low mean annual flow (as compared to other major rivers), a higher percentage of its water is exported from its basin than from any other river in the United States. Mean annual precipitation is about 250 mm/year, 95% of which is depleted by evapotranspiration. Mean January temperatures vary from -5°C in the North to near 13°C in the South; in July, some areas register mean temperatures of 13°C and 35°C, respectively.

Four scenarios of climate change were postulated and the mean annual runoff (Q_s) was compared with the present mean annual runoff (Q_p) averaged over all the meteorological stations within the Lower Colorado River Basin. The results are shown in Table 1. They indicate that should the climate become warmer and drier, the runoff in the Lower Colorado River Basin will be reduced to less than half of the present. Undoubtedly, this will cause very serious socio-economic stresses. The greatly reduced runoff would lead to greater groundwater mining, resulting in even faster declining water levels. The increased costs of pumping groundwater may result in the abandonment of irrigated lands.

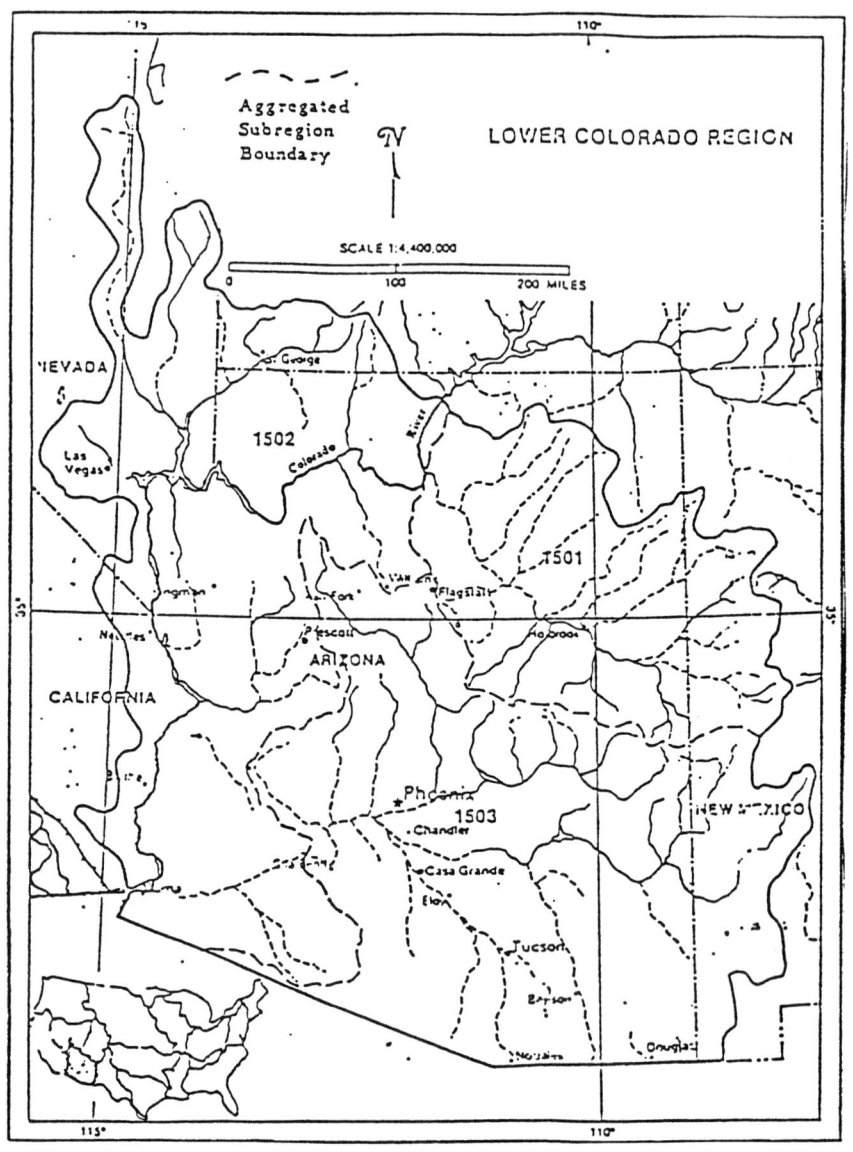

Figure 3. The Lower Colorado River Basin. Source: Stockton et al., 1989.

TABLE 1. Estimated Ratios $\bar{Q}s/\bar{Q}p$ for climate change scenarios.

Scenario		$\bar{Q}s/\bar{Q}p$
1	warmer and drier	0·44
2	cooler and wetter	1·69
3	warmer and wetter	0·98
4	cooler and dryer	0·98

DISCUSSION

A significant change in climate can affect regional water resources and result in socio-economic and environmental impacts that can become public issues. Decision makers who formulate policies regarding the development and utilization of regional water resources and managers implementing those policies will probably raise a number of key questions in their attempts to address the effects of climate change on water resources (Chagnon, 1987). As mentioned before, initial stages in the study of climatic changes involved simulations of large-scale weather systems using general circulation models (GCM's). Subsequently, higher resolution models were developed. Recently, a mesoscale model version 4 (MM4) was formulated, using a 60 km mesh. This model was used to simulate the climate in the western U.S. with considerable success (Dickinson et al., 1989). The measure of success is expressed by the fact the predicted mean rainfall using the MM4 model and historical meteorological data. It differed within a factor of 2 of the corresponding measured values.

SUMMARY

The problem of forecasting climatic changes and their influence on regional water resources, especially in the Western United States, has a long lead-time which can be expressed in terms of decades (or even longer) (Dickinson, 1990). This is rather fortunate, because modelling the comportment of regional water resources under a range of scenarios of global climate change is an activity that began only recently. Current climate models yield significant results only in a qualitative sense for surface hydrology. We can reasonably expect, however, that improved and more sensitive hydrometeorological models at the meso-scale will be forthcoming. If we will not be able to forecast accurately changes in climate, at least we will be in a position to estimate possible outcomes of different scenarios.

REFERENCES

Chagnon, S.A, Jr. (1987). *An Assessment of Climate Change, Water Resources and Policy Research.* Water International 12° 69-76.

Dickinson, R.E. (1990). *Managing Water Resources Under Conditions of Climate Uncertainty. Institute of Atmospheric Physics*, University of Arizona, Tucson, AZ, USA.

Dickinson, R.E., R.M. Errico, F. Giorgi and G.T. Bates (1989). *A Regional Climate Model for the Western United States.* Climate Change, 15: 383-422.

Flaschka, D., C., W. Stockton and W.R. Boggess (1987). *Climatic Variation and Surface Water Resources in the Great Basin Region.* Water Resources Bulletin, 26(1): 47-57.

Gleick, P.H. (1986). Methods for Evaluating the Regional *Hydrologic Impacts of Global Climatic Changes*. Journal of Hydrology, 88: 97-116.

Gleick, P.H. (1989). *Climate Change, Hydrology and Water Resources*. Reviews of Geophysics, 27(3): 329-344.

Idso, S.B. and A.J. Brazel (1984). *Rising Atmospheric Carbon Dioxide Concentrations May Increase Streamflow*. Nature, 312: 51-53.

Matalas, N.C. and M.B. Fiering (1977). *Water-Resource Systems Planning, Climate, Climatic Change and Water Supply*. National Academy of Sciences. Washington, DC, pp. 99-102.

Nemec, J. and J. Schaake (1982). *Sensitivity of Water Resource Systems to Climate Variations*. Hydrological Sciences Journal, 27(3): 327-343.

Revelle, R.R. and P.E. Waggoner (1983). *Effects of Carbon Dioxide-Induced Climatic Change on Water Supplies in the Western United States. Changing Climate*, Report of the Carbon Dioxide Assessment Committee. National Academy Press. Washington, DC, pp. 419-432.

Stockton, C.W., D.M. Meke and W.R. Boggess (1989). *Geohydrological Implications of Climate Change on Water Resource Development*. Report submitted to the U.S. Army Corps of Engineers, Laboratory of Tree-Ring Research, University of Arizona, Tucson, AZ, USA.

SOME REMARKS ON UNESCO'S PROGRAM IN HYDROLOGICAL EDUCATION UNDER IHD / IHP

Wilfried H. Gilbrich
Division of Water Sciences
UNESCO
Paris 75700, France

ABSTRACT

An account is given of the results of educational program of UNESCO within the framework of the International Hydrological Decade (IHD), (1965-1974), and of three first phases of the International Hydrological Program (IHP), (1975-1989), as well as an outlook on the expected results of the present program. The report highlights the training courses held or sponsored by UNESCO and it refers to the publications issued. Critical remarks are made on the impact of UNESCO's program on developing countries.

INTRODUCTION

The present paper is a short excerpt of a report entitled *25 years of UNESCO's program in hydrological education under IHD/IHP* to be shortly published by UNESCO. The complete report which contains information on all working groups, expert panels, training courses and related statistical material will be mailed to the participants of the Symposium.

AN APPRAISAL

Certainly, after twenty-five years of a hydrological educational program in UNESCO, one can look back on quite impressive figures - over fifty meetings, two dozen publications, more than a hundred experts participating in working groups and panels, and about ten thousand people who have undergone a training program. However, one should not lose sight of the world-wide dimensions and compare it with the quite unknown number of books published, of teachers and students involved in hydrological and water-related courses, at all levels and all over the world.

What is perhaps more striking is the fact that hydrological education has become a world-wide concern, in all of its facets, from on-the-job training to formal education, from the technician level to summer schools for professors, from pure classical hydrology to its variations in geology, agriculture, meteorology, geography, engineering, biology, chemistry, environmental subjects, etc.

The value of the program can also be assessed when considering the fact that a UNESCO program has left its narrow confines and today is a worldwide activity - with, and more often without, UNESCO's involvement. This development, possibly accelerated as a result of funding shortcomings within the United Nations system, corresponds perfectly with UNESCO's philosophy of a catalytic function. The aim must be that the program continues without the United Nations system: only if it is fully absorbed by the world community can it attain its full justification and vitality. The fact that Member States and international associations have become involved in hydrological education shows the relevance of a program which started with a small international working group and a handful of postgraduate courses. While in the beginning, the bulk of training activities could be recorded, today nobody knows the complete dimensions of training activities. Certainly, one could argue that this development would have come anyway, but there is no doubt that the IHD and IHP have been one of the dynamic mechanisms leading to today's state-of-the-art.

This report has been written in order to provide a historical record, in order to thank those persons and institutions who helped the program to be executed and to grow. UNESCO is much indebted to them. The report, however, is also intended to encourage teachers, organizers, donors, institutions, Member States and international organizations to continue and to expand hydrological education and to make it a truly world-wide movement both in industrialized and developing countries.

When analyzing the statistical material used for the report one cannot ignore the fact that more activities have been performed by and in industrialized countries, although largely oriented towards the needs of the developing countries. What is required in the future is an increased participation of developing countries, a situation which can only be attained through a concerted venture between the hydrologically and financially advanced countries and the developing regions. This is a giant program which would exceed the budget of international organizations. The present phase of the IHP, and also development programs in general outside the United Nations system, can only be successful if the mobilizing effect of the past twenty-five years attains the dimensions of the real needs of the world. The success of future programs will be measured by the rectification of the imbalance between hydrologists required and the population. The population growth adds to the challenge and any rise in the standard of living will focus on water. In the future, the water problems will increase globally and training of hydrologists will become more and more an indispensable requirement to ensure life for future generations. Man's attitude as an ignorant consumer must convert into skill.

SOME REMARKS CONCERNING THE STATUS OF HYDROLOGICAL EDUCATION PRIOR TO THE INTERNATIONAL HYDROLOGICAL DECADE

The foundation, in 1923, of the International Association for Scientific Hydrology shows that hydrology was already considered nearly three quarters of a century ago as an independent field of studies. Geographers and geologists, as well as hydraulic engineers, widely contributed to that field.

Yet hydrology did not enter as an independent subject into university curricula but it was considered as a subject auxiliary to water resources development. In the university curricula hydrological material could be found as part of water resources development subjects, such as irrigation or hydraulics, or as part of courses in physical geography and geomorphology. In the years before the International Hydrological Decade (IHD) started, the growing need to develop also marginal water resources initiated many important hydrological studies, and gradually at various universities, hydrology started to become an independent subject. At the beginning of the IHD, this had already resulted into the foundation of a few postgraduate programs in this field. The first textbooks dealing with modern hydrology appear in the 1920s. At the beginning of the IHD their number was still limited and they seemed not always to have kept pace with the latest developments. However, by the time the IHD began, there were already some new developments in this respect. The inception of the IHD came at the right time. The hydrologists as a separate professional group started to evolve in various countries. Rightly, the Coordinating Council for the IHD considered education to be one of the most important instruments by which hydrology could be promoted and they considered it to be on a par with research activities.

THE ROLE OF HYDROLOGICAL EDUCATION WITHIN THE IHD

The IHD was conceived as a scientific program. For its execution, the Coordinating Council established a large number of projects to be executed by Member States, non-governmental organizations or by individually appointed rapporteurs. However, nine major fields of water sciences had been selected to be dealt with by internationally composed working groups. Their expected outcome was research reports, preparation of scientific meetings (symposia, seminars), monographs and guidebooks.

UNESCO is, however, an organization for Science and Education and the Coordinating Council felt that the scientific program of the Decade needed to be supplemented by an education component. This component should help to transfer research into application and practice. It should also help engineers, geographers, etc. to become hydrologists. While training as such was considered a task basically for Member States and less so for UNESCO, due partly to budgetary reasons, the working group established by the Council was to provide guidance to Member States, universities and teachers in the form of policy issues and printed guidance material.

The Council foresaw the great needs of developing countries which at that time were generally still very young nations without adequate hydrological services and lacking practically all hydrological personnel at whatsoever level. In establishing its working group on hydrological education, the Coordinating Council laid the foundations for a world-wide program which resulted in numerous publications and most successfully in a great number of national and international training courses. Looking back, one can say that the level and extent of hydrological activities of today are the fruit of the educational program launched in 1965.

SUBJECT MATTER OF HYDROLOGICAL EDUCATION

The subject matter of education is one of the fundamental characteristics of teaching hydrology in the same way as many other branches of science. For a long time hydrological education has not had, and even in these days it does not appear to have a strictly circumscribed, throughout the world uniform subject matter. Some parts of hydrology are overlapped by marginal sciences, among others meteorology, geology, geography, engineering sciences; other parts e.g hydraulics, hydromechanics developed into independent branches of sciences, while a substantial part of their scope of knowledge continues to play an important role in hydrology. The limitation of the subject matter varies in some cases by country, many times by author, not to mention the different stages of development of the science of hydrology in each country.

In consequence of the above, the first significant step in the interest of the development of hydrological education had to be the establishment and limitation of the subject matter. Besides the limitation and unification of the subject matter, a very important problem to be solved concerning the development of hydrology and hydrological education was the elaboration of a terminology uniform by languages. Significant steps have been made in this field during the last years. Nevertheless, a lot of tasks remain to be solved, because an unambiguous, accurate terminology is one of the indispensable conditions of the efficiency of teaching hydrology.

The domain and scope of knowledge of hydrology in general do not agree with the subject matters of the hydrological education at different levels. The subject matter is usually less in range, even in cases of the highest level of education, than the entire scope of knowledge of hydrology. The efficiency of education depends to a great extent on the adequate selection and assessment of the subject matter. For this reason the Working Group on Education has greatly contributed to the development of the subject matter of hydrology also by:

- assessing and reviewing the curricula and syllabi of hydrological education;
- elaborating syllabi for teaching some of the more important chapters of hydrology, guides to some hydrological works of prominent significance e.g. syllabi for determination of characteristic discharges, drawing up forecasts, investigations on subsurface waters and subsurface water management.

By this activity the Working Group on Education set examples for the elaboration of curricula and syllabi of other chapters of hydrology, furthered the realization of curricula and syllabi suitable to local circumstances of the countries, and greatly contributed to shifting the main point of the subject matter from descriptive hydrology to an endeavor to explore the relationships between the phenomena, quantitatively characterize the processes, and satisfy the practical needs to a greater extent.

It is necessary to emphasize particularly the above outcome of the activities. Incontestably, there are still numerous undiscovered domains concerning the hydrological cycle, the state of rest and various phenomena of the movement of water. For this reason descriptive hydrology will continue to be studied in the future. Nevertheless, a mere cognition of, or a description of the hydrological processes and phenomena are usually not enough to fulfil the ever increasing tasks of society. In addition to the qualitative connections of the phenomena, their quantitative characteristics should also be known; the characteristic elements of the processes, the range of their changes, the interrelationships between the characteristic elements should be revealed. In general a tabular or graphical account of the relationships is not sufficient, an analysis is also indispensable.

The curricula and syllabi elaborated by the Working Group on Education have greatly contributed to increasing the importance of the role of related sciences, such as selected branches of mathematics, chemistry, biology, general physics, geomorphology, geodesy, soil science, soil mechanics and water management in water science in general, and in hydrological education in particular, in accordance with the demands of hydrology.

The growing importance of the role of related sciences in hydrology is closely related to the increased demands of society on water resources and consequences of this are the endeavors to establish analyzed relationships in hydrology. Obviously, for solving more complicated problems, it is necessary to have a larger number and more accurate measurement results, more refined logical and mathematical methods.

METHODOLOGY IN TEACHING HYDROLOGY

Besides the subject matter, the method of teaching is another very important characteristic of teaching sciences. Attention has been called to the fact that for the efficient teaching of hydrology, as a practical science, the earlier generally applied, almost exclusively verbal methods are insufficient. By means of textbooks the descriptive parts of the subject matter can generally be attained by the trainees without oral explanations. The teachers' work can be concentrated on explanations about some parts of the material, revelation of relationships, and mainly, practical training.

Additional means in the teaching process are:

- laboratory measurements, experiments, investigations, including the use of various models with a view to working on the principle of relations between hydraulic processes, on the basis of analogies, etc.,
- field measurements and observations made on experimental and representative areas,
- observations and investigations on hydrological processes not realized for experimental purposes but occurring in nature,

in up-to-date teaching of hydrology.

The science of hydrology is closely related to its applications. Therefore, in up-to-date teaching practical methods should receive an adequate role. In assessing the teaching methods light has been thrown on some problems connected with the determination of the role of the hydrologist and attention has been called to the dependence of the methods of teaching hydrology (according to subject matter) on the level of education. Evidently, both the subject matter and the method of teaching ought to be different in cases of research hydrologists or hydrological technicians.

SOME RESULTS CONCERNING THE THIRD IHP PHASE

The International Conference on Hydrology and the Scientific Bases for the Rational Management of Water Resources was held in Paris from 18 to 27 August 1981. One of its aims was to evaluate the progress of the first and second phases of the IHP and to prepare for the third phase (1984-1989). With regard to education and training, the Conference, in general debate, made the following statement concerning the first and second phases:

"Education and training was considered to be of the greatest importance and should be given the highest priority. The UNESCO postgraduate program was appreciated in terms of the variety of its subjects and the increasing number of trainees.

The uneven language and geographical distribution of postgraduate courses with respect to the location of the courses and the countries of origin of the participants was regretted and it was recommended that steps be taken to permit a greater number of countries to participate in the scheme. Higher and postgraduate training institutions for the specific conditions of tropical Africa should be established.

It was stressed that each training activity should aim at increasing the number and quality of national staff at professional and technician level. While the postgraduate courses scheme had developed well in general, it was felt that there is still very much to be done at higher and middle technician level. It was agreed that technicians were best trained locally since working requirements and conditions differ in each country. Several delegates reported on programs to train technicians and local workers. It was requested that teaching programs be less academic and more practical. In line with this, instrumentation and equipment delivered to developing countries should correspond to the existing training programs so that proper use and maintenance could be ensured.

It was recognized that the execution of such training programs requires a large input from all partners involved: the host country, donor countries and international organizations. It was stressed that close cooperation is imperative if good results are to be achieved. Cooperative programs, both in training and education as well as in the scientific programs, can best be carried out where the donor country has a sufficient knowledge of the hydrological and socio-economic conditions in the recipient country, or where the cooperating countries have similar socio-economic conditions."

With regard to the planning of the third phase, the Conference

"stressed the great need for education and training in IHP-III and the complementary activities of UNESCO for 1984-1989. In particular, the new emphasis on middle and higher level technician training was welcomed as this training, it was stated, formed in many countries a "bottle neck" in the development of water resources. The Conference also stressed the need for establishing regional technician training centers in order to provide the large number of technicians required.

With regard to graduate and postgraduate education and training, the Conference noted with satisfaction the continuing trend, visible in IHP-III, towards the introduction of the concept of integrated, rational water resources assessment and development into these programs.

Although general satisfaction was expressed at the complementary activities of UNESCO in the field of education and training, such as the organization of courses, assistance in setting up educational institutions in developing countries, etc., it was generally felt that these should be expanded considerably. In this respect, assistance in the setting up of regional training centers and the organization of roving seminars was requested. The need for a greater number of fellowships to be awarded to specialists and middle-level technicians was stressed."

The outline plan, in its main objectives referred to education and training:

'to promote education and training in hydrology and other disciplines related to water resources management, with increased emphasis at the technician level, in order to strengthen the endogenous capacity of Member States to solve their water problems.'

More specifically, the outline plan devoted one section out of four to education and training:

Education and training activities - They cover all aspects of water sciences and are directed at all levels from middle-level technicians through undergraduate to postgraduate. Two main programs will be followed: (l) hydrology education for the training of specialized personnel (middle-level and postgraduate), and (2) general water resources education with emphasis on the integrated aspects of water resources management (all levels from technicians to graduate engineers and also to planners and decision makers). A more flexible approach with regard to the method of teaching or transferring knowledge will be promoted. While UNESCO will continue to sponsor an international network of training courses, functioning on a regular basis, the organization of *ad hoc* courses and seminars, primarily at regional level (in developing countries) and, if possible, linked with field projects, will be encouraged. A program of the IHP "traineeships" (including in-service training) and "professorships" based on arrangements with the National Committees concerned will also be developed.

Comparative methodologies for public information and the promotion of public participation in the proper utilization, protection and conservation of water resources - Although there are many approaches available for the involvement of the public in water resources planning and development, it is not an area without controversy. Yet it is quite clear that in many water resources activities, the public must be involved if the programs are to be successful. In fact, many planners feel that planning and development cannot only be done for the public, but must also be done with the public. Public participation, however, of necessity involves public education in the various aspects related to the economical use of water, protection against pollution and natural hazards, etc. The results of these studies will present alternative concepts and procedures for raising the level of public awareness so that the public can be profitably involved in the proper utilization, protection and conservation of water resources.

Scientific information systems - The emphasis here is on the scientific and technical information, and not on the operational exchange of data. The area is concerned with the methodological principles for the establishment of such information systems at national, regional and global levels. It will bring together experts who will provide, through case studies and examples, information on alternative and complementary systems which can be used by institutions interested in developing an information system.

Methods for the effective transfer of knowledge and technology related to water resources, and for the evaluation of their impacts in developing countries - The need for effective programs to transfer knowledge and technology requires that an assessment be made of results achieved by IHP activities in that area.

NETWORK OF UNESCO-SPONSORED POSTGRADUATE COURSES

During the third phase of the IHP, further courses were established or already existing ones were incorporated into the network. The result (Annex II) was a better topical and geographical coverage but shortages remained in the French, Spanish, Arabic and Russian languages.

During the third phase, some of the momentum was undoubtedly lost. One reason was the reduction of the UNESCO budget during the last years of the phase which meant that not all courses received financial contributions and that even the support provided was stopped or reduced. The sharp depreciation of the U.S. dollar and the increased costs of international air travel coming at the same time as a result of the oil price movements, was another factor. UNESCO therefore acknowledges the help rendered by the host countries of the courses, to make up at least part of the losses.

The number of students trained exceeded 500 annually and today a great number of hydrologists and water engineers in developing countries have participated in a UNESCO-sponsored course.

Also, during the third phase of the IHP, a number of problems continued to remain unsolved. The financial problems have already been mentioned and without long-term commitments from industrialized countries, some courses in poorer countries will find it increasingly difficult to maintain a reasonable output or even to survive. Another problem is coordination. For financial reasons, no meeting of course directors could be held (the last one was in 1968) and a conference is foreseen only for the fourth phase of the IHP.

Although all courses award a diploma at the end of the course, or at least a certificate, these documents lack world-wide official acknowledgement as a career aid. The IHP Council has raised this problem at several of its sessions without, however, response from Member States.

As a positive development, UNESCO has noted the increasing interest of nongovernmental organizations in hydrological education as well as the growing number of bilateral arrangements between industrialized and developing countries. It is now being recognized that training and education is a particularly efficient development aid and the transfer of knowledge and technology has become part of many aid schemes.

Most of the UNESCO-sponsored postgraduate courses had been conceived on aspects of quantitative hydrology. During the third IHP phase, however, environmental topics became more and more important. Financed by UNEP, UNESCO contacted a number of courses with a wide topical and geographical coverage and carried out a survey to find out to what extent they had included environmental aspects in their curricula. UNESCO prepared a short technical paper *Integration of environmental aspects in water resources engineering education* published by UNEP and UNESCO in 1988.

AN OUTLOOK

This report has been written at the very beginning of the fourth phase of the IHP, prior to any results becoming visible. A brief look at this phase must however be provided in order to avoid the wrong impression that UNESCO's program in hydrological training and education terminated with the end of the third phase of the IHP, in 1989.

Preparation for the fourth phase started as early as 1987 when the Third UNESCO/WMO International Conference on Hydrology and the Scientific Bases of Water Resources Management (Geneva, 16-20 March 1987) discussed the priorities of future activities and when it elaborated recommendations for the contents of the fourth IHP phase. With regard to training and education, the Conference stated:

'High priority in general was accorded to the Education, Training and Public Information Sub-Program. It recommended the development of posters and other popularized material to illustrate man's influence on water resources, the provision of water-resources training to economists and lawyers, the inclusion of aspects of water-saving methods in the training of engineers and higher technicians and increased training in urban hydrology. The Conference recommended that, in the execution of this Sub-Program, UNESCO should play a more active role in guiding the international postgraduate course system, promote pairing of universities and training institutions, give particular emphasis to the training of trainers and, while keeping the guidance material general at global level, include more detail at regional and national levels in the light of the particular situations and requirements.'

The fourth phase will firstly emphasize technician training by providing guidance material for course organizers, both organizational and didactic, and by creating regional networks. As an innovation, university curricula will be developed for different degrees of water-related instruction within the whole study program, ranging from hydrology as an auxiliary subject to hydrology as the target subject. A new approach in postgraduate education will be developed which will foresee a differentiation in duration from specialized short courses to third cycle courses ending with an acknowledged diploma. A further project will be devoted to continuous education and special efforts will be made for hydrological instruction at primary and secondary school level, for the general public and for the special group of politicians and decision-makers. This short summary shows that the fourth phase is not simply an extension of the third phase but is innovative.

The success of the IHD and of the first three phases of the IHP will inspire all persons involved in the execution of the fourth phase to improve the level of performance, to maintain the substance inherited and to develop imaginative innovations.

ANNEX I

LIST OF PUBLICATIONS AND REPORTS

I - During the International Hydrological Decade, 1965-1974

Technical Papers in Hydrology

- No. 6   Textbooks on hydrology, 1970
- No. 6/II   Textbooks on hydrology, 1974
- No. 10   Curricula and syllabi in hydrology, 1972
- No. 11   Teaching aids in hydrology, 1974

Technical Documents in Hydrology

- SC/WS/432   Equipment for training in hydrology, 1972
- SC/WS/434   International courses, fellowships and scholarships in hydrology, Third edition, 1972
- SC/WS/434   International courses, fellowships and scholarships in hydrology, Fourth edition, 1974
- SC/WS/581   The progress in hydrological education since the inception of the IND, 1974

II - During the first two phases of the IHP, 1975-1983

Technical Papers in Hydrology

- Teaching the systems approach to water resources development, by L. J. Mostertman, No. 25, 1983, 20p.
- Curricula and syllabi in hydrology, second edition, Chief editors Satish Chandra and L.J. Mostertman, No. 22, 1983, 112 p.
- Experimental facilities in water resources education, Chief editor R.A. Lopardo, No. 24, 1983, 84 p.
- Teaching aids in hydrology, second edition, Chairman U. Maniak, Editor P.W. Jowitt, No. 27, 1985, 76 p. and 1 map.

Technical Documents in Hydrology

- Teaching the application of computers in water resources studies by 1. Herrera and R.A. Yates Smith, 1983, 49 p.
- Fourth regional training course for hydrology technicians, Lusaka (1982), UNESCO, 1983, 30 p.
- International courses, fellowships and scholarships in hydrology, fifth edition, UNESCO, 1978, 62 p.
- International courses, fellowships and scholarships in hydrology, sixth edition, UNESCO 1983, 66 p.
- Lecture Notes of the UNESCO/NORAD Third Regional Training Course for Hydrology Technicians (Kenya 1977), edited by K.D. Grey, 1979, 214p.

III - During the third IHP phase, 1984-1989

- Fifth regional training course for hydrology technicians, 1984.
- International colloquium on the role of micro-computers in hydraulic and hydrological research and education, 1985.
- UNESCO-sponsored postgraduate course in hydrology, seventh edition, 1986.
- Evaluation of the UNESCO-sponsored postgraduate courses in hydrology and water resources, by N.B. Ayibotele, LJ. Mostertman and U. Maniak, 1988.
- Model curricula for courses in hydrology and water resources by U. Maniak, 1988, as an annex to (4).
- Lecture notes of the UNESCO/NORWAY fifth regional training course for hydrology technicians, edited by G.P. Jones, 4 volumes, 1988.
- Notes de cours de formation pour techniciens en hydrologie, 3 volumes, 1989.
- Integration of environmental aspects in water resources engineering education, UNESCO/UNEP, 1988.
- Model Curriculum for short-term training courses for senior hydrology technicians, by U. Maniak, 1988.
- Effective on-the-job training in hydrology by R. Allaburton (in print).
- Integrated planning and management of water resources (guidance material for courses for engineers, planners and decision-makers), edited by S. Bruk and S. Dyck, 1990.

ANNEX II

LIST OF THE UNESCO-SPONSORED POSTGRADUATE HYDROLOGY COURSES

Place	Subject of Course	Duration	Frequency	L*
ANKARA (Turkey)	Sediment technology	4 weeks	annually in June	E
ARGENTINE Buenos Aires, Santa Fé Mendoza, San Juan	General hydrology with emphasis on groundwater	6 months	Inquire	S
BARCELONA (Spain)	Groundwater hydrology	6 months	annually January-July	S
BELGIUM	Hydrology and hydrogeology	10 months	annually, begins in October	F
	- *French language programme*			
	- *English language programme*	1 or 2 years	annually, begins September	E
BELGRADE (Yugoslavia)	Water resources engineering	3 months	annually	E
BIRMINGHAM (United Kingdom)	Water resources engineering in developing countries	9 months	Oct. 1990	E
BRAZIL	Water resources management			P
BUDAPEST (Hungary)	Hydrology	6 months	annually from January	E
CAIRO (Egypt)	Environmental hydrology for arid and semi-arid zones	2 months May-June	annually	E
CRICA (Central America and the Caribbean)	Changing subjects (for subject and date inquire with organizer)	4 weeks	annually	S
CRICA (Central America and the Caribbean)	Changing subjects (for subject and date inquire with organizer)	4 weeks	annually	S

*E = English, F = French, P = Portuguese, R = Russian, S = Spanish

ANNEX II continued

Place	Subject of Course	Duration	Frequency	L*
CRICA (Central America and the Caribbean)	Changing subjects (for subject and date inquire with organizer)	4 weeks	annually	S
DAR-ES SALAAM (Tanzania)	Water resources engineering	18 months	annually begins 1 October	E
DELFT (Netherlands)	Hydrology	11 or 18 months	annually	E
GALWAY (Ireland)	Hydrology	1 year	annually begins in October	E
GRAZ (Austria)	Groundwater tracing techniques	5 weeks	1991, 1993, etc. October	E
GUATAMALA	Hydraulic resources	11 months	annually	S
KENSINGTON (Australia)	Hydrology, covering principles, practices and applications of surface and groundwater hydrology	3 months	annually	E
LAHORE (Pakistan)	Water resources management. Various options: - postgraduate - M. Sc. - M. Phil	12 mo. 16- 112 mo. 2 years	annually beginning in Sept.	E
LAUSANNE (Switzerland) (in conjunction with Neuchatel)	Hydrology	15 months	annually beginning in Oct.	F
NEUCHATEL (Switzerland) (in conjunction with Lausanne)	Hydrogeology	15 months	annually beginning in Oct.	F
LISBON (Portugal)	Operational Hydrology	2 months	annually	P

ANNEX II continued

Place	Subject of Course	Duration	Frequency	L*
MADRAS (India)	Hydrology and water resources engineering	1 year	annually mid-August	E
MADRID (Spain)	General and applied hydrology	6 months	annually from January	S
MONASH (Australia)	Hydrology and water sciences	1 year	annually	E
MONTPELLIER (France)	Hydrology of fractured rocks	2 weeks	13-21 September 1990	F
MOSCOW (Russia)	1990: Hydrological forecasting in national economy 1991: Formation and study of groundwater resources	2 months	annually begins in June	E R
NANJING (China)	Hydrology (advanced)	2 months	Special announcements	E
NEWCASTLE-UPON-TYNE (United Kingdom)	(a) Hydrology (b) Water resources	1 year	annually from October	E
OUAGA-DOUGOU (Burkina Faso)	(a) Mobilization of water resources; (b) Agriculture hydraulics (c) Sanitary engineering	9 months 9 months 11 months	annually annually annually	F F F
PADOVA (Italy)	Hydrology	6 months	annually from February	E
PRAGUE (Czecho-slovakia)	Hydrological data for water resource planning	6 months	1990, 1992, etc. from February	E
ROORKEE (India)	Hydrology (and several additional options)	1 year	annually beginning mid-July	E

ANNEX II continued

Place	Subject of Course	Duration	Frequency	L*
U.S.A.	Techniques of hydrologic investigations for international participants	2 months	Special announcements	E
WALLINGFORD (United Kingdom)	Estimation of hydrological variables		Special announcements	E

ANNEX III

IHP-IV - SUB-PROGRAME

EDUCATION, TRAINING, THE TRANSFER OF KNOWLEDGE AND PUBLIC INFORMATION

THEMES AND PROJECTS

Theme E-1: Education and training of senior technicians

- *Project E-1-1* : Education systems for higher hydrological technicians
- *Project E-1-2*: Improvement of training programs for both technicians and their supervisors through teaching material and courses
- *Project E-1-3*: Regional networks of technician training centres concerned with water resources
- *Project E-1-4* : Comparison of textbooks for hydrology technicians

Theme E-2: University education

- *Project E-2-1:* Model curricula for water-related courses in university programs
- *Project E-2-2* : Cooperative arrangements on water programs among educational institutions
- *Project E-2-3* : Comparison of water resources textbooks for undergraduate students

Theme E 3: Postgraduate training

- *Project E-3-1*: Improvement of the system of post-graduate courses in hydrology and water resources through better topical, geographical and language distribution

Theme E-4: Continuing education

- *Project E-4-1* : Policies for and establishment of continuing education systems

Theme E-5: Public education and information

- *Project E-5-1*: Introduction of water-related subjects in primary and secondary education
- *Project E-5-2* : Use of mass media for disseminating information on the rational use of water
- *Project E-5-3* : Development of reports for decision-makers and legislative bodies on water resources for sustainable development in a changing environment

SOME MUSINGS ON HYDROLOGICAL EDUCATION

J.E. Nash
Department of Engineering Hydrology,
University College Galway,
Galway, Ireland

ABSTRACT

The traditional view of hydrology as a technology founded on the natural sciences is reviewed and the seeming slow progress commented on. The status of hydrology among the sciences is examined and a distinction drawn between hydrology as a mere application of more basic sciences and as a science with its own domain. The dual role of the hydrologist as a scientist and a technologist follows and the necessity for involving interdisciplinary teams in the larger problems of hydrology is recognized. Appropriate structures for the education of hydrologists emerge and are considered.

INTRODUCTION

It is fashionable to decry the limited progress which has been made in hydrology over the past forty years and many hydrologists have engaged in soul searching to find the cause of this partial failure. The distinguished President of the IASH, Vit Klemeš, with his customary wit and erudition, has become pre-eminent among the critics of our profession and of our training establishments. It is of course a good thing to undertake such self examination and criticism and indeed most hydrologists being, usually, humble engineers are content to accept this criticism and responsibility for our limited success. Destructive criticism alone however is not sufficient. We must diagnose the cause of the trouble and take steps to improve matters and this is where we begin to disagree among ourselves.

The report of the IASH-UNESCO Panel on the education of hydrologists, following opinions that have been expressed often and widely, suggests two not identical, but related, causes of the present sad state of hydrology.

1. Hydrology taught by engineers in engineering departments of universities is usually problem orientated and constrained in scope by the engineering discipline concerned. The technology is built in ignorance of, or at best neglectful of, the scientific principles on which it should be founded.

2. The science of hydrology, as a branch of geoscience, has not been given its rightful place in geoscience departments of universities and therefore

the scientific basis on which the technology should rest has not been developed adequately.

Among those who hold these views, there is usually a concomitant assumption, not always stated but implied, that the fault lies with the engineers - though why engineers should be blamed for the alleged neglect of the geoscientists is not clear. No doubt a share of the blame, if blame there be, should be attributed to those of us who are responsible for the teaching of hydrology, especially in the UNESCO sponsored international courses. I feel however that the criticism in general may be a little naive and founded on an inadequate appreciation of the complexity of hydrology, which at the same time can be a science, a domain of application of more basic sciences and a technology, or the intellectual equipment of a profession, and the corresponding demands which this complexity implies in the educational sphere.

THE STATUS OF HYDROLOGY AMONG THE SCIENCES

Any science is a body of related knowledge, pursued and acquired in a generally agreed way - the scientific method. In some domains, the term science is applied to mere classification of species or observations, or even to a description of what is in the domain. In others - the "harder" as distinct from the "softer" sciences - the emphasis is on analysis and deduction, and reason rather than observation is the primary faculty used in expanding the body of knowledge. The term science is also applied to the manner in which knowledge is obtained and expanded, as well as to the body of knowledge itself. In this sense, science is an activity of the intellect rather than a mere compilation of knowledge in a prescribed domain.

Hydrology might be defined as the knowledge of the occurrence and behavior, particularly the movement, of water in the natural environment. If we restrict this knowledge to mere description of where and how water occurs, hydrology would be a soft science, a matter of classification, advanced by mere observation and would not be very interesting, though it might be useful. On the other hand, if the knowledge referred to implies an understanding of the laws of nature relevant to the watery domain, hydrology as a basic science would seem to have little room for activity, at least at the practical level, since these laws are already well understood.

Not being a basic science, and not wishing to be classified as a mere categorization, hydrology, if scientific, would seem to be so because it provides a domain of application wherein basic scientific knowledge is applied to explain or predict phenomena. One might however question whether such an application should be called hydrology or be known rather by the name of the basic science which is applied. The application of physical principles to produce knowledge in the domain of water, might give rise to a body of knowledge called hydrology but the activity would be physics.

If only one basic science were involved, the terms hydrology and hydrologist would be unnecessary, except to designate the compiled knowledge and the domain of application of the basic science. Given, however, that the application of a number of basic sciences is involved, the role of the hydrologist is widened and hydrology as an applied science acquires many facets.

EMPIRICAL HYDROLOGY

One might imagine that, in these circumstances, the main role of the hydrologist would be the interdisciplinary one of assembling the relevant scientific principles and tools of analysis and applying these in the required context. This would be a very important role, akin to that of the conductor of an orchestra who assembles the different instrumentalists, defines their activities without usurping them, controls their interaction and ensures an harmonious whole. There is however another scientific role for the hydrologist which tends to give hydrology a special status. At the catchment and higher scales, the complexity of the boundary conditions often renders it impracticable to apply even well known natural principles to obtain solutions to real life problems. The obvious expedient of taking spatial averages is not always available either. Relationships between averages are not necessarily the same as those between point values, as consideration of the relationship of rainfall to runoff and infiltration immediately shows. There is thus a legitimate role, and indeed a need, for the hydrologist to seek, by observation and experiment, empirical relationships at the catchment and higher levels, rather than to rely on their synthesis from basic physical laws. The method of this empirical, parametric engineering or "real" hydrology (Nash, 1973) is that of a researcher in any basic science, where progress is made by hypothesis formulation, testing and modification within the appropriate domain, rather than by merely applying a more basic science. Thus, along with the interdisciplinary role, the hydrologist acquires a research role differing only from that of the basic scientist in the level of application, viz., the catchment rather than the particle.

I suggest that it is this two-fold role, this dependence on two pillars, which distinguishes the work of the hydrologist from that of the physicist, chemist or botanist engaged merely in the application of his science in the domain of water. Both pillars are essential. Exclusive reliance on one can lead to disaster.

It is probable that engineering hydrologists have tended to rely excessively on the empirical approach. Perhaps because of their training as engineers, they have acquired a respect for, and a reliance on mathematics as a tool, to the neglect of the accumulated knowledge of relevant basic sciences. It is surely, however, the business of the physicist, chemist and botanist to demonstrate how to use the principles of their sciences to obtain answers to the day to day problems of hydrology. We hydrologists are prepared to learn, to be convinced, but in the meantime we cannot wait but must make progress by the use of the tools we have and can command. In doing so, we may be encouraged by reflection on the empirical development of other technologies, e.g., our understanding of the phenomenon of resistance to flow in pipes and open channels. Until approximately one hundred years ago, the role of the conduit roughness in turbulent flow was almost completely discounted, but when the importance of roughness was recognized empirically the simple relationship known as the Chezy-Manning equation which is adequate for all practical purposes was quickly found. Subsequently, boundary layer theory leading to the logarithmic velocity distribution and the experiments of Nikuradse produced the "rough and smooth pipe laws" and the Colebrook-White equation - a remarkable development, intellectually satisfying, broader in its application than the Chezy-Manning formula, but not really more useful in the domain of fully developed turbulence. If our predecessors had been differently trained, Manning and Chezy might not have discovered what we now call the Colebrook-White equation but they certainly would not have simply waited for the development of fluid mechanics to provide a good physical basis for their work. The lesson, of course, is that we must depend on our own resources and make such progress as we can in the prevailing circumstances of knowledge.

If we have been neglectful of the possibilities of developing hydrology as an application of more basic sciences, this does not imply that there is something wrong in adopting to the macro relationships of hydrology the method of analysis of experiments and observations appropriate to basic sciences. It is not for this that we must be blamed, but rather for excessive concentration on the development of tools and for our failure to appreciate the importance of accuracy and adequacy in the observations to which these were applied. We have tended to be careless in the measurement of our basic quantities; the accuracy of rainfall measurements is still suspect, and we have failed to obtain a method for the direct measurement of evaporation as a vertical vapor flux. We have been content to use the concept of the catchment as a control volume, into which, and from which, the mass and energy fluxes are conservative, but we often neglect the real possibility of water leakage from and into the catchment. We have not always tested our hypotheses, nor do we normally examine the errors resulting from their application to obtain indications for further modification. On the contrary, we have tended to settle for any hypothesis which provides a fair reproduction of observed behavior. We have on occasion departed from all consideration of observations and concentrated on the refinement of the tools themselves, thus creating the subject of "blackboard hydrology" - a field of study which though providing many opportunities for superficial brilliance, has little or no prospect of ever being relevant to actual hydrology. This subject remains with us today. A most recent manifestation has been the tendency to express catchment behavior in probable terms even when no probable concept is involved. The instantaneous unit hydrograph has become "the probability density function of the waiting time". Blackboard hydrology proceeds by the adoption of new clothes rather than more solid achievement and by and large, the participants at international conferences are reluctant to assume the responsibility of decrying the practice.

Reflecting recognition of hydrology as an interdisciplinary subject, there has been in recent years an increasing reliance not on hydrologists, trained as such, but on teams of scientists trained in more basic disciplines, to whom are entrusted major research and development projects in hydrology. This development is most natural and commendable. There is of course a role for the hydrologist in such teams, but it must be admitted that this role diminishes in importance the further the problem being tackled is beyond existing experience. There remains of course the coordinating role - that of the conductor of the orchestra, for which the experience of the hydrologist should render him particularly fit. I think it is unlikely that the major problems of hydrology will, henceforth, be entrusted exclusively to hydrologists. Instead hydrologists will have to learn to work with and perhaps coordinate the work of interdisciplinary teams which will be assembled for specific purposes or for general hydrological research. The alternative of creating a Renaissance-type hydrologist, competent in all the basic sciences and experienced in their application, is to ask too much at least for the immediate future.

THE EDUCATION OF HYDROLOGISTS

Perhaps unique among the practitioners of applied sciences, hydrologists have not generally enjoyed an accepted, well-defined, educational preparation. Instead, hydrology is looked upon as a specialization within a number of wider disciplines, civil engineering, agricultural engineering, forestry, etc. These specializations differ from one another and are limited by the subject matter of each parent discipline.

It is probably true that most of the pioneers of hydrology, particularly those distinguished hydrologists of the immediate post war period, had little undergraduate training in hydrology and probably very little formal training in hydrology at any level. The ranks of hydrologists have always been replenished by a drifting in from other disciplines, and it must be recognized that many who came to hydrology in this way brought with them a consuming interest, a lively intelligence and sometimes an acquaintance with technologies which were relevant but previously unused in hydrology.

This however is not an orthodox way in which to build a profession. It would be better for hydrology if its distinct status were recognized and its practitioners trained in an appropriate manner, though not necessarily at the undergraduate level. The employment opportunities for hydrologists are probably too limited to justify the career commitment that an undergraduate course dealing exclusively with hydrology would imply. However, there is no reason why graduates in the physical sciences generally (in various mixes) should not become hydrologists through subsequent specialization by way of postgraduate courses. Astronomers are so trained; so generally speaking are geophysicists, using the term in the narrower sense. Geologists, however, are usually required to make a commitment at the undergraduate level. Perhaps because their subject is relatively descriptive, a less intensive training in the basic sciences is sufficient thus leaving room for the inclusion of some geology in undergraduate curricula. Hydrologists, however, have to learn a wide range of basic scientific material, become familiar with the scientific method and acquire the technological expertise of a profession. It is perhaps not surprising that the somewhat haphazard educational system which has evolved rather than been designed, for the education of hydrologists, has partially failed to meet these extensive requirements. The IASH-UNESCO Panel to which I referred above, distinguished between scientific hydrology and scientists on the one hand, recommending that they should be trained in university departments of geoscience, and applied hydrology and professional hydrologists on the other, recommending that "they should continue to be trained in postgraduate courses which should however provide an increased content of basic sciences and a greater variety of hydrological sub-fields. ..... efforts should be made to ensure that the developments in hydrological science achieved in geoscience departments are made available to the applied hydrologist, typically in engineering departments. Close contact should be established (between the two training systems)".

Without wishing to detract in any way from my commitment to that report, I confess that my present thinking would be to prefer a single hydrological stream (only exceptionally at the undergraduate level) normally drawing from graduates in engineering and science and providing for longer and more scientific training in the relevant basic sciences, but recognizing also the specific science of hydrology referred to above as the second pillar. I think that the defect in our present postgraduate courses lies largely in the inadequate preparation of the entrants and the inadequate duration of the courses themselves. If we could rely on obtaining good honors graduates in any of many combinations of science subjects or in engineering, and if we had these not for a single year or a year and a half, but for a two or three years, I believe we could overcome all the present difficulties and in time the standards would rise so that the graduates would be capable of fulfilling both the scientific and professional roles and the continuation of both through teaching.

Where an undergraduate training is feasible, I would consider that this might be provided as an option within the general civil engineering or environmental engineering framework. With a greater emphasis on physics and chemistry, some introduction to botany, about the present amount of geology, some geophysics and hydrology in the narrow (or basic) sense, a very good training could be provided in a typical four year degree programme if room were found in the syllabi, by renouncing the structural engineering elements and other, optional, courses which are, typically, provided in contemporary civil engineering programmes.

Engineering hydrologists trained to this level in their undergraduate courses would be eminently suitable for higher training as hydrologists even in relatively short postgraduate courses. Moreover they would not lose their designation as civil (or environmental) engineers, thus preserving their wider job suitability. Indeed, I would feel that such graduates, within the general civil or environmental engineering fields, would be at least as well trained for general employment in those fields as are the typical present graduates trained on a surfeit of structural mechanics to a level which very few ever use.

Awareness of the Environment

I would like to finish these musings with some reference to the necessity to inculcate an awareness of the environment during the training of hydrologists. The work of the hydrologist may often and severely impinge on the environment. There may be consequences outside the immediate concern or interest of the hydrologist which on that account may be neglected. This is not to say that there is another science - environmental science - whose practitioners must be given a veto on water resources development or indeed on any development. An adequate training for a general purpose environmental scientist would require a very long period of scientific training indeed and students of wide interests and abilities. If it is difficult to train hydrologists, it would be even more difficult to train environmental scientists to any useful level. Yet we do need an environmental awareness not only in hydrology but in many activities.

Acceptance that what we mean by an "environmental awareness" is a concern for the total effects of our work or proposals, rather than a concern limited to our own immediate interests, suggests that this might be supplied by extending the concern of the specific professional rather than creating a new profession of environmentalist. When the Directors of some UNESCO sponsored international postgraduate hydrology courses were asked by UNEP to consider, as an experiment, the inclusion of an environmental component in their courses, it was suggested that this should be done through

(1)   the inclusion of a specific environmental impact course;

(2)   emphasizing environmental effects in all of the courses being taught.

I have no quarrel with the second suggestion, except to say that not all subjects could be taught in a manner involving a consciousness of environmental effect. I do however feel that it is not possible to define a suitable course to meet the first suggestion. I feel that the requirements of such a course would be so wide, and to be useful so deep, that there would be room for nothing else in a typical postgraduate hydrology course. The cuckoo of the environment would push the legitimate hydrological offspring out of the nest. I believe that the solution must be sought in a different direction. Hydrologists must become aware of environmental impact through the deepening and widening of their interests as hydrologists. It is not necessary, or possible, to become everything else, or even something else in addition to becoming hydrologists. The better we are as hydrologists, the more accurately will we foresee the consequences on the environment of our works and proposals, and if our general education is adequate we will realize the necessity to inform or consult with experts in other areas and to inform appropriate authorities. The solution lies not in the creation of a new science, profession or discipline and certainly not a band wagon, but in the extension of the competence of professional hydrologists in their own domain through greater acquaintance with the natural sciences and the scientific method.

REFERENCES

Nash J.E., P.S. Eagleson, J.R. Philip and W.H. van der Molen *The education of hydrologists (Report of the IASH-UNESCO Panel),* Hydrological Sciences Journal 35, b, 12/1990.

Nash J.E., *Real Hydrology* Report no. 20, Institute of Hydrology, Wallingford, Oxon, U.K.

EDUCATION IN WATER RESOURCES UNDER CONTINUAL EVOLUTION IN THEIR PROBLEMS AND IN SOCIETY'S ATTITUDES AND DEMANDS

Vujica Yevjevich
Professor Emeritus of Civil Engineering
Colorado State University
Fort Collins, Colorado 80523, USA

ABSTRACT

Evolution in information, technology, human needs and society's attitude and demand, require adjustments in education of water resources professionals. Professionals are either specialists or generalists. Nine cases of evolution in water resources problems and solutions demonstrate how they influence the needs for an improved education. The increased pollution and resulting efforts to protect environment has created controversies which significantly influence the approaches for water resources development, conservation, control and protection. Demands for decrease and control of pollution have transformed planning and operation of water resources systems. The release of gases into atmosphere eventually leads to climatic change, with river runoff considered attractive for monitoring this change, and water resources development helping to counteract the negative aspects of the change. Aging of water resources structures poses new technological and economic challenges to water resources professionals. Pressures to extract the maximal benefit at the minimal cost from existing water resources systems require the well educated specialists of many disciplines. As the society may not tolerate some high risks of water resources projects, structures and systems, the risk abating and optimization have been put on social agenda in many countries. With time, increased clashes occur between opposite interests, proponents and opponents of water resources projects, which require efficient application of conflict resolution methods. Requests for reallocation of water rights are current in several parts of the world, which need efficient solution methods and approaches. Because of versatile and increased trends in pollution worldwide, strategies for procurement of drinking water should change in many cases. Resulting complexities in solutions of these nine water resources aspects, problems and needs should lead to adjustments in future education of water resources professionals.

1. Classic Education and Selection of Professionals for Water Resources Activities

The classic education of professionals for water resources activities is based on a fundamental principle, namely of orienting the involved professionals to become either the relatively narrow specialists or the broad generalists. That will likely continue to be a necessary approach because of an ever-increasing complexity of water resources systems and problems. Specialists have come from various but limited number of scientific and technologic disciplines, with hydraulic and environmental engineering being in a kind of the center of needed specialization. Generalists have come from any of a broad variety of disciplines.

Specialists in hydraulic engineering, considered as a part of civil engineering, had to undergo a very detailed education in fluid mechanics and hydraulics. That discipline enabled them to treat properly the movement of water in nature, and along, over, through, around and beneath the hydraulic and other structures. They needed the most advanced knowledge in hydrology, on laws and regularities of distribution of water in space and time. That enable them to assess the characteristics of water supply and of hydrologic extremes in nature. They needed fundamental knowledge on geology, soil and rock mechanics, and the other aspects of geotechnics. They had to be versed in geophysical methods of investigation, in order to acquire information on environment in which a water resources system was to be created and operated. The knowledge of materials and principles of their use was a further aspect of the specialist's education. The design technology usually happened to be the highest level of specialist's education. It involved safety, risk and economics of decisions on composition and dimensions of structures in a system. They had to know how to assess water quality and quantity demands, how to match properly supply and demand by water transfers in time and space, and how to analyze the economic aspects of water resources projects.

The other important specialists involved with water resources development included hydrometeorologists, hydrogeologists, mechanical and electrical engineers, biological and chemical water quality specialists, agronomists, foresters, economists, water law specialists, recreationists and many other professionals for specific problems of water resources projects. In recent decades, the environmental specialists, particularly ecologists, geographers, chemists, biologists and others became involved with the specific aspects of water resources projects. The list of all narrow but marginal specializations involved with the particular aspects of water resources projects would be relatively long.

It may be a safe assertion that leaders in water resources planning and operation had to be most often professionals as the self-educated generalists. In developing countries, they usually came from engineering profession, often from hydraulic engineering. In some countries these engineers even attained the highest political position of prime ministers, because of services made to population as leaders in water resources. In developed countries, they usually evolved from any specialization related to water resources activities, if an individual had the leadership qualities. The particular help may have been a degree from a school on management, economics or administration. Two or more master degrees, one in engineering and another in management or economics, may have propelled an individual with general education to such a position. The versatile experience in variety of water resources systems and problem solutions usually helped. In practice, these generalists have come to prominence by their capabilities to integrate talent and specialization of various kinds. They must have an instinct for human qualities and weaknesses. They need a good grasp of complexities of water resources systems and problems. They should know how to resolve conflicts and to make compromise of opposite requests or interests. They must know how to relate to various kinds of people in general public and to professionals.

2. Evolution in Society's Attitude and Demand, with their Effects on Education of Water Resources Professionals

As a society evolves in particular ways at different times, with new attitudes and demands on water resources, so the education of professionals must also evolve. The adjustment in educational curriculum for new profiles of professionals should always precede the projected need of new types of specialists and generalists in water resources activities whenever feasible. Several fundamental evolutions related to water resources have occurred in the last 25-50 years, or can be safely projected to happen in the near future. They already require adjustments in profiles of water resources professionals.

Water resources development implies that change in nature must occur. Solutions of related problems require structures for water transfer in space from places of supply to places of demand. The water transfer in time is needed from weeks or months of surplus in supply to weeks or months of deficit in demand. The change in water energy potential and the change in water quality from those available in nature to those imposed by water demand are also necessary. Any developmental change in nature is also defined as the environmental change. The relationship of society to these changes has evolved in such a way that often any change may be conceived as an undesirable impact on nature, to be eventually opposed by environmental movements. It is progressed to the point that many water resources projects of sound economic and environmental solutions are routinely opposed and as a consequence projects are delayed or abandoned. To resolve these high controversies all around the world, the well educated professionals, both as specialists of various kinds and as very progressive generalists, are needed. To accomplish this task, education must also be tailored to these new problems.

Society was willing, or was forced, to pay the cost of extraction or synthesis of chemicals needed for industrial and agricultural products or for services, because the cost was built into the price of a product or a service. Society was not asked for, or compelled to, pay the eventual cost of harmless disposal of various remnants of manufactured products or of services made. Neither it had to pay the price of avoiding harmful effects in disposing products and accessories after their use. Remnants, discarded products and accessories were simply dumped into the environment or temporarily stored in various, usually unsafe and cheap, ways. Then the natural process of degradation in time released them into the general environment, namely into air, water, soil, rocks and biomass. Thus, the modern industrial age compounded manyfold the old human process of polluting environment and making the other damages. The 1950's years are usually considered as the watershed at which people became fully aware that environmental problems could no more be neglected without a heavy price. That awareness also affected planning of water resources development, conservation, control and protection. With time, significant controversies arose between water resources development and environmental protection. This is, or will be, affecting education of all professionals active in water resources.

The emission of industrial gases into atmosphere, including the carbon-based gases (carbon dioxide, methane and others), are found to endanger the ozone layer of atmosphere, to produce acid rains and to eventually warm up the lower layer of atmosphere by the greenhouse effect. All these consequences are considered by the majority of investigators as harmful, with a multitude of proposals advanced how to mitigate or eliminate these effects. Acid rains affect forests and water quality of lakes, rivers and aquifers. General prediction by the atmospheric models claim that the greenhouse warming phenomenon will affect the agricultural and water resources systems, mainly in negative ways. While the prediction of ozone layer threat and the acid rain occurrence seems justified, prediction of threatening danger of the carbon dioxide greenhouse effect is not yet accepted as definitive by a part of community of climatologists and environmentalists. Climatic change with their effects on water resources systems and the future development of water resources has become the most recent topic to be seriously considered by specialists on water resources and environment. These topics will likely occupy many water resources planners and will influence the formation of future professionals, either specialists or generalists.

The unavoidable aging of water resources structures and systems, after about 50-150 years of service, has created numerous not only technical but also economic and safety problems in all the countries of the world. Billions of dollars are needed to replace or overhaul the urban water supply, drainage and sewage treatment and removal systems. Dams, weirs, canals, pipes, wells, locks, levees, hydromechanical equipment and machines, river training structures, require worldwide either the expected costly outright replacement or the regular but substantial overhaul. This cost is in a tough competition for funds with investments into the new water resources systems. These mature structures and systems pose already many problems for which the classic education of water resources specialists and generalists may not provide knowledge for the accurate and inexpensive solutions.

Trends and pressures are unavoidable to "squeeze out" as much benefit from the existing water resources structures and systems as theoretically feasible, once they were finished and in operation. They require such an advanced knowledge and a particular accuracy in solutions, which the ongoing education often does not provide. In other words, the expectation is often generated in many institutions, society and with investors that modern information theory, systems analysis, operational research, computer technology, forecast technology, expert systems and other contemporaneous innovations and improvements would be able to do what the classic technologies of planning, design and operation have not been able to accomplish. Though the ongoing educational curricula usually covers these advanced technologies, their several aspects and usefulness in practice are still controversial between theoreticians and practitioners.

The more advanced an economy, the less ready a society is to accept high risks. As water resources projects involve various types of events which carry with them the unavoidable risks, pressures continually build up to decrease those risks at the least expense to society. These requests are well justified in order to lower risks whenever impacts of potential risk producing events threaten an ever increasing population, wealth and investment. Risk abating is a new speciality which deserves a better position in education of specialists than now. Complexity in assessing risks and diversity in approaches to finding the optimal risk in their abatement at any stage of economic and demographic development require very well educated water resources professionals.

Most water resources projects in the world are in public domain. These projects are often conceived as largeness of government to be tapped by individuals or groups. It is not surprising that many individuals and institutions have become tempted to maximally benefit either from future products of these projects, or from compensation at the maximum possible level for any damage, property expropriation or inconvenience. Multiple controversies arise between the purposes of these projects and the real or construed interests of involved parties. Litigations often make both, a delay in realization of a project and an increase in its overall cost. In the final analysis, both lead to a decrease of the benefit-cost ratio, or in the net difference of benefit and cost. The evolving discipline of conflict resolution is an integration of solutions of a myriad of cases of such controversies in various domains of development of natural resources and the solution of societal problems. Somewhere along the educational process an opportunity should be available for water resources professionals to obtain full insight into this new discipline of conflict resolution. It may be well compensated by a fast implementation of projects and their lower costs.

Water in nature is limited in its availability. Many areas of the world have already reached the state that total water or its hydropower potential have been already allocated through governmental decisions, concessions or contracts. This state of affairs may become a barrier to further economic and social progress. New societal or economic needs for water may than be difficult to satisfy, if there is no well-defined mechanism for the reallocation of water rights. The reallocation may be carried out either through market forces by considering water as a commodity, namely to be freely sold, or water rights to be purchased or revoked by the government and reallocated to new water purposes. These transfers of water rights require the most advanced knowledge of the way how to resolve of variety of related political, economic, technical and legal problems.

The prevailing hypothesis of people and professionals in relation to supply of safe drinking water is that springs and aquifers represent the best sources of that water. In many cases of industrial advanced societies this assumption may be no more valid. Some of these springs and groundwaters already belong to the most polluted sources of water. This fact must then lead to the change in attitudes and concepts, as well as in the education of specialists in water resources and sanitary engineering.

The classic education in water resources seems to have left the above nine areas of needed education for water resources professionals to be mastered in practice by a trial-and-error method. The main assumption in this approach may have been that formal education should essentially cover only those disciplines and their subjects which can not be easily mastered by the day-to-day practical work. The work experience, special courses within water resources institutions or consulting firms, the continuing education by special programs or courses at learning institutions and the self-education, seem to have been used as the ways to solve this educational problem. To some extent it was successfully done, though many ongoing problems with water resources development and its controversies may imply the opposite conclusion.

The above described nine subjects are looked at in the further text from the viewpoints of complexities and diversities of solutions and educational needs. These nine subjects are: changes in environment by water resources development, environmental pollution, repercussion of climatic change on water resources and their structures and systems, aging of structures and systems, better operation and utilization of existing systems, risk abatement problems, clash of interests with conflict resolution in water resources development, reallocation of water rights and needed change in strategies of drinking water supply. Singling out these nine topics does not mean that several other areas of evolution with water resources development do not merit a proper attention in education. Education is conceived here in its formal and informal components. The continuing education outside of regulated formal education is particularly considered as an increasingly attractive vehicle to build such capabilities in the community of water resources professionals, that the needed water resources development, conservation, control and protection may be smoothly performed in the future.

3. Controversies between Water Resources Development and Protection of Environment

The evolution of environmental movements has gone from the simple goal of protecting environment, with a search for a proper balance between that protection and economic growth, to a fulfillment of visions of social engineers on how the society should develop and be organized. They oppose most of classic purposes of water resources development and their implementation, though these water resources developments may in most cases be considered as sound environmental activities (building reservoirs with recreation; treatment of waste waters; maintaining clean rivers, lakes and aquifers; supply of clean water). Controversies between the environmental protection and water resources development, conservation, control and protection have increased recently to include nearly every aspect in using these natural resources for the betterment of humanity. These controversies have become philosophical, political, social, economic, ecological, aesthetic, archaeological, cultural, technological, or simply of the operational nature.

The main philosophical controversy between the involved individuals, groups and institutions refers to the type of relationship which humans should have with nature, namely whether nature should fully control humanity, or humans should also partially control nature. Political, social and economic controversies result from concepts on how to develop water resources without the detrimental impacts on environment, or that benefits of this development significantly outweigh the eventual negative effects on environment. Ecological controversies are based on the premise that any intrusion or change in water environments may, or definitely will, alter the ecological balance, and that it most often becomes detrimental. Aesthetics is the most difficult aspect of controversies, since the lake may be more beautiful to a viewer than a running muddy river, or the opposite, and a canyon may be considered much more valuable beauty than meadows, plains or hills. Preservation of archaeological sites and cultural monuments may collide with basic premises of water resources activities. Technologic controversies are related to the use of new or old methods or equipment which may damage or alter the environment. Or, the way how water resources structures are operated or measures implemented may be adversely reflected on the environment.

Major impacts of water resources projects on the environment, as sources of controversies and litigations, result on water quantity side from water storage with inundation of land, induced changes in fluctuation of water flow and water level, changes due to coping with floods and droughts, activities that use water head for hydropower, diversion of water from rivers, lakes and reservoirs, decrease of flows with their detrimental effects, and similar activities. On the water quality side, the present state of affairs may be changed by river dredging, sediment increase or decrease, use of water to evacuate pollutants or sewage from cities, industries, mines, roads, thus altering water quality which becomes environmentally detrimental. Combined quantitative-qualitative changes created by water resources projects are often unavoidable, since any quantitative change in water regime may affect water quality and the ecological balance. It should be understood that changes in nature by water resources projects are both beneficial and detrimental to the environment. Among the beneficial aspects are the preservation of natural beauty, protection of ecological balance, enhancement of recreational values of various natural assets, protection of water quality, protection of habitats for wildlife and fish, and similar impacts which are important for a healthy environment.

Abundant literature is available on various aspects of environmental changes, positive or negative, as the results of human activities, especially in developing and utilizing the natural resources. Myriads of cases of controversy, legal litigations and resolutions by arbitration or negotiation present the general picture of the state of relationship. Already the specialized individuals and firms in water resources serve as legal or technical experts to courts and arbitration panels. However, one rarely finds a systematic presentation of past cases of controversy between the water resources development and the protection of environment. Neither it gives a systematic review how these controversies have been resolved in the past. Neither the available literature gives yet an exhaustive listing of all types of effects of water resources development on the environment, which might become controversial. Nor it gives all the general changes in the environment (say through urbanization, land use, deforestation and similar activities), which either occurred in the past or have potential to happen in the future, with the significant effects on water resources regimes and developments.

Projects of dams and reservoirs have been abandoned or not approved for construction because of resistance by environmentalists for various reasons. Diversions of water, especially of the transmountain types, have been stopped. Dredgings have been also fought against. Drainage of swamps has been successfully resisted. Location of structures have been changed or their sizes decreased. Flood control projects have been opposed or modified. The list of controversies and defeats of water resources projects are numerous. What all this means for the performance of water resources planners and designers is that the new era of environmental consciousness and militancy in opposing water resources projects could be only resolved and counteracted, whenever feasible, with good arguments by adding a new dimension in the education of water resources professionals. The trend in education must then be "an environmentally sound water resources planning, design, construction, maintenance and operation." To do that, special courses based on the best written texts, or the general professional books, respectively for the formal and informal educational components, should produce the environmentally sensitive water resources professionals.

4. Water Resources and Pollution of Environment

Water in nature contains dissolved minerals and biological matter, which come mainly from the surface, soil and rock phases of the water cycle, apart from the atmosphere. Most sources of drinking water for humans had the tolerable mineral contents of non-detrimental compounds until recently. The major problem in treating waters required the removal of the biological matter, especially of viruses, bacteria, planktons and remnants of dead plants and animal species. The primary and secondary treatments of waters from nature, with filtration and chlorination or ozone treatment, have been sufficient to produce the safe drinking water. With industrialization and a continual increase in the use of chemicals in industry, agriculture and various services, these chemicals find their ways into waters of nature. Airborne or coming via surface and underground ways, the water chemical contents became with time as important as the biological pollutants have been in the past. In many cases the water has to undergo the tertiary treatment, namely the removal of chemicals. This fact made the treatment of water for drinking purposes more expensive than when only the secondary treatment was sufficient. Many new chemicals, introduced into the nature by human activities, are toxins, carcinogens, poisonous compounds, and as the other noxious or detrimental materials.

Many rivers have become large sewers. Aquifers have been polluted. Groundwaters adjacent to rivers were affected by a regular exchange of water with polluted rivers. Limestone karst water systems and aquifers have often been used for sewage and other waste removal by dumping them into sinkholes, thus polluting not only water but also the walls and bottoms of underground channels, caverns and rock fissures. In some cases the surface pollutants migrate during the rain or melting of snow into these karst systems. The experience with pumping out of the polluted waters from aquifers in the United States of America is very instructive. These aquifers were polluted by leakage of chemicals from dumps of industrial chemicals or from garbage deposits. To clean aquifers, pumping of water out of them was undertaken in a large number of cases. Results have been usually disappointing. The concentration of pollutants after a long and expensive pumping have been significantly reduced, however to be again restored approximately to the original concentration after the pumping was interrupted for a sufficient time. The only explanation could be that pollutants have been stored in underground on surfaces of solid particles from which the aquifer is made. Similarly, sediments full of polluting chemicals, which have been deposited on bottoms of lakes, reservoirs, ponds, karst caverns, estuaries and seas leak pollutants for a long time, regardless of inflow of new sediments without these polluting chemicals.

The last quarter of a century has been characterized in industrial countries by the major activity of cleaning waters and water environments from pollutants. It is anticipated that another half a century will be needed to accomplish the general goal of relatively clean waters and clean water environments of rivers, lakes, reservoirs, ponds, aquifers, estuaries, coastal waters. All will, however, depend on the leaking behavior of myriad of dumps of buried industrial waste containers, and of large dumps of urban wastes, regardless of safeguards undertaken. The major problem will likely be the pollution by agricultural chemicals, because it will be decided by a compromise between protection of the environment and feeding of the expanding world population.

Water quality problems and their solutions have now outpaced the classic sanitary engineering activities of treating waters to become drinking water or suitable water for industrial and other uses, as well as treating sewage waters, and waste waters after various uses. Good water quality in nature has become the symbol of a healthy environment, not only for humans but also for animals and plants. To accomplish this task, the advanced and comprehensive water quality monitoring has become a necessity for good planning and implementation of measures to attain a healthy water environment. Even a new hydrologic science or subdiscipline of hydrology is being shaped at present. Namely, "water quality hydrology" has become concerned with investigations of processes in nature and the nature's responses to various human interventions, positive or negative, which lead to the given water quality characteristics as they are distributed in space and time. This new hydrologic subdiscipline should produce the necessary information on water quality, while the various existing or emerging technologies in treating waters will represent a new dimension in water resources planning, design, construction, maintenance and operation.

The formal education of water resources professionals has always included the course curricula on water quality and groundwater subjects, however this latter subject essentially studied from the geological, geophysical, geochemical, hydrologic, hydraulic and water utilization viewpoints. The excessive groundwater pollution, its cleaning and further needed protection, have been added as the new significant aspects of water resources tasks and activities in the last quarter of the century. The experience with rehabilitation of polluted aquifers has been the major practical educational vehicle, though recently more formal and informal courses worldwide have meant a full attention to education of professionals. It is quite likely that the future balance between the protection of aquifers from agricultural pollution and the cheapest production of food and fiber will require the well educated specialists in groundwater cleaning and protection.

5. Climatic Change and Water Resources Development

The overall relationship between the eventual climatic change and the general water resources activities may be divided into three major groups: (i) Whether river runoff may be used as the most reliable variable and process which would help to identify or discriminate how much the climatic change has occurred; (ii) What influences if any the climatic change has and will exercised on water resources, first on water in nature and then on the existing water resources systems and structures; and (iii) Whether, where, how and how much the water resources systems and technologies could help to mitigate or eliminate the general negative consequences of the eventual climatic change.

Current claims on climatic changes refer to temperature and precipitation. Outputs of atmospheric or atmospheric-oceanic computer-based models are predicting at present that arid regions of the world will become drier (with greater temperature and smaller precipitation than now). Also, they predict that the general greenhouse warming up of the atmosphere will melt some permanent ice and snow, and thus raise the ocean level. All these expected changes have yet to be properly monitored and unmistakenly proven. If these predictions came to be true, their effects on water resources must be assessed and the corresponding measures undertaken to mitigate them. If significant relations exist between water resources development and the consequences of climatic change, and they could be quantitatively established, water resources development may in turn become one of the most important countermeasures in alleviating these general consequences of warming up.

As the river runoff integrates precipitation and evaporation, it may serve as the monitoring stochastic variable on whether the effect of eventual warming increases or decreases the net water budget of a river basin. Only in case the change in precipitation is equal to the change in evaporation in a river basin, runoff could not detect any change. By parallelly studying precipitation over a river basin, this particular case can be also detected. The World Meteorological Organization has therefore attempted to use river flows as an eventual control variable of climatic change. At present, the German Hydrological Service gathers and stores for WMO data on runoff of the selected river gauging stations from all around the world.

The use of runoff as the monitoring random variable and process faces the main problem of errors in data: random, systematic and sampling errors, as well as the non-homogeneity in data caused by versatile human activities and disruptions of nature. Monthly runoff values seem less reliable as the detection variable than the annual values, mainly due to many seasonal water flow regulations in large river basins. Critical aspects for the assessment of accuracy of the eventually detected change are: (i) Selection of gauging stations with the longest and most accurate data; (ii) Feasibility of the eventual correction for the identified non-homogeneity in data; and (iii) Selection of the most appropriate change-discriminating statistical methods and techniques. As an example, the long record gauging station of the Rhine River at Basle, Switzerland, with instrumentally obtained data for 183 years (1908-1990), does not show any significant change in the annual river flow. Similarly, the Gota River in Sweden, with the similarly long and reliable record of annual flows, shows neither a significant change. Many rivers in the world already are gauged for 100 years or more. Some of them may be safely selected as having the reliable annual runoff series for the purpose of climatic change detection.

The world has invested tremendous capital into agricultural productivity, industrial infrastructure and various water resources systems. This economic infrastructure maintains the standards of living and supports the ongoing civilizations. The essential question here becomes how the claimed ongoing or forthcoming climatic changes would affect this infrastructure in general, and water resources in particular? The arid areas (such as the Great Plains of the United States, the Prairies of Canada, the arid lands of Mexico, the Pumpa of Argentina, and the arid lands of other parts of the world) have attained a relatively high levels of agricultural production. If it comes out to be true, that these areas would become much warmer and much drier than at present because of climatic change, the agriculture would suffer enormously. The main question becomes then should all the nations with agriculturally productive arid regions start immediately to plan and implement massive irrigation projects, even with water diversion from large rivers hundreds and thousands of kilometers away? The dilemma then becomes, either to completely stop further increases in greenhouse warming with tremendous investments and efforts, which may be politically and economically nearly impossible, or to use only a small portion of these investments to stabilize agriculture production in these large arid areas at a still higher level of productivity than at present?

Some countries are finding already economical to develop irrigation in their semi-humid and humid regions for the purpose of stabilizing the agricultural production at the level of production of the best of the years even during dry years. Why should not then be economically justified for countries to stabilize the agricultural production in arid regions at the optimal but highest levels, and in the same time to mitigate the consequences of the eventual climatic change? Furthermore, should the outputs of existing water resources systems be revised according to predicted climatic changes, with a decrease or an increase of the expected future average production? Should the economic aspects of these systems be completely revised? Should the measures be immediately implemented to avoid the eventual economic hardships for the owners of these systems? To answer positively to these questions, decision makers must have a very hard evidence that the climatic change will definitely occur, if it is not already occurring.

Prediction of the forthcoming raise of ocean level because of the greenhouse warming of the lower atmosphere poses a fundamental dilemma. Namely, whether defense of coastal areas should be planned and implemented now? Similarly, whether the coastal water resources systems and structures should be immediately adjusted to this predicted change? Or, should one trust the claim that all costs involved with the decrease of warming should be proportionally much smaller than the cost of these adjustments, made when one has already full confidence in the predicted forthcoming raise of the ocean level? These are tough questions to be reliably answered.

Proposals are made on governmental levels now, to significantly decrease emissions of carbon-based gases to fight the greenhouse warming. However, the opposite hypothesis should be also investigated, namely that non-noxious carbon-based gases in the air will significantly increase the future agricultural and forest production, as the geologic history and recent experiments testify. The alternative to the large investment and losses because of reduction of these emissions is to allow these gases to increase, with warming up problems to be solved by the three essential types of action, not only to fight the consequences of emission of gases and greenhouse warming, but also to obtain some other multiple benefits. They are: (i) To reduce only the noxious and detrimental gases emitted into the air by the industrial and energy production, which threaten the ozone layer and create the acid rain; (ii) To increase massively the irrigation worldwide, especially in arid regions, say from the present about 300 million hectares to the future 750-1000 million hectares, as well as to increase the other water supplies, thus to transfer water from oceans to continents and keep ocean level lower; and (iii) To significantly increase the water stored in various unproductive spaces at continental surfaces and in their underground, thus to also transfer water from oceans to continents. These three types of actions will remove the ozone layer threat and the acid rains, but also would avoid the fall of agricultural production of arid lands and the threat of raising of ocean level.

The budget of water retained on continents and islands is related to budgets of water in atmosphere and oceans. Reservoirs, ponds, increase of lake and aquifer levels, irrigation and other water supplies, represent an increase in continental water budget and a decrease of ocean level. Overpumping of aquifers, decrease of lake levels, and drainage of swamps have the opposite effect. The first developments seem of much larger effect on the continental land surfaces than the second. This change of water budget on continents because of human activities has received a relatively little attention, though data for this type of studies are already available. Future activities such as building of reservoirs, recharge of aquifers, irrigation and other water supplies, will represent a decrease of the ocean level.

Apart from the ongoing needs for water storage, many special projects may significantly increase the water stored on continents with the corresponding sea level decrease. Special projects of water storage would include: (i) use of large continental depressions for large reservoirs (such as Qattara, Dead Sea, etc.), with production of energy, sea water minerals, change in micro climate; (ii) building of immense reservoirs in distant cold regions for hydropower and then hydrogen production, as clean energy sources; (iii) creation of large reservoirs in desertic region whenever feasible (cheap inundated land, water available close by for diversion to reservoirs, irrigation, hydropower, change of microclimate, etc.); (iv) artificial recharge of large aquifers by water diversion (such as the potential recharge of the Ogallala aquifer of the Great Plains of USA by waters from the Upper Missouri or the other rivers); and (v) building of large reservoirs for water storage for irrigation of the additional 450-700 million hectares.

To accomplish the above gigantic tasks, eventually assigned to water resources professionals and to both the generalists-planners and the specialists-designers, their educational level should be significantly raised. The reason is simple. Problems to be solved will be much more complex and difficult, either technologically or economically or environmentally than most of the ongoing problems. To prove that the water resources route in solving the eventual warming-up problems was much more attractive from many standpoints, particularly environmental and economic, than to just stop using the fossil fuels as the energy sources, needs the best planning and technological brains that could be mastered. First, it must be proven that the hypothesis, of solving the major consequences of the eventual greenhouse warming of lower atmosphere by water resources developments and a large number of special projects, should be accepted. Second, it should be proven that the water resources alternative is much less costly on the long run than the alternative with the major efforts to stop burning of fossil fuels and replacing those energy sources by the much more costly alternatives. Even if it comes out that forecasts of the size of climatic change came out to be exaggerated, the water resources alternative might be justified only by all the other benefits that it would produce.

6. Aging of Water Resources Structures and Systems

The simple premise, namely that each structure and each system must have its finite life, and that it will age with time, is the sound assumption which planners and designers should always respect and keep in mind in their activities. One can ask an appropriate question, namely how many planners and designers of the new systems and structures, respectively, have seriously taken into account in what way the systems and structures would be rehabilitated once they have sufficiently aged, either from the safety or from the production and operation standpoints? The aging is not only the result of the usual wear and tear processes, namely of corrosion and erosion, but it also occurs by fatigue and general deterioration of materials, break down of connections between components, obsolescence of equipment, various breaks and failures, geotechnical creeping failures, etc. If the concrete is only about 100 years old as the construction material, does anybody could guarantee that it will serve 200 or 300 years? Did anybody envision in design of water supply and sewage treatment and removal systems in Boston, or New York, or Mexico City, how they will be rehabilitated or replaced in the most economically, environmentally and technologically sound ways, once they have been declared as deteriorated?

Social infrastructures, consisting of buildings, highways, railroads, bridges, airports, harbors, dams, weirs, canals, locks, wells and others, need systematic overhaul, rehabilitation, repair and regular maintenance. It is easy to give the precedence to investment into the new infrastructures at the expense of maintaining the existing ones at the full safety and operation states. Many water resources structures and systems, especially the urban water resources systems, are in such a poor state of aging, that treated water is massively lost, its contamination often unavoidable, repairs sketchy and insufficient. The classic dilemma may be then whether these systems should be occasionally patched up as the need arises, or they should be completely replaced. And if the replacement comes out to be the optimal solution, how the new system should avoid shortcomings of the old one? And, how to take into account all the characteristics of sound environmental solutions, the use of advanced technology at the reasonable cost, and the smooth operation with the well conceived maintenance techniques? All these tasks require not only the classic education of water resources professionals, but also some new information and special technologies needed in overhauling and upgrading of the existing infrastructures.

The solution of educational problems associated with rehabilitation of aged or aging water resources structures and systems looks most attractive by an on-the-site or informal education. For that purpose, internal courses on various specific aspects of rehabilitation of aged structures within the operational and maintenance agencies or consortia may be the most effective way to provide for the competent work. For the most difficult aspects of rehabilitation or replacement of the aged systems and structures, the special advanced courses at high learning institutions would likely give more insight into the critical aspects of this work than the narrowly conceived internal courses of agencies and consortia. This would be especially appropriate when good and comprehensive books on these subjects become available as the course texts.

7. Extraction of Maximal Benefit from Existing Water Resources Systems

Expectations of general public to extract the maximal benefit from the existing governmental water resources systems, or of shareholders of private companies the benefit from their water projects, require serious efforts by professionals. The objective should be the extraction of all the potential benefit from a system or a project with the minimal operational and maintenance cost. The underlining premise is that the new or evolving information on water supply, water demand and the state of the system, the evolution in the society's attitudes, the innovation in technology and change in environmental requirements would justify expectations. Difficulties in raising the capital for additional capacities of existing or new systems often require from water resources professionals to undertake the responsible task of proving that existing facilities have been fully utilized, and conservation methods could no more decrease water or energy demands.

The next step in the sequence of solving the problems of matching demand and supply should follow, namely the expectation that the existing systems and capacities may be economically enlarged. Only when the most trusted professionals clearly document that all alternatives of expansion, improvement and streamlining of operation have been exhausted, the public will not object to using taxes or bond issues, or the shareholder to further invest money, for the new water resources system or project. Here comes the classic dilemma between improvement of the existing and building of the new.

Problems in extraction of maximal benefit from a system or a project, with the minimal operational and maintenance cost, result mainly from the potential shortcomings made in planning, design and construction and from an insufficient analysis of economics and safety of the system or the project. These problems may also be generated by the change in original information, technology and environmental laws and solutions. It often may occur that all the components of a system were not properly sized to function at the same capacity, because component of the minimal capacity dictates the system's productivity. New technological methods may show the potential for the economical increase of benefit and some cost decrease. Automation, mechanization, miniaturization, computerization, and the application of other innovations have been shown to accomplish some of these expectations of the public and/or shareholders.

Therefore, it should be a current practice of any operational organization of water resources systems or projects to routinely review all their aspects of performance occasionally. Particularly, this review should include the objective of increasing production and benefit while decreasing their cost, say by doing it every five years, or more or less often depending on the system's or project's characteristics. The main objective should always be to improve or maximize the benefit-cost ratio, or their difference, especially by using forecasts of water supply and water demand, as well as the most advanced operational technologies.

To extract the maximal benefit from a system or a project, often special investigations and applied research are required for specific aspects of the state and performance of that system or project. Operational organizations, run-of-the mill consulting firms, headquarters of governmental agencies and main offices of companies or corporations may not have the capacity or know-how or both, to successfully undertake those investigations or the needed applied research. Therefore, teams of selected specialists from institutions of research, technology development, design and operation may produce the most effective solution, if led by a good generalist. The ongoing formal and informal education of water resources professionals may or may not include the essential principles of how to review the state and the performance of the existing systems or projects for purposes of maximization of the benefit and minimization of the cost. These principles should be a part of any advanced continuing education of decision makers who are responsible for the general operation of important systems or projects. Particularly, the role of analysis of past performance and data on future operation, the effect of forecasts, the role of systems analysis, the experience with the behavior and specific demands from users of the system's products and similar aspects of the system, deserve the full attention in any review of performance and state of the system. In this approach, one uses the power of the human brain and all new data and innovated technologies in order to increase the benefit-cost ratio, rather than to invest into the completely new facilities.

8. Estimation and Abatement of Risks

Water resources structures and systems are inherently subject of many risks, either internal or external. All natural disasters may affect a structure or system (such as earthquake, flood, drought, landslide, avalanche, hurricane, etc.) as the external source of risk. Failure of materials, failure of foundations, miscalculation of dimensions, fatigue phenomenon, represent the internal source of risk. The design and decision process starts from the simple and sound hypothesis, namely that in most cases of these risks it is nearly impossible to completely avoid them, though it is always possible to decrease them with higher cost of problem solution. Therefore, there must always be a problem of how to optimize the solution between the level of the final design risk and the cost of accomplishing it. Nobody can prove that any design earthquake or any design flood could not be exceeded.

Assumptions, requirements, data and other information inputs into the risk optimization process may change with time. In many cases, the growth of wealth, endangered by a failure of a water resources structure, affects the risk/cost optimization equation. Simply, the potential damage to the new wealth from the design-risk event may be significantly greater than the one originally assessed. Therefore, the risk level should be revised and where technically and economically feasible also reduced to the new economically optimal risk level.

The main problem may consist of difficulties to physically decrease a risk without a large cost. The best example may be the designed and constructed spillways at many large dams in the United States of America. New calculations of needed spillway capacities now would require reconstructions which may exceed the total cost of 20 billion dollars. Planners of dams and designers of those flood evacuation spillways and outlets did not even dream in the past that their calculations, designs and constructions must change in the future because of various evolutions, innovations, change in risk tolerance by people and change in information. Otherwise, their design in the past would be quite different, more flexible to allow for the future revision of design-risk event.

Optimal social risk and risk tolerance belong to the dynamic category of water resources projects. It means that the risk level should be decreased with time as required by the new risk acceptance factors, tough in some cases it may be allowed to increase with time. In practical terms, design of risk-level acceptance should allow for the most economical change of this level, when new circumstances require it. The design of structures for their flexible adjustment to future conditions, with the most economical solutions, is a challenging task for water resources professionals. The resistance to earthquakes could be increased if shown that risk is too great for a society to continue living with them. Levees can be raised and capacities of spillways and outlets increased if design flood risk could no more be tolerated. Similarly, flexibility to adjust may be provided for the other sources of the risk.

The set of solutions of risk problems in water resources include several technologies. First, a reliable assessment of types of risk events and their underlying probability distributions must be made. Second, proper methods should be selected and used for economic and social optimization of design risks. Third, the evaluation of new factors, with information increase or revision, should be carried out occasionally, which would require a decrease of design risks. Fourth, a good understanding, and when feasible the proper quantification, of the social dynamics of change in risk tolerance. Fifth, the practical implementation of risk decrease measures requires a good knowledge and experience. And, finally, methods should be available or developed for treating the complex phenomenon of combination of various sources of risks into an overall risk of a water resources structure or system. This set of needed solutions requires also a wide knowledge of risk phenomena and methods of their treatment. For that purpose, professionals in water resources need either formal or informal education of decision making under the conditions of risk and various uncertainties related to risk problems and solutions.

9. Conflict of Interests in Water Resources Projects

Most water resources projects consist of three types of interested parties: (i) those who have right to any kind of benefit, whether they contribute anything substantial to the project or not; (ii) those who may suffer from the insufficient compensation for expropriation, damage or inconvenience; and (iii) those who simply want to benefit in one way or another from public or private investment into water resources projects (namely those who want "to share in the pie"). The first two groups are the legitimate partners in a project. The third group may be realistically considered as composed of participants of marginal interests in project assessment and in public hearings, with questionable demands or claimed interests. This later group may use any environmental, social and political argument, problem or concern, the construed damage or inflated interest rights, in order to be included into the final discussions affecting the decision on how to distribute compensations or future benefits. The most important aspect of any evaluation of interested parties in the project is to divide them into these three groups.

Definitely, planners of water resources projects must have clear criteria on how to classify interested parties into the above three groups. One lives now in an age in which a resolute person or a group of persons, with financial backing, can find a myriad of reasons to criticize or challenge a project. Thus, they intend either to delay the approval and implementation of the project, or to force the decision makers for that person or group to be included as an interested party to benefit from the project in one way or another. The public participation in hearings on project approval, while very attractive from the viewpoint of defense of public interests, carries with it also the third type of interested parties. Often they are the negative side of the otherwise constructive approach to protection of public interests. As time is money in many types of projects, any delay in project implementation may represent a loss to those who are the legitimate interested parties and ready to contribute their share to the success of the project.

It is not surprising that government, state administration, local authority, international and national financing organization, and other administrative bodies for project approvals have developed specific procedures of how to carry out public hearings, how to obtain claims and statements of interests, and how to carry out the decision making process. However, to plan a project, usually there must be dominant purposes for the project to be constructed, and these purposes should have their major representatives. Otherwise, there would be no plan and no proposal for implementation of the project. These major interested parties have all the benefit in exhausting all the potential claims, stated interests and public objections and requests in hearings on water resources projects. Especially this approach is useful for the purpose of avoiding the future litigation and delay.

Rarely a major water resources project is approved for construction without first resolving the inevitable controversies, conflicts of interests, dissatisfaction with compensation, public and environmental opposition and even the legal action. Therefore, the decision making in approving and implementing water resources projects is often a conflict resolution process, with the coordination and compromise of interests. With time, complexities of this process and diversities of solutions have significantly proliferated, making any fast decision unlikely.

Professionals of water resources development, conservation, control and protection must then be fully acquainted with procedures of treating the project approval phase, with methods of a fair distribution of future benefit, cost, compensation and rights. In this way, a new water resources administrative speciality has been slowly created. It may be filled either by the technical personnel who has specialized in those procedures, or by the legal, administrative, economic or social sciences specialists, who have specialized for that particular aspect of the entire process of development and implementation of water resources projects. Included in these specializations may be also the education on most appropriate methods of resolving conflicts of interests, either by legal avenue, by arbitration or simply by a negotiation process.

10. Reallocation of Water Rights

Water as the natural resource is considered in nearly all the countries of the world as being in the public domain or property. Therefore, central, intermediate or local governments have taken over the task to govern the general use of water resources and water power, and to regulate or implement their development, conservation, control and protection. Any activity in water resources, not performed directly by various levels of government, are usually considered as concessions to public, semi-public and private institutions, and to individuals, however for specified time and specified conditions. They are usually conceived as and called "water rights."

Water rights usually depend on doctrine of how they can be acquired or granted, which doctrine is usually valid for a country or a region of a country. Because the amortization of investment in projects and the concept of ongoing depreciation of assets are often tied to the economic or physical lives of water resources structures and systems, concessions or grants of water rights are given by government for the periods ranging from 25 to 100 years. Rarely they are given for less than 25 or more than 100 years. These water rights then become economic values or capital assets. These rights may be either denied by the government according to the concession or grant stipulations, or they may be allowed to become a commodity, to be eventually sold or exchanged at the capital market.

Rights to use water or water power for any purpose may be fixed in the sense that only governments may reallocate them, or that they may be reassigned or sold by the owner of water rights to another owner or to another purpose. In this latter case, water or water rights are conceived as market commodities. In cases of government being the only vehicle to give or reallocate water rights, concessions or reallocations of these rights are often difficult to grant without a proper public procedure. Public cries or legal challenges become often expressed with the claim that the rights seeking organizations or individuals are "plundering the national or common natural resource," or that they do not sufficiently compensate the society for the benefit granted. The approach of considering water rights as the market commodity is simple and fair in many instances. The highest bidder for the grant of water rights, or the highest offer to purchase the existing water rights through reallocation of these rights as the market commodity, lead usually to the best solution. The concessioner then "does not steel our water or our water power" since they are bought under the competitive market conditions.

Granted water rights in case of scarcity of new water to be allocated by governments may become an obstacle to further economic and social development of a region. Grants of water power rights to electric power companies, governmental or private, for long periods of time (say 50-l00 years) may create a crisis situation with water supply of population, industry, agriculture, recreation and other valid purposes of water use. Similarly, water rights granted or acquired by large agricultural ranches or cooperatives of farmers may become an obstacle to water supply of growing cities, towns and rural communities. Therefore, sooner or later the problem of reallocation of water rights comes to the fore. Examples of buying the entire large land ranches by cities in the United States of America, not for the land but for their water rights, are the best illustration of the fortcomeng water reallocation problems.

To avoid political problems and infighting in the case of government being the only but administrative vehicle for water rights reallocation, the most efficient way to solve these problems is to give the water rights the status of market commodity. Water or water rights can be sold at a market price, thus the market becomes reallocation vehicle instead the bureaucrats and politicians. This approach may be also used as an efficient way to solve the problem of water diversion from river basin to river basin, or from state to state, or from country to country. Simply, exporters of water will be selling cubic meters of water in the same way as the electric power companies are selling kilowatthours of electric energy in bulk.

Water and water rights reallocation will become more and more a common practice in many regions with time, especially in arid areas with limited water resources. In this domain of water resources activities, professionals have yet to develop the standardized complex approaches and methods for an efficient transfer of rights. The education of professionals for the solution of such problems will likely be most attractive by publishing books on the systematic ways of solutions, with the abundant number of instances and examples of how these problems have been solved in various regions and countries of the world. Then, special continuing education courses may replace learning on the spot by a much broader approach to these problems.

11. Evolutionary Change in Water Supply Strategies

It may be of interest to review the history of evolution of using sources of supply of drinking water in the last couple of centuries. It will show how the use of these sources has been imperceptibly affected by the ever-increasing pollution of water in nature by humans. It may also indicate from where this water supply will be most likely obtained in the not-so-distant future. As a consequence, it will also point out in what direction the education of professionals in water supply and development of water resources may evolve.

The modern technology took over the ancient water supply strategy, namely to look first for springs of clean water with relatively persistent low flows. It is sufficient to review locations of coastal cities all around the Mediterranean Sea to prove this statement. In most cases, those locations have been selected either exactly at, or close to, the large springs. Or, springs have been relatively close to cities to permit an easy conveyance of water to public fountains. Because of geological conditions of carbonate rock formations all around the Mediterranean, the large and persistent karst springs, among the other favorable conditions, permitted the establishment of large cities. The next source of water for the coastal, but particularly for the non-coastal human agglomerations, from the old times until very recently, have been wells dug into the relatively shallow aquifers, especially in the coastal and riverine alluvial aquifers. Apart from efforts of digging wells and insuring their stability, the clean and often sufficient quantities of water were thus obtained.

Springs and aquifers with wells have been preferred as sources of best drinking water for a long time. When the technology of treating water developed at the beginning of industrial age, lake waters and low flows of rivers, after the primary and the secondary water treatments (mainly by filtration and chlorination), became the third and fourth dependable sources of potable water. By an imperceptible but continual increase of water pollution in all the continental water environments, especially underground, rivers and lakes, the evolution of strategies for drinking water supply took several turning points. By further progress of treating waters to make them potable, especially the secondary treatment in removing the biological pollutants, and the tertiary treatment in removing the undesirable dissolved chemicals, nearly each other potential water source became feasible to become drinking water. Only the cost of providing the untreated water and the cost of treating it would decide which water source will be used for a water supply project. Then the key supply constraints became water availability and cost of treatment. To solve the problem of availability, large aquifers and water storage on rivers with sufficient average water flow became the most attractive water supply sources. To solve the problem of cost, the close-by waters and the cases for which only the primary and secondary treatment was needed became the prize sources of water.

The airborne pollutants affected the water supply strategies, namely that even the previously cleanest spring and aquifer waters became often loaded with heavy metals and the other toxic chemicals released by industry, agriculture and cars. When "naturally clean waters" in the Rocky Mountains in USA showed contents of undesirable chemicals, whose provenience could only be explained by emissions of the Californian industries and cars, and the Arizona's smelters, the airborne pollution became evident. Similarly, the increased acidity of water of lakes, rivers and aquifers in the Eastern United

States and in Canada could be only explained by the coal-fired thermal power plants and industries of the American Midwest. Those emissions became a continually aggravating problem.

Buried or unburied, stored industrial waste of polluting chemicals and proliferating city garbage dumps have started with time to leak liquids into many aquifers in the United States of America and elsewhere. Then, the main strategy of supplying drinking water from springs and aquifers came into question. Professionals started to challenge the main strategy of leaning heavily on springs and aquifers as sources of potable water. Many rivers became also polluted by industries, advanced agriculture and various service activities. A large number of rivers during low flows became sewers, evacuating the garbage of modern societies. By an interchange of water between those rivers and the adjacent alluvial aquifers, aquifers became also polluted, adding to the pollution by agricultural chemicals used at surfaces of these aquifers. Many cities in Europe and USA obtain now their water from such aquifers.

Enormous expenditures have been needed in industrial countries to clean polluted waters and rivers, as well as lakes and aquifers. They wait to be cleaned also in industrializing and developing countries. However, this task is handicapped by the lack of investment for such purposes. High penalties are continually paid in health, work productivity and quality of life of the population of these countries. Examples are the Eastern European countries, Soviet Union, India, Indonesia, Brazil, China, Mexico, and others. Waters can be cleaned by stopping further inputs of pollutants. However, not so for rivers, lake and aquifers. Deposited sediments, full of pollutants at bottoms of river channels, lakes and underground karst channels and caverns leak continually these pollutants into the new clean inflow water. It is easiest to clean rivers than aquifers. Each flood helps to move sediments and expose pollutants to be carried away by the clean water. The intermediate position is for lakes and underground channels. The alluvial and rock fissure aquifers are most difficult to clean once they have been polluted.

Toxic chemicals and organic matter adhered to particles and walls of fissures in polluted aquifers, apart of their concentration in water. Also, they slowly accumulate in their finest primary or secondary porosity. Thus, a decrease in permeability also may occur. When the pollution stopped and cleaning of already polluted aquifers started, say by pumping polluted water out of the aquifer, the high concentration of pollutants started to decrease. However, as soon as pumping is interrupted for a sufficient time, the concentration of pollutants usually returns close to the original one at the restart of new pumping. This is a current experience in several cases in the United States of America, with the country's efforts to clean the highly polluted aquifers by pumping out its polluted waters. Namely, tightly trapped pollutants are as slow to be released into the pumped water as they were slow in their original deposition. The enormous total surface of particles of alluvial aquifers, the large total surface of walls of primary and secondary porosity and fissures in rock aquifers, and the tremendous volume of small pores in both types of aquifers, can absorb a very large quantity of pollutants and retain them for a long time. Therefore, the most persistent and dangerous pollution of all water environments may be the polluted aquifers.

The already classic approach to supply the potable water in a region was to tap their water sources in the following order of source preference: springs, groundwater, lake water, river low flows, regulated river flows, directly collected rainfall, already used but recycled water, desalinated brackish and then desalinated sea water, thus going from one to the other until each previous source is exhausted. That strategy was usually dictated by how clean is water in nature, and the cost of water transport and treatment. The massive pollution of waters in nature seams to dictate a change in the above strategy on the preferred sequence of sources.

The storage of water in lakes and reservoirs in upstream parts of river basins for the purpose of potable water supply, with seasonal or interannual flow regulation, may come out to be a safer and more feasible source of water, on the long run, than the previously preferred water sources of springs, aquifers, lakes and river low flows. Simply, these upper parts of river basins may be easily protected from industrial and agricultural pollution. The concentration of airborne pollutants in waters of these lakes and reservoirs may be decreased so much by mixing in these large bodies of flood waters of very low or negligible concentration of pollutants with lowest flows of a large concentration of airborne, surface and underground originated pollutants. Besides, these bodies of water can satisfy some other water resources purposes, if they are compatible with the main purpose of potable water supply. Simply, the avoidable or unavoidable pollution of environments in general, and of water resources environments in particular, leads to a revision of strategies in procuring the safe potable water to human agglomerations.

If the safe potable water becomes difficult or uneconomical to provide from classic sources, even with additional tertiary treatment, the only attractive solution may be to produce potable water industrially. That means, if pollution of water environments in the world continues with the ongoing pace, water from any source would be completely distilled or all undissolved and dissolved matters removed from it by other means. Then the desirable chemical composition to water will be industrially produced. That new commodity of the market-sold industrially prepared water may then have various chemical compositions, lake Water Type A, B, C, D, etc. Each person would then find in the supermarket the type of water what his or her health criteria may dictate. Are the "mineral waters" or "mountain spring waters," sold in bottles in many supermarkets around the world, the precursors of this inevitable phenomenon of the future, if pollution trends could not be reversed?

The education in water supply and water treatment technologies may require revisions and additions. Planning the comprehensive multistructure, multipurpose and multisource development, conservation, control and protection of water resources in nature will more and more require the well educated professionals, both generalists and specialists. At the present junction of evolution of potable water supply strategies, the education must be not only self-generated by the working experience, but also through the systematic continuing education at the working and high education institutions.

12. Educational Dilemmas in Water Resources

The knowledge in water resources related disciplines continually increases as in all the other technical and scientific disciplines. Also, the new information and evolution in attitudes and demands of human societies require novel approaches and new solutions to old and new water resources problems, all based on new knowledge. However, the capacity of human brain for learning and the use of the best educational methods have clear limitations.

Therefore, specialists must more and more restrict their specializations to narrower and narrower areas, while generalists must broaden their areas of encyclopedic knowledge. In the distant future, the trend in the first case may be the classic limit paradox, namely that specialists will know everything about nothing, and in the second case that generalists will know nothing about everything. To avoid this pitfall of the trend towards the paradox, several steps must be undertaken in education of water resources professionals.

First, the new knowledge often makes obsolete the curricula of formal and informal educational courses. Therefore, the major principle should be that whenever a new teaching material is introduced into a curriculum, the old one must be trimmed by deleting and condensing its less important material. Second, whatever may be learned more efficiently and economically at the working place should be removed from the curricula of formal educational courses. Mainly those subjects should be retained, which are learned much more efficiently and economically in schools or in the formal continuing education. Third, by using the best laboratory, computer and other learning tools and methods, the educational potential should be increased within the prescribed time and expenditure which are available for that education.

Conclusions

The analysis of educational aspects of water resources, under the continual evolution in water resources problems and in societies' demands and attitudes, leads to the following major conclusions:

1. Water resources problems are changing with time because of availability of new information, advent of new technologies and new needs, which require new solutions.

2. Attitudes and demands by societies also change with time, thus imposing new approaches and solutions to the old and the new water resources problems.

3. Professionals of water resources disciplines have become divided by necessity into two major groups, specialists and generalists, with each group needing change in education because of evolution in problems, attitudes, demands and technologies.

4. The advent of new and complex water resources problems, as the nine cases selected and discussed in the previous text demonstrated, requires many future changes either in formal institutional or in informal institutional or on-the-spot continuing education of water resources professionals.

2 PERSONAL COMPUTING IN EDUCATION AND TRAINING

TRANSFERRING PERSONAL COMPUTER MODELS TO POTENTIAL USERS

Thomas N. Debo
Professor, School of Public Policy
Georgia Institute of Technology,
Atlanta, Georgia 30332, U.S.A.

ABSTRACT

Many engineers have been trained and educated to practice hydrology and water resources using simple formulas and nomographs. These methods have been accepted for the estimation of peak flows and simple hydrographs to design culverts, storm drains, and other drainage and flood management facilities. Today in many urban areas the engineer is called upon to analyze complex urban drainage systems consisting of networks of drainage pipes, storage facilities, and other conveyance systems, where simple formulas and nomographs will not give adequate results. As a result the use of computer models for hydrologic and water resource analysis is becoming more popular and many municipalities across the United States are beginning to require their use. The problem facing educators today is how to educate the practicing engineer to use the models and provide classroom instruction for students now enrolled in colleges and universities. This paper describes the experience of giving workshops to professional engineers over the past ten years. These workshops have concentrated on transferring the use of computer models to potential users. Included are examples of different techniques used to introduce users to the models, the experience of "hands on" use in the classroom, problems encountered, and support needed after the classroom experience.

KEY TERMS: Workshops; Personal Computer Models; Technology Transfer; Water Resource Education

INTRODUCTION

Until quite recently, engineers and designers have been able to analyze and design urban stormwater management facilities (i.e., culverts, detention storage) using simple formulas or nomographs. Since most of these facilities were designed as single elements within the drainage system with little concern for their effect on the system these techniques were seen as adequate. Recently, urban drainage ordinances and regulations are requiring hydrologic and hydraulic studies to analyze the interaction of the different facilities within the urban drainage system and the effects that different facility designs will have on this interaction. This level of design and analysis goes beyond the capability of the simple formulas and nomographs and requires the engineer to utilize computer models. As a result computer models capable of being run on personal computers have been developed for most engineering applications ranging from simple hydrologic models to detailed hydraulic models for the design of culverts, bridges, energy dissipators, etc.

One of the major problems in the rush to utilize computer models for urban drainage design and analysis is how to effectively transfer these models to potential users without loosing the engineering judgement that is essential for the proper design of drainage and flood control facilities. In other words, how to train the engineers to use the models as design aids rather than "black boxes" to produce answers acceptable to the local regulatory agency.

This paper will document the experiences gained from ten years of giving workshops to professional engineers and planners which involved the use of simple and complex computer models for urban drainage analysis and design. Many different models have been used in the workshops ranging from complex proprietary hydrologic models utilizing continuous simulation to public domain models for the design of individual drainage facilities. The models also range from very expensive private models to public models available at minimal cost. In addition, some models were only available to the users in executable versions (compiled) while source codes were available for others.

THE WORKSHOP FORMAT

Although people could be trained to use computer models in several ways, the workshop format is the most popular. In this format, participants spend from one to five days in a classroom where the theoretical background for the model is presented, model operation is discussed, and then the participants either see a demonstration of the model or they actually use the model on computers provided at the workshop.

Model Demonstration Only

Because of the high cost of providing computers for each participant or pairs of participants, many workshops limit the model use to a demonstration of the models and their capabilities. By using a liquid plate projection system the instructor can project the screen of the computer through an overhead projection system onto a screen so all participants can view the input and operation of the model. This allows the instructor to demonstrate how to input data, edit data, and run the model for different options. Model results can be sent to the screen so potential users can see how the results will be presented and options available. Utilizing this format solves several potential problems.

• Only requiring one computer saves a considerable amount of money which allows the fees for the workshop to be kept much lower than if many computers were required.

• Renting computers for local workshops often leads to hardware problems including compatibility with software needs, breakdowns of equipment, and problems with graphical and other output devices.

• Having participants working on individual computers often requires more than one instructor to assist in the operation. This again adds to the cost of the workshop.

• Requiring space and facilities to handle many computers limits the locations where workshops can be held.

Thus there are many advantages to limiting the workshops to demonstrating the use of the models without having participants actually using the models.

"Hands On" Use Of Models

If sufficient computers can be made available so all participants at a workshop can gain some experience in using the model, several benefits will be provided

• Participants will gain "hands on" experience in using the model on simple applications where needed data are supplied. This is especially important for data input, editing of data, and utilizing some of the options available within the model.

• Experience has shown that when users actually get to use the model, they leave the workshop with more confidence in using the model and are more likely to use the model after completing the workshop.

• Potential problems in using the model can be detected within the workshop where proper instruction can be obtained. This can save the participants a lot of time and frustration when they use the model on their computer system after the workshop. This can also save the instructor the time that might be needed to assist users after the workshop.

One major problem in providing a "hands on" experience, especially for complex models, is that it is necessary to provide needed data for workshop examples and often necessary to require the users to make vague assumptions since there is not time to fully analyze the design situations or visit potential facility sites. This can lead to participants leaving the workshop with the idea that using the models requires a number of vague assumptions and guessing of model variables and parameters. Thus it is important for the instructor to make the workshop examples as realistic as possible and provide maps, slides of the facility site, and other materials to allow participants to make informed engineering judgments similar to actual designs.

DOCUMENTATION

Many of the available models for use by engineers will provide accurate answers if properly used, are relatively easy to use once the user understands the specific needs of the model, and incorporate many options that can be used to validate the output and final results of the model. What is often lacking is good documentation to assist the user in applying the model and analyzing the results. Often persons attending a workshop will return to their job and it may be weeks and even months before they will attempt to correctly use the model. Good documentation is essential if they are then expected to use the model without further instruction. Following are some of the elements of the documentation that are extremely important.

Loading The Model - Detailed instructions should be given on how to load the model on different computer systems. These instructions should include loading the model on a hard drive (use of subdirectories for model storage and data storage), needed changes to the computers config.sys and autoexec.bat files, storage and computer configuration requirements, and any hardware requirements related to graphical or other outputs. If possible, the model should accomplish as many of the software requirements as possible (i.e., creating subdirectors, changing config.sys and autoexec.bat files).

Typical Data Input - Documentation should include examples of typical data input for a range of applications. These examples should include figures showing what will appear on the screen during the data input operations. This will allow the user to compare the computer screen output with the documentation to be sure that data are being input correctly. This will also help to give the users confidence that they are using the model correctly.

Example Problems - Giving several detailed example problems with figures showing data input, model selection menus, data summary screens, and output results will allow the user to work through the problems and check to be sure the model is working correctly on that particular computer system.

Background Information - The documentation should give the user information on what engineering procedures are being used so that proper engineering judgments can be used in analyzing results and deciding on input values. If the model requires the user to input values for different variables and parameters, sufficient information should be given to assist in the selection of values. The documentation should be in a format so the user can find items of interest quickly, so that instructions are clear and easy to follow, and incorporate numerous pictures and graphs to assist with model operations and analysis of results.

PRE-WORKSHOP EXPOSURE

Often when people attend workshops where computer models are explained and demonstrated, they become overwhelmed with the amount of material that is presented. Also, not being familiar with the models being demonstrated makes it difficult for them to know what possible problems they might encounter in using the models and what application questions might arise. What works well to alleviate some of the problems is to provide copies of the models and documentation to the users before the workshop and ask them to load the models on their systems and work through the example problems. This allows them to attend the workshop with a much better understanding of the models and their use. Also, participants come with much better questions concerning how to use the models for specific applications, limitations of the models, requirements for data input, etc. Some pre-workshop exposure also allows the participants to gain more from the workshop presentations since they are familiar with some aspects of the models.

Dividing the workshop into two parts has worked well in several applications. The first part is usually a half day presentation of the model with a demonstration of its application. Then the users are given a period of time to use the model on their systems following the documentation and example problems. The second part of the workshop is then summary of the model's use, demonstration of more advanced applications of the model, and answering questions that the participants have from their experience in using the model. Participants in this type of workshop tend to ask much more in-depth questions about using the model, and comprehend more of the workshop instructions than if no exposure to the model is given. This type of workshop works quite well when the workshop is being given to an agency such as a city or county where the instructor can travel to the location rather than asking participants to attend two separate workshops.

SUPPORT

The workshop format will only be effective in providing initial instructions on how to use the model and answer certain questions concerning the models use, limitations, and possible applications. It is important to provide some continuing support after the workshop where participants can obtain assistance to answer specific questions concerning:

• the use of the model on a particular computer system,

• particular application problems which might affect data input or interpretations of model results,

• errors encountered in using the models, and

• questions arising after the participants gain experience with using the model

Support is necessary so that participants do not get discouraged with using the model as the result of errors that could be quickly corrected. In addition having some source to contact for questions will assist in using the models as designed and avoiding incorrect use and interpretations of model results. Although supplying model support can be time consuming and troublesome for the instructors of workshops, it is also a good source for the instructors to learn what problems participants are having when they try to use the models. This information can be used to improve workshop presentations and the model's documentation. Thus a continuing two way communication between the instructors and participants can be a valuable resource for all involved.

EXAMPLE PROBLEMS

An important part of transferring computer models to users is providing good example problems for workshop presentation and documentation. Example problems should be as realistic as possible and reflect the type of data and design constraints that will be encountered when the models are used for actual designs. Thus some of the example problems will need to be complex in order to cover the options available within the models and possible site characteristics. It is also important that the problems be designed for the types of problems encountered by particular users. Thus if a culvert design problem were being developed for use by a city engineering department, a site where a 48 culvert would be needed would be appropriate. If an example were being developed for a state agency, a site where a large double-box culvert would be needed might be more appropriate. Example problems should directly relate to the types of designs encountered by the users.

If possible, example problems should show how different options within the models can be used for design and/or analysis. A hydrologic analysis problem might involve estimating peak discharges and hydrographs using several methods available within the model or evaluating different levels of development or different channel characteristics.

Sufficient data should be given for each example so that model users can use these examples to test the model on their system and gain some experience with using the models. Also, complete output should be given to allow users to compare their output with the documentation.

INTERNAL MODEL ASSISTANCE

Model developers can provide some internal model assistance to help users use the model. Following are some of the items that could be incorporated within the model.

On-Screen Help - Many models provide an on-screen help option where the user can access the help while using the model. This allows the user to obtain instant assistance while running the model and can be effective in answering specific questions. Some models have been developed where on-screen help was the only source of assistance for the user and a documentation manual was not provided. For beginning model users, on™screen help should not be viewed as a substitute for a good documentation manual. Both are helpful but the documentation should be viewed as the major assistance source.

Error Catching Routines - Model users can become very frustrated if committing simple errors in using the model results in run termination and sending the model back to the computer system prompt with an error message such as "error in line 1087". This type of error message does not tell the user what the problem is nor does it give the user a chance to correct the error without terminating the computer run. Thus, users can spend a considerable amount of time inputting data and have the run terminated and data input lost because they did something as simple as not turning on a printer. Models should include an error catching routine which has several functions.

• The routine can determine what the error is and give the user a message that will describe the error (i.e., file name not found, is the printer turned on, the printer is out of paper)

• The routine can stop the model when an error is encountered and allow the user to correct the error without terminating the run. Thus if the printer is out of paper the user can load the paper and press a key to continue with the execution of the model.

• Error catching routines also help with the communication between the user and anyone trying to give assistance, because the user will know what error is encountered. As an example, if a path error is encountered the person giving assistance will not have to search the source code for a particular line of code but can respond to the error message detected by the user.

Error catching routines are not difficult to incorporate within most models and can be effectively used to assist with most of the common errors that will be encountered.

Access To Source Codes - Some models are given to users with copies of the source code. The source code of many public domain models is available for the asking. If the source code is written in a language familiar to the user, or a source code such as BASIC which is pretty easy for most users to understand, users can sometimes use the source code to determine what the model is calculating and how that fits with their particular application. This type of assistance is usually for the advanced user but can be a valuable aid for specific application of some engineering models. It is often important for the engineer to know what procedures, formulas, etc., the model is using in order to make good engineering judgments for some design and analysis applications. If the entire source code is not available, portions which give the procedures and formulas used may be available.

For some models (i.e., hydrologic models) it may be necessary for the user or user agency to make changes to the model for local application. To accomplish this the user may need the source code so changes can be made and compiled for local use. In this case the user will need copies of the source code and detailed instruction or assistance in making appropriate changes and modifications.

On-Screen Editing Capabilities - One of the major efforts in using a computer model for engineering design and application is inputting data and editing the data once input to the model. If data input operations are too difficult, if it is difficult to change or edit data to correct mistakes, add additional data, or change data values, users will soon get frustrated and find alternative means to provide the needed design information. Thus to assist in the transferring of models, data operations should include on-screen editing capabilities. This should allow users to quickly get a screen printout of the data being used and allow users to enter the data set to make changes and additions. Forcing users to re-input major portions of the data set should be avoided in most cases.

CONCLUSIONS AND RECOMMENDATIONS

Transferring personal computer models to potential users is not an easy process. Experience has shown that many workshop participants complete the workshop but leave with insufficient training, knowledge, and confidence to use the model. This results in dissatisfaction with the model, the workshop, and the instruction given. The user then either reverts back to methods which are familiar or seeks another model which is easier to use or where the transfer process is better implemented. Ideally workshops designed to transfer personal computer models to potential users should involve as many of the following items as possible.

• Complete demonstration of the model and all options.

• Some "hands on" experience in using the model during the workshop to gain familiarity and confidence in using the model.

• Complete documentation of the model including relevant background information, operation of the model, and example applications.

• Pre-workshop exposure to the models so participants can come to the workshop with some experience in using the model and some basic background information.

• User support so that workshop participants have some source to direct questions after the workshop is complete and participants attempt to use the models.

• Example problems to assist in the initial use and application of the model.

In addition, models should have capabilities to assist in the transferring process by including on-screen help, error catching routines, and on-screen editing capabilities. For some models it will also be helpful if the source code is available to users. All of these items will make the transfer process easier and increase the probability that potential users will become successful users of the models in the engineering design and analysis process.

CASCADE ELEMENT NUMBERING FOR GIS-BASED DISTRIBUTED PARAMETER HYDROLOGIC MODELING:

Processing Raster Digital Elevation Models to Derive a Hydrologically Ordered Computational Sequence for Overland Flow Modeling

Michael B. Smith and **Mitja Brilly**
Civil Engineering Department
Hydraulics and Hydrology Section
University of Ljubljana
28 Hajdrihova Ulica
61000 Ljubljana, Yugoslavia

Abstract

A group of previously developed processing steps for digital elevation models has been expanded to include the automatic numbering of raster cell elements within a hydrologic cascade. The tools are a series of Fortran computer programs which produce a hydrologically ordered connectivity matrix for input into a distributed parameter model for overland flow computations. Coupling of the numbering algorithm with a rainfall-runoff model to generate runoff hydrographs for experimental watersheds demonstrates the utility of the method. The algorithm is an important link between digital elevation models and GIS-based distributed parameter hydrologic models.

INTRODUCTION

Processing digital elevation models to derive hydrologically important information is neither new nor uncommon. In fact, many commercially available GIS packages routinely offer options for many types of DEM processing. Standard options for DEM processing include steps for watershed boundary delineation, slope angle and aspect computations, elevation interpolation from points or contours, cut and fill estimates, and filtering operations.

Other researchers have developed their own processing methodologies and assembled them into "toolboxes" of analysis utilities. These include procedures to analyze grid cell DEMs and TIN models. TIN models have received significant attention in recent years, while grid cell elevation models continue to be popular because they can be easily coupled to remotely-sensed data structures.

Distributed parameter hydrologic models have been held to be more accurate than lumped parameter models in that they attempt to quantify the spatial variation of various parameters within the watershed. However, accounting for spatial variations of hydrologically significant parameters requires the use of large data bases and thus computers with high memory capacity and fast processing speeds. Recent advances in microcomputer technology have facilitated higher processing speeds and operating systems which are not bound by previous computer memory limitations. Thus, distributed parameter hydrologic models are now being used in the microcomputer environment in connection with geographic information systems (Johnson, 1988).

One of the necessary input parameters for distributed parameter modeling is the cell-to-cell connectivity scheme. When utilizing a Kinematic overland flow scheme or a cascade of linear or non-linear reservoirs approach, the computations must proceed in the correct hydrological sequence. This means that before any cell is examined and a rainfall-runoff transformation is performed, all cells upstream of the current cell must be analyzed. In addition, distributed parameter modeling requires that this sequence be followed within each time step. When watersheds are small or when cell sizes are large, the connectivity matrix can be derived by hand. However, when large watersheds are examined or larger numbers of cells are involved, an automatic procedure is needed. The purpose of this paper is to describe an automatic method for numbering grid cell elements for distributed parameter hydrologic modeling.

BACKGROUND

Jenson and Dominque (1988) present a detailed description of conditioning procedures and analyses to be applied to digital elevation models. Depression detection and filling, flow direction computations, and assigning flow accumulation values are conditioning procedures used to create data sets for further analysis. These conditioned data sets include a depressionless digital elevation model in which each cell has assigned to it an outflow direction. Thus, each cell has a path to the watershed outlet or data set edge.

Using these conditioned data sets, operations such as watershed delineation, automatic sub-watershed delineation, and determination of watershed linkages are performed. The derived algorithms were tested on several large watersheds and good agreement was achieved between computed and actual topographic structure.

For digital elevation models represented by triangulated irregular networks (TIN), Gandoy and Palacios (1990) present methods for the automatic numbering of unit elements. These procedures are used to number river segments as well as overland flow elements flowing to river channels.

Van Deursen and Kwadijk (1990) also developed a series of programs for deriving hydrologically significant information from grid-type digital elevation models and assembled them within a hydrological toolbox. Procedures were derived for interactive pit and depression removal and for defining drainage paths. Also included in the toolbox are hydrological building blocks or sub-models that the user can select. Thus, the user selects not one hydrological model but instead composes a model to suit individual needs and project objectives.

APPROACH

Preliminary processing

The methods presented here are generally based on the conditioning procedures described by Jenson and Dominque (1988) to develop a depressionless digital elevation model. For the purposes of this paper, it is assumed that a digital elevation model has been processed to remove pits and depressions and that a flow direction data set has been derived. Flow directions are assigned on the basis of greatest downhill slope away from the current cell x and are specified using the format of Greenlee (1987) shown in Figure 1.

64	128	1
32	x	2
16	8	4

Figure 1. Flow direction codes for cell x.

To determine the watershed draining to a user specified outlet cell, a watershed growing procedure is used. First, the algorithm examines all cells neighboring the selected outlet cell. Those cells flowing into the outlet cell become the preliminary watershed drainage area. In a recursive procedure, the neighbors of this starting group of watershed elements are examined to see if they flow into previously detected watershed cells. Those cells contributing to the watershed area are designated as watershed cells. When no neighbors of existing watershed cells can be found that flow into the watershed, the drainage area is considered to be fully defined. As an example, Table 1.a presents the DEM subset used by Jenson and Domingue (1988), while Table 1b shows the subsequent direction data set. Cells forming tile border of the data set are given direction values leading away from the interior. Figure 2 presents pictorially the direction values. Using the watershed grow procedure, the drainage area for outlet cell (11,9) is outlined in Table 1.c. While the watershed grow procedure was developed by the first author, any other means to define the watershed boundary in a raster format may be used.

Also required for the numbering algorithm is a neighbor data set, in which each cell is assigned an integer value denoting the number of inflowing neighbor cells. Table 1.d shows the derived neighbor data set. Using the direction data set, the neighbor algorithm determines the number of inflowing neighbors for each cell and also locates start cells, or those cells into which no neighboring cells flow. Most often, these start cells form the border of a watershed. However, local maxima within a watershed also form start cells. Since no neighboring cell flows into them, these start cells form the beginning of overland flow paths and are thus named start cells. Start cells appear in Table 1.d as those cells having a value of zero and in Figure 2 as cells having solid outlines. Cells having a value of 2 or more are called junction cells.

TABLE 1. A Numeric example of the analysis procedures.

Table 1.a - Depressionless DEM Subset used by Jenson and Dominque 41988).

column

row	1	2	3	4	5	6	7	8	9	10	11	12
1	778	765	750	740	747	759	765	766	769	776	786	795
2	770	758	745	737	741	751	753	761	777	789	802	814
3	777	763	747	736	735	743	750	767	787	806	820	832
4	786	767	750	737	733	739	752	767	785	797	808	822
5	794	773	756	741	733	733	744	759	772	779	789	806
6	799	782	763	750	737	733	733	745	757	767	782	801
7	802	788	771	761	751	736	733	738	751	764	779	798
8	799	790	780	772	762	746	733	737	754	770	784	794
9	811	799	787	771	757	741	728	730	745	765	779	783
10	823	807	790	774	762	748	733	725	733	750	764	763
11	830	814	801	787	776	761	743	728	725	737	748	751
12	822	818	811	801	791	776	757	739	726	725	735	751

Table 1 .b - Flow direction data set for the depressionless DEM.

column

row	1	2	3	4	5	6	7	8	9	10	11	12
1	64	128	128	128	128	128	128	128	128	128	128	1
2	32	2	2	4	8	16	16	32	32	64	64	2
3	32	2	2	4	8	32	16	32	32	64	64	2
4	32	2	2	2	8	32	16	16	16	8	16	2
5	32	2	2	2	4	8	32	16	16	16	16	2
6	32	2	1	2	128	4	8	32	16	16	32	2
7	32	1	1	1	2	128	8	32	32	32	32	2
8	32	1	1	1	1	2	8	8	32	16	64	2
9	32	1	2	2	2	2	4	8	32	16	16	2
10	32	2	2	1	1	2	2	4	32	16	16	2
11	32	1	1	1	1	1	2	128	4	32	16	2
12	16	8	8	8	8	8	8	8	8	8	8	4

TABLE 1. Continued

Table 1.c - Watershed draining to outlet cell (11,9).

row	1	2	3	4	5	6	7	8	9	10	11	12
1	-	-	-	-	-	-	-	-	-	-	-	-
2	-	2	2	4	8	16	16	32	32	-	-	-
3	-	2	2	4	8	32	16	32	32	64	-	-
4	-	2	2	2	8	32	16	16	16	8	16	-
5	-	2	2	2	4	8	32	16	16	16	16	-
6	-	2	1	2	128	4	8	32	16	16	32	-
7	-	1	1	1	2	128	8	32	32	32	32	-
8	-	1	1	1	1	2	8	8	32	16	64	-
9	-	1	2	2	2	2	4	8	32	16	16	-
10	-	2	2	1	1	2	2	4	32	16	16	-
11	-	1	1	1	1	1	2	128	4	32	-	-
12	-	-	-	-	-	-	-	-	-	-	-	-

Table 1.d - Neighbor data set for the derived watershed.

row	1	2	3	4	5	6	7	8	9	10	11	12
1	-	-	-	-	-	-	-	-	-	-	-	-
2	-	0	1	1	0	0	1	1	1	-	-	-
3	-	0	1	1	4	1	1	1	0	0	-	-
4	-	0	1	1	4	1	0	0	0	0	0	-
5	-	0	1	2	3	2	1	1	0	2	0	-
6	-	0	2	1	2	3	2	1	1	2	0	-
7	-	0	1	1	1	2	3	2	2	2	0	-
8	-	0	1	0	0	0	2	1	0	0	0	-
9	-	0	0	1	2	2	2	2	1	0	0	-
10	-	0	2	2	1	1	2	5	1	1	0	-
11	-	0	0	0	0	0	0	1	3	1	-	-
12	-	-	-	-	-	-	-	-	-	-	-	-

TABLE 1. Continued

Table 1.e - Values of the variable *Inflow* for each junction cell in the watershed.

column

row	1	2	3	4	5	6	7	8	9	10	11	12
1	-	-	-	-	-	-	-	-	-	-	-	-
2	-	0	0	0	0	0	0	0	0	-	-	-
3	-	0	0	0	4	0	0	0	0	0	-	-
4	-	0	0	0	7	0	0	0	0	0	0	-
5	-	0	0	3	12	2	0	0	0	2	0	-
6	-	0	2	0	2	16	2	0	0	2	0	-
7	-	0	0	0	0	2	24	6	4	2	0	-
8	-	0	0	0	0	0	25	0	0	0	0	-
9	-	0	0	0	4	5	30	0	2	0	0	-
10	-	0	2	3	0	0	2	36	0	0	0	-
11	-	0	0	0	0	0	0	0	38	0	-	-
12	-	-	-	-	-	-	-	-	-	-	-	-

Flow Path Delineation

In general, the process of element numbering consists of following overland flow paths from each start cell to the watershed outlet. The algorithm makes many passes through the watershed, tracing overland paths from start cells to the outlet. As each path is traced, two different types of path segments are assembled. Start paths begin with a start cell and end with the first detected junction cell. Junction paths begin with a junction cell and end at the next downstream junction cell. Values are assigned to each junction cell depending on the number of times the algorithm has traced an overland path through it to the outlet. These values are used later to reorder the path segments into the proper hydrological order.

For a watershed having n start cells, the algorithm makes n passes through the drainage area. Pass number one begins with the algorithm tracing a path from the first start cell using the directions stored in the direction data set. This first path is assigned a path of number one. Upon reaching the first junction cell, the algorithm ends path number one and begins path number two. All cells in the start cell flow path are numbered and cell coordinates are stored in Fortran variables as follows:

variable(path number, cell number) = cell i coordinate

variable(path number, cell number) = cell j coordinate

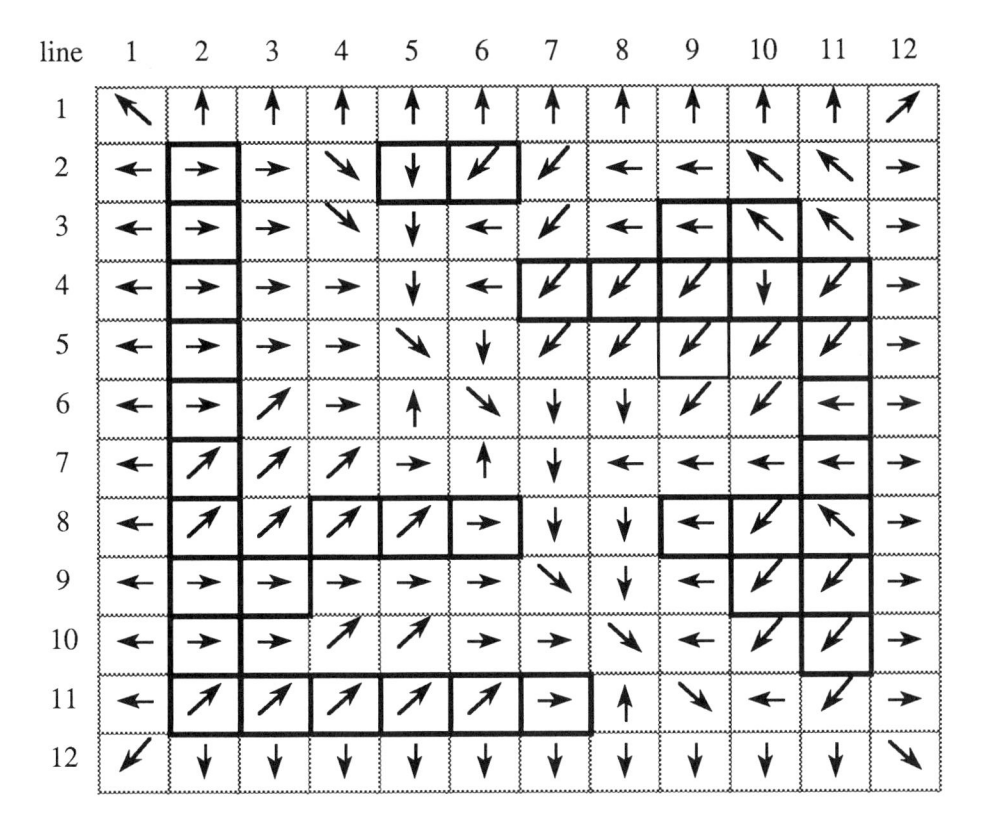

Figure 2. Pictorial representation of the flow directions listed in Table 1.b.

For path number two, the algorithm assembles cells into junction cell paths until the next downstream junction cell is reached. Cell coordinates are stored in a manner similar to start paths.

Each time the algorithm reaches a junction cell, a new path number must be assigned because the presence of a junction cell indicates upstream cells whose hydrologic influence must be considered before continuing downhill. At each junction cell, the algorithm also updates a counter named *inflow* indicating the number of passes that have proceeded through the cell. Thus, the junction cell nearest the outlet cell will have the highest value of *inflow* which is also equal to the number of start cells in the watershed. While each start cell has associated with it a path number, each junction cell is assigned both a path number and an *inflow* value.

Processing continues in pass one until the algorithm reaches the outlet cell. At this point, pass two is begun and the algorithm traces the overland path beginning with the second start cell. Cells are assembled into the start path and junction paths as previously described. However, during the second and all subsequent passes, an additional operation is performed on each junction - cell. If the algorithm has previously passed through the junction cell i.e., if the *inflow* value is one or greater, then no junction cell paths are assembled, as that path number and all cell coordinates have previously been established and assembled. However, the *inflow* value for each junction is incremented as the path is traced to the outlet. Upon completion of the nth pass through the watershed, the *inflow* values shown in Table 1.e result. It should be noted that the values increase as one moves towards the outlet. Since in this example there are 38 start cells, the algorithm has made 38 passes through the drainage area. Thus, the *inflow* value for the outlet is also 38.

Path Segment Ordering

It is important to note at this point that cells are not individually ordered as such, but are located within path segments which themselves are ordered. Within each path segment, however, each cell is ordered according to its proper place in the path.

By definition, start cells have no uphill hydrologic contribution. Thus, within the group of start cell paths, each path has the same importance as all other start cell paths. Therefore, there is no need to place start cell paths into any specific order. Table 2 lists in the cells comprising each start path.

TABLE 2. Listing of start cell coordinates

Path	Cell No.	Cell Row	Coordinates Column	Path No.	Cell No.	Cell Row	Coordinates Column
1	1	2	2	36	1	7	11
	2	2	3		2	7	10
	3	2	4	38	1	8	2
	4	3	5		2	7	3
11	1	2	5		3	6	4
	2	3	5		4	6	5
12	1	2	6	40	1	8	4
	2	3	5		2	7	5
13	1	3	2		3	7	6
	2	3	3	42	1	8	5
	3	3	4		2	7	6
	4	4	5	43	1	8	6
14	1	3	9		2	8	7
	2	3	8	44	1	8	9
	3	3	7		2	8	8
	4	4	6		3	9	8
	5	4	5	46	1	8	10
15	1	3	10		2	9	9
	2	2	9		3	9	8
	3	2	8	47	1	8	11
	4	2	7		2	7	10
	5	3	6	48	1	9	2
	6	3	5		2	8	3
16	1	4	2		3	7	4
	2	4	3		4	6	5
	3	4	4	49	1	9	3
	4	4	5		2	9	4
17	1	4	7		3	9	5
	2	5	6	52	1	9	10

TABLE 2. Continued

19	1	4	8		2	10	9
	2	5	7		3	10	8
	3	5	6				
20	1	4	9	53	1	9	11
	2	5	8		2	10	10
	3	6	7		3	11	9
22	1	4	10	54	1	10	2
	2	5	10		2	10	3
25	1	4	11	57	1	10	11
	2	5	10		2	11	10
26	1	5	2		3	11	9
	2	5	3	58	1	11	2
	3	5	4		2	10	3
28	1	5	9	59	1	11	3
	2	6	8		2	10	4
	3	6	7	60	1	11	4
29	1	5	11		2	10	5
	2	6	10		3	9	6
32	1	6	2	61	1	11	5
	2	6	3		2	10	6
34	1	6	11		3	10	7
	2	6	10	64	1	11	7
35	1	7	2		2	11	8
	2	6	3		3	10	8

Final determination of the flow sequence for junction cell segments is accomplished by compiling an ordered list of junction cells and storing the path number associated with each. Ordering is dictated by the final *inflow* value of each junction cell. Thus, a junction cell having an inflow value of three would have its associated path number stored in the third position or level of the ranking variable according to the following Fortran assignment statement:

rank(level,counter) = path number assigned to junction cell

Since it stores the path number, which is in turn linked to cell coordinates, *rank* serves as a link between the proper hydrological order and cell coordinates. The variable level varies from 2 to n, the number of start cells. Flow path numbers associated with start cell segments are not stored within the *rank* variable.

Within a watershed, there may exist many junction path segments which exist at the same hydrological level. This concept is similar to stream ordering, in which many stream segments can have the same order. Within *rank,* the variable *counter* stores the number of path segments having the same hydrological level. Table 3 lists in hydrological order each junction path and each cell within each path.

Table 3. Listing of Junction Cell Coordinates in Hydrologic Order

Level	Counter	Path No.	Cell No.	Cell Row	Coordinates Column
2	1	18	1	5	6
			2	6	6
2	2	23	1	5	10
			2	6	9
			3	7	8
2	3	33	1	6	3
			2	5	4
2	4	39	1	6	5
			2	5	5
2	5	21	1	6	7
			2	7	7
2	6	30	1	6	10
			2	7	9
2	7	41	1	7	6
			2	6	6
2	8	37	1	7	10
			2	7	9
2	9	45	1	9	8
			2	10	8
2	10	55	1	10	3
			2	10	4
2	11	62	1	10	7
			2	10	8
3	1	27	1	5	4
			2	5	5
3	2	56	1	10	4
			2	9	5
4	1	2	1	3	5
			2	4	5
4	2	31	1	7	9
			2	7	8
4	3	50	1	9	5
			2	9	6
5	1	51	1	9	6
			2	9	7
6	1	24	1	7	8
			2	7	7
7	1	3	1	4	5
			2	5	5
12	1	4	1	5	5
			2	6	6
16	1	5	1	6	6
			2	7	7
24	1	6	1	7	7
			2	8	7
25	1	7	1	8	7
			2	9	7
30	1	8	1	9	7
			2	10	8
36	1	9	1	10	8
			2	11	9
38	1	10	1	11	9

In the context of a distributed parameter hydrological model, the information contained within the *rank* variable serves as a driver to dictate the order of computations for cell paths whose level is two or higher. In essence, all of the path number and cell coordinate information is contained in linked lists which are traced during each time step. Figure 3 presents a generalized set of Fortran nested doloops which recall the coordinates of each cell in hydrological order. The call statements represent calls to subroutines to extract hydrologically important parameters from other data bases and then perform a rainfall-runoff transformation.

```
           do 1000 t=1 to max time by time step
             do 900 i=2 to number of start cells
               do 800 j=1 to number of paths in each level

                 pathnumber = rank(i,j)
                 number of cells in path = numcell(pathnumber)
                 do 700 k= 1 to number of cells in path
c                  recall cell coordinates
                   cell i coordinate = variable(pathnumber, k)
                   cell j coordinate = variable(pathnumber, k)


c                  Hydrologic Model
                 call hydrologic parameters (celli, cellj, parameters)
                 call runoff (parameters)


700                          continue
800                        continue
900                      continue
1000                   continue
```

Figure 3. Generalized Fortran Procedure for Recalling Each Watershed Cell in Hydrological Order

APPLICATION

Testing of the numbering algorithm involved coupling the method with a rainfall-runoff model to generate runoff hydrographs. A cascade of non-linear reservoirs was employed to transform rainfall amounts into runoff. During each time step, the rainfall-runoff transformation is applied to each cell in the order dictated by the derived sequence. Runoff generated from one cell becomes inflow to the next cell in the sequence. Details of the hydrological model are not presented here but since the method is quite well known, the reader is referred to Huber et al (1988) and Green (1984) for more information.

Data was taken from an experimental watershed located in the United States. Figure 4 shows the topographical arrangement of the site. Rainfall-runoff measurements were taken from a publication of the U.S. Department of Agriculture (USDA 1966). Using the contour lines in Figure 4, a digital elevation model was derived. Subsequent processing according to the above steps resulted in the direction data set in Figure 5. The watershed was modeled as a matrix of 15 meter by 15 meter cells. Combining the automatic numbering algorithm with the hydrologic model produced the hydrographs shown in Figure 6. It can be seen that the model accurately reproduces the measured hydrographs.

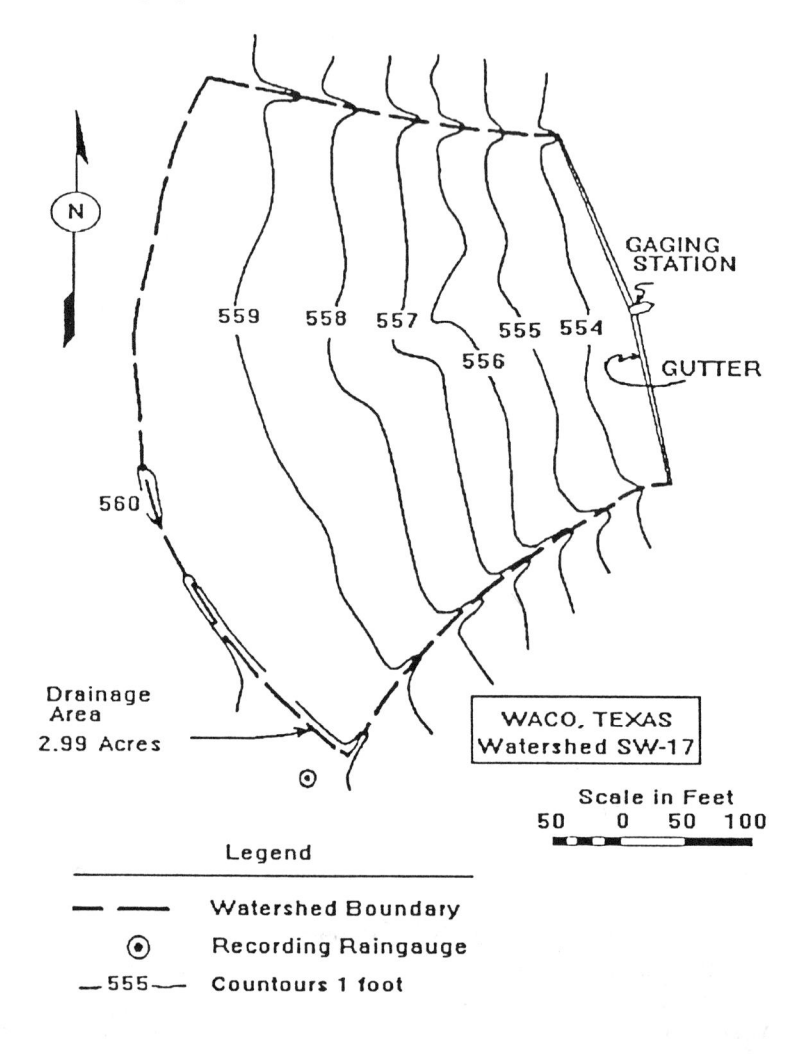

Figure 4. Generalized layout of the experimental watershed in Waco, Texas USA.

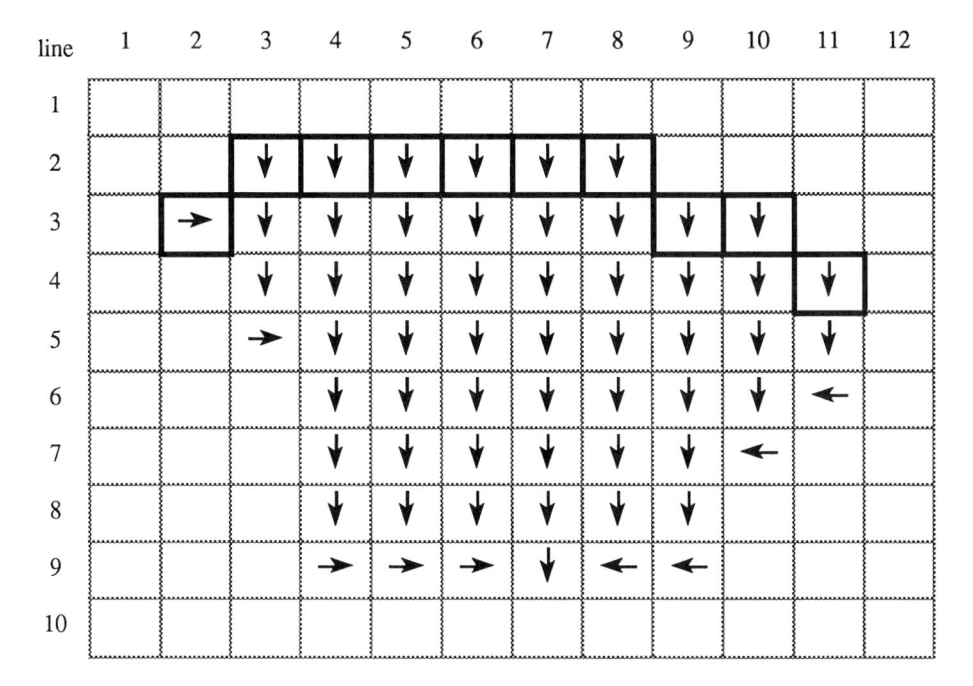

Figure 5. Grid cell representation of the experimental watershed in Waco, Texas USA. Cell size is 15m. by 15m.

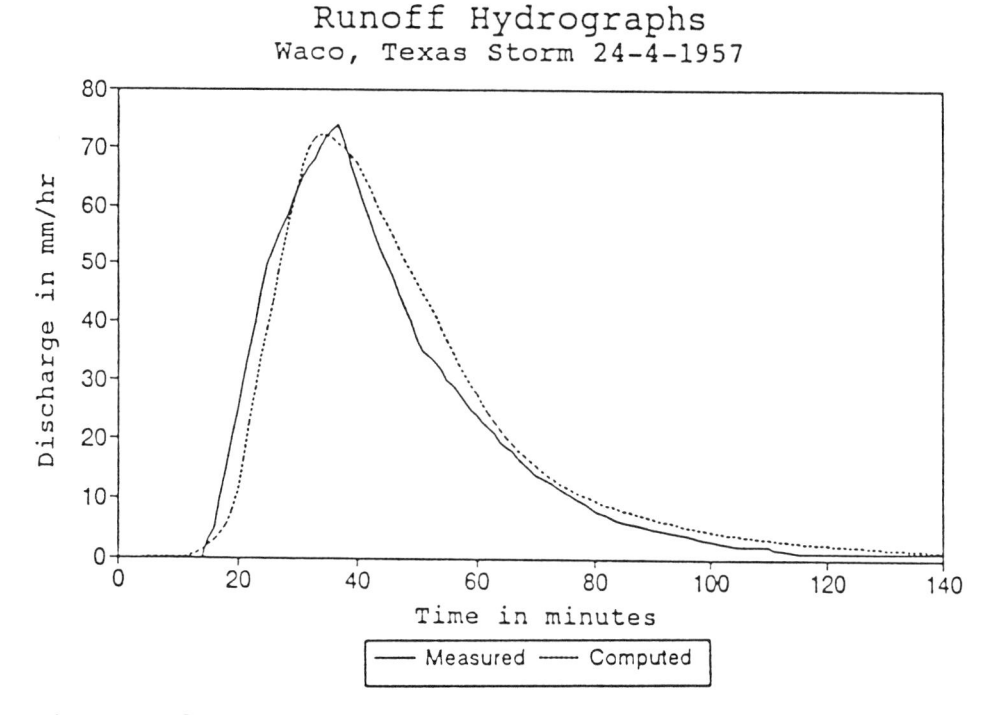

Figure 6. Computed vs. measured runoff hydrographs for the experimental watershed.

CONCLUSIONS

Proper ordering of elements is required for proper watershed runoff simulation. An algorithm has been developed that computes a hydrologically ordered flow sequence of grid cell elements for input into a distributed parameter hydrological model. Coupling the algorithm with a rainfall-runoff model accurately reproduced measured hydrographs for an experimental watershed. The algorithm serves as a useful link between digital elevation models and GIS-based distributed parameter hydrologic models.

REFERENCES

Bernasconi, W.G., and Velez, O.P., 1990. *Automatic cascade numbering of unit elements in distributed hydrological models.* Journal of Hydrology, vol. 112, pp.375-393.

Green, I.D.A., 1984. *WITWAT stormwater drainage program* - version II. report no. 2/1984. University of the Witwatersrand, Republic of South Africa, pp. 12-20.

Greenlee, D.D., 1987. *Raster and vector processing for scanned linework.* Photogrammetric Engineering and Remote Sensing, vol.53, no. 10, pp. 1383-1387.

Huber, W.C., Dickenson, R.E., and Barnwell, T.O., 1988. *Storm Water Management Model, version 4 users manual.* U.S. Environmental Protection Agency, Athens, Georgia, pp. 448-489.

Jenson, S.K., and Dominque, J.O.,1988. *Extracting topographic structure from digital elevation data for geographic information system analysis.* Photogrammetric Engineering and Remote Sensing, vol. 54, no. II, pp. 1593-1600.

Johnson, L.E., 1989. MAPHYD - *A digital map-based hydrologic modeling system.* Photogrammetric Engineering and Remote Sensing, vol 55, no. 6, pp. 911-917.

U.S.D.A Agricultural Research Service, 1963. *Hydrologic data for experimental agricultural watersheds in the United States, 1956-1959,* Miscellaneous Publication no. 945, U.S. Govt. Printing Office, pp. 42.28.1-42.28.5.

Van Deursen, W.P.A., and Kwadijk, K.J., 1990. *Using the watershed tools for modeling the rhine catchment.* Proceedings of the First European Conference on Geographical Informational Systems, Amsterdam, The Netherlands, pp. 254-264.

AN INFORMATION SYSTEM ON WATER RESOURCES

M. L. Mercader and **J. A. Salas Plata**
Centro Nacional de Consulta del Agua (CENCA)
Instituto Mexicano de Tecnologia del Agua (IMTA)
Paseo Cuauhnahuac 8532 Col. Progreso, Jiutepec,
Morelos, México.

ABSTRACT

This paper emphasizes the importance of the systems and services of bibliographic information in activities related with water sciences. It describes some considerations on the participation of users and institutions in the information process. Likewise, it informs about the existence and activities of a National Center of Water Information, at the Mexican Institute of Water Technology, and describes the services offered. The need of an information net in Mexico dealing with the subject is discussed, as well as its advantages on a short term basis. A list of data bases is included.

"Knowledge comes about in two ways we either know a subject on our own account, or else know where we can find information about it." (Samuel Johnson (1775))[1]

INTRODUCTION

Ever since the 18th century, human knowledge has been so widely diffused that knowledge, in its ultimate form has become an axiom, according to the apothegm of Samuel Johnson. Water is vital for humanity and apparently is the most abundant resource. However, accessibility to it, demands of an ever-increasing economic investment and a more complex technical-scientific knowledge in a moment in which availability is reaching its limits. In such conditions, access to information which aids in the solution of such complex problems, becomes almost fundamental.

However, the complexity in the interaction of the manifold components of water-related systems, makes it difficult to find simple responses to most of these problems. In order to solve them, multi-disciplinary cooperation among professionals is required. Information systems are the only option which make a quick and easy way to be informed about recent findings in applied and basic research possible. Nevertheless, in Mexico this task is expensive.

Although the principles for the production and use of information are the same for all fields of knowledge, water sciences require systems which define information needs, as well as techniques for storage and retrieval. One of the

---

[1] Samuel Johnson (1709-1784). English Poet, assayer, reviewer, journalist, and lexicographer was one of the most prominent men in the 18th century's English Literature.

objectives of this paper, is to invite users to acknowledge information as a never ending resource for the retrieval of knowledge, and that it is the basis needed to start any research, planning, management or education and related activity. In it, the process of information of the point of view of the final user, mainly from the point of view of the directors, specialists and students of water sciences, is considered. Therefore, a second objective pursued is diffusion of services included in this purpose, at the information center mentioned within the content of this paper.

IMPORTANCE OF USERS IN INFORMATION SYSTEMS

Assuming that users and people who provide information are the same, a positive attitude which contributes to the increase of information resources in water sciences throughout the country is required. Each final user should be a future information provider, which means that she or he is aware of the importance of existing information and the available methods for a successful information search. Furthermore, all potential users should be trained in order to develop an awareness of the value of information as part of their culture.

As a third objective, we make some suggestions to improve current information systems. We specially recommend that courses should be developed at the educational and training institutions, as well as through seminars and conferences as part of a program to train the users in obtaining the information.

THE NATIONS CENTER OF WATER INFORMATION (CENCA)

The Mexican Institute of Water Technology (IMTA) offers information services through the Center of Water Information (CENCA)[2] at Jiutepec, Morelos. It has water-related bibliographic data bases at the national and the international level.

Objectives

- To provide a better information service on water related topics.
- To store copies of documents written in Mexico in water sciences.
- To participate in creating and developing a water-related national bibliographical data base, and to make it available at an international level.
- To accomplish search online in data banks, to locate information on specific topics in water sciences as well as to reduce the delivery time of solicited documents.
- To keep or to establish a telecommunication system among the national water-related institutions.
- To construct a national information net in water sciences in order to integrate the most important specialized collection of water documents in Mexico.
- To establish a data base which contains hemerographic information available at CENCA, and lead users to a quick access to it.
- With the aid of micro-computers, CENCA could distribute information through CD-ROM.

---

[2] Paseo Cuauhnahuac 8582, Colonia Progreso, C.P. 62550, Jiutepec, Morelos. Telephone 91 (73) 19-49-99 ext. 140 to 145, Fax 194361.

INFORMATION SERVICES

Data bases

Currently CENCA has catalogued the water-related information in data bases with 12,000 records, called IMTA. It also has a documentation data base of grey of fugitive literature (unpublished documents). We therefore invite all authors who wish to be included in this data base to send a copy of their papers, in order to make them available at a national level for all users interested. (The reference data base has 2,500 records)

At CENCA the access to 350 international information data banks with more than 200 million references can be attained. Furthermore, it has specialists in information on water sciences for an efficient management of bibliographical retrieval searches (BBR'S). At the end of this paper, a list of the best known data bases in service for users is presented.

Another important service is the universal availability of water-related publications through the inter-library loans. This constitutes one of the ideals to have in mind in order to increase cooperation for its accomplishment.

Bibliographical Search

- Access on line to monographic materials and grey literature of CENCA's material.
- Bibliographical retrieval search in international data banks.

Alerts

- IMTA-TC is a bimonthly publication containing indexes of serial publications (journals) which are received by CENCA.
- IMTA-BIB is a document published irregularly, which presents bibliography on specific topics.
- IMTA-LERTA is an information sheet published irregularly which presents citations and summaries of articles or documents on potable water, waste water, water quality, meteorology, hydrology, irrigation and drainage.
- Acquisition Bulletin. It publishes the latest most important books, received by CENCA.
- Periodical Publication Bulletin. Published irregularly, presents the latest journals received by CENCA.
- Catalogue of CENCA's Periodical Publications. It is an annual publication of periodicals.

OTHER SERVICES

- Acquisition of national and international books and journal articles.
- Inter-library loans. CENCA has made 90 agreements with other data bases.
- Reading room
- Reference service institutions. It permits the location of documents which are not found in the CENCA's collection.
- Request attention. Integration of information packages on specific topics.
- National map collection.
- Photo duplication of technical papers and reports.

NEED FOR A DOCUMENTATION INFORMATION NETWORK IN WATER SCIENCES

Institutions devoted to technological research and teaching tasks in the field of water sciences, is dispersed throughout the national territory. This situation hinders access to easy information which these users require. The fundamental problem is shortage of special libraries or information centers with specialized, current and organized collections in this area .[3]

Unfortunately, information centers or libraries in Mexico haven't always been given the importance and strategic position as given to scientific and technological developments. To contribute to the solution of this problem, CENCA has started a network of information units at the domestic level. In the first phase of of such net, collaboration agreements with the general and regional National Water Commission's (Mexico) (CNA) managing offices, were signed. In the second phase, we hope to extend its scope to other academic and public offices of the water sector.

The objective is to direct the CENCA's information services to users at their work centers. This purpose is attained through the information units. The communication infrastructure for information requests has been established. We expect to develop a system for sending information through private special delivery of documents to users. This special delivery will work as a cooperative network, on the base of each individual unit's participating with its bibliographical and human resources.

CONCLUSIONS

CENCA is in the transition phase between a specialized library and an information center. The difference among them is that the latter not only fulfils the collection function, but also it can perceive the specific needs of information activities, and acts as a link between information and final users of the institution to which they belong. In order to evaluate the functionality of these new information centers, an inventory of the existing infrastructure, the specific needs of its directors, the available resources and the strategies of the institution, are needed.

THE WATER-RELATED DATA BASES

AQUALINE

Type: Reference (bibliographic)
Major subjects: Contains citations on world-wide literature on every aspect of water, wastewater and the aquatic environment. Topics include groundwater, surface water, wastewater treatment, instrumentation, control and computing, resource development and management, water sampling and analysis, water treatment, distribution systems, potable water, water quality, river management, sludge utilizations, tidal waters, sewerage systems and the other water-related topics.
Coverage: International

---

[3] According to an analysis of international associations related to water sciences, CENCA contains an average of 25,000 volumes of specialized collections.

Online: ORBIT Search Service
Descriptions: hydrometry, water quality, water management, surface hydrology, groundwater, urban hydrology, watershed management.

COMPENDEX

Type: Source (textual-numeric)
Major subjects: Contains citations on the world-wide literature in engineering and technology. The water-related topics are: civil engineering, water and waterworks, pollution of ocean and underwater technology and fluid flow.
Coverage: International.
Online: BRS (COMP), BRS Colleague (COMP), Centre de Documentation de L' Armement, (CEDOCAR), CAN OLE, Data-Star, Dialog, ESA-IRS, knowledge index, (engineering literature index), orbit search services.
Descriptions: surface hydrology, environment.

FLUIDEX

Type: Reference (bibliographic)
Major subjects: Contains citations on world-wide literature related to behavior and applications of fluid mechanics, ports and harbors technology, flow measurement, control of rivers and flood problems, flow dynamics, mixing and separation, energy storage and conversion, fluid power, dredging, civil engineering hydraulics, computational and mathematical techniques, jet cutting and clearing, fluid control and instrumentation, pumping and pipeline technology.
Coverage: International

Online: Dialog
Descriptions: hydrometry, hydraulics, water quality surface hydrology.

PASCAL: BATIMENTS, TRAVAUX PUBLICS

Type: Reference (bibliographic)
Major subjects: Contains literature references in
hydraulic works. Includes civil engineering topics related to bridges, preys, maritime structures, sewers and water supply.
Describers: surface hydrology, urban hydrology, water management.

WATER RESOURCES ABSTRACTS

Type: Reference (bibliographic)
Major subject: Contains citations and abstracts to scientific and technical literature on water-related aspects of the physical, social and life sciences. Topics include the nature of water and water cycles, water quality management and protection, water resources planning and engineering works.
Coverage: International
Online: Dialog

Descriptions: Environment, water quality, surface hydrology and water management.

WATERLIT

Type: Reference (bibliographic)
Major subjects: Contains literature reference in sciences of the water. Includes hydrology, liminology, ecology, residual waters and pollution, desalinization, engineering and construction and management of the water.
Describers: surface hydrology, water quality and water management.

PHI

Type: Reference (bibliographic)
Major subjects: Contains scientific and technical literature references in hydrology. Includes topics related to the hydrological cycle, erosion, mathematical models, water management, geohydrology, education and information for technical personnel in hydrology.
Describers: surface hydrology, geohydrology, education, technology transfer, management of hydraulic resources.

ACKNOWLEDGEMENTS

The authors wish to acknowledge the authorities of the Mexican Institute of Water Technology, specially Guillermo Ortega, Professional Development Coordinator, for the opportunity to diffuse information concerning CENCA. We would also like to acknowledge Clara Levi, who spent hours of her time reading and correcting the English draft of this document.

REFERENCES

Mercader. M. (1986). *Red de unidades de información. Instituto Mexicano de Tecnologia del Aqua*, Morelos. 12p. ilus.

Nieuwehhuysen, P. (1989). *Scientific and Technical Water-Related Documentary and Information Systems*. IHP UNESCO, Paris 52p.

Garcia, R. (1988)-. *Informe del Centro de Consulta del Aqua. Instituto Mexicano de Tecnologia del Aqua*, Morelos. 6p.

Willard, M. A. and P. Morrison. (1988). *The Dynamic Role of the Information Specialist. Two Perspectives*. Special Libraries, vol.79, num. 4, pp. 271-276.

Thury, E. M. (1989). *From Library to Information Center. Special Libraries*, Winter 1989, vol. 79, num. I., pp. 21-27.

FLODRO: A User-Friendly Personal Computer Package for Flood and Drought Frequency Analyses for Education and Training

Jose A. Raynal-Villaseñor
Water Resources Program
Universidad Autonoma de Chihuahua
P.O. Box 1528-C
31160 Chihuahua, Chih., Mexico

and

Carlos A. Escalante-Sandoval
Water Resources Program
Universidad Nacional Autonoma de Mexico
P.O. Box 70-256
04510 Mexico, D.F., Mexico

ABSTRACT

The most recent advances in flood and drought frequency analyses are shown through the use of a personal computer package, structured to be used in an interactive and easy way. The computer package is designed as an effective tool for education and training purposes in such fields as hydrology. FLODRO has been shaped to have the minimal memory requirement and the graphs are printed by a common printer. The computer program has been applied successfully to train students coming from countries of Latin America and Africa.

INTRODUCTION

A subject of paramount interest in planning and design of water works is that which is related to the analysis of flood and drought frequencies. Due to the characteristic that design values, in both flood and drought analyses, are linked to a return period or to a non-exceedance or exceedance probability, the use of mathematical models known as probability distribution functions is a must.

Among the most widely used probability distribution functions for hydrological analyses are the following, [Kite(1988), Matalas(1976) and Salas and Smith(1980)]:

a) For flood frequency analysis: normal, log-normal with 2 and 3 parameters, gamma with 2 and 3 parameters, log-Pearson type III, extreme value type I and general extreme value.
b) For drought frequencies analysis: log-normal with 3 parameters,

gamma with 3 parameters, Weibull, extreme value type I and general extreme value.

In the light of the personal computer applications in education and training in all the fields of science, a personal computer program was designed to take care of flood and drought frequency analyses, providing a wide number of options for models to be used. The resulting code has been named FLODRO, as it will be referred herein. This paper contains the key features of FLODRO and two examples, one for floods and one for droughts. They are included to show the main results that FLODRO can supply to users.

FRAMEWORK OF FLODRO

FLODRO is written in GWBASIC[TM1] BASIC compiler compatible with IBM[TM2] personal computers. The interactive mode in which FLODRO is written makes it to have a high user-friendly component. In any step, the user has control on the processes that the program executes, from data input to printing of results of the analysis. The personal computer package FLODRO has the structure shown in Figure 1.

```
                                  ┌─ INFORMATION
                                  ├─ NORMAL
                                  ├─ LOG-NORMAL 2 AND 3
                                  │  PARAMETERS
                     ┌─ FLOOD ────┤  GAMMA 2 AND 3
                     │            │  PARAMETERS
                     │            ├─ LOG-PEARSON TYPE III
                     │            ├─ EXTREME VALUE TYPE I
                     │            └─ GENERAL EXTREME VALUE
       FLODRO ───────┤
                     │            ┌─ INFORMATION
                     │            ├─ LOG-NORMAL 3
                     │            │  PARAMETERS
                     │            ├─ GAMMA 3 PARAMETERS
                     └─ DROUGHT ──┤  WEIBULL
                                  ├─ EXTREME VALUE TYPE I
                                  └─ GENERAL EXTREME VALUE
```

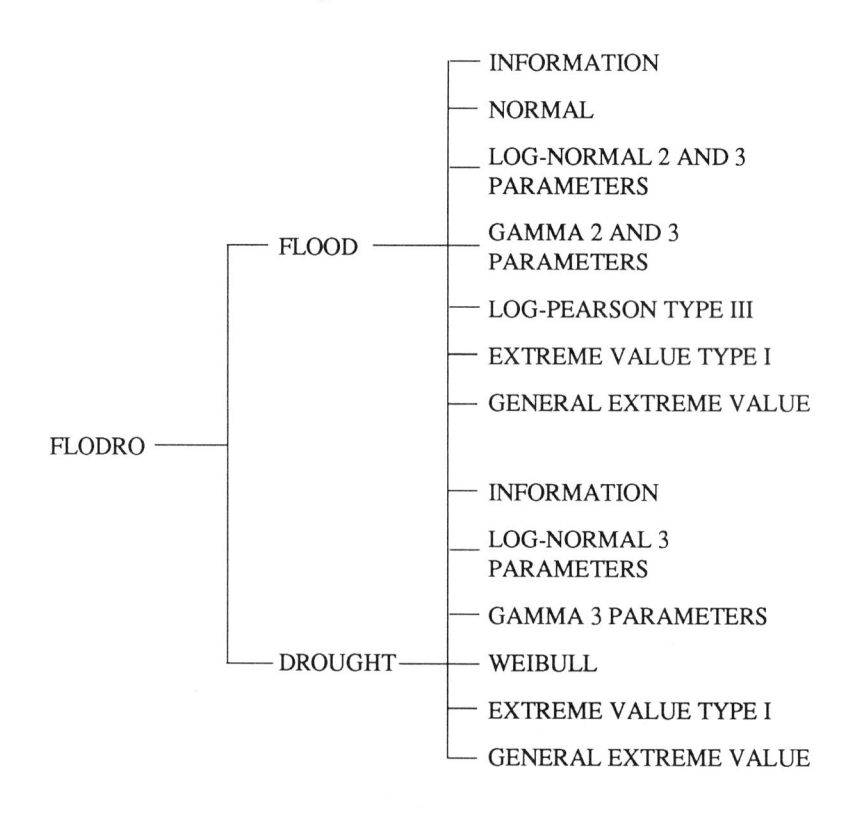

Figure 1. Framework of computer package FLODRO.

---

[1] GWBASIC[TM] is a registered trademark of Microsoft Corporation.
[2] IBM[TM] is a registered trademark of International Business Machines.

All the probability distribution functions mentioned in the previous section are contained in FLODRO. FLODRO is divided in two independent computer programs: FLOOD and DROUGHT. In the FLOOD computer program, the flood frequency analysis is performed by the use of seven probability distribution functions, as shown in Figure 1. In the DROUGHT computer program, the drought frequency analysis is performed by the use of five probability distribution functions, as shown in Figure 1.

Both programs can perform the required computations to obtain:

a) Estimation of parameters, by the methods of moments and maximum likelihood in FLOOD and moments in DROUGHT.

b) Computation of probability distribution function for sample values or for any other data provided by the user.

c) Computation of probability density function for sample values or for any other data provided by the user.

d) Inverse of the probability distribution function for a fixed number of values or for any other values provided by the user.

e) Confidence limits for design events, by the methods of moments and maximum likelihood in FLOOD and moments in DROUGHT.

f) Goodness of fit tests based on the standard error of fit, Kite(1988), and based in a graphical comparison between the empirical and theoretical probability distribution and density functions.

These options are shown in Figure 2.

OPTIONS
- INFORMATION
- ESTIMATION OF PARAMETERS
- COMPUTATION OF DENSITY FUNCTION
- COMPUTATION OF CUMULATIVE DISTRIBUTION FUNCTION
- INVERSE OF CUMULATIVE DISTRIBUTION FUNCTION
- COMPUTATION OF CONFIDENCE LIMITS
- GOODNESS OF FIT TESTS

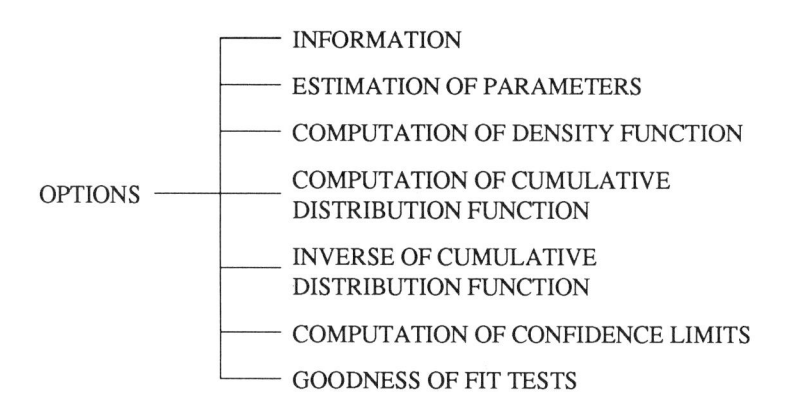

Figure 2. Options of analysis in computer package FLODRO.

Personal computer program FLODRO was designed to use minimum of memory and computer peripherals. Each computer program FLOOD or DROUGHT have less than 360K, so there is no need to have a hard disk to run any of such programs. The graphs provided by FLOOD or DROUGHT are printed by a common printer. There is no need to use costly plotters to get these graphs on paper. These features make FLODRO very suitable in programs of hydrology education and training, particularly in developing countries, and in continuing education.

NUMERICAL EXAMPLE

Gauging station Villalba was selected to analyze the annual floods and the one-day low flows, in the period of record 1939-1981, using the Log-Normal 3 parameters probability distribution function and the method of moments. The parameters obtained by the use of FLODRO are:

a) For floods:

Location parameter = - 55.74

Scale parameter = 0.64

Shape parameter = 5.77

Mean = 355.41

Standard deviation = 393.98

Skewness = 3.62

Standard error of fit = 222.21

b) For droughts:

Location parameter = - 0.39

Scale parameter = 0.20

Shape parameter = - 0.34

Mean = 0.33 ; Standard deviation = 0.15

Skewness = 0.64

Standard error of fit = 0.02

The graphical displays provided by FLODRO are given in Figures 3, 4, 5, 6, 7 and 8.

CONCLUSIONS

A personal computer program is presented for flood and drought frequency analyses for purposes of education and training. The computer code was applied successfully to train students coming from Latin American and African countries, showing the user-friendly component of such computer code, given that most students have not have any previous computer experience. Due to the minimum requirements of central memory and computer peripherals that the personal computer program has, as it has been shown in this paper, makes it a versatile tool to train students or technical personnel in the field or with a personal computer without a hard disk or a plotter.

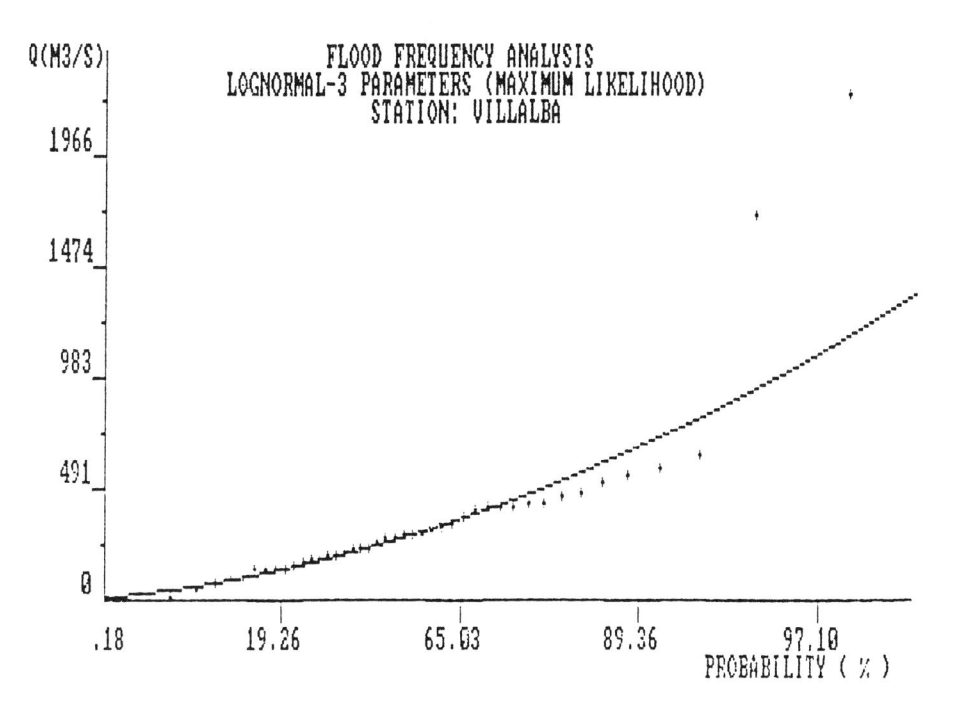

Figure 3. Flood frequency curve for station Villalba.

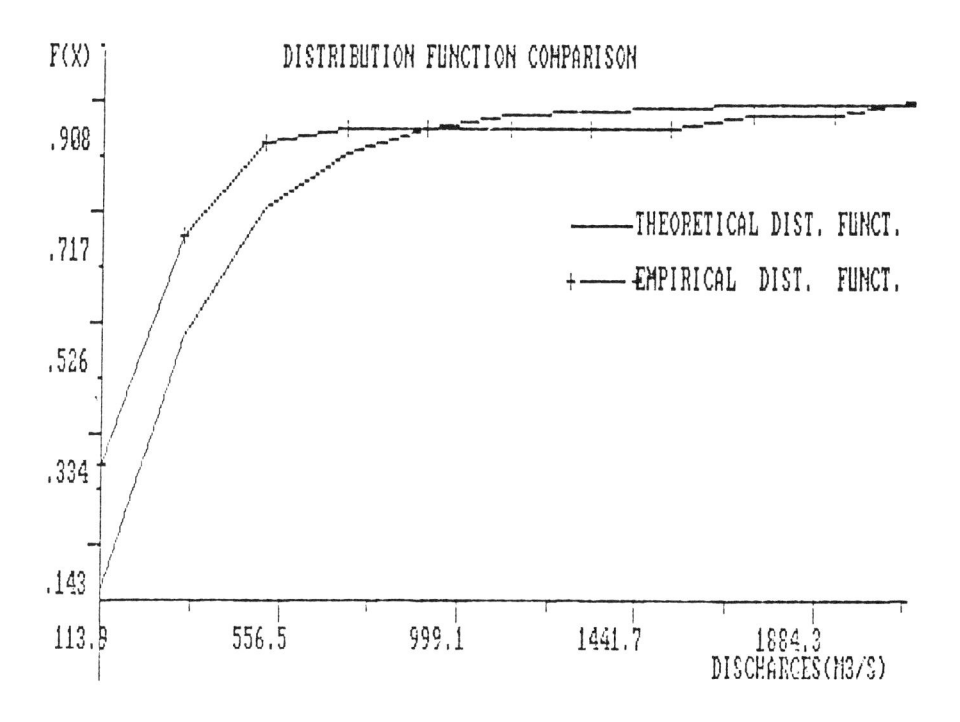

Figure 4. Distribution function comparison for station Villalba.

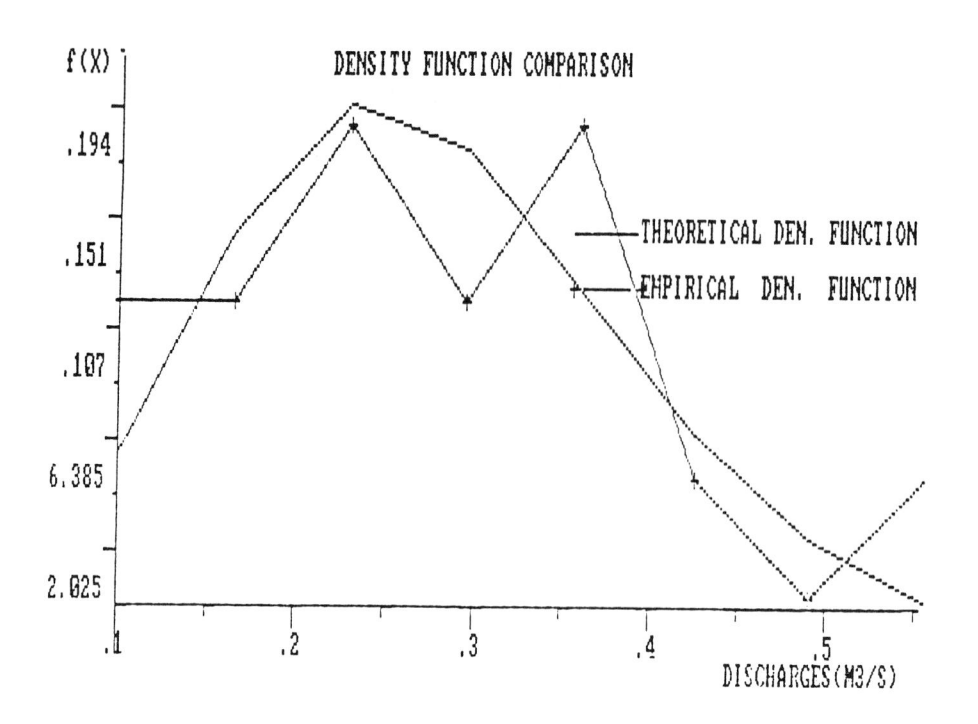

Figure 5. Density function comparison for station Villalba.

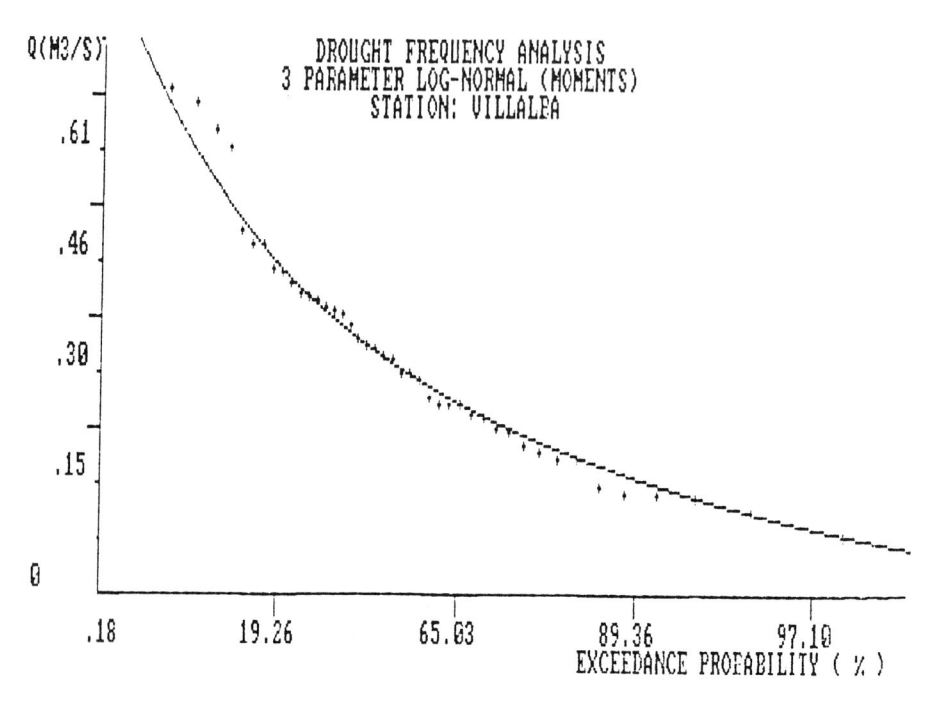

Figure 6. Low-flow frequency curve for station Villalba.

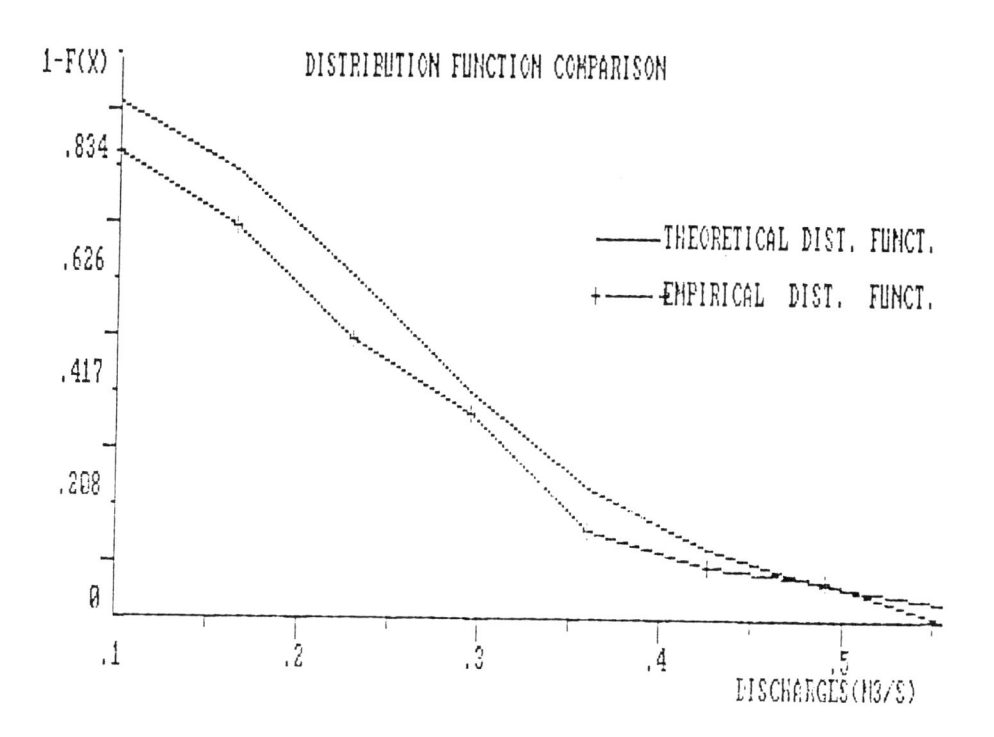

Figure 7. Distribution Function Comparison for station Villalba.

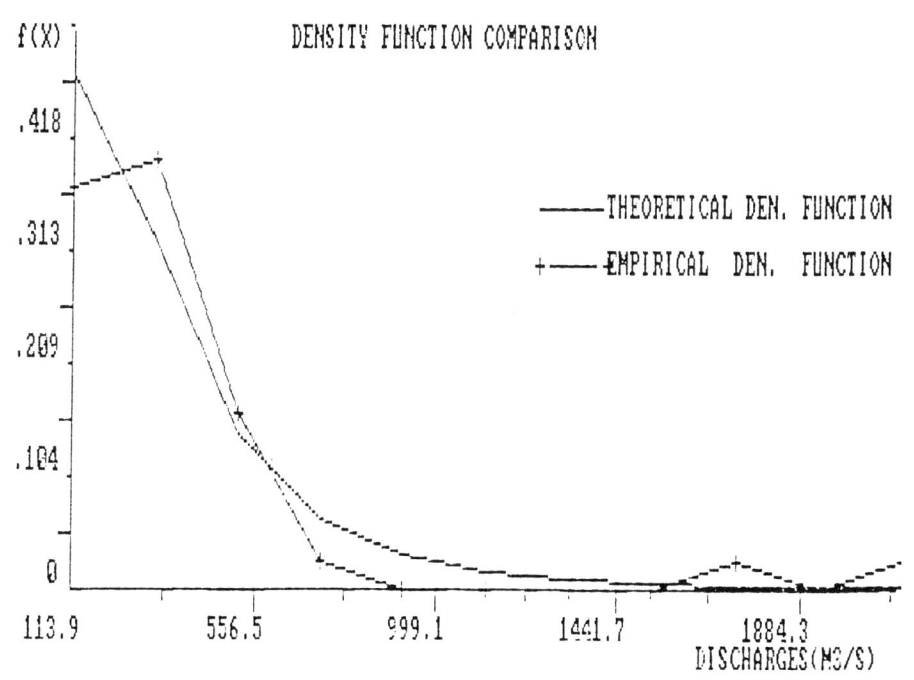

Figure 4. Density function comparison for station Villalba.

ACKNOWLEDGEMENTS

The authors wish to express their deepest gratitude to the Graduate Studies Divisions of Universidad Autonoma de Chihuahua and Universidad Nacional Autonoma de Mexico, respectively, for their support given to produce this paper.

REFERENCES

Kite, G.W. (1988). *Flood and Risk Analyses in Hydrology*, Water Resources Publications, Littleton, Colorado.

Matalas, N. C.(1963). *Probability Distribution of Low Flows, Statistical Studies in Hydrology*, Geological Survey Professional Paper 434-4, pp A1-A27.

Raynal, J.A. and Escalante, C.A.(1989). FLODRO: USER'S MANUAL.

Salas, J. D. and Smith, R. (1980). *Computer Programs of Distribution Functions in Hydrology*. Colorado State University, Fort Collins, Colorado.

SHIFT: A PC-ORIENTED DISTRIBUTED HYDROLOGIC MODEL BASED ON IRREGULAR TRIANGULAR FACETS

O.L. Palacios-Vélez and B. Cuevas-Renaud
Centro de Hidrociencias
Colegio de Postgraduados
Montecillo, Méx., México, 56230

ABSTRACT

SHIFT (Sistema Hidrodológico de Facetas Triangulares) is a computational system that allows for: a) creation, edition and visualization of a watershed Triangular Irregular Network (TIN) Digital Elevation Model (DEM), b) input and interpolation of soil, riverbed and rainfall data, and c) calculation and routing of runoff in all the facets and reaches. The TIN-DEM model is constructed from a set of points, where the slope changes abruptly. Afterwards, the drainage network is automatically identified as consisting of those edges with converging slopes and an interactive editor allows addition or deletion of points to eliminate network discontinuities. Soil characteristics and rainfall data are interpolated by means of a procedure based on the minimization of the bending energy of a thin plate. In order to calculate and route the runoff, the system determines the routing sequence of river segments and for each one of them identifies the facets forming the contributing area and determines a cascade of overland flow planes. Then, for each element and time interval the system calculates the infiltration and routes the resulting runoff by a numerical solution of the kinematic wave equation. This information is saved and the user can see the hydrograph for any facet or reach.

INTRODUCTION

The development of physically-based distributed models is a relatively new trend in hydrological modeling, facilitated by the dissemination and improvement of computer technique. Beven (1985) discusses the nature, main characteristics, present limitations, and problems of the distributed models. He also mentions four major areas for the potential application of these models:

a) Forecasting the effects of land-use change;

b) Forecasting the effects of spatially variable parameters and inputs,

c) Forecasting the movements of pollutants and sediments; and

d) Forecasting the hydrological response of ungauged catchments.

The most significant difference between the distributed and "lumped" models is that the distributed models consider the spatial variability of the land use, topography, soil and rainfall data. As a consequence the distributed models offer the capability of forecasting what happens practically at any point within the catchment, unlike "lumped" models which only provide outlet results. The cost of this advantage is an increased information requirement, mainly soil and rainfall data, a more complicated model construction, which is important when the number of unit elements is high and increased computer costs.

Presently several distributed models are already being applied to real-world problems or are reaching the testing stage. Probably the best known one is the Système Hydrologique European (SHE), developed in Denmark, France and Britain (Abbott et al., 1986a, 1986b).

Obviously, wider use of distributed models will be facilitated by the availability of more "user-friendly" systems that can be run on (advanced) personal computers.

The aim of this paper is to describe the main features of a distributed model, called SHIFT (Sistema Hidrológico de Facetas Triangulares), that unlike SHE and other distributed models, is based on a watershed model constructed by a network of non-overlapping irregular triangular facets, which better approximate the topography. SHIFT also has a series of "user-friendly" features and can be run on a PC, which is intended to facilitate its use. Technical details and computer operation are explained by Palacios and Cuevas (1990a, 1990c).

DESCRIPTION OF SHIFT

SHIFT is an integrated hydrological model that includes:

a) The interactive creation and edition of a watershed topographic model.

b) The input and interpolation of soil, river-bed and rainfall data.

c) The calculation of runoff in all the facets conforming the watershed model, as well as in all the reaches of the drainage network.

The most relevant and distinctive features of these operations are described in the following. Creation and Interactive Edition of the Topographic Model.. The topographic model is created on the basis of a set of "surface-specific" points (Peucker et al., 1978), that is, points where the topographic slope changes abruptly. The topographic domain is then partitioned into a network of non-overlapping Delaunay triangles (a Delaunay triangle is formed by joining three Thiessen neighbors), using an algorithm that is described in Palacios and Cuevas, (1990b). One useful feature of this algorithm is that it provides for the deletion of points without total network reconstruction, something that is important for an interactive editor, as will be explained later.

In a second step the drainage or river-course network is identified as composed by those triangular edges with converging slopes. Often the drainage network results with artificial discontinuities, as has been pointed out by Gandoy and Palacios (1990). In order to eliminate such discontinuities it may be necessary to re-sample (move) some points, that is delete some points and then add new ones, probably with a slightly different elevation. These operations are greatly facilitated by an interactive editor with which the model builder can see immediately on the computer screen the result of a proposed change.

Once the drainage network is free of discontinuities a cascade of reaches and a cascade of triangular facets are defined. These cascades are used to route the runoff by means of the kinematic wave equation. The runoff routing through the basin model is carried out by a recursive procedure that starts in the higher model elements and descends until finally reaching the outlet. The only condition for a valid calculation sequence of model elements, is that when analyzing a given element (triangular facet or reach), all of the upstream neighboring elements should have already been analyzed. This calculation sequence is called hydrologic or kinematic cascade. SHIFT uses an algorithm that is able to identify a kinematic cascade of river-course segments developed by Gandoy and Palacios (1990).

Once a cascade of reaches is defined, then for each reach its contributing triangular facets are identified and a specific cascade is also defined. Both operations are carried out simultaneously by a second algorithm also developed by Gandoy and Palacios, (1990).

Input and Interpolation of Soil, River-Bed and Rainfall Data

SHIFT requires the knowledge of the roughness coefficient, the saturated hydraulic conductivity, the effective net capillary drive coefficient (Smith and Parlarnge, 1978), the saturation, the initial water content and the hyetogram in all of the unit elements forming the watershed model. These data, known in certain locations from field measurements and raingauge stations, are interpolated for all the model elements. The interpolation procedure is based on a spline surface that minimizes a quantity that is, in a first approximation, equal to the bending energy of a "thin elastic plate" forced to pass through the data points. This method, developed by Duchon (1976) and widely used by French researchers (Dubrule, 1984; Level et al., 1987) avoids the drawback of uncontrolled oscillations arising when polynomial interpolation is used.

The river-bed width should also be known for all the reaches. SHIFT assumes that this value is measured in some places and then interpolates it to all the reaches, assuming that there is a linear relationship between the river-bed width and the contributing area. This value was automatically calculated for all the reaches of the topographic model.

Runoff Calculations

Probably the most rigorous method for making the runoff calculations in drainage networks is through the solution of the Saint-Venant equations. These equations are solved separately and in an alternating fashion. First, the Saint-Venant equations are solved for the main river-course, considering the confluences as point sources with known discharge from the previous time interval. Second, the equations are solved for each tributary, considering the outlet into the main river as a boundary of known water depth from the previous time interval. This method is applied recursively for higher order branchings, and a similar procedure is applied for the overland flow. Obviously this method is highly complicated and time-consuming even for simple drainage networks, let alone for more complex ones.

Among the simpler methods to carry out the runoff calculations, the kinematic wave approximation seems specially interesting. In this case the complexity of the calculations is reduced to the recursive solution for a single element (triangular facet for the overland flow or reach for the channel flow) with the only condition that the input coming from the neighboring upstream element(s) be known, since the "backwater" effects are not considered by the kinematic wave equation.

At this point it is important to remark that considering that the soil and rainfall data are usually known in each facet only with a low level of approximation, it has seemed reasonable to carry out the overland flow calculations only for an average length of the water paths through the facet. This is equivalent to transform the triangular facet into a rectangular one, with the same area, the same steepest slope, but only one length of the (potential) water path: the average one. On the other hand, it would have been impossible to try to calculate the overland flow for any possible path of the runoff through one facet and through a network of facets.

The infiltration is calculated by the Smith-Parlange (1978) equation, that can be written as

$$f = K_s / (1 - e^{-F/B}) \text{ ; or} \qquad (1)$$

$$F = K_s t + B\left[1 - e^{-F/B}\right] \qquad (2)$$

Where:

- f : infiltration capacity,
- F : accumulated infiltration,
- K_s : effective saturated hydraulic conductivity,
- t : time after ponding,
- B = $G(q - q)$,
- q : saturated water content,
- q : initial water content,
- G : effective net capillary drive,

$$G = \frac{1}{K_s} \int_{-\infty}^{0} K(\psi) d\psi . \qquad (3)$$

In order to take into account the fact that the water rarely covers the whole surface of a unit element, and following Woolhiser et al., (1989), an assumption was made that the inundated area linearly varies, up to a critical point, with the calculated water depth.

When rainfall intensity is greater than the infiltration, or when there is an input from the neighboring upstream element, the runoff is calculated and routed by the kinematic wave equation. For a typical length increment we can write the following continuity equation:

$$V_e - V_s = \Delta V_\alpha + \Delta V_i \qquad (4)$$

Where:

- V_e : input volume in Δt time,
- V_s : output volume,
- ΔV_α : change in storage (above soil surface), in Δt time,
- ΔV_1 : change of infiltrated volume.

$$V_e = \left[wQ_{i-1}^j + (1-w) Q_{i-1}^{j-1}\right] \Delta t + \left[wq^j + (1-w)q^{j-1}\right] \Delta t \, \Delta x \qquad (5)$$

$$V_s = \left[wQ_i^j + (1-w) Q_i^{j-1}\right] \Delta t \qquad (5')$$

$$\Delta V_\alpha = \left[\phi h_{i-1}^j + (1-\phi) h_i^j\right] \Delta x - \left[\phi h_{i-1}^{j-1} + (1-\phi) h_i^{j-1}\right] \Delta x \qquad (5'')$$

$$\Delta V_1 = \left[\phi_z Z_{i-1}^j + (1-\phi_z) Z_i^j\right] \Delta x - \left[\phi_z Z_{i-1}^{j-1} + (1-\phi_z) Z_i^{j-1}\right] \Delta x \qquad (5''')$$

Where:

- Q : discharge,
- q : lateral inflow-rate infiltration,
- Δx : finite difference length increment,
- h : water depth,
- Z : infiltrated depth,
- w : space weighting coefficients.
- ϕ ϕ_z : space weighting coefficients.

We use the well known depth-discharge equation:

$$Q = \alpha h^\beta \; ; \; \text{or} \qquad (6)$$

$$h = (Q/\alpha)^{1/\beta} \qquad (6')$$

Where:

$$\alpha = \frac{bS^{1/2}}{n}$$

$$\beta = \frac{5}{3}$$

- b : channel width,
- n : Manning's coefficient
- S : slope

Combining the previous equations, after some simplifications we get:

$$Q_1^j + A\left[Q_1^j\right]^{1/\beta} = B \qquad (7)$$

Where:

$$A = \frac{(1-\phi)\Delta x}{w} \frac{\Delta x}{\Delta t} \left(\frac{1}{\alpha}\right)^{1/\beta} \tag{8}$$

$$B = \frac{v_e - \Delta v_i}{w\Delta t} - \frac{(1-w)}{w} Q_i^{j-1} - \frac{\Delta x}{w\Delta t}\left[\phi h_{i-1}^{j} - \phi h_{i-1}^{j-1} - (1-\phi)h_{i-1}^{j-1}\right] \tag{9}$$

Observe that we solve equation (7) for the discharge, instead of the water depth. The advantage of this approach is that at the boundaries, when passing from one element (facet or reach) to the neighboring downstream element, the discharge, unlike the water depth, maintains the continuity, regardless of changes in the slope, Manning coefficient, rainfall intensity or hydraulic conductivity.

Equation (7) is solved iteratively by using a Newton-Raphson scheme. For iteration k+1 we have:

$$\left(Q_i^j\right)^{k+1} = \left(Q_i^j\right)^{k} + \left(\Delta Q_i^j\right)^{k+1} \tag{10}$$

Where:

$$\left(\Delta Q_i^j\right)^{k+1} = \frac{v_e - v_s - \Delta V_\alpha - \Delta V_i}{w\Delta t + \Delta x (1-\phi)\left(\frac{1}{\beta}\right)\left(\frac{1}{\alpha}\right)^{1/\beta}\left[Q_i^j\right]^{(1-\beta)/\beta}} \tag{11}$$

The proposed scheme is robust enough to allow the description of different flux forms: runoff formation due only to rainfall, runoff routing (without rainfall) and their combinations. The same procedure is used for the overland and for the channel flow computations. The only difference is in the meaning of the lateral input "q"; for the triangular facets it is the rainfall minus infiltration and in the reaches it is the runoff from the converging triangular facets forming the reach minus the river-bed infiltration.

SHIFT saves the results of all the computations and when they are completed the user can interactively choose any facet or reach in order to observe its hydrograph.

APPLICATIONS

During the development of the system and in order to test its modules, especially those where the overland flow is calculated, the information of a small watershed was used. This watershed is located within the Walnut Gulch Experimental Watershed, operated by the USDA-ARS in Southeastern Arizona. The watershed area is around 3600 m^2 and its main characteristics are described by Goodrich et al.(1988). There is a raingauge close to the watershed centroid and it is assumed that the rainfall is uniformly distributed within the area.

From a watershed contour map 40 points, where the topographic slope changes abruptly, were selected and a 81 triangular facets with 14 reaches model was constructed. Figure 1 shows a 3D representation of the watershed. The triangular facets have been superposed.

In order to study the general behavior of the model, some real rainfall events were selected and the obtained hydrographs were compared with the observed runoff. Figure 2 shows the calculated and the measured hydrographs corresponding to a 40 minutes rainfall event.

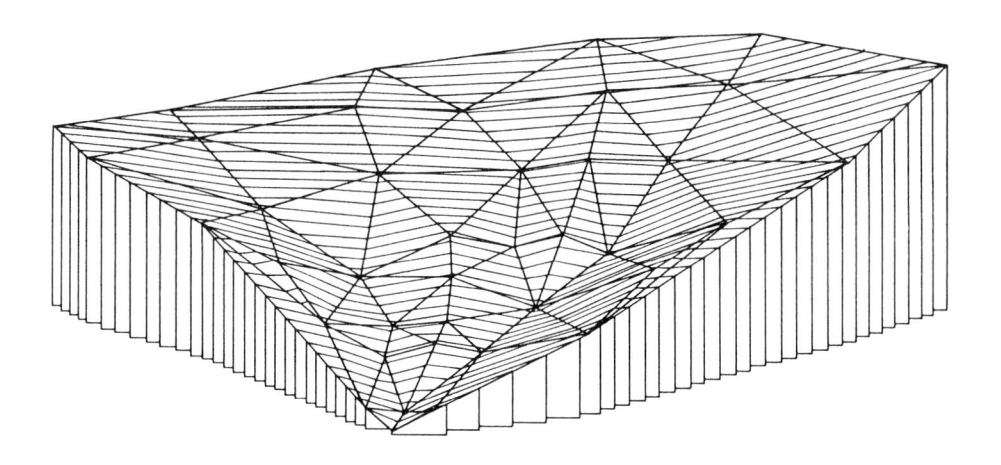

Figure 1. 3D Representation of the Lucky Hills experimental Watershed (Tombstone, Az).

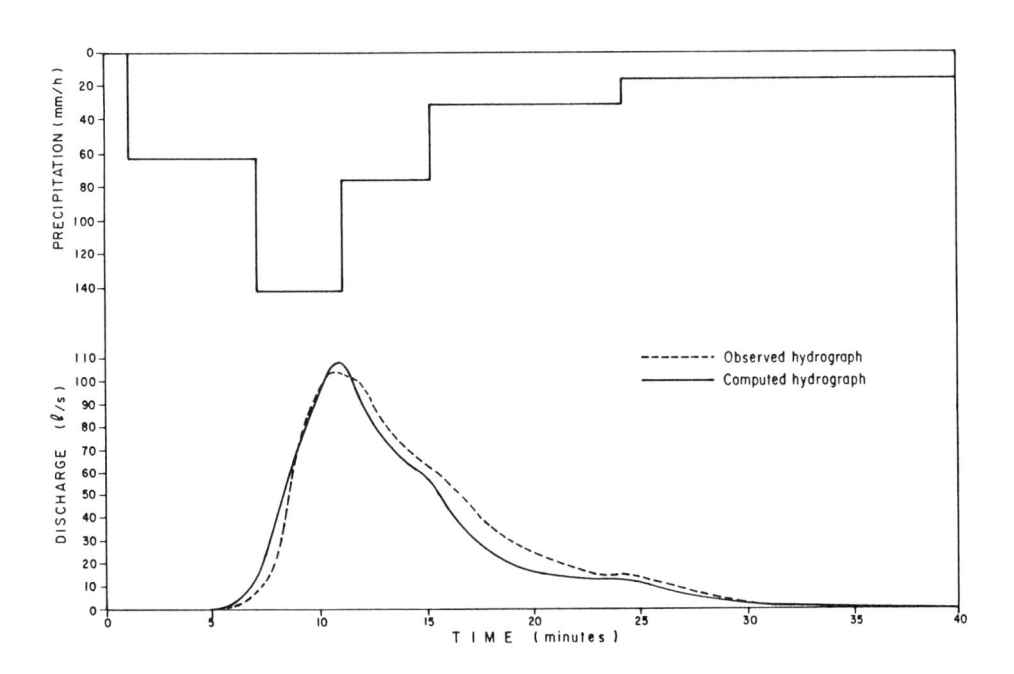

Figure 2. Calculated and measured hydrographs of a 40 minute rainfall event.

DISCUSSION

The present version of SHIFT is a very simple one that lacks a groundwater module, which is essential in many cases. SHIFT does not calculate the soil water redistribution and evapotranspiration and hence is unable to carry out a continuous simulation. It is an "event model" and hence it requires the knowledge of the initial water content for each event simulation. Another limitation of the present version of SHIFT is that it does not consider the existence of ponds and reservoirs.

However, all these limitations are superable and future versions of the system may include the corresponding modules to overcome such deficiencies. Much more important are other fundamental problems, such as those mentioned particularly by Beven (1989).

The distributed models need the value of several parameters and input variables (roughness, hydraulic conductivity, saturation, initial water content, etc.) at each unit element (triangular facet or reach). This situation may pose an important economic limitation in many cases. However, if it is necessary to optimize those parameter values by comparison of observed and simulated responses a more important problem arises, since "many different combinations of parameter values may give equally acceptable results" (Beven, 1985).

Whether in spite of all of these fundamental problems the distributed models will be able to produce valuable hydrologic predictions is something that remains to be seen. Some preliminary results (Bathurst, 1986) seem encouraging and probably this is why some other distributed models are being developed. Anyhow, to predict the influence of the variability of soil properties and rainfall (at the watershed level) in the resulting runoff may be difficult and not very accurate with the present distributed models, but it is entirely out of the question with models lumped to the catchment scale.

As mentioned before, in distributed models the basis for all the hydrologic computations is the topographic model of the watershed. Moore et al. (1988) mention three principal types of digital topographic models: a) triangular irregular network (TIN), b) square-grid network and c) contour-based network. Peucker et al. (1978) showed the advantages of the TIN models over the square-grid ones. Contour-based models partition the watershed into a series of interconnected parallel one-dimensional finite element cells. However, "this approach needs at least an order of magnitude more points in contour line form than in regular grid form to adequately describe the elevation surface and it is computationally slower than the grid cell approach" (Moore et al. 1988). It should be also noted that the definition of the lines of steepest slope is a time-consuming process. On the other hand, the runoff calculations may be easily performed, since the cells are ordered in cascades without influence from lateral cells, although some merging of stream tubes do occur, because of the converging water paths.

In the TIN models the water paths cross the triangle network in a way that at first does not seem tractable for runoff computations because of the many mergings and branchings. In these models it is relatively easy to find the lines of steepest slope (Palacios and Cuevas, 1986). Since these lines can be determined it is easy to define which triangles are upstream or downstream in regard to a given triangle. After this, as was shown in a previous section, the definition of cascades of planes and reaches is straightforward and the hydrologic computations (using the kinematic wave equation) may be performed. We then conclude that our proposed way of creating (and eventually editing) a TIN watershed model facilitates the automatic handling of the runoff computations in this kind of networks, something that will contribute to a wider use of TIN models, which present many advantages over other kind of topographic models.

One of the advantages of the distributed models is that they allow to carry out sensibility analysis of the involved parameters. In different tests we found that the initial water content, the hydraulic conductivity and the roughness coefficient have the main influence. The initial water content defines the hydrograph starting time as well as the pick time. The hydraulic conductivity influences the runoff volume and the roughness coefficient affects the hydrograph shape.

Since SHIFT is an interactive system it gives an immediate answer to the changes in parameters proposed by the user, greatly facilitating in this way the sensibility analysis.

ACKNOWLEDGEMENTS

Advantage is taken of this opportunity to acknowledge the researchers who have participated in this project. William Gandoy-Bernasconi, José Pimentel-López and Eduardo Chávarri-Velarde worked in the hydrologic module. Luis Rendón Pimentel developed the infiltration sub-module. Pablo López-Antezana participated in the development of the interpolation procedure and in the module to capture rainfall data. Jesús Chávez-Morales took part in the general design of the system and José Antonio Pedraza-Oropeza was of great help in developing some graphic routines and user-friendly features of the system. Juan Avila-Alcibar helped to test the programs and Guadalupe Ortiz Candia wrote the various manuscripts.

The authors would like to make special mention of Dr. David A. Woolhiser and Dr. David C. Goodrich, from the Aridland Watershed Mgmt. Res. Unit, USDA-ARS, Tucson, Az, with whom many parts of the project were discussed and from whom many suggestions were received. Working meetings with Dr. Woolhiser and Dr. Goodrich took place with a financial support from the USDA-OICD and the Mexican Ministry of Agriculture. (SARH-DGAI).

REFERENCES

Abbott, M.B., J.C. Bathurst, J.A. Cunge, P.E. O'Connell and J. Rasmussen, 1986a. *An Introduction to the European Hydrological System-Systeme Hydrologique Europan*, "SHE", 1: History and Philosophy of a Physically-based, Distributing Modelling System. J. of Hydrology, 87, 45:59.

Abbott, M.B., J.C. Bathurst, J.A. Cunge, P.E. O'Connell and J. Rasmussen, 1986b. *An Introduction to the European Hydrological System-Systeme Hydrologique European*, "SHE", 2: The Structure of a Physically-based, Distributed Modelling System. J. of Hydrology, 87, 61:77.

Bathurst, J.C., 1986. *Physically-based Distributed Modelling of an Upland Catchment Using the Systeme Hydrologique European*. J. of Hydrology, 87, 79-102.

Beven, K., 1985. *Distributed Models, in Hydrological Forecasting*. Edited by M.G. Anderson and T.P. Burt., John Wiley & Sons Ltd., 405-435.

Beven, K., 1989. *Changing Ideas in Hydrology-The case of Physically-based Models*. J. of Hydrology, 105, 157:172.

Duchon, J., 1976. *Interpolation des fonctions de deux variables suivant le principe de la flexion des plaques minces*. Revue Française d'Automatique, Informatique et Recherche Opérationnelle. Vol 10, No. 12, 5:12.

Dubrule, O., 1984. *Comparing Splines and Kriging. Computers & Geosciences* Vol. 10, No. 2-3, 327:338.

Gandoy, B.W. and O. Palacios-Vélez, 1990. *Automatic cascade numbering of unit elements in distributed hydrological models*. J. of Hydrology, (112), 375: 393.

Goodrich, D.C., Woolhiser, D. A. and Sorooshian S., 1988. *Model complexity required to maintain hydrologic response*. ASCE National Conference on Hydraulic Engineering, Colorado, Springs, Colo., Aug 6-10.

Level T., G. Bastin, C. Obled, and J.D. Creutin, 1987. *On the Accuracy of Areal Rainall Estimation: A Case Study*. Water Resour. Res., 23(11). 2123:2134.

Moore, I.D., J.C. Panuska, R.B. Grayson and K.P. Srivastova, 1988. *Application of Digital Topographic Modelling in Hydrology*. ASAE Proc. of the Intern. Symposium on Modeling Agricultural, Forest and Rangeland Hydrology, Chicago, Ill., Dec. 12-13, 447:481.

Palacios-Vélez O. and B. Cuevas Renaud, 1986. *Automated river-course, ridge and basin delineation from digital elevation data* J. Hydrology, 86, 299:314.

Palacios-Vélez O. and B. Cuevas Renaud, 1990a. SHIFT: *Sistema Hidrológico de Facetas Triangulares,* Manual Técnico y de uso. Colegio de Postgraduados, Montecillo, Méx. México.

Palacios-Vélez O. and B.Cuevas Renaud, 1990b. *A dynamic hierarchical subdivision algorithm for computing Delaunay triangulations and other closest-point problems*. ACM TOMS, Vol. 16, No. 3, September, 1990, 275:292.

Palacios-Vélez O. y Cuevas Renaud, 1990c. SHIFT: *A distributed runoff Model Using Irregular Triangular Facets*. Submitted to J. of Hydrology.

Peucker, T.K., R.J. Fowler, J.J. Little and D.M. Mark, 1978. *The Triangulated Irregular Network*. Procc. of the ASP-ACSM Symp. on DTM's. St. Louis, Missouri, May 9-11, 516:540.

Smith, R.E. and J.Y. Parlange, 1978. *A parameter-efficient hydrologic infiltration model*. Water Res. Research. Vol. 14, No. 3, 533-538.

Woolhiser, D.A.; R.E. Smith and D.C. Goodrich, 1989. KINEROS, *A Kinematic runoff and erosion model: Documentation and User Manual* U.S.D.A., ARS.

3 TECHNOLOGY TRANSFER

THE TRANSFER OF TECHNICAL INFORMATION IN THE WATER RESOURCES ARENA: TRUST AMONG COMPETING SOURCES

Dennis L. Soden

Janet S. Conary

and

Jerry L. Simich
Department of Political Science
University of Nevada, Las Vegas
Las Vegas, NV, USA 89154

ABSTRACT

The water resource issue is one which may be characterized as scientifically complex and technical in nature. The degree of trust which exists among competing providers of information is important in gaining insight into how different policy process actors respond to complex environmental issues. This paper looks at variation in positions held about sources of technical information among the general public, activists and policymakers utilizing data collected in the State of Florida, USA.

INTRODUCTION

The challenge of offering education in the water resources arena in light of the scientific and technical nature of the issue raises many questions and concerns which policymakers must address if they are to effectively manage the often too scarce supplies of water. Increasingly, it has become evident that various political and social forces in the policymaking process are the drivers of program development, in contrast to technological developments which hallmarked water resource development in the past. More often than not these are group forces, especially in western democracies, who undertake a number of education efforts in order to forward their perspective of the "public interest" pertaining to water resource use.

Through their efforts, special and general interest groups seek methods of educating the general public, other groups and policymakers. In doing so, they may be best advised to search for patterns of preference about sources of information, particularly those patterns which identify preferred sources of technical and scientific information about complex issues such as water resource development.

Less than complete agreement exists among students of public policy concerning the definitions of groups, be they interest groups, pressure groups, special or general interest, or lobbies (See, for example Garson, 1978). For our purposes we are addressing groups who have a political concern relating to water resources and actively seek to disseminate their information. We recognize that interest groups have purposes other than political and that associations engage in a wide range of activities. However, in the water resource area decisions made about water are classic clashes over scarce resources, are extremely political, and see groups actively disseminating information in order to educate policy process actors.

In this political environment, providers of information must be trusted if they hope to be successful. Who do individuals trust in the policy process associated with water resources? The technical and scientific complexity of the water resources issue is well documented (Pierce and Lovrich, 1986) and suggests problems may occur when the public is involved in the decision process. It is proposed that more knowledgeable individuals are able to dominate the process because of the information accrued to them as a result of their positions. Such may be the case with individual experts or very concerned elected and appointed officials (Freeman, 1974). Thus, it becomes important to ascertain which sources of information are most trusted by actors in the policy process attendant to water resources. In order to investigate this area of policymaking in the water arena, this study examines trust in technical information providers who are major actors in the education of citizens, other groups, and elected and non-elected officials. Moreover, education efforts lead to better informed participants in the policy process and give them the ability to choose the options best suited to their individual preferences. Knowledge of preferences for some providers of this information over others should, it is proposed, enhance our understanding of how we maximize these education efforts.

METHODS AND MEASURES

This study explores the views of the general public, its activist subset and policy experts about a set of natural resources issues in the State of Florida, USA. The results presented are based on a mail survey questionnaire distributed to the three samples. For the general public, the survey was sent to 1700 residents of the State of Florida. The surveys were distributed in proportion to the percentage of residents who live in a county; all counties in Florida were included. If a county has 10 percent of the population, 170 surveys were assigned to it. The sample was generated by the random selection of names from Florida telephone directories, with every available directory utilized. Some individuals identified through the sampling process could not be contacted, resulting in 311 undeliverable questionnaires. The original sample was thereby reduced to 1389 who were surveyed using a three-wave mailing in the Spring of 1988. Of the 1389, 699 or 50.3 percent responded to the survey.

The activist data set pertains to a subgroup within the general public who demonstrated the highest levels of political participation in the natural resources issue area. This group comprises a sample of 207 individuals obtained from the general public sample who recorded the highest levels of political activity in regards to natural resources in the State of Florida. The activists were identified on the basis of an index composed of eight items relating to involvement in natural resource issues. A lead-in question asked: "Have you ever tried to influence a decision about the use of natural resources in Florida in any of the following ways?" Individuals who answered yes to five or more of these activities were identified as "activists" within the general population. (The scale of reliability [Cronbach's Alpha] for the activism index is .781) The expectation in using this group is that the activist group is the most likely element of the public to be highly attuned to public policy debates in the area of natural resources. As such, these individuals are likely to be the first elements in the public to act out their roles of advocacy in behalf of their interests. From the 699 general public respondents, 207 or 29.7% are categorized as "activists" in the analysis.

The results presented with respect to policy experts are based on the mail survey questionnaire sent to two sets of respondents. The first set included 250 policy experts in Florida who recorded membership in professional organizations with a natural resource emphasis (i.e., American Society for Civil Engineers, American Planning Association). These individuals were contacted via a two-way survey (an initial mailing and a follow-up), unlike the general public, because of a higher response rate after two-waves. The second set was made up of the 160 members of the Florida State Legislature who were surveyed via a three-wave approach. These two sets were combined to develop a set of policy experts we refer to as environmental professionals (Soden and Conary, 1990). In all, 410 surveys were distributed. Nineteen surveys were either undeliverable or rejected, while 208 were returned, resulting in a combined effective response rate of 53.2 percent.

TRUST IN SOURCES OF TECHNICAL INFORMATION: FINDINGS

The major aim of this study is to identify the degree of trust which exists in providers of technical information in the water resources issue area. Much of the discussion in the scholarly literature about this issue focuses on public involvement, mandated in the United States by the National Environmental Policy Act of 1969. It concerns the role of the public and its need to obtain the requisite scientific and technical information so that they can compete with activists and policy experts (Soden, 1990). The role of the activists relates to pluralism (Truman, 1951) and concern about which groups and individuals the general public is likely to rely upon for the information they need to assess complex technical questions. The role of the policy expert, in this study reported as environmental professionals, centers largely around whether they use different sources of information and exact policy concurrence because of their positions (Pierce et al., 1987).

The first issue to be considered is to view the general level of trust in competing providers of technical information. Table 1 illustrates that four groups are seen as having considerable trust among the general public, activists and policy experts. College/University Educators receive the highest index scores for both samples, 84.5 for the general public, 87 for the activists and 89.7 for the policy experts. This group is followed by the National Park Service, 81.5, 80.6 and 83.3 for the general public, activists and experts respectively. The Florida Department of Natural Resources, the Department of Environmental Regulation, Water Management Districts, Technical and Scientific Experts, along with the Environmentalists all obtain index scores in excess of +50 from all three samples. The least trusted group sources of technical information are Labor Unions and Developers/Construction

TABLE 1: Trust in Group Sources of Technical Information

Among the General Public, Activists and Policy Experts Question: Many groups may supply technical information about water resources. How much trust do you have in the technical information supplied by each of the groups listed below?

Group	Response Percentages				
A Great					
Business					
General Public	16.5	42.8	35.5	02.4	- 21.5
Activists	15.0	38.6	42.5	02.9	-08.2
Environmental Professionals	09.7	30.2	53.5	01.9	+15.5
Environmentalists					
General Public	02.6	12.0	51.2	31.2	+67.8
Activists	01.9	13.0	50.7	31.9	+67.7
Environmental Professionals	01.3	14.8	58.7	22.6	+65.2
Developers/Construction Co.					
General Public	38.1	40.9	16.0	01.4	- 61.6
Activists	33.3	44.0	19.8	01.0	- 56.5
Environmental Professionals	23.2	47.1	25.8	03.9	- 40.6
College/University Educators					
General Public	01.6	04.3	45.8	44.6	+84.5
Activists	01.4	03.9	39.6	52.7	+87.0
Environmental Professionals	00.6	03.9	50.3	43.9	+89.7
Farmers					
General Public	04.7	28.2	51.1	09.9	+28.1
Activists	06.8	34.8	49.3	08.2	+15.9
Environmental Professionals	07.1	32.9	56.8	01.9	+18.7
Fishing Industry					
General Public	09.6	28.5	47.9	10.3	+20.1
Activists	08.7	29.5	51.7	08.2	+21.7
Environmental Professionals	08.4	26.5	56.1	07.7	+28.9
National Park Service					
General Public	01.1	06.3	41.1	47.8	+81.5
Activists	02.4	06.8	44.9	44.9	+80.6
Environmental Professionals	01.9	06.5	46.5	45.2	+83.3 1
Outdoor Recreation Advocates					
General Public	03.9	23.6	55.5	12.9	+40.9
Activists	03.9	25.6	55.1	13.5	+39.1
Environmental Professionals	02.6	23.9	63.2	09.0	+45.7
Industry					
General Public	14.9	27.9	39.9	10.4	+40.9
Activists	18.8	28.5	39.6	07.2	- 00.5
Environmental Professionals	14.2	36.8	36.8	06.5	- 07.7
Labor Unions					
General Public	52.9	33.6	08.9	00.6	- 77.0
Activists	54.1	33.3	09.7	00.0	- 77.0
Environmental Professionals	49.0	38.1	10.3	00.0	- 76.8

TABLE 1: Continued

State Legislators					
General Public	20.0	39.8	35.3	01.7	- 22.8
Activists	17.4	35.7	44.0	01.9	- 07.2
Environmental Professionals	11.6	36.8	49.0	01.9	+02.5
Timber Companies					
General Public	30.5	36.3	25.6	02.6	- 38.6
Activists	29.0	37.7	26.6	02.9	- 37.2
Environmental Professionals	23.9	41.3	29.0	03.9	- 32.3
Water Management Districts					
General Public	05.2	17.5	53.2	19.9	+50.4
Activists	05.3	16.9	51.7	24.6	+54.1
Environmental Professionals	01.9	08.4	56.8	32.3	+78.8
Public Utilities					
General Public	16.0	39.1	36.6	04.9	- 13.6
Activists	15.5	36.2	42.0	05.3	- 04.4
Environmental Professionals	10.3	31.6	50.3	07.1	+15.5
Dept. of Natural Resources					
General Public	03.0	07.7	46.9	39.5	+75.7
Activists	03.4	08.2	38.6	48.3	+75.3
Environmental Professionals	01.9	05.8	41.9	50.3	+84.5
Dept. of Environmental Regulation					
General Public	03.4	12.6	48.1	32.2	+64.3
Activists	03.9	12.6	44.0	37.7	+65.2
Environmental Professionals	01.9	11.6	46.5	40.0	+73.0
Dept. of Community Affairs					
General Public	10.9	27.0	44.1	11.9	+18.1
Activists	07.7	27.5	46.4	05.5	+26.7
Environmental Professionals	05.8	20.0	47.7	24.5	+46.4
Federal Agency Representative					
General Public	08.9	26.5	50.2	10.2	+25.0
Activists	07.2	19.8	57.0	14.0	+44.0
Environmental Professionals	03.2	18.1	60.6	16.8	+56.1
Local Govt. Representative					
General Public	10.4	34.3	45.8	06.0	+07.1
Activists	08.2	30.4	53.1	07.2	+21.7
Environmental Professionals	04.5	25.8	55.5	13.5	+38.7
Technical & Scientific Experts					
General Public	02.7	07.7	47.5	39.5	+76.6
Activists	01.4	05.3	46.9	45.4	+85.6
Environmental Professionals	00.6	01.9	48.9	48.4	+94.3

*Index is the sum of those responding "Some" and "A Great Deal" minus the sum of those responding "None" and "Not Much".

Companies, each with scores in excess of -60 among at least two sets of respondents. These low scores are not unexpected since these would be groups who place economic incentives above environmental interests in the pursuit of their collective goals and are not expected to be among the most trusted sources of technical information about natural resource issues.

Beyond recognizing general patterns which exists about trust in sources of technical information, it is also important to realize that while information sources may receive about the same average trust among the general public, activists and experts, their distributions about the mean may, in fact, be quite different. As previous research has pointed out, "The most politicized interests in a policy area would be expected to exhibit the greatest differentiation about mean scores." In this regard, the standard deviation of trust scores for each group source of information is reported in Table 2. Across all groups there exists disagreement about the trust in potential information providers. Among the general public, Industry and the State of Florida's Department of Community Affairs recorded high deviation (1.06 and 1.0, respectively). Several groups also score high on potential for conflict among the general public based on standard deviation scores of .9 or better, namely environmentalists, college/university educators, farmers, National Park Service, Timber Companies, Water Management Districts, Public Utilities, Department of Natural Resources, Department of Environmental Regulation and Federal Agencies. It is these providers who may face the toughest test in gaining acceptance for their educational efforts among the general public, and as a consequence see this provision challenged at one extreme and well-accepted at the other.

TABLE 2: Level of Differentiation in Trust of Sources of Technical Information

Information Source	General Public	Policy Activists	Experts
Business	.84	.80	.70
Environmentalists	.90	.86	.81
Developers/Construction Companies	.82	.79	.80
College/University Educators	.91	.83	.71
Farmers	.92	.78	.72
Fishing Industry	.93	.84	.80
National Park Service	.92	.78	.69
Outdoor Recreation Advocates	.89	.81	.70
Industry	1.06	1.02	.97
Labor Unions	.74	.71	.71
State Legislators	.86	.80	.74
Timber Companies	.93	.91	.87
Water Management Districts	.96	.87	.72
Public Utilities	.90	.84	.80
Dept. of Natural Resources	.91	.87	.69
Dept. of Environmental Regulation	.96	.91	.73
Dept. of Community Affairs	1.0	.93	.92
Federal Agency Representative	.94	.86	.76
Local Government Representative	.88	.78	.76
Technical & Scientific Experts	.88	.73	.63

a. The entry is the standard deviation of trust evaluations given to that particular source.

Among activists and policy experts, similar patterns are in evidence. The highest scores in each instance are recorded by Industry (1.02 and .97 for activists and policy experts, respectively). Overall, activist record more deviation about nearly every group thereby suggesting their conflict over trustworthiness of sources. Activism is not novel in the U.S. political system and the record of the "environmental movement" clearly supports a major concern for the information provided by competing group sources. Policy experts, for a number of reasons report less conflict about sources, possibly as a result of higher education levels, better access and more experience in weeding out some sources over others.

Other accounts for variations about trust for these education actors exist in the extant literature. One well accepted explanation is that individuals trust those sources with whom they have compatible values (Soden, 1990). Based on compatibility with political, social and environmental orientations, it has been proposed that the costs of information acquisition and assessment of information reliability are reduced (Greenwald, 1977). In light of this, and the evidence presented in this study, it may well be that conflict is reduced when information providers are already accepted as supporting beliefs, both personal and perhaps professional (Soden, et al., 1988). Inversely, conflict is heightened as group providers attempt to educate those holding non-sympathetic values.

CONCLUSION

Education efforts via technical information dissemination by groups has a distinct impact on the policymaking process. Group education efforts clearly enhance the democratic process, but need not be expected to unite individuals with varying predispositions. Knowledge transfer may well lead to enhanced group positions and better positioning by groups on the water resources agenda, an important consideration for those policy experts and activists in the water policy arena.

Given the plethora of group providers which exist, there are obviously multiple pathways for education of the general public, its active subset and policy experts. The message provided by the data described here is clearly only a first-step towards understanding a very complicated question of group activity in the public and civic education process. The findings do, however, provide some clues about groups which may have a better chance of gaining broad acceptance as opposed to facing pressure about the "goodness" or "trustworthiness" of their information. Hopefully, the clues will provide some information which will increase the efficiency of the education process thereby generating concern which will lead to the best policies for managing our water resources.

REFERENCES

Freeman, D. (1974) *Technology and Society*. Markham: Chicago, IL

Garson, G.D. (1978) *Group Theories of Politics*. Sage Publications: Beverly Hills, CA.

Greenwald, C. (1977) *Group Power: Lobbying and Public Policy.* Praeger: New York, NY.

Pierce, J. and Lovrich, N. (1986) Water Resources, Democracy, and the Technical Information Quandary. Associated Faculty Press: Millwood, NY.

Pierce, J., Lovrich, N., Tsurutani, T. and Abe T. (1987) *Environmental Policy Elites' Trust of Information Sources.* American Behavioral Scientist. 30 (6): 578-596.

Soden, D. (1990) *Managing Florida's Coastal Resources: Technical Complexity and Public Attitudes.* Florida Sea Grant College: Gainesville, FL.

Soden, D., Lovrich, N., Pierce, J. and Lamb, B. (1988) *Public Involvement in Natural Resource Policy Processes: A View From The Inside-Out.* The Environmental Professional. 10 (4): 304-316.

Soden, D. and Conary, J. (1990) *Trust in Sources of Technical Information About Coastal Resources Among Environmental Professionals.* Presented at the meeting of the National Association of Environmental Professionals. June 1990, San Antonio, TX.

Truman, D. (1951) *The Governmental Process.* Knopf: New York, NY.

INTERNATIONAL TECHNICAL INFORMATION EXCHANGE AND TRAINING - SOME EXPERIENCES OF THE SWISS NATIONAL HYDROLOGICAL AND GEOLOGICAL SURVEY

M. Spreafico
Service Hydrologique et Geologique National
CH - 3003 Bern, Switzerland

and

R. Grabs
Deutsche Gesellschaft fuer
Technische Zusammenarbeit (GTZ)
(German Technical Agency)
D - 6236 Eschborn, Germany

ABSTRACT

In this paper, three selected projects of technical collaboration and technology transfer are briefly described. The projects were selected in a way that - in the opinion of the authors - representative examples for international cooperation in hydrology are presented. The example of the implementation of the Dilution Method in surface hydrology in Nepal demonstrates some basic principles of an efficient bilateral technology transfer. In the example of the International Commission for the Hydrology of the Rhine River Basin it is demonstrated, how a successful cooperation in an international river basin is organized and implemented. The example of the Working Group Hydrology of the Regional Association VI of WM0 is chosen to present the information exchange and cooperation in a region with the assistance of an international organization.

INTRODUCTION

Our society is making ever increasing use of water resources, in particular for drinking water supply, agriculture and for industrial purposes. In order to meet the increasing demand, a rationalized and optimized management of water resources is indispensable. This however, can only be achieved on the basis of high-quality hydrological information and well trained and experienced manpower. The acquisition of hydrological information requires great efforts in data acquisition in often adverse natural environments, data processing and analysis of hydrological variables. The development and operational use of often complex measuring instruments, methods and mathematical models exerts an increasingly high pressure on finances and the training of personnel. These preconditional efforts are quite so high, that many countries can simply not afford the costs involved in the development and implementation of new technologies. This leads to the fact, that water resources planning is often based on inadequate hydrological information and planning is sub-optimal which is more so regrettable, as water is a scarce commodity in many parts of the world and its harnessing and use a heavy burden on national economies.

To improve this situation, it is necessary to intensify and institutionalize bilateral and international cooperation. Despite the progress achieved in the past years through the efforts of international organizations like WMO and UNESCO, scientific organizations like IAHS and a great number of bilateral projects, a lot remains to be done and negative as well as positive examples teach us good lessons. In the following paragraphs, three projects are put forward which - in the view of the authors - seem in principal to be adequate to secure a sustainable technology transfer in hydrology.

BILATERAL TECHNOLOGY TRANSFER IN A TECHNICAL COOPERATION PROJECT

Since 1987, the Federal Republic of Germany -through the German Technical Agency is implementing a technical cooperation project with the Kingdom of Nepal in the field of Snow and Glacier Hydrology. The purpose of the project is the establishment of a measuring service for snow and glacier hydrology in the high Himalayas with the long-term objective to simulate and forecast the snow and icemelt runoff for water resources projects. In the course of the project, it became evident, that a specialized technology had to be selected and introduced to quantify discharges in steep, fully turbulent remote high mountain rivers, fed to a large extend by snow and glacial meltwaters. Key questions were:

1. Can a new, rather complex technology, which has not been in use in this country, be absorbed by the personnel of the Snow and Glacier Hydrology Unit in the Department of Hydrology and Meteorology?

2. Is the technology adapted in a way, that it can be used in the field by relatively less educated field staff and the laboratory operated in Kathmandu?

3. Is the technology sustainable in the context of routine operations by indigenous personnel, scarce financial resources and dependency on imports of operating materials and spare parts?

A sensitive approach had to be chosen to tackle these problems:

- A competent participating institution had to be found

- The technical aspects and the training components had to be adapted to the specific conditions in Nepal

- A long-term involvement by the donor-agency (GTZ) and technical backstopping by the participating institution (LHG) had to be envisaged.

The Swiss National Hydrological and Geological Survey (LHG), operating in a country with largely comparable hydrological conditions and with decades of experience in the use of a special dilution method (the Tracer Method) in hydrology which was found to be best suited to the conditions in Nepal- agreed to cooperate in the framework of this project.

By the method used by the LHG, a known quantity of initial tracer solution of a fluorescent tracer (Sulforhodamine G) with a concentration C1 is injected into the river water over a specific period of time. The injection time must be calculated in such a manner, that an evenly diluted concentration C2 flows through the entire sampling cross-section of the river during a specific time (Figure 1). If the weight of the marking substance passing through the injection cross-section of the river is equal to the weight of the tracer passing through the sampling cross-section, then the following formula (Eq. 1) is obtained:

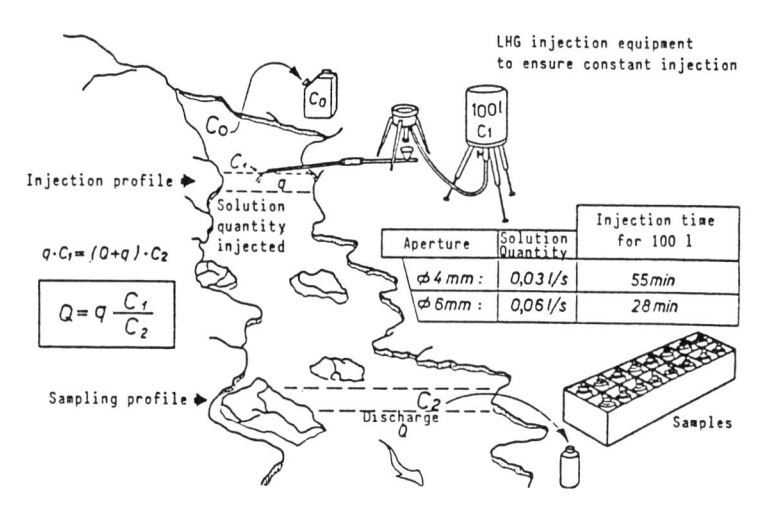

Figure 1. Scheme of the Tracer Dilution Method used by the Swiss National Hydrological and Geological Survey.

$$Co \times 0 + q \times C1 = C2 \,(0 + q) \tag{1}$$

If Co is very small and q is negligibly small with respect to 0, then:

$$Q = q \times \frac{C1}{C2} \tag{2}$$

whereby:

- Co : Natural concentration of tracer in river water
- 0 : Discharge in the river
- q : Constant quantity of tracer solution injected
- C1 : Concentration of injected tracer solution
- C2 : Tracer concentration in the sampling cross-section

The following criteria must be met, if the LHG tracer method is to be used:
- The discharge must be approximately constant during the measuring procedure
- The entire quantity of tracer which is injected must flow through the sampling cross-section
- The tracer must be well dispersed at the sampling point. This means, that the same quantity of tracer must flow past each point of the sampling cross-section

As indicated above, this technology is not used routinely in the region, so no trained personnel was available. Even elsewhere, this technology is by no means commonly used in hydrological services. To achieve the objectives as outlined above, a 10-day theoretical training course in tracer hydrology was held by the German Agency for Radiation and Environmental Research to introduce the principles of the method to the staff of the Snow and Glacier Hydrology Unit (SGHU). Subsequently, the LHG was contracted in 1990 with the following principle term of reference:

The personnel of the Snow and Glacier Hydrology Unit of the Department of Hydrology and Meteorology in Nepal has to be trained in such a way that - with the necessary field equipment delivered and the tracer laboratory established - its members can independently and operationally execute all field and laboratory works which are necessary to determine the discharge in high mountain rivers and establish the water level-discharge relationship with tracer hydrological methods.

To meet these objectives, the following tasks have been carried out :

1. Acquisition of tracer hydrological instruments and operating materials (Figure 2). Full use was made of the technical experience of the LHG so that identical instruments were procured, which have been in use for several years at the LHG. Where necessary, the components of the system were adapted to the Nepalese conditions, especially with respect to safety of handling and minimizing operating errors.

2. Before the establishment of the tracer laboratory, the complete system was assembled at the LHG, pre-calibrated and tested to check any problem that might come up beforehand; special spare part kits were compiled to meet on-site requirements in Nepal.

3. An Operation Manual has been compiled which, in a step-by step approach, explains all procedures in the field and the laboratory for the operational use of the tracer method. Without compromising in accuracy, the procedures were simplified and edited in view of the introduction of this new technology into the Nepalese environment.

4. Right from the beginning of the establishment of the tracer laboratory in Nepal, the Nepalese personnel was actively integrated to obtain first-hand, on-the-job experience in this technology.

5. During a two-week practical training period, the personnel of the SGHU was trained in small, closely supervised groups in all aspects of field and

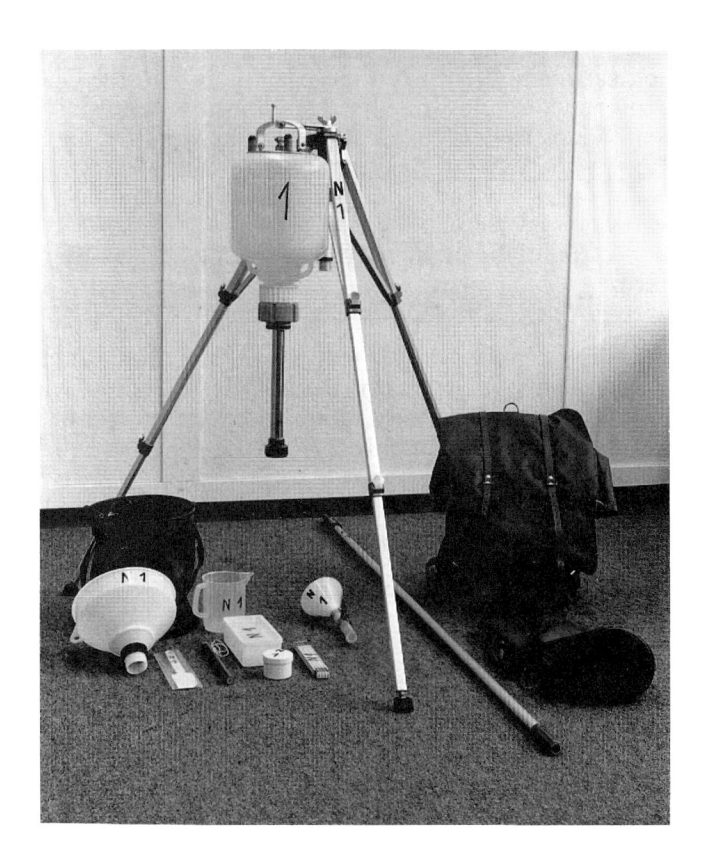

Figure 2. Tracer injection equipment with MARIOTT-bottle.

laboratory works. The training was followed by a practical examination under real field/laboratory conditions.

6. Each staff under training was supplied with a set of manuals and additional materials presented during the training course. A special challenge was the very diverse educational level of the staff trained which ranged from tenth-grade school leaving certificate to Ph.D. trained personnel in the same group. Good experiences were made with the extensive use of audiovisual teaching materials.

Currently, the LHG is assisting the GTZ-Project with continuous support of the SGHU in terms of calculation of operating expenses, supply of operating materials and technical advice, should difficulties arise during the lifetime of the project. To monitor the accuracy of the measurements and the overall performance of the tracer laboratory and field works, cross-checks of measurements are made at the LHG. To implement the specific Nepalese experiences during the use of the tracer technology, to incorporate new developments at the LHG and to make up for shortcomings in practical and theoretical knowledge of the SGHU staff, a short-course in practical tracer hydrology is planned to hold in 1991/92

In cooperation with the GTS-expert, the SGHU-staff is using now the tracerhydrological method on a routine basis both - in the field and in the laboratory, with encouraging results. Neighboring countries with similar hydrological problems have taken an interest in the works of the SGHU.

Generally, - in the view of the authors - the following prerequisites and requirements are necessary for a successful bilateral technology transfer in a technical cooperation project :

Efforts and costs of bilateral projects can only be justified, when vital aspects concerning the long-term sustainability of project activities have been bilaterally discussed in detail. Such aspects include:

- Continued interest in the results of project activities (here: discharge of snow and glacier fed rivers of the high Nepal Himalayas) expressed not only by the target groups, but also by the project personnel and - with a sense of responsibility, by the superior authorities and politicians.

- Long-term commitment of counterpart personnel which has been trained, financial resources and working infrastructure (offices, laboratory space, etc.) to the project on behalf of the counterpart agency.

- Long-term commitment of technical backstopping including technical advice, some financial resources and continued other active support in post-project phases on behalf of donor agencies and collaborating institutions.

- The hydrological conditions should be comparable in executing bilateral projects which include technology transfer components or - at the very least - the technical advisers must have long standing experience of every detail of the new technology to be transferred under situations, which are comparable to the conditions in the recipient country.

- It is usually difficult to find institutions to participate on a medium - to - long term basis for such kind of projects as personnel is bound to a project and therefore is not available for other activities for which the institution may stand responsible as is the case with the LHG. It is therefore important, that the participating institution gains also from its cooperation.

The participating agency gains experience in the technology transferred, when the technical experience made by the project-agency is incorporated in improvements of the the technology itself. This greatly helps to further develop new technology and are a precondition for its transferability to other countries.

Since adapting hardware, training materials etc. to the specific country conditions can be very time consuming, involving high costs which are not always fully covered by donor agencies. It is desirable, that adapted, transferred technology packages have a multi-use capability. This can be achieved in several ways, e. g. bilateral technical assistance in another country, execution of regional training courses and/or implementation of the technology into the HOMS - System of WMO (HOMS = Hydrological Operational Multipurpose Subprogramme).

COLLABORATION AND TECHNOLOGY TRANSFER WITHIN RIVER BASINS

In the framework of the working Group Hydrology of the Regional Association VI (Europe) of WMO a report has been produced, which covers the subject of international cooperation in hydrology in international river basins (Spreafico, 1986). Besides the description of selected bilateral and multilateral hydrological projects in Europe, the collaboration in international commissions in large river basins has been closely examined. The report also includes general principles for international collaboration in the field of water resources management and recommendations.

Representative for a multitude of other projects, the work of the International Commission for the Hydrology of the Rhine River (CHR) shall be outlined below. The CHR was founded in 1970 within the framework of UNESCO's International Hydrological Decade with the following tasks:

- Support of cooperation between hydrological institutes and services active in the catchment area of the Rhine River

- Executing hydrological studies in the Rhine Basin and exchange of research results

- Promoting the exchange of hydrological data and information in the Rhine Basin as the real time data and discharge forecast data

- Development of standardized methods for collecting and processing hydrological data in the Rhine riparian countries

The organization of the commission is shown in Figure 3. Planning and coordination of the work is undertaken by the permanent representatives, which meet twice a year and are supported by a permanent secretariat. The work is undertaken by an editing committee, working groups and rapporteurs, assisted by the secretariat.

In the framework of the Commission, a large hydrological monography of the Rhine River Basin has been published. Amongst others, working groups on the standardization and processing of data and on hydrological forecast have been installed. Tasks for the rapporteurs are: Quantitative precipitation forecasts for the Rhine River Basin, analysis of drought (e.g. drought of 1976) and floods (e.g. floods of 1983 and 1988), probabilities of floods and low waters, representative basins, areal precipitation, effects of forests on the hydrology of the river basin. Important current projects are: changes in the discharge regime; descriptions of the impact of human activities on the Rhine discharge; determination of the effect of changes in land use and climate on the discharge regime of the Rhine), sediment (improvement and standardization of methods to measure suspended load and bed-load transport, description of sediment characteristics of the river) and determination of travel times within the Rhine River.

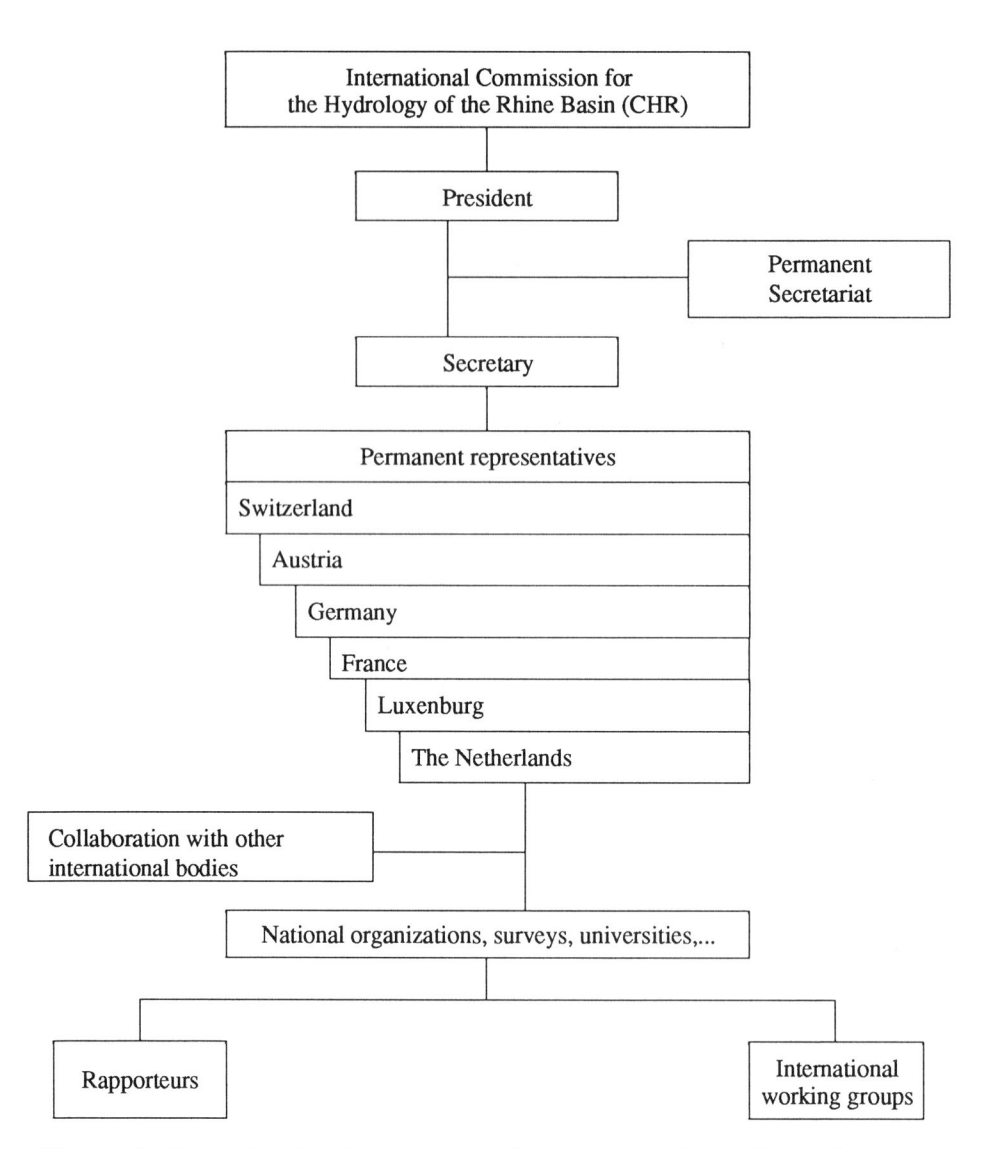

```
┌─────────────────────────────────┐
│   International Commission for  │
│ the Hydrology of the Rhine Basin (CHR) │
└─────────────────────────────────┘
              │
        ┌───────────┐
        │ President │──────────────┬──────────────────┐
        └───────────┘              │  ┌────────────────┐
              │                    └──│   Permanent    │
        ┌───────────┐                 │   Secretariat  │
        │ Secretary │                 └────────────────┘
        └───────────┘
              │
┌─────────────────────────────────┐
│    Permanent representatives    │
│ Switzerland                     │
│   Austria                       │
│     Germany                     │
│       France                    │
│         Luxenburg               │
│           The Netherlands       │
└─────────────────────────────────┘

┌──────────────────────┐
│ Collaboration with other │
│ international bodies  │
└──────────────────────┘
              │
┌─────────────────────────────────────────┐
│ National organizations, surveys, universities,... │
└─────────────────────────────────────────┘
         │                            │
┌──────────────┐            ┌──────────────────┐
│  Rapporteurs │            │   International  │
│              │            │  working groups  │
└──────────────┘            └──────────────────┘
```

Figure 3. Organizational structure of the International Commission for Hydrology of the Rhine River Basin.

During the last few years, several accidents have occurred, where the waters of the Rhine were polluted. At a meeting in December 1986, the respective ministers in charge of the adjacent countries of the Rhine instructed the CHR to develop methods to forecast travel times and transport of dissolved material in the river. A group with experts of the CHR and the International Commission for the Protection of the Rhine against Pollution has developed a transport model which is able to forecast the travel time and the concentration of pollutants in the Rhine. The model is suited for real-time application and is integrated in the Alarm and Warning System of the Rhine.

The latter project serves as an example for the collaboration of two international commissions, working in different fields in an international river basin.

Conclusions from the collaboration in the CHR:

- The overall proven political willingness for close international cooperation serves as firm ground for all other institutionalized collaboration in hydrology of international river basins.
- For the collaboration in an international river basin like the Rhine, expert commissions working in different specific fields are appropriate.
- Existing legislation, institutional structures and infrastructures in countries bordering water courses are sometimes an obstacle to collaboration. On the other hand, the existence of special laws concerning hydrology and the existence of national operational hydrological services is of an advantage.
- It is of great importance, that the Permanent Representatives in the CHR are the chiefs of powerful and effective institutions. As the financial resources of the CHR are very limited, the Permanent Representatives have to be concerned with the task providing the financial resources needed for projects and personnel of the CHR through the active support of member countries. This often delicate task is greatly facilitated, when projects and tasks are selected, which are of acute interest for as many member countries as possible and whose implementation is of high priority as e.g. the flood warning and pollution alarm systems.

REGIONAL COLLABORATION AND KNOW-HOW TRANSFER IN THE FIELD OF MODELLING THE WATER CYCLE

The recent programmes of the Regional Association VI Working Group on Hydrology of WMO are good examples for cooperation and information transfer in hydrology. There are several projects elaborating basic informations about observation networks and hydrological know-how in member countries. A special project in this context is called "Operational Hydrological Models". In this project, the owners of operational models use data sets placed at someone's disposal by other countries for calibration purposes. Data sets which are simulated by the calibrated model are sent back to collaborating institutions, who evaluate the results. The objectives pursued by these activities are twofold:

To allow the model owners judgement on the range of applicability of their models, and to allow data owners to choose types of models which best meet their requirements.

In the framework of this project, a cooperation has been developed between the Royal Meteorological Institute of Belgium (RMI) and the Swiss National Hydrological and Geological Survey (LHG). In Belgium, a detailed, operational water-bilance model has been developed (BULTOT et al. 1976; Figure 4). As an example for its wide range of applications capability, the effects of the increase of atmospheric carbondioxide on basin discharge can be simulated.

The quantification of such changes in the water bilance of river basins, caused by human interference is also of great interest for Switzerland. Therefore, a project was implemented between the two agencies as outlined below:

The LHG collected and supplied all necessary input parameters for the IRMB-model from the river Murg basin - one of the representative basins of Switzerland. For the calibration of the model, the LHG supplied for a period of five years all measured hydrological variables. The RMI computed the water bilance of the basin and simulated the basin runoff for the consequent two years with the calibrated model. The LHG compared the simulated with the actual discharges, and after discussions with RMI, improvements of the model components were implemented.

With the improved water-bilance model, RMI could compute the effects of a doubled atmospheric carbondioxide concentration on the runoff in the river Murg basin.

In the view of the participating institutions, such kind of international, institutional collaboration has the following mutual advantages:

- The development of such a complex model is extremely costly and time consuming and the calibration and actual use of the model requires great experience. A "Do-it-yourself" development of a comparable model by the LHG would have required approximately equal efforts and costs in addition to the costs and efforts for data acquisition; a take-over of the model by LHG would have incurred the costs for the purchase and would have required user-training for several months. In the view of the LHG, the collaboration with the RMI was the most cost-effective way.

- The acquisition of input data for such a complex water-balance model requires great technical, personal and financial efforts. Therefore, in many cases such kind of models cannot sufficiently be tested under various hydrological conditions. Subsequently, this leads to difficulties in the simulation of discharge forming processes, which have not been examined. The IRMB model had been developed for Belgian hydrological basin conditions. Therefore, it was of great interest for the RMI to find out to what extend the model could describe a hydrologically very different river basin. Through the additional experiences gained, an improvement of the model has been rendered possible. For possible applications of the model in other river basins these experiences and consequent model improvements are an important step forward.

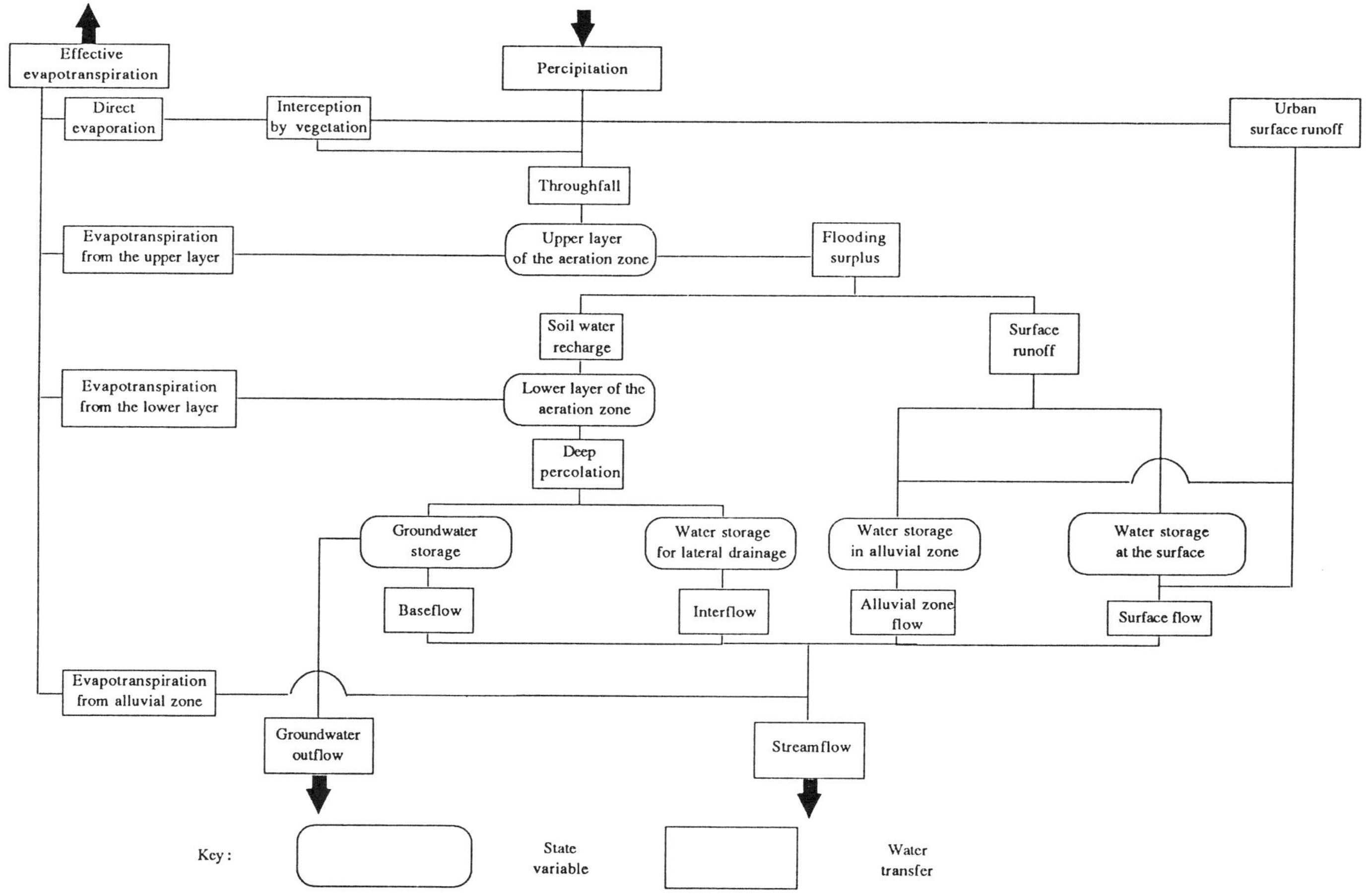

Figure 4. Structure of the IRMB-Model (Bultot, 1976).

125

CONCLUDING REMARKS

The previous examples have shown three principally feasible ways to effectively disseminate knowledge and experiences, technologies and technical know-how in hydrology. In the view of the authors, the common denominator of all approaches described here can be summarized:

The political will for bilateral and/or multilateral collaboration must materialize in strong and effective institutions which by their structure and organization are capable to absorb and operationalize new techniques and know-how in accord with the specific hydrological conditions and social structures. Where these institutions do not have this capability, projects with the purpose of institution building have to precede those hydrological projects, which rely heavily on administrative and managerial capabilities of the collaborating institution.

Sustainability of a project can only be reached, if the continuity of available trained personnel to the project, maintenance of equipments and project infrastructure and sufficiently allocated finance to a project could be secured. In many cases, this would suggest a long-term commitment by donor agencies and collaborating institutions to a project.

Vital for a continued political will and the sustainability of a project is the continued demand for the results or outputs of the projects. Besides demand for results, common, shared interests of the participating institutions, whereby each party gains from the project purpose directly or indirectly, are an especially strong and welcomed motivation for a successful project implementation.

REFERENCES

Bultot, F. and Dupriez, G.L., 1976. *Conceptual hydrological model for an average-sized catchment area.* Journal of Hydrology, 29, pp. 251-292.

Deutsche Gesellschaft fuer Technische Zusammenarbeit (GTZ), 1988. *Objective - oriented project planning. An introduction to the method.*

Spreafico, M., 1986. *Hydrological projects in international river basins.* Technical report of the Working Group Hydrology of the Association VI of WMO.

SPECIAL WATER RESOURCES OUTREACH PROGRAMS

Dr. M.H. Watt

and

Mr. J. H. Hannaham
D.C. Water Resources Research Center
University of the District of Columbia
4200 Connecticut Avenue, N.W.
Washington, D.C. 20008

ABSTRACT

By far, the most challenging aspects of education and training in the field of water resources are the process of technology and information transfer. In order to be effective, these processes must target professionals, students, decision makers and the public. The authors provide a highlight summary of their experiences and some of the lessons learned during the process of designing either ad hoc or institutionally related public enrichment programs. The paper also briefly highlights the environmental education programs of Historically Black Colleges and Universities (HBCU's), an option that many pre-college students will select for their higher education.

INTRODUCTION

Environmental problems and related issues are gaining in attention at local, national and international levels. Corresponding, there is a growing appreciation at all levels of the need to increase public understanding of the natural environment and to advance and develop environmental education.

All are concerned with potential and actual threats to human health and overall environmental quality associated with a broad range of conventional and toxic contaminants in the air, water and on the land. On an international scale there is growing evidence of problems such as global warming, ocean pollution and species diversity which all pose serious threats to human health, the quality of life and the economic vitality of urban areas as well as they do to the natural balance of rural areas.

A major effort will be required at all levels in the world community to inform and educate the public about the natural and built environment as a prerequisite to gaining public support of adequate measures for environmental education and training. The Universidad Autonoma De Chihuahua is to be congratulated for organizing this "International Symposium on Hydrology and Water Resources Education and Training: The Challenges to Meet at the Turn of the XXI Century" and the "Second North American Water Management Seminar". Each attendee at this symposium/seminar will gain a fuller understanding and appreciation of water related education and training and effective approaches and solutions learned which may then be applied or adapted to the particular environmental problems and issues confronting us at home.

As you are aware, the United States is a singularly unique country in that its population is a microcosm of the world's population. Its great strength and vitality is generated by the fantastic infusion and interaction of the talents and creativity of a diverse people of all colors, ethnicities, cultures and religions.

This paper is concerned primarily with the efforts of one institution, the D.C. Water Resources Research Center (D.C. WRRC) located in the city of Washington, D.C. to address several specific water and environmental education needs and concerns of a predominant African-American population.

As is the case with many other urban communities, the level of awareness and understanding of water issues is low relative to suburban and rural communities. The Center offers an extensive program of technology transfer including seminars, workshops, symposia, field trips and publications directed to the scientific community. Nevertheless, it was felt that special emphasis was needed to address pre-college youth and the public. Several water education intervention programs were developed to fit specific targeted groups. Over the years, these have been incorporated into the Center's Technology Transfer Program.

In addition, the Center has developed links with Historically Black Colleges and Universities (HBCU's), attempting to encourage and reinforce their environmental education program development and to strengthen cooperation and collaboration between them. These HBCU institutions are important elements in the international education network through their enrollment of large numbers of foreign students, primarily from the Third World countries.

This paper provides a summary of several education/training projects sponsored by the Center, directed to pre-college youth, university students professionals and the public. In addition, a brief overview is given to show the scope of undergraduate and graduate environmental education programs conducted at HBCU institutions.

A program of technology transfer was designed by the D.C. WRRC to increase the communication of technical and scientific knowledge and to promote a general understanding of water resources problems. Under this program the DC-WRRC:

- provides advice and assistance to local and regional governmental bodies;
- convenes conferences, symposia, workshops, and seminars;
- maintains a library of more than 4,000 water resources documents in all fields, from all the states and federal agencies;
- publishes technical reports distributed nation-wide, as well as to the Water Research Scientific Information Center (WRSIC) and the National Technical Information Service (NTIS);
- publishes a quarterly newsletter "Water Highlights";
- presents special awards for outstanding pre-college student water research projects.

Identification of the Target Audience for Dissemination

The target audience for the dissemination of information includes the following three levels:

- Administrators, managers, and government decision makers for the purpose of problem identification and water management policy issues. The Center is a member of several local and regional committees and commissions. It also represents the DC government to the Interstate Commission on the Potomac River Basin (ICPRB), to the Chesapeake Bay Scientific and Technical Advisory Committee (STAC), and the D.C. Soil Conservation District,
- The universities' scientific faculties and other experts through its publications, seminars and conferences, and
- The general public, including youth groups through conferences, exhibits, and public tours.

Research Training

The Center encourages student involvement in these projects, thereby enabling them to enhance their knowledge of water resources and helping them to improve their capabilities as water problem solvers. Ultimately, these students will develop careers in management, research, or a technical field related to water resources.

The Center recruits its students to assist in research projects, primarily from the University of the District of Columbia which is basically an undergraduate institution and from the other affiliated area universities which have graduate programs.

At the Center, students are an integral part of the research program. They participate in a wide range of activities under the direction of faculty who serve as principal investigators. These activities include field work, literature searches, laboratory analyses, and even independent analysis of a particular aspect of a major research project. An example of duties is shown as follows:

The student functions as assistant to the WRRC Project Researcher in the performance of the following duties:

- Assist in conducting library and literature search.
- General office work, including typing, organizing, filing, copying, etc.
- Assist in general technical research work.
- Collect data, measurements, data computation and analysis.
- General investigation.

The Center recruits a number of undergraduate and graduate students as research assistants, physical science technicians, and education technicians. While the majority of the students are paid with funds from research project grants, a number of them are paid through the Work-Study Program administrated by the Financial Aid Office of the University.

For the undergraduates: their background encompasses environmental science, biology, fishery, computer science, and business. Their involvement in the program will enable them to learn the basics of hydrology and water quality, field sampling techniques, compilation and analysis of data.

For the graduates: their duties involve literature research, data analysis, computer modeling and report writing. Table 1 gives an estimate of the student numbers and their distribution in the different fields from 1973 to 1988.

Table 1. STUDENT TRAINING ACCOMPLISHMENTS OF DC-WRRC (from 1973 to 1988)

TRAINING CATEGORY	Under-graduate	Master's Degree	Ph.D. Degree	Total
Chemistry	24	7	2	33
Engineering				
•Agricultural				
•Civil	12	8	4	24
•Environmental	1	3	1	5
•Soils				
•Systems	2			2
•Other: Admin.		1		1
Geology	1			1
Hydrology		1		1
Agronomy				
Biology	9	7	3	19
Ecology	18	4	1	23
Fishery, Wildlife and Forestry	2		2	
Computer Science	3			3
Economics				
Geography				
Law	1			1
Resources Planning	1		1	2
Other: Nursing	1			1
TOTAL	73	33	12	118

Internship

The Center cooperates with local DC area environmental and water resources agencies. The Center assists in placing student-interns to work during the summer in these agencies:

- Washington Council of Governments (COG)
- Interstate Commission on the Potomac River Basin (ICPRB)
- Department of Consumer and Regulatory Affairs (DCRA)
- Department of Public Works (DPW)

The students gain valuable experience as trainees and are exposed to a variety of field experiences.

I. SPECIAL SCIENCE PROGRAM FOR STUDENTS

In 1982, a group of science professionals from government, academia, and the local schools met to discuss their concerns with limited success of D.C. high school students as contestants in national and regional science fair competitions. It was decided eventually to establish the Special Science Program for Students, to facilitate collaboration with the junior and senior high schools and to support and encourage science oriented students in grades 7-12 to meet the challenges of such contests as the annual Westinghouse Science Talent Search as well as other similar national and regional events.

Student participants in the program were invited from among the winners in the various categories in the annual D.C. Science Fair in grade 7-12. Mentors were recruited from faculty at local universities and federal agency science facilities in the metropolitan Washington, D.C. area. Most of the mentors selected were African-Americans, both male and female, in order to keep with the intent to provide strong and effective role models for the students who were primarily African-American as well.

Program coordination between students, mentors, science teachers, and parents was lodged in the Center's Director and the Director of the D.C. Science Fair. During the first year of the program approximately 35 students were enrolled, 20 of whom were actively engaged with mentors in project preparation. Students represented both public and private schools, although the public schools were home to a majority of the students in the program. Important supporting roles were performed by several science teachers and a number of parents and relatives of participating students. Approximately 80% of the student participants were female.

General group meetings of students and mentors were held beginning in the fall, shortly after the start of the school year. Meeting were usually hosted at a mentor's facility and were primarily intended to identify student science project interests, to match up mentors with students requesting guidance, to report on progress with individual science projects, to exchange ideas, to participate in tours of science facilities of host mentors, and to share special programs, such as invited talks by guest scientists and mentors. Mentors coordinated their efforts with participating students and the students' science teachers. Parents and teachers also attended and made valuable contributions during the course of these group session which were held on Saturdays.

Student participants did very well in the D.C. Science Fair competition following the start of the program (1983-1984). Several were repeat winners in major science categories and/or recipients of honors and special awards. Overall, female students did exceedingly well in the first and in subsequent D.C. Science Fair competitions, taking virtually all major honors gained by student program participants.

After 1985, the Special Science Program for Student was formally incorporated into the Center's technology transfer program for administrative support previously lacking during the ad hoc initial start up years. However, the program, though retaining its student - mentor structure, became less broad in scope across all science disciplines and more oriented to providing guidance to students interested in research projects in the environmental and related engineering disciplines. The Center's Principal Investigators and staff assumed larger mentorship roles beginning with this transition.

D.C. Science Fair Winners continued to be invited to participate in the student-mentor program and interested new students were referred to the expanding pool of professional mentors representing a diversity of science, engineering, and social science disciplines. The main difference this time was that the close personal coordination and group assessments which were features at the beginning of the program were no longer feasible. Nevertheless, the Center continued to maintain computer-based mailing lists of all student winners who were periodically notified of special science activities and events in the area.

Among these events were tutorials hosted by the Center at the University and invitations to participate in special student programs at professional science organizations during their annual conferences in Washington, D.C. The Smithsonian Naturalist Center also joined with the Center in the sponsorship of special science programs for participating students and welcomed students and their mentors to share the Nautilus Center facilities as a meeting place and as a resource in project research and preparation. The Center's student participants are regularly invited to meet the Westinghouse Science Talent Search Program national finalist each year when they exhibit their projects in Washington, D.C. prior to the final selection of the top prizes.

II. D.C. WATER RESOURCES RESEARCH CENTER SPECIAL AWARD FOR WATER RESEARCH

The D.C. Science Fair continued to provide a stimulus for the Center to seek ways to reach and recognize students who showed interest and who were motivated to undertake research projects in the environmental sciences. In 1987, the first Special Award for Water Research was established by the Center. Award certificates and prizes were presented for the best student science projects at the Science Fair in the area of water research. Prior to establishing this Special Award, the Center identified outstanding student water projects and offered assistance to these students, encouraging them to enter their projects in special regional or national science fair competitions, such as the World of Water Award (WOW) sponsored by the National Marine Education Association (see Figure 1).

Recently, a 10th grade student recipient of the Center's Special Water Award presented his research results at a professional symposium sponsored by the Center. This student presented his findings and has had them included in the Symposium proceedings which were recently published. Other student winners of the Special Water Award have exhibited their research projects at the annual D.C. Riverfest celebration and at student research exhibitions sponsored at the University for undergraduates.

Additionally, the Center participates in the Annual Thomas L. Ayers Awards Ceremony to honor outstanding student conservation projects at DC Public Schools as a member of the Soil and Water conservation District.

Figure 1. World of Water Award (WOW) sponsored by the National Marine Education Association.

III. ANACOSTIA RIVER BASIN LABORATORY PROJECT

As part of the "Anacostia Month" commemoration beginning in 1987, the Center established a program known as the "Anacostia River Basin Laboratory Project for Students". The Center's several ongoing year round field research investigations in the Anacostia River Basin are offered to provide assistance to interested students and teachers who wish to develop and use direct exposure to field research to enhance their understanding and appreciation of environmental science subject matter. This program is intended to stimulate greater awareness and understanding by students concerning environmental problems existing within the Anacostia River and their solutions through scientific and engineering study and experimentation. Twelve schools - elementary through senior high school - in the District of Columbia have responded to the Center's invitation to participate in this project. This effort is viewed as complimentary to the foregoing science enrichment programs and provides an additional avenue for access by students and teachers to environmental science activities in the field.

Examples of ideas provided for the Laboratory Project by principal investigators in the areas of Chemistry, Physics, Biology are indicated in the followings:

Chemistry

- Study the effects of various substances (metal ions, organic compounds, etc.) on growth of Hydrilla.
- Study the effects of varying temperatures on growth of Hydrilla
- Study the effects of varying light levels on the growth of Hydrilla.
- Note: Hydrilla-submerged aquatic vegetation.

Physics

- **Land Pollution**-Select small tributaries and study the erosion pattern of their drainage areas in regards to concentration of eroded soil from exposed areas.
- Select exposed areas with steep slopes and observe the erosion rate. The erosion rate can be measured by simply using yard sticks.
- **The Debris From Streets** -The quantity of debris produced by human beings on streets are not known in great detail by engineers. To advance this knowledge more data needs to be collected.
- Select some section of streets and periodically count debris in each section. Also sweep a portion of the section and weight the soil and other smaller particles.
- Study the effects of debris on flooding streets.
- Sediment deposits on the Anacostia-After each flood a cross section of the Anacostia River at several places can be surveyed to observe the continuous change in the river bed.

Biology

- Specific observation of the presence/absence of aquatic submerged vegetation and fish activity at different seasons at one general area. Record date, time and weather condition.
- Do a vegetation gradient study starting from the low level of the riverbank towards the upper level or inland, to identify the vegetation harbored cross sectionally.
- Carry out a survey on the plain folk's perception of the condition of the river. Do this by walking along the river and interview the sport fisherman, picnicker, and/or anyone else using the grounds for recreational purpose. Prepare a questionnaire with questions such as what fish have been caught, any sighted dead fish, how the area has changed over the years, condition of the river, etc.

IV. URBAN ENVIRONMENTAL SUMMER STUDIES PILOT PROGRAM

A pilot Urban Environmental Summer Studies Program for 5th and 6th grade D.C. Public School students was initiated by the Center in 1988 in collaboration with faculty members in the College of Life Sciences at U.D.C. The Center's contribution to the program enabled these students to receive an introduction to field and laboratory water monitoring techniques and to visit local water and treatment facilities.

V. THE CENTER'S PUBLIC EXHIBITS AND DEMONSTRATION PROGRAM

The relocation of the Center in 1987 to new and spacious facilities in the Minor Building made it possible to develop water resources demonstrations and exhibits for the benefit of the general public as well as scientific community. An Urban Water Museum component is currently in the design stage. A wide variety of activities and programs including special lectures, film and video showings and special exhibitions of D.C. historical water equipment and related memorabilia will be regularly featured. Ongoing student science enrichment programs are expected to derive substantial benefit from access to these facilities and adjacent laboratory spaces which will be made available for limited use in student science project development.

VI. HISTORICALLY BLACK COLLEGES AND UNIVERSITIES (HBCU's)

The historically and predominantly black institutions are a vital national resource and the backbone of African-American leadership. These institutions have produced upwards of 70 percent of all African-American graduates of colleges since the inception of the nation. In the future, they will produce in excess of 300,000 college graduates every ten years. More than 50 percent of the nations's African-American business executives and elected officials are graduates of HBCU's colleges, as are 75 percent of African-American Americans with Ph.D. degrees, 75 percent of military officers, 80 percent of African-American Federal judges and 80 percent of African-American physicians. HBCU's, founded to serve those who have been severely crippled by slavery and poverty, have continued through the years to elevate disadvantaged youth to creative citizenship. The Center has attempted to encourage the HBCU's participation in water research and related curriculum development. More recently, the authors have developed linkages with other HBCU's institutions to conduct joint research projects. Internationally, the Center is interested in developing cooperative relationships with other universities and agencies.

Table 2 illustrates environmental and related course offerings and degrees granted by HBCU institutions which represents a significant and ongoing contribution to the cadre of skilled professional manpower pool in the United States.

Table 2. A Listing of HBCU's Offering Majors in Environmental Related Studies and Their Distribution According to Degree Type.

MAJORS	Pre-professional Study	Certificate	Associates	Bachelors	Masters	Doctorate
Agriculture	-	-	4	6	7	-
Air Pollution	-	-	1	-	-	-
Biochemistry	-	-	-	3	1	1
Biology	I	-	9	70	13	1
Botany	-	-	-	3	-	-
Chemistry	-	1	6	64	3	2
Earth Science	-	-	-	2	-	-
Ecology	-	-	1	4	1	1
Engineering	5	-	7	51	6	1
Environmental Science	-	-	2	2	2	1
Fisheries	-	-	-	2	-	-
Forestry	-	-	7	1	-	-
Geography	-	-	2	11	1	-
Geology	-	-	-	3	-	-
Horticulture	-	-	-	5	-	-
Landscaping	-	-	-	2	1	-
Law (Environmental)	2	-	-	-	2	*2
Marine Biology	-	-	2	7	-	2
Microbiology	-	-	-	-	-	1
Natural Resource Mgmt.	-	-	1	6	2	-
Natural Science	-	-	-	2	1	-
Plant and Soil Science	-	-	-	4	2	-
Poultry Technology Mgmt.	-	-	-	1	1	-
Rural Development	-	-	-	1	-	-
Sanitation Technology	-	-	-	1	-	-
Science	-	-	5	12	8	-
Water Quality	-	-	2	-	-	-
Wildlife Mgmt.	-	-	-	1	-	-
Zoology	-	-	-	2	-	1

*This is a Professional Degree not a doctorate per say

Compiled Iron information supplied by NAFEO

CONCLUSION

Environmental resources, i.e. water, soil and the atmosphere are the basis for human existence and survival. Understanding the environment and knowing how to protect these resources are essential duties of all governments and all people. Minorities are often the first to suffer the consequences of environmental degradation because in the cities where they are concentrated environmental problems are most acute and yet most often ignored.

For more than a decade, the D.C. Water Resources Research Center has explored different approaches with varying degrees of success in an attempt to expose young people to practical uses of science methodology to solve problems and to broaden their appreciation of science and engineering career options.

Students involved in the Center's programs have been recruited from a variety of activities where they had been able to show interest and motivation to work on science projects or to learn about particular science subjects. The city-wide science fair proved to be a fertile area to match aspiring young scientists with adult profession mentors and role models who could provide guidance and encouragement leading to greater achievements and personal satisfaction in problem solving and in competition with their peers. The achievement of their goals relation to prestigious national and regional science project competition must be accompanied by a more structured and integrated long term program effort in partnership with the local school system and environmental agencies and organizations.

Nevertheless, continued exploration by the Center has yielded a variety of options and approaches that fit directly into its mission related technology transfer and information dissemination programs-enabling environmental science and water resources related efforts to be directed to the public generally and young people in particular.

The diversity of students, combined with the variety of the environmental fields requires creative multifaceted technology transfer and information dissemination systems. The transfer mechanisms can provide a significant part of the answers to public awareness and understanding. There are a multiplicity of options and methods which are well suited to the diffusion of knowledge in the environmental fields. Audio, video, computer systems, conferences, open exhibits, hands on clinics or one on one mentor relationships are well established instruments.

Urban centers such as Washington, D.C. possess rich human and institutional resources which when combined with good will, imagination and dedication can be turned into instruments which can serve to improve science literacy and improve public understanding and appreciation of both the challenges and opportunities presented by science and technology in our daily lives.

The authors recommend that in devising plans and strategies for improved environmental education and training that appropriate actions should be taken to address issues of minority participation in all fields of environmental science and environmental technology.

REFERENCES

The DC Water Resources Research Center. *FY 90 Annual Final* Report. DC WRRC Report No. 88. DC Water Resources Research Center, Washington, DC, USA.

Field, R.J., 1989. *Black Natural Resources Managers: Why. Where and How,* Presentation to the Southeastern Association of Fish and Wildlife Agencies Annual Conference, St. Louis. Missouri, USA.

The National Association of Equal Opportunity in Higher Education (NAFEO), 1989. *An Inventory of the Capabilities of the Historically Black Colleges and Universities and Other Minority Institutions (HBCUs/ MIs).* Washington, DC ,USA.

Watt, M.H. August 1983. *Views on U.S. Water Research and Technology Transfer.* DC WRRC Report No. 53. D.C. Water Resources Research Center, Washington, DC, USA.

4 RESEARCH and EDUCATION and TRAINING

SEASONAL VARIATION OF RAINFALL WATER IN SOIL

R. D. Valdez-Cepeda
Unidad Regional Universitaria de Zonas Aridas
Universidad Autónoma Chapingo
Apartado postal No. 8
C.P. 35230 Bermejillo, Durango, México

M. R. Almeida-Martínez
CENID RASPA, INIFAP-SARH
Apartado postal No. 41
Cd. Lerdo, Durango, México

S. Rubio-Díaz
CIFAP Zac., INIFAP-SARH
Apartado postal No. 18
C. P. 98500 Calera de V. R., Zacatecas, México

ABSTRACT

The regionalized variables theory helps to describe the autocorrelation between data corresponding to geographic space or time interval. Also, autocorrelation level is a valuable tool to derive precise and unbiased estimations of the variable within the sample unit. The autocorrelation is defined through the statistical semivariance, $\sigma(h)$, estimated for each interval of distance or time. In addition, the drift, $D(h)$ allows to identify the nested structure of the treated variable. In this research work the purpose was to define the time interval (days) of maximum dependency and the periodicity of the variable soil water (as head in mm) in a cultivated peach field under rainfall condition. Data corresponds to soil depth of 0-30 cm registered by gravimetric method for Palmas Altas, Jerez, Zacatecas, México. The data shows an autocorrelation between smaller 110 days interval, but two months is the maximum dependency interval. The drift allowed to identify the periodicity of the variable as seasonality.

INTRODUCTION

In general, the values of the variables of agronomic, ecologic and hydrologic interest trend to be of similar magnitude as the distance decrease, in space and time that separates them. There is a known variability through space and time, which by different methods can be determined. In fact, a close analogy between space and time is recognized, at least at one dimensional analysis. Time series analysis has been based on the autocorrelation and autocovariance. The purpose of this research work was to illustrate the regionalized variables approach and its use in order to define the autocorrelation level and the periodicity of the soil water as head, in mm.

REGIONALIZED VARIABLES THEORY

Autocorrelation

If the autocorrelation level within data is unknown the possibilities to obtain a behavior pattern of a variable and its dependent processes are lessened. Under these assumption the theory of the regionalized variables is a valuable tool (Webster, 1985) because the theory assumes Eq. 1 as a model of variation.

$$z(x) = \mu + \in(x) \qquad (1)$$

Where $z(x)$ is the value of the property at position x within a domain; μ, is the mean value in that domain; and the $\in(x)$ is the dependent random component with zero mean and variance defined by Eq. 2.

$$\text{var}[\in(x) - \in(x+h)] = E\{[\in(x) - \in(x+h)]^2\} = 2\sigma(h) \qquad (2)$$

Where the intrinsic hypotheses implies to expect the same degree of difference in the property at any two places h apart, whatever the measured values of the property were. Consequently Eq. 3 defines the semivariance as a function of h, the lag, in one dimension.

$$N(h) \; \sigma(h) = 1/2 \, N(h) \sum_{i=1}^{N(h)} [z(x_i) - z(x_{i+h})]^2 \qquad (3)$$

Where $z(x_i)$ is the measured value at point i; $z(x_{i+h})$ is the measured value at point x_{i+h}; and $N(h)$ is the number of couples or differences for the interval h. The obtained curve between $\sigma(h)$ versus the lag h is called semivariogram.

The semivariogram represents the percentage change of the variable with respect to h and its behavior describes the variation pattern according to the magnitude, scale and general form or structure. Therefore, all the above is based in terms of the following parameters: range, A, or interval in which dependency between data exists; nugget variance, Co, or variance not detected by the analyzed data; sill or total variance, C; and identified variance with the data, C1. Webster (1985), Burgess and Webster (1980) and Vieira et al. (1983) recognized that the sill is found when the dispersion is finite.

Trangmar et al. (1985) express that the trends are identified by examination of semivariograms when periodic variation is observed as a whole effect, which is indicative of non-monotonic growth of the semivariance with distance.

Periodicity

Vieira et al. (1983) reported that the drift, D(h), for each lag h can be estimated by Eq. 4.

$$D(h) = 1/2 \, N(h) \sum_{i=1}^{N(h)} z(x_i) - z(x_{i+h}) \qquad (4)$$

Equation 4 is valid only when the semivariogram detects periodicity ought to changes or nested structure of the variable with position through the expected values (Eq. 5).

$$E[z(x)] = m(x) \tag{5}$$

Then the theory assumes that Eq. 1 must be changed by replacing the mean, μ, by the more general, m(x), given in Eq. 6.

$$z(x) = m(x) + \in (x) \tag{6}$$

Webster (1985) suggest that the quantity m(x) represents the trend which is known in regionalized variable theory as the drift, D(h). However, D(h) is described commonly as in Eq. 4, because the dependent random component is defined by Eq. 2.

The obtained curve between each D(h) versus lag h identifies the periodicity in terms of seasonality (periods smaller than a year time) or cycling (periods bigger than a year time) of the variable.

Temporal and space variability

The soil water quantity is a function of some factors as evapotranspiration, rainfall, water holding capacity of the soil, and others. In some earlier research, Valdez-Cepeda and Romo-Gonzáez (1989a) reported that the evaporation has an experimental behavior pattern because the maximum dependency through experimental range, A, is near 60 days for the locality of Palmas Altas, Jerez, Zacatecas. Valdez-Cepeda et al. (1990) and Valdez-Cepeda and Romo-Gonzáez (1989b) found out that water content in surface soil shows a structure of its variability when analyzed as a time series. In this last work they reported the following experimental values for range, A=59 days; C=31; Co=4.44. Also, the theoretical semivariograms obtained through an adjusted least square procedure (p = 0.05) presented the following values: Linear model, A=77 days, C=372, Co=23, and R^2=0.84; spherical model, A=95 days, C=366, Co=10 and R^2=0.82; exponential model, A=59 days, C=441, Co=0 and R^2=0.81; and gaussian model, A=86 days, C=382, Co=54 and R^2=0.75. The above results were derived from a weekly sampling data.

The semivariograms have been utilized to obtain the structure of the variation for agronomic, ecologic, hydrologic and agrometeorologic variables (Vieira et al., 1983). Some examples have been reported by Bos et al. (1984) for phosphate soil, Campbell (1978) for soil sand content, Webster (1985) for soil stone content, Robertson (1987) for ecological aspects and Vieira et al. (1983) for surface temperature.

The potential use of this approach has not been well developed to undertake studies to identify the periodicity of variables, although in hydrologic studies is common to work this aspect. In similar way, the hydrologist obtains the periodicity by using moving average technique (Campos-Aranda, 1987).

STUDY CASE

Data

The source data was generated by kriging method and calculated as a regular grid with daily lag increments and reported by Valdez-Cepeda (1990), but the original data was obtained by weekly sampling during 1984 for soil 0-30 cm layer, on cultivated peach trees field, under rainfall condition at Palmas Altas, Jerez, Zacatecas. The soil water content variable was registered by gravimetric method and for this study was transformed to head and reported in mm.

Analysis

The semivariogram and the drift curves were estimated (p=0.05) by using computer algorithms reported by Robertson (1987).

Autocorrelation. Figure 1 shows that the theoretical range, A, lies between 80 and 110 days, but the experimental range is of 60 days, this means that the maximum dependency is within intervals of two months. This results coincide to those reported by Valdez-Cepeda and Romo-Gonzáez (1989b) and

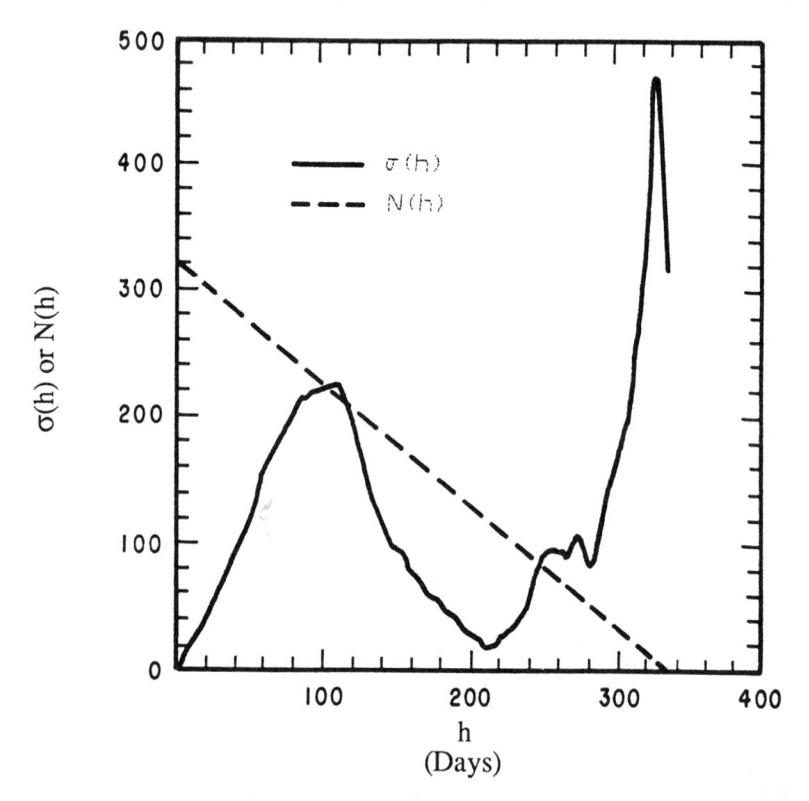

Figure 1. Experimental semivariogram with hole effect and its relationship with the couples, N(h), for the variable surface soil water as head in mm. Palmas, Altas, Jerez, Zacatecas, México. 1984.

Valdez-Cepeda et al. (1990) supporting evidence that there is a correlation between the structure of the variability of soil water content and its similar of evaporation (Valdez-Cepeda and Romo-González, 1989a) for the locality of Jerez, Zacatecas. The nugget variance, Co, has zero value which means that the total variance has been explained by the accounted data, then the daily registered sampling is sufficient for this analysis. The sill, C, is big if the complete semivariogram is considered, but this is not convenient since the last semivariance values are of deterministic kind because they are function of a very small number of couples. In the same Fig. 1 the relation of number of couples and the semivariance values are shown. There is appreciable hole effect in the semivariogram, which means continuity of this variable during a year.

Periodicity. Figure 2 shows that the variable has a seasonal behavior. The two first seasons identified are approximately of 110 days, each one of them. The soil moisture content variable shows decrement values until intervals of 85 days are reached, and increment values until reaching intervals of 88 days; Figure 2 provides this information, because the drift, D(h), trends to increase up to the 85th day, and trends to decrease down to the 173th day. This is derived from Eq. 4 described above. The behavior or increment-decrement change coincide with the theoretical range, A, reported by Valdez-Cepeda and Romo-González (1989a) for the gaussian model.

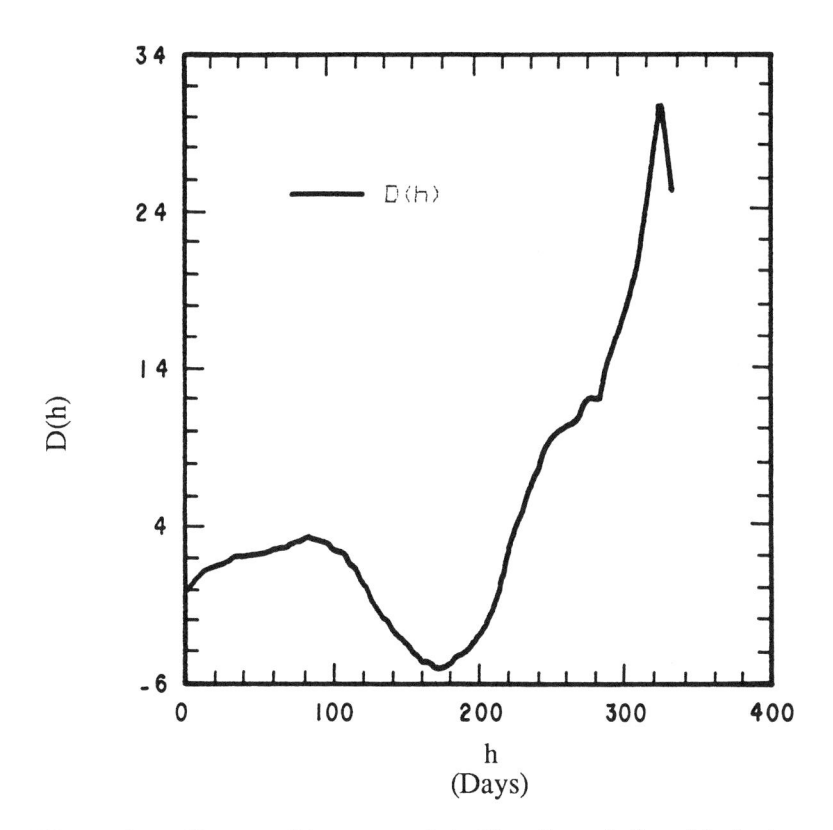

Figure 2. Seasonality, appreciated by the relationship between the drift [D(h)] and the lag (h) as days, for the variable surface soil water as head in mm. Palmas, Altas, Jerez, Zacatecas, México. 1984.

REFERENCES

Bos, J., M. E. Collins, G. J. Gensheimer and R. B. Brown (1984). *Spatial variability for one type of phosphate mine land in central Florida.* Soil Sci. Soc. Am. J. 48:1120-1125.

Burgess,T. M. and R. Webster (1980). *Optimal interpolation and isarithmic mapping of soils properties.* I: The semivariogram and punctual kriging. J. Soil Sci.31:315-331.

Campbell, J. B. (1978). *Spatial variation of sand content and pH within single contiguous delineations of two soil mapping units.* Soil. Sci. Soc.Am. J. 42:460-464.

Campos-Aranda, D. F. (1987). *Procesos del ciclo hidrológico.* Edit. Universitaria Potosina, UASLP. SLP, México.Vol. 1. Tomo 1/2.

Robertson, G. P. (1987). *Geostatistics in ecology: Interpolating with known variance.* Ecology 68(3):744-748.

Trangmar, B. B., R. S. Yost and G. Uehara (1985). *Application of geostatistics to spatial studies of soil properties.* Adv. Agron. 38:45-94.

Valdez-Cepeda, R. D. (1990) *Estimación del agua en el suelo.* Terra: (en prensa).

Valdez-Cepeda, R. D. y J. R. Romo-González (1989a). *Variabilidad temporal de la evaporación.* In: Vergara, M. A., G. Alcántar y A. Aguilar (Eds.). Memoria del XXII Congreso Nacional de la Ciencia del Suelo. C. P. Montecillo, Méx. p. 34.

Valdez-Cepeda, R. D. y J. R. Romo-González (1989b). *Variabilidad temporal del agua en el suelo.* In: Memorias de la segunda reunión nacional deagroclimatología. Universidad Autónoma Chapingo. Departamento de Irrigación. Chapingo, Méx. pp.240-247.

Valdez-Cepeda, R. D., J. R. Romo-González y S. Rubio-Díaz(1990). *Variabilidad temporal del agua de lluvia captada en parcelas de Duraznero.* In: Tovar, J. L. y A. Legaspi (Eds.). Memoria del 1er. Simposium Nacional Captación (in situ) del agua de lluvia y manejo de escurrimientos superficiales a nivel parcela. UAZ-CP-CONACYT y SMCS, A. C. Zacatecas, Zac., México. pp. 95-105.

Vieira, S. R., J. L. Hatfield, D. R. Nielsen and J. W. Biggar (1983). *Geostatistical theory and application to variability of some agronomical properties.* Hilgardia 51(3):1-75.

Webster, R. (1985). *Quantitative Spatial Analysis of Soil in the Field.* Adv. Soil Sci. 3:1-70.

TIME-SERIES MODELLING AS A TOOL FOR EVALUATING AN IRRIGATION DECISION IN ADVANCE

C. Hernández-Yáñez
CENID-RASPA
Apartado Postal No 41, Cd.
Lerdo Dgo., México

ABSTRACT

When water is scarce, an irrigation decision should be taken very carefully. In general, a farmer or any other decision maker must decide whether to irrigate or not within a certain period of time. To assist the decision maker, for the irrigation management in a beef production system, a time-series irrigation model was developed. The model was calibrated, in part for La Región Lagunera conditions. A good agreement between the estimated and real reference evapotranspiration (ETr) and precipitation (P) was obtained. Moreover, results indicated that by using time intervals of more than seven days, the prediction error for soil water status is increased. The model, can be used mainly in two ways: (1) to give advice to irrigators in advance about irrigation activities and (2) to teach farmers and technicians about the sensitivity of the production system to certain components (irrigation, economics, animal, crop).

INTRODUCTION

It is well known that arid and semiarid regions do not have enough water. Nevertheless, human population is growing the fastest in these parts of the world. Therefore, more food is required in order to satisfy human needs. Taking the above situation into account agricultural production must be approached in an optimal way. Although people can take protein from vegetables, animal protein is usually preferred because of the essential amino acids that it provides; therefore, meat from domestic animals is needed for human nourishment.

In order to obtain a faster weight gain in northern Mexico, livestock should be fed on irrigated pastures. These pastures are usually alfalfa (Medicago sativa) fields. However, alfalfa is generally produced only during the hot weather season. Therefore, during the winter season there is not enough animal food because alfalfa production decreases. Consequently, farmers need to plant other kinds of pastures.

In these regions, during the winter season, livestock are fed with a suitable crop which can be grown during the cold winter conditions (e.g. rye grass, Lolium multiflorum).

A Short Duration Grazing System (SDGS), in conjunction with an irrigation system, constitutes a good combination that may better control the environmental variability that characterize an animal production system (Anez Reverol, 1985). Through the time, the combination of grazing pastures with irrigation has been used without carefully considering factors related to the management of the soil-plant-animal system, and as a consequence the results sometimes are not good enough or they are site-specific. During the past few years, research (Hernandez, 1978, 1979; Salinas and Martinez, 1976) has been done in order to determine rye grass response to different levels of irrigation, and animal stocking rate; nevertheless, to the writer's knowledge, no research has been done in which both concepts have been combined. In animal research the most important element is the animal response to the environmental conditions. Nevertheless, the conditions where the animal is developed is subject to a high temporal variability which is mainly affected by weather. Due to that variability the farmer has to deal with uncertainty in order to get the proper management decisions.

Because of uncertainty of pasture environment, understanding the soil-plant-animal system requires study for several years, and at several locations. One fast and inexpensive way to evaluate some of the ideas (i.e. changes in the environmental medium to which the animal is subjected) is by computer modeling (Kundu et al., 1982). If the major environmental factor is irrigation, the resulting simulation model may be used by researchers, planners, consultants, equipment suppliers and farmers in order to make meaningful comparisons between different systems and/or the effects of different irrigation-related management practices (King et al., 1987). In order to obtain a reliable response to controlled variables, crop and animal models must reproduce the dynamic irrigation environment, and they must be combined with a method of systematically evaluating the alternative strategies to find the optimal strategy. Some of the modeling methods used to evaluate irrigation strategies under uncertainty are stochastic dynamic programming (Bosch et al., 1987), linear programming, dynamic programming or their combinations (Udeh and Bosch, 1982). Due to uncertainty of the production system, the principal objective of this research was development of a dynamic stochastic model in order to aid the irrigation decision maker in advance in his/her own decision.

MODEL DEVELOPMENT

General Structure

The developed model assumes that the system production is well managed in all its components (fertilization, planting date) except in irrigation water. The model was built up from four general programs or submodels: (1) data, which reads and stores into a proper file the general input information; (2) evapotranspiration, which computes the historical ETr using a certain number of years of historical weather data (it has been written with three different ET equations: Evaporation (Hill et al., 1983), Hargreaves (Hargreaves et al., 1985), and Penman-Monteith (Allen et al., 1989)); (3) parameter generation, which computes the ETr and precipitation statistical parameters; and (4) decision-maker. This last submodel is the biggest in the model due to its management of the information generated by previous submodels, and because it advises the model user with respect to the soil water status and irrigation necessities in three time intervals in advance from the current date. A time interval is defined as the number of days in advance that the model user wants to predict the irrigation needs. After the user of the model decides to irrigate or not to irrigate on those dates (time intervals), an economic evaluation is done taking as a reference the next grazing event; if the user of the model decides to irrigate, the economic evaluation is done and compared against no irrigation. Although the model works in advance for three time intervals, the real time interval is a function of the remaining time from the current day to the next grazing event minus a soil drying period of time.

Outputs are statistical parameters that represent the mean, standard deviation and confidence limits ($\ddagger$ = 0.05) for a 20-year generated ETr and precipitation period. It is considered that the crop growing season is divided into several stages (grazing events), which are model user-defined.

Generation of ETr and Precipitation

In order to generate synthetic ETr and precipitation, P, data, for a certain number of years, the model uses an AR(1) model (Salas, 1980) and a two states Markov chain model (Richardson, 1981), respectively. In the case of precipitation, once computed a wet event, the rainfall amount is computed by the model using a two-parameters gamma distribution (Richardson, 1982).

System Simulation

Once generated the ETr and P data for a certain number of years, (in this case it is 20 years), the option 1 requests determination of the current day. With that date, the model computes and shows a soil water content, SWC, assuming that at the first simulated day, the soil is at field capacity, and using a general soil water balance criterion on a daily basis. If the model user knows the real SWC, he/she can accept or reject the model proposed SWC. Using this input for the SWC data, the model computes and shows the average SWC and the soil water status, one, two and three time intervals in advance from the current date. Taking into account this soil information on the water content the model requests for an user irrigation decision, which is evaluated at the next grazing event. The evaluation is done in terms of grass dry matter yield, beef yield, and the economic terms. The grass yield is computed using the Doorenbos and Kassam (1979) model, where the actual transpiration and potential transpiration (computed according to Hill et al. (1987) procedure) are used instead of the actual ET and potential ET, respectively. Beef production is computed in the model following the MacNeil et al. (1987) criterion combined with Charles-Edwards' (1987) model. The MacNeil et al. (1987) model is directed to wildland systems simulation, while Charles-Edwards' model (1987) is a general framework analysis to simulate the dynamic nature of a controlled grazing system. The grazing efficiency, term Eg, is computed using the Anez Reverol (1985) equation. Finally, the economic analysis is computed using the following equation

$$G = -Cf + ii [P\ Yb - Egt] \qquad (1)$$

where G is the net profit ($/ha) during the evaluation period (from current date to next grazing event); Cf is a capital recovery term ($/ha); P is the beef unit sale price ($/kg); Yb is the beef production during the evaluation period (kg/ha); ii is the present-worth factor that is computed as $[1/(1+i)]^j$, $j=1,...,ng$, where i and ng are the periodic interest rate and number of grazing events during the growing season, respectively; and Egt is the total system expenses during the same evaluation period ($/ha). The total expenses term is computed as the sum of energy cost ($/ha), animal supplementation cost ($/ha) (the model deals with either supplementation or not supplementation), irrigation cost ($/ha), fixed or constant cost ($/ha), and animal management cost ($/ha). Irrigation cost is computed as the sum of operation, maintenance and the periodic/yearly equipment cost plus taxes. Fixed costs, are considered as the sum of initial animal cost, field rent, fertilization, seeding bed preparation, etc., ($/ha). Animal management costs are the expenses for medicines, electrical fences, salt and others minerals and the proper animal management expenses, etc. ($/an/year).

The gross amount of applied water is defined as a percent of the needed water to raise the root zone to field capacity (soil water replacement) divided by a randomly generated irrigation-application efficiency (Eq. (2))

$$Eag = Easd \; Rnd + Eam \qquad (2)$$

where Eag is the generated irrigation efficiency; Easd the corresponding Ea standard deviation; Rnd a standard random normal number; and Eam is the mean irrigation efficiency. The model assumes that the mean and standard deviation are the same for the different grass resting periods and that there is no difference between those parameters from one irrigation to another. The model assumes that the generated Ea value applies to different soil water replacement water depths.

RESULTS AND DISCUSSION

Predicting Irrigation Necessities and Its Economic Analysis

The model, gives two kinds o information to the model user; one of them is the forecasted values for i^{th+1}, i^{th+2}, and ith time interval in advance of the water balance components (precipitation, evapotranspiration, and soil water content), taking as a reference the current date i. Besides those data, it shows the soil water status referenced to the soil water limit for irrigation. In this case it is considered as 0.50 of the difference of field capacity and wilting point. The another kind of information given by the model, is the economic evaluation of the user model irrigation decision. Due to that irrigation decision made by the user according to the forecast water balance components, his/her decision is a real function of the model forecasting capability. The model, using only one seed number (any generated random number is a function of that seed number), was run by using three different time intervals in advance. The results are shown in Table 1. A portion of an irrigation treatment used by Hernandez (1979) was taken as a reference. The time intervals of 3, 7 and 14 days were used. The dates (cumulative days from planting) in Table 1 correspond to the days where irrigation was applied to that irrigation treatment. It is such that the soil water content at the irrigation date was at field capacity (336 mm). Because of the lack of real information for soil water content for a rooting depth at 120 cm, information was used for only 90 cm in this case.

TABLE 1. Real (R) and Estimated (Es) Soil Water Content (mm) at Different Dates and Time Interval.

	Date						
Time in	7		107		126		
Advance	R	Es	R	Es	R	Es	D
3	327*	319**	322	313	317	310	24
7	295	305	291	286	285	282	20
14	247	271	245	233	237	226	47

D = Sum of absolute deviations.
* Soil water depth in a 90-cm soil layer.
* Average estimated soil water depth (based on the 20-year generated data)

Even thought the estimated soil water content has the implicit uncertainty component there exist a clear tendency of closeness of results when the time interval in advance is shorter. According to Table 1, forecasting soil water status more than 7 days in advance tends to have a higher absolute deviation, D, in respect to the real value. In this case, the resulting predicted water contents tend to be lower than the real values. If the model is run several times with different seed numbers some of the forecast results may have values higher than the real water contents. In any case, as the time interval increases the D value will show a similar tendency than in Table 1. In order to evaluate the user's irrigation decision, the model was run under the supposition that the model user has decided 14 days in advance to irrigate, taking as a reference the current date. The economic evaluation is made by the model at the next grazing event (Nge) from the current date. Input information from La Region Lagunera, México as shown in Table 2 was used.

Table 3 shows the obtained results. According to Table 3, grass yield for irrigation is closely similar to its potential values for each stage (3360, 4060, 3500 and 2100 kg/ha). Without irrigation a reduction in grass yield due to the lack of irrigation water to the crop is observed. Beef production shows the same tendency as the grass yield for irrigation in comparison with no irrigation, but the net profit does not have the same trend. During the first evaluation event, Np for no irrigation is nearly the same as Np for irrigation. It is because the irrigation decision was taken when the soil water content was 12 millimeters over the irrigation limit. In this case, the increment in beef production due to irrigation does not justify the irrigation cost. Thereafter, the reduction in Yb due to no irrigation makes Np for irrigation to be higher than Np for no irrigation. Because the economic analyses is done in advance of one grazing period, this economic analysis does not account for the cost of the antecedent soil water content. The model user can make such analyses at any time in order to decide in advance whether to irrigate or not. This analysis was made using a constant irrigation efficiency, Ea, but it can be randomly generated using Eq. (2).

TABLE 2. Input Data Used in The Model.

Variable	Value
SOIL INFORMATION	
Field Capacity (mm/m)	373.0
Welting Point (mm/m)	193.0
Texture Factor	5
CROP INFORMATION	
Last Grazing Day	212
Grazing Number	5
Crop Transp. Coefficient	0.87
Maximum Rooting Depth (cm)	120.0
Days to Max. Root. Depth (days)	70
ANIMAL INFORMATION	
Stocking Rate (animals/ha)	10-20
Mature Cow Weight,WMA, (kg)	509[1]
Initial Steer Edge (days)	320
Initial Steer Weight (kg)	180
Supplement Alternative	no
COST INFORMATION	
Animal Sale Price ($/kg)	2.0
Annual interest rate (%)	15.0
Cattle Management Index ($/an-yr) 30.0	
Labor Irr. Cost ($/8-hr period)	5.5
Others	500.0[a]
DATE AT EACH GRAZING EVENT (Cum. Days)	
First	100
Second	128
Third	156
Fourth	184
Fifth	212
POTENTIAL YIELD PER GRAZING (kg of DM/ha/day)	
First	30[3]
Second	120
Third	145
Fourth	125
Fifth	75
IRRIGATION STATISTICS	
Mean Ea (%)	43
Standard Deviations Ea (%)	13
Table 2. (continue)	6
PUMPING SYSTEM INFORMATION	
Efficiency (%)	40-60
Flow (l/sec)	35
Total Dynamic Head (m)	25-157

[1] From MacNeil et al. (1987)
[2] From Pair et al. (1975)
[3] From Hernandez (1978, 1979)
[4] From Hernandez (1985)
[6] From Moreno and Cervantes (1988)
[a] Means the sum of field rent, fertilizer cost and seeding bed preparation cost

TABLE 3. Average Economic Results for an Irrigation Decision Made 14 Days in Advance at Several Dates.

	Evaluation Event			
	1	2	3	4
Date i (cum.day)	103	131	159	187
Nge Date (cum.day)	128	156	184	212
SWCi (mm)	448	448	448	448
Steer Weight (kg)	181	195	213	237
SWSi+2*in (mm)	12	-8	-18	-30
Animals/ha	15	15	15	15
Irrig. Eff. (%)	43	43	43	43
Results:				
With irrigation:				
Wir (mm)	449	542	556	570
Yg (kg/ha)	3360	4055	3461	2076
Yb (kg/ha)	253	275	259	156
Np ($/ha)	292	312	262	51
Not irrigation:				
Wir (mm)	0	0	0	0
Yg (kg/ha)	2931	3149	2607	1587
Yb (kg/ha)	235	244	210	92
Np ($/ha)	297	297	215	-24

SWCi = Soil Water Content at date i^{th} (Field Capacity for a 120-Soil Layer);
SWSi+2*in = Soil Water Status at Date i^{th} Plus Two Times the Time Interval (14 days); Its Value is Taking as Reference the Soil Water Limit to Irrigate.
Yb = Beef Production;
Np = Net Profit;
Eg = Grazing Efficiency;
Wir = Applied Irrigation Water

Test of the Model

In order to test the model, results from Salinas and Martinez (1976) were taken, consisting of 15-steer liveweight data during the grass growth period. Because these researchers did not actually report how field irrigation was managed, the more frequently irrigation practice used in La Region Lagunera was used. This typical irrigation scheme consists of four irrigations from planting to first grazing and afterward, one irrigation after each grazing. Table 3 shows the results regarding to a user's irrigation decision made 14 days in advance from the current date. In all cases, the current date was three days after a grazing event which is the date that normally the farmer applies irrigation. That table shows the information of irrigation made 14 days in advance and no irrigation. In other words, this information equals to application of two or one irrigation after a grazing event. Results from no irrigation (one irrigation after the grazing event) in terms of current steer weight in kg (beef production, Yb, divided by the stocking rate plus the antecedent steer weight) shown by Table 3 were used as comparison with the real values reported by Salinas and Martinez (1976). Table 4 shows the minimum and maximum simulated results from the model, using a 20-year generated period and the confidence limits ($\alpha = 0.05$) computed from the real data.

Taking an irrigation as a reference, the model tended to underestimate the steer weight during the third evaluation event, while taking two irrigations, in all evaluation events, the results fell within the 95 percent confidence limits. In general, the results showed good agreement with the real case (one irrigation). Those discrepancies observed mainly in the third event may be explained by following reasons: (a) the irrigation management used in the simulated data is really different to that used in the experiment;

TABLE 4. Estimated Minimum and Maximum Steer Liveweight (kg) and Confidence Limits Computed from Salinas and Martinez (1976).

			Evaluation Event			
			1	2	3	4
Min	1		196.2	211.0	227.7	242.2
	2		197.8	213.3	230.2	247.3
Max	1		197.5	211.5	228.7	247.6
	2		197.8	213.4	230.3	247.4
Lower	Lim		190.0	207.6	229.5	240.0
Upper	Lim		199.2	220.7	245.3	248.4

(b) the plant-animal relationships taken from the literature do not represent sufficiently well the case of irrigated pasture management; and (c) the model does not account for the implicit animal heterogeneity. All the plant-animal relationships used in the model have been developed under the rangeland conditions.

SUMMARY AND CONCLUSIONS

A time series model was developed to plan irrigation activities on a pasture-animal production system. The model evaluates and compares in economic terms the irrigation decisions taken by the user of the model in one, two or three time intervals in advance, against no irrigation. A good agreement between the real and the simulated steer liveweight data was observed for a stocking rate of 15 animals/ha.

REFERENCES

Allen, R. G. 1986. *Sprinkler irrigation project design with production functions*, J. of Irrig. and D. Eng. 112(4): 305-321.

Allen, R. G., Jensen, M. E., Wright, J. L., and Burman R. D. 1989.*Operational estimates of reference evapotranspiration*, Agronomy J. 81(4): 650-662.

Anez Reverol, D. C., 1985. *Optimal water allocation in pasture under sprinkler irrigation and short duration grazing.*, Dissertation Presented to Utah State University, at Logan, Utah.

Borg, H., and Grimes, D. W. 1986. *Depth development of roots with time: an empirical description.*' Transactions of the ASAE, 29(1): 194-197.

Bosch, D. J., Eidman, V. R., and Oosthuizen, L. R. 1987. *A review of methods for evaluating the economic efficiency of irrigation*, Agricultural Water Management, 12(3): 231-245.

Charles-Edwards, D. A., Tow, P., and Evans, T. R. 1987. *An analysis is of the growth rates of pasture and animal production*, Agricultural Systems, 25(4): 245-259.

Doorenbos, J., and Kassam, A. H. 1979. *Yield response to water*. FAO Irrigation and Drainage Paper No 33, Food and Agriculture Organization of the United Nations, Rome.

Haan, C.T. 1986. *Statistical methods in hydrology*. Iowa State University.

Hargreaves, G. L., Hargreaves, G. H., and Riley, J. P. 1985. *Irrigation water requirements for Senegal River Basin.*, J. of Irrig. and Drainage Eng. Division ASCE 111(3): 265-275.

Hernández, Y.C. 1978. Cuándo y cuánto regar el ballico anual (Lolium multiflorum. Lam), Research Report, CENAMAR-SARH, Mexico.

Hernández, Y. C. 1979. *Cuándo y cuánto regar diferentes variedadesde ballico anual*, Research Report, CENAMAR-SARH, Mexico.

Hernández, Y. C. 1985. *Eficiencias de riego en riego por superficie en la Región Lagunera*, Research Report, PRONAPA- INIA-SARH, Mexico.

Hill, R. W., Johns, E. L., and Frevert, D. K. 1983. *Comparsion of equations used for estimating agricultural crop evapotranspiration with field research*, Bureau of Reclamation, U.S. Department of Interior.

King, B. A., Sauer, B. W.. and Busch, J. R. 1987. *A simulation model procedure for on-farm irrigation system planning,* 21st Century. Proceeding/Irrigation and Drainage Div/ASCE Portland, Oregon. July, 28-30.

Kundu, S. S., Skogerboe, G. V., and Walker, W. R. 1982. *Using a crop growth simulation model for evaluating irrigation practices*, Agricultural Water Management, 5(3): 253-268.

MacNeil, M. D., Jenkins, T. G., Rice, R. W., and Koong, L. J.1987. *Animal component, SPUR, simulation of production and utilization of rangelands*, United Department of Agriculture. Agr. Res. Serv. Dec., 1987.

Martínez, P. R. A., and Martinez, J. C. 1976. *Determinacion dela carga animal optima en zacate ballico anual (Lolium multiflorum) y avena (Avena sativa) variedad opalo*, Research Report, CIANE-INIA-SARH, Mexico.

Moreno, D.L., and Cervantes, G. I. 1988. *Aspectos economicos dela productividad del agua subterranea en la agricultura*, Research report, CENID-RASPA-INIFAP-SARH, Mexico.

Richardson, C. W. 1981. *Stochastic simulation of daily precipitation, temperature, and solar radiation*, Water Resources Research, 17(1): 182-190.

Richardson, C. W. 1982. *A Comparison of three distributions for the generation of daily rainfall amounts*. Statistical Analysis of Rainfall and Runoff, V.P.Singh., Water Resources Publications, Fort Collins, Colorado.

Salinas, G. H., and Martinez, P. R. A. 1976. *Determinacion de lacarga optima economica de novillos en pastoreo de zacateballico anual (Lolium multiflorum Lam)*, Research Report, CIANE-INIA-SARH, Mexico.

Sánchez, V. 1985. *Caracteristicas generales del acuifero en la Region Lagunera, Memorias del II Ciclo Internacional de Conferencias*. Aprovechamiento de Aguas Subterraneas en la Agricultura, IATEM, CONACYT, Torreon Coah., México.

Udeh, C. W., and Bush, J. R. 982. *Optimal irrigation management using probabilistic hydrologic and irrigation efficiency parameters*, Transactions of the ASAE, 25(4): 954-960.

SUPPORT OF AGROMETEOROLOGY TO MANAGEMENT OF WATER RESOURCES

Dr. D.F. Campos-Aranda
Faculty of Engineering
Universidad de San Luis Potosi
78290 San Luis Potosi, S.L.P., México

ABSTRACT

The objective of agricultural meteorology, the reach of quantitative agroclimatology and the scope of operational agrometeorology are presented, as an introduction to antecedents of the general plan proposed. Then, the approaches given are described in detail. These are: diffusion program, investigation projects and specific studies. Immediately, it is explained how the simulation crop model will be utilized, overcome the difficulties imposed by the necessity of daily climatic data, that is, when the long records are not available or are not easy to obtain. At the end, the proposed studies in the Villa de Reyes agricultural irrigation area, distant 50 km from San Luis Potosi city, are formulated, which have the main objective of minimizing water consumption, to be able to assign more water for domestic and industrial uses.

INTRODUCTION

Objective of Agricultural Meteorology

In general terms, the agricultural production is still dependent on weather and climate despite the impressive advances in agricultural technology over the last couple of decades. Therefore, knowledge of available environment resources (climate) and the expected conditions from the soil up to the lower atmosphere provides the guidance for decisions in planning of agricultural systems, for example in the choice of land use, the selection of crops and farming patters, the design of irrigation and drainage schemes, the modifications to the environment (frost and hail protection, windbreaks and greenhouses), and so on.

In accord with the WMO(1981), the primary objective of agrometeorology is to give a practical approach towards integrating the agricultural ecosystems and the climatic resources into research and development programs to increase and stabilize agricultural production.

Quantitative Agroclimatology

The agroclimatology has been transformed in a discipline eminently quantitative in the last years. For example, it is now possible to make estimations of potential and real yields of each specific crop. Also it is feasible to obtain the advance information on crop prospects and is possible to formulate the harvest forecasts. Previous estimations can be realized each with several techniques. For example, the potential yields can be estimated with the climatic index of agricultural potentiality (Turc, 1972), or with the procedures of agro-ecological zones project of FAO (ONUAA, 1981) and the International Institute for Land Reclamation and Improvement of Wageningen, the Netherlands (Feddes et al., 1978; Doorenbos and Kassam, 1979). The actual yields can be estimated with the Hargreaves production function (Hargreaves, 1975) or by applying the harvest index of FAO, to the potential yield estimation.

Operational Agrometeorology

Detailed real-time estimates of meteorological variables are important for tactical decisions in short-term planning of agricultural operations. The application of pesticides, protection against adverse weather and freezing temperatures, application of sprays and fertilizer by aircraft, sun-drying of certain fruits, and so on, are activities that can be made or delayed in accord with the weather conditions (Robertson, 1983).

On the other hand, other main application of agrometeorology is in modeling of crop growth. Growing a crop is complex. Some activities, such as planting or seeding, are always needed. The others like irrigation, fertilization and spraying fungicides are optional.

Penning de Vries et al. (1989) stated that a crop model is a simple representation of a crop, used to study crop growth and to compute growth responses to the environment. Crop models can be distinguished as descriptive and explanatory models, the former defines the behavior of a system in a simple manner. They reflect little or none of the mechanisms that are the cause of this behavior. An explanatory model consist of a quantitative description of the mechanisms and processes that cause the behavior of a system. An explanatory crop growth model contains descriptions of distinct processes as photosynthesis, leaf area expansion and tiller induction, so that the growth is a consequence of these underlying processes.

GENERAL APPROACHES

Diffusion Program of Agroclimatology

In this program the dissemination documents to the general public and the normative papers to the agroclimatic studies (Campos, 1990a, 1990b) are made. In the former the following themes are included: importance, scope, benefits and state of art of the agroclimatic studies. In the latter: the themes are oriented to standardizing the execution or development of field investigation, and the analyses of both climatic and phenological data.

Investigation Projects

The studies of rain fed agricultural regions are oriented to the evaluation of their climatic characteristics, with the main objective to adapt their agriculture to those particularities, to obtain the best production and to reduce the hazards of adverse meteorological conditions. This is the case of the studies realized in the high plateau and mid-zone of San Luis Potosi state (Campos, 1989; Perales and Hernandez, 1989).

On the other hand, the analyses of zones with irrigation, full or partial, have them as the main objective to make maximum use of rain, minimizing the irrigation and for that reason, the cost, mainly when water was supplied by pumping. Moreover, as Hargreaves et al. (1989) indicated, the areas of good quality lands for crop production frequently far exceed those that can be irrigated from developed or developable water supplies. Then, the responsible people for planning and designing the irrigation projects may need a method or criteria for deciding on the most acceptable degree of deficit irrigation or the probable benefits from supplemental irrigation to rainfall.

The agricultural development planning can be significantly improved by the use of explanatory models for comparing the probable yields from rain-fed agriculture with those obtained when one, two or more supplemental irrigations are applied. Moreover, the crop yield models can provide a useful tool for evaluating the relative benefits from different crop production practices.

Specific Studies

In the conflict areas, mainly between the irrigation and domestic or industrial water supply, the approach is to obtain the same economic benefits with other more remunerative crops but with lower water requirements, likewise feasible to growth, in accord with the climatic and soil conditions. This approach will give more water to supply the domestic or industrial uses.

In the change and development of new crops, the agroclimatic studies will give the spectrum of possible crops and the basic characteristics about their water consumptions. The application of explanatory models makes it possible to obtain the benefits from the conjunctive use of rain and irrigation, evaluating the differences between crop production under rainfall conditions and potential crop production with the application of one or more irrigations, and also evaluating the benefits from different crop production practices in each of them.

USE OF EXPLANATORY CROP MODELS

Problems and Solutions

The analyses realized in the agrometeorological studies with tendency to obtain the minimum water requirements of crops, make use of a mathematical model of growth and development simulating crop or explanatory model, which can probe very different schedules of irrigation and practices, with the support of daily weather data available. At present, there are explanatory models for the main crops, as for example: cotton (Stapleton et al., 1973), winter wheat (Maas and Arkin, 1980), potato (Ng and Loomis, 1984), maize (Jones and Kiniry, 1986), spring wheat (van Keulen and Seligman, 1987) and sorghum (Rosenthal et al., 1989).

All the above models, including the plant growth (PLANTGRO) developed by Hanks (1974, 1985), use the daily meteorological data as climatic input, therefore it required great computer capacity to their application, but more important is the fact that not always the long records are available or easy to obtain the daily climatic values. For these reasons weather simulation or generation models have been developed, such as the weather generator (WGEN) model described by Richardson and Wright (1984) and the weather maker (WMAKER) model presented and used by Samani et al. (1987).

The WMAKER model requires the mean monthly values of potential evapotranspiration, temperature, number of rainy days, rainfall amounts, and standard deviations of the monthly data. Hargreaves and Samani (1988) pointed out the advantage of this model over other weather generating models, because of its ability to generate daily data without the requirement of local calibration. Although the WGEN model provides good estimates, its application is limited to the availability of local climatological parameters which are not available outside the United States of America. Whereas the WMAKER model requires little local calibration and uses a fairly simple monthly data base. For these reasons it was selected for the use in the studies described.

Proposed Studies

Their main city and the Villa de Reyes valley, distant 50 km, in the San Luis Potosi state are the zones with more conflict in the use of water, both with total water supply originating in the pumping from the same aquifer, which is overdraft, mainly in the zone of San Luis Potosi city.

In the city, in accord with collected local information and the work of Sanchez and Rojas (1990), the agricultural area is approximately 2,570 hectares dispersed around the city, the main crops are maize, alfalfa and in minor scale vegetables. The annual water consumption by domestic uses is about 60 Mm^3 and for industry 15 Mm^3. The population estimated is half a million and the number of industries is 200.

In the Villa de Reyes valley, the consumptions are 5 Mm^3, 25 Mm^3 and 80 Mm^3 for domestic, industrial and agricultural uses, respectively; with fifty thousand inhabitant, two industries and 6,000 hectares. The industries are one thermoelectric and one paper manufacture. The Villa de Reyes total agricultural valley, include the Jaral de Berrios area in the Guanajuato state, with 10,000 hectares under irrigation, therefore their annual water consumption is approximately 120 Mm^3. These figures point out the need to optimized irrigation mainly in the agricultural areas of Jaral de Berrios and Villa de Reyes, with the approaches stated in above descriptions. The objective is to obtain the answers as to the annual crop to each irrigation schedule, and make a probabilistic analysis to establish the yield associated with the specific hazards. Then, the cost analyses will lead to the best solutions in benefits and economy of water. These savings of water will be utilized for domestic and industrial uses in the San Luis Potosi city, to avoid or to lessen the overdraft of the aquifer.

REFERENCES

Campos-Aranda, D.F.(1989). *Primera estimacion del potencial agricola del Estado de San San Luis Potosi por medio de indices climaticos.* 2a. Reunion Nal. de Agroclimatologia U.A.Ch. Texcoco. pp. 80-91.

Campos-Aranda, D.F.(1990a). *Propuesta de Normas para la elaboracion de estudios agroclimaticos.* Submitted for publication to Ingenieria Hidraulica en Mexico. 42 p.

Campos-Aranda, D.F.(1990b). *Hacia la normalizacion de los estudios agroclimaticos.* Aprovechamiento del agua y los fertilizantes en las regiones aridas de Mexico S.M.C.S. Comarca Lagunera. pp 47-72.

Doorenbos, J. y Kassam, A.H.(1979). *Efectos del agua sobre el rendimiento de los cultivos.* Estudio FAO: riego y drenaje 33. Roma, Italia. 212 p.

Feddes, R.A., Kowalik, P.J. and Zaradny, H.(1978). *Simulation of field water use and crop yield.* Centre for Agricultural Publishing and Documentation. Wageningen, the Netherlands. 178 p.

Frere, M. y Popov, G.F.(1980). *Pronostico de cosechas basado en datos agrometeorologicos.* Estudio FAO: produc. y protec. vegetal 17. Roma Italia. 66 p.

Frere, M. y Popov, G.F.(1986). *Pronostico agrometeorologico del rendimiento de los cultivos.* Estudio FAO: Produc. y protec. vegetal 73. Roma Italia. 194 p.

Hanks, R.J. (1974). *Model for predicting plant yield as influenced by water use.* Agron. J., 66, 660-665.

Hanks, R.J. (1985). *Soil Water modelling.* Hydrological Forecasting. John Wiley and Sons, Ltd. England. pp 15-36.

Hargreaves, G.H. (1975). *Moisture availability and crop production.* Trans. ASAE, pp. 980-984.

Hargreaves, G.H. and Samani, Z.A. (1988). *Estimation of standard deviation of potential evapotranspiration.* J. Irrig. and Drain. Engrg., 114, 1, 175-180.

Hargreaves, G.H., Samani, Z.A. and Zuniga, E.(1989). *Modeling yields from rainfall and supplemental irrigation* J. Irrig. and Drain. Engrg., 115, 2, 239-247.

Jones, C.A. and Kiniry, J.R.(1986). *CERES-Maize, a simulation model of maize growth and development.* Texas A-M University Press, College Station, Tex. 194 p.

Maas, S.J. and Arkin, G.F.(1980). *TAMW: A wheat growth and development simulation model.* Texas Agricultural Experiment Station, Temple, Tex. 124 p.

Ng, E. and Loomis, R.S.(1984). *Simulation of growth and yield of the potato crop.* Centre for Agricultural Publishing and Documentation, Wageningen, the Netherlands. 147 p.

Organizacion de las Naciones Unidas para la Agricultura y la Alimentacion. (1981). *Informe del proyecto de zonas agroecologicas.* Informe sobre Rec. Mundiales de suelos 48/3. Roma, Italia. 253 p.

Penning de Vries, F.W.T., Jansen, D.M., ten Berge, H.F.M. and Bakema, A.(1989). *Simulation of ecophysiological processes of growth in several annual crops.* Centre for Agricultural Publishing and Documentation, Wageningen, the Netherlands. 271 p.

Perales-de la Cruz, M.A. y Hernandez-Alatorre, J.(1989) *Efectos de las temperaturas en variedades de maiz en la zona media de San Luis Potosi.* 2a. Reunion Nal. de Agroclimatologia. U.A.Ch. Texcoco. pp. 413-419.

Richardson, C.W. and Wright, D.A.(1984). *WGEN: A model for generating daily weather variables.* U.S.D.A., ARS-8, 83p.

Robertson, G.W.(1983). *Weather-based mathematical models for estimating development and ripening of crops* T.N.-180,WMO-No.620. Geneva, Switzerland.99 p.

Rosenthal, W.D., Vanderlip, R.L., Jackson, B.S. and Arkin, G.F.(1989). *SORKAM: A grain sorghum crop growth model.* College Station, Texas A-M University and Agronomy Department, Kansas Agricultural Experiment Station. 205 p.

Samani, Z.A., Hargreaves, G.H., Zuniga, E. and Keller, A.A. (1987). *Estimating crop yields from simualted daily weather data.* Appl. Engrg. in Agric., 3 (2), 290-294.

Sanchez-Lara, M. y Rojas-Aguilar, A.(1990). *Estudio de factibilidad integral para la reutilizacion de las aguas residuales de la ciudad de San Luis Potosi,S.L.P.(primera etapa).* 11o Congreso Nal. de Hidraulica. Zacatecas, Zac. Tomo I, 36-47.

Stapleton, H.N. Buxton, D.R., Watson, F.L., Nolting, D.J. and Baker, D.N.(1973). *COTTON: A computer simulation of cotton growth.* College of Agriculture, The University of Arizona. 124 p.

Turc, L.(1972). *Indice climatique de potentialite agricole.* Supplement au Bulletin de L'Association Francaise pour L'Etude du Sol, 2, 81-102.

van Keulen, H. and Seligman, N.G.(1987). *Simulation of water use, nitrogen nutrition and growth of a spring wheat crop.* Centre for Agricultural Publishing and Documentation, Wageningen, The Netherlands. 310 p.

World Meteorological Organization.(1981). *Guide to agricultural meteorological practices.* WMO-No.134. Geneva Switzerland. Second edition.

FORECASTING METHODS APPLIED TO ESTIMATION OF WATER STORAGE IN THE LÁZARO CÁRDENAS RESERVOIR IN THE LA LAGUNA REGION, MEXICO

Rafael Figueroa-Viramontes
FAZ-UJED
Apartado No 142
Gómez Palacio, Durango, México

Leopoldo Moreno-Díaz and Ricardo Almeida-Martínez
CENID-RASPA, INIFAP-SARH
Apartado 41
Cd. Lerdo, Durango, México

ABSTRACT

The La Laguna region is devoted mainly to agriculture, being one of the more important in whole México. The irrigated surface amounts to 175,000 ha; 58% of this land utilizes water which is provided by the Lázaro Cárdenas reservoir and a regulatory pond called the Fransisco Zarco. The rain water is highly variable, annually and monthly. Considering the 50 years record of monthly data, the standard deviation for September of 457.4×10^{-6} m^{-3}, with a coefficient of variation of 0.776, shows large variability. Therefore, the forecast of water storage state is difficult. If irrigation schedule depends on water levels in reservoir, then the robust forecast must be developed with a sufficient reliability and an easy use. Seven forecast techniques were analyzed, comparisons between them were made considering the square root of the sum of square deviations with respect to real values, considering the 50 years period of monthly data. Regression polynomial analysis, Fourier series, smoothing curve, MMM, normal, lognormal, and the first order Markov model were utilized. As a primary result, Fourier series was best suited to data available. For the above procedures and in a didactic manner, algorithms in BASIC for PC (IBM compatibles) were developed.

INTRODUCTION

Forecast techniques applied to water management programs provide assistance for both the producer and those who plan the water control schedule. The water storage of the reservoir depends on rainfall. Therefore, historical records of rain and runoff during the long periods of time enable forecasts which can be done by different methods.

Irrigation program depend on reliable method to predict the total water available, for the La Laguna Region. The Lázaro Cádenas reservoir provides

58% of agricultural water needs for irrigation. The water stored in the reservoir has a great variability, which is measured by the coefficient of variation of 0.121 for the monthly data. Under such conditions water management programs present inherent difficulties. On the other hand, recent technology allows the development of computer programs which facilitate calculation and data utilization in order to assist water use planning and its distribution as a support decision tool. Also, some computer programs help technicians to forecast variables such as rainfall runoffs and investigators to predict the future application by modifying and enriching the proposed methods and programs.

The purpose of this study is to present seven forecasting techniques which utilize the original data for the La Laguna Region, in order to establish the selection criteria for their utilization. Another purpose was to develop computer programs in BASIC to facilitate calculations, estimate values, and accommodate data according to the specific method.

GENERAL PROCEDURE

Monthly runoffs measurements of the Lázaro Cárdenas reservoir were analyzed, included the period 1939-1988. The methods used were: regression polynomial analysis, Fourier series, smoothing curve, MMM, normal, lognormal and the first order Markov model. Normal and lognormal PDF were complemented with xy for the best fit. The MMM transformation technique was used to test for normality.

Polynomial regression analysis

Method - The polynomial regression is commonly used to relate two or more variables, where the least square method is applied for estimation purposes. Its mathematical expression is given by Eq. 1.

$$y_i = \beta_0 + \beta_1 x + \beta_2 x^2 + \ldots + \beta_0 x^n + \varepsilon_i, \text{ with } N(0, \sigma^2) \quad (1)$$

where $N(0, \sigma^2)$ indicates that error, are normally distributed and are independent. For each value of x there is a value of y with the normal distribution. Méndez-Ramírez (1976) provides a more explanatory and comprehensive text for the application and use of statistical linear regressions.

The 1939-1988 period included 600 monthly runoff values. These data were sorted in such a way that calculation could be done separately for each month. Then, data was obtained for each month, for the corresponding 50 years. These values for some months were found to be independent variables. Regression analysis was run by utilizing different polynomial models of various orders in x_i.

Results - For the regression models of various orders the coefficient of determination for each one was computed. The corresponding R^2 were: second order, 0.09; third order, 0.20; fourth order, 0.20; fifth order, 0.17; and sixth order, 0.26. According to those results, an inconsistent increase in R^2 was obtained. Therefore, this approach was not recommended for the analysis of data, because of their small coefficients of determination and inconsistency.

To illustrate the above results, the average monthly runoff data were used by the same procedure of polynomial regression analysis, as the 12 other records of data. Figure 1 shows the tendency of the various orders, 2th, 4th, 6th and 8th order. Also, some negative values were obtained in the estimation of runoff. Both, the coefficient of determination and the estimated values are not reliable because of the averaging procedure, a practice commonly used to show the averaged monthly data with time.

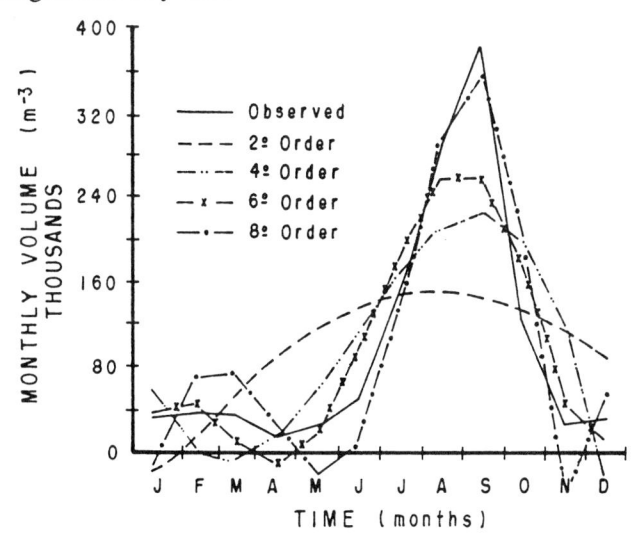

Figure 1. Polynomial regression estimates for different orders and their relation with the monthly values, 1939-1988, of runoff of the Lázaro Cárdenas Reservoir of the La Laguna Region, Coah., Dgo., México.

Fourier Series

Method - Little and Jackson (1979) point out that Fourier series is a type of regression which relates a variable with time and its periodicity in fixed intervals. There are two main methods for calculating the Fourier series. In this case an abbreviated form of Eq. 2 was used.

$$y = \alpha_0 + \alpha_1 \cos Cx + \beta_1 \sin C_x + \ldots + \alpha_o \cos nC_x + x^n + \beta_o \sin nC_x \qquad (2)$$

where x is time in arbitrary initial setting, C is a constant equal to 360° divided by a number of units in a cycle. Different runs were done considering the first order of the fifth order calculation using the 600 records.

The calculated values by Eq. 2 were compared with the real monthly runoff data. The differences, given in terms of least square fit, provided the error term.

Results - The selection method for the best calculation was the square root of the sum of square of deviations (SSD) in 10^{-6} m-3. The results of SSD were: for the first order, 173.6; second order, 163.6; third order, 159.1; fourth order, 157.5; fifth order, 157.2. The last order is considered the best fit.

Smoothing curve

Method - This technique is based on the moving average, the general calculation procedure is given by Eq. 3.

$$S^{(n)}_t = a \cdot S^{(n-1)}_t + (1 - a) S^{(n-1)}_{t-1} \qquad (3)$$

where S_t is the smoothed value, a is the smooth constant being equal to 2/(N - 1), N = interval value, n is smoothing order.

Results - After analyzing several sizes of interval, considering each 5-months increment up to 45 months, the best fit was that of 45 months with constant a = 0.04. Figure 2 shows the relationship of the constant "a" obtained by the method of square root of the sum of squares of deviations. The value a = 0.04 was selected because there is a tendency of the square root of the sum of squares of deviation, to increase above 0.04.

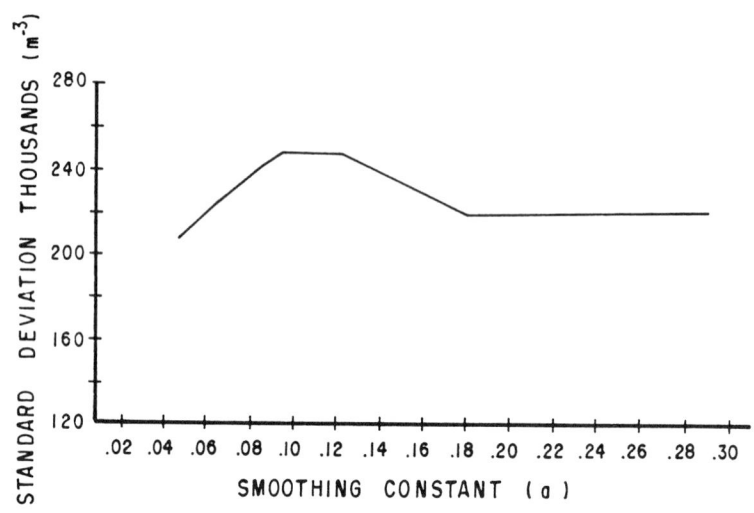

Figure 2. Smoothing constant values related to the square root of the sum of squares of deviations (SDD) of the runoff, 1939-1988. the Lázaro Cárdenas Reservoir of the La Laguna Region, Coah., Dgo., México.

MMM Transformation

Method - This method consists of transforming the original data into the trigonometric expressions (Moreno-Díaz and Santamaria, 1982). The triple M, MMM, is given because the mean, mode and median are considered. These are central tendency estimates.

Results - The square root of the sum of squares of deviations, considering the total 600 records, was 166.34, at the confidence 50% level. For each month (in calendar order from January to December), the estimates were 17.2, 13.3, 16, 9.7, 9, 33.3, 83.4, 240.4, 225.8, 75.1, 15.2, 13.3 in 10^{-6} m^{-3}. In Fig. 3 the pattern of volume of water is shown for the occurrence in different months in the averaged year, for both, the estimated and real values.

Normal and lognormal

Method - This technique assumes that monthly runoff was distributed normally or lognormally. Therefore, logarithmic transformations were done. The function that characterizes the normal distribution is given by Eq. 4, whose integral determines the probability

$$y = 1/\sqrt{2\pi} \; e^{-1/4 z^z} \qquad (4)$$

where y is the normal ordinate, with known constants of π and e; and z is the standardized variable.

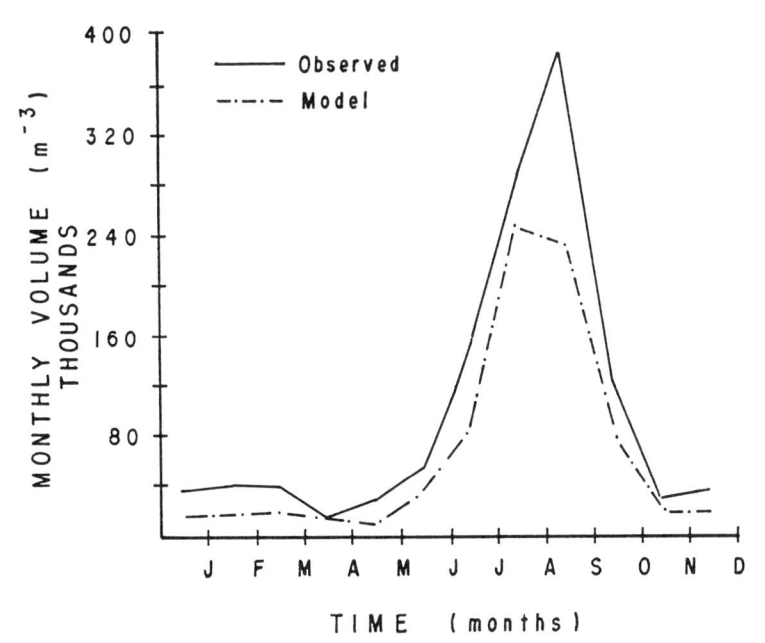

Figure 3. Monthly runoff volume of the Lázaro Cárdenas Reservoir 1988, at the 50 percent confidence level. The La Laguna Region, Coah., Dgo., México.

Results - The best fit was obtained for the lognormal distribution, if compared with normal PDF, because four months were under 0.95 confidence level. Meanwhile, the normal PDF showed only one month under the same confidence level. The result was according to the χ^2-test. Figure 4 shows the real values against those estimated. The greatest variability is observed in September. The square root of the sum of squares of deviations for all 600 records were 186.5×10^{-6} m^{-3}.

First-order Markov chain

Method - This technique considers the runoff with two components, one deterministic and the other random. This condition according to Linsley et al. (1977) may be represented by Eq. 5

$$Q_{i,j} = Q_{m,j} + R_j \; \sigma_j/\sigma_{j-1} (Q_{i-1,j-1} - Q_{mj-1}) + t_i \cdot \sigma_j \sqrt{1-R^2_j} \quad (5)$$

where $Q_{i,j}$ is runoff for jth month and ith year; $Q_{m,j}$ is the mean runoff monthly volume; R_j is the serial correlation coefficient between Q_j and Q_{j-1}; σ_j is the standard deviation and t_j is the random variable.

Results - A normal process was used to generate the t_j variable, the square root of deviations, 204.8×10^{-6} m^{-3}, was one of the greatest.

SYNTHESIS

All the above techniques were tested considering the square root of the sum of squares of deviations (SSD). Using the criteria of smallest SSD value to biggest SSD for all the techniques analyzed, the following order of methods is obtained: Fourier series, fifth order, 163.7; MMM transformation, 50% confidence, 166.3; regression polynomial, second order, 183.5; lognormal, 50% confidence, 186.5; Markov chain, 204.8; and last, smoothing curve, quadratic form, 206.4. From the above results it is considered that the Fourier series, with the smallest SSD, offers the best method to relate the runoff variable with respect to time. The complete data, the BASIC programs for PC (IBM/XT) computer of the 7 analyzed techniques, as the development of the didactic examples, are included in Figueroa-Viramontes (1990).

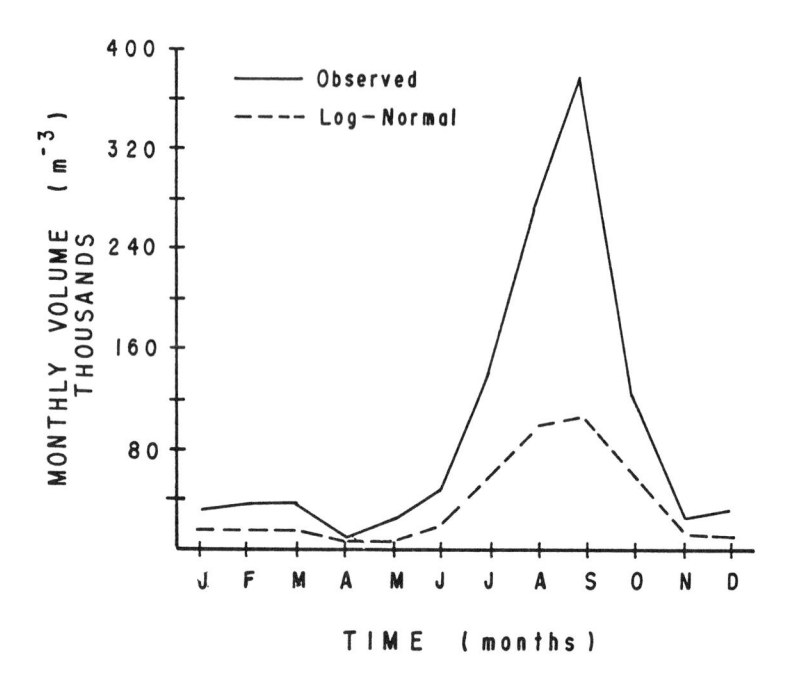

Figure 4. The runoff estimates, at the 50 percent confidence level, and their relation with time under lognormal technique, 1939-1988. the Lázaro Cárdenas Reservoir of the La Laguna Region, Coah., Dgo., México.

REFERENCES

Figueroa-Viramontes, R. (1990). *Evaluación de Algunos Métodos de Predicción Aplicados a las Aportaciones Mensuales a la Presa Lázaro Cárdenas, Comarca Lagunera.* M. C. Thesis, Universidad Juárez del Estado de Durango, Facultad de Agricultura y Zootecnia. Venecia, Durango, México, 94 pp.

Méndez-Ramírez, I. (1976) *Modelos Estadísticos lineales.- Interpretación y aplicaciones.* Conacyt, México, 140 pp.

Moreno-Díaz, L., E. Santamaria (1982). *Aspectos cuantitativos del uso de agua para riego de la presa Lázaro Cárdenas en La Región Lagunera, Coah., y Dgo.* CENAMAR-DGDUR, SARH (Mimeographed).

Linsley, K. R., A. M. Kohler, L. H. J. Paulhus (1977). *Hidrología para ingenieros.* McGraw-Hill de México.

Little M., H. T. and F. Jackson Hills (1979). *Métodos Estadísticos para Investigación en la Agricultura.* Trillas, México.

EDUCATION, TRAINING AND RESEARCH AT THE HYDROSCIENCE CENTER OF THE COLEGIO DE POSTGRADUADOS

L. Rendon-Pimentel and R. Fernández-González
Centro de Hidrociencias
Colegio de Postgraduados
Montecillo, Mexico, Mexico, 56230

ABSTRACT

The Colegio de Postgraduados (Postgraduate College) is an education and research institution in agricultural sciences. The Hydroscience Center of the Colegio de Postgraduados has as objectives education, research and training in the agricultural water use. This Center gives the Master in Science degree to its regular students. The educational program is composed of the regular and the special courses. The research program is formed by several research projects carried out by professors, researchers and students. The training program consists of short courses and training in special activity. The academic staff includes eight professors, seven researchers and three research assistants.

INTRODUCTION

The Colegio de Postgraduados is an educational, research and training institution in agricultural sciences, dependent on the Ministry of Agriculture and Water Resources in Mexico. It has 11 centers on campus located at Montecillo and Chapingo, Mexico, and 4 regional centers at the states of San Luis Potosi, Puebla, Veracruz and Tabasco.

The Hydroscience Center is located on the campus at Montecillo, Mexico, and was founded in 1959 as a section of soil-plant-water relationships of the Soils Department. Later in 1968, it was given a new category as an Irrigation and Drainage Department at the Colegio de Postgraduados. Finally, the department turned into centers, and the name changed to Hydroscience Center.

A program on agricultural meteorology started in 1986 within the Center. The Center of Hydroscience offers a master in science program and soon it will offer a doctorate program.

This paper gives information about the organization of the Center, its educational areas and the research program, including some statistical data about students and graduated students.

EDUCATION AND RESEARCH

The Hydroscience Center has five areas of education and research, called sections: the Water in the Soil-Plant-Atmosphere System, Saline and Alkali

Soils and Water Management, Irrigation Engineering, Drainage Engineering and Water Resources Engineering. Besides the Center chairman for each section there is a research professor as head, several more professors, researchers and office and field personnel.

Educational program at each section includes the regular and special courses, and courses of other sections from other centers. It offers three academic periods: Spring, from January to May; Summer, from May to July; and Fall, from July to December. Spring and Fall class periods are given in 18 weeks, while Summer is given in only 6 weeks. Regular courses are listed on Tables 1 to 3.

TABLE 1. Courses of the water in the soil-plant-atmosphere system, irrigation engineering and drainage engineering sections.

Name	Code	Credits	period
The Water in the soil-plant-atmosphere system I	HID-601	3	Spring
The Water in the soil-plant-atmosphere system II	HID-602	3	Fall
The water flow trough non-saturated soils	HID-605	3	Summer
Surface irrigation engineering	HID-611	3	Fall
Pressure irrigation engineering	HID-612	3	Spring
Agricultural drainage	HID-621	3	Spring
The flow in porous media	HID-623	3	Fall

TABLE 2. Courses of the saline and alkali soils and water management section.

Name	Code	Credits	period
Salinity soils of irrigated lands	HID-631	3	Fall
The soil salt effect on the plants	HID-632	3	Spring
Chemical analysis of salty and sodic soils	HID-633	3	Spring
The water quality in agriculture	HID-636	3	Summer

TABLE 3. Courses of the water resources engineering section.

Name	Code	Credits	period
Introduction to systems analysis	HID-641	3	Fall
Operation of irrigation systems	HID-642	3	Spring
Systems engineering of water resources	HID-643	3	Fall
Numerical methods	HID-645	3	Fall
Advanced hydraulics	HID-646	3	Spring
Operation of hydraulic structures	HID-647	3	Fall
Hydrology	HID-652	3	Spring
Hydrogeology	HID-653	3	Fall
Water resources economy	HID-660	3	Spring
Economic engineering	HID-661	3	Summer
Design of small hydraulic structures	HID-665	3	Summer

According to the Colegio de Postgraduados normatives, during the first academic period, which is the spring, the graduate student selects his Academic Advisory Council taking into consideration his Academic and professional background. In general the student selects courses offered at the Soil Science and Statistics Centers. To consolidate his academic background the student with the advise of his committee selects some special courses.

In relation to seminars offered by the Hydroscience Center, the student must take at least two. These seminars are oriented to research work that the student carried out under the supervision of his advisor. It is one of the most important part of requisites to obtain the master of science degree. Each student has to complete 24 credit units, including seminars and both regular and special courses.

The research program in each section includes research lines and within each of these lines there are research projects carried out by professors, researchers and graduate students.

The main research lines under way, are shown on Table 4. In order to get the approval of every research program, each year the professors and researchers submit to the Academic Committe of the Center their research project proposals. The Academic Committee is the authority at the Center.

At the beginning of the second academic year every regular student must submit for approval his proposal of the research project to his Academic Advisory Council. Later, he must give an oral presentation to the academic staff of the Center. This research project will be used to write the thesis which is a requisite to obtain the Master of Science Degree. Usually the program needs two years to complete all the requirements to obtain the Master of Science Degree.

TABLE 4. Main research line of Hydroscience Center.

Section	Research line
Saline and Alkali Soils and Water Management	Leaching of saline soils
	Improvement of sodic soils with gypsum
	Cationic exchange in salty soils
	Reserve evaluation of salts in salty soils
	Plant response to salinity
Water Resources Engineering	Planning and operation of irrigation systems
	Mathematical models applied to operation of irrigation systems
	Automation in irrigation systems
Irrigation Engineering	Surface irrigation engineering
	Pressure irrigation engineering
	Hydrodynamic of soil characteristics
Drainage Engineering	Hydrologic modeling of rainfall-runoff relationship
	Field drainage assays for improving water conditions for sugar cane crop
Water in the Soil-Plant-Atmosphere System	Physiological parameters and their relations to drought periods
	Transpiration retardants
	Production models at different soil moisture levels at several phenological stages
	Comparative study of models to estimate consumptive use
	Cropping methods in wheat production to optimize the use of water.

TRAINING

Training programs are prepared under request by private and public institutions. We offer practical training or workshops to transfers knowledge and technology generated by our research program. This training is offered to farmers, technicians and professionals. Sometimes, national or international institutions ask for short courses on a special subject and those are given on campus, in the regional centers or in any other institution throughout the country. In these cases a professor is responsible for the planning, organization and supervision of the course. Table 5 shows some short courses given during 1989 and 1990.

TABLE 5. Short courses given during 1989 and 1990. Planning, operation and Ministry of Agriculture

Name	Institution
International course of surface irrigation and technical assistance irrigation	Agency for International Development. Dominican Republic.
Planning, operation, conservation and efficient water use in irrigation systems	Water National Commission. Mexico.
Planning, operation and efficient water use in small irrigation systems	Ministry of Agriculture and Water Resources, Mexico.
Rice irrigation in tropical humid zones	Government of Tabasco State. Mexico.

Name and Subject	Institution
Angel Reynaldo Rey Garcia. The soil moisture control using neutron scatter method.	Research Institute of Irrigation. Cuba.
Augusto Medinaceli Ortiz. Water Resources Engineering	F.A.D. Bolivia

ACADEMIC STAFF AND FACILITIES

At present, the academic staff includes eight professors, seven researchers and three research assistants working full-time at the Center. From them seven have Ph. D. degree and eight have M.S. degree. From the seven with the Ph.D. degree, three studied in U.S.A., two in U.S.S.R. and two in France. From the academic staff six belongs to the Research National System sponsored by the Mexican Government.

To support education, training and research activities, the Center has three laboratories: salinity, water-soil-plant relationships and computation, an agricultural meteorology station and an irrigation engineering experimental plot. The salinity laboratory has an absorption atomic electrophotometer and modern equipment to do chemical analysis of soils and water. The water-soil-plant relationship laboratory is equipped with instrumentation to do physical soil analysis and to measure the plant water states even in the field. The computer laboratory has nine personal computer, one HP-3000 system with plotter and three laserjet printers. The agricultural meteorology station is equipped with an undisturbed weighing lysimeter and is possible to register the main agro-meteorological variables. The irrigation engineering experimental plot has the main infrastructure to conduct experiments by different irrigation methods: trickle, sprinkler, furrow, border and surge irrigation.

IMPACTS OF HYDROSCIENCE CENTER

During its 31 years of work, the Center has graduated 126 students, 60% Mexicans and the rest of them from 11 countries, mainly from Latin America.

In Mexico the graduates work covers mainly the needs of the Ministry of Agriculture and Water Resources, for the irrigation areas, also as professors at all the state universities, as well as for banks and private companies.

Research projects carried out at the Center or at the irrigation areas have allowed the development of laboratory methodologies, irrigation equipment, irrigation scheduling of the main irrigated crops, mathematical models for watershed and water management and water application methods.

Some Hydroscience Center results are: constant head infiltrograph for field infiltration, water quality parameters to classify water effluents for irrigation, suction ceramic capsules for underground water application (hydraulics, design and construction), mathematical models for planning and management of water in an irrigation system, watershed runoff models to simulate the available volumes of water for use in surface irrigation models.

The staff members have published a large number of technical papers, several books like: Introduction to Operation Theory of Irrigation Systems, by E. Palacios-Velez and A. Exebio-Garcia; Manual for Small Hydraulics Structures and Projects for Irrigation and Cattle Watering, by Hydroscience Center staff; Salinity of Irrigated Soils: Identification, Control, Improvement and Plant Adaptation by E. Aceves-Navarro, and Water in Soil-Plant-Atmosphere System (first draft), by R. Fernandez Gonzalez.

ROLE OF RESEARCH IN WATER SCIENCES AS A CATALYZER OF EDUCATION AND TRAINING IN SOME DEVELOPING COUNTRIES

M. Abu-Zeid
Water Research Center
Il Cairo, Egypt

A. Hamdy
Mediterranean Agronomic Institute
Bari, Italy

C. Lacirignola
Mediterranean Agronomic Institute
Bari, Italy

ABSTRACT

Research is a major catalyzer of education and training in developing countries. Research priorities are usually set according to development needs of a country or sometimes to solve specific problems. Adoption of technology may also require research. There are some difficulties associated with organizing research programs oriented towards development questions. Graduate training programmes consistently face the problem of working with standard approaches that are successful in helping students to become efficient researchers able to make meaningful contributions to resolution of water resources and related management problems in their countries. Continuous feedback and revision of education and training programmes to improve the concepts are necessary. The paper discusses the need to consider major research findings and issues in training and educational programmes. Few examples are given where the role of national and international institutes is stated and discussed. Donor agencies to developing countries are urged to assist in initiating applied research for education in subjects related to the country priorities. Different models are given where joint supervision of research and training proved to be successful.

INTRODUCTION

Experience from a higher education indicates substantial benefits when training, research and the provision of advisory service are combined. A research component provides new information to feed into the training function, which otherwise tends to become tradition bound. Furthermore, combining a research function with training may increase the programme appeal to competent staff who may not wish to be associated with a training programme alone. Another element of importance is that research and training staff are faced with practical problems and have the opportunity to put their ideas into practice.

It appears that when irrigation training and research are combined at the national level, the former strengthens the latter; but the reverse may not occur. This is because in many countries irrigation research capacity is even more limited than training capacity, so the research mandate may retard training rather than strengthen it. Furthermore, traditional irrigation research has tended to focus on physical and biological effects of water use, not on operational and management decisions. That focus does not support the innovative training activities needed by irrigation departments to overcome their performance shortcomings in a changing environment. Most of the developing countries, especially the poorest ones, are facing major constraints in food production; appropriate technology consisting of all mechanical, physical, sociological and other resource manipulation that enable these countries to attain increased productivity is called for. This can be achieved through the support of a combined training and research programme aimed at the accumulation of the know-how required for development. This paper will focus on the way to improve cooperation for agricultural research in developing countries with emphasis on the role of the International Center for Advanced Mediterranean Agronomic Studies (ICAMAS), in particular Bari Institute, on the research and training development in the Mediterranean Region.

PLANNING AND MANAGING RESEARCH IN DEVELOPING COUNTRIES

Unfortunately, research facilities and programmes in developing countries are not well established, and few are yet on a par with those in developed countries. The greatest deficiencies include excessive fragmentation of research activities among governmental agencies, the low priority assigned to research by governments, and inadequate institutional structures for research and extension (World Bank, 1981). Research staff in developing countries are often small, have not a balance of disciplines, and usually lack adequate budgets. In many cases there is no planning or management to direct the scarce resources available towards the most appropriate research priorities.

Agricultural Research in the Mediterranean Countries

A complete analysis on the situation in the 13 Mediterranean Member Countries of ICAMAS (Algeria, Egypt, Spain, Malta, Tunisia, Morocco, Lebanon, Turkey, Yugoslavia, Portugal, France, Italy and Greece) is given through two seminars: the first about the Agricultural Research, Istanbul December 1986, and the second about the Agronomic training in Mediterranean Countries, Rabat, March 1987. Both seminars were organized by ICAMAS with the support of the Directorate General of Science (DGXII) Commission of the European Community. In view of the separate national reports presented by each member country about the research infrastructure, programmes, manpower involved, budgets, institutions facilities, difficulties and the future prospects an analysis of National Agricultural Research

Systems (NARS) in the Mediterranean region was prepared by Casas (1988). He states that until now NARS of Mediterranean countries have had relatively little in the way of exchange programmes. The bilateral relations that have been mostly developed have involved primarily either neighboring countries in the North or both northern and southern countries that have historical links. But even these have remained quite limited and sometimes even less developed than those with non Mediterranean countries.

Multilateral relations initiated by the International organizations such as the FAO, ICAMAS, ICARDA, etc. are still the exception to the rule. As a result, Mediterranean NARS are poorly known to each other. Moreover, the infrastructure of research in the member states of ICAMAS is completely different from the Northern part of the Mediterranean Sea where agricultural research is already well organized and of high order of competence with respect to the southern part where renovation, reorientation and reorganization of research according to the national individual country plans are a must. However, due to the similarity in the problems the Mediterranean countries are facing, the agronomic research is becoming increasingly important, and it is now recognized that the right way to bridge the gulf between the Northern and the Southern shore of the Mediterranean sea is through the establishment of proper links of bilateral or multilateral cooperation.

ICAMAS and research improvement in the Mediterranean countries - the recent evolution of lCAMAS towards a greater integration with non-European Mediterranean countries has made it possible to achieve the rather important objectives of bringing together, at the same level, 13 countries and inter-governmental organizations such as the OCED, the Council of Europe, the EEC, the FAO and the Arab League, for the purpose of examining the agricultural problems of area. But this evolution also calls for a new ICAMAS policy in training, teaching and research to meet the needs of the member countries. ICAMAS plays an important flexible role through its four International Institutes (in Bari, Montpellier, Saragoza and Chania) in improving the qualifications of professional staff in the Mediterranean countries working in agricultural and rural development. The goal is to develop and maintain a group of well trained, competent scientists in appropriate research disciplines, in problem solution and interpretation of national and international scientific advances for the benefit of national development.

Given the existence of differences between various countries that cannot always be mitigated over the short term, and the will to work together to overcome them, ICAMAS, through its operational institutes, has a difficult task in setting and grading up its training as well as research programmes aimed at satisfying the real needs of rapidly evolving countries in which great progress has been accomplished and great efforts are under way for perfecting. Equally so, research programmes should be tailored to the specific problems faced by the Mediterranean Region and aim at the highest quality. As the creation of ICAMAS was meant to improve cooperation between Mediterranean Countries, research programmes of the center and its institutes gave priority to activities likely to promote such initiatives (research network, comparative studies, overall analysis of the Mediterranean region). Scientific activity is not limited to the creation or operation of networks. It also takes place through the organization of Mediterranean seminars which can constitute the starting point for inter-Mediterranean cooperation through networks or which make evaluation of the existing network activities possible.

Training and Research: Bari Institute Contribution. - Research is unquestionably a necessity for higher education. It contributes to the continuous education of teachers/researchers and in many countries, it determines their careers. In addition to the continuing education of instructors, research objectives include the training of students and the development of Mediterranean agriculture. These goals may be complementary in some cases, or they may be competitive. Training in Mediterranean Countries must work out a consistent rational link between science and practice, thereby reconciling concern for the scientific reputation of teachers/researchers with the objectives of the agricultural development of the country. Certain topics are specific to the Mediterranean region, for example: Irrigation, Management and development of conventional and unconventional water resources.

Bari-MAI one of the operational institutes of ICAMAS, will be taken as an example to elucidate the role of research in water science as a catalyzer of education and training in some developing countries. One of the main programmes Bari Institute is dealing with irrigation, a subject which is of primary importance and interest for the whole Mediterranean area. The programme is mainly based on Irrigation techniques, planning and management for a two year duration. In the first year a teaching, technical and practical programme is carried out to cover the main irrigation aspects (Agronomy, Hydraulics and Socioeconomic aspects) with the participation of nearly 40 candidates the majority from the developing Mediterranean countries.

The programme, covers 1100 hours: 580 hours are for the theoretical and teaching part corresponding to 52% of the total teaching activities; 520 hours are for practical activities including laboratory work, drawing up of small and medium irrigation projects and technical visits and they account for 48% of the teaching activities. The philosophy behind this first year programme is the preparation of well trained technicians having a better understanding of the variable aspects of irrigation, capable of following up irrigation in their home countries on both scientific and technical basis.

This type of training is completely absent in the Mediterranean countries and, more to the point, it is urgently needed to fill the big existing gap between the planners and specialists of this sector. The training programme starts with a heterogeneous group of candidates with different specializations (Agronomy, Soil Science, Hydraulics, Economics and Geology) in an effort to have at the end of the programmea technical irrigation engineer with a better understanding of all the different aspects of irrigation, able to talk to and exchange views with partners of different specialization. In addition, this training programme is run by professors of notable and long experience from the Mediterranean region, European countries and others all over the world. This enables the participants not only to be acquainted with the experience in both the Mediterranean countries and other countries, but also to be informed of the latest up-date innovation and knowledge in this field. The second part of the programme for a master degree also lasts one year.

This programme is directed to research and is only open to those candidates who attended the first year teaching programme and obtained the post-graduate specialization diploma (DSPU) with a very high grade (Excellent). The selected candidates participate in the individual research programme carried out by the Institute which covers eleven major subjects of vital importance to the Mediterranean countries (unconventional water resources practices and management; supplementary irrigation for cereals and winter crops, irrigation scheduling, hydraulics of irrigation and drainage network and others) (Fig. 1).

The programme as a whole gives priority to the Mediterranean countries not only in terms of the number of participants, (Fig. 2), but also relative to the subjects included in the programme. The programme extended its activity covering not only the Mediterranean region but other continents too. On the top was Africa with 50% of the fellowships, followed by Latin America 20%, Europe (15%) and Asia (13%) (Fig. 3). The research programme mainly aims at the development of the human resources through the preparation of the researchers who can share the national research programmes in their countries. The master programme is supervised with the participation of professors from the Mediterranean universities and scientific institutions. Through this channel a concrete cooperation was established between scientists and researchers from different Mediterranean countries.

In view of the above, we can state that Bari-MAI is following a training policy that combines both education and research. The teaching programme is periodically evaluated and graded up in view of the results obtained from the research programme. Some subjects and materials were eliminated from the teaching programme and substituted for others that are more directly related to research requirements.

The above said standard programmes may be of considerable importance for development, but they don't exhaust the possible forms of cooperation with member countries of the Mediterranean region. In order to establish permanent link between researchers of this area, who are often culturally, structurally and technologically isolated, another line of research was set up by Bari-MAI and realized in cooperation with the scientific institutions and universities of the Mediterranean region. It covers items of global importance and interest for the majority of Mediterranean countries. The research is followed up by organizing round tables and seminars held by Bari Institute with the participation of the researchers involved in this programme to discuss the results, to exchange ideas and opinions and to plan for the future.

Research programme applied and adaptive versus strategic research - Collaborative research between developed and developing countries of the Mediterranean region has to be developed. Such development could have many forms: research plus accompanying development projects, support to research programmes of Institutes or laboratories, research to generate knowledge, including thesis research, etc. For the maximum benefits of cooperation to be achieved through applied research some basic principles should be in mind.

The first concerning the strength of national research system in developing countries. This includes the training of manpower to build up scientific skills and methodologies; research stations and laboratories and comprehensive research organizations, as well as partnership between scientists or laboratories working together for solving problems of common basic interest.

The second pursues a research topic that coincides with the priorities of developing countries. In this connection Bari-MAI coordinated a pilot project based on an integrated approach on the reuse of drainage water for irrigation in the Fayoum area (over 16,000 feddans) in Egypt. The project lasted for three years and was realized in cooperation with the Water Research Center with a financial support of the Italian Ministry of Foreign Affairs and the Egyptian Ministry of Irrigation.

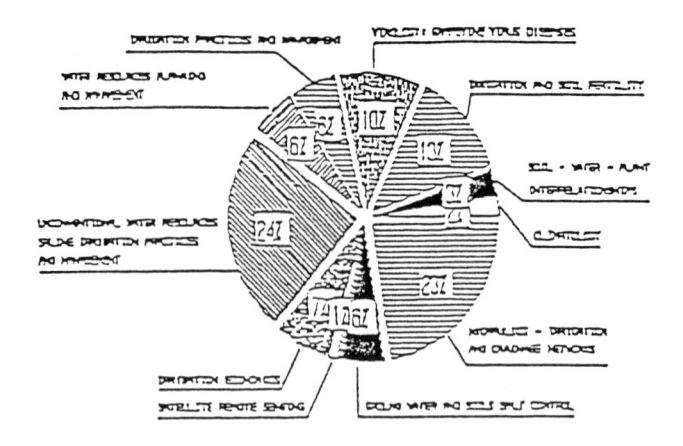

Figure 1. Percentage distribution of subjects.

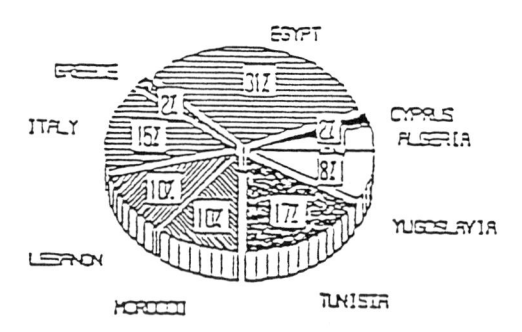

Figure 2. Percentage distribution of candidates per Mediterranean Countries.

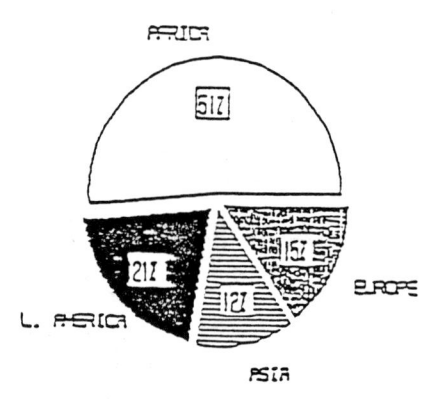

Figure 3. Master program % distribution for different continents.

In spite of the fact that the project was quite complex from the organizational point of view, and although with the limits of a pilot project, the experience gained was highly positive in terms of research development, planning, organization of research infrastructure (facilities and research manpower) as well as the disciplines of national teaching and training programmes. Moreover, methodologies and practices of proven and confirmed viability and efficaciousness will allow the extrapolation of data and forecasts for the preparation/implementation of agricultural development programmes and activities not only in Egypt but also in other Mediterranean countries and areas with similar problems or conditions.

Conclusions and perspective remarks - Research and its results have a definite role on the orientation, modification and updating of teaching and training programmes. This could be sounder by combining research with teaching and training programmes to achieve fruitful and successful interactions between research and teaching, particularly in the developing countries where research needs an effective policy formulation and coordination by creating a full operational and effective national research structure. This most likely has to be developed and tested in poorer agricultural area of the Mediterranean region. Research collaboration and exchange of experience would benefit both developed and developing countries.

In this respect, ICAMAS and its four operational institute played an important role in developing research, educational and training programmes and in creating proper links for cooperation among the Mediterranean countries.

The rapid changes taking place in various sectors of agro-food system also increased the importance of recurrent or continuous education. Consequently, Institutes of ICAMAS will have to expend and orient their programmes:

- their teaching and training programmes should be a complementary factor to the knowledge acquired in the universities of Mediterranean member countries, they must evolve in order to preserve this complementarity and in order to keep up with a post-graduate level; the number of very specialized and short monographic courses meant either for professionals (in education, research, agricultural development) or students should be increased.

- the highly specialized monographic courses should be organized in collaboration with universities and scientific institutions in member countries;

- research and education should be supported by a very efficient information system. The Institutes must go on in creating data banks, by proposing reference methodologies and by organizing Mediterranean documentation network. Finally, the policy of ICAMAS and its institutes should be directed towards the establishment of successful networks categorized according to their purpose which range from information exchange to collaborative planning, implementation and monitoring of research activities. These networks should be of equal benefit to all the participants of the Mediterranean countries.

REFERENCES

Arnon, I. 1968 . *Organization and administration of agricultural research.* Elsevier Publishing Company Ltd. Amsterdam - London - New York.

Boyazoglu, I. 1984. *Prospective inventory of the requirements of Greek Agriculture with special reference to agronomic research.* Report EUR 8653 EN, FR.123 pp.

Casas, I. ed. 1988. *Agricultural research in countries of the Mediterranean region.* Proceeding of the Istanbul seminar, December 1986. In "Options Mediterraneennes", ICAMAS, Paris, 190 pp.

Casas. I. 1988. *An analysis of national agricultural research system in the Mediterranean region.* Proceeding of the Istanbul seminar, December 1986, in "Options Mediterraneennes", ICAMAS. 157-171

Elz. D. ed. 1984. *The planning and management of agricultural research.* The World Bank, Washington, D.C., U.S.A., 143 pp.

F.A.O. 1989. *Research cooperation in agriculture between European and developing countries,* 92 pp. and annexes.

Hervieu, B. ed. 1988. *Agricultural training in countries of the Mediterranean region.* Proceeding of Rabat seminar, March/April 1987. In "Options Mediterraneennes", lCAMAS, Paris, 249 pp.

ICAMAS - MAI B 1990. *Master programme. Ten-year activities 1981- 1990,* 87 pp.

The World Bank, 1981. *Agricultural research. Sector policy paper,* Washington, D.C.

The World Bank, USAID, 1989. *Irrigation training in the public sectors. Guidelines for preparing strategies and programs.* Washington, D.C., 24 pp. and annexes.

THE INTEGRATED SOIL AND WATER IMPROVEMENT PROJECT TRAINING PROGRAM

M. Abu El-Magd
Training Director
SNC Inc.

F. El-Nagar
Egyptian Training Director
EPADP

J.S.A. Brichieri-Colombi
Canadian Team leader
SNC Inc.

M.A. Makhlouf
Egyptian Project Manager
EPADP

P.D.Box 281, Mansoura, Egypt

ABSTRACT

This paper describes the training program of a Canadian funded project in Egypt (ISAWIP). The program has a budget of about $1,500.000 Canadian Dollars. Its objectives are to improve the capabilities and performance of project personnel (400 staff) and to ensure a lasting transfer of technology. The process has been one of assessing staff training needs, providing structured training courses and programs and following up with well supervised on-the-job training. The main areas of introduction of new technologies have been polyethylene pipe production for subsurface drainage, surveys and mapping using electronic total station technology, drainage and irrigation design, computer aided design and drafting "CADD", geographical information system (GIS), multi-media production and desk-top publishing. The paper discusses the experience gained in implementing the ISAWIP training program and the advantages and disadvantages of the different training approaches utilized in the project.

INTRODUCTION

The Integrated Soil and Water Improvement Project (ISAWIP) is a joint undertaking of the Governments of Egypt and Canada. The project is located in the eastern area of the Nile Delta (Fig.1). The goal of ISAWIP is to increase agricultural output of the project area (35,000 ha) through an integrated approach consisting of improvements in irrigation, drainage, soil and agricultural extension. One of the project objectives is the introduction and use of new equipment and technologies to achieve this goal.

Significant areas of agricultural land in the River Nile delta have become waterlogged and salinized. ISAWIP is reversing the deterioration process in the project area by installing a comprehensive subsurface drainage system, improving the surface drainage and pump stations, treating problem soils, increasing efficiencies of the irrigation delivery system and strengthening the ability of the farm population to take advantage of improved conditions. The project is the first in Egypt to attack all the interrelated problems in a coordinated manner by the agencies responsible for soil and water improvement.

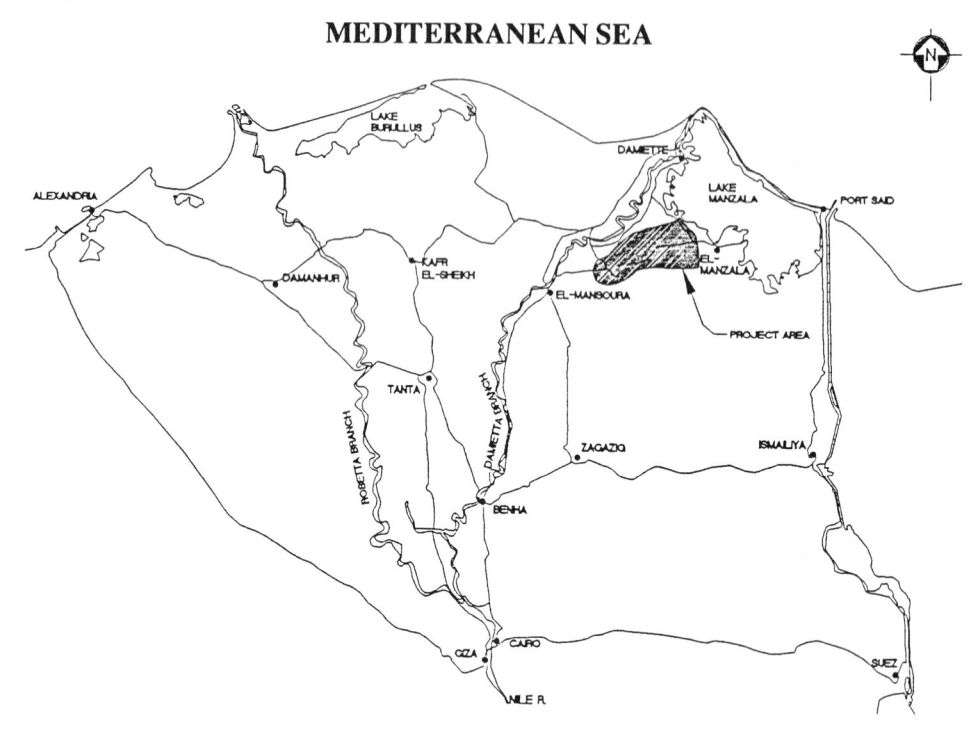

Figure 1. Project Location

The project has established a task force methodology using modern management techniques that can be replicated in other areas. The high degree of efficiency of the protect comes from using computer-aided design and drafting (CADD technology) including electronic total station surveys, digitized data handling and computer plotting of construction drawings, information processing of soils and agricultural data using a geographical information system (GIS) and multi-media production of agricultural massages to the farmers.

To support the introduction and use of new technologies, the project is supported by a fully developed training program. The training program is discussed in details in the following sections. Also, the experience gained in implementing the program, and the advantages and disadvantages of the different training approaches utilized in the project are summarized.

A SYSTEMS APPROACH FOR TRAINING

A major objective of the ISAWIP training program is to enhance human resources by building in new knowledge and skills that will lead to positive changes in behavior. Human resource development is more than offering courses in the hope that they will be helpful, it considers overall objectives, identifies needs and plans to allocate resources to meet these needs effectively and efficiently. To do this effectively, a number of questions were addressed. They include:

- What type of training and development should be offered?
- Who gets training?
- Who will supply the training and development?
- How is the training and development evaluated?

To answer these questions a four phase training model (Cherrington 1987) was used. This model, shown in Figure 2, is described briefly below:

(a) **IDENTIFICATION OF SPECIFIC TRAINING NEEDS:**

Training needs are an outgrowth of project objectives, which determine what functions must be carried out and the general knowledge and skill requirements, to perform these functions successfully. These general needs are made more specific by examining specific job functions and the personnel responsible for them.

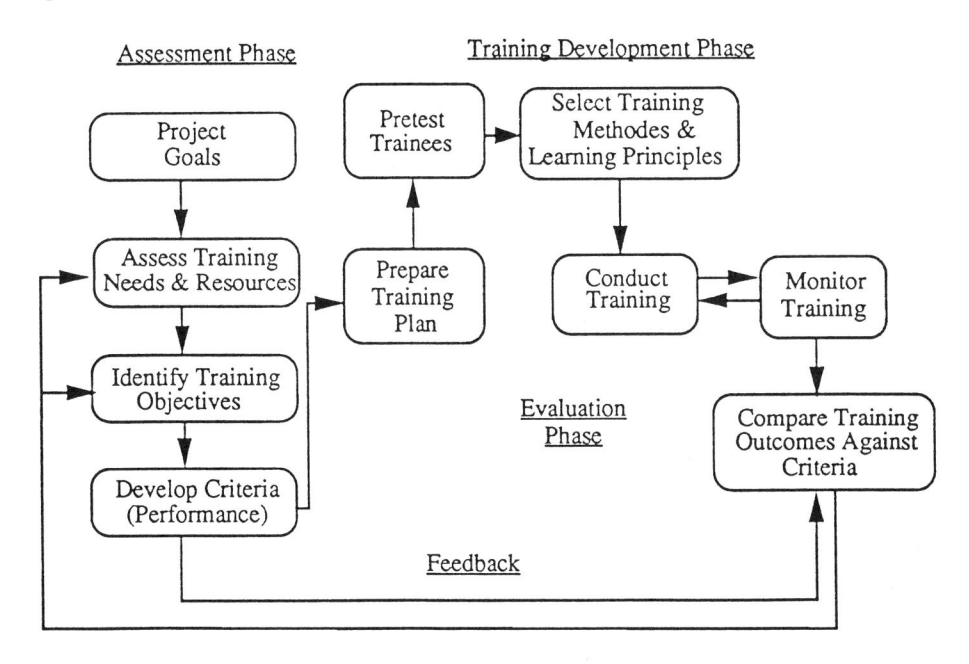

Figure 2. Training Model

Detailed needs assessment questionnaires were prepared in Arabic and English and distributed to all staff (about 400). Interviews with 4 of the staff were carried out to discuss their training needs and career development objectives. Table 1 shows the breakdown of GOE project staff by gender and education based on the analysis of the information, a detailed human resource development plan was prepared which included a career development path for the GOE staff.

TABLE 1. Gender and education of GOE staff.

COMPONENT	Education			Gender		
	Tech. Dept	Univ.	H School	Male	Female	Total
Drainage	12	23	12	46	1	47
irrigation	3	17	0	20	--	20
Agriculture Extension	9	108	60	153	24	177
Soil	5	60	30	50	45	95
Admin & Others	7	30	26	45	18	63
Total	36	238	128	314	88	402

Table 2 summarizes the main functions which had to be provided by the GOE staff, the skills required, and the training programs needed in order to complete the activities of the project using new technologies. Training programs were required to cover all functions of the four major components of the project (drainage irrigation, soil improvements and agricultural extension).

TABLE 2. The tasks and skills required and training program provided.

Tasks	Skills required	Training provided
(a) DRAINAGE AND IRRIGATION		
1. Topoqraphic Surveys and Mapping		
Basic survey of ground control network of over 750 benchmarks for horizontal and vertical control	Basic survey techniques - levelling - traversing - quality control	Basic Surveying course
Topographic surveys	Use of Electronics Total Stations (ETS) survey equipment	• Basic computer skills • Use of ETS equipment

Table 2. Continued

Constructions surveys	Layouts with network using coordinate geometry	Advanced surveying / computer

2. Design

Drainage design	• English • Understanding of drainage theory and practice • Concepts of Hydraulics • Computer applications	• English as a second language. • Basic computer skills • Design course offered by Canadian & Egyptian University staff • Irrigation Engineering • Water balance course
Basemap preparation design maps covering project area based on orthophotography	Digitization	Basic CADD course
Design computations: calculations of drain pipe capacity, size, grade and location	Computer applications CADD	Advanced computer including programming. Advanced CADD courses

3. Construction and Implementation

Construction supervision and management	Surveying for layout using horizontal coordinate geometry	Advanced survey and computer courses
	Surveying for quality control and inspection	Construction inspection courses
	Contract management	Construction management course
Formation of water user groups	Group dynamics, on farm water management practice	- Water user groups course - Computer applications - Agriculture extension course
Operation and maintenance of pump stations	- Safe operation maintenance management	- Preventive maintenance of pump stations

Table 2. Continued

Main Canal Automation	- Water balance - Hydraulic modelling - Systems - Engineering - Programming	- Hydraulic modelling application - Advanced programming of PLC - Communication and system engineering course

(b) SOIL IMPROVEMENT

Land levelling activity	- Basic survey skills	- Laser levelling - English as a training second language
Soil field studies	- Agriculture, soils basic knowledge soil morphology	- Soil field training course - Computer application courses
Soil and plant tissue analyses	- Basic soil fertility information	- Soil fertility & plant analyses
Macro and micro nutrient and analyses	- Soil chemistry, soil physis, plant physiology	- Soil fertility & plant analyses course
Work shop management and maintenance	- Basic engineering background	- Effective operation of the workshop
Operation and maintenance of heavy equipment	- Preventive techniques - Management practices	- Safe operation of heavy equipment. - Management course

(c) AGRICULTURE EXTENSION

DSCC print room operation	Basic printing techniques: • Operation of print presses • printing formats • papers	• Printing Types • Offset • Dark room operation • Colour operation • Mounting • Print press operation
Production of audio programs	Sound Recording interview production cassette duplication group listening	• Research and operations • Manuscript preparation • Narration • Tape speed correction • Basic maintenance of studio equipment • Listening group formation

Table 2. Continued

Use of desk top publishing in creative service production	Orientation of Apple operation system and utilities	• Introduction to computer concepts • Familiarization with hardware and software • Learning mouse & scanning skills
Apply training & visit system	- Principles of training and visit systems - Management techniques	• Training & visit course • Management training
Production of Video Programs	- Script writing - Shooting - Editing - Duplication	• Basic video course • Advanced video course

(b) PREPARATION OF A HUMAN RESOURCE DEVELOPMENT PLAN:

A comprehensive human resource development plan has been prepared to address the identified training needs. The plan has the following characteristics to be effective:

- Sensitive to cultural considerations.
- Consistent with the overall objectives of the project.
- Flexible enough to meet individual needs.
- Cost effective and efficient.

Basic courses in English as a second language and computer skills were emphasised in the early stages of the training program. Although the project was largely implemented using English, many training were implemented in Arabic using qualified instructors from Egypt. Knowledge of English was essential for advanced computer courses and training provided by Canadian instructors.

The plan developed was for a series of training courses. The training courses were offered at successive levels with enough time between each for assimilation before proceeding to next level. Training programs were carried out before and during the period of each activity. The rate of progress and the quality of work produced were initially poor, but improved dramatically as the staff gained knowledge and skills, reinforced by immediate application in an on-the-job situation.

(c) DELIVERY OF TRAINING AND DEVELOPMENT ACTIVITIES:

The implementation of the resource development plan reflected the characteristics listed before. Modifications were made during the delivery stage to meet new developments or anticipated changes. The plan used a variety of techniques to support training and encouraged transfer of training to the job; such as the use of full-time local trainers and training institutes, short technical courses run by Canadian and Egyptian universities staff, training courses, and attendance at conferences and seminars in Canada and USA.

The activities of the training program are grouped into three elements:

1. Training Facilities: Two fully equipped training centers were established in Mansoura with full-time computer trainers. A technical library with over 600 books has been created.

2. Training and Development Courses: To facilities the transfer of new technologies, intensive courses in English and basic computer skills have been offered. Short technical courses in design of subsurface drainage systems and automated engineering survey and mapping using electronic total technology were offered to the design and survey groups, following by courses on construction management and supervision.

Different programs are offered to improve the managerial skills of the staff. These programs are divided to top and middle management and line supervisors. To ensure these programs are sensitive to cultural considerations a Canadian and an Egyptian management consultant prepared and conducted the courses.

3. Documentation: Training manuals (Arabic/English) were prepared for all the training courses with examples related to work problems.

4. On-the-Job Application: In the practical applications, a period of three months was allowed for familiarization with the drawing office procedures, electronic filing systems, quality control and progress reporting under the guidance of Canadian engineers. Then an incentive program was introduced which provided payments on the basis of area designed. This provided a very effective system of rewards to who applied their-training most usefully.

(d) EVALUATION OF TRAINING IMPACT:

The effectiveness of the training was assessed using observable or measurable data wherever possible. This allowed for modifications to provide for objectives that were not achieved. Evaluation was done using the following criteria:

- Reactions: How well did the trainees like the program?
- Learning: To what extent did their trainees learn and retain the information presented in the program?
- Behaviour: To what extent did the behaviour of the trainees change to achieve the program objectives?
- Results: What final results were achieved back on the job?

Evaluation is carried out for every course covering the content, organization, discussion, relevance, group activities, amount learned, instructors and facilities. Table 3 shows average overall evaluation results for basic computer, advanced computer, English, technical and management courses. To make sure that the trainees master and retain the skills presented in the program, each course has supervised practice time and a manual with work related problems. The bottom line is that the GOE staff are now using state-of-the art equipment and producing high quality work and it is done on time.

TABLE 3 Average overall evaluation of training programs.

Program	Average Overall Evaluation*
Basic Computer	3.9
Advanced Computer	3.75
English	3.75
Technical	3.5
Management	3.6

Computations are based on the following ratings scale

Excellent 4   Good 3
Fair 2   Poor 1

CONCLUSION and DISCUSSIONS

Although all the training courses were offered after working hours the attendance in the computer courses was 100% and in all other courses from 90 to 95%. The ISAWIP training program was successful for the following reasons

- Each course was designed to satisfy specific training objectives. These objectives were closely related to the trainees' work.

- Most of the courses were offered in-house with supervised practice time.

- Additional training was provided for the stars of each course (train the trainer program).

- Manuals were prepared and distributed for each course with examples related to work problems.

- Motivation was built into the structure of our training program. Training allowances, prizes and certificates were features of the program designed to promote motivation.

The key to success has been to make training relevant to the needs of the project, so that trained individuals have tasks to which they can immediately apply their newly acquired skills, using the sophisticated equipment the project has made available.

And success there has been. Engineers who had scarcely seen a computer when assigned to the project are now using state of-the-art CADD equipment to produce high quality drainage designs at speeds which are comparable to those achieved anywhere in the world. This also applies in all activities of the ISAWIP project.

REFERENCE

Cherrington, D.J. *Personnel Management.* Wm. C. Brown Publishers, Dubuque, Iowa, U.S.A. Second Edition, 1987.

MATHEMATICAL MODEL FOR MANEUVERING SINGULARITIES IN AN IRRIGATION CANAL NETWORK

Benjamin de Leon Mojarro
Investigador Docente, Colegio
de Postgraduados, Montecillo, Edo.
de Mexico. C.P. 56230

ABSTRACT

A method to represent maneuvers for regulation structures using the Saint-Venant's complete model is proposed. The procedure calculates the discharge and water level variations downstream and upstream of a singularity. Essentially, the method uses a combination of two schemes: the finite differences (implicit or explicit), and the method characteristics. The procedure was applied to a 25 km long irrigation canal with 9 regulation gates. The obtained results were satisfactory from the point of view of modeling.

Introduction

The nonpermanent flux modeling in open conducts presents three basic problems, that without categorization are: the solution of the partial differential equations which describe the governed water movement, the selection of a numerical scheme to allow the representation and treatment of singularities (geometric discontinuities), and finally the representation of the variation of geometric characteristics in those points where singularities are located.

Since the 1950's with the appearance of the electronic calculations, a great number of numerical algorithms have been developed to solve the equations established in 1871 by the French mathematician Barré de Saint-Venant. Therefore, there are many technical and scientific publications which present the treatment of problems related with the water flux in open conducts, through the solution of such equations. However, as it is known in the case of differential equations there are solutions, and not always methods of solution, so that each situation requires a particular study.

On the other hand, and according to the hypothesis on which the equations are based, they are valid in pools where the transport vectors are geometrically uniform, situation which seldom occurs in reality. In fact, whether it is natural or artificial vectors, such as irrigation canal networks, sewage or urban networks. In all cases, control structures are required to allow the regulation of some variables: volume, discharge or water level and consequently, the speed and the hydraulic area.

To achieve this control, hydraulic structures like weirs, gates, etc. are required. These structures constitute geometric discontinuities at the points where they are located. Evidently, these physical obstacles break the hydraulic continuity and avoid the application of the Saint-Venant's equations. In all points of the transport vectors, and in such cases a pair of equations should be introduced, which allow passing from one side to the other of the singularity.

The proposed solutions to this problem vary, from the individual treatment for each pool limited by a pair of singularities, through the introduction of a law that defines its functioning, to the use of a tangential approximation to the exact function that defines the singularity at each time step.

When the singularities are static (weirs), this is the last alternative to facilitates the analysis of various pools of canals which are connected in series. However, when singularities show temporal variations (gates), the tangential approximation gives errors which are cumulative, because in each time step or at each instant of variation, the error between the tangential approximation calculated and the precise function is added to the variables calculated (discharge and water level).

In the next paragraphs, a methodology to represent the maneuver of the singularities in a Saint-Venant's model will be developed.

MATHEMATICAL MODEL OF SAINT-VENANT.

In a pool of a uniform canal and under the Saint Venant's hypothesis (1871), the one dimensional flux can be represented by a pair of differential equations. These equations represent the mass and quantity of movement conservation, which can be expressed as follows:

continuity equation

$$\frac{\partial Q}{\partial x} + \frac{\partial z}{\partial t} = q \tag{1}$$

dynamics equation

$$\frac{\partial Q}{\partial t} + \frac{\partial (QV)}{\partial x} + gS\frac{\partial z}{\partial x} = -gSJ + KqV \tag{2}$$

where:
- Q = discharge L^3T^{-1}
- S = hydraulic area L^2
- T = time T
- $K = 1$ si $q < 0$
- $K = 0$ si $q > 0$
- V = mean speed in S LT^{-1}
- J = Slope of energy line
- L = Width of the free water L
- g = gravitational acceleration LT^{-2}

z = water level   L

q = lateral inflow L^3T^{-1}/L

x = distance   L

As it has been mentioned, there are graphic methods Craya (1945), and numeric algorithms Wylie (1969), Abbott (1961), Preissman and Cunge (1961), Thirriot (1961), Favre and Nahas (1961), Cunge and Wegner (1964), Strelkofft (1970), Pochat (1980) etc., to solve these equations.

REPRESENTATION OF SINGULARITIES

In those points where a geometric discontinuity is located the equations (1) and (2) are replaced by a pair of equations to transmit the information from one side to the other, these equations are:

continuity equation

$$Qa = Qb$$

where: Qa = discharge upstream of the singularity

           Qb = discharge downstream of the singularity

It is assumed that sections a and b are located immediately upstream and downstream of the singularity, so the lateral contribution "q" can be neglected, since the distance is very short.

dynamics equation

$$F(Qa, Qb, Za, Zb, h) = 0 \tag{4}$$

where: Za = upstream water level of the singularity

           Zb = downstream water level of the singularity

           h = aperture or position of the singularity

If the singularity is static, a tangential approximation to the equation (4) allows to assimilate the Eq. (2), and the solution below the singularity is approximated by

$$\frac{\partial F}{\partial t}(Qa, Qb, Za, Zb, h) = 0 \tag{5}$$

$$\frac{\partial F}{\partial Qa}\frac{dQa}{dt} + \frac{\partial F}{\partial Qb}\frac{dQb}{dt} + \frac{\partial F}{\partial Za}\frac{dZa}{dt} + \ldots$$

$$\ldots + \frac{\partial F}{\partial Qb}\frac{dZb}{dt} + \frac{\partial F}{\partial h}\frac{dh}{dt} + 0 \tag{6}$$

It is clear that if a temporal variation of any of the variables in equation (4) has not been programmed, equation (6) will represent an important difference according to the magnitude of the variation.

The difference between (4) and (6) can be highly significant only when the singularities are maneuvers. In such case, the tangential approximation is not enough and a form of provision of this variation is required; in other words, an estimation of the magnitude of the maneuver.

MANEUVERS AT SINGULARITIES

Singularities can define the boundary conditions, external and internal. The last represents the problems mentioned, and we will refer to them in the following paragraphs.

According to equation 3, the following hypotheses are assumed:

1.- the consecutive discharge of a maneuver is constant

2.- the lateral inflow is negligible $q = 0$

3.- the losses due to friction are negligible: $J = 0$

Under these hypotheses, equations (1) and (2) are expressed in the following way:

$$\frac{\partial Q}{\partial x} + L\frac{\partial Z}{\partial t} = 0 \tag{7}$$

$$\frac{\partial Q}{\partial t} + \frac{\partial (QV)}{\partial x} + g S \frac{\partial z}{\partial x} + 0 \tag{8}$$

To reduce the internal boundary condition problem to the calculus of a limit, it is convenient to take the discharge Q and the width Z as dependent and independent variables respectively, and to eliminate the spatial and temporal variables, since the singularity is located in one fixed distance (x) and on the other hand, it is assumed constant discharge after the maneuver. This allows to express the system (7) and (8) through an ordinary differential equation in terms of dQ/dZ, then: from equation (7) we obtain:

$$\frac{\partial x}{\partial t} + \frac{1}{L} + \frac{\partial Q}{\partial Z} \tag{9}$$

if equation (8) is multiplied by dx/dz, we obtain:

$$\frac{\partial Q}{\partial t}\frac{\partial x}{\partial z} + \frac{\partial (QV)Q}{\partial z} + g S = 0 \tag{10}$$

substituting (9) in (10) and $QV = Q/S$ we obtain:

$$W(dQ/dZ) = \frac{1}{L}\left(\frac{\partial Q}{\partial t}\right)^2 - \frac{2Q}{S}\frac{dQ}{dZ} + \frac{Q^2}{S^2}L - gS = 0 \qquad (11)$$

In this second grade equation, the main solution is the equation:

$$\frac{dQ}{dZ} = (V \pm C)\, L \qquad (12)$$

where: $C = (g\, S/L)^{1/2}$

C = celerity of the perturbation waves caused by the maneuvers at singularity.

A second solution is $dQ/dZ = 0$, situation which occurs in the absence of the maneuver, in this case the term is

$$(Q^2/S^2)\, L - g\, S = V^2 L - C^2 L = 0$$

Since the velocity and celerity have the same value, because in the singularity the flux correspond to the critical flux.

Equation (12) related to Eq. (4) allows the estimate of the magnitude of maneuver at singularities, by obtaining:

$$dQ = dF(Qa, Qb, Za, Zb, h) \qquad (13)$$

In equation (13) the value of dQ is estimated with some procedure according to the irrigation needs, then with the singularity equation the variation of the F variables are obtained, and therefore the value of dZ in equation (12). The values for V, C, and L in the same equation are obtained from the general solution of equations (1) and (2) for the increased discharge dQ. The discrete expression of equation (11) is:

$$\frac{1}{L_i^{n+1}}\left[\frac{\Delta Q}{\Delta Z}\right]^2 - 2\frac{Q_i^{n+1}}{\left(Q_i^{n+1}\right)}\left[\frac{\Delta Q}{\Delta Z}\right]\left[\frac{Q_i^{n+1}}{S_i^{n+1}}\right]^2 L_i^{n+1} - g\, S_i^{n+1} = 0 \qquad (14)$$

where:

$$Q_i^{n+1} = Q_i^n + \Delta Q$$

$$S_i^{n+1} = f\left(Q_i^{n+1}\right)$$

$$L_i^{n+1} = f\left(Q_i^{n+1}\right)$$

$$n+1 = t + \Delta t$$

i = distance from singularities

Equation (12) represents the propagation of perturbation waves upstream and downstream of the singularity. This equation, in terms of the theory of characteristics, defines the properties of the flux along the characteristics:

$$\frac{dx}{dt} = V \pm C \qquad (15)$$

equation (12), while the extreme point is situated:

$$\frac{dQ}{dz} = \frac{QL}{S} = VL$$

corresponding to a minimum value whose value is:

$$W(VL) = -gS = -LC^2$$

The following scheme shows the graph of the function

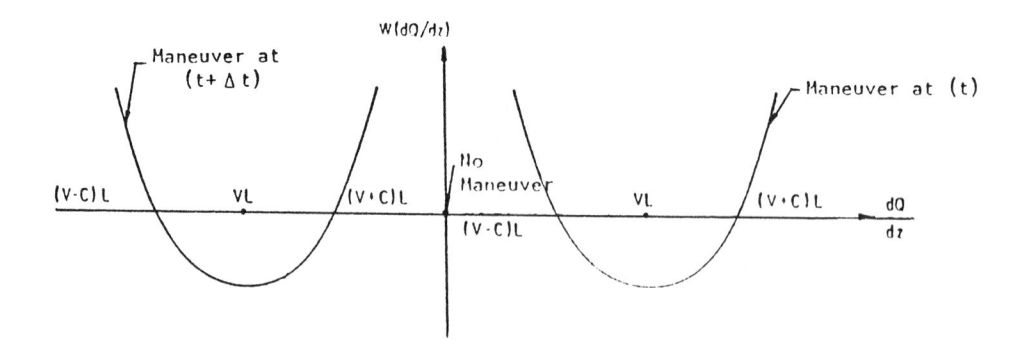

RESULTS

With the proposed methodology a model of an irrigation canal was constructed. The canal had 9 regulation gates installed along 25 km, with different transversal sections and with a capacity of 13 m³/s. The hydraulic operation of the canal represented by Eqs. (1) and (2), linearized by an implicit scheme of finite differences and solved by the method of double sweep. Figure 1 shows, the results of the maneuvers in a gate whose characteristics are: width = 4.5 m, coefficient of discharge = 0.53, discharge = 7.25 m³/s, upstream water level = 2.29 m, downstream water level = 2.02 m, aperture = 1.32 m.

These results are satisfactory from the point of view of modeling, since the hydraulic analysis of various pools of canal, connected in series, can be done simultaneously, which allows to study the problem of regulation of canals.

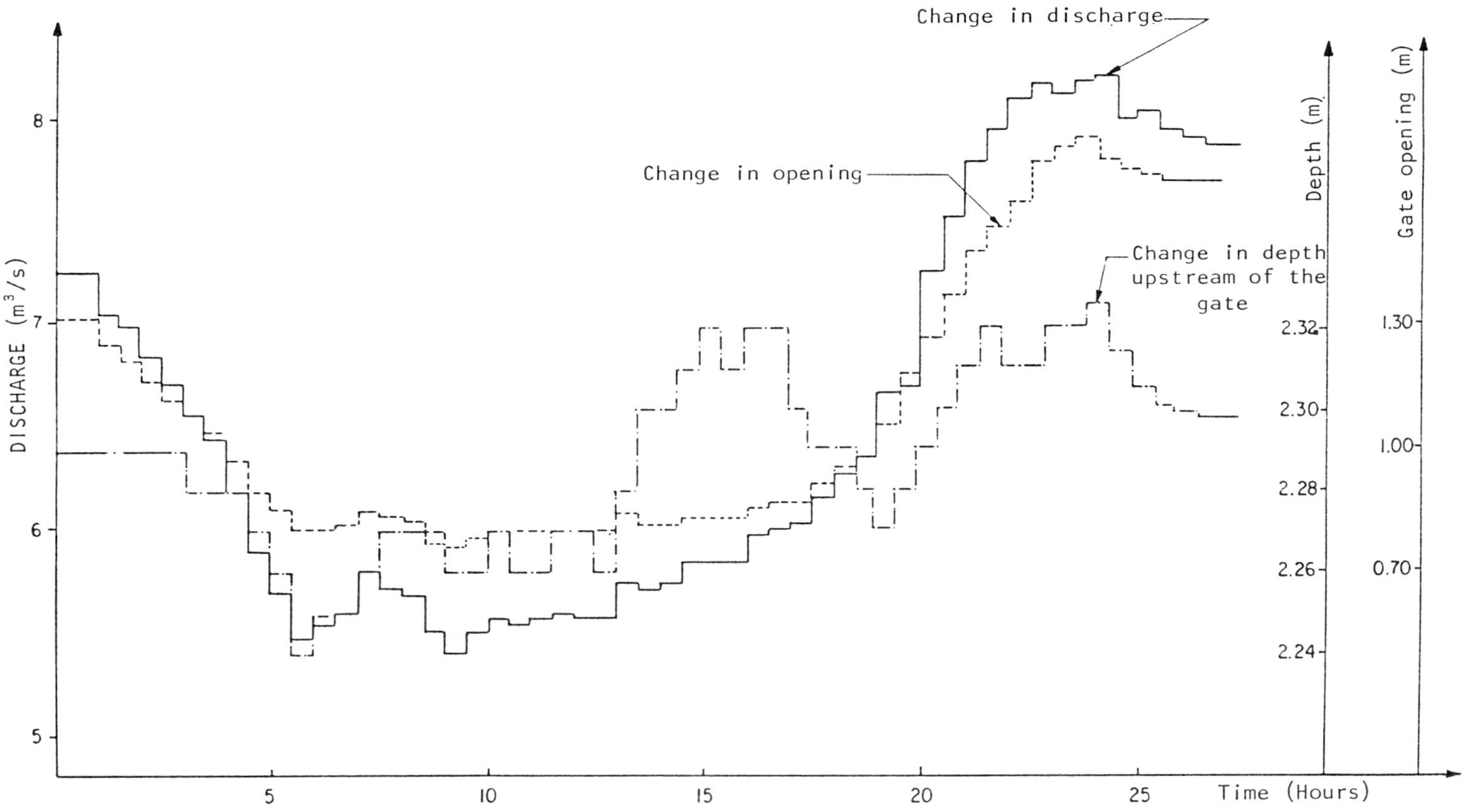

Figure 1. Maneuver sequence at the gate.

CONCLUSIONS

Equation (14) is locally valid and its solution can be handled easily by the general method of solution to equations (1) and (2).

Modeling of the propagation phenomena of discharge in irrigation canals can be only approximated. However, through the proposed methodology, it is possible to represent acceptably the temporal variation of regulation structures.

REFERENCES

Abbott B. 1961. *De l' étalement d'un fluide sur un autre*. La Houille Blanche. No. 5. Francia.

Craya A. 1945. *Calcul Grafique des régimes variables dans les canaux*, La Houille Blanche. Francia.

Cunge y Wegner 1964. *Intégration Numérique des équations de Saint-Venant par un Schéma implicite de différences finies*. La Houille Blanche. No. 1. Francia.

Favre y Nahas, 1961. *Etude Numérique et experimentale d'íntumescences a forte courbure du front*. La Houille Blanches. No. 5. Francia.

Preissman et Cunge 1961. *Calcul du mascaret sur machine electronique*. La Houille Blanche. Francia.

Pochat R. 1980. *Ecole d'été de Mécanique des fluides*. Hanoi.

Strelkofft. 1970. *Numerical Solution of Saint-Venant Equation*. Journal of Hydraulics Division. HyL.

Saint-Venant B.A.C.J. 1871. *Thérie du mouvement non permanent des eaux, avec applicatión aux crues des rivierès et l'introduction des marés dans leur lit*. Comptes rendus des séances de l'Académie des Sciences. Vol. 73: 147-154 et 237-240, Paris. Francia.

5 NATIONAL WATER PLANS

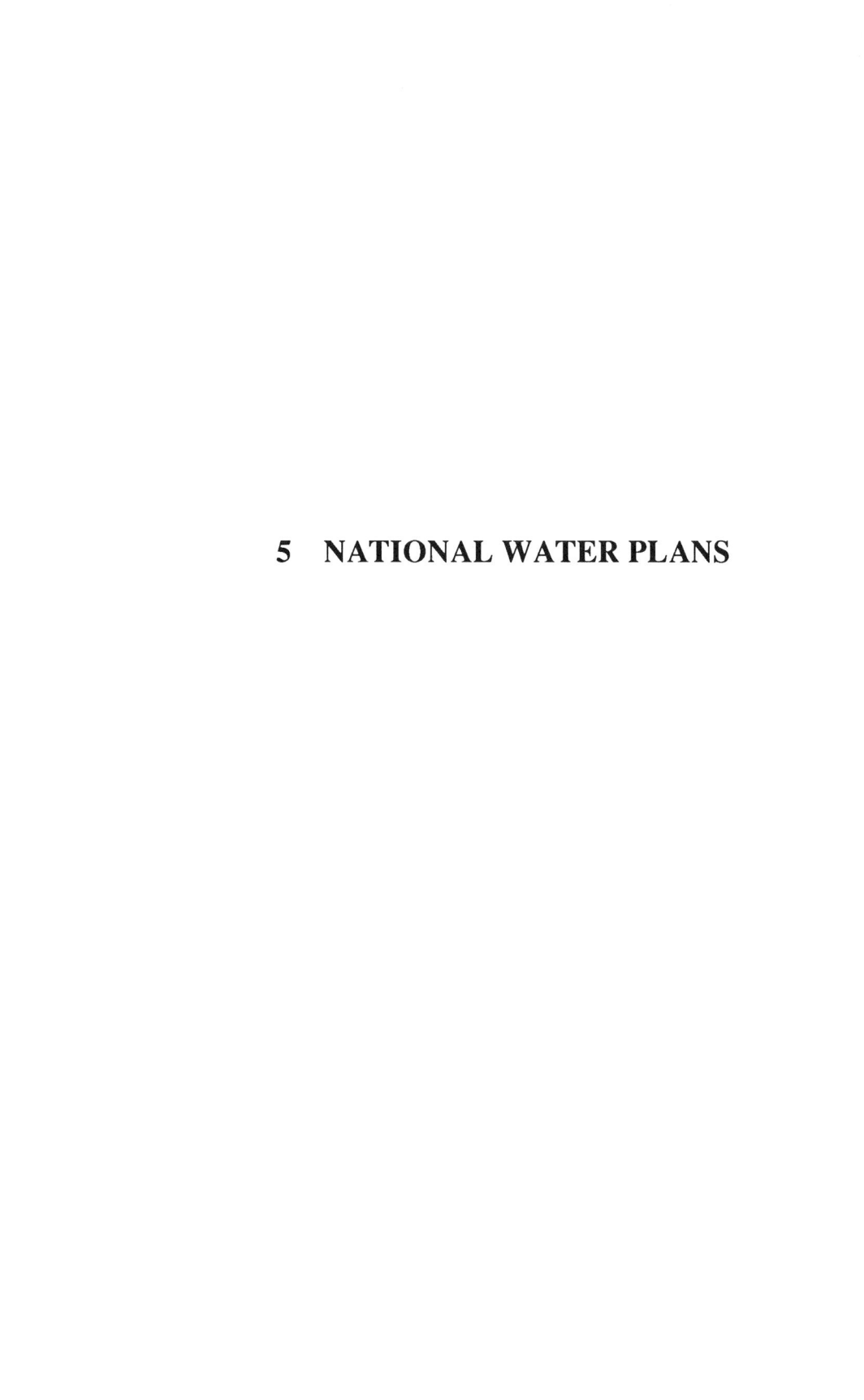

PARTICIPATION IN STATE AND LOCAL GROUND-WATER ORGANIZATIONS - A PROGRAM OF MUTUAL BENEFIT TO PUBLIC AGENCIES AND THEIR PROFESSIONAL EMPLOYEES:

A Case History of the Colorado Ground-Water Association

Judith L. Hamilton
Ground Water Branch
U.S. Bureau of Reclamation, Denver Federal Center
Denver, Colorado 80225

ABSTRACT

Local ground-water organizations are a valuable means for employees of public agencies to increase their technical knowledge and their capabilities in developing plans and programs while providing good public and professional relations for their agency's projects. The Colorado Ground Water Association is a very successful example of these organizations, with an active program of technical meetings, field trips, committee activities, publications, and public awareness programs. The Bureau of Reclamation has actively encouraged participation by its employees in the Colorado Ground Water Association and has benefitted from this participation in a number of ways.

In the United States, ground-water professionals in several localities have formed State associations which supplement activities of national and international ground-water organizations. These local groups have the advantage of being able to concentrate on local problems and conditions and thus can be very effective not only in enhancing the professional expertise of their members but also in educating public officials and the general public on local matters involving ground-water use, quality, and protection. Because they are not tied to any national organization, such groups have considerably more freedom to deal with local situations than might be the case with a local section of a national association. Participation of employees in these local groups can be very advantageous for public agencies not only for the technical information their employees obtain, but also because the associations developed with personnel from other organizations facilitate the operations and programs of the agencies. A further advantage of such groups is that their operating expenses are considerably lower, on a per-member basis, than most national professional organizations. Since few public agencies reimburse their employees for membership dues, low membership fees encourage participation by many employees who have a limited budget for professional society dues.

The Colorado Ground-Water Association (CGWA) has been a very successful example of these local groups. CGWA, which was formed in 1981 as an outgrowth of a local hydrogeology study group, has attracted a membership of almost 400 consultants and other private sector hydrologists, Federal, local and State employees, and water attorneys. The broad base of its membership contributes to a good exchange of ideas and a variety of projects. The group has had an active program involving professional meetings on various aspects of ground water, participation in governmental commissions and planning organizations, monitoring of water-related bills being considered by the State legislature and providing technical input for legislative committees, and supporting programs which aid the public in understanding ground water issues. Because of the expertise of its members in many aspects of ground water, CGWA is recognized as a valuable source of information and advice for both State and local groups concerned with ground-water use or regulation.

Recognizing it as a valuable resource, many Federal and State agencies encourage their employees to participate in CGWA. The Bureau of Reclamation is one of these. Reclamation is a Federal agency which operates more than 350 water storage reservoirs in the Western United States. It provides irrigation water to about 10 million acres of land and municipal water to about 25 million people. Although most Reclamation projects focus on surface-water supplies, many of those supplies are used conjunctively with ground-water resources. Further, the relationship of ground and surface waters is a growing concern in Reclamation's program including such diverse areas as ground-water recharge, toxicity issues, and maintenance of wetlands through shallow aquifer recharge. Thus, the participation of Bureau of Reclamation personnel in the Colorado Ground-Water Association is of benefit to the agency by creating an additional avenue for maintaining professional contacts and associations in an area of critical importance to Reclamation.

The Bureau of Reclamation has participated in the Colorado Ground-Water Association in several ways. Many of the employees of Reclamation's Ground Water Branch are members of the group, and several have served as officers or presented papers at the monthly meetings. Participation in the committees, such as the microcomputer committee, has enhanced the technical knowledge of the employees, and the skills acquired in planning workshops and meetings contributes to the ability of the employees in similar activities on the job. In addition, several of the field trips have been to areas where Reclamation has active projects. Both Reclamation employees and outside professionals have benefitted from the opportunity for personal inspection of Reclamation projects.

The basic program of the CGWA consists of monthly meetings with a technical program. A monthly newsletter keeps the members informed of the Association activities as well as other items of interest to ground-water professionals. Committees meet on an as-required basis. One or more workshops are given each year, and an annual field trip is made to some area in Colorado. The annual business meeting combines announcement of new officers and presentation of awards with a social meeting.

The technical meetings are often on some project in Colorado, and aid in acquainting members with various aspects of Colorado hydrology and geology. Other programs deal with new techniques in ground-water investigations, such as methods of determining aquifer parameters, kriging, or hazardous waste investigations. Members are encouraged to present talks on their projects. This provides an opportunity to improve speaking skills in friendly surroundings, and gives the audience a chance to learn of projects in other areas. Several of the projects described have been in foreign countries; because some of Reclamation's work is abroad or involves foreign trainees, the opportunity for Reclamation employees to learn about these projects enhances their skills in working with foreign nationals.

The newsletter is one of the most useful methods of disseminating information, especially to those members who attend the monthly meetings only infrequently. Initially the newsletter was put out by volunteers; however, as the size of the newsletter increased, it became increasingly difficult to find volunteers with sufficient time available. A paid editor now coordinates the publication, incorporating articles prepared by officers and committee chair persons and special interest articles, and also takes care of the mailing. Advertising in the newsletter offsets the additional costs of the paid editor. Typically a monthly newsletter contains an announcement of the monthly meeting and of any upcoming workshops or special activities, the President's letter, a list of the Board of Directors and Committee Chairpersons with their telephone numbers, a calendar of meetings related to ground water to be held by various groups, summaries of new publications in ground water, advertisements from suppliers and service firms, and a membership application form to encourage new members.

Committee work is an important part of CGWA activities. The standing committees include micro-computers, ground-water protection, legislative activities, membership, by-laws and program. There are also several ad-hoc committees involved in specific projects of CGWA. With a local organization such as the Colorado Ground-Water Association, all activities originate within the group, rather than being mandated or encouraged by some national organization. Thus, the activities of the committees are ones of particular interest to the group, encouraging active participation.

The various committees of CGWA have different aims. The microcomputer committee is primarily for the dissemination of knowledge to its members. In contrast, the ground-water protection committee has as a major goal educating the general public. It co-authored a publication on ground-water protection which was widely distributed, and is active in the State Health Department's wellhead protection area committee. The legislative committee serves a dual purpose of informing the membership of proposed legislation and educating the State Legislature on the technical aspects of the proposed laws. The activities of the legislative committee have influenced much of the legislation related to ground water in the State, and have enabled considerably more participation by knowledgeable professionals in proposed legislation than would be likely on a strictly individual basis. Since many public agencies deal extensively with public advisory committees, the skills gained in participating in CGWA committee activities can aid considerably in the employees' work.

The Association, through its committees, also engages in activities which are designed to benefit students and potential students in ground-water, as well as the general public. Among these activities are the Harlan Erker Scholarship, which is in honor of a former President of the Association who was killed in an airplane accident during his term of office. The scholarship is awarded to an undergraduate or graduate student who is pursuing studies on some aspect of Colorado ground-water hydrology. At the end of the school year, the student presents a summary of work accomplished, often in the form of one of the monthly talks. In addition, the Association participates yearly in local and/or State science fairs, giving awards to outstanding exhibits related to ground water. The Association will also be participating in the Children's Water Festival, a program designed to acquaint fourth and fifth grade elementary school children with water in Colorado. While benefits are very long term, such activities aid public agencies as well as the profession as a whole by encouraging students to pursue studies in water resources development.

Another committee project which has been a long term one, but is scheduled for completion next year, is the publishing of a Colorado Groundwater Atlas. It will contain both maps and articles describing the various aquifers throughout the State.

A very valuable benefit of membership in the Association is the opportunity to attend its workshops. Generally one or two workshops are held every year. Subjects have included hands-on operation of microcomputer programs, aquifer tests, vadose zone hydrology, time management, and applications of new ground-water legislation. In addition, the Association participates actively in the annual Denver, Colorado, GeoTech Conference on computers in geology and engineering.

The yearly field trip is also an important event. Field trips are usually a one-day, but sometimes two-day event. Several of the field trips have included guidebooks, which give employees of public agencies an opportunity to publish articles on their projects and aid in disseminating information on these projects to the general public as well as to ground-water personnel. One of the recent guidebooks, on the San Luis Valley of Colorado, has been very popular recently because of the interest of a commercial group in developing and exporting water from the Valley. Reclamation is extensively involved in water in the San Luis Valley, and contributed an article to the guidebook on the Programmable Master Supervisory and Control System (PMSC) for the Closed Basin Project. Other articles in the publication have been very useful to Reclamation personnel in other work on the Project.

An important aspect of any professional group is the opportunity for socializing. This provides a medium for exchange of ideas on an informal basis and enhances working relationships. Informal get-togethers after the monthly meetings usually involve discussion of the meeting subject or other work. The annual Christmas party gives an opportunity to find out what projects many other members are working on. Public agency employees can utilize these meetings to get better acquainted with personnel from other agencies and from the public sector who are working with them on projects. Since it is usually easier working with friends and associates than with strangers, such social events can lubricate the wheels of joint activities.

Much of the work of the Association is done by a number of members each contributing small but important amounts. However, CGWA tries to recognize its members and other ground-water professionals who have made especially important contributions. The annual meeting is an opportunity to present awards to these people. The Association awards include certificates of appreciation, special awards of outstanding service, and the Robert E. Glover Award. The Glover Award, named in honor of a Bureau of Reclamation employee who pioneered in mathematical applications, is given to a member of the Colorado ground-water community who has made an outstanding contribution to the advancement of ground water. Several employees of public agencies have been the recipients of this award, enhancing the reputation not only of the individual but also the employing agency.

The Colorado Ground-Water Association illustrates the effectiveness of a local group in addressing issues which are particularly pertinent to it. The benefits to public agencies of encouraging participation in such a group include not only greater technical capabilities of the employees, but also more effective associations on projects of joint interest and better public awareness of the agency's activities. The success of the CGWA should encourage others to establish similar organizations which will supplement national and international ground-water groups. The benefits the Bureau of Reclamation has realized from participation of its employees in CGWA activities is an incentive to other agencies to provide active support to such groups.

WATER CONSERVATION EDUCATION AND OUTREACH IN THE U. S.

Cynthia Dyballa
Office of Policy Analysis (PM-221)
U.S. Environmental Protection Agency
401 M St., SW
Washington, D. C. 20460

ABSTRACT

This paper describes efforts for water conservation and outreach in the U.S., directed at both the general public and at local government officials who implement these programs. Case studies of federal, state and local programs are presented. Education and outreach, while not alone sufficient to achieve water savings, are critical components of any successful water conservation program. A range of techniques clearly targeted to particular audiences appears more effective than broad-based blanket coverage. Higher level agencies should emphasize technical assistance to local officials, to provide them with the best experience available.

INTRODUCTION: THE NEED FOR WATER CONSERVATION

Interest in water conservation in the U.S. has grown dramatically in recent years. Some individual communities initiated programs back in the 1970's. Today, from Boston to Honolulu, in small communities and large cities throughout the U. S., water conservation programs have been initiated. Most programs are implemented at the local level. And most of them rely heavily, in some cases exclusively, on education and outreach to achieve results.

Why this renewed interest? Water conservation is increasingly viewed as a possible solution to an array of community environmental and economic problems. Several areas of the U.S. have experienced drought conditions in recent years, including the populous northeast and California. Rising costs of drinking water and wastewater treatment and facility construction have raised concern. Development of large new surface water projects is increasingly difficult due to increasing concerns over their environmental impacts. And water quality concerns, such as wastewater discharges to surface water and the impact of overpumping on groundwater, are increasingly on the minds of communities.

THE ROLE OF EDUCATION AND OUTREACH

In the U. S., education and outreach efforts, to modify water-using behavior and solicit voluntary participation, are a key method of implementing water conservation programs. Other common means of achieving water conservation are regulatory programs and mandates, and economic incentives such as pricing. In extreme situations, such as drought, user restrictions can also bring about reduced water use.

Reliance on voluntary efforts raises the issue of selecting the most effective approach to conduct outreach and education activities for different audiences. A second issue is the question of whether public education alone can stimulate water conservation, or whether it works best as a complement to incentive and regulatory programs. A third issue is how communities are informed about what others are doing, and what the role of higher level governments is in facilitating this exchange.

This paper is not a formal or comprehensive survey of federal, state and local programs. Rather, it's selective: we seek to highlight a few of the issues involved, and showcase examples of what works. Opinions expressed are those of the author, not of the U.S. Environmental Protection Agency (EPA) or any of the agencies and programs described.

OVERVIEW OF OUTREACH AND TRAINING APPROACHES AND AUDIENCES

Reaching the Public

The most common audience for water conservation information is the general public. A variety of techniques are available. More conventional techniques include leaflets, billstuffers, and posters. Use of the media can spread a message quickly and broadly. Educational programs and special events are common and useful. Individual assistance by telephone is also a common approach (Beecher, 1989; Maddaus, 1987).

Individual assistance at the home or place of business, through on-sight water audits, is a new and growing area of interest. Visible demonstrations of the effectiveness of water conservation techniques, particularly xeriscape gardens, are increasingly popular (CDWR, 1989).

Reaching Community Leaders

Reaching the community leaders that implement the programs is another audience and a crucial one. This arena is largely the province of higher level government, wholesale water suppliers, and national organizations such as the American Water Works Association.

Published manuals on water conservation program implementation aimed at the concerns of local officials are widely available, as are materials local officials can use in working with the public. Workshops and seminars on specific water conservation techniques are another common technique. Several software programs make it easier for local officials to make water conservation choices.

Techniques common in other fields, such as peer-to-peer exchange and demonstration grants from higher level governments, are less frequently offered. Water conservation information is often presented in the context of training and assistance on drought preparedness, and wastewater and drinking water treatment.

Messages

A water utility, municipality, or higher level government may choose to promote public education for any of several reasons. They might wish to increase voluntary participation in other programs; to explain a difficult policy, such as price increases or user restrictions; to modify consumer behavior; or to deliver general information about the need for water conservation, and impart an understanding of why it is important.

Effective public outreach is targeted outreach. Targeting a specific audience, such as industries, high water users, school children, or a particular neighborhood, and tailoring the message to them, is most effective (MWRA, 1990).

DELIVERY OF CONSERVATION EDUCATION PROGRAMS

As most outreach and education programs in the U.S. are locally based, local governments have the most direct experience in this area. But some state and federal agencies have recently entered the picture, in an effort to influence more local governments to undertake these programs. Some wholesale water suppliers have undertaken programs as well. This section highlights a few of the more successful or unusual programs delivered by these different agencies.

EPA has recently exhibited a renewed interest in water conservation. Two other federal agencies with efforts in municipal or agricultural water conservation include the Army Corps of Engineers and the Bureau of Reclamation.

Several state outreach and training programs target communities as well as the public. California has the most extensive program. A Texas program is run through the State Water Board, which issues permits for new water withdrawals and system expansions. New York State's program is primarily regulatory, based on a statewide requirement for local water conservation plans. New York has issued a manual on water conservation practices for local government, covering such basics as leak detection, metering, and pricing (Nechamen, 1989). The Illinois Dept. of Transportation conducts drought preparedness workshops for local officials, presenting largely water conservation information.

CASE STUDIES: FEDERAL STATE AND LOCAL PROGRAMS

EPA Programs

EPA has recently increased its efforts in water conservation, focusing on several areas: 1) technical assistance, primarily to communities; 2) education, primarily for local officials but also for the general public; 3) research on the effectiveness of new water-saving technologies; and 4) integration of water conservation into ongoing EPA programs. An in-house Water Conservation Task Force coordinates EPA's strategy for implementation. This year the program received its first major infusion of funds. Several aspects of the program are highlighted in this section.

Computerized Education - EPA has supported the revision of California's Waterplan personal computer program for a national audience. Waterplan assists a community in selecting the most appropriate water conservation measures, and in estimating the costs and benefits of those measures. Waterplan can be used with minimum training (CDWR, 1989).

EPA's Region V Office in Chicago has issued a series of personal computer programs, in conjunction with Purdue University. The Residential Water Conservation Program (Blank, 1990) is designed to teach consumers about home water conservation. The on-site wastewater treatment program, primarily for local officials (Stuve, 1988) has a section on water conservation alternatives. A program on water-efficient landscaping may be available as soon as October 1991.

Another widely available federal (not EPA) computerized program, sponsored by the Army Corps of Engineers, is the IWR-MAIN model (Dziegielewski, 1989). IWR-MAIN assists a community in projecting its long-term water demand, based on information about the community such as water prices, household income, housing stock, and the relative size of water-using sectors. The model can serve as a complement to Waterplan. As IWR-MAIN is a very complex model, to use it currently requires training.

Workshops - By the end of 1990, EPA will have conducted three major workshops on water conservation. The first, in Tucson in Feb. 1990, primarily for EPA staff focused on the range of water conservation techniques available. The second this May, in cooperation with two other federal agencies, the Bureau of Reclamation and Dept. of Agriculture, will address the relationship between agricultural water conservation and environmental protection. A third, co-sponsored with the National Governors' Association, will aim at transferring information and successful programs among states.

Outreach - EPA is working to incorporate water conservation information into regular EPA programs, including small communities outreach through the Offices of Drinking Water and Municipal Pollution Control, the National Small Flows Clearinghouse, and outreach to Indian tribes. Reprints of existing materials (NWF, 1989) and preparation of a few new ones for local officials and consumers accompany this effort. The National Small Flows Clearinghouse has available a bibliography of water conservation literature (NSFC, 1989).

EPA's Region V Office has built water conservation information into its regular training on wastewater and drinking water for Indian tribes in its area. Several tribes have begun local residential retrofit programs, as a result of exposure to water conservation techniques at the workshops and ongoing extensive technical assistance. Two tribes have already successfully completed programs (Krause, 1991).

A State Program: California

No other state has a program the scope and size of California's Department of Water Resources (CDWR). High growth, recurrent drought, and competing demand are the reasons for this program. Through the many services of its regional offices, DWR reaches a variety of audiences: the public, industry, agriculture, and local government.

For example, CDWR utilized outreach techniques to help implement a state legislative requirement for community water management plans, including a water conservation component. This requirement applies to over 300 public water suppliers in the state. CDWR offers workshops and individual assistance to water suppliers. In addition, a series of manuals for local government illustrates how to run different types of conservation programs.

CDWR has also pioneered the application of personal computers to water management decisions. CDWR has invested in development of the Waterplan software package to assist communities in determining the costs and benefits of water conservation for their situation (CDWR, 1989). Other software currently available includes Agwater for agriculture, and irrigation scheduling software for large scale landscape water management.

Wholesale Water Supplier Programs

Massachusetts Water Resources Authority - Providing 46 communities and 2.5 million people in the metropolitan Boston area with water supply and wastewater treatment services, MWRA is among the nation's largest water utilities. From 1971 to 1989, MWRA annual withdrawals from its reservoir source exceeded safe yield by 8-12%, stimulating interest in water conservation to achieve long-term balance. Several years of dry weather in the 1980's accelerated MWRA conservation efforts (MWRA, 1989).

MWRA's program is among the more aggressive in the country. Education, training and outreach programs focus on both the public and the member water suppliers. MWRA programs avoid broad-based, glossy outreach efforts in favor of highly targeted to particular audiences and geographic areas. Special efforts include public and low-income housing residents, tenants, and industry (MWRA, 1990).

Educational efforts for member communities include installing ultralow-flow toilets as demonstrations in municipal buildings, and workshops for municipalities on rate setting to encourage water conservation. The workshops were designed in part to implement an MWRA rule prohibiting declining block rates for members.

One of the country's most extensive industrial water conservation programs provides education and technical assistance to a variety of businesses and industries in the metropolitan area. A pilot program provided water conservation audits to 35 representative facilities. These were followed by a series of technical workshops for other facility managers and engineers, case studies, and manuals of conservation recommendations for various industries. Results so far in the two year old program: over 500 companies and institutions attending workshops, and 48% implementation of recommendations in the first audits. Over time, this could result in up to 10% reduction in system-wide non-domestic use (McGrath, 1990).

Metropolitan Water District - MWD supplies water to 27 member agencies, indirectly serving 14.5 million people in southern California, including Los Angeles (MWD, 1990). Five years of increasingly severe drought and rapid population growth have led to an expanded program. MWD's program combines outreach and economic incentives for member communities, and public education.

In the drought of 1977, a 100% surcharge to communities exceeding their water allotment, plus extensive public education and distribution of free retrofit materials, yielded 12-15% savings (MWD, 1990). MWD evaluated their intensive three-month paid advertising campaign in the drought summer of 1988, and found a short-term 8% reduction in water use (CDWR, 1989).

A Local Projects Program in place since 1981 to fund wastewater reuse, has proven popular. A Water Conservation Credits Program, begun in 1988, offers to buy the water savings of effective local conservation programs. By April 1990, eight programs were approved for 8, 000 acre feet a year. Almost all of these eight projects had strong outreach components (MWD, 1990).

Two Local Retrofit Programs

Many of the most successful community water conservation programs include outreach and education as a key component (Grisham and Fleming). Rather than survey the full range of local public education programs, we will illustrate the importance of outreach and public education to two residential retrofit programs. The most successful residential retrofit programs focus on one neighborhood at a time, with extensive outreach and education to motivate participants.

San Jose, California achieved remarkable results in their retrofit program, one of the largest completed to date in the U. S.(an estimated 220, 000 households). Their approach: door-to-door delivery of water conservation materials, with follow-up home visits in a neighborhood. Participation is entirely voluntary, and residents installed their own devices.

In the pilot phase, effective installation rate was 80% of households; in the full scale program, 77%. Per household indoor water savings were 13-17%, total indoor water savings 10-11%. Extensive outreach partly accounts for this success (Jordan, 1990).

The MWRA conducted a pilot program comparing depot and direct home visit methods of retrofitting residences. The depot method achieved 21% participation rate and 0-3% water savings. The direct home visits, accompanied by intensive community outreach and in-home education and installation of materials, were far more successful: 58% participation and 8-10% savings. Based on these results, MWRA will conduct a system-wide residential retrofit program (MWRA, 1990).

WATER SAVINGS FROM EDUCATION AND OUTREACH

Quantifying the water savings resulting from education and outreach techniques has proven difficult. Earlier literature reports measurable water savings; much of it reports short-term savings achieved during droughts, where higher motivation can yield good results temporarily (Bruvold, 1979).

Waterplan estimates a 1% annual water use reduction from public information programs, assuming a 25% participation rate (CDWR, 1989). On a statewide list of best management practices for California water utilities, public education is listed as a required program, but savings are not attributed to it.

This is borne out in the more sophisticated energy conservation field, where evaluations have shown that simple information programs (including information pamphlets, hotlines, videos, and appeals to conserve) achieve net or gross savings of 0.2% (Collins et al 1985).

DISCUSSION AND CONCLUSIONS

At the start of this paper, we introduced three issues. What are the most effective approaches to outreach and education for different audiences? Is education and outreach by itself enough to achieve conservation results? And, how can communities get the information they need to conduct successful water conservation programs?

Effective Approaches for Outreach and Education

Experience to date has shown that the most effective outreach and education programs are ones that develop a clear message, target the audience to reach, employ a variety of techniques, and include as much individual direct contact as possible (Maddaus, 1987; CDWR, 1989; Smith, 1990) Basing the message on the perceptions of the recipients is important as well (Bauman, 1990). The relative success of retrofit programs that target neighborhoods, involve community groups, and visit individual homes is one illustration of this.

The Role of Outreach and Education

Most water conservation practitioners agree that outreach and education are necessary components of a successful program (Beecher, 1989; Grisham and Fleming, 1989; Maddaus, 1989; Maddaus, 1987). An outreach and education program by itself, without any other measures, is not likely to be effective in achieving water savings. Such a program may serve other objectives, such as public relations, but by itself it may not save any water.

On the other hand, a successful community water conservation program will most likely include public education, to stimulate interest and participation in the program. For example, one key to the public's acceptance of user restrictions, perhaps the most difficult conservation measure to accept, is public education (Beecher, 1989).

Again this is well-documented in the energy conservation field. A recent survey of over 200 electricity conservation programs operated by U.S. electric utilities found that many of the most effective energy conservation programs (commercial and industrial) combine financial incentives with in-depth education and technical assistance. Programs with financial incentives alone were generally not as successful (Nadel, 1990).

Outreach to Local Officials

In the U.S., outreach by higher level government to local officials who must implement these programs is uneven. Only a few of the 50 states have such programs for water conservation. Some wholesale water suppliers emphasize technical assistance or education for their member communities. The American Water Works Association is attempting to fill this gap for water suppliers.

Federal programs are just beginning. The U.S. Congressional Research Service (Copeland, 1989) recommended that the federal role is one of education, as well as research and financial assistance for program implementation.

The limited experience with outreach to local officials on water conservation programs suggests the importance of linking outreach and education with a strong motivation to participate. One motivation, as noted earlier, for California's extensive outreach program is the statewide requirement for water management planning. Other states, such as New York and Massachusetts, have employed regulatory requirements to motivate local governments toward conservation. Recurring drought and rising costs provide non-regulatory but strong motivation to participate. Wholesale water suppliers that offer a combination of technical assistance and regulatory or financial incentives may illustrate this point as well.

There is a need in the U.S. for increased higher-level outreach technical assistance to local officials on water conservation issues. With rising drinking water and wastewater treatment costs, this is especially true. This outreach may be most effective in combination with other outreach efforts on water issues, such as wastewater and drinking water, and drought preparedness.

REFERENCES

Bauman, D. and J. Simms. *The Social Acceptability of Water Conservation. In Conserv 90 Proceedings.* NWWA. August 1990.

Beecher, J. *Compendium on Water Supply. Drought and Conservation.* National Regulatory Research Institute. Oct. 1989.

Blank, M. J. *Residential Water Conservation.* Purdue University, 1990.

Bruvold, W. *Residential Response to Urban Drought in Central California.* Water Resources Research. 1979.

California Dept. of Water Resources, Office of Water Conservation. *Designing a Public Information Program for Water Conservation. Water Conservation Guidebook No. 3.* October 1984.

California Dept. of Water Resources. *Managing Limited Urban Water Suppliers: Conference for California Water Agencies.* November 1989.

California Dept. of Water Resources. *Agreement Reached on Urban BMP's*. Water Conservation News. December 1990.

California Dept. of Water Resources. *Waterplan*. October 1989 (two volumes and computer discs).

Collins, N., et al. *Past Efforts and Future Directions for Evaluating State Energy Conservation Programs*. Oak Ridge National Laboratory, ORNL-6113, 1985.

Copeland, C. *Water Conservation: Options for the Residential Sector*. Congressional Research Service. Sept. 1989.

Dziegielewski, B. and J. Boland. *Forecasting Urban Water Use: The IWR-MAIN Model*. Water Resources Bulletin. Feb. 1989.

Grisham, A. and W. Fleming. *Long-Term Options for Municipal Water Conservation*. AWWA Journal, March 1989.

EPA. Office of Wetlands Protection. *Water Supply Alternatives Workshop*. Feb. 1990. NOTE: Formal proceedings are not available. Copies of papers presented can be obtained from OWP, address.

Jordan, B. *San Jose: A Retrofit Success Story*. Brown & Caldwell, 1990.

Krause, A. *Indian tribes report*.

Maddaus, W. *Water Conservation*. American Water Works Association. 1987.

Massachusetts Water Resources Authority. *Draft Drought Management* March 1989.

Massachusetts Water Resources Authority. *Long Range Water Supply Plan*. Jan. 1990.

McGrath, L and M. Pinkham. *Demand Management for Industry - Clearing the Hurdles to Implementation*. Water Conservation News. Dec. 1990.

Nadel, S. *Lessons Learned: A Review of Utility Experience with Conservation and Load Management Programs for Commercial and Industrial Customers*. New York State Energy Research and Development Authority, April 1990.

National Wildlife Federation. *A Citizen's Guide to Community Water Conservation*. 1989.

National Small Flows Clearinghouse. *Computer Search on Water Conservation and Reuse*. WWBLCM-11. 1989.

Nechamen, W. *Water Conservation Manual for Development of a Water Conservation Plan*. 1989.

Smith, C. *Social Marketing Strategies to Sell Water Conservation Programs. In Conserv 90 Proceedings.* NWWA. August 1990.

Stuve, M. et al. *Principles of On-Site Wastewater Treatment.* Purdue University. 1988.

U.S. Environmental Protection Agency, Office of Wetlands Protection. *Water Supply Alternatives Workshop.* February 1990. Formal proceedings not available; contact Office of Wetlands Protection for copies of papers presented.

ACKNOWLEDGEMENTS

The author gratefully acknowledges the assistance of Chris Connelly of the Bruce Co., who provided background research and general support in preparing this paper.

NATIONAL URBAN DRAINAGE PLAN MANAGEMENT

Levent Yilmaz
Technical University of Istanbul, Turkey
Civil Engineering Department, Hydraulic Division
Maslak, Ayazaga, Istanbul, Turkey

ABSTRACT

Education and training in hydrology and water resources at the universities has an important effect on the economic life of a country and its development. Because no one conceives the real development of a country without a satisfactory hydrologic and water resources problems training of engineers. It must be a real coordination of hydrology and water resources education and practical training in industry for planning manpower. The migration of people from rural to urban areas, particularly in underdeveloped or developing countries, increases at a rate which stretches the resources of the city managers. Over 60% of the South America's population is expected to live in urban areas by the end of this century. Such rapid growth of cities leads to near impossible demands on services such as water supply and drainage, waste disposal and communications. Drainage of sewage and storm water is vital to reduce the spread of disease and to reduce economic losses. For example, urban drainage in developed countries may be out of sight and out of mind because of the lack of education and training in hydrology and water resources, as far as the general public is concerned. For other countries the lack of effective drainage may be a grim fact of life. There is no doubt that managers of many large cities, particularly in the Far East, are grappling with these issues and realize that they need to come together so as to pool the expertise and experience, and where possible, to promote more effective ways of improving their drainage and flood control in the 21st century.

INTRODUCTION

Drainage is a particularly welcome development because each city in the last analysis has to be responsible for its own drainage. Although many lessons can be learned from hydrologic and water resources education, each city has to maintain and upgrade its drainage within the particular social, political and economic conditions.

It is of common knowledge that implementation of powerful analytical methods to predict the behavior of hydraulic structures has been made possible both by an increased understanding of hydraulic phenomena involved in the study of water resources problems and by an exceptionally rapid increase of computing capacities. However, the greater accuracy required in the analysis of hydraulic phenomena points to the convenience of a continuous use of hydraulic models for the study and design of water resources hydraulic works.

Education in hydrology is feasible for engineers, surveyors, agricultural scientists, meteorologists, foresters, soil conservationists and hydrogeologists. The special education for hydrologists must include statistics and basic computing hydraulics, special lectures, excursions and various demonstrations to suit the needs of environmental protection.

The common core should be composed of the following subjects:

i. the detailed study of processes along the water cycle, including the runoff, atmospheric circulation, precipitation, interception, infiltration, storm runoff, evaporation, evapotranspiration, surface-groundwater interactions, and land use:

ii. the occurrence of groundwater, aquifer types, regional groundwater basins, extraction techniques, groundwater mapping and exploration; and

iii. the soil-water-salt-plant relationship; the analysis and design of irrigation systems, irrigation system management, economics, law and politics of irrigation.

The following objectives of education and training in hydrology and water resources were selected:

a) to improve the scientific understanding and increase the awareness of the complex dynamics governing human interaction with the total water resources system;

b) to strengthen the efforts to study, explore and anticipate the social change which affects the environment and the consequences for humans of this environmental change;

c) to identify the broad social strategies to prevent or mitigate the undesirable impacts of global climate change, or to adjust to changes that are already unavoidable;

d) to analyze the policy options for dealing with the global environmental change and promoting the goal of a sustainable development.

In pursuit of these goals, the program is to undertake several activities, including those initiatives:

(1) to foster a global network of scientists and other concerned parties, and to encourage this network -- in collaboration with the other relevant research activities -- to engage in research directed towards the dynamics of human interactions related to water resources systems;

(2) to undertake the selected core research projects, central to the purposes of the program;

(3) to develop the new appropriate information systems and methodologies that will enable the execution of a research program

of this scope;

(4) to propose procedures and techniques for assisting in the transfer of research findings into the water resources terms; and

(5) to promote the educational efforts devoted to human activities having significant effects on water resources.

EDUCATION IN URBAN WATER MANAGEMENT AND SUSTAINABLE DEVELOPMENT

Considering the collective expertise, engineers should focus on sustainable development of water resources recognizing that the generic concept covers many other spheres of human activities as well, including population dynamics, food supply, energy, industrial development, urbanization, global economy, international law, and institutional arrangements. This restriction is feasible as long as the engineer recognizes that the other spheres provide inputs to, or restrictions on, water resources management. With the above qualification, it may be easier to reach a consensus on what sustainable development means. Water management is generally defined as a complex of activities and measures designed to satisfy human needs and social demands concerning water in an optimal way. Thus, water resources management strives to meet demands of economic development and utilization of water resources and to create an optimum living environment which protects society against harmful effects of water. The primary objectives of water resources management include the selection of combination of services to be produced from specific water resources and an efficient provision of such services within the overall goals and policy constraints. The adjective "integrated" has various meanings reflected in the literature on this subject, including spatial, temporal, administrative, and functional integration. In this connection, the functional integration is the most important one and the other forms should be viewed as prerequisites of a rational functional integration.

With the above definitions in mind, the engineer can state that sustainable development in relation to water resources is synonymous to integrated management of water resources. Pressures of development of water resources generally arise from certain uses of water resources or as a result of such uses. Examples of such activities include interferences with the water cycle, ecosystem, and habitat; transport and disposal of polluted effluents; and the ever increasing demands for water supply. Impacts of such activities manifest themselves by floods, droughts, groundwater drawdown, water diversions and export, pollution, and extinction of species. The above water uses and their impacts are considered in integrated water management and their acceptance or development of remedies can be evaluated. Thus, integrated water management deals with all concerns of sustainable development of water resources and inputs of other spheres of human activities can be introduced in the form of constraints.

The preceding discussion indicates that, in relation to water resources, the concept of sustainable development is not something completely new, but more or less another name for an earlier formulated concept. Integrated water resources management and sustainable development require the use of a rational, analytical planning approach, in which the system analysis is used to predict the problems, solutions, actions and their consequences. It should be also recognized that the adaptive approach (i.e. reacting and finding solutions to the immediate problems) is not necessarily crude or backward; it is an admission that future scenarios affected by political pressures and other factors, are unpredictable, with an acceptable uncertainty.

Thus, there are relatively few examples of comprehensive integrated water resources management (or sustainable development) implemented in practice. Such examples can be found in areas with limited water resources and a high degree of their utilization - e.g. potable water supply in Israel and the Netherlands. Furthermore, implementation of the concept of sustainable development requires the adoption of a systems approach to water management planning. Although the literature on the subject is plentiful, the measurable contribution to water resources management is marginal. The systems approach consists of a number of steps such as needed awareness, problem definition, definition of goals and objectives, development of alternative solutions, selection of alternatives, decision making, implementation and post evaluation. Note that besides exchanges in the runoff peak regime, urban development will increase volumes of runoff (with contaminant channel erosion), depress the groundwater tables, produce non-point source pollution of the receiving waters, and urban population will contribute to the point source pollution (discharges of treated waste effluents).

SOME DEVELOPMENTS AND BASIC PROBLEMS

The principle of calculating minima or maxima subject to constraints has been known for a long time. The multiplier method by Lagrange, for example, was developed before modern science-based engineering started. Nevertheless, classical mathematical procedures for finding minima or maxima subject to constraints have not significantly influenced water resources design procedures.

The limited application of these procedures is caused by the restrictions they imposed in practice. The first obstacle was computational extravagance. A second limitation was that only problems with a special structure can be solved. For the Lagrange's method, for example, only differential functions can be dealt with and the equational system, which is part of the procedure, easily becomes insoluble if the variables appear in higher powers. Practically speaking, there were not many design problems which could be solved by these mathematical tools.

The situation changed with the development of computers and operations research in the middle of this century. Today, extensive mathematical problems can be solved by high speed computers, and operations research offers solution procedures for an impressive variety of problems. Although there are still many mathematical problems for which a satisfying solution algorithm is not yet available, operations research in connection with computers today is used very successfully for many design problems.

The application of linear programming to water distribution systems dates back to Labye (1966) who presented a linear programming model for branched networks, where the flow rate is given for all pipes. For a given flow rate the slope of the hydraulic grade line (HGL) is constant for each one of a set of alternative diameters. For each alternative diameter, the pressure head loss depends linearly on the length of the pipe. This principle became fundamental for most subsequent linear models for branched as well as for looped water distribution systems. A linear programming formulation for a looped distribution system is presented in von Dobschütz (1976).

Besides linear models, numerous other models were developed for branched and looped networks as well. A review can be found in Shamir (1974) and Alperovits and Shamir (1977). The achievable optimum depends on the preselection of certain parameters as for example the flow distribution. The various models therefore strive for improvements by applying iterative or non-linear procedures. However, the application of non-linear models is still hampered by computational extravagance.

Whereas mostly the minimization of cost was considered to be the objective of the application of operation research, less attention has been paid to technical improvements. Hydraulically complex design problems, which may impose considerable difficulties in finding at least one feasible solution satisfying all design criteria simultaneously, became easily solvable. This is of particular importance for developing countries, where many large scale water distribution systems have to be designed from the very beginning.

In model-based design procedures for sewerage and drainage systems two categories can be distinguished. The first deals with the alignment of sewers or stormwater pipes and the location of treatment plants. Design problems to be solved in this category are routing of canals, determining the number of treatment plants, and assigning catchment areas to individual treatment plants. The catchment areas may be parts of a greater city or of smaller communities in rural areas. The problem briefly can be described as designing primary sewerage and drainage systems for large cities and regional waste water management systems.

The second category is the design of collection systems with a fixed or at least far-reaching fixed sewer alignment. Instead of the alignment the sewer levels and the lift of pumping stations are to be determined by the design procedure. There is a decisive difference between the two categories with respect to the flow rate. In the first case the flow rate in each individual pipe section is unknown and a variable of the design model. In the second case the flow rate is known or can at least be calculated from design procedures such as the rational method. This also implies completely different solution procedures. The first problem results in a concave minimization problem, a problem category which still imposes some difficulties in solving practical problems. For the second category dynamic programming became the main solution calculus.

Summarizing the model-based design of water distribution systems as well as of waste-water collection systems, the following two basic problems can be distinguished:

(1) finding the optimal flow distribution; and

(2) designing the system for a given flow distribution.

Finding an exact solution for the flow distribution problem is still impossible or extravagant, and approximative procedures therefore became the preferred methodology for practical applications. For a fixed flow distribution the slope of the hydraulic grade line or the pipe becomes constant for each individual diameter allowing the application of the powerful linear or dynamic programming calculus.

CONCLUSIONS

The need for a valid basis for incorporating sediment quality standards into wet weather criteria was recognized. Much progress has been made in understanding the sources of urban pollution and in developing cost-effective engineering solutions. Education also showed that there is still scope for optimizing quality performance of engineering solutions. They also showed that there is still scope for optimizing quality performance of engineering solutions. Sewers can be designed to minimize sedimentation. Overflow design can help to retain and attenuate pollution loads. Real-time control can minimize spill volumes. It is also necessary to view sewerage systems at the total network scale rather than from the end of pipe discharge.

REFERENCES

Alperovits, E. and Shamir U. (1977). *Design of optimal water distribution systems*. Water Resources Research 13. No.6,885-900.

von Dobschütz, L. (1976). *Die optimale Dimensionierung vermaschter Versorgungsrohrnetze. Proceedings in Operations Research*. 6,593-602. Physica-Verlag, Würzburg-Wien.

Labye, Y. (1966) *Etude des procedes de calcul ayant pur but de rendre minimal le cout d'un reseau de distribution d'eau sous pression*. La Houille Blanche. 5,577-3.

Shamir, U (1974) *Optimal design and operation of water distribution systems*. Water Resources Research, 10. No. 1, 27-36.

World Commission on Environment and Development (1987). *Our Common Future*. Oxford University Press, Oxford, U.K.

SPILLS ON OPEN WATERS, A CAUSE FOR CONCERN - THE NEED FOR ACTION TO PREVENT THEM

Walter A. Lyon
University of Pennsylvania
20 Clifton Road
Camp Hill, Pa 17011

INTRODUCTION

In the Spring of 1986 the Technological Committee of the INTERNATIONAL JOINT COMMISSION began a series of four workshops to address the topic of the Humans-Machines interface which it believed was the fundamental cause of most spills. From these workshops emerged a much better understanding of what is needed to do about spills and how devastating the major spills would be for the people and the ecosystem of the Great Lakes.

The problems and the principles which apply to spills on the Great Lakes also apply to the other open waters such as rivers, canals and estuaries used for water-borne transportation, then lakes and reservoirs. For the objectives of this paper, from the term "open waters" tributaries and enclosed coastal waters such as ports and harbors, where spilled oil or chemicals may be successfully collected, are excluded. Also excluded from this paper is the subject of spills from fixed facilities. The concentration is on the transportation related spills which are more typical for open waters.

There are five reasons why a major spill of a toxic chemical on open waters would be a catastrophic event and why prevention of spills is so important:

1) MANY OPEN WATERS ARE TRAPS

The hydraulic retention time of Great Lakes is not expressed in terms of days, as the case is with a flowing stream. However, it is often expressed in terms of weeks, months or even years. The retention time of the Lake Michigan is 100 years. The retention time of Lake Erie is approximately two years.

2) LARGE VOLUMES OF TOXINS ARE BEING SHIPPED BY VESSELS

Large volumes of petroleum and the other toxic chemicals are being shipped by vessels on the waters of the Great Lakes. A recent draft report by the State of Michigan indicates that the Michigan ports handled 2.4 millions short tons of petroleum products in 1987. During that year 5 million short tons passed through the Michigan waters. The largest single category is gasoline which is both toxic and carcinogenic.

During the same year 5.4 millions short tons of hazardous chemical products were shipped through the Michigan waters and 432,000 short tons of hazardous chemical products were handled at the Michigan ports. The volume of these products is huge and the dangers are comparable.

The advents of Superfund and RCRA and similar laws in Canada have greatly increased the distances which hazardous wastes are being shipped. While this presents a hazard for land transportation it is a much more serious hazard for water transportation.

3) WATER TRANSPORTATION IN ITS PRESENT FORM IS ACCIDENTS- PRONE

When compared with the commercial aviation the water transport system uses the obsolete navigation practices, which are accidents-prone and present high probabilities of occurrence of catastrophic events. This point is best expressed in Chapter 6 of the book "Normal Accidents", by Yale Professor Charles Perrow. Among the conclusions he says:" Marine transport appears to be an error-inducing system, where perverse interconnections defeat safety goals as well as operating efficiencies."

The use of water transport in its present forms exposes the drinking water users of the Great Lakes to an unacceptable level of risk. The high standards which are traditionally applied to drinking water source protection elsewhere, do not, for historic, economic and political reasons, apply to the Great Lakes. In many drinking water reservoirs even the recreational uses are prohibited, not to speak of transportation of hazardous substances.

4) MAJOR OPEN WATER SPILLS CANNOT BE CLEANED-UP BECAUSE CONTINGENCY PLANNING WILL NOT WORK FOR SUCH SPILLS

A spill of a toxic chemical in the open waters of the Great Lakes could not be cleaned up at all and could do serious irreversible damage to one of the many drinking water supplies which serve over 30 million people and to the ecosystem. Experience has shown that at best only about 20 percent of the oil in major spills in open waters can be collected or cleaned up.

Therefore, contingency planning is not a viable option for chemical and major oil spills in open waters because the major oil spills cannot be cleaned-up economically and successfully. The same is true for nearly all the chemical spills.

Spill prevention should be given a higher priority than contingency planning.

SETTING PRIORITIES FOR SPILL PREVENTION - A FIRST STEP

5) AT A TIME OF SERIOUS BUDGET LIMITATIONS ANY PREVENTION PROGRAM NEEDS TO TARGET FIRST THE HIGH PRIORITY ISSUES.

Spill prevention is a complex subject. It includes such diverse topics as vessel manning, navigation, drug abuse, fatigue, excessive automation and a broad diversity of other topics relating to human behavior and technology.

Present data systems are highly fragmented and unreliable. In order to set priorities we need reliable data about the relative importance of these causes of spills. Such data is not now available.

Setting a goal of reducing the number of spills on endangered water bodies by one-half every three years might work.

Once we have good data to help set priorities for spill prevention programs, we can set a goal of cutting the number of spills by one half every three years. That type of management goal would encourage implementation of effective preventive measures. It would gradually reduce the serious risk of catastrophes.

There is a need for an examination of transportation policy. That examination should essentially answer the following two questions:

a. "What is the safest mode of transportation for oil and toxic substances?" That question examines the level of risk inherent in the alternative modes of transportation such as highway, railway, pipeline and water, and relates the transportation risks to the economic and geographic conditions and considerations.

b. "How can the transportation systems be made safer?" Would, for example, the installation of the better navigation command and control systems and shifting to safer forms of transportation for hazardous substances be a wise policy? The engineering and human requirements to make the transportation system safer should be addressed in the answer to that question.

Summary

The present forms of water transport of toxic chemicals on the Great Lakes and other open waters, using the inappropriate and obsolete forms of navigation control systems, present the people and the ecosystem with the high probability of chemical catastrophes.

The present emphasis on contingency planning is inappropriate and leads to a false sense of security. It should promptly be changed to spill prevention.

KEYWORDS: Spills, prevention, Great Lakes, water, transportation, human factors

6 PROGRAMS FOR EDUCATION AND TRAINING

TOWARDS ESTABLISHING "WATER RESOURCES ENGINEERING" AS AN UNDERGRADUATE ENGINEERING-DEGREE PROGRAM

Ünal Öziş
Professor, Dr.-Ing.
Civil Engineering Department
Faculty of Engineering and Architecture
Dokuz Eylül University, İzmir 35100 Turkey

ABSTRACT

Hydraulic structures have been built at least during the last five millenniums, without any proper scientific knowledge, but using technology as an art. Hydraulics became more and more a science during only the last few centuries. This "hardware" line, having always the "construction" of an engineering work in mind, was and still is, well incorporated into "civil engineering" programs. The development of the economics as a science and of computers as a powerful tool, opened up new horizons for hydrology and water resources, still badly incorporated into undergraduate civil engineering programs. This "software" line, having the "decision" of construction or operation of an engineering work in mind, will presumably lead to the emergence of "water resources engineering" as a new discipline with a distinct undergraduate engineering-degree program. The new discipline, depending heavily on "civil engineering" and "economics", to some extent on "environmental" and "industrial" engineering, will then appear as "the" profession for solving the world's water-related problems, pressed into the unusually short time limits of a couple of decades.

INTRODUCTION

The fast increase in the world's population and the even faster growth of the socioeconomic development in especially the so-called developing countries, will require an almost complete exploitation of the world's water resources before the middle of the next century.

The development of water resources through the implementation of hydraulic works for the beneficial use of water as well as for protecting from the damages of water, has actually two backbones: (1) the "hardware" one, resulting from the fluid mechanics and hydraulics line; (2) the "software" one, resulting from the hydrology and water resources line; both lines having still art and science aspects.

It is actually the most complex branch of civil engineering, has close relations with other branches of civil engineering and important interrelations with other disciplines. Figure 1 shows only the major areas of them.

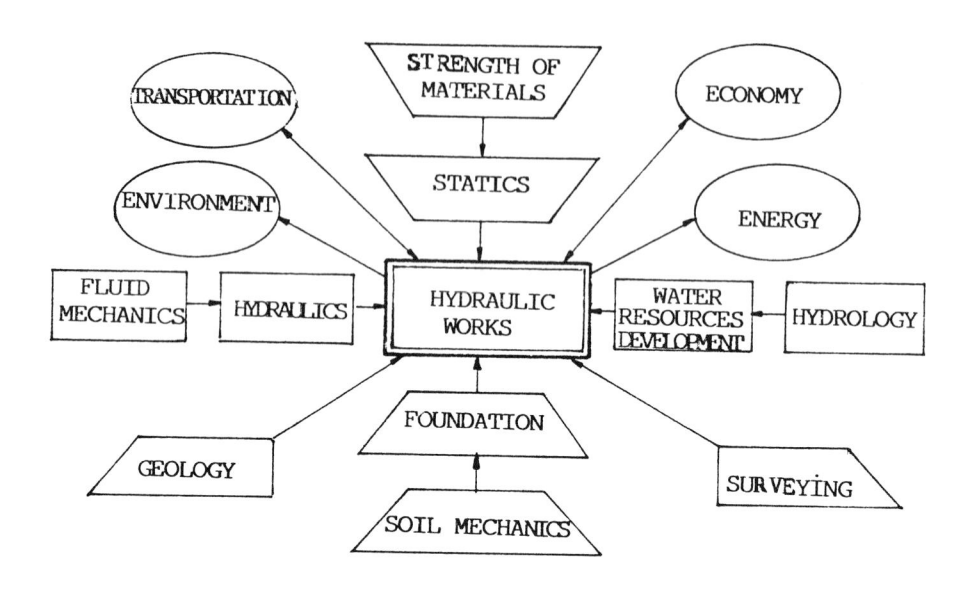

Figure 1. Major interrelations of hydraulics engineering with other subjects (Öziş and Akyarli 1984).

Without any proper scientific knowledge, men built hydraulic works at least during the last five millenniums, where the Nile, the Mesopotamia, the Indus and the Hoang-ho valleys witnessed the early hydraulic civilizations (Wittfogel 1957) and countries like Turkey may be considered as open-air museums of remains of hydraulic works throughout the ages (Öziş 1987). That technology was rather an "art", where the construction of a dam was "both and experience as well as an adventure".

The roots of the positive sciences go back to Ionia in Western Anatolia during the middle of the 1st millennium B.C. (Saraş 1971); got significant contributions from the Islam World during the Middle-Age (Özdaş 1981); flourished after the Renaissance during the XV-XVI. centuries A.D.; and hydraulics became more and more a science during the last few centuries (Rouse and Ince 1957). Parallel to the evolution of civil engineering education, water resources technology has become one of the major components of it. This technology, based primarily on the science of fluid mechanics and hydraulics, enabled that the construction of a dam "is still an experience", but should "no more be an adventure".

The development of economics as a science and of computers as a powerful tool, led to the rapid development of hydrology and water resources development, although its roots go almost four millenniums back into history (Biswas 1970; Chow 1976). These subjects are still lacking an important place in undergraduate civil engineering programs, often represented by a simple course on hydrology; whereas detailed treatment of the subjects are considered as a matter of graduate programs.

In the near future, quantitatively as well as qualitatively limited water resources on one hand, and limited investment resources on the other hand, may lead either to give ample place to subjects related to hydrology and water resources development in undergraduate civil engineering programs, or to the emergence of "water resources engineering" as a new discipline, as experienced in the last decades with "industrial engineering" or "environmental engineering".

However, even in this case, the construction of a dam will remain "to be an experience", although "definitely not an adventure". The analysis, design, construction and operation of water resources systems will heavily depend upon related "sciences", but there will always be an important component of "art" in water resources technology.

WATER RESOURCES EDUCATION IN ACTUAL CIVIL ENGINEERING PROGRAMS

Undergraduate Programs

Subjects related to hydraulics/water resources field of civil engineering usually consist of a series of compulsory courses (namely Fluid Mechanics, Hydraulics, Hydrology, Hydraulic Works/Structures) and certain elective courses.

Furthermore, at most institutions, an undergraduate student has to prepare a "graduation project" during the last semester; carried out under close supervision of the instructor, providing a forum of master-apprentice cooperation. This project is another opportunity for those students wishing to go deeper in water resources engineering.

As an example, the related part of the undergraduate program of the Civil Engineering Department of Dokuz Eylül University is given in Table 1, the list of elective courses in Table 2.

TABLE 1. Hydraulics-technology-related compulsory courses at the undergraduate civil engineering program of the D.E.Ü. in Izmir.

Sem.	Course	h./s.w.	Sem.	Course	h./s.w.
4	Fluid mechanics	4	7	Elective courses	12
4	Hydrology	4	7	Hydraulic works II	3
5	Hydraulics	6	8	Elective courses	6
6	Hydraulic works I	5			

TABLE 2. Hydraulics-technology-related elective courses at the undergraduate civil engineering program of the D.E.Ü. in Izmir.

Course h./s.w		Course h./s.w	
Computer-aided hydraulic design	4	Water supply and sewerage	12
Applied hydrology	4	Coastal and harbor structures	4
Dams	4	Flood control	2
Irrigation and drainage	4	History of water resources technology	2
Water power	4		

It should be noted, that this program is giving to the student a quite large opportunity of selection among elective courses; in most existing programs in the world, the total credit for elective courses is far less than that cited in this program.

Graduate Programs

A number of universities offer graduate programs in civil engineering, with special emphasis on hydromechanics and/or water resources.

As an example, the graduate programs of Dokuz Eylül University towards M.Sc. and then Ph.D. degrees in civil engineering, with two options in hydraulics technology: (a) hydromechanics and hydraulic works, is shown in Table 3: (b) hydrology and water resources, in Table 4.

The student is required to attend a total of 20 credit-hours for M.Sc. and of 15 credit-hours for Ph.D. degrees, with the possibility of selecting among major and minor subjects. Furthermore a master-thesis for M.Sc. and a doctoral-thesis for the Ph.D. degrees are compulsory.

TABLE 3. Courses at the graduate program in hydromechanics and hydraulic works of the D.E.Ü. in Izmir.

Course h./s.w		Course h./s.w	
Applied mathematics	3	Flow through porous media	2
Hydromechanics	4	Embankment dams	4
Boundary layer theory	2	Coastal structures	4
Concrete dams	4	Water resources economics	4
Fluid dynamics	4		

TABLE 4. Courses at the graduate program in hydrology and water resources of the D.E.U. in Izmir.

Course	h./s.w	Course	h./s.w
Applied mathematics	3	Stochastic hydrology	4
Hydromechanics	4	Karst water resources	4
Evaluation of hydrometric data	4	Reservoir theory	4
Modelling of hydrologic processes	2	Water resources economics	4
Water resources planning	2	Water resources systems analysis	4

TENTATIVE PROPOSAL FOR AN UNDERGRADUATE PROGRAM TOWARDS WATER RESOURCES ENGINEERING

A tentative proposal for an undergraduate program towards a B.S.- Degree in "Water Resources Engineering" is given in Table 5; the total hours per week per semester being 32 for each semester.

TABLE 5. Tentative proposal for an undergraduate program towards water resources engineering.

Sem.	Course	h./s.w	Sem.	Course	h./s.w
I	Mathematics I	4	II	Mathematics II	4
	Probability and statistics	2		Statics	4
	Physics	4		Chemistry	4
	Hydrogeography	2		Technical Drawing II	4
	Technical Drawing I	4		Engineering Geology	4
	Computer Programming	4		Hydrometeorology	2
	Ecology	2		History of Water Technology	2
	Macroeconomics	2		Operations Research	2
	Introduction to W.R.E.	2		Humanities	6
	Humanities	6			
III	Mathematics III	4	IV	Mathematics IV	4
	Strength of Materials	4		Construction Materials	4
	Surveying	6		Hydrogeology	4
	Water Quality	4		Basic Hydraulics	6
	Fluid Mechanics	4		Hydrology	4
	Engineering Economy	4		Systems Analysis	4
	Humanities	6		Humanities	6

TABLE 5. Continued

Sem.	Course	h./s.w	Sem.	Course	h./s.w
V	Hydraulic Transients	4	VI	Dams	4
	Hydraulic Systems	4		Conduits	4
	Weirs	2		Reservoir Theory	4
	Hydrological Models	4		Water Supply and	
	Soils Engineering	6		Sewerage	6
	Structural Engineering	6		Irrigation and Drainage	4
	Humanities	6		Transportation	
				Engineering	4
				Humanities	6
			VIII	Water Resources	
VII	Water Power	6		Management	6
	Flood Control	4		Water Right	2
	Melioration and			River Basin	
	Navigation	4		Development	4
	Water Resources			Electives	4
	Economics	4		Graduation Project	10
	Financing	4		Humanities	6
	Electives	4			
	Humanities	6			

This program retains the humanities and the bulk of the engineering science part of actual civil engineering program, with certain modifications in mathematics; shifts to earlier semesters the compulsory courses and adds most of the actual elective undergraduate courses and many graduate courses in hydraulics and water resources engineering as compulsory ones; discards several structural and transportation engineering specific courses; adds certain courses of the operations research line of industrial engineering and water quality line of environmental engineering, as well as some multi-disciplinary courses in the geography-geology-meteorology line.

CONCLUSION

The Need For An Undergraduate Program

The first question to be answered is whether the world needs undergraduate "water resources engineers" to solve the ever increasing water-related problems; especially due to the fast increase in the population and to the even faster growing need of exploiting the water resources.

The country of the author is experiencing with the implementation of the South-east Anatolian Project, developing Euphrates and Tigris basins in Turkey (Öziş 1982, 1983; Harmancioğlu and Öziş 1983; Öziş a.o. 1989, 1990), an outstanding example of such activities, with nation-wide as well as international impacts.

A civil engineer, selecting water-oriented courses at the undergraduate level and deepening himself through a M.S. program in water resources engineering, appears to remain the more conservative preference, both from the viewpoint of the person as well as of the job.

Unfortunately, financial problems lead the young engineers to enter the profession as early as possible and leave hardly any opportunity for graduate studies. On the other hand, limited capacities for graduate-level training with regard to sophisticated theses especially in developing countries, might be a bottleneck for the recruitment of such engineers in appropriate numbers. In both respects, an undergraduate program towards the B.S.-Degree in "Water Resources Engineering" would appear to be the optimum solution.

Type of The Program

Because of the rather interdisciplinary nature of water resources engineering, the tentatively proposed program in Table 5 enhances the "software" (hydrology and water resources) aspect, though with due respect to the "hardware" (hydromechanics and hydraulic structures) aspect.

Due to the multi-faceted nature of the subjects, this program has not great flexibility for shifting its priorities, since it incorporates only 8 hours/sem. week elective courses, divided in the last two semesters.

An alternative would be a more "hardware"-oriented program, depending much heavily on the civil engineering program, as experienced during the early stages of environmental engineering. In any case, the author believes that it should be appropriate to "loudly think" about establishing of "water resources" as an undergraduate engineering program, in order to avoid hastily-taken inefficient decisions.

ACKNOWLEDGMENT

The author gratefully acknowledges the exchange of views with his colleagues of the Hydraulic Sciences Branch of the Civil Engineering Department at the Dokuz Eylül University, Izmir, Turkey. Further acknowledgment is due to Mrs. Senel Ekmekáiler for the typing of the manuscript and to Mr. Birol Kaya, M.S.C.E. for transferring it into the diskette.

REFERENCES

Biswas, A.(1970): *History of Hydrology*. North Holland, Amsterdam.

Chow, V.T.(1976): *Hydrology in Asian civilizations*. Water International, 1/2, 7 0.

Harmancioğlu, N. and Öziş, Ü. (1983): Dynamics of water resources development: Lower Euphrates case in Turkey. Application of Systems Analysis on Water Resources Development, Nato Workshop Proceedings (ed.: M.Bayazit), (May 30-June 3, 1983), pp. VIII/1 1.

Özdaş, N. (1981): Kongre açilis konuşmasi. İ.T.Ü. Birinci Uluslararasi Türk-İslam Bilim ve Teknoloji Tarihi Kongresi, Proceedings, Istanbul, V.V, pp. 7 1.

Öziş, Ü. (1982): Aménagement de la Basse Euphrate en Turquie. Travaux, 565, 68-72 - Ausbauplan des unteren Euphrates-Beckens in der Türkei. Die Wasserwirtschaft. 72, 207-210 - The development plan for the lower Euphrates basin in Turkey, National Resources and Development, 16, 73-82.

Öziş, Ü. (1987a): Su mühendisliği tarihi açisindan Anadoludaki eski su yapilari. Dokuz Eylül Üniversitesi Mühendislik- Mimarlik Fakültesi, N. 73 (2.ed.), Izmir.

Öziş, Ü. (1987b): Ancient water works in Anatolia. Water Resources Development, 3/1,55-62.

Öziş, Ü. and Akyarli, A. (1984): Hydraulics engineering education and research in developing countries : case study of Turkey. World Conference on Education in Applied Engineering and Engineering Technology, Köln, Sp. preprint, 8 p.

Öziş, Ü.; Özel, İ (1989): Karakaya dam and power plant. Int. Water Power & Dam Construction, 41/7, 20-24.

Öziş, Ü.; Basmaci, E.; Harmancioğlu, N. (1990): Atatürk nears completion. Int. Water Power & Dam Construction, 42/9,126.

Rouse, H. and Ince, S. (1957): History of hydraulics. University of Iowa, Institute of Hydraulic Research, Iowa City.

Saraç, C. (1971): İyonya pozitif bilimi. Ege Üniversitesi Arkeoloji Enstitüsü N.1., İzmir.

Wittogel, K.A. (1957): Oriental despotism : a comparative study of total power. Yale University Press. New-Haven.

WATER RESOURCES MANAGEMENT: A CHALLENGE FOR EDUCATORS

N. S. Grigg
Colorado Water Resources Research Institute
Colorado State University
Ft Collins Colo USA 80523

ABSTRACT

During the 20th Century "water resources management" has developed as an interdisciplinary field requiring solutions of technical and political problems. Education in water management for engineers and executives is essential to aid in finding solutions. General and technical education with realistic project oriented courses are needed at the undergraduate level. Graduate programs must impart competence in water resources engineering, respond to complexity with the systems approach, deal with unstructured problems by bringing the real world into the classroom, and impart competence in and understanding of communication skills and the need for coordination, cooperation and ethics.

WATER RESOURCES MANAGEMENT: A GLOBAL CHALLENGE FOR EDUCATION

At a conference such as this it should not be necessary to reiterate the importance of water resources management for the advancement of economies and societies and the preservation of the environment. It also is safe to assume that readers of this volume understand the critical linkage between education and improvements in water resources management.

To summarize these points, water resources problems are among the world's most important issues. Emphasis is on drought-induced water supply problems, water pollution, flood disasters and lack of safe drinking water and sanitation. A survey by the writer revealed that media reports of water crisis focus primarily on water shortage and pollution (Grigg, 1985). A long list of related problems includes: slowness of projects, agricultural subsidy costs, cost allocation conflicts, navigation problems, effectiveness of planning and economic evaluation, water for energy, high water bills, interbasin transfer conflicts, financing problems, institutional problems, dam safety, flooding and stormwater problems.

What can education contribute to the solution of these difficult socio-technical problems? The political systems of some nations are overwhelmed with water-related problems, and other nations, including the US, work against difficult odds to develop water policies that work. Obviously, education is not the whole answer. However, education may be the investment and the program area with the greatest promise for helping.

Educators can contribute to the solution of these problems through effective, integrated programs of water resources management education. The purposes of this paper are to provide an overview of current educational programs, to diagnose the problems faced, and make suggestions for improvements in curricula and programs. The paper deals with management issues and is not primarily concerned with education in technical subjects.

PROBLEMS FACED IN ACHIEVING EFFECTIVE WATER RESOURCES MANAGEMENT

It is my belief that the factors behind lack of success in water resources management can be explained by complexity, conflict and competence. Complexity is due to technical and political factors. Conflict arises through jurisdictional and value disputes; it requires three more "C's" to solve: communication, coordination and cooperation. Competence refers to the extraordinary degree of competence that is required to unravel the complex mysteries of water resources systems and deal with conflict. Thus the model of water resources management features two main problems, complexity and conflict, and four solutions: competence to unravel complexity and communication, coordination and cooperation to provide harmony and deal with conflict. Altogether six "C's" are involved and each can be addressed to some extent in water management education.

To design educational systems we must begin with a clear goal: to manage water effectively. However, the term "water management" is broad and requires focus to facilitate discussion.

Viessman (1990) states that water resources management "... embraces planning, design, construction, operation, and maintenance" and that its ingredients include "... technological capability, social attitudes, economic realities, political viewpoints, and environmental goals." A UNESCO report on water management education (Dyck, 1990) states that "Water resources management (WRM) unites the totality of conditions and means for the assessment and planning of water resources and water demands, the rational use, comprehensive monitoring, effective protection, and conservation of water resources." Clearly, water resources management is a broad activity, encompassing many problems and disciplines of knowledge.

For instructional purposes I developed a definition that recognizes that management involves both programs and facilities and that both man-made (hydraulic structures) and natural (eg., rivers, aquifers) systems are to be managed. It defines a water resources system, lists water control facilities and environmental elements, and delineates the purposes and tasks of water resources management:

Water resources management is the application of management programs and water control facilities to control natural and man-made water resources systems. Water control facilities include: conveyance systems, diversion structures, dams and storage facilities, treatment plants, pumping stations, wells, and appurtenances. A water resources system is a combination of water control facilities and environmental elements that work together to achieve water management purposes. The purposes of water resources management may be expressed as the following services to people, farms, industries and the environment: water supply, wastewater and water quality management, storm and flood water control, hydropower, transportation and water for the environment, fish and wildlife and recreation. Environmental elements involved in water resources systems include: the atmosphere, catchments, stream channels, aquifers, lakes, estuaries, seas and the ocean. The tasks of water resources management are: planning, design, construction, implementation and operations and maintenance of water control systems.

My experience rates the severity of water management problems in this order: political, financial, legal, technological. Political problems involve the many conflicts that arise in water management. Financial problems are to find, allocate and control the funds to manage water. Legal problems are caused by the rigidity of legal systems and result in constraints on water management. Technological problems abound; they include all of the issues described in the definition of water resources management given above. Each of these categories of problems involves complexity and conflict and must be attacked through educational programs.

EDUCATIONAL PROGRAMS IN WATER RESOURCES MANAGEMENT

UNESCO's (1990) report describes the available and required educational programs for integrated planning and management of water resources. It lists the categories of those needing education as: professionals working full time in water resources management; professionals working occasionally in the field; planners and policy analysts whose work includes water issues; managers with portfolios that include water; policy makers and decision-makers; non-professionals involved in implementation and operation of projects; and laymen participating in the water management process.

This list of participants in water management education involves both a spectrum and a hierarchy. The spectrum includes different sectors of society: professionals and managers from different disciplines and industries, and the public. The hierarchy includes different levels within each sector of the spectrum. For example, within a particular sector of water management such as a water supply organization, the levels include: executive and policy, management and engineering, and operations. Educating the public includes levels from schoolchildren to sophisticated adults. The full tableau of educational needs is thus a table; the columns are the different sectors, professions, and interest groups, and the rows are the different levels.

While it is necessary to have effective water management education within the full tableau described, the focus in this discussion is on the executive and management levels within the water industry itself. It can be argued that this part of the water management tableau is the most critical to making systems work and to solving the most urgent problems. A recent task force of the American Public Works Association, assessing the education problems of public works managers, reached this conclusion as it regards infrastructure systems in general, including water (American Public Works Association, 1990).

To understand the career tracks of engineers and managers we can examine typical water management organizations. It has been my observation that in the US three basic types of organizations dominate the water industry: operating water agencies such as water management utilities and districts; regulatory organizations such as state government agencies; and federal government agencies such as the Corps of Engineers. There are also many former or future water managers working in the private sector and in various other organizations, but they are too diverse to describe here. Other countries will have different experiences, but the differences are not great.

It can be said that there are three "typical" tracks to management within water organizations: engineer to manager to executive (engineering track); non-engineer to manager to executive (public administration or political track); operator to manager (rise through the ranks track). The career tracks to management still lead mostly through engineering, but other disciplines are increasing their influence. A survey by the American Public Works Association showed that public works managers are increasingly coming from disciplines other than engineering. It is my belief that educational programs for the engineering track can begin at the BS level, while the other tracks can be accommodated at the graduate level and through continuing education.

To prepare water managers to deal with the six "C's" presented earlier (complexity, conflict, competence, communication, coordination and cooperation) it is clearly necessary to provide at the same time a high level and broad educational foundation. Is this asking too much? It is a dilemma facing much of education today, particularly education in fields of technology and management.

At the undergraduate level responses have centered on the need for "general education," with the goal to prepare graduates in several key areas of competence. At my university the fields covered in this program are: communication and reasoning, natural science, arts and humanities and behavior and social science. At the undergraduate level this requirement provides at least an exposure to fields that relate to the "C's".

At the graduate level the engineering profession has recognized the need for broader education for water managers. In the 1970's the American Society of Civil Engineers inaugurated the Water Resources Planning and Management Division to recognize the need to consider non-technical objectives in water resources management.

Goodman (1976), representing a committee on education and training of this division, traces the literature about education for water resources planning, a subset of the broader field of water resources management. He shows that thinking about the unique educational requirements of planners goes back to the 1960's. Quoting one unpublished report from 1963 Goodman notes a definition of water resources planning as "the process of selecting from among all feasible alternatives the plan that offers the optimum economic and social values within the constraints set by pre-established planning criteria and goals." Goodman preferred a definition that included the identification and evaluation of water resources, and the planning of projects that utilize and control water. Goodman goes on to state that in addition to having a background in engineering and science, the practitioner of the field should have knowledge in the fields of social science, law and other aspects of planning.

More recently, a task committee of ASCE (1990) reported a survey of practitioners' attitudes about water resources education. Key conclusions related to management include: need for communications skills and increasing the breadth of degree programs. The report actually suggests replacing the undergraduate requirement in electrical engineering with a course in business and management.

Education in water resources management is not unlike the educational problem in the broader field of infrastructure management (Grigg, 1988). The problem is not mainly technical; it is a management challenge, and managers do not have to be engineers. Grigg and Fontane (1990), in describing educational programs in infrastructure management, suggested that either infrastructure needs are not being met, or that they are being met with less civil engineering input than the profession would like. Infrastructure systems are complex technically and politically, and success in managing them requires special talents exercised in an interdisciplinary environment by engineers, managers and policy makers.

A founder of the profession of public works management put the situation this way: "Engineering capability alone is insufficient for these multidimensional purposes. Engineering and other specialized skills must be complemented by public affairs and managerial competencies. These include capacity to deal with the gamut of social, economic, environmental and political factories inherent in planning, policy resolution and program implementation. Practitioners are needed who can integrate public works systems and subsystems into urban and national development programs" (Stone, 1974).

The tasks of engineers working on infrastructure are planning, designing, constructing and operating. But there is more to infrastructure management than just getting the facilities planned, built and operated. There is a high level of dependence on politics, finance and project management. ASCE recognizes this; a conference recently concluded that "The principal conclusion ...from this...examination of our profession is that carefully crafted planning coupled with leadership and action at all levels is essential" (ASCE, 1988). The leadership and action can take care of some of the problems of communication, cooperation, coordination and conflict management.

While technical aspects of civil engineering in the US are excellent, infrastructure problems call for different skills. What is needed is to redirect parts of the curriculum into making civil engineers better leaders of interdisciplinary teams that deal with infrastructure. It is the same challenge referred to by Donald Stone. The key word is to "integrate", or in Stone's words: "Practitioners are needed who can integrate public works systems..." This is a real challenge and does not call for more technical courses but for what we call in engineering education "synthesis". In this case what is needed is not to synthesize mechanical systems but socio-technical systems. This will be the key to unraveling the complexity of water resources systems.

To lead in infrastructure management, students need to learn about interdisciplinary efforts in areas of policy, finance and organizational arrangements. There is not time in a four-year undergraduate curriculum for special courses on these, but they can be introduced in interdisciplinary project-oriented courses and strengthened at the graduate level.

At Colorado State University we offer both MS and PhD degrees in the field of water resources planning and management. To participate in this program the student must come from an engineering background or take prerequisites. Afterwards the programs require competence in the basic fields of water resources engineering (hydraulics, hydrology, water quality) and in planning and management, computer-aided water management and the policy sciences (economics and political science). This is a popular program which deals with a wide variety of subjects falling into the broad field of planning and management.

SUMMARY AND SUGGESTIONS FOR IMPROVEMENTS IN PROGRAMS

Any suggestions about needed improvements in water management education can only point in directions, not provide comprehensive solutions. The problem space is simply too large. Nevertheless, some directions can be indicated.

Education may not be the whole answer to the difficult problems of water resources management, but it may be the investment with the greatest promise.

If the factors behind lack of success in water resources management can be explained by the "C's", how can engineers, managers and executives be educated to deal with them? At the undergraduate level the use of general and technical education coupled with realistic project oriented courses seems the best response. This is the approach taken today and, while improvements are needed, they are being addressed within the context of engineering education.

At the graduate level there is opportunity to respond to the needs of the spectrum and pyramid of water management participants identified earlier, particularly to those engineers and managers needing further education. New degree tracks may be needed to enable managers with undergraduate engineering, science and maybe even liberal arts degrees to advance through programs leading to masters degrees in engineering or management with emphasis on water resources management. At the PhD level programs may be needed to prepare graduates for work in research or analysis of complex systems and problems.

Any of the programs will have to deal with the "C's" of water resources management if they are to contribute.

They will have to begin by assuring that graduates are competent in the basic and applied areas of water resources management.

They will have to respond to complexity with the systems approach, including both the analysis of complex unstructured problems and the use of computer-aided problem analysis.

Dealing with unstructured problems requires bringing the real world into the classroom, perhaps using the case study approach as is done in some business education. This problem needs further attention by educators and practitioners if the gap between the classroom and the real world is to be narrowed.

Gaining skills in computer-aided water management involves modeling, database management and geographical information systems. Students are eager to improve their skills in these areas, and when provided with the right tools and good learning environments, they make considerable progress.

Graduates will have to gain competence in the harmonizing "C's" (coordination, cooperation and communication) with courses and training in communication skills and interdisciplinary teamwork. Disciplinary barriers need to broken down. Much of the conflict in water resources problems involves communication problems.

Perhaps the greatest need is for training in ethics. Without ethical approaches to problem solving with the public interest in mind, no education or training program can help to solve the severe problems facing water resources managers today.

REFERENCES

American Society of Civil Engineers (1988). *Civil Engineering in the 21st Century.* New York, NY.

American Society of Civil Engineers (1990). *Task Committee on Water Resources Education and Training*, J. Water Res. Planning and Mgmt. Div., ASCE.

American Public Works Association (1990). *Task Force on the Education of Future Public Works Employees, Final Report*, Chicago, IL.

Dyck, S. editor (1990). *Integrated Planning and Management of Water Resources.* UNESCO, International Hydrological Programme, Paris.

Goodman, A. S. (1976). *Education and Training in Water Resources Planning.* J. Water Res. Planning and Mgmt. Div., ASCE.

Grigg, N. S. (1985). *Water Resources Planning*, McGraw-Hill, New York, NY.

Grigg, N. S. (1988). *Infrastructure Engineering and Management.* John Wiley & Sons, New York, NY.

Grigg, N. S. and Fontane, D. G. (1990). *Infrastructure and Civil Engineering Education.* ASCE Conference on Education of Civil Engineers, Las Vegas, NV.

Stone, D. C. (1974). *Professional Education in Public Works/Environmental Engineering and Administration.* American Public Works Association, Chicago, IL.

Viessman, W. Jr. (1990). *Water Management: Challenge and Opportunity.* J. Water Res. Planning and Mgmt., Vol 116, No. 2.

UNIVERSITIES, INTERNATIONAL AGENCIES AND WATER RESOURCES EDUCATION

Ronald M. North
Institute of Natural Resources
The University of Georgia
Athens, GA, USA 30602

ABSTRACT

Universities train and educate people for work in the system and for useful, satisfying lives. Water resources is one of several fields of training that has long term employment prospects but draws its trained professionals from many fields of study and disciplines, few of which are described as water resources. International agencies provide substantial funding opportunities for training in water resources but not many universities offer the needed or required courses of special content, level or intensity. If water resources training is to be improved, universities, water agencies, and international agencies must work out solutions that match training needs with the training resources, programs and facilities.

OVERVIEW

Universities view themselves as repositories of talent, expertise, experience, programs and facilities for the training of international students in many fields, particularly in water resources. Universities also view themselves as the appropriate legitimizers (certification authorities) for the programs students need in order to seek employment in a specific discipline or field. How well do universities serve for international training in water resources planning and management? Probably, very well for long-term studies such as advanced degrees. Probably not very well for the immediate needs of developing nations and international funding agencies.

International agencies view themselves as providing substantial training of both students and practicing professionals. Most international funding programs include an education and/or training component although it is given low priority in practice.

Exceptions are made in agencies where provisions are made for short-term, specialized training designed to compliment the project planning and/or design/investment objectives. Many of these water resources projects are contracted to international firms or consortia of universities in which training is not the highest priority nor the main focus of their work. The uncertain tenure of specialized short courses in water resources makes it difficult for those in the consulting business to keep up with their availability. Conversely, the short-term nature of most internationally funded projects makes it equally difficult for universities and other organizations in the training business to develop adequate and appropriate courses. Short courses and specialized training programs are often geared to needs of existing technical and policy issues and these may not be appropriate for host countries. There are some possible solutions.

One or more of the professional/academic associations could organize a task force to pool resources and to create a clearinghouse for water resources training needs and the available training resources. Associations co-sponsoring this conference would be an excellent starting point. This task force could provide training programs on a pre-planned basis to meet the more significant and prevailing needs for intensive training in water resources. Ideally, the development of an international program of water resources training would involve substantial representation from a number of nations, both developed and developing. Any successful program will require a meeting of minds between those who can offer training programs and those who have need of training programs. A good description of water resources training needs might be that of "NICHE TRAINING". Universities should offer short courses that fill the gaps or "NICHES" for those employed or expecting to be employed in the water business. Traditional hydrology and engineering would be included but other aspects such as management, finance and planning should be added.

The principle international funding agencies for water resources development and management include the World Bank, the Asian Development Bank, the United Nations Development Program, the U.S. State Department: Agency for International Development (AID) and the Trade and Development Program (TDP), the Overseas Development Authority (ODA) in Great Britain, and other national agencies. The Bureau of Reclamation in the Department of the Interior, the Corps of Engineers in the Department of Army, and the Environmental Protection Agency of the U.S. offer limited opportunities. The United Nations Development Program (UNDP), Food and Agriculture (FAD), and other U.N. Agencies sponsor and finance training programs through various departments such as Technical Cooperation and Development (DTCD). The common thread through most of these efforts is not water resources training but water as required for health, economic development, agriculture, etc. Therefore, we as universities and faculties must deal with more than our particular specialty to meet the broader needs of international collaboration in water resources training. It is extremely difficult to put together a competitive proposal when the funding agency looks strongly at the ability of the managing firm to be able to provide substantial manpower from its internal organization. There is not much hope for proposals submitted in which most of the working team is assembled from various sources and backgrounds. Such assemblages of diverse backgrounds usually work very well if they are given sufficient time together on location. The funding agencies view this as expensive start-up time. Thus, we in the Universities are left to generate our own interaction programs on a small training and faculty resources scale where the full support of our are not available to do the proper training job in a field such as water resources.

The water resources business is a substantial economic endeavor. However, it never seems to rank at the same importance as roads, schools, telecommunications, and electricity/gas services. Water and sewer services, for most cities and for most states, do not achieve the same status in budgets as the sister utilities and services. From an economic point of view we could ascribe most of this to the under-pricing and under-valuing of water services, especially the sewage and waste disposal. It is a major industry but we do not have in most university systems a well defined field for training persons in water resources management. Most of the programs are centered in civil or environmental engineering with a few hydrologists being trained in schools of forest resources and departments of earth sciences/geology. Most of the people are technically well trained but they lack depth in the areas of planning, policy, management, financing, personnel, and related areas of managing complex water resources systems. NICHE training is needed to supplement the existing technical backgrounds.

PROPOSED SOLUTIONS

The international agencies that fund water resources projects usually include a training component in their projects. The U.S. A.I.D. programs are developing more intensive approaches to natural resources policy and management training (specifically a program called EPAT - Environmental Policy Analysis and Training). The UNPD funded programs of the future will include more substantive specialized training components consisting of intensive short courses for small groups (10 - 15) or individuals. Other agencies such as World Bank and the Regional Development Banks, are recognizing the necessity for intensive training of local people in both technical and managerial functions. Obviously, we need more research and training money for water resources students and professors in the universities. Less obviously, we need to focus our available funds so they can be used more effectively. This could be accomplished by developing a few regional centers for water resources training, among the North American universities. These centers should include those where professors and students work consistently on technical and management problems specific to the water resources business. We should work to focus more frequently on the mainstream issues where training is badly needed. More importantly, we should focus on making the training programs available to domestic and international participants who are in the water resources business. This focus on information exchange would make it much easier for North American and other universities to cooperate with each other and with private firms where all might benefit from sharing expertise and training.

It seems evident that four or five well funded university centers focused on solving water management/development problems could make a greater contribution to their universities and to their economies through training and research than we are now doing. The importance of water to all makes it a great medium through which several disciplines can be focused. These would include engineering, earth sciences, social sciences, management and other disciplines that could bring contributions to the table to address water management issues.

The best possibility for strengthening water resources training and research exists in the professional societies and other organizations that deal with water resources. Many people in the water business are familiar with the professional societies such as ASCE (and its divisions - EED, WRPMD, IDD, WPCOED), CNA, AGM, AMH, AWRA, AGU, IWRA, UCOWR and others involved in this symposium.

Some of these organizations have an international committee and an education and public service committee that could function as initiator or task force to develop training programs. Each organization needs to expand its role in international education and research in water resources by enlarging its membership and by encouraging university administrators to give more attention to the water resources business in their universities. We should use these organizational ties to learn more about water resources programs in other nations, particularly in North America. We could improve our international exchange of faculty and students through existing exchange organizations such as the National Science Foundation (NSF), CNA, National Academy of Sciences, Council for International Exchange of Scholars, and similar organizations. We have done this, to some extent, by recruiting and sponsoring water resources faculty to spend their sabbaticals with federal agencies in the U.S. Intergovernmental Exchange Programs.

Many universities are under-utilizing their water resources faculty and facilities as a result of structural problems in funding for water resources research and an equally deplorable problem of structural constraints within the universities. Now that we know this situation exists, we need to work as professionals in water resources to improve our lot regarding international research and training in water resources. Organizations such as those sponsoring this symposium can be very effective in expanding our opportunities and our horizons regarding water resources issues, regarding our training needs, and regarding the social/economic importance of the water business.

If I could leave you with a specific issue for this group, it would be to identify and categorize water development and management processes in member nations that are represented in this symposium. Such a project would do much to familiarize all of us with national water resources issues and it could lead to improvements in international, trans-boundary water management. It could also open up more opportunities to learn how our neighbors address their water management problems. We see this often in where one state does a good job on a particular water management problem and their experience is quickly passed on to others.

INTERDISCIPLINARY EDUCATION IN WATERSHED SCIENCE: A NATURAL RESOURCE PERSPECTIVE

C. Hawkins, J. Dobrowolski, J. McDonnell and M. O'Neill
Watershed Science Unit
Utah State University
Logan, UT., U.S.A., 84322-5210

ABSTRACT

Natural resources managers will face profound challenges in the next decade and beyond. Many of these challenges will require expertise in watershed science: global change effects on the quality and quantity of water falling on wildland ecosystems, degradation of riparian systems, acidic deposition, cumulative effects of multiple impacts on wildland watersheds. We believe that these issues can be better addressed from a natural resources perspective that is interdisciplinary in nature and that explicitly recognizes linkages between physical, chemical and ecological components within watersheds. Despite these requirements, only three U.S. institutions offer undergraduate and graduate degrees in watershed science. Producing the type of managers and researchers that will be needed requires that new and existing programs recognize watershed science as a main focus of undergraduate education by establishing: (i) multidisciplinary faculty capable of collaborative research on watershed issues, (ii) curricula that provide multidisciplinary training in watershed sciences, and (iii) extension services that can meet the increasing demands for watershed information and rapidly disseminatie technical knowledge to user groups.

INTRODUCTION

We define watershed science as the interdisciplinary study of the physical, chemical, and ecological interactions in a drainage basin that affect the quantity, quality, and ecological integrity of water resources. We view watersheds as a **fundamental natural resource** unit, because watersheds are distinct landscape features within which water interacts to influence forest, range, and aquatic ecosystems. Watershed scientists use their skills to study how water interacts with other ecosystem components and to manage the often conflicting uses of water within natural drainage basins.

The emphasis of watershed science is on the management and use of water within basins rather than its use and management outside of a basin. Watershed scientists are concerned with defining water-mediated interactions between hillslope, riparian, and aquatic ecosystems; quantifying the movement of water through different geophysical and ecological pathways within basins; and managing the impacts of logging, grazing, mining, waste disposal, and recreation on these systems. This emphasis places watershed science firmly within a natural resources context and distinguishes it from engineering programs that emphasize the management of water yield and delivery for downstream purposes (e.g. irrigation, flood control).

Challenges Facing Watershed Science in the 1990's

Natural resource managers will face profound challenges in the next decade and beyond. Many of these challenges will require expertise in watershed science to address such issues as:

1. What are the physical, chemical, and ecological processes governing streamflow generation, and how do they influence water chemistry and stream ecosystem function? The age, origin, and pathway of runoff production is poorly understood in many areas. Furthermore, we have very little understanding of how these factors operate across different spatial scales. Understanding these processes is critical, if we are to address the specific issues facing watershed scientists described under items 2 - 6 below.

2. Global and regional climatic change associated with global warming may significantly affect the quantity and quality of water falling on wildland ecosystems. This issue is so important that the U. S. Global Change Research Program has been directed to shape national research policies of EPA, USGS, NASA, DOE, and other agencies. We currently have a poor understanding of the consequences of such changes for natural resource values in the Intermountain West and have exceptionally poor predictive capabilities. Effective management of natural resources in a changing environment will depend on how well we can anticipate the timing, chemistry, and quantity of water reaching basins and the retention of water within those basins.

3. Riparian ecosystems have been identified as perhaps the most critical, most sensitive, and most abused ecological component within watersheds. Riparian ecosystems directly influence runoff production by affecting the retention and water yield from basins. They act as important buffers within basins to slow down the loss of soils and nutrients associated with erosion. Riparian vegetation provides critical habitat for many species of wildlife and directly affects the quality of fish habitat in streams by influencing channel morphology and water quality.

4. Many basins in the Intermountain West and elsewhere are potentially sensitive to acid precipitation. Acidification can alter both the productivity of hillslopes (forest and range vegetation) and that of aquatic ecosystems. Conserving and managing the resources within basins receiving acid precipitation will require an understanding of the fundamental ways acidic compounds interact with natural soils.

5. Wildland basins are increasingly being used for a variety of purposes.

In some cases, the effects of single impacts are well understood, but practically nothing is known about the cumulative effects of multiple impacts. The study and quantification of cumulative effects has been identified as a priority issue by the U.S. Forest Service and other national and international agencies. Because the cumulative effects of different disturbances will almost always be mediated through water, watershed scientists should take an active lead in both defining their effects and recommending management strategies to minimize their effects.

6. As the human population continues to grow, increasing and multiple demands are being made on an effectively diminishing supply of water. Managers will be asked to supply greater quantities of water for downstream uses at the potential expense of natural resource values within basins. Management decisions will depend on the understanding of what minimal, critical flows are necessary to maintain wildland water quality.

We believe these issues can be better addressed from a natural resources perspective that is interdisciplinary in nature and that explicitly recognizes linkages between physical, chemical, and ecological components within watersheds. To produce the type of managers and researchers that will be needed in the 1990's requires that watershed science programs:

1. Establish a multidisciplinary faculty capable of collaborative research on watershed issues,

2. Offer a curriculum that provides multidisciplinary training in Watershed Science, and

3. Provide an extension service that can meet the increasing demands for watershed information and rapidly disseminate technical knowledge to user groups.

WATERSHED SCIENCE AT UTAH STATE UNIVERSITY

Background

At Utah State University, Watershed Science has the status of a primary discipline for which the student is prepared by mastering its broad scientific and natural science basis. The Watershed Science Unit was started in 1974 in response to a growing need by resource management agencies for personnel trained in the management of water resources associated with wildland ecosystems. At that time, increasing consumptive and recreational demands were being placed on wildland water resources: Because the College of Natural Resources recognized that both use of and demands on water resources transcended traditional departmental boundaries, the unit was explicitly conceived as an interdepartmental program between the departments of Forestry and Outdoor Recreation and Range Science (Figure 1). It was designed to be distinctly different in both objectives and scope from programs in engineering.

```
                COLLEGE
                   OF
                NATURAL
                RESOUCES
               /         \
         FOREST          RANGE
        RESOURCES       SCIENCE
         |               |
         |_ HYDROLOGY    |_ HYDROLOGY
         |               |
         |_ WATERSHED    |_ WATERSHED
            MANAGEMENT      MANAGEMENT
```

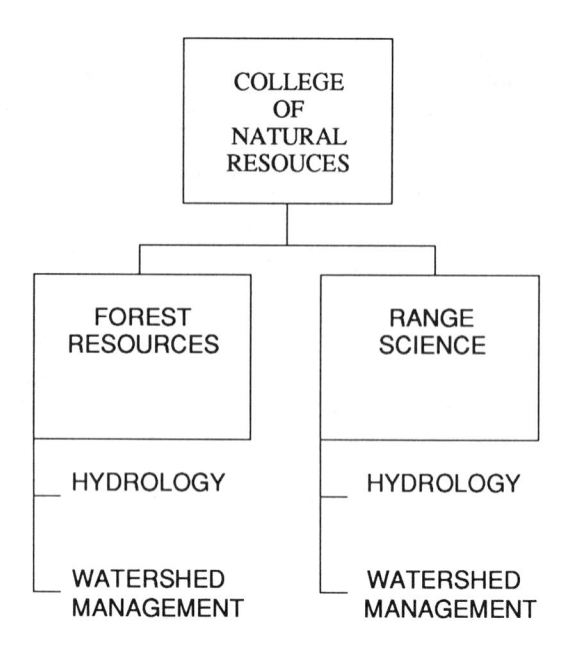

Figure 1. The Watershed Science Program in 1980

The original objectives of the Watershed Science Unit were to administer undergraduate and graduate programs in Watershed Science (BS, MS, and PhD) and a Watershed Management emphasis (BS). Both the curricula and research interests of Unit faculty were strongly focused on surface hydrology, with an emphasis on management for water production. Faculty research included modeling of rainfall, runoff, erosion, and infiltration, and the Watershed Science curriculum emphasized hydrology, water quality, and instrumentation. Completion of the BS in Watershed Science qualified students as hydrologists by U.S. Civil Service standards. The Watershed Management degree allowed undergraduates in either Forest Resources or Range Science to tailor their training toward water related topics. Courses were completed in Watershed Science, in addition to those required for the BS in either Forest Resources or Range Science.

The program was successful as measured by both the number of graduates placed in hydrology positions within resource management agencies and the extracurricular research support secured by faculty. Because of its relatively narrow focus on surface hydrology, the program was less successful in addressing issues that required collaborative, interdisciplinary research.

Current Status

The current Watershed Science program is more diverse and productive than it was 10 years ago (Figure 2). The program has grown through the addition of faculty interested in a variety of watershed related problems in addition to surface hydrology. The addition of these faculty and the changing nature of water related issues in wildland ecosystems catalyzed a self-evaluation of the program in 1985, from which the following recommendations were made:

```
                    ┌─────────────┐
                    │   COLLEGE   │
                    │     OF      │
                    │   NATURAL   │
                    │  RESOUCES   │
                    └──────┬──────┘
        ┌──────────┬───────┴────────┬──────────┐
┌───────┴──┐  ┌────┴─────┐  ┌───────┴──────┐  ┌┴────────┐
│ FISHERIES│  │  FOREST  │  │  GEOGRAPHY   │  │  RANGE  │
│   AND    │  │RESOURCES │  │     AND      │  │ SCIENCE │
│ WILDLIFE │  │          │  │EARTH RESOURCES│ │         │
└──────────┘  └──────────┘  └──────────────┘  └─────────┘
```

Fisheries and Wildlife:
- LIMNOLOGY
- STREAM ECOLOGY
- WETLAND ECOLOGY

Forest Resources:
- BASIN GEOMORPHOLOGY
- SNOW DYNAMICS
- SUBSURFACE HYDROLOGY
- WATER LAW

Geography and Earth Resources:
- CLIMATOLOGY
- METEORLOGY
- FLUVIAL GEOMORPHOLOGY
- GIS
- REMOTE SENSING

Range Science:
- SUBSURFACE HYDROLOGY
- WATERSHED MANAGEMENT

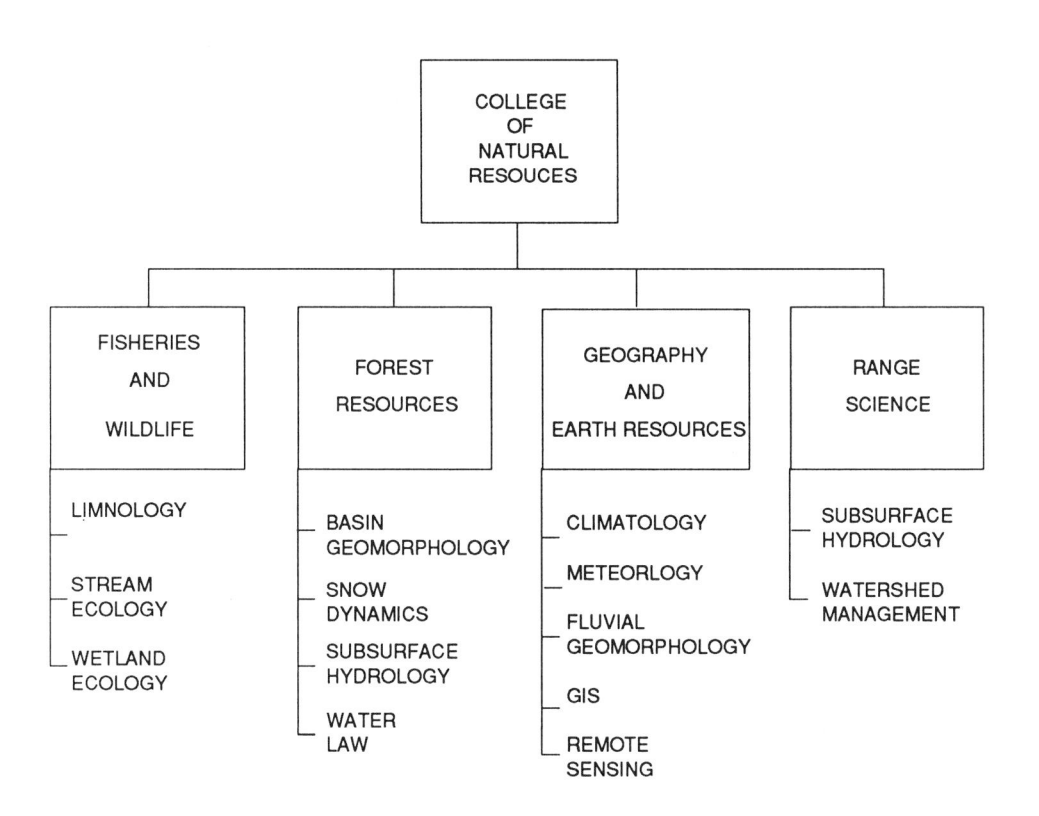

Figure 2. The Watershed Science Program in 1990.

1. A formal restatement of the nature of watershed science was needed that more accurately reflected current water resource issues,

2. Additional faculty should be included whose professional interests would complement, broaden, and strengthen the program,

3. Both the undergraduate and graduate curricula should be revised and expanded in scope to emphasize more than surface hydrology (Figure 3), and

4. The program's structure and responsibilities within the College of Natural Resources should be clarified.

Approximately 14 faculty in the College of Natural Resources at USU have professional interests in some aspect of watershed science. In addition, both agency collaborators and faculty associated with the Utah Water Research Laboratory (College of Engineering) are affiliated with the Unit. The program has maintained its historical strengths in hydrology and watershed management, while greatly expanding in other areas. The recent addition of Geography and Earth Resources to the College of Natural Resources provided expertise in fluvial geomorphology, remote sensing, geographic information systems, meteorology, and climatology. Faculty with a watershed perspective in Fisheries and Wildlife contribute expertise in how lake, stream, and wetland ecosystems are linked to and respond to watershed alteration. Water on the landscape is the common denominator that unites the interests of these faculty.

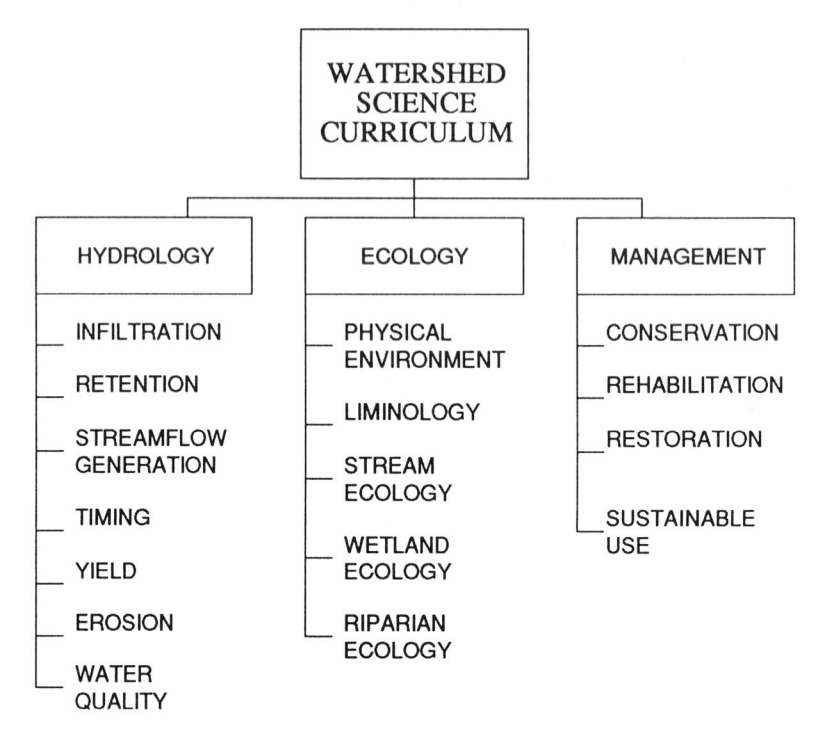

```
                    WATERSHED
                    SCIENCE
                    CURRICULUM

    HYDROLOGY           ECOLOGY            MANAGEMENT

    INFILTRATION        PHYSICAL           CONSERVATION
                        ENVIRONMENT
    RETENTION                              REHABILITATION
                        LIMINOLOGY
    STREAMFLOW                             RESTORATION
    GENERATION          STREAM
                        ECOLOGY
    TIMING                                 SUSTAINABLE
                        WETLAND            USE
    YIELD               ECOLOGY

    EROSION             RIPARIAN
                        ECOLOGY
    WATER
    QUALITY
```

Figure 3. Watershed Science Curriculum.

CONCLUSIONS

Education is a critical component of the Watershed Science Unit at Utah State University. The Unit is one of only three programs in the United States that offers degrees in Watershed Science. Students can pursue BS, MS, and PhD degrees emphasizing hydrology, ecology, or management. These options focus on different aspects of watershed science and are designed to provide the flexibility necessary for an interdisciplinary program.

The goal of the Watershed Science Program at Utah State University is to be a Center of Excellence for watershed studies. The program possesses a multi-disciplinary faculty that actively collaborates in both teaching and research. It offers an interdisciplinary curriculum to meet the needs of both students and society. The program is also moving to build an active extension program capable of rapidly disseminating information to private and public users. Finally, the Unit has research programs at state, national, and international levels that are addressing many of the issues now challenging watershed conservation and management.

EDUCATION AND TRAINING IN HYDROLOGY - SOME PROBLEMS FROM A WMO PERSPECTIVE

Dr. John C. Rodda
World Meteorological Organization,
Geneva, Switzerland

ABSTRACT

As the start of the 21st century approaches, the World is facing a growing number of issues of increasing complexity, including a large number where water is concerned. For water and its uses and abuses enter into so many aspects of modern civilization. Water is needed for drinking, power production, carriage of wastes and for a lot of other purposes. Water is a hazard, killing more people and damaging more property each year than other natural disasters. Water is vital to the maintenance of natural ecosystems of this planet, such as those of the tropical forests, the wetlands and the arid regions.

Fundamental to the outcome of many, if not most, of these issues is the science of hydrology, with its applications to water resources planning and management and its importance to the protection of the aquatic environment. Global issues, such as those surrounding the likelihood that by the middle of the next century many parts of the world will be short of water as the available resource is fully utilized, are paralleled by others on regional, national and local scales. Important to some is the possibility of climatic change and the accompanying sea level rise.

The demands for hydrology to be applied to various of these water issues, either alone, or as part of the effort of a scientific team, requires a ready supply of professional hydrologists. While global arrangements to educate and train hydrologists at all levels have evolved in an ad hoc fashion over the last 40 years, which attempts to meet these requirements both nationally and internationally, there is currently concern that these arrangements do not really match the needs.

There is the criticism (Nash et al. 1990) that education for the advancement of the science is at fault: there is also anxiety (WMO/Unesco 1991) that human resources development and training is not meeting the needs for professionals versed in the basic skills of operational hydrology, such as water resources assessment. Perhaps this concern also points to the difference between the hydrological community in the developed and the developing worlds. In the former the numbers of hydrologists being educated is generally not the problem, it is more the appropriateness of the curriculum to the profession of hydrology that is being questioned.

Has not hydrology advanced far enough as a science in its own right to free courses from the constraints of teaching just the applications of civil engineering or geology? In the latter it is both the nature of the educational background of hydrology and the numbers of hydrologists being produced which are subjects of concern.

As the report on water resources assessment capabilities indicates (WMO/Unesco 1991), there are a number of hindrances to the attainment of a staff of fully trained professional hydrologist which are summarized below:

(1) recruitment or retention of staff, particularly trained staff, is often difficult, in the face of the competition from the better conditions of employment in industry, or even in other countries;

(2) staff responsible for management of WRA programmes commonly often have technical backgrounds and little formal training in management; they are therefore not always able to make optimum use of available resources, or argue for increased resources;

(3) training programmes at all levels are too often hindered by a lack of well qualified educators, suitable syllabi or educational equipment and materials which are appropriate (e.g. in the right language);

(4) technical training must be founded on an adequate level of secondary education, but even this cannot be provided in all countries. Increasingly, training in mathematics, physics and computing will be required, even at technician level, to make full use of available technology;

(5) training must be recognized as a continuous process, with staff requiring regular refresher courses to ensure their familiarity with developing technology.

There is also the point that there is no clear career path leading from the education system in many developing countries into the hydrology and water resources area, as there is for other professions e.g. the medical profession. In addition to water resources assessment activities, such a staff would, of course, be involved in combatting floods and in counter-measures against pollution, erosion and in various other problems.

However the skills necessary to these tasks make the hydrologist attractive to other employers. Indeed the difficulties of attracting and retaining staff against the competition from private industry is one of the main obstacles to proper staffing levels. This is obviously an important point for consideration, particularly in the developing world where the brain drain from the public sector to the plusher pastures of private industry is most marked and serious. However this problem of competition amongst employers is not usually addressed where education and training is discussed, yet it is in part responsible for the chronic shortage of hydrologists in the developing countries, particularly in the hydrological services.

2. HYDROLOGICAL SERVICES

The hydrological services of the world are those bodies of government who together perform the range of activities concerned with water resources assessment, flood forecasting and warning and the other duties that together cover the field of operational hydrology. They normally have responsibilities for:

- assessing a country's water resources (quantity, quality, distribution in time and space), the potential for water-related development, and the ability of the supply to meet actual or foreseeable demand;

- planning, designing, and operating water projects,

- assessing the environmental, economic, and social impacts of water resources management practices, existing and proposed, and planning sound management strategies;

- assessing the response of water resources to other, non-water sector activities, such as urbanization or forest harvesting;

- providing security for people and property against water-related hazards, particularly floods and droughts.

They are involved in both surface waters and groundwaters and in the quality aspects of these waters, as well as these with quantity. Figure 1 outlines the main activities of the hydrological service, but of course, there are considerable variations in the form of the service, as well as in the responsibilities from country to country.

The INFOHYDRO Manual (WMO 1987) lists the bodies responsible for the hydrological service in more than 130 Members of WMO and details of their range of activities. These vary widely from country to country (Rodda and Flanders 1985). However a prime task is the operation and maintenance of the national hydrological network and the gathering of the data from the network by various means, such as by the use of DCPs and satellites.

Most hydrological services are concerned with the education and training of their staff both on the job and in more formal circumstances. Obviously the educational qualifications of candidates for positions is one factor which determines their level of entry to the service, but this concern is usually centered more on enhancing the capabilities of the existing staff. Many services provide training for new entrants and additional education which may be in areas separate from hydrology, such as management and marketing. Nevertheless the bulk of the effort lies within the field of hydrology and the subjects important to it, such as mathematics, statistics, hydraulics, geology, chemistry and physics. Indeed one of the problems facing both educationalists and those wanting to be educated is the wide range of subjects that have to be included in the normal hydrological curriculum at the different levels.

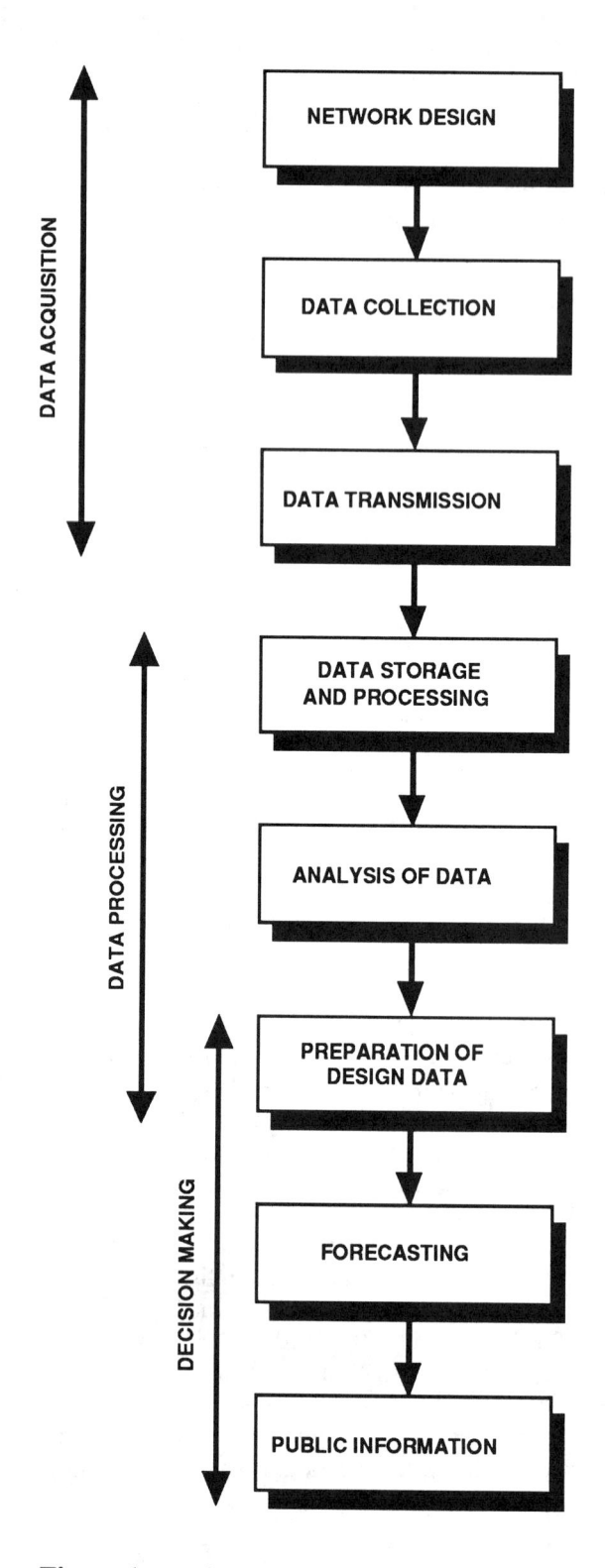

Figure 1. Activities of a hydrological service.

3. ASSESSING THE NEEDS

The achievement and maintenance of a highly educated and well trained population is one of the fundamental responsibilities of governments. Hence nations, international organizations and like bodies are urged to give the highest priority to education and training in their programmes. In the water area, the Mar del Plata Action Plan (UN 1977) makes the appropriate recommendations in paragraphs 73 to 76 the most important being:

74. Countries should accord priority to conducting surveys to determine national needs for administrative, scientific and technical manpower in the water resources area. Law-makers and the public in general should be informed about and sensitized to this problem.

75. Training programmes should be implemented to give water management planners an understanding and appreciation of the various disciplines involved in water resources development and utilization; to provide professional, technical and skilled manpower in hydrology, hydrogeology, hydraulics, social, biological and health sciences and water desalination; and to provide managers for water resources systems. Operators for water distribution and for treatment plants and monitors for water quality installations. Extension services at the farm level should also be organized.

Like so many other well intended actions, their results overall have rarely reached the goals that were intended. However some valuable progress has been made in certain fields, in a number of countries and through different international initiatives such disparities between the gains and losses have produced a very inhomogeneous scenario for education and training in hydrology between both the developed and developing worlds and between one region and another. Take as an example, the findings of the WMO/Unesco Water Resources Assessment (WRA) Report (WMO/Unesco 1991) for the countries of the UN Economic Commission for Africa (ECA):

"Some countries have achieved a good degree of training of WRA staff (both in number and level), but there are large differences, and only in a few countries is the education and training infrastructure adequate. The situation has improved particularly for engineers and professionals up to first degree level, especially in the more developed English-speaking countries, and to a lesser extent for senior technicians. However, environmental subjects, planning, and resource management require more attention, and there is a need for greater integration of training in the various sub-areas of water.

Planning of special education programmes at the national level is difficult, because of the lack of resources and of national human resource planning at the broader scale. Essentially, there seems to be an inability to mobilize the existing educational resources to develop courses which are relevant to changing needs.

In several countries, there is a "brain drain" of experienced staff because of poor conditions of service and remuneration, both to private sector employment and to better paid posts abroad.

Primary needs include the continual strengthening and reorientation of education programmes, the development of the potential which several universities and institutes offer for postgraduate and senior technician training, in-service training for junior technicians and observers, the teachers and materials needed for these areas, and the integration and broadening of water-related education and training."

Indeed in several ECA countries, the number of professional staff in the hydrological service has sunk to less than 10 and the situation is extremely serious. African hydrological services in crisis (WMO 1990) is one assessment of the position, which is also characterized by lack of funds and an absence of the means for collecting data, analyzing it and applying it. These findings have been reinforced by those of the ongoing World Bank/UNDP Sub-Saharan Africa Hydrological Assessment Project, which is producing a country by country picture of the situation in the hydrological service.

The WMO/Unesco Report found the situation in other regions generally better than that for Africa with, as might be anticipated, the more satisfactory conditions within the ECE Region. However, even in the ECE, there were great contrasts in the education and training needs across the Region and concern in many countries that certain specialist skills were lacking amongst professional hydrologists.

One example was the trend towards commercialization of activities which was placing a new emphasis on selling the capabilities of the hydrological services and on the search for customers. Another was the need to introduce the use of remote sensing into the activities of the hydrological service and hydrology generally (Table 1), with the appropriate education and training (Barrett et al. 1988). Table 2 shows the recommendations for education and training for all five UN regional commissions, for ECLAC conditions have aggravated a shortage of staff and progress towards their academic advancement at all levels.

While these gaps and deficiencies in human resources are relatively simple to list, it is not such a simple matter to assess the number of hydrologists required nationally at the different levels of skill. These requirements will obviously vary from one national hydrological service to another, dependent on the duties involved and on other factors. However one Unesco/WMO Manual (Unesco/WMO 1988) has resulted in an assessment of the numbers of professional and technical staff needed in relation to the size of the population of a country (Table 3).

The study did not go on to show how existing staff levels match these requirements, but it is an easy matter to postulate that many countries, including a number in the developed world, fall short of these standards. As an alternative for one sector of activities, the staffing requirements were estimated for maintaining the hydrological network (Table 4). The educational needs were farther defined by estimating that in a stable situation, the education should be capable of producing approximately 15% of the corresponding number of staff of the hydrological service and related agencies. This figure would allow for a moderate development of activities and replacement of personnel resulting from movement of staff, promotion, retirement and death. For developing countries the education system was taken to mean both the national and international educational establishment.

TABLE 1. Identified needs for education and training in satellite remote sensing for hydrology in the UK (from Barrett et al., 1986).

CLIENTELE:	Post-graduate	Mid-Career	Senior management	Civil engineering consultants and engineering hydrologists	Technical staff from operational organizations
TYPES OF COURSES:	One-year MSc	Post experience courses and workshops (5 days to 6 weeks)	Short introductory courses (1-5 days)	Disseminated training courses and workshops, within water authorities, civil engineering firms etc. (5 days-1 month)	One-year training and retraining courses
SIZE OF MARKET: (per year)	5-25 persons	10-100 persons	10-50 persons	5-10 courses or workshops	5-75 persons
STAFF TIME: (teaching and preparation for each course)	1 man-year for preparation and teaching	10 days-10 weeks	5-25 days	3 man-days per 1 day of course or workshop	150 man-days
FACILITIES REQUIRED:	Image processing systems; hydrological and meteorological monitoring instruments, e.g. Agrometeorological stations; computer graphical output devices; meteorological and hydrological ground monitoring equipment	User friendly image processors; hydrological data processors and computer graphical output devices	General range; case studies illustrating the range of potential uses; image processing systems; integration with existing data sets, etc.	Image-processing and hydrological data processing facilities and demonstration materials; hands-on workshop facilities and processors; hardware models; usual hardcopy materials; interactive video/digital processing facilities	As wide a range as possible of current top technology, as for postgraduates
TRAINING DATA SETS (e.g. NOAA, Landsat etc.)	Landsat MSS; Seasat SAR; Nimbus, Meteosat etc. NOAA AVHRR to coincide with catchment rainfall data etc. Ground truth: all available	Basic and practical project-orientated aircraft and ground data	Proven types of data, regardless of source	NOAA/Landsat digital data and NRSC leaflets. Choice related to particular needs	As wide a range as possible, from all currently available sources
COSTS (Approx.)	c. £5K per person. Total costs c. £20K to £100K per year + hardware	£0.5-£5K per person	£0.2-£1K per person	£0.2-£1.5K per person	£5-£7.5K per person

Table 2. Recommendations for education and training for all five UN regional commissions.

Recommendations for areas of education and training where improvements are needed	ECA	ECE	ECIAC	ESCAP	ESCWA
• staff training programmes	X		X	X	X
• improve public WRA awareness	X	X	X	X	X
• better WRA employment conditions			X	X	X
• strengthen WRA technical training	X		X		X
• more training in automated equipment				X	X
• more co-operation in training	X			X	X
• improve management skills of staff	X				X

TABLE 3. Requirements for professionals and technicians in the water-resource field.

Natural and economic characteristics of the country	Professionals per million inhabitants	Technicians per million inhabitants
Low economic development; simple hydrological regime; no major problems in water use	5	30
Average conditions	15	80
High economic development; complicated hydrological regime; great problems in water use; multiple use of water	40	200

TABLE 4. Manpower requirements for collection. Processing and analysis of surface water data.

Item	Professionals	Technicians Senior	Technicians Junior	Observers
I Hydrometric stations	-			
- field operations and maintenance	1	5	5	100
- data processing, analysis and interpretation	2	3	3	-
- supervision	0.5	-	-	-
Subtotal	3.5	8	8	100
II Rainfall and evaporation stations				
- field operations and maintenance	0.5	2	2	100
- data processing, analysis and interpretation	1	2	2	-
- supervision	0.25	-	-	-
Subtotal	1.75	4	4	100

Notes:
1) Many observers work part time or on a voluntary basis.

2) The same field staff often performs the tasks included in all items I and II.

3) Topographical and hydrographical characteristics and ease of access condition manpower needs in field and maintenance operations. Therefore, the figures shown will have to be adjusted in each case.

4) It is convenient for each country to carry out the evaluation on the basis of this table, taking into account the present and recommended operating conditions of its hydrometric, precipitation and evaporation stations. It will be possible to determine the future manpower needs by means of the subsequent table comparison by observing the expected growth percentages during a given period.

4. ATTEMPTING TO MEET THE NEEDS - THE WMO RESPONSE

Education and training has featured prominently amongst the several programmes of WMO since its inception in 1950. Presently the WMO Education and Training Programme contains a significant effort in hydrology and hydrometeorology, while ways of increasing and improving this effort are currently being developed. The main expression of this effort are the educational publications of the Organization (Table 5) and, more obviously, the training courses, seminars and workshops organized by WMO, together with those organized by other institutions which are co-sponsored or supported by the Organization. Nearly 30 such events, attracting support from WMO took place in 1988, 1989 and 1990.

TABLE 5. Operational hydrology - training publications (Blue Series)

WMO 258	Guidelines for education and training of personnel in meteorological and operational hydrology 1984 (3rd Edition). English, French, Spanish.
WMO 364	Vol. II part 5. Hydrometeorology Compendium of meteorology for use by Class I and Class II meteorological personnel. 1984.

These ranged from established postgraduate university courses, such as the course held at the University of Roorkee, India, to one of training workshops, such as those on the hydrometry of large rivers held in Venezuela and on sediment transport measurement which was convened in China. About 100 fellowships are made available each year by WMO in the field of hydrology and hydrometeorology to support attendance at these regular and established courses, while funds are provided to participants for other training events from several alternative budgetary sources. Where a technical assistance project is underway, for instance, some of its funds may be employed for study tours, on the job training and also for the fellowships referred to earlier.

Some may be used to provide training material, such as that produced by WMO, including WMO components. In fact, several highly successful training workshops have been based on HOMS components where technology transfer has been an integral part of the course. In a recent example, a HOMS workshop was held in November 1990 at the Regional Meteorological Training Centre in Nairobi when data bases and data processing was the subject, with attention focussed on the HYDATA component.

To improve its assistance to meteorological and hydrological services and to anticipate future needs, WMO maintains close links with Members, with the education and training community and with bodies which offer funding. To define requirements more precisely, WMO circulated a questionnaire to

Members in 1989 to enquire about the present status of education and training in meteorology and hydrology and to seek information on future needs. Analyses of the 91 replies will provide the basis for determining the thrust for education and training in WMO for the future.

One initiative being promoted within this framework is the postgraduate diploma course in hydrology that it is proposed to launch at the Regional Meteorological Training Centre Nairobi in 1991. This course, it is hoped, will provide some of the professionals currently lacking in the hydrological services of the region. Similar initiatives are to spring from the improved definition of education and training needs in the fellowship area and in manpower development for hydrological services. Many of these activities will of course, take place in partnership with other bodies, such as Unesco, and in connection with other initiatives such as technical assistance projects.

5. CONCLUDING REMARKS

Although the start of formal training in hydrology does not seem to have been chronicled, the first university courses are known to have started early in the 20th Century. The content of these courses was somewhat restricted by comparison with today's far reaching syllabi. Nevertheless, the science of hydrology was placed firmly on a secure foundation. It is hoped that the current activities in education and training will be as appropriate to the demands placed on the science of hydrology in the next century.

REFERENCES

Nash J.E., Eagleson P.S, Philip J.R, and Van Der Molen, W.H., 1990 *The Education of Hydrologists.* Hydrological Sciences Journal 35 pp 597-607

WMO 1987 INFOHYDRO Manual - Hydrological Information Referral Service Operational Hydrology Report No. 28.

Rodda J.C. and Flanders, A.F., 1985 *The Organization of Hydrological Services in Facets of Hydrology II.* (Rodda J.C. Ed). John Wiley Chichester pp 413-441

WMO/Unesco 1991 Water Resources Assessment-Progress in the Implementation of the Mar del Plata Action Plan and a Strategy for the 1990's (in press). WMO,/Unesco

UN 1977 Mar del Plata Action Plan, United Nations Water Conference, Mar del Plata, Argentina 14-25 March 1977

Barrett E.C.,Herschy R.W. and Stewart J.B., 1986 *Satellite Remote Sense Requirements for Hydrology and Water Management from the mid 1990's in Relation to the Columbus Programme of the European Space Agency.* Hydrological Sciences Journal 33. pp 1-17.

WMO 1990 *African Hydrological Services in Crisis,* WMO Bulletin, 39 pp 296 - 298

Unesco/WMO 1968, *Water Resources Assessment Activities a Handbook for National Evaluation.* Unesco/WMO 116p.

A QUARTER OF A CENTURY: THE INTERNATIONAL COURSE FOR HYDROLOGISTS, DELFT, THE NETHERLANDS

Mamdouh Shahin
Senior Lecturer in Water Resources
Engineering, International Institute
for Hydraulic and Environmental
Engineering, Nieuwelaan 76, 2611 RT,
Delft, The Netherlands

ABSTRACT

Since 1966 the International Institute for Hydraulic and Environmental Engineering, Delft, The Netherlands has been organizing an International Course for Hydrologists. This paper surveys the performance of 644 participants representing 90 countries along a span of 24 years, from 1966-67 until 1989-1990. The aim is to assess the competence of each participant to successfully follow the study programme embodied in the course. Emphasis is given to the differences caused by the country of origin and the educational and practical backgrounds. Finally, the restructuring of the course, to begin in October 1991, is reported and discussed.

BACKGROUND INFORMATION

The International Course for Hydrologists, Delft, The Netherlands, was established in 1966 to facilitate the dissemination of know-how in hydrology and related subjects needed for the International Hydrologic Decade (1965-1974) and the subsequent International Hydrologic Programmes.

The course is held annually and lasts eleven months. The number of participants in the period 1966 to 1990 totaled 644 (609 males, 35 females), with an average of 27 per year.

An applicant to the course is academically admitted if he/she holds a recognized university degree in hydrology or any related discipline. Applicants for a Dutch fellowship should have at least three years of experience and not be older than 39 years of age.

The study programme consists of lectures, exercises, group work, laboratory and field work, and field trips in The Netherlands and abroad. The participants take examinations in some selected subjects. If the results are satisfactory the participant sits for a general examination at the end of the year. If the result of this examination is also successful the participant is awarded a diploma and is entitled to put Dip. HY after his name. The diploma work is considered equivalent to the course work for an M.Sc. degree. Since

1986 a participant who obtains his/her diploma with high scores can get an extension of six to eight months to complete his/her M.Sc. thesis.

Since the course began, except from 1975 to 1980, the compulsory subjects of the study programme have been the same for all course participants. The subdivision of the course in those years into scientific and operational hydrology did not prove to be satisfying and was therefore abolished.

DATA USED IN THE ANALYSIS

The data used in this analysis comprise the name of each participant, country of origin, birth date, university background, and experience before participation in the course. Also, the performance during the course year is considered.

The countries have been grouped geographically for the analysis. According to this grouping Western, Central, Eastern Europe and the British Isles form the region of Europe. Africa consists of all countries on the African continent except Egypt. The latter together with Syria, Jordan, Iraq, Saudi Arabia, Yemen, Iran and Turkey are referred to as the Middle and Near East. The remaining countries of Asia and the Far East are referred to as Asia. The United States of America and Canada are considered one region, whereas South and Central America and the Caribbean Islands form another region.

Table 1 summarizes the number of participants per country and region. The number of participants per course year, those with engineering background and those without engineering background and the percentage of those who have obtained the diploma are included in Table 2.

ANALYSIS

Annual Number of Participants

The period from 1966-67 up to 1989-90 can be divided into two equal periods, each 12 years in length. The first period has a mean of 25 participants per year and standard deviation of 10. The second period has a mean of 29 and standard deviation of 2. These figures clearly show that the annual mean in the second period is 19% more than in the first one, whereas the variation in the latter period is only 25% of that of the first one. The rapid increase in the number of participants in the early years was followed by a decrease, till a rather stable number has been reached due to the setting up of more or less similar courses in other parts of the world. Of much importance here is the availability of fellowships. Since the average number of participants, P, per year is about 27, and the number of fellowships, F, is about 20, one can conclude that

$$P \approx 1.35 F \qquad (1)$$

Country of Origin

Most of the participants come from anglophonic countries and to a lesser extent from Latin American countries. The contribution of the (originally) francophonic countries of 0.6% is definitely negligible. Participants of the last 24 courses have come from 90 countries belonging to the six geographic regions already defined in the previous section. The countries and the corresponding regions are listed in Table 1. Africa (21 countries) has been

TABLE 1 - Number of participants per country and per region

Africa		Asia		Europe		South America*	
Country	No	Country	No.	Country	No.	Country	No.
Algeria	1	Afghanistan	4	Austria	1	Argentina	2
Botswana	1	Bangladesh	23	Belgium	1	Barbados	1
Burkina Faso	1	Bhutan	1	Czechoslovakia	15	Belize	1
		Burma	19			Bolivia	6
Cameroon	1	China	20	Finland	1	Brazil	6
Ethiopia	6	Hong Kong	1	Germany	4	Chile	1
The Gambia	1	India	34	Greece	10	Colombia	8
Ghana	5	Indonesia	32	Hungary	2	Costa Rica	2
Kenya	10	Japan	4	Italy	3	Cuba	2
Mauritius	1	Khmer Rep.	1	Netherlands	4	Dominican Republic	1
Mozambique	2	S. Korea	15				
Nigeria	11	Laos	1	Poland	2	Ecuador	3
S. Africa	1	Malaysia	12	Portugal	2	Guatemala	2
Sierra Léone	1	Nepal	4	Romania	6	Guyana	2
		Pakistan	13	U.K.	8	Honduras	1
Somalia	4	Philippines	38	Yugoslavia	8	Jamaica	3
Sudan	24	Singapore	3			St. Lucia	1
Swaziland	1	Sri Lanka	26	Total	67	Mexico	3
Tanzania	23	Thailand	28			Nicaragua	4
Uganda	6	Vietnam	7	Middle & Near East		Panama	1
Zaire	1					Peru	5
Zambia	6	Total	284			Salvador	3
Zimbabwe	1			Egypt	26	Trinidad & Tobago	2
				Iran	22		
		North America		Iraq	8	Venezuela	2
				Jordan	9		
		Canada	2	Saudi Arabia	3	Total	62
		U.S.A.	3	Syria	18		
				Turkey	28		
				Yemen	3		
Total	108	Total	5	Total	117	Fiji Isl.	1

* Including the Caribbean and Central America

TABLE 2. Percentages of participants with and without engineering backgrounds and success in each group

Course Year	Course participants No.	% success	Participants with engineering background No.	% of total	% success	Participants without engineering background No.	% of total	% success
1966-67	6	83.3	6	100	83.3	0	0	
1967-68	14	85.7	14	100	85.7	0	0	
1968-69	19	84.2	14	73.7	85.7	5	26.3	80.0
1969-70	36	72.2	27	75.0	77.8	9	25.0	55.5
1970-71	35	65.7	24	68.6	70.8	11	31.4	54.5
1971-72	42	66.7	27	64.3	70.4	15	35.7	60.0
1972-73	24	79.2	19	79.2	78.9	5	20.8	80.0
1973-74	28	71.4	20	71.4	75.0	8	28.6	37.5
1974-75	20	80.0	16	80.0	87.5	4	20.0	50.0
1975-76	27	81.5	21	77.8	85.7	6	22.2	66.7
1976-77	22	81.8	18	81.8	83.3	4	18.2	75.0
1977-78	21	76.2	16	76.2	87.5	5	23.2	40.0
1978-79	31	93.5	30	96.8	96.7	1	3.2	0
1979-80	33	84.8	29	87.9	93.1	4	12.1	25.0
1980-81	31	61.3	27	87.1	66.7	4	12.9	25.0
1981-82	28	71.4	22	78.6	86.4	6	21.4	16.7
1982-83	27	81.5	22	81.5	95.5	5	18.5	20.0
1983-84	27	77.8	21	77.8	85.7	6	22.2	50.0
1984-85	31	54.8	23	74.2	60.9	8	25.8	37.5
1985-86	33	66.7	23	69.7	73.9	10	30.3	50.0
1986-87	26	69.2	21	80.8	71.4	5	19.2	60.0
1987-88	26	73.1	24	92.3	78.3	2	7.7	50.0
1988-89	28	67.9	19	67.9	68.4	9	32.1	66.7
1989-90	29	75.9	22	75.9	81.8	7	24.1	57.1
	644	74.1	505	78.4	80.4	139	21.6	51.1

represented by 108 participants or about 16.8% of the total, Asia (20 countries) by 284 participants or 44.1% of the total, Europe (14 countries) by 67 participants or 10.4% of the total, the Middle and Near East (8 countries) by 117 participants or 18.2% of the total and Central and South America (24 countries) by 62 participants or 9.6% of the total. Only 5 participants came from North America (USA and Canada) and none from Tasmania, except one participant from the Fiji Islands.

From Table 1 it can be observed that 26 countries (29% of the total) are represented by just one participant, and 13 countries (14.5%) by two participants each. The five leading countries in the number of participants are: Philippines 38, India 34, Indonesia 32, and Thailand and Turkey, 28 each. This means that the participants of these five countries alone represent one-quarter of the whole population.

The strong differentiation in the number of participants between one country and another can be attributed to the:

i - variation in the number of applications for admission and/or a fellowship from the different countries

ii - rules issued by the Dutch fellowship-granting agencies

iii - fellowships allocated by the various organizations for the kind of training given at Delft, and

iv - the availability of similar training courses in hydrology in other countries (e.g. Ireland and Belgium).

STUDY PROGRAM

The contents of the study programme are broken down into two semesters. In either case, the first term usually consists of compulsory subjects, a few elective subjects, a few field trips, first order exercises (equivalent to examinations) and written examinations. The second term consists of a few more compulsory subjects, many more elective subjects, second-order exercises, field and laboratory work, reexaminations, group work, field trips in The Netherlands and abroad, and a general examination.

Examples of compulsory subjects taught in the course are: hydrology, meteorology, groundwater flow, geology and groundwater recovery, river hydraulics, statistical analysis, applied informatics, and mathematics.

Examples of elective subjects are: deterministic hydrology, stochastic hydrology and coastal hydrology. Each elective subject earns the participant a number of credit points. The participant is free to choose his package of elective subjects, provided that the sum of the credit points does not fall below a specified total. Often the participant chooses certain subjects in order to fulfil the requirements of the group work he/she wishes to carry out.

Group work deals with actual hydrologic situations. A group of participants (4-6) work together to solve problems which exist in a given area. Each participant also works out an individual problem. The group work helps the participants apply theoretical know-how to cases of practical interest.

EVALUATION OF THE RESULTS

Every participant must pass examinations in certain subjects in order to obtain the diploma. Additionally, first-order exercise work has to be completed and is considered equivalent to an examination subject. The same applies to the group work and the average mark of all second-order exercises.

The participant has to score satisfactory marks in all mentioned items to qualify for the general examination. He/she is awarded the course diploma if all marks are satisfactory, or if just one mark falls to almost satisfactory. Those who earn the diploma with an average of 75% or higher are admitted to the M.Sc. programme, where they spend at least six months writing a thesis on a chosen topic. Those who fail to fulfil the requirements for the examinations, yet perform satisfactorily in other course activities, are awarded a Certificate of Attendance.

Table 3 includes the percentage of participants who have obtained the diploma.

TABLE 3. Percentage of participants per country and per region who obtained the course diploma

Africa		Asia		Europe		South America*	
Country	%	Country	%	Country	%	Country	%
Algeria	0	Afghanistan	25	Austria	100	Argentina	100
Botswana	100	Bangladesh	70	Belgium	100	Barbados	100
Burkina Faso	100	Bhutan	0	Czecho-slovakia	100	Belize	0
Cameroon	0	Burma	89	Finland	100	Bolivia	50
Ethiopia	50	China	95	Germany	100	Brazil	83
The Gambia	0	Hong Kong	100	Greece	50	Chile	100
Ghana	80	India	79	Hungary	100	Colombia	50
Kenya	80	Indonesia	78	Italy	67	Costa Rica	100
Mauritius	100	Japan	100	Nether-lands	100	Cuba	50
Mozambique	100	Khmer Rep.	100	Poland	100	Dominican Republic	100
Nigeria	45	S. Korea	0	Portugal	100	Ecuador	100
S. Africa	100	Laos	1	Romania	67	Guatemala	50
Sierra Léone	100	Malaysia	100	U.K.	100	Guyana	100
Somalia	25	Nepal	100	Yugoslavia	88	Honduras	0
Sudan	84	Pakistan	67			Jamaica	100
Swaziland	100	Philippines	761	Total	84	St. Lucia	100
Tanzania	83	Singapore	100			Mexico	100
Uganda	100	Sri Lanka	100	Middle & Near East		Nicaragua	50
Zaire	100	Thailand	93			Panama	100
Zambia	50	Vietnam	43	Egypt	73	Peru	80
Zimbabwe	100			Iran	45	Salvador	0
		Total	81	Iraq	38	Trinidad & Tobago	100
				Jordan	33	Venezuela	100
		North America		Saudi Arabia	0		
		Canada	100	Syria	61	Total	71
		U.S.A.	67	Turkey	46		
				Yemen	0		
Total	72	Total	80	Total	51	Fiji Isl.	0

Time Variation of the Percentage of Diplomas Obtained

The data listed in the third column of Table 2 are plotted as a time-series (Figure 1). The plot of this series can be approximated to a cyclic wave mounted on a linearly falling trend, which can be expressed by the equation

$$D' = 80.7 - 0.44 t \qquad (2)$$

where D' is the ordinate, in percent, of the trend line and t is the abscissa, which is the number of the course year (t=1 for 1966-67, 2 for 1967-68, ... 24 for 1989-90).

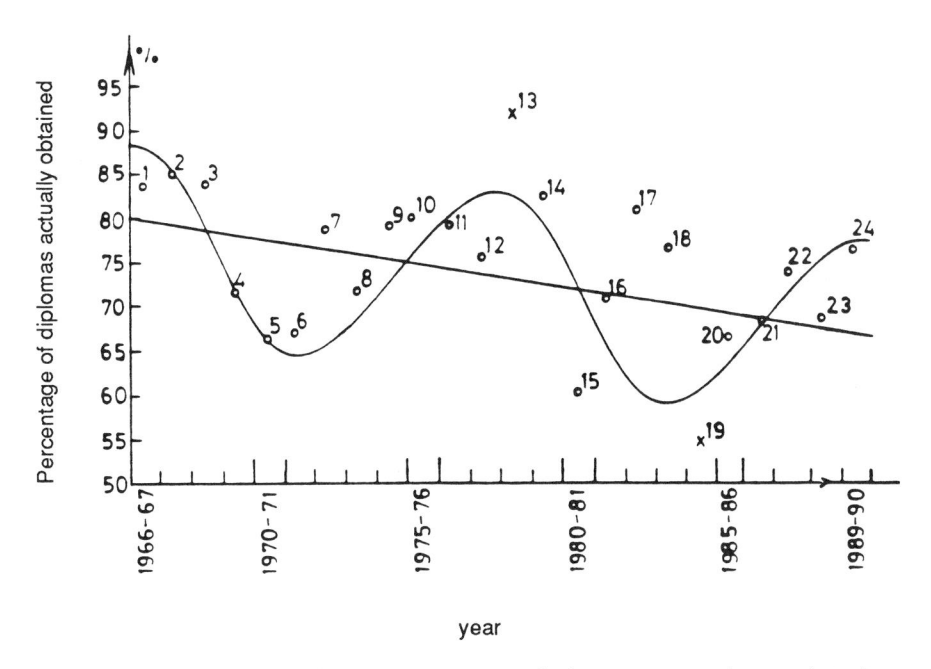

Figure 1. Variation of the percentage of diplomas obtained with time.

The heavy scatter of the points, especially in the second half of the series, does not justify the search for an exhaustive expression for the cyclic component in the series. A smooth curve, however, has been fitted to median and moving average points, with less emphasis on those years of extremely high and extremely low results. The cycle shows two trough points, spaced 14 years apart, with a peak point halfway. The rise of the peak point above the trend line, and the fall of each trough point below the same line, each amounts to 9%.

A further look to Tables 2 and 3 will show that two factors play a decisive role in the overall result: the country from which the participant comes, and the educational and practical background of the participant.

Country and Regional Variations

Table 3 shows that 84% of the participants coming from Europe obtain the diploma (54 out of 67), 81% from Asia (231 out of 284), 80% from North America (4 out of 5), 72% from Africa (78 out of 108), 71% from Central and South America (44 out of 62) and 51% from the Middle and Near East (59 out of 116).

Whereas the percentage of success in obtaining the diploma is low for the Middle and Near East participants, the favorable results extend themselves beyond Europe to several countries in Asia. Asian countries with more than 10 participants each score between 78% (Indonesia) and 100% (Sri Lanka).

Using the weight assigned to each country (Table 3) the number of diplomas for each year has been estimated. The percentage of diplomas estimated, pD_{ec}, is plotted against the percentage of diplomas actually obtained pD_a, and a straight line has been fitted (Figure 2). This line can be described as

$$pD_a = 2.546 (pD_{ec} - 44.06) \tag{3}$$

for the full length of the record. Excluding the years with extremely high and extremely low results, Eq (3) becomes

$$pD_a = 1.755 (pD_{ec} - 30.87) \tag{4}$$

bringing the coefficient of correlation from 0.608 to 0.686.

Equations (3) and (4) should be used only for prediction purposes and not as an argument against admission of applicants from specific regions.

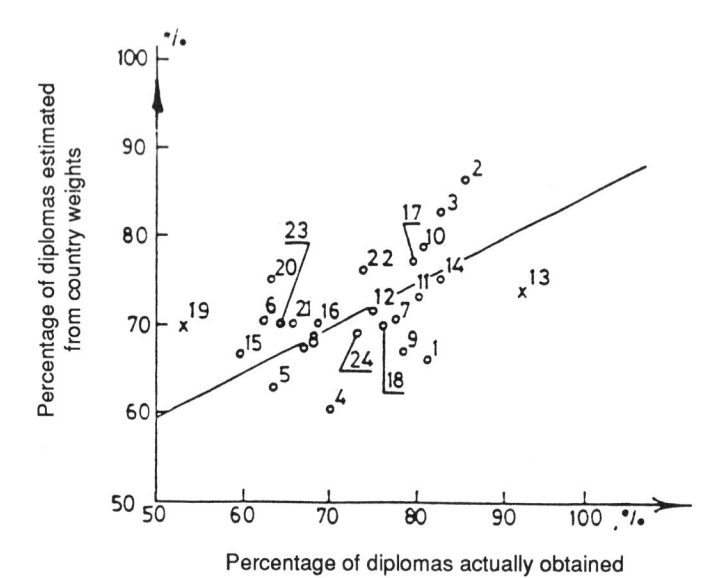

Figure 2. Percentage of estimated diplomas versus percentage of diplomas obtained.

Background Variation

The participants of the last 24 years can be subdivided into two general groups as far as their university education and practical experience are concerned. These are the engineering and the non-engineering background groups. The engineering group is mainly comprised of civil and agricultural engineers, hydrologists, mathematicians and physicists. The non-engineering group consists mainly of geologists, meteorologists and geographers. The percentage of diplomas obtained each year by the course participants (both backgrounds) is plotted versus the percentage of participants with an engineering background. After excluding a few points, a curved line has been fitted to the remaining points (Figure 3). This graph clearly shows that the overall result improves with an increasing percentage of participants with an engineering background. The averages for the 24 courses are: 74.1% for both groups combined, 80.4% for the engineering group (78.4% of the total) and 51.1% for the non-engineering group (21.6% of the total). In other words, the expected percentage of participants who will receive the diploma, pD, can be roughly expressed by the equation

$$pD = 80.4 P_e + 51.1 P_{ne} \tag{5}$$

or
$$pD = 51.1 + 29.3\, P_{ne} \tag{5'}$$

where P_e and P_{ne} are the ratios of the participants with engineering and non-engineering backgrounds, respectively.

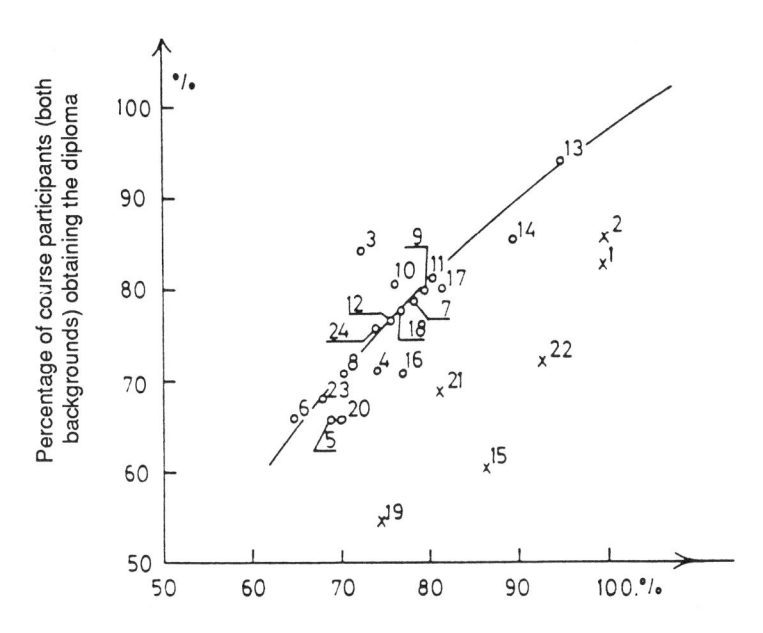

Percentage of participants with engineering background

Figure 3. Percentage of diplomas obtained versus percentage of participants with an engineering background

EVALUATION OF THE COURSE

In the previous sections we have tried to evaluate the response of the participants to the course requirements. It is essential to highlight the extent to which the current course is preparing the participants for the changing task of the hydrologist.

Changing Domain of Hydrology

Developments in the field of hydrology during the last decades have been caused by the increasing interference of man in the hydrological cycle. The repercussions of the human activities may better be predicted using simulation techniques.

The increased demand for quality water did not only increase the need for more basic research in the field of hydrology but it also resulted in significant developments in its related discipline of water resources planning and management. This discipline has at its disposal recently developed tools such as geographical information system (GIS), remote sensing techniques, and database management systems.

Hydrology is an applied geophysical science. Some of the participants study hydrology as a fundamental subject to increase their knowledge in a relevant field of research. The remaining participants continue to work as consulting engineers or government employees after completing their studies.

Restructuring of the Current Course

The new structure, which is to be implemented in October 1991, consists of three branches, each covering a specific discipline. These are: surface water hydrology, groundwater hydrology and water resources management.

Surface Water Hydrology - includes topics such as engineering hydrology, agricultural hydrology, deterministic and stochastic hydrology, hydrological modelling, river hydraulics, erosion and sedimentation, etc. These basic subjects are unavoidable for the proper design of hydraulic engineering works.

Groundwater hydrology - this branch embodies three main activities: hydrogeology, geohydrology including groundwater modelling, and groundwater chemistry. Emphasis should be on groundwater quality.

Water resources management - includes systems analysis, simulation and optimization techniques, policy and economic analyses, institutional development and environmental assessment.

The first two branches will provide a somewhat deeper specialization in surface water and groundwater hydrology. The water resources management branch, on the other hand, will tend to serve a broader field.

CONCLUSIONS AND RECOMMENDATIONS

i. The number of applicants to the course has remained almost stable for the last ten years. Nearly one out of three or four applicants receives a Dutch fellowship.

ii. The percentage of participants obtaining the diploma each year varies with time. The variation assumes the form of a cycle superposed on a falling trend.

iii. There is a distinct difference in the level of competence between the participants of the different geographic regions and between the participants of the different countries within each region.

iv. Participants with an engineering background have proven to be more able to successfully follow the course than those without an engineering background.

v. The success among the female participants (35 in total) is 76%. This percentage is almost the same as that of the male participants (609 in total), which is 74%.

vi. There seems to be a pressing need for a preparatory course for hydrologists, at least from certain countries. The same applies to applicants without an engineering background. Such a course must precede the international one.

vii. It is recommended to implement the planned restructuring of the current course in order to help every hydrologist carry out his/her tasks satisfactorily.

HYDROLOGY AND WATER RESOURCES EDUCATION AND TRAINING: THE CUIDES RESPONSE

John S. Miller, PH.D
University of Arkansas at Little Rock
Little Rock, Arkansas 72204

ABSTRACT

Since 1986 CUIDES (The Inter-American University Council for Economics and Social Development) has been working to establish a mechanism to encourage and facilitate the exchange of water resources expertise and technology in the Americas. As a first step toward establishing a focus on global water resources, CUIDES has inventoried water resources management expertise, in the Americas. The data base is being used to identify water resources issues, individuals and organizations who have expertise in water resources and a willingness to share that expertise internationally. The next phase involves exchanges, hemispheric conferences, seminars and the development of a innovative water resources curriculum. A key aim of CUIDES is to sharpen understanding as to ways in which universities, businesses, governments and research institutes can work together to address water related development issues on an inter-American scale. This includes research programs, exchanges and demonstration projects the CUIDES member institutions can undertake through cooperative efforts. Experience has shown that the networks that develop out of a joint action provide a basis for long-term shared commitments to address common stop-gap, solutions. Fresh insights are obtained by examining the same issue in a different cultural and economic setting.

HYDROLOGY AND WATER RESOURCES EDUCATION AND TRAINING: THE CUIDES RESPONSE

INTRODUCTION

Since 1986 the Office of International Programs at the University of Arkansas at Little Rock (UALR), the Land Stewardship Project at UALR and the Arkansas Water Resources Research Center at the University of Arkansas at Fayetteville (UAF) have been working to establish a mechanism to encourage and facilitate the exchange of expertise and technology in the Americas. In 1987 the Center for Urban Water Studies at Southern Methodist University (SMU) became a partner with UALR and UAF. CUIDES (The

Inter-American University Council for Economics and Social Development), the Autonomous University of Guadalajara (UAG), the International Water Resources Association and the University of Illinois, Water Resources Center began working with the consortium in 1988. In 1989 the Institute for Natural Resources at the University of Georgia became a partner.

Our work in establishing a mechanism for international exchange has been guided by several principles. First, given finite resources, a desire to contribute to the resolution of any hemispheric problem dictates a focus on a few, perhaps one hemispheric issue. And second, if there is a special focus on a single problem, it should be one of particular import for the inter-American region. Inter-American water resources represent a set of problems and issues of major consequence for both industrial and developing countries in the Americas.

The set of problems encompassed under the label water resources involves issues that are interdisciplinary in nature. One finds health related, economic, financial, scientific, technical, legal, ethical, social, political, religious, and aesthetic water problems and issues. Consequently, within universities, water issues research and expertise span school, college and department lines and outside the university they cross business sectors and agency lines and relate to people in a very broad range of disciplines and professions.

Water's interdisciplinary nature requires that if universities are to address water resources issues effectively, they must organize their resources campus-wide and link-up with other universities, the state and private sector. Consortia, such as CUIDES, can play a key role in encouraging and supporting such interdisciplinary linkages which focus attention and resources on inter-American issues.

WATER AS A GLOBAL AND HEMISPHERIC ISSUE

Water is certainly an issue of global and hemispheric importance. Today's water resources problems are global and interdependence is both a problem and a solution. Venezuela's President, Carlos Andres Perez, in an interview with *Time* magazine, identified three problems that effect the North and South equally: debt, drug trafficking and the environment. These three fundamental problems, Perez said, demand a broad and constructive dialogue in the hemisphere (Time, 1989).

An examination of current reliable data on world water resources makes interdependence clear. (Repetto, 1985; World Watch Institute, 1987, 1989, 1990 and 1991; World Resources Institute, 1989 and 1990) Solar energy and water maintain the life support systems on earth. Out of a total water volume of approximately 1.4 billion cubic kilometers, more than 97 percent is ocean water, unsuitable for human use. Of the three percent of the earth's water that is fresh, an estimated 77.2 percent of this is in "cold storage," frozen in ice caps and glaciers. Most of the remaining supplies of fresh water--22.4 percent--is groundwater and soil moisture. This leaves only a very small amount of surface freshwater--0.35 percent contained in lakes and swamps and less than 0.01 percent in rivers and streams. Obviously freshwater is a limited resource.

The hydrologic cycle does not spread water around in an equitable manner; it is unevenly distributed around the globe. In a general sense the world is divided into water surplus and water deficit regions. Most of Africa, much of the Middle East, the western United States and northwestern Mexico, parts of Chile and Argentina, and all of Australia are areas of severe water deficits.

The relative amount of water available for use in a particular area is also limited by the size of the population; the larger the population, the more people there are competing for water resources. In some areas of our hemisphere increased and competing demands have reached critical levels. Future projected growth in population will likely result in increasing cases of water shortage.

I think it is safe to predict that globally, and in the inter-American region, managing water demand, instead of increasing supplies, will become extremely important over the course of the next two decades. Water efficient technologies in agriculture and industry, along with conservation and water reuse strategies must be developed and widely used if a water crisis is to be avoided, especially in water-poor regions (Vlachos, 1990).

In fact, in September, 1989, in Costa Rica, the United Nations Development Program (UNDP) representatives from 24 Latin American and Caribbean countries met and agreed that there would be three priorities for UNDP in the 1990's: restoring growth in Latin America, a commitment to human development, and the protection and regeneration of the region's vast and diverse natural resources.

CUIDES RESPONSE

I do not think there is any doubt in any of our minds that water related issues will remain at the top of the political, economic, development and health agendas in the Inter-American Region. The nature and extent of water interdependencies has placed the inter-American region in the forefront in facing up to many of the dilemmas of development related to the unequal distribution of water resources. From our perspective, the good news is that water resources expertise in the region and the water problems we face, have placed our hemisphere in the forefront globally in addressing many of the dilemmas of development related to water resources. This coincidence of issues, concerns and expertise provides us with unlimited opportunity to play a role in addressing hemispheric and ultimately world water resources issues through planning, training, education and exchange.

As a first step toward establishing a focus on global water resources, the Arkansas Water Resources Research Center, the Land Stewardship Project and UALR's Office for International Programs in cooperation with CUIDES have inventoried water resources management expertise, research and needs in Arkansas, the Southwest and West Central Mexico (Jalisco). Nearly 300 individuals are listed in the data base representing a wide range of water related fields. Each of these individuals has indicated an interest in traveling to Latin America or hosting a Latin American colleague in the US or vice versa.

The data base is being used to identify water resources problems and individuals and organizations who have expertise pertaining to water related problems or issues and a willingness to share that expertise internationally. The first exchange took place in June 1988 when Dr. John S. Miller presented a week long seminar on Negotiation and Mediation in Guadalajara at the invitation of the Autonomous University. The second exchange took place in October 1988 when a five person team of water resources experts traveled to Guadalajara and Lake Chapala, Mexico to consult with local water officials and Autonomous University faculty on a wide range of water issues and proposals.

In April, 1989, Dr. Mike Collins of SMU, Dr. Andy Covington, of UALR, and Dr. Miller, at the invitation of the Universidad Regiomontana in Monterrey, Mexico made presentations at a CUIDES seminar on Water resources Issues in Mexico. Dr. Jose Reyes Sanchez, Chairperson of the Department of Irrigation, Autonomous University of Chapingo, at the invitation of Drs. Collins and Miller, visited Texas and Arkansas in December, 1989 as part of a USAID funded exchange arranged by the consortium. In January 1990, Dr. Miller and Dr. Ronald North, Director of the Institute for Natural Resources participated in the International Symposium on Water Management hosted by the Autonomous University of the Yucatan, Merida, Mexico.

Building on the exchanges and the information on needs and expertise contained in the data base, the next phase involves additional exchanges, hemispheric conferences and seminars, and the development of a innovative water resources curriculum. Based on discussions which took place in Tegucigalpa, Honduras, at the International Seminar on Water Resources Management, sponsored by CUIDES, UALR and the Autonomous University of Honduras, technical and engineering skills are abundant in Latin America. Management and leadership skills, however, are underdeveloped. The same is true in the United States, only on a smaller scale.

For the management of water and the management of increasingly large and complex water using systems, very little can be found in Latin America or the U.S. in the way of the systematic preparation in hydrology for water resources managers. Courses in hydrology that are offered are not usually directed toward management, but rather toward the scientific and technical aspects of water. (Grogan, et.al., 1988; Johnston, et.al, 1988). Specifically we have found some of the same deficiencies uncovered by Terence Lee in a United Nations study reported in the September 1988 issue of *Water Resources Development* (Lee, 1988):

1. vagueness in the decision-making system, commonly resulting in excessive slowness in reacting to management issues;

2. reductionism, or a tendency to reduce the definition of the water management system to the construction of physical water control and distribution works;

3. a preoccupation with the solution of immediate, short-run and local issues at the cost of a longer view of operational and economic efficiency;

4. the adoption of a generally passive management style;

5. the maintenance of inappropriate or obsolete management structures and style;

6. a need to fully consider that water systems are important social institutions as well as productive enterprises;

7. a failure to fully consider and appreciate the social impact of project decisions and the ethical dilemmas posed by some decisions.

What we found in Latin America in terms of water management and administration skills is also true in the US. There are few courses and fewer degree programs in the US which emphasize water management. Based on our discussions we believe hydrology education in the US and Latin America does a poor job in preparing graduates to deal with nontechnical issues and nontechnical professionals they encounter on the job and with the rapid pace of change that is occurring in the environment in which hydrologists operate.

The practice of hydrology does not depend on turning in homework like assignments, but on the completion of projects on time. Such projects require not only mastery of the technical disciplines, but also command of verbal and written communication skills, administration and management skills and an ability to think critically.

Further, few hydrologists remain strictly within their original disciplines after 8-10 years or so. Successful hydrologists move into management, consulting and/or open their own business. They then must work directly with other professionals, regulatory agencies, businesses and the general public. In other words higher education in hydrology must assist in preparing graduates for managerial and administrative leadership and social responsibility.

No one questions the need for a foundation in science, engineering and hydrology fundamentals. What we find in Latin America and the US, however, is a need to devise an integrated multi-disciplinary educational curriculum that while continuing to develop an essential base of engineering and hydrologic knowledge, would require students to synthesize information, transfer ideas from one environment to another, communicate effectively, formulate approaches to complex problems, locate and appreciate new information and perspectives and understand other people and their priorities and values.

In response to these needs in Latin America, CUIDES is preparing a concept paper on the feasibility of a multi-disciplinary water resources management/administration program. This concept paper will also serve as a point of departure for discussions concerning the feasibility of establishing a CUIDES Water Studies Center at a CUIDES member institution in Latin America.

A second initiative focuses on training. Dr. Ronald North, Director of the Institute for Natural Resources at the University of Georgia, Dr. Michael Collins, Director of the Urban Water Center, Southern Methodist University, and Dr. Miller have prepared a list of short courses which can be offered through CUIDES member university continuing education programs or integrated into the current curriculum. These short courses focus on the water technician or engineer as a **manager** and can lead to a permanent CUIDES supported program in the field of Water Resources Management for cooperating universities.

Examples of some of the proposed courses include:

PLANNING AND DECISION MAKING

Economic Decision Theory
Water Resources Project Planning and Development
Environmental and Social
Impact Assessment

WATER RESOURCES PROJECT OPERATION AND MANAGEMENT

Devising Operating Rules for Reservoir Operations
Water Distribution Operation and Control
Water Supply Planning and
Development

WATER QUALITY MANAGEMENT AND CONTROL

Strategies of Pollution Control
Social Impacts of Environmental Degradation
Recycling and Reuse of
Municipal and Industrial Wastes

AN AGENDA FOR ACTION

To be viable, a university focus on any global issue requires a commitment from faculty in many fields and the leadership of the Rector/President. Likewise, due to limited resources and expertise, such an undertaking must include support and participation from the private and public sectors and other colleges and universities. A key aim of CUIDES is to sharpen understandings as to ways in which universities, businesses, governments and research institutes can work together to address water related development issues on an inter-American scale. A second and closely related purpose is to further develop a water resources agenda. That is, research programs, exchanges and demonstration projects the CUIDES member institutions can undertake through joint and other cooperative efforts.

What has become apparent over the past several decades is that international exchange and cooperation can benefit all those concerned with water related issues. Exchanges and seminars facilitate the development of agendas for collective action and assist in identifying priorities for action. Experience has shown that the networks that develop out of joint action provide a basis for long-term shared commitments to address common problems, as opposed to short-term stop-gap solutions. Fresh insights into our own domestic problems are obtained by examining the same issue in a different cultural and economic setting.

Finally, it is important to remember we do not inherit the land and water from our ancestors, we borrow it from our children. Wise management of our water resources and the protection of water quality are intimately linked to a number of objectives we all share for our hemisphere: the alleviation of poverty, achievement and maintenance of sustainable economic growth, promotion of public health, attention to the pressures of rapid population expansion, and the ensuring of long-term political and economic stability. UALR Chancellor James Young, President of CUIDES, has challenged CUIDES membership to become partners in developing a "global leadership institute." Chancellor Young's vision is supportive of and a natural outgrowth of CUIDES efforts thus far in Water Resources Management.Clearly, the challenges we face in water resources management in this hemisphere can be met only if concerted efforts are made. Our hope is that the work we have begun will facilitate such a response. As we begin I am reminded of the words of the great Indian political and spiritual leader Mohandas K. Gandhi:

"The means may be likened to a seed, and there is just the same inviolable connection between the means and the end as there is between the seed and the tree."

CUIDES looks forward to working with its inter-American friends as we together develop our plans and see this seed germinate and mature.

REFERENCES

Day, H. (1989). "Water Resources Educational Issues: The United States and Developing Nations," *Water Resources Bulletin,* Vol. 25, No. 6 (Dec): v-vl.

Grogan, William R., L.E. Schachterle and C. Lutz. (1988). "Liberal Learning in Engineering Education: The WPI Experience," in P. Hutchings and A. Wutzdorff (eds.), *Knowing and Doing Through Experience,* New Directions for Teaching and Learning, No. 35. San Francisco: Jossey-Bass.

Lee, Terence R. (1988). "The Evolution of Water Management in Latin America," in *Water Resources Development,* Vol. 4, No. 3, September: 160-168.

Johnston, Joseph S., Susan Shaman and Robert Zensbrey (1988). *Unfinished Design:* The Humanities and Social Sciences in Undergraduate Engineering Education, Association of American Colleges.

Repetto, Robert (ed.) (1985). *The Global Possible.* Yale University Press: New Haven.

World Resources Institute. (1988-91). *World Resources,* Basic Books, Inc.: New York.

World Watch Institute. (1989-91), *The State of the World,* W. W. Norton and Co.: New York.

Vlachos, E. M. (1990). "Water, Peace and Conflict Management," *Water International,* Vol. 15, No. 4: 185-188.

THE VADOSE ZONE: AN EDUCATIONAL FRONTIER IN HYDROLOGY

J.M.H. Hendrickx,
F.M. Phillips, J.L. Wilson, and R.S. Bowman
Hydrology Program
Department of Geoscience
New Mexico Tech
Socorro, NM 87801

ABSTRACT

Education and training in hydrology are emphasizing the study of groundwater hydrology and surface hydrology. Especially in arid regions such as New Mexico, the core of the hydrology curriculum was formed by groundwater hydrology. Recent concern for the quality of groundwater and a growing awareness of the limited supplies of groundwater have induced an interest in the study of groundwater contamination and recharge processes in the vadose zone. Therefore, education and training in vadose zone hydrology become more important and hydrology curricula should reflect this shift in emphasis. In this paper we present evidence that the vadose zone has been somewhat overlooked by hydrology educators. Then we depict a few examples of the importance of vadose zone hydrology in arid regions and describe in which manner the Hydrology Program at New Mexico Tech expanded its emphasis from pure groundwater hydrology to a program which addresses not only ground- and surface water, but also the processes in the vadose zone.

INTRODUCTION

Worldwide there is growing concern about the quantity and quality of water which is needed for the provision of irrigation water, industrial water and drinking water for ever increasing populations. Not only in arid regions but even in temperate climates good quality water is becoming a scarcer commodity.

For example, a national survey in the Netherlands identified more than 4000 sites where soil and groundwater might already be polluted by hazardous wastes. Because many of these sites are situated in the infiltration areas of groundwater pumping stations for public water supplies, the quality of the groundwater is deteriorating faster than previously has been assumed (Ginjaar 1989). In many developing countries, surveys can often not be conducted so that groundwater pollution remains hidden. In Quetta Valley (Pakistan) the quantity of water is already a serious problem but it is expected that the increasing population of man and animal will cause a major quality problem in the near future. Unfortunately, the deterioration of groundwater quality can only be deducted from Total Dissolved Solids because bacteriological and chemical analysis are limited. The T.D.S. values increased from 500 ppm in 1973 to 1000 ppm in 1980. In 1986, water samples collected near areas with a pollution source exhibited a T.D.S. range between 1500 and 3250 ppm (Ghory 1986).

These examples show that the filtering capacity of the soil in the vadose zone between the soil surface and groundwater is often not sufficient to safeguard the quality of the groundwater. Therefore, it is necessary for the protection of the quality of the groundwater to take into account the processes which affect the flow of water and the transport of contaminants through the vadose zone.

Although many studies in the vadose zone deal with problems related to groundwater quality, it should not be overlooked that the processes in the vadose zone also play an important role when water quantity is an issue. Often groundwater is managed with insufficient knowledge of recharge rates which may result in a decrease of the groundwater table depth when excess quantities of water are pumped out the aquifer. Even relatively small decreases may have a large ecological impact in situations where capillary rise provides water to natural vegetation or agricultural crops during periods with a soil moisture deficit. In the Netherlands there is concern that lowering of the relatively shallow groundwater table may result in permanent damage to natural ecosystems and cause yield reductions of agricultural crops. In more arid regions where a deep groundwater table is used to supply water for irrigated crops, lowering of the groundwater table through overpumping may cause pumping costs to increase to a point where profitable agriculture becomes very difficult. This has happened in the Central Valley of California, in Arizona, and on the High Plains of New Mexico and Texas where the Ogallala Aquifer was overpumped.

In many irrigated areas of the world rising water tables are a concern, because these cause valuable lands to become saline and sodic. For example, in the Indus Valley in Pakistan near Faisalabad the water table depth decreased from approximately 20 m to close to the surface in approximately fifty years (Ahmad and Chaudhry 1988). In the Draa Valley of Morocco the water table depth decreased from 6 m in the sixties to less than 1 m in the eighties (Bazza 1990). Such undesirable decreases of water table depth could be prevented by improved water management based on an understanding of hydrological processes in the vadose zone.

In the field of surface water hydrology a good understanding of the physical processes in the vadose zone will help to quantify the mechanism of infiltration and subsurface runoff (Anderson and Burt 1990).

The objective of this paper is to present evidence that the vadose zone is an educational frontier in hydrology and to show in which manner the Hydrology Program at New Mexico Tech addresses this educational challenge.

DISCUSSION OF VADOSE ZONE HYDROLOGY IN TEXTBOOKS

To obtain a reasonably unbiased view of the attention which vadose zone hydrology receives from educators we decided to evaluate a number of hydrology textbooks. The criteria for selection of these books were:

(A) the word hydrology should be in the title, but without indication that the book is dealing with 'groundwater hydrology' or 'surface hydrology' (i.e. such titles were omitted);

(B) the book should be written as a textbook for students with an interest in hydrology (i.e. proceedings and advanced treatises were also omitted);

(C) the book should be available at New Mexico Tech.

Criterion (A) indicates implicitly to the potential readers that - according to the title- the book claims to deal with all aspects of hydrology. Therefore, one may expect a proper introduction to groundwater, surface water, and vadose zone hydrology. Criterion (B) makes sure that the authors discuss all the basics which they consider important for hydrology without omission. Criterion (C) was a logistical necessity.

In each book we counted the number of pages which were dealing with water retention and water movement through the vadose zone. Next, we expressed this number as a percentage of the total number of pages in the book so that we could compare different texts. The results of this survey are given in Table 1. Although we do not claim to have conducted a scientific survey, the data indicate clearly that the vadose zone receives less attention than it deserves. Only the books of Eagleson, Gray and Ward discuss in some detail the processes of water storage and movement in the vadose zone. None of the books include a complete discussion of solute and contaminant movement through the vadose zone. Therefore, we conclude that educators so far have for the most part neglected to include the physical processes in the vadose zone into hydrology textbooks. Because many undergraduate hydrology students will not be exposed to more hydrology than the average textbook offers, the omission of vadose zone hydrology in textbooks may lead to the neglect of vadose zone processes in the real world.

Two reasons may explain why the vadose zone did not procure the attention which it deserves. First, many authors of hydrology textbooks written before the eighties opted not to include discussions of groundwater contamination through the vadose zone and considered the net outcome of the recharge or capillary rise processes in the vadose zone as a given quantity. This view is expressed, for example, by Kazmann (1972, p. 157): "Of only minor concern to the groundwater hydrologist is subsurface water that moves in response to capillary forces, water that moves under conditions of partial saturation (vadose water) in porous media above the zone of saturation, or water bound to the internal groundwater hydrology program. It is felt that these examples are typical for many arid and semi-arid zones in the world.

Unstable Wetting Fronts in the Vadose Zone: In many different environments one-dimensional models have predicted negligible risk of groundwater contamination due to sufficient residence time in the vadose zone. However, it is found now that significant pollution of the groundwater has occurred where these models predicted none. The surfaces of a soil or rock complex by the forces of molecular attraction. It is only when, under special circumstances, such water adds to or subtracts from the main body of groundwater that it becomes briefly, the object of study". Second, there was and is not much hydrological information available on the unsaturated subsoil below a depth of approximately 1.2 meters -this depth is the survey depth used in most soil surveys all over the world - so that many authors did not have

TABLE 1. Discussion of Vadose Zone Hydrology in Textbooks.

Year	Title	Authors	Total No. of pages (TN)	Pages on Unsat. Flow (UP)	UP/TP
1928	The Elements of Hydrology	A.F. Meyer	522	6	.01
1957	Engineering Hydrology	S.S. Butler	350	18	.05
1970	Dynamic Hydrology	P.S. Eagleson	462	45	.10
1971	Regional Hydrology Fundamentals	R.A. Deju	204	2	.01
1972	Modern Hydrology	R.G. Kazmann	370	3	.01
1973	Handbook on Principles of Hydrology	D.M. Gray (Ed.)	570	55	.10
1975	Principles of Hydrology	R.C. Ward	360	50	.14
1975	Hydrology for Engineers	R.K. Linsley, M.A. Kohler, and J.L.H. Paulhus	482	16	.03
1975	Hydrology for Engineers and Planners	A.T. Hjehmfelt and J.J. Cassidy	210	5	.02
1976	Systematic Hydrology	J.C. Rodda, R.A. Downing, and F.M. Law	399	35	.09
1985	Hydrology	H.M. Raghunath	482	15	.03
1988	Applied Hydrology	Ven Te Chow, D.R. Maidment, and L.W. Mays	572	25	.04
1989	Introduction to Hydrology	W. Viessman, G.L. Lewis, and J.W. Knapp	780	14	.04
1990	Hydrology	R.L. Bras	643	43	.07

sufficient material to write about. We feel that this second reason is more important than the first one. Bannink et al. (1988) and Hendrickx et al. (1988a, 1990) show in which manner qualitative information of soil surveys can be used to quantify agrohydrological processes but unfortunately most soil surveys do not survey below a depth of 1.2 to 1.5 meters.

On the other hand, most geohydrological surveys go much deeper but without the detail needed to quantify water movement in the vadose zone. As many transient hydrological processes seem to occur in the vadose zone below a depth of 1.5 meters, there exists a major gap of physical data for quantification of the hydrological processes in the vadose zone. This gap caused the vadose zone to be a twilight zone in hydrology. Fortunately, nowadays soil physicists are leaving the root zone to dig deeper into the vadose zone and hydrologists are departing the capillary fringe into the lower part of the vadose zone. The results of these efforts are reflected already in the hydrological journals and it is expected that new hydrology textbooks will have the material to discuss vadose zone hydrology adequately.

EDUCATION IN VADOSE ZONE HYDROLOGY AT NEW MEXICO TECH

The hydrology program at the Department of Geoscience of the New Mexico Institute for Mining and Technology is primarily concerned with education and research in groundwater hydrology. The first two directors of the New Mexico Tech hydrology program were Mahdi Hantush and Charles E. Jacob, the founders of modern well hydraulics. Their terms of office covered the first 16 years of our existence, from 1954 until 1970. In the seventies and eighties the program was directed by Lynn Gelhar who, with Allan Gutjahr, led the development of the field of stochastic groundwater hydrology. In 1984 John Wilson replaced Dr. Gelhar as director of the hydrology program.

Many important papers in the field of groundwater hydrology were written in Socorro, including most of Hantush's fundamental contributions to well hydraulics and the theory of leaky aquifers, and Gelhar and Gutjahr's papers in stochastic groundwater flow and pollutant transport. These publications indicate that groundwater hydrology was and is the main emphasis of the hydrology program. Nevertheless, the developments in groundwater hydrology made it necessary to expand the study of vadose hydrology in our program. Therefore, we want to present in this section a few vadose zone studies which are carried out at New Mexico Tech to support our cause for these cases of groundwater contamination is presumably the occurrence of preferential flow paths in the vadose zone.

Such preferential flow paths can be caused by macropores such as cracks in swelling soils or old root channels, spatial variability of hydraulic conductivity, or by the occurrence of unstable wetting fronts. A stable wetting front is a horizontal wetting front which moves downward without breaking into fingers. The behavior of such a front can be simulated with one-dimensional computer models. Unstable wetting fronts start out as horizontal wetting fronts which under certain conditions break into 'fingers' or 'preferential flow paths' as the front moves downward, much like rain running off a sheet of glass breaking into streams. These fingers facilitate the transport of contaminants to the groundwater at velocities many times those calculated if a stable horizontal front is assumed. For example, Hendrickx et al. (1988b) measured in a bromide tracer experiment that after five weeks with 120 mm precipitation bromide concentrations in the groundwater are six to thirteen times higher under unstable wetting fronts than under stable wetting fronts.

The conditions under which unstable wetting fronts in field soils form are not yet fully understood. Recently developed soil physical theories (Glass et al. 1989; Hillel and Baker 1988; Philip 1975a,b; Raats 1973; Tabuchi 1961) and experimental evidence (Glass et al. 1987; Hendrickx et al. 1988; Hendrickx et al. 1989; Hill and Parlange 1972) indicate that fingers caused by unstable wetting fronts will occur in water repellent soils and in layered soils where the hydraulic conductivity increases with depth. For non-ponding infiltration in dry homogeneous soils without layering some theories predict fingers to occur (Raats 1973) and some theories predict fingers not to occur (Philip 1975a). Experimental evidence however, shows that fingers do indeed occur in single layered homogeneous soils during non-ponding infiltration (Hagerman et al. 1989; Selker et al. 1989). It appears that the occurrence of fingers is especially likely in dry soils such as found in New Mexico and elsewhere in the arid regions of North America.

For example, Hendrickx et al. (to be published) found that 400 mm natural precipitation in an initial dry wettable sand wetted only 15% of the total soil volume. The remaining 85% of the soil was not wetted and remained dry. Jan Hendrickx and his graduate students are conducting field and laboratory experiments to determine in which manner unstable wetting front theories can be applied for the prediction of wetting front instabilities in New Mexico's dry desert soils.

Chemical Aspects of Preferential Flow Processes in the Vadose Zone: For the past eight years, Robert Bowman and his graduate students have conducted experiments on non-ideal flow and transport in field soils under irrigated agricultural conditions. The research has shown that, under intermittent ponding (the primary water application method in arid region agriculture), mean downward velocities of recharge water can exceed (by a factor of two to five) velocities calculated from classical miscible displacement theory.

This behavior has been observed even in unstructured soils which show no evidence of cracks, wormholes, or other macroscopic structural features usually associated with non-ideal flow. We have conducted quantitative studies with nonreactive water tracers as well as qualitative visualization experiments using sorbing dyes. Based on this work, we believe that preferential flow paths develop on a microscopic scale in non-structured media due to slight differences in pore configurations and/or due to instability-induced fingering when irrigation water invades drier subsoil (Bowman and Rice, 1986a; Rice et al., 1986).

A major current area of interest is how such preferential flow affects the behavior of reactive chemicals, i e. those which are subject to processes such as sorption and degradation. Generally, reactive chemical behavior is evaluated in laboratory experiments, and the derived parameters (such as sorption coefficients) incorporated into transport models to predict solute fate in a defined flow regime. Our work indicates that, at least for sorption, laboratory derived data can be used to accurately predict reactive solute transport even under preferential flow conditions if the flow regime is adequately characterized (Bowman and Rice, 1986b).

Application of Isotopes in Vadose Zone Hydrology: Although vadose zone hydrology has in general been neglected, the neglect is even more severe when the vadose zone in arid regions is considered. One of the reasons for this is the very slow rate of soil-water processes under the dry conditions in desert soils. Research and education at New Mexico Tech has attempted to address this problem by using environmental tracers for the movement of water in arid vadose zones. The use of 36Cl as a tracer for soil water was developed at Tech in the 1980's (Phillips et al., 1988). Both 36Cl and 3H are radionuclides released into the atmosphere by nuclear weapons testing in the 1950's and 1960's. Tritium (3H) is incorporated into the water molecule whereas 36Cl is a conservative solute.

Our studies (Phillips et al., 1987; Phillips et al., 1988; Phillips et al., 1990) have shown that even though the main pulse of tritium entered the soil one decade after the 36Cl pulse, the tritium is found deeper in the vadose zone. This difference in transport is attributed to thermally-driven vapor transport of the tritiated water and suggests that vapor transport may be much more important in desert soils than has been previously thought. The importance of vapor transport has been supported by subsequent stable-isotope studies (Knowlton 1990). The most recent isotopic tracing work by Fred Phillips and his graduate students has suggested that modern recharge rates through desert soils in the American Southwest are more than an order of magnitude less than during the most recent glacial period and that the vadose zone regime is still adjusting to the shift in climatic boundary conditions. These results may aid in prediction of the effects of human-induced global climate change.

Application of Micromodels for the Study of Multiphase Flow: Micromodels are physical models of a pore space created by etching mirror image pore patterns onto two glass plates, which are then fused in a furnace. The pattern is two dimensional, although the pores are three dimensional. Flow and transport can be observed visually on both bulk and pore scales; and recorded on film or videotape. The models can be used in research and education to improve understanding of basic processes. For example, a model of the vadose zone would start with a vertically orientated water saturated micromodel, that is drained with air. The resulting water or moisture distribution can be recorded and qualitatively analyzed using image processing.

John Wilson and his graduate students use micromodels to study simultaneous flow of water and non-aqueous phase liquids (NAPL) in the vadose zone. In these studies the NAPL is introduced at the top of the model and the NAPL redistribution is observed. Various remediation schemes can be tested. In one case we contrasted the behavior of "spreading" and "non-spreading" NAPL's, such as gasoline and carbon tetrachloride, respectively. The spreading NAPL forms a thin film between the capillary held water and the air, whereas the non-spreading, NAPL coalesced into isolated pockets and tiny lenses floating at the air-water interface (Wilson, 1990). Mass transfer coefficients, important to remediation approaches, such as vacuum extraction, must certainly be different for spreading and non-spreading NAPL's. We also observed a greater propensity for gravity fingering of the non-spreading NAPL, caused by the somewhat lower capillarity associated with the non-spreading behavior. The non-spreading NAPL behavior is similar to the behavior of infiltrating water into a hydrophobic soil.

SUMMARY

In this contribution we have presented evidence which helps explain the neglect of vadose zone hydrology in many hydrology textbooks and shown that a good understanding of the processes in the vadose zone is necessary for proper management and protection of groundwater quantity and quality. The vadose zone studies conducted in the hydrology program at New Mexico Tech are examples of investigations relevant for arid and semi-arid zone hydrology programs.

REFERENCES

Ahmad, N., and G.R. Chaudhry. 1988. *Irrigated Agriculture of Pakistan*. Publ. Nazir, Lahore, Pakistan. pp. 600.

Anderson, M.G., and T.P. Burt. 1990. *Subsurface Runoff*. In: M.G. Anderson and T.P. Burt (Eds.), *Process Studies in Hillslope Hydrology*, John Wiley and Sons, New York. pp. 365-400.

Bannink, M.H., J.M.H. Hendrickx, and B.J. Bles. 1988. *Quantitative Evaluation of Large Areas in Respect of Vulnerability to Moisture Deficit*. Soil Survey and Land Evaluation 8:47-63.

Bazza, M. 1990. *Salinity Problems in the Draa Valley of Morocco: Urgent Need for Drainage*. Proc. Symposium on Land Drainage for Salinity Control in Arid and Semi-Arid Regions, Cairo, Egypt. Febr. 25 - March 2, 1990. pp. 76-88.

Bowman, R.S. and R.C. Rice. 1986a. *Transport of Conservative Tracers in the Field Under Intermittent Flood Irrigation*. Water Resour. Res. 22:1531-1536.

Bowman, R.S., and R.C. Rice. 1986b. *Accelerated Herbicide Leaching Resulting From Preferential Flow Phenomena and its Implications for Groundwater Contamination*. p. 413-425. In Proc. FOCUS Conf. on Southwestern Groundwater Issues, 20-22 Oct. 1986, Phoenix, AZ. Natl. Water Well Assoc. Dublin, OH.

Ghory, M.S.K. 1986. *Pollution in Groundwater of Quetta Valley (Pakistan)*. Hydrogeology Project, WAPDA, Quetta. pp. 10.

Ginjaar, L. 1989. *Opening Address*. In: G. Jousma, J. Bear, Y.Y. Haimes, and F. Walter. Proc. Intern. Conf. on Groundwater Contamination: Use of models in decision-making, Amsterdam, The Netherlands, 26-29 October. pp. 3-5.

Glass, R.J. T.S. Steenhuis, and J.-Y. Parlange. 1987. *Water Infiltration in Layered Soils Where a Fine Textured Layer Overlays a Coarse Sand*. Proc. Int. Conf. for Infiltration Developm. and Applic., Jan 5-9, Hawaii.

Glass, R.J., T.S. Steenhuis, and J.-Y. Parlange. 1989. *Wetting Front Instability: 1. Theoretical Discussion and Dimensional Analysis*. Water

Resour. Res. 25:1187-1194.

Hagerman, J.R., N.B. Pickering, W.F. Ritter, and T.S. Steenhuis. 1989. *In Situ Measurement of Preferential Flow*. ASCE National Water Conference and Symposium, Newark, Delaware. pp. 10.

Hendrickx, J.M.H., L.W. Dekker, M.H. Bannink, and H.C. van Ommen. 1988a. *Significance of Soil Survey for Agrohydrological Studies*. Agric. Water Manage. 14:195-208

Hendrickx, J.M.H., L.W. Dekker, E.J. Van Zuilen, and O.H. Boersma. 1988b. *Water and Solute Movement Through a Water Repellent Sand Soil With Grasscover*. pp. 131-146. In: Wierenga, P.J. and D. Bachelet. 1988. Validation of flow and transport models for the unsaturated zone: Conference Proceedings; May 23-26, 1988 Ruidoso, New Mexico. Research Report 88-55-04 Dept. of Agronomy and Horticulture, New Mexico State University, Las Cruces, N.M. 545 p.

Hendrickx, J.M.H., M. Akram Chaudhry, J.W. Kijne, M. Sadiq, and Iqbal Raza. 1990. *Soil Physical Measurements for Drainage Design in Arid Regions*. Symposium on Land Drainage for Salinity Control in Arid and Semi-Arid Regions, Febr. 25-March 2, Cairo, Egypt. Vol. 2:124-134.

Hill, D.E., and J.-Y. Parlange. 1972. *Wetting front instability in layered soils*. Soil Sci. Soc. Am. Proc. 36:697-702.

Hillel, D., and R.S. Baker. 1988. *A descriptive theory of fingering during infiltration into layered soils*. Soil Sci. 146: 51- 56.

Kazmann, R.C. 1972. *Modern hydrology*. Harper & Row, New York. pp. 365.

Knowlton, R.G. 1990. *A stable isotope study of water and chloride movement in natural desert soils*. Ph.D. thesis, New Mexico Institute of Mining and Technology, Socorro, New Mexico, U.S.A.

Philip, J.R. 1975a. *Stability analysis of infiltration*. Soil Sci. Soc. Am. Proc. 39:1042-1049.

Philip, J.R. 1975b. *The growth of disturbances in unstable infiltration flows*. Soil Sci. Soc. Am. Proc. 39:1049-1053.

Phillips, F.M., Mattick, J.L., Duval, T.A., Elmore, N., and Kubik, P.W. 1988. *Chlorine-36 and tritium from nuclear weapons fallout as tracers for long-term liquid and vapor movement in desert soils*. Water Resour. Res. 25:141-145.

Phillips, F.M., Davis, S.N., and Kubik, P.W. 1990. *A proposal to use chlorine-36 for monitoring the movement of radionuclides from nuclear explosions*. Ground Water Monitoring Review 10(3) 106-113.

Phillips, F.M., Mattick, J.L., and Duval, T.A. 1987. *Implications of bomb-^{36}Cl and tritium studies for ground water recharge and contaminant transport through the vadose zone*. In Ground Water Management (Proc. 32nd Annual New Mexico Water Conf Albuquerque, 5-6 Nov., 1987)

New Mexico Water Resources Research Institute Report Number 229, Las Cruces, p. 124-130.

Raats, P.A. C. 1973. *Unstable wetting fronts in uniform and nonuniform soils.* Soil Sci. Soc. Am. Proc. 37:681-685.

Rice, R.C., R.S. Bowman, and D.B. Jaynes. 1986. *Percolation of water below an irrigated field.* Soil Sci. Soc. Am. J. 50:855-859.

Selker, J.S., T.S. Steenhuis, and J.-Y. Parlange. 1989. *Preferential flow in homogeneous sandy soils without layering.* Paper No. 89-2543, Am. Soc. Agric. Eng., Winter Meeting, New Orleans. pp. 22.

Tabuchi, T. 1961. *Infiltration and ensuing percolation in columns of layered glass particles packed in laboratory* (In Japanese, with a summary in English). Nogyo dobuku kenkyn, Bessatsu (Trans. Agr. Eng. Soc., Japan) 1;13-19.

Wilson, J.L. 1990. *Pore Scale Behavior of Spreading and Non-spreading Organic Liquids in the Vadose Zone.* Proceedings of Subsurface Contamination by Immiscible Fluids, IAH, (Calgary, Alberta, Canada).

ON THE STATUS OF EDUCATION AND TRAINING IN THE HYDROLOGIC SCIENCES, JAMAICA, WEST INDIES

J.R. Nuckols
Department of Environmental Health
Colorado State University
Fort Collins, Colorado, USA 00523

ABSTRACT

As we go into the 21st century, more and more third world nations will make environmental protection a priority in their national agenda. Education and training programs in the hydrologic sciences are essential to achieve these national goals. The purpose of this paper is to assess the evolution and status of education and training in the hydrologic sciences in the island nation of Jamaica, West Indies. The paper also explores the issue of international political boundaries as a barrier to technology transfer and knowledge applications, and what measures can be taken to overcome this problem.

BACKGROUND

I want to set the record straight from the beginning of this paper that I do not pretend to be an expert on the educational system in Jamaica. Indeed, this paper should be viewed as an attempt by a professional in the field of hydrologic sciences to ascertain the status of education, in a global context, for his chosen field. In this effort, I have tried to determine how this status was achieved, placing it in the context of a world view, and to share my personal observations and philosophy as to the issues that beg to be addressed as we enter a new era in global politics.

Jamaica is in many ways an ideal laboratory from which to study the hydrologic sciences. From the perspective of an earth scientist, it is a natural system with well-defined boundaries. Jamaica is one of four larger islands in the Northern Caribbean Sea and is located about 90 miles south of Cuba and 490 miles southeast of the United States of America. Although small in geographic terms, approximately 4,350 square miles, the island has abundant water resources. Native indians first called the island "Xamayca," "land of wood and water" (Lawson, 1977) 80% of the island receives an annual rainfall of between 50 and 100 inches, with the mean annual rainfall being 78 inches. By personal account, no less than 65 fresh water streams drain the surface of the island.

Historically, the major drainages have been described as "teeming" with aquatic life (Strachan, 1910). The major river basins head up in rugged interior mountains with elevations ranging from 2,000 to 7,000+ feet. The coastal areas into which these rivers drain vary from coral reef ecosystems to swampy, mangrove—fringed wetlands. The human population of the island is approximately 2.5 Million. Generally speaking, the land-use in each river basin can be described as sparsely populated agricultural lands in the headwaters, with population density increasing as the rivers approach the coastal zone.

From the perspective of a social or political scientist, or an educational planner, Jamaica also serves well as a model for study as a Third World country. The human population in Jamaica primarily descends from a slave population with African roots emancipated under British law in the mid-19th Century. The country obtained independent nation status in 1962. This population evolved under the rule of adherents to a European world view based on the belief that the unbridled exploitation of nature was the inalienable right of individuals (Beaty and Johnson, 1971). Jamaica is hardly alone in terms of suffering this exploitation nor in seeking political from the world powers which instilled this view.

Between 1945 and 1970, virtually the entire colonial world was to rise up, demand, and secure political independence. Flags of independence were to rise in more than 100 national capitals with a total population exceeding 11.5 billion people (Manley, 1982). If today we add the events that are transpiring in Eastern Europe, the significance of change in world order is impressive, to say the least. The purpose of this paper is to explore possible consequences of this change in terms of needs for education and training in the hydrologic sciences. Jamaica will be used as the model for analysis of these consequences.

STATUS OF EDUCATION AND TRAINING

Like most of the other colonial populations worldwide, education was almost entirely neglected, with the exception being the minority population of the ruling class. In the Eighteenth Century, some charitable education was provided to the local poor by the wealthy residents. However, "poor" in this case meant as a rule poor white or slightly coloured children (Black, 1972). With regard to slaves, the only external training they received (or were allowed) was such as would increase or improve their labor (ibid). The term "external" was used because there appears to be increasing evidence that an "internal" education process was ongoing within the slave population during the Colonial Period (Alleyne, 1988). Although much of this training was in regards to religious and cultural aspects of their African heritage, it should not be ignored in consideration of educational goals for the society that evolved from this period.

Emancipation in 1838 did little to improve the education of the masses in Jamaica primarily due to the cost of education, which was out of reach for most of the population. By 1883 it was estimated that less than 10% of the population was literate (Black, 1972). In 1892 elementary education was free and conditions began to improve. It was about this time that the development of technical education had its beginning (ibid).

As recently as 1973, secondary and higher education was still beyond the economic grasp of much of the population because they required tuition fees in order to operate. In 1957 the Jamaican government began a program of competitive scholarships for students to enter grant-aided schools. This provided for some 20% of the approximately 10,000 slots in secondary education schools to be filled from the general populace (Black, 1972). In

1973, the Manley administration expanded the program to pay for approximately 90% of the available slots. Even with this program in place, however, it is estimated that in 1973 this program provided an educational opportunity for only approximately 24 of the some 45,000 eleven year-olds who competed (Manley, 1982).

The lack of educational opportunity in Jamaica becomes even more acute when specific consideration is given to the hydrologic sciences in higher education (college and technical schools). In this paper the term "hydrologic sciences" is defined as those sciences necessary to provide integrated study of water resources issues. The most definitive works found in the research of this paper on this subject was a survey of Jamaican science and technology research institutions by the Jamaica National Planning Agency (JNPA), published in 1976 and a series of surveys concerning the University of the West Indies, Mona (UWIM), published in the 1980's (Stone, 1983; Stone 1985). These documents indicate that in Jamaica there is one university, UWIM, and approximately thirteen research institutes outside the university which provide education and/or training opportunities in fields related to the hydrologic sciences.

The JNPA study concluded that Jamaica has a severe shortage in the supply of trained scientists and technicians in fields related to the hydrologic sciences. The paucity of individuals trained in these sciences becomes even more apparent when you consider the distribution of these professionals as illustrated in Table 1 (from JNPA, 1976). The table shows that research and education in the university sector is highly skewed to the physical sciences, with virtually no representation in the engineering sciences or hydrology. The private sector accounts for approximately 30% of these professionals, indicating a residual professional to total population ratio of 85.6 per million in the public service sector of the hydrologic sciences. In comparison, the World Plan calls for a professional to population ratio of 400 per million for all science and technology.

The University of the West Indies at Mona was established in 1948. It was originally a university college awarding University of London degrees. It is now an independent university with a majority of its faculty being West Indian. The student enrollment at the University has grown from 600 in 1959 to approximately 4500 in 1987. The results of the Stone survey studies (Stone, 1983; Stone, 1985) indicate that the University has a poor, but improving, self and public image in terms of teaching and research. In his studies, Stone surveyed a cross-section of Jamaicans concerning their perception of the University.

The results of one part of the survey in which the participants were asked to compare teaching, research, and scientific expertise capabilities of the UWIM faculty in comparison with faculties of similar sized universities in the U.S.A. and Britain are presented in Table 2. In his study, Stone reported that the most outstanding faculty were considered to be in the medical sciences with 45-67% of the respondents, with the natural sciences lagging far behind with 5-9% of the respondents. Engineering was not even mentioned as a category. One conclusion of the study: "UWI academics do not apparently have a self image of the institution having either generated scientific or policy expertise or applied research which has been of importance in Jamaica" (Stone, 1983). When these same academicians were asked what should be done to remedy this problem, 28% responded that more varied programs including engineering should be developed (ibid).

TABLE 1. Distribution of Professionals by Scientific Discipline and Sector of Performance, 1973.

Discipline	Statuatory Bodies	Private Business	University	Government
Physical and Natural Sciences				
Biology	1		1	1
Botany	1			
Chemistry	46	45	19	14
Geography			6	
Geology			6	14
Hydrology				5
Meteorology				1
Zoology	1		17	
Engineering Science and Technology				
Agricultur.	2			
Chemical	2	28	1	
Civil	3	10		
Geologic.		1		
Sanitary				5
Agricultural Science and Technology				
Ag. Chemistry				8
Agronomy	9	4	4	5
Earth Sci				
Forestry				4
Soil Science	2	1		37
TOTAL	67	89	54	93

TABLE 2. Comparison of UWIM Faculty Performance With Equivalent Universities in USA and Britain (as % agreeing with statement).

Category	UWIM Better 1982	UWIM Better 1985	UWIM Similar 1982	UWIM Similar 1985	UWIM Inferior 1982	UWIM Inferior 1985
Teaching	15%	49%	58%	52%	27%	1%
Research	3%	17%	15%	51%	81%	32%
Scientific Expertise	1%	26%	20%	46%	78%	29%

Both the JNPA study and the Stone surveys cited three prevalent factors in the lack of educational and training opportunities in science and technology in Jamaica. One explanation is the "brain drain" of students from the Jamaican population to more affluent countries. Stone reported that even with the increased confidence in UWIM's faculty expressed in the three year interim between his surveys (see Table 2), 63 of those surveyed still preferred an overseas education for their children. The main reason offered was that UWIM does not offer a wide enough range of courses in technology and professional skills. A second factor cited was a phenomenon known as "internal brain drain".

In this case, industrialization under the country's attempt to "catch up" to the developed world has resulted in a migration of scientific talent to the private sector, in most cases a multi-national corporation. With a limited pool of adequately trained professionals, siphoning of this talent by the private sector results in a deficiency in the professionals who might otherwise have been enticed into the public science and technology system. For example the statistics in Table 2 show that 75% of professional positions in engineering science and technology are held in the private sector. The JNPA report (1976) also reported that in 1973 there was a vacancy rate of 15% of positions in the physical and natural sciences, and a 17% vacancy rate in the engineering sciences. In each case the percent of vacancies in job sectors other than private enterprise was 92% and 78%, respectively. These statistics indicate that most of the professional positions in these fields are held in the private sector, and that the private sector has significantly less problems with filling vacancies.

Last, but certainly by no means least, is the factor of the lack of financial resources to fund an appropriate science and technology program. Over the period of 1971 through 1973 total expenditure for science and technology in Jamaica was estimated to average only $9.5 million (Jamaican currency) with 22% expended within private enterprise (JNPA, 1976). In today's U.S. dollars this would reflect an annual expenditure in the public sector of less than $1.5 million excluding inflation since 1973. It should also be noted that only about half of this figure is actually invested in research and development (ibid). This figure amounted to about 0.7% of Jamaica's Gross National Product (GNP) for 1973. This figure is considerably less than the percentage of GNP recommended by the World Plan (ibid).

The history of education in Jamaica is not all doom and gloom. There are some success stories. One is the Marine Lab, now located at Port Royal. This facility was established in 1891 and has developed a world-class research program in marine biology. The Jamaican Agricultural Society, now associated with the Botany Department at UWIM has published a scientific journal since 1897. And in 1960, the Government of Jamaica established a Scientific Research Council, which has published a scientific journal since at least 1972.

DISCUSSION

The logical question is "what is the underlying reason for the lack of an adequate science and technology system in Jamaica?". One might first want to assume that there is an inadequate pool of students from general population. However, students who graduated from UWIM and were employed in private enterprise at the time of the Stone surveys were found to be (on a scale of 10) competent (7), intelligent (7), to possess an ability to learn and develop (8), and leaders with a good attitude (6) (Stone, 1983).

The reason the system is inadequate lies not within the intellectual resources of the population, but rather within the political struggle of a newly freed nation trying to define its cultural identity. This is the basic underlying factor in the status of scientific education and training throughout the Third World, and must be addressed in the development of any plan for enhancing educational opportunities in any area of study, including the hydrologic sciences. Components of this political struggle include world view, economic order, and the development of intellectual alliances.

It has been noted that studies of contemporary Jamaica have failed to come to grips with two fundamental aspects of Jamaican culture: its value system (or ethos) and its world view or cognitive orientations (Alleyne, 1988). These are the aspects of culture that impinge most on political ideology and clash most with the culture and technology of modernization (ibid). As pointed out earlier in this paper, the only education afforded the colonial population for two hundred plus years during the dark ages of slavery was the passing on of cultural and religious values within the slave community.

It has been suggested that in premodern Jamaica, the world view was based more on natural events (ibid), and that in all phases of life in the traditional community the concept of "oneness," with the universe, the community, and self was the essence of "truth" in life (Lewin, 1974). This is a markedly different world view from that held by the North American and European powers of the Second World. In fact, in many cases these world views have historically either been ignored or treated as obstacles to "modernization" (Alleyne, 1988). We must come to grips with this world view if we are ever to advance the state of scientific knowledge in the Third World.

In order to achieve this requires that this world view be examined from a different perspective. They must be viewed as positive attitudes, and not as the negative reactions they have historically been assumed to be. We must remember that "truth" is also the essence of science, as dictated by the scientific method. Paraphrasing Glascow (1985), the appreciation of science (by traditional people) can only be achieved by allowing science to take its role beside arts and religion as a fundamental part of a country's cultural tradition. Incorporation of this world view into our educational plan does not contradict development, it enhances it.

Another factor affecting the status of scientific education and training in Jamaica and the Third World is global economic order. In these nations there is a growing awareness that the world's economic structure was established by the imperial powers of the colonial period, and works substantially to the advantage of those who possess industrial strength, technological superiority and market and financial control (Manley, 1982). The economies of these nations are at a marked disadvantage in these categories due to their roots as colonies. Their industries were developed to serve foreign interests as opposed to a national interest. European and North American influence in Jamaica is now stronger than ever, although the island is politically independent (Alleyne, 1988).

This economic colonization has drawn strong criticism. It has been stated that in Latin America, for every dollar of net profit by a U.S. interest, 52% leaves the country even though 78% of the initial investment funds came from local sources (Manley, 1982). In addition to a capital and natural resource drain, it also limits the development of a science and technology system for the host country.

Science and technology become synonymous with export potential, and much of the human and financial scientific resources of the host country are expended in developing this manufacturing sector at the expense of the development of a national science program geared to the requirements of the citizenry of that country. Such a program does not serve to enhance either the economic plight of the ordinary people, nor does it serve to increase their educational opportunities. This form of technology transfer is known as the

"Puerto Rico" model, which has been demonstrated to be an abysmal failure (Manley, 1982).

After more than 40 years of subscribing to the model, the Puerto Rican people suffered 25-40% unemployment, 62% were dependent on welfare for food, and there existed a serious migration problem. In the meantime, 80% of the Puerto Rican economy was owned by U.S. multinationals, and foreign capital controlled 90% of the assets in manufacturing, 70% in banking and finance, and 90% of all retail sales in the country (ibid).

The real problem of development as stated by Glasgow (1985) is not so much to increase production, as it is to increase the capacity to produce, a capacity which is really inherent in all people. It arises out of their capacity to control their own environment, because they have the training and confidence to solve the problems they encounter. A prerequisite for this control is the ability of the trained scientific specialists in the society to adapt foreign technologies to local needs, and to innovate. Development of such an educational program requires the support of the international scientific community.

A final component in the struggle for equitable educational opportunity in the Third World is the development of intellectual alliances. In an intellectual alliance, participants freely exchange thoughts, ideas, research, and applications. Such an alliance is perhaps more readily adaptable to the hydrologic sciences than many areas of science and technology where economic or defense interests might make such alliances more problematic. Historically, the industrial countries have been criticized that one means by which they maintain their colonial powers is through their capacity to control education - the transfer of knowledge (Manley, 1982).

Perhaps the "Puerto Rico" model is a good example of this. On the other hand, Third World countries have historically been very hesitant to seek collaboration with and assistance from foreign scientists, who could provide a great deal of experience and know-how in the development of a strong research and educational program. To secure the opportunities that the formation of intellectual alliances within the scientific community could have, means we must begin to identify an agenda in which cooperation between the "old" world and the "new", North and South, will be mutually beneficial. Educational cooperation may not be truly "development" oriented in the long run if it inhibits a recipient country's capacity for self-determination, or if it alienates individual scientists only because of their country of residence.

CONCLUSION

The main aim of education should be to increase knowledge, know-how, and capabilities of the world's citizens so they may meaningfully contribute toward the process of development (McIntyre, 1987). As stated so nobly by Manley (1982), "collective self-reliance among Third World countries must become more than a slogan, ... it is an important step on the long hard road to economic independence". My charge to you as colleagues and educators in the hydrologic sciences is that we too must create a collective self-reliance among ourselves. A self-reliance based on the premise that each country has the right to prosper intellectually, and that we as a collective voice should strive to insure these rights. One means by which we can achieve this goal is to enhance the educational opportunities in our science, unfettered by the ideological, political, and economic differences between our governments.

REFERENCES

Alleyne, Mervyn C. 1988. *Roots of Jamaican Culture*. Karia Publishers. Bridgetown, Barbados, West Indies.

Beaty, J. and 0. Johnson, 1971. *Heritage of Western Civilization*. Prentice Hall, Camden, NJ, U.S.A.

Black, Clifton v. 1972. *The Story of Jamaica*. Collins Publishers, St James Place, London.

Casslyn, R., R. Jolly, J.W. Sewell, and R. Wood. 1982. *Rich Country Intoret and the Third World*. Overseas Development Council, London.

Coke, L. 1974. "Science for the People: The Management of Science and Technology in the West Indies". *Caribbean Quarterly*, Vol 20, No. 2.

Glasgow, Joyce. 1985 "Scientific Literacy - Its meaning and its importance for Jamaica". *Caribbean Quarterly*, Vol. 31, No. 3 & 4.

JNPA, Jamaica National Planning Agency. 1976. *Survey of Jamaican Science and Technology Research Institutions*, Editor: Juan Carlos Gamba, Dept. of Scientific Affairs, Organization of American States, Washington, D.C.

Lawson, L.A. 1977, in *Proceedings of the Eighth Annual Conference of Caribbean Water Engineers*, Sept. 19-22, 1977, New Kingston, Jamaica. Caribbean Council of Engr. Organizations.

Lewin, Olive. 1974. "Folk Music Research in Jamaica" in *Black Communication: Dimensions of Research and Instructions*, ed. J. Daniels. Speech Communication Association, New York.

Manley, M. 1982. *Jamaica, Struggle in the Periphery*. Writers and Readers Publishing Cooperative Society Ltd. London.

McIntyre, A. 1989. "Developing Centres of Excellence through North/South Linkages in Higher Education." *Journal of Social and Economic Studies*, Vol. 38, No. 2. Institute of Social and Economic Research, University of the West Indies.

Proceedings of the symposium on Environmental Studies in Jamaica, May 25-26, 1979. Chemistry Dept. University of the West Indies, Mona.

Stone, Carl. 1983. "Public Opinion Perspectives on the University of the West Indies". *Caribbean Quarterly*. Vol 29, No. 3 & 4, P.21-39.

Stone, Carl. 1985. "The Jamaican Public and the University of the West Indies." *Caribbean Quarterly*, Vol. 31, No. 3 & 4.

Strachan, A.F. 1910. *With Rod and Line in Jamaica*. Werner Laurie. London.

Turner, A.D. 1974. "Science in the 70's - Observations on Science Education in Jamaica." *Caribbean Quarterly*. Yol 20. No. 2. June, 1974.

HYDROLOGICAL EDUCATION IN A DEVELOPING SOCIETY: PERSPECTIVES FROM AN AFRICAN UNIVERSITY

Brian K. Rawlins
Department of Hydrology
University of Zululand
KwaDlangezwa 3886
South Africa

ABSTRACT

The Department of Hydrology was established at the University of Zululand in 1986 in response to a perceived need for suitably trained hydrologists in the country. The syllabus at undergraduate level attempts to offer a broad grounding in the subject over a two-year period. The honors course (first-year postgraduate level) allows for specialization in various fields. Though the syllabus is a fairly conventional one, it does attempt to address the country's specific hydrological needs. Because of a limited staff quota, and because of the potential it offers for interactive learning, computer and video-based education is increasingly being incorporated into what was originally a more formal course consisting of lectures and practicals.

INTRODUCTION

The establishment of hydrological expertise in South Africa has taken place in a similar manner to that of many newly developed countries. The early years were characterized by direct input from foreign countries (notably Britain) in association with local incentives for the immigration of qualified personnel. Until 1945, the economy of the country was mainly based on agricultural production and extraction industry. Development of water resources to meet the demands of these industries was directed primarily at solving individual problems as and when they occurred.

Rapid industrial development since 1945 has put increased stress on the readily available water resources. In addition, the political isolation which affected South Africa increasingly from the 1960s reduced overseas involvement. These were the prime factors that led to the establishment of a locally based hydrological education program. By a rather haphazard process, different universities and technical colleges incorporated various aspects of hydrology into existing courses, while government departments contributed improvements at the technical level. Subsequently, university departments expanded their courses to encompass both broader and more involved aspects of hydrology and water resources management. In these departments, as well as in other bodies, developments with a locally specific emphasis took place in both pure and applied research fields.

With the arrival of the 1990s, and the imminent prospect of a 'new South Africa', the country's hydrological community can now assess its role from a more global perspective. Serious water resources problems facing us include catering for the large and rapidly expanding industrial and urban centers, and addressing the needs of impoverished rural communities which have thus far received scant attention.

This paper highlights present and expected future trends in South African water demands. It considers the state of hydrological education in South Africa, and then describes the attempts of the Department of Hydrology at the University of Zululand to produce hydrologists competent to respond to these trends in facilitating the planned management of water resources in the country.

THE IMPORTANCE OF HYDROLOGY IN SOUTH AFRICA

Water resources management in South Africa is of considerable importance since water is both scarce and unevenly distributed. South Africa is essentially a semi-arid country with a mean annual rainfall of only 500 mm. This figure however disguises the great spatial variability of rainfall within the country. Very arid desert regions in the west comprise 21% of the surface area and receive average rainfall of less than 200 mm/year, whereas in the subtropical eastern regions average a rainfall of over 2000 mm/year (Department of Water Affairs, 1986). The availability of water is further complicated by the irregular temporal nature of the rainfall and by high evaporation rates. Seasonally, most of the country receives rainfall only during the summer months with a prolonged dry season occurring from April to September. The regular occurrence of droughts lasting several years puts further stress on these meagre resources. Consequently, water resources management has been directed at creating sufficient reservoir storage to enable yields to be sustained over long periods.

The industrialization of South Africa has thus far proceeded with little regard for the availability of water. The mining base of the economy, centered around the Johannesburg gold reef, is not in a particularly water-rich area. Around this area mining activities have led first to the development of heavy industry and power generation and second to the establishment of numerous light industries. The corresponding increase in water utilization has tapped locally available water resources to the limit. Continued industrial expansion has been possible only by the construction of large and costly inter-basin transfer schemes which transport water from the well-watered regions of Natal and Lesotho. Decentralization policies have been initiated by the Government to alleviate the situation, however as yet they have only had limited success. Consequently, the function of South African water resource management is to meet the rapidly increasing industrial and domestic water demands where and when they occur.

The rural areas of the country are notoriously impoverished and over-populated. As a consequence of the apartheid system, many people live in remote areas which are generally deficient in water. Water supply to these areas has thus far been developed only on a small scale and sanitation technology is rudimentary. For decades this sector of the country has been largely ignored; however it is now gaining increasing attention due to current political changes.

The focuses of future development of South Africa's water supply should thus be twofold. The urban and industrial centers which have relied on high technology solutions in the past will continue to require 'first-world' hydrological expertise, especially in the application of water conservation measures, the recycling of effluent and the development of inter-basin transfer schemes. The rural areas, in which reticulated water and sewage networks are often unfeasible, require the introduction of alternative strategies to address their water needs. Development schemes currently in progress include spring protection measures, gravity fed supply networks, low cost drilling methods, hand pump design, and the improvement in sanitation technology.

In order for South Africa to implement this twofold development strategy, personnel trained in many fields will be needed. At present, the small hydrological community is mainly specialized, through training and employment, in addressing 'first-world' problems. The need for a broader base in terms of expertise is essential.

HYDROLOGICAL EDUCATION IN SOUTH AFRICA

In South African universities, departments of agriculture, geography, engineering and geology developed hydrological courses with different hydrological emphases. Until recently, these universities have catered exclusively for 'white' students with first-world backgrounds and aspirations. Course structures are conventional and similar to those found elsewhere in the developed world. Government departments, notably those responsible for water affairs, forestry and agriculture, have addressed the need for qualified hydrologists and hydrological technicians by conducting in-house training schemes and encouraging further study. Regular courses aimed at practising hydrologists and engineers in the private sector are also offered by various bodies.

Existing university courses focus on high technology solutions to complex water resources problems. The need for development and training in lower alternative technology solutions to the problems of the underdeveloped sectors of the country have been recognized mainly by development agencies but training in these fields has as yet not been implemented on more than a small scale.

Zululand University and its Department of Hydrology

The University was founded in 1960 as part of the segregated tertiary education system then in existence in South Africa. Although it is now fully open and autonomous, the majority of students come from the poor and still segregated school system. It is common for students to have had little or no exposure to modern facilities, and many school teachers are under-qualified. The sciences suffer greatly in this system as the weak infrastructure and the lack of finance often preclude the establishment of laboratories. Enrollment in the Faculty of Science at the University is consequently low, forming less than 10% of total student numbers.

The language of instruction is English. Although this allows the students access to internationally published material and a cosmopolitan teaching staff, the disadvantage is that almost no students are first-language English speakers. This leads to difficulties in student comprehension both generally during lectures and specifically when complex scientific terms are used.

While the University does conduct courses aimed at improving English proficiency, these courses are unfortunately not specifically designed for science students.

The University of Zululand has recognized the need for the hydrological training of black students who through circumstance are unable to enrol in the 'white' universities. The initial aims of the Department were to duplicate course structures found elsewhere and to provide additional training in fields specific to rural communities.

Hydrology was first taught in 1986 and student enrollment fluctuated between three and fifteen students during the past five years. Dropout rates have been low, so that the Department has produced eleven graduates to date. After graduation, at least five students have continued their studies at honors level either at the University of Zululand or elsewhere. Other students have entered employment with government departments or private concerns, most notably the mining industry where geohydrological expertise is in great demand.

Syllabus taught Undergraduate courses follow the system whereby students will study four subjects in their first year, three in their second year and two 'major' subjects in their final year. Hydrology is presented only at second- and third- year levels. Students who major in hydrology can opt to have as their co-major any of the wide range of subjects offered by the Science faculty. Geology, Mathematics and Geography are the most commonly selected co-majors, though Botany, Chemistry and Biochemistry have also been chosen.

The admission requirement for Hydrology is the passing of the requisite number of first-year science courses for progression to the second-year level. This proves to be an effective academic filter, though it does produce hydrology students with varied scientific backgrounds. The course is consequently structured to accommodate both mathematically and non-mathematically grounded students. The second year concentrates on process studies, which cover the main components of the hydrological cycle in generally descriptive terms (Table 1). Basic mathematical principles are included, and students are encouraged to enrol for additional mathematics courses. The main objective of this course is to encompass the complete range of hydrological topics and thus to provide the student with a solid grounding for further studies.

To progress to the third-year Hydrology course, students must pass in first-year mathematics, statistics or physics. At third-year level, selected hydrological topics are covered in greater detail with emphasis on the application of problem solving techniques (Table 2). The objectives of this course are to equip the graduate in hydrology for study at postgraduate level or for employment, usually at technician level, either by government departments or by the private sector.

In South Africa, an honors degree is usually required for a student to be employed in a professional capacity. The hydrology honors course at the University of Zululand allows for specialization in accordance with individual interests and academic background. The admission requirement to honors level is a mark of at least 60% in both major subjects at third-year level. The hydrology honors course is conducted over one year and comprises a number of options of which four are selected by the student (Table 3). This selection is made in consultation with Department staff, the main criteria being balance

TABLE 1. Second-year Syllabus

Introduction	Definition; Scope; Hydrological cycle; Chemical composition/properties of water
Climatology	Composition of the atmosphere; Radiation laws; Energy and radiation balance at the earth's surface; Weather systems over southern Africa.
Precipitation	The rain process; Types of rain; Rainfall measurement; Interception.
Evaporation/Eva-potranspiration	Energy balance and turbulent transfer theory; Penman-Monteith equation; Potential and actual evapotranspiration; measurement.
Surface water	The runoff process; measurement; Horton and Hewlett runoff models; Factors affecting runoff; Hydrograph separation; Floods and flood alleviation.
Soil moisture	Infiltration theory, Processes, Factors affecting infiltration; Moisture storage; Measurement; Unsaturated flow principles.
Groundwater	Origins and occurrence of groundwater; Hydrological properties of porous media; Design, construction and operation of wells; Groundwater quality and pollution.
Water Quality	Erosion and sediment yield; solute transport; water analysis; pollution; eutrophication; water and waste water treatment.

TABLE 2. Third-year Syllabus

Stochastic hydrology	Probability theory; Probability distributions; Parameter estimation; Probability plotting; Frequency analysis.
Water Resources	Water resources of southern Africa; Demand/supply management; Reservoir yield analysis. Management of ground and surface water resources; Conjunctive use schemes.
Hydraulics	Fluid dynamics; Bernoulli's equation; Open channel flow and structures; Flood routing.
Groundwater	Groundwater movement; Groundwater and well hydraulics; Geological and geophysical investigation techniques; Artificial recharge; Saline intrusion.

TABLE 3. Honors Syllabus

Applied Hydrology	The stochastic hydrology course conducted at third-year level is expanded and developed with the introduction of advanced techniques and applications.
Groundwater Studies	Geohydrological techniques are studied at an advanced level, special attention is given to geohydrological problem solving for anisotropic and non-homogeneous aquifers.
Water Quality	A range of water quality related topics are presented, aspects of pollution and water treatment are covered in detail.
Water Resources Management	Integrated water resources planning and management techniques are studied, additionally covered are systems analysis application techniques.
Computer Applications in Hydrology	The use of computer-based mathematical models are studied to solve both surface and groundwater hydrological problems.
Elective topic	Depending on staff availability, additional courses on topics such as hydrometeorology, environmental hydrology, and remote sensing may be selected. It is also possible for subjects conducted by related departments such as geology, geography or mathematics to be included in the course as this option.

of the course and the student's grounding and ability in his or her chosen options. In addition to the options which are presented by means of lectures, seminars and assignments, an independent research project is undertaken which forms the basis of a mini-thesis.

Teaching methods Teaching methods at all levels are based on formal presentation of material by means of lectures and practicals. The student will, at undergraduate level, have about 9 formal contact hours per week. Further study is structured to include assignments, reading of additional literature, informal consultation, and video- and computer- based tuition and revision.

The lecture courses are primarily designed to provide the student with a framework. Topics are presented in sufficient detail for the student to grasp the basics then to study independently in greater detail. The lecture system in theory allows for staff and students to interact and for specific problem areas to be highlighted and expanded. Unfortunately, language difficulties and student reluctance to respond to prompts and questions tend in practice to impair this system. Learning by rote seems to have been so thoroughly inculcated in the schools that students are unable easily to break away from a process of direct absorption and regurgitation of facts.

Practical experience is provided in parallel with the lecture course both in the laboratory and in the field. It is possible here to break down language and status barriers and so encourage a less structured lecturer-student relationship and more of a one-to-one situation. Over the course of two years it is noticeable how students gain confidence and become more responsive.

The recent introduction of both computer-aided teaching methods and videotaped instruction programs has benefited the Department to a remarkable degree. Though at present commercially available packages are mainly restricted to topics designed for non-hydrological courses, they have proved useful for the teaching of mathematical and geographical concepts. Available computer packages guide the students through theoretical concepts and then allow self-assessment by means of multiple choice questions. Progression through the programs is possible only when the concepts have been adequately understood. Students have access to the computer system at times suitable to them and the instructor can, at any stage, review each student's performance.

Applications programs relating to hydrological topics such as hydraulics, mathematical modelling and water resources management are at present successfully being used in practical classes. This success can perhaps be measured by the enthusiasm of the students to experiment and interact with the programs, an enthusiasm which would be difficult or even impossible to engender by other means.

It is hoped that with the increasing availability and suitability of such programs, the formality of the lecture system with its inherent disadvantages can ultimately be replaced by a freer system in which the lecturer acts as guide and mentor. Students should thus gain the requisite knowledge more efficiently and personally. For advanced courses, the use of computers not only is an essential teaching tool but also provides valuable exposure to the type of work likely to be encountered after graduation.

Future prospects and requirements. Course content and structure are continually undergoing revision in response to both hydrological developments and student feedback. At present the course is being considerably modified to accommodate computer use and to link practical applications more closely to theoretical concepts. The students' weak educational background demands that they be given more individual attention than their counterparts elsewhere. Regular assignments and tests consequently are conducted to ensure that the basics have been mastered before progress is made to more advanced topics. Being thus responsive to different class needs, the depth to which topics are dealt with has varied from year to year. The introduction of computer-aided instruction and revision techniques is expected to make the formal course more uniform. Individual students will thus be able to spend more time on topics with which they have difficulty without adversely affecting the formal course.

Hydrological aspects relevant to the rural sector of the country have, thus far, only been tentatively incorporated into the syllabus. Students perceive 'alternative' hydrology quite definitely as inferior or second-rate hydrology. Their aim is to compete with hydrologists from the mainstream universities. As a consequence, such issues have only been introduced in the groundwater, water resources management and water quality sections of the course. It will take a change in student aspirations to allow for the introduction of specific courses addressing rural needs, these courses will probably only be feasible at honors level.

Moves to incorporate computer-aided learning have been restricted by the availability and the suitability of commercial software packages. While Department staff are in any event likely to write programs specific to their purposes, our task would be greatly facilitated and the quality of education we can provide be greatly improved if we could draw on contributions from the hydrological community at large.

CONCLUSIONS

The current state of hydrological education in South Africa is relatively healthy. There is however, a severe shortage of experienced personnel in both the public and private sectors, a shortage which cannot rapidly be redressed by local training. In consequence positions that would normally be occupied by experienced personnel are being given to newly qualified hydrologists. This situation is likely to continue well into the future, although attention being given now to addressing the staff requirements of the next century, the situation should see a progressive improvement. Until South Africa can attain such local independence, the importation of hydrological expertise will be essential.

Though small in staff and student numbers, the contribution made by the Department of Hydrology at the University of Zululand to meet the needs of the future is substantial, not least because it is drawing on the previously untapped black community. Future political changes within South Africa, which should lead to a more equitable distribution of resources amongst all its citizens, will certainly be enhanced by our efforts.

ACKNOWLEDGMENTS

The author would like to express his appreciation to the University of Zululand, especially to other members of staff of the Department of Hydrology and to the Research Committee who have made it possible for this paper to be written and presented. Special thanks are also due to my wife, Myrtle Hooper, for her editorial expertise, and for her helpful suggestions.

REFERENCES

Department of Water Affairs, (1986). *Management of the Water Resources of South Africa.* Government Printer, Pretoria, Republic of South Africa.

NATIONAL AND INTERNATIONAL TRAINING INSTITUTES AND THEIR ROLE IN IMPROVING WATER RESOURCES DEVELOPMENT AND MANAGEMENT IN DEVELOPING COUNTRIES

M. Abu-Zeid
Water Research Center
Cairo, Egypt

A. Hamdy
Mediterranean Agronomic Institute,
Bari, Italy

C. Lacirignola
Mediterranean Agronomic Institute,
Bari, Italy

ABSTRACT

In most developing countries, water sciences and applications are taught only in Engineering Colleges. Very little about plant-soil-water relationships and interactions is given. On the other hand, Agricultural Colleges may deal, if any, in a very general way with water and the hydrologic cycle. Graduates from these two disciplines may face serious short-comings when they get involved in agricultural water management programs. In most cases, attempts have failed so far to complement educational programs at the University level to satisfy basic needs in water, agronomic and soil sciences. Sustainability of development and environmental considerations add a new dimension. Some national and international training institutes have played a great role in filling in the gaps. This paper discusses such gaps for some developing countries and gives examples of the Water Research Center in Egypt, as a national organization, and Bari Training Institute of ICAMAS (Italy) as an international center. Evaluation of training programs confirms the need for a multidisciplinary approach and proved encouraging for their impacts on national water management programs.

INTRODUCTION

People are the real wealth of a nation. The basic objective of development is to create an enabling environment for people to enjoy creative lives. This can be achieved through human development which concerns not only upgrading of human capabilities but also using these capabilities as human potential which will be wasted if not polished and used. Trained educated people are in a better position than others to take their share in developing their countries as they have better access to information gained through training.

Therefore, a strong and efficient training program is vital to maximize productivity, as high-quality training produces better productive professionals. The most successful technical cooperation requires that programs focus on training issues. This will broaden the basis for more effective national capacity-building through the exchange of experience and the transfer of knowledge.

The welfare of a country is expressed, in a way, in the self-satisfaction of its nutritive requirements from the available natural resources. Water has for long been considered as the most precious of all natural resources. The earth's water supply is constant and awareness with the scarcity of water resources is limited. Water resources development and management has thus become a must where science and technology play a crucial part in this respect.

In most developing countries, there are some difficulties associated with organizing research programs oriented towards water resources development and management. This is due to lack of researches and researchers who are able to contribute to the resolution of water resources and related management problems in their countries. Therefore, National and International training Institutes play an important role in filling in such gaps.

TRAINING AND RESEARCH NEEDS IN THE AREA OF AGRICULTURAL WATER MANAGEMENT FOR DEVELOPING COUNTRIES

The first step towards developing successful agricultural water management programs is education. Training and research are the major catalyzers of education. In most developing countries, water sciences and applications are taught only in Engineering Colleges. Graduates face shortcomings when they get involved in agricultural water management programs. In many cases, attempts have failed so far to complement educational programs at the University level to satisfy the basic need in water, agronomic and soil sciences. Sustainability of development and environmental considerations add a new dimension.

In some developing countries, there continues to be an acute lack of trained national personnel and the expansion of human capabilities has been grossly inadequate. The concept of both short-term and long-term training is appropriate to strengthen the human potential and the national institutions.

Moreover, in other developing countries, there is a fairly large number of studies which have led to major advances in water sciences and applications. Yet there are some difficulties associated with applying research programs, and the problem of applying the results of studies in the broadest context and transferring results from research in the field still remains.

Training and research work is needed to upgrade human capabilities. A prerequisite to research activities is the awareness that there is a problem that requires resolution. This awareness ensures the definition of the problem and its formulation, objectives and constraints. In order to maximize the probability of deriving a solution, identifying research needs is a necessary step in the direction of current and future problems. Investigative research work is also needed to better understand and formulate alternative solutions to the water resources development and management issues and conflicts, and to evaluate each alternative.

ROLE OF NATIONAL AND INTERNATIONAL TRAINING INSTITUTES

National and international institutes play a great role in providing the necessary training. Graduate training courses and on-the-job training are accomplished by using materials, information and resources provided by various water-related groups, research and developmental initiative. This effort involved the preparation of courses and activities for each grade level in the field of water resources development and management.

On the national scale, an adequate number of personnel ought to be trained to develop their management, engineering and technical skills, in order to contribute to the resolution of water resources and related management problems. On the other hand, appropriate training and research institutions ought to be established to carry out such challenging tasks.

THE WATER RESEARCH CENTER IN EGYPT

As a national organization, the Water Research Center (WRC) in Egypt provides a variety of venues which promote proactive participation on the part of the researchers. In addition, it is created in a cooperative effort between government and researchers.

The Water Research Center of Egypt presently consists of eleven Research Institutes that read like a list of the problems facing Egypt's irrigation improvement and water development:

- Water Distribution and Irrigation Systems Research Institute.
- Drainage Research Institute
- Hydraulics and Sediment Research Institute.
- Water Resources Development Research Institute.
- Weed Control and Channel Maintenance Research Institute.
- Ground Water Research Institute.
- High Aswan Dam Side Effects Research Institute.
- Mechanical and Electrical Research Institute.
- Survey Research Institute.
- Construction , Soil Mechanics and Foundations Research Institute.
- Coastal Protection Research Institute.

At first glance to WRC's eleven Research Institutes, work plans appeared to have adopted materials which were not only avant-grade but also extremely ambitious.

One of the major objectives of the Water Research Center is to outline and implement long-term policies for managing the water resources in Egypt in order to cope with national demands. The Center also aims at solving the technical and applied problems associated with the general policy for irrigation and drainage.

Moreover, the Center is concerned with investigations and research work connected with the extension of agricultural land and water resources assessment. It attempts to find a means for utilizing the water resources of the country in the most efficient and cost-effective manner. The organizational chart of the Water Research Center is presented.

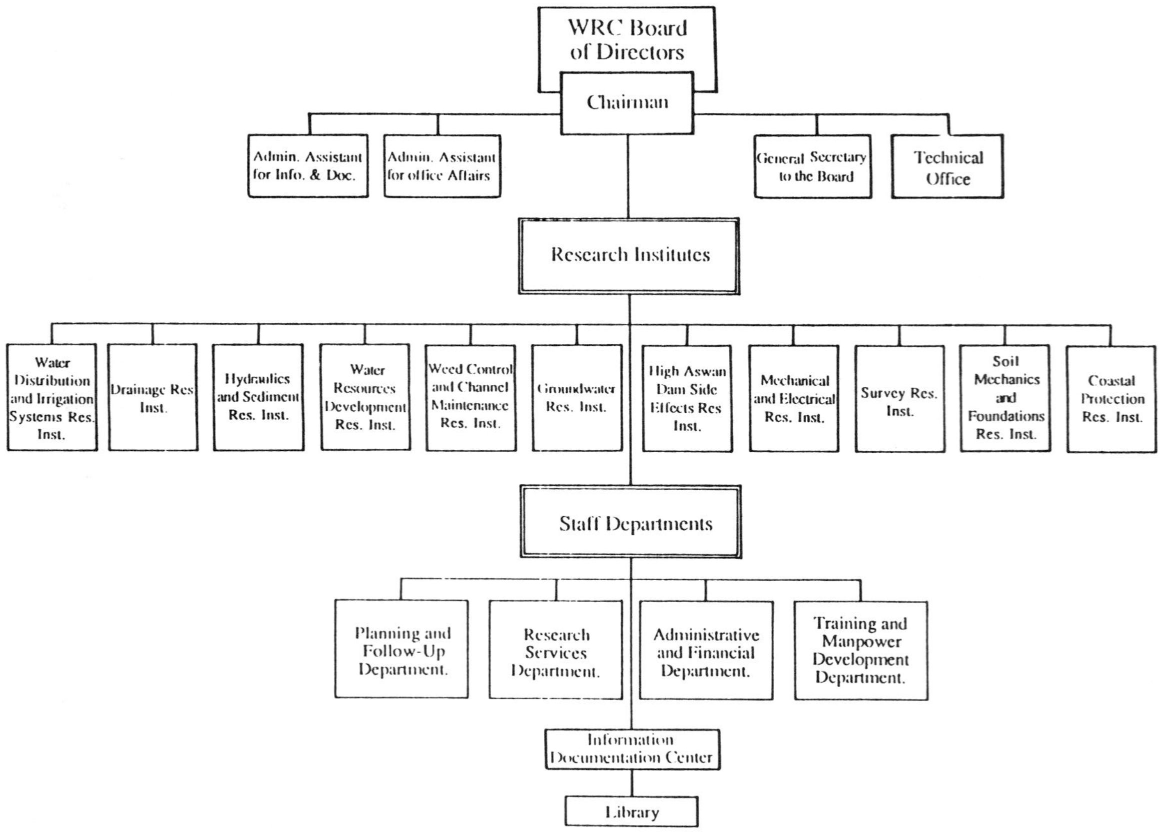

Organizational Chart of the Water Research Center

WRC plays not only a national role but also an international one. On the local scale, WRC from its inception, has worked to strengthen the research programs of its eleven institutes. On the international scale, WRC has established wide-scale communications with several international bodies. Interrelations with such foreign authorities involves technology transfer, training, employee exchange programs, conferences and seminars, field trips and similar activities. Training plays an important role to cope with the rapid worldwide development in the field of water resources management. In order for the WRC to carry out its current and anticipated obligations efficiently, a Training and Manpower Development Department was established by WRC in 1982. This department is the nucleus for the currently established National Irrigation Training Institute.

THE NATIONAL IRRIGATION TRAINING INSTITUTE (NITI)

The overall objective of NITI is to improve the efficiency of the agricultural irrigation system and to remove key constraints to increase production. The specific role of NITI is to provide training for all levels of employees within the Ministry of Public Works and Water Resources as a means of maximizing their job capacity and performance, and to provide training in the field of water resources development and management for other developing countries. The NITI philosophy is based on the following assumptions:

- The acquisition of proper work attitudes, skills and knowledge will lead to greater efficiency, productivity and job satisfaction.
- In-service training is necessary to help workers in the field keep abreast of technological changes, new methods and processes, and state-of-the-art equipment. It is also concerned with their total growth.
- Institutionalized training is a cost-effective means for providing quality instruction in an organization such as the Ministry of Public Works and Water Resources.
- The instructional programs should take the learners from where they are and help them achieve the highest levels commensurate with their inherent abilities. The program makes provisions for individuals to progress at their own rates and provide remedial and advanced activities for those who need them.
- Hands-on instruction helps learners acquire a better understanding of theoretical and conceptual knowledge. Concomitantly, a better understanding will enhance the ability to apply concepts and increase memorization.
- The use of multi-media instruction is encouraged because it makes the presentation more interesting, makes the subject matter more understandable, and improves retention of information.
- The training program is more effective when workers are able to return to their work places and put into use what they have learned.

Since mid-1982 NITI has provided training to 3,500 employees of whom 2,700 were engineers and 800 were technicians, plus a fairly large number of trainees from developing countries. Technical study tours were organized for senior staff members from Sudan, Bangladesh, Yemen, China and other African and Asian countries.

One of the training components is to develop and implement a Monitoring, Evaluation and Feedback Program (MEF) for the Training Center and its Satellites. Such a program is vital to building and maintaining quality training, with respect to both the instruction methodology and the instructional materials. It monitors the results of the training, evaluates the training effectiveness against specified objectives, and finally provides feedback to the Departments of Instruction and of Curriculum Development as the basis for improvement and quality training sustainance.

MONITORING, EVALUATION AND FEEDBACK PROGRAMS (MEP)

Monitoring, evaluation and feedback are vital to the achievement and maintenance of quality in any program; but they are particularly critical to any educational or training endeavor. Some of the roles MEP program plays in quality control for training are the refinement and improvement of:

- The instructional process and methodology.
- The course content and organization.
- The instructional materials.
- Instructor characteristics and performance.
- Trainee achievement and interest.
- On-the-job trainee performance after training.
- The trainer/trainee relationship.
- Training management.
- Selection process for training candidates.

The better the quality of the training program, the more effectively the human resources will perform to achieve its goals.

The MEP programs involve collecting information in seven consecutive steps for evaluation of training impact and quality. Data is obtained from the instructors, the trainees and the supervisors of the trainees - the trainees being the primary source. The seven steps are: Course Demographics; Pre-Assessment; Interim Evaluation; Post-Assessment; End-of-Course Evaluation; Training Impact Assessments at six months and two to three years after the course.

The MEP evaluation producers include: data collection, primarily by questionnaire; analysis of results and preparation of recommendations; and feedback provided to the units responsible for the quality of the various aspects of the training process primarily Curriculum Development and Training of the Trainers.

A survey on the impact of off-shore training courses has taken place. The survey indicated that the attitudes of trainees were strongly positive towards the training and its aspects, such as: its value in terms of technical development; its providing skills and techniques directly related to the job; the relevance of the training content to the job; recommendation of the training to others; and overall impression of the training institution. Trainees and their supervisors were asked to give two or three aspects of the training which were most useful to their current jobs. These were categorized, counted and ranked. Under the "General Irrigation Engineering" heading, the most highly ranked items were: New Techniques and Technology; Use of Computers in Irrigation; and Design of Irrigation Structures. Under the "Specific Irrigation Engineering" heading, the aspects in order of ranking were: Operation and Maintenance; Laboratory and Field Measurements; Land Reclamation and

Rehabilitation; Conservation of Water; and Reuse of Water. Under the "Irrigation Management" heading, the highest ranked aspects were: Related Non-Engineering Aspects of Irrigation; On-Farm Management; Project Planning; and Management Principles. Trainees and supervisors were in substantial agreement in their response.

Trainees and their supervisors were also asked to provide suggestions for improving the program in the future. Their responses were again categorized, counted and ranked. Three major categories were apparent from the responses, namely: Preparation for Off-shore Courses; Improvement of Off-shore Course Procedures; and Dissemination of Course Benefits in Egypt. Two major factors were apparent under the first category "Preparation for Off-shore courses": Matching of trainee needs with course content; and pre-course orientation in Egypt. Under the "Course Procedures" category the rankings were: More time for courses, trainee needs matched to course objectives; courses stress applications; applications should apply to Egypt; increased field studies, number of courses, and number of trainees. "Dissemination of Off-shore Course Benefits in Egypt" consisted of two main suggestions: Required preparation of a training report by each trainee for his/her supervisor; evaluation of the potential benefit of the course and its dissemination to the appropriate authorities. Trainees and their supervisors were again in substantial agreement.

Suggestions were requested for courses, present and future, which are needed for professional development. The three major categories were: Irrigation Engineering, Irrigation Management and Miscellaneous. The top items in order of ranking under Irrigation Engineering were: Computer Applications to Irrigation; New Techniques and Technology; Operation and Maintenance; and Design of Irrigation Structures. Under Irrigation Management were: On-Farm Management, Non-Engineering, Aspects of Irrigation Management and Project Planning and Design.

THE MEDITERRANEAN AGRONOMIC INSTITUTE OF BARI (ITALY)

The Bari Institute was created in 1962 as one of the four training Institutes of the International Center for Advanced Mediterranean Agronomic studies. The other Institutes are located in France, Spain, and Greece. The Bari Institute originally dealt with training in the area of land development and rural equipment with special reference to irrigation. Later on, given the prime importance of water problems in the Mediterranean basin, the Bari IAM became essentially a training Institute in irrigation and water management as of 1978.

Since 1984, the Institute has expanded its fields of specialization to the subject of plant protection. So far more than 1500 trainees have taken the courses given at Bari; 70% of them coming from the Mediterranean basin.

The Institute provides teaching at the post-graduate level which is both original and complementary to the training provided in national institutions. Three types of cycles are organized for the trainees:

a) Cycle of specialization, over a period of one academic year lasting nine months, sanctioned by the post-graduate specialization diploma.

b) Cycle of advanced training (or Masters Cycle) lasting over a period equivalent to two academic years, sanctioned by the Advanced Studies diploma.

c) The training sessions of short cycles lasting less than nine months and are sanctioned by a certificate of participation.

Furthermore, the Bari IAM has played an important role in the training of technicians and specialists upon request from local and regional government and public agencies.

The students benefit from teacher support throughout their training and for the completion of their personal work. Teaching is provided by permanent professors, or visiting staff of high technical level that have contributed to developing or renewing scientific thought in their countries. The diversity of these teachers, chosen in consideration of their competence and professional experience makes it possible for the participants to confront different schools of thought, and contributes to the development of the agriculture sectors in their countries.

SUMMARY AND CONCLUSIONS

Post-graduate training is essential in areas of water management and water resources. Very few undergraduate institutions provide the multi-disciplinary basic training required. Monitoring, evaluation, and feedback programs are important for the success of the training programs. In both Egypt (WRC) and Bari (Italy) two institutions have been created to provide training for national specialists and trainees from Africa, Middle East, and other developing countries. Programs in different areas of water management, water resources and land reclamation have been conducted for many years. The exchange of teachers, experience and training programs among these two institutions have proved very successful. They present an excellent model of national and international institutions that are devoted towards achieving sustainable agricultural development in developing countries.

REFERENCES

Abdelsalam, M. and Fahim A. 1987. *Training as a Tool to Improve Water Management in Egypt.* ICID. Thirteenth Congress Q41 R13.

Abu-Zeid, M., Hamdy, A., and Lacirignola, C. 1991. *Role of Research in Water Sciences as a Catalyzer of Education and Training in some Developing Countries.* Paper presented at the International Symposium on Hydrology and Water Resources Education and Training, Mexico.

Hervieu, B. ed. 1988. *Agricultural Training in Countries of the Mediterranean Region.* Proceedings of Rabat Seminar March/April, 1987. Options Mediterraneennes, ICAMAS, Paris.

Ministry of Public Works and Water Resources of Egypt, 1989. *The Monitoring, Evaluation and Feedback Program for the MPWWR* Training Center, Technical Report MPWWR, Egypt.

The World Bank, USAID, 1989. *Irrigation Training in the Public Sector. Guidelines for preparing strategies and programs.* Washington, D.C. 24 pp and annexes.

A HYDROGEOLOGICAL SURVEY IN MEXICO

J. Joel Carrillo R.
Instituto de Geofisica
UNAM, C.U. Coyoacan
04510, MEXICO D.F.

Oscar A. Escolero F.
Gerencia Aguas Subterraneas
CNA, Nuevo Leon 210
06100, MEXICO D. F.

ABSTRACT

A national inquiry was made to define the availability of professionals engaged in groundwater related activities mainly agronomists, surveyors, hydrologists, petroleum engineers, physicists, chemists, geophysicists, mathematicians, civil and geological engineers. Out of these groups civil and geological engineers are the most numerous. Two groups can be made in terms of education. The most ample is lead by undergraduates; the second one is at a postgraduate level with a remarkable small number of fully qualified professionals in groundwater hydrology.

Postgraduate professionals had been educated either in Mexico or at the foreign universities. From the former, graduates at M.Sc. level are few (5) and one at doctoral level; their engagement in groundwater education and training is non-existent. Postgraduates from foreign countries are more engaged in undergraduate and postgraduate teaching of groundwater related subjects; doctoral level is only encountered in mathematical modelling, geophysics, stratigraphy, statistics, etc., but rarely with a comprehensive background in hydrogeology. An important percentage of professionals with higher degrees in groundwater are working outside hydrogeology, for example in mining, as stock brokers and other business professions.

Diffusion of professional activities by means of publications is rather weak and hardly represents an average of one paper per five working years of a researcher. The educational/training differences between people doing research on groundwater and professionals in the problem areas, is outstanding. Education and income are not strictly related. Taking into account the surface of the country, and without considering the number of problems to be defined, and population, there is an extremely small number of professionals available in groundwater related sciences. There is not one full time hydrogeoiogist per state on the average. An appropriate number of personnel at a suitable level of education, capable to define a problem, submit a solution and supervise the process of optimal management in groundwater resources are needed.

To improve the situation and to increase the number of Mexican nationals in the groundwater profession, the education and training in groundwater related sciences are required, best through a nation-wide program that acknowledges interconnection among education, research, management and the appropriate jobs.

INTRODUCTION

The problems of groundwater in Mexico are twofold: quantity and quality. In many instances what appears to be the problem is only a symptom that may be due to several factors. The appropriate solution needs a proper definition of mechanisms which control the groundwater regime in the area of interest. This challenge can be solved with the aid of a hydrogeologist working in an interdisciplinary environment.

At present time, groundwater is a water source of high competition. Towns, industries and agriculture are sharing the same problems of water supply, depletion of aquifers and water contamination from sea water and waste disposal. When considering the future development of the country an appropriate number of efficient professionals in groundwater is required. In developed countries the aim is for one hydrogeologist per 100,000 inhabitants (Jacob Bear, personal communication, January, 1987). Mexico has a population of about 80,000,000 people.

METHODOLOGY

A national inquiry was made to define the availability of professionals engaged in groundwater related activities. A questionnaire (Fig. 1) was distributed to educational institutions, private companies and government agencies (including CNA) by two main groups: CNA (Comision Nacional del Agua) and UNAM (Universidad Nacional Autonoma de Mexico). Distribution of the questionnaire was accompanied by direct telephone communication with individual hydrogeologists. The results of this survey were then compiled into a *DBASE III PLUS* data base.

NAME _____	GROUNDWATER COURSES DATES AND SUBJECT _____
PROFESSION _____	NAME OF COMPANY AND ADDRESS _____
UNIVERSITY _____	POSITION IN COMPANY _____
GRADUATION DATE _____	NUMBER OF
THESES TITLE _____	PUBLICATIONS _____
HIGHER DEGREE _____	FIELD OF INTEREST IN GROUNDWATER _____
GRADUATION DATE _____	TEACHING ACTIVITIES
DIPLOMA _____	IN GROUNDWATER _____
GRADUATION DATE _____	SEX _____

Figure 1. Questionnaire presented to professionals engaged in groundwater activities.

It is important to emphasize that professionals engaged in drilling, well construction and maintenance activities were out of reach, due to their large number and wide-spread distribution.

RESULTS AND CONCLUSIONS

The results of the survey are shown in Figures 2 to 9. The majority of the people that were contacted are of the male sex, due perhaps to the fact that most of the engineering careers are male orientated. However this is not a feature unique to Mexico (Fig. 2).

Figure 3 shows the outstanding involvement of geological and civil engineers in groundwater related activities. However, there are hydrogeological activities carried out mainly by (surface water) hydrologists, petroleum engineers, physicists, geophysics, mathematicians, geographers among others. As it is shown in Figure 4, a large percentage of professionals

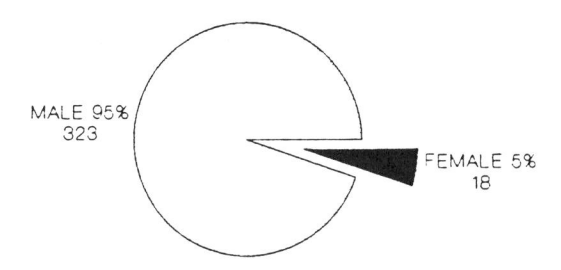

Figure 2. Relation of Professionals (by sex) engaged in groundwater.

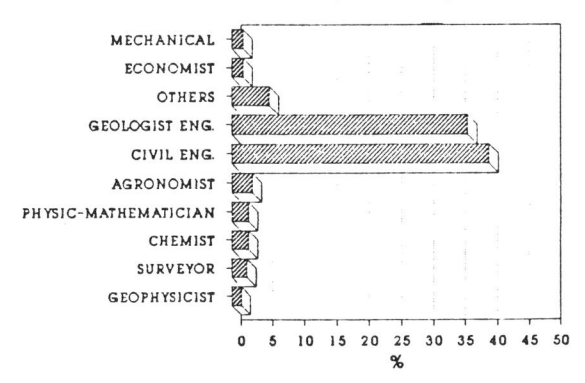

Figure 3. Original education of professionals engaged in groundwater.

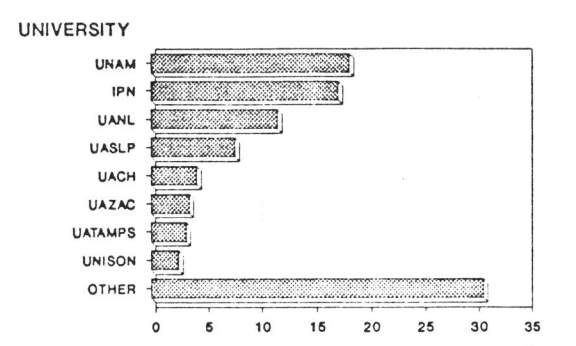

Figure 4. Center of education of Professionals engaged in groundwater.

obtained their bachelor degree from the UNAM and the IPN (Instituto Politecnico Nacional).

Figure 5 shows the professionals with a complete bachelors degree. It is important to mention that the big percentage attend courses of informative nuture (Division de Educacion Continua, Facultad de Ingenieria, UNAM) rather than those that cover specific problems, such as hydrogeochemistry, pumping tests analysis, stable isotopes, flow modelling, etc.

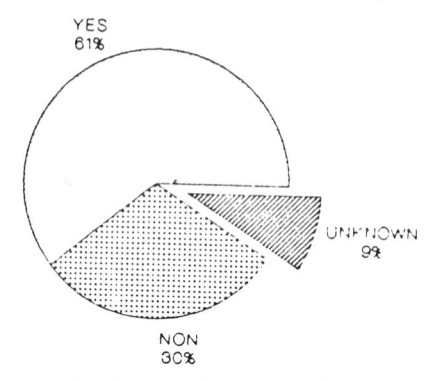

Figure 5. Fully graduated and non-graduated professionals.

Two groups of professionals according to their education can be distinguished. The most ample is lead by undergraduates; the second one is at a postgraduate level with a remarkable number of professionals without a proper education in hydrogeology. Postgraduate professionals (see Figures 6 & 7) have been either educated in Mexico or in foreign universities. From the former only five graduates have obtained an M.Sc. degree and those were from one institution, the Universidad Autonoma de Nuevo Leon (the M.Sc. programme here has since been discontinued). No Mexican national has yet obtained a doctoral degree in hydrogeology from a Mexican institution. However, one professional has a Ph. D. degree in hydraulics of groundwater modelling. Currently there are only two institutions in Mexico that provide groundwater related courses, the Faculty of Engineering at the University of Chihuahua and the Institute of Geophysics in UNAM. Postgraduates from Mexican universities have no academic activities at universities or in teaching hydrogeology. All have taken positions with government agencies or in industry.

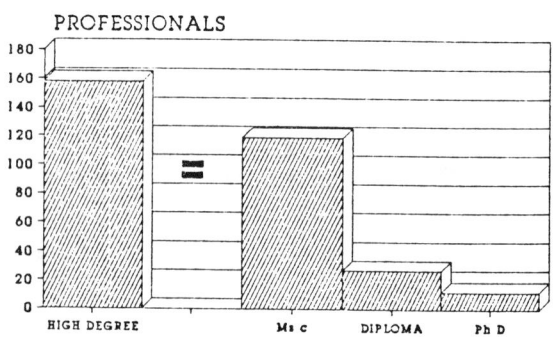

Figure 6. Number of professionals that participated in MsC and PhD training.

PHYLOSOPHY DOCTOR 10
24%

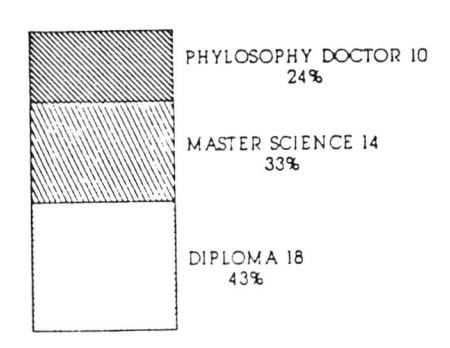

MASTER SCIENCE 14
33%

DIPLOMA 18
43%

Figure 7. Number of professionals with a higher degree working in groundwater.

There are professionals with a higher degree other than in hydrogeology, working in groundwater, because the reduced number of post-graduates in this field is not enough to cope with the present problems (Fig. 8). As far as post-graduates from foreign countries are concerned, they are mainly engaged in undergraduate and postgraduate teaching of groundwater related subjects. There are nine professionals with M.Sc. level that work on specific topics such as (surface water) hydrology, isotopes, hydrogeochemistry and hydrogeology (see Fig. 9) and there are nine professionals with doctoral degrees with their fields of interest in mathematical modelling, geophysics,

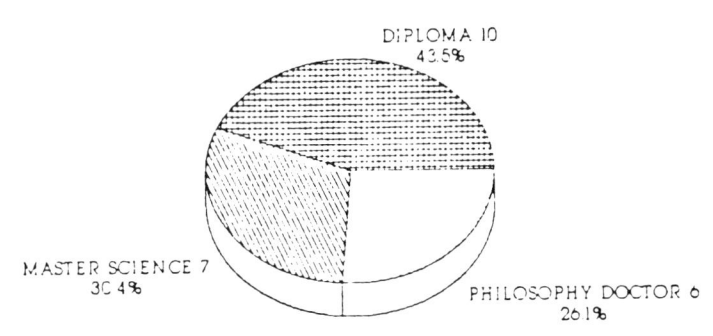

DIPLOMA 10
43.5%

MASTER SCIENCE 7
30.4%

PHILOSOPHY DOCTOR 6
26.1%

Figure 8. Number of fully qualified professionals in groundwater.

DRILLING
G.W. PROSPECTING
HIDROLOGY
G.W. R. EVALUATION
M. MODELLING
GEOPHYSICS
ISOTOPES
HYDROGEOCHEMISTRY
CONTAMINATION
ADMINISTRATION

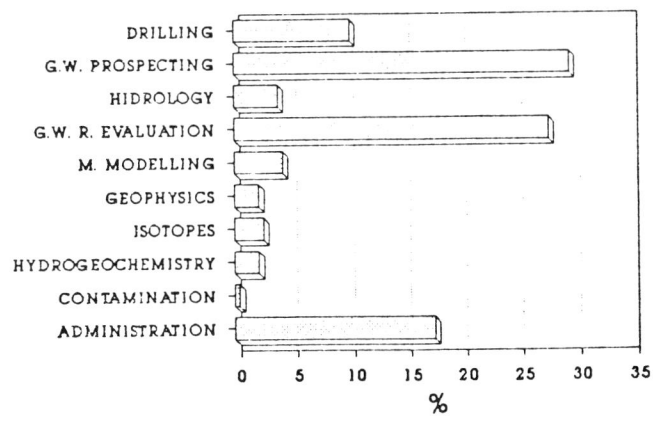

0   5   10   15   20   25   30   35
%

Figure 9. Main field of interest of professionals in groundwater.

stratigraphy, geology, (surface water) hydrology, geostatistics. Few have a comprehensive background in hydrogeology. An important number of professionals with a higher degree in groundwater are working in different fields.

The diffusion of professional activities by means of publications is rather weak and hardly represents an average of one paper per five working years per person. Basically, people who publish, work or have had academic activities at universities. Most publications are made in local journals. There is strong evidence that outside the universities they hold little value. Consequently, the education and training differences between people doing research on groundwater and professionals in the problem areas are striking. Normally, curriculum vitae and income are not directly related.

At present, there is not an appropriate number of personnel with a suitable level of education to *define a problem, submit a solution and supervise the processes of optimal* management of groundwater resources. Evidently, there is a strong need for a program that will integrate education and job availability through a scheme of incentives. This program should be put into perspective of the acute present and future groundwater problems in Mexico. The number of professionals with a thorough knowledge of processes controlling groundwater, for example sea water intrusion, over-exploitation and contamination, falls far below the number of personnel needed to cope with the present problems. Therefore, the situation in an immediate future will further deteriorate if the number of properly trained professional hydrogeologists remains low.

Abbreviations used in figures

UANL, Universidad Autonoma de Nuevo Leon

UASLP, Universidad Autonoma de San Luis Potosi

UACH, Universidad Autonoma de Chihuahua

UAZAC, Universidad Autonoma de Zacatecas

UATAMPS, Universidad Autonoma de Tamaulipas

UNISON, Universidad de Sonora

EFFICIENCY OF PRACTICAL SHORT TIME TRAINING COURSES IN HYDROCHEMISTRY-HYDROGEOLOGY AT UNIVERSITIES OF DEVELOPING COUNTRIES

J. Bundschuh
Institute of Geology and Paleontology
University of Tübingen
Sigwartstr.10, D-7400 Tübingen
Federal Republic of Germany.

ABSTRACT

Assistant professorships in the fields of hydrochemistry and hydrogeology at universities in Pakistan and Argentine gave opportunity to the author to test the efficiency of different comprehensive one-month training courses for post-graduate students, hydrogeologists, chemists and engineers working at water supply organizations. In general, there is a deficiency of practical training at universities of developing countries. To solve this problem, special training courses were given, based on experiences and made during the advanced studies course entitled "Hydrogeology and Engineering Geology of Tropical and Subtropical Regions" at Tübingen University (Germany). They were attended by students of developing countries. The results of investigation program concerning the groundwater quality of Peshawar Valley (Pakistan), were discussed with the participants after finishing the hydrochemical courses at the university.

INTRODUCTION

Nowadays, we live at a time when the anthropogenic pollution of ground- and surface waters is of great importance. Furthermore, in many agricultural areas, the use of unsuitable irrigation water causes rising salification problems. For these facts, it is absolutely necessary for hydrogeologists and engineers working in this subject to have enough hydrochemical knowledge.

The high deficiency of practical training at universities of developing countries is found in the fields of hydrochemistry and hydrogeology, because they are the comparatively new fields of teaching and investigations in those countries. Some exceptions excluded, hydrochemistry is not offered in subjects taught at universities of developing countries. If it is offered, in most of cases, only the theoretical lectures of the related subjects are given. As typical in many developing countries, such as Argentine and Pakistan, the fast growing industries and agriculture cause an increase in demand for drinking, industrial and irrigation water. Simultaneously, the amount of sewage water and general wastes are rising. The pollution of ground- and surface water is increasing. To ensure water supply in the future, it is necessary to protect groundwater resources. Therefore, hydrochemical-hydrogeological knowledge are absolutely necessary. To solve the problems of this nature, different intensive practical training courses of the duration of one month each on these subjects were carried out at the universities of Peshawar/Pakistan (1988) and Salta/Argentine (1990 and 1991). The courses are based on experience gained during the advanced studies course entitled "Hydrogeology and Engineering Geology of Tropical and Subtropical Regions" at the Institute of Geology in Tübingen, West Germany, where students of many developing countries participated.

The above-mentioned "Advanced Studies Course" is presented briefly. This course at the Geological Institute of Tübingen University lasts a year. It is attended by both, the foreign and German participants of eight persons each, which have finished their regular studies in geology (diploma, M.S., or licenciado). The course language is English. The lectures and practical training courses as well construction, regional hydrogeology, applied hydrochemistry, soil mechanics, technical reports, raw material, tunnelling, surveying, geophysics, geothermics, road construction and hydraulic engineering are given by professors and lecturers of different German universities and persons from industry. Having foreign and German students studying alongside each other proved to be a most stimulating experience. Additionally, the common study of participants from different continents shall support the intercultural understanding and the willingness for partnerships of cooperation. The new ideas and points of view made for much vivid discussions that raised many a doubt about the ongoing ways of thinking. The main objective of the "Advanced Studies Course" has been to train postgraduate students of geology of developing countries and Germans in the fields of applied hydrogeology and engineering geology in tropical and subtropical regions. The courses are intended to improve the basic requirements of of technical and economic missions in developing countries.

COURSES

The courses entitled "Applied Hydrochemistry", "Calculation Methods in Hydrochemistry" and "Introduction to Groundwater Modeling" are composed of lectures, practical exercises, computer work, laboratory work and field work. The aim of the first course "Applied Hydrochemistry" is to get fundamental knowledge of practical hydrochemistry. The course includes lectures (60 hours), laboratory exercises (80 h), 5 field work days and the preparation of reports. After finishing this course, participants should have sufficient knowledge to carry out self-reliant water analysis for the most important chemical compounds contained in natural water samples and to interpret the analysis data in the hydrogeological sense.

In the course "Calculation Methods in Hydrochemistry", the participants sould learn how to use hydrochemical and physical analysis of data of water samples to do hydrochemical calculations and to interpret the results within a global hydrogeological framework. Calculations of chemical equilibria of multiphase and multi-component systems found in ground and surface waters are carried out. The use of stability fields (Eh-pH diagrams) and the calculations of corresponding redox systems are of special practical interest. The optimal choice of suitable hydrochemical procedures and the correct use of special evaluation methods for different scopes of duties and problems are handled in details. The correct use of modern hydrochemical computer programs is taught. Hydrochemical calculations of examples similar to natural ones and of real case studies are carried out and discussed. The participants are trained to solve hydrochemical problems on their own.

The course "Introduction to Groundwater Modeling" should train the participants to simulate the groundwater flow and the propagation of pollutants in groundwater using the numerical computer programs.

Participants of courses held in Argentine, consisting of postgraduate students and employees in hydrogeology and chemistry, showed more interest than the average student did at the university in Tübingen (Germany). Both, geologists and chemists had no knowledge in practical field work. Additionally, geologists had no experience and knowledge of laboratory work. Additionally, there was another drawback. The first report, written by participants, showed that all of them had great problems to review, to discuss and to evaluate the results obtained during the field- and laboratory work. The first reports have contained only descriptions. This deficiency, namely that participants were not able to interpret hydrochemical results and analysis data of water samples, can be explained by the fact that neither at schools nor at universities the thinking, interpreting and discussing the interpretation results were taught. During these courses, this deficiency was removed quickly. Participants recognized soon that interpretation and discussion of facts are of great importance.

Carrying out hydrochemical and hydrogeological field investigations in Pakistan and Argentine, together with participants of the courses, students showed that most of them have learned to use the knowledge obtained at the above mentioned courses by using them to make hydrochemical investigations, to estimate the quality of water for different purposes, to recognize sources of pollutions and to give ideas on how to protect ground- and surface waters against pollution. These examples of practical training in using the concrete field examples and tasks have shown an excellent way of learning.

Basing on the first course given in Peshawar/Pakistan, a hydrochemical investigation program was carried out, where special hydrochemical and hydrogeological investigations related to the problems in the vicinity of Peshawar as salification and pollution were carried out. Thereby, it could be recognized that this type of practical training with concrete tasks and exercises leads to an optimal learning success. The fact that contacts with some students who participated at the courses have existed up to this day, shows, that, at least some students, acquired useful information, both at the theoretical and especially at the practical level. That information was a base for applying the more difficult analyses of their own hydrochemical and hydrogeological problems. The scientific results of investigations, carried out in Peshawar Valley, are presented in the following chapter.

EXAMPLE: PESHAWAR VALLEY (PAKISTAN) AND ITS GROUNDWATER QUALITY

Summary

Groundwater in the marginal areas of the Peshawar Valley is little mineralized and is of good quality. It consists of alkaline earth freshwater with hydrogen-carbonates prevailing. Toward the center of the Valley the degree of mineralization increases and the hydrochemical composition changes forming the alkaline freshwater which is either hydrogen-carbonatic or sulphatic-chloridic. This gives rise to the salination problems, rendering groundwater of this part of the Peshawar Valley unsuitable as drinking water. Moreover, it should not be used for irrigation as it is used nowadays.

Introduction

Increasing demands for drinking, irrigation and industrial water on the part of five million people living in the Peshawar Valley requires that additional water sources of satisfactory quality be tapped. Moreover, long neglect of the hydrochemical composition of groundwater supplies has led to salinization of both water and soil in at least some parts of the Peshawar Valley. Accordingly a comprehensive training scheme and investigation program on these and related hydrochemical groundwater problems were launched at the National Center of Excellence in Geology at the University of Peshawar, Pakistan. The combination of a one-month training course backed up by two months of field work, proved to be especially successful. It gave participants the chance to become familiar not only with the theory and the measuring methods, but also with the hydrogeological features of the area under investigation. Areas of the Peshawar Valley containing either suitable or unsuitable groundwater could be determined by the chemical composition of groundwater and its level of mineralization.

Area of Investigation

Geography and geology - The Peshawar Valley is located in the northwestern part of Pakistan. It covers an area of approximately 8000 km^2 (Fig. 1). The topography ranges from 270 m above sea level in the center of the basin to 460 m at its margins. The mean annual precipitation ranges from 330 mm to 600 mm. The mean annual air temperature in Peshawar is 23 °C. Peshawar Valley - a structural depression - consists of a sandy plain with an undulating relief. It is nearly completely surrounded by mountainous regions of metamorphic and sedimentary rocks, except at its southeast boundary facing the Indus Valley. Peshawar Valley is filled with alluvial sediments of quaternary age with a thickness amounting up to several hundred metres. The lithological composition of alluvial fill varies in both vertical and horizontal planes.

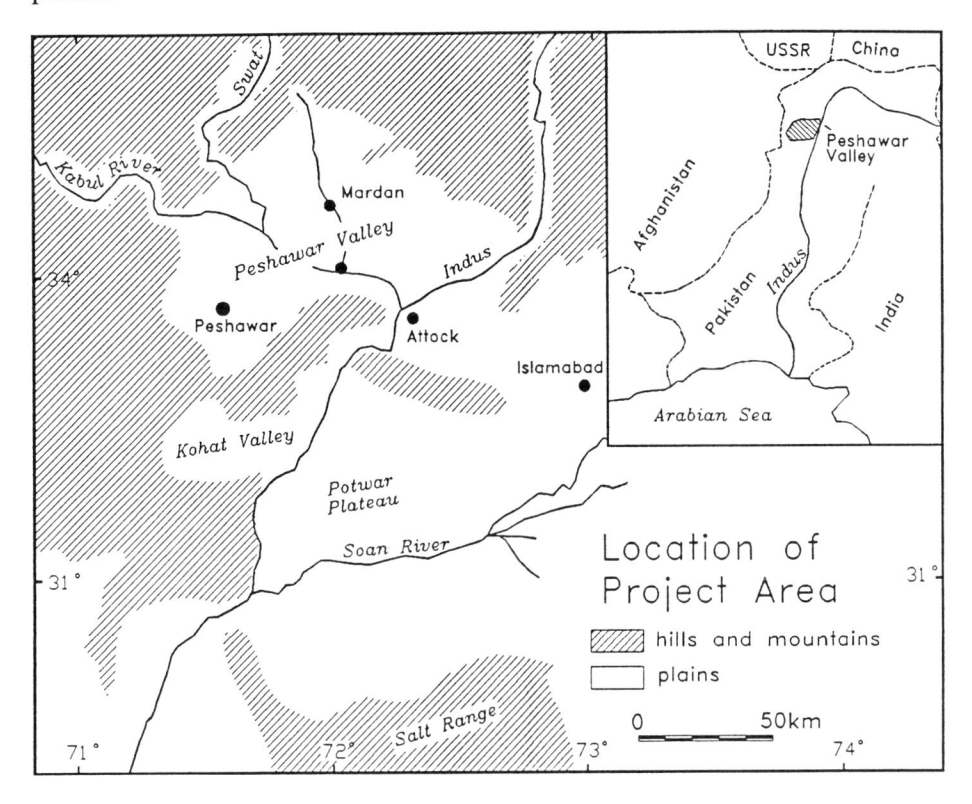

Figure 1.

Surface Water

The calcium-hydrogencarbonate waters of rivers are of low mineralization. Their electrical conductivity values range between 250 and 500 µS/cm. Because of low incidence of mineralization the surface water can be used for irrigational purposes.

Hydrogeology

The uppermost and, for the most part, unconfined aquifer in the Peshawar Valley is the most important one. It consists of alternating layers of clay, silt, sand and gravel, and is exploited by numerous dug and drilled wells of various depths. The depth of groundwater table is more than 5 m deep near the surrounding mountains and decreases to values less than 1.5 m deep in the center of the basin (Fig. 2). In combination with irrigational salification of soil and groundwater due to evaporation has to be expected. Using the map of the groundwater level above the sea level, it is apparent that there is a general groundwater flow from the margins of the basin towards the center with an average gradient of about 0.004. In the center, both the slope of the groundwater table and, in close dependence, the velocity of the groundwater flow decrease approaching zero.

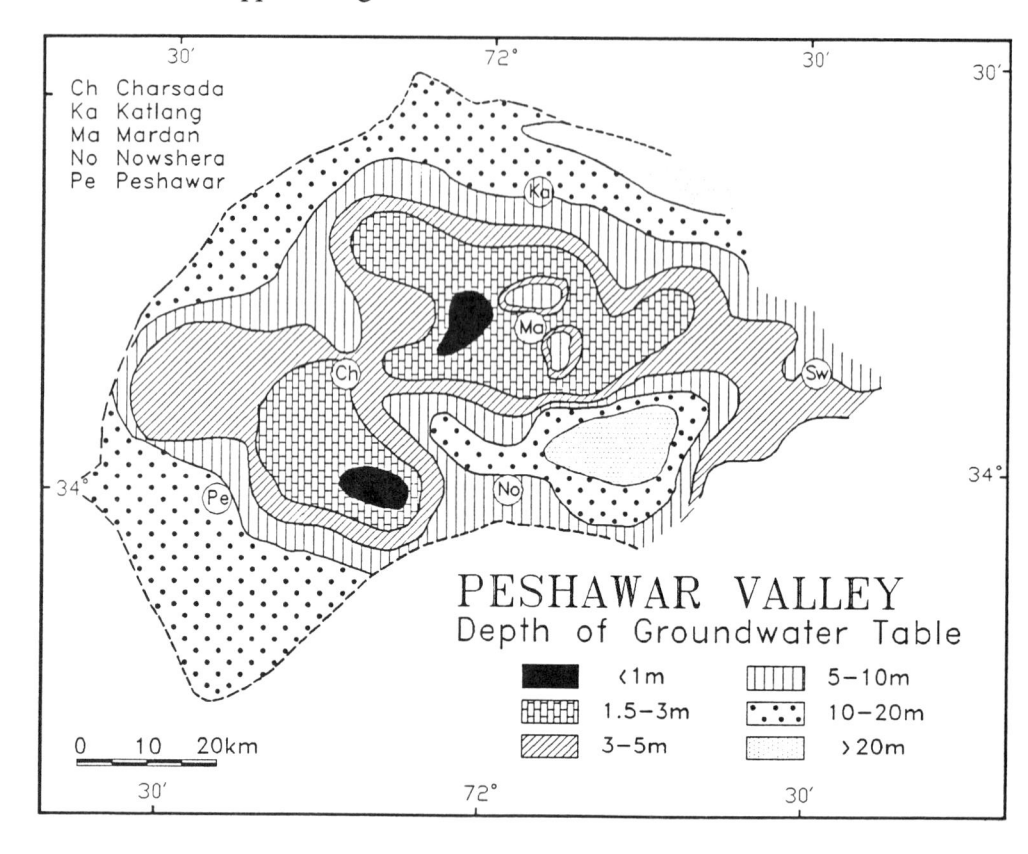

Figure 2.

Hydrochemistry

The hydrochemical investigations comprise measurements of groundwater temperature, electrical conductivity, pH-value, dissolved oxygen content and a chemical water analysis performed at the University of Peshawar.

Electrical conductivity - The regional distribution of electrical conductivity - a general index of mineralization - shows values ranging from less than 800 µS/cm at the margins of the Peshawar Valley up to 7800 µS/cm in its center (Fig. 3). The distribution of electrical conductivity corresponds to the depth of the groundwater table: the shallower the groundwater table, the higher conductivity. During its flow into the center of the basin the groundwater dissolves ions from sediments of the aquifer. Moreover, additional ion enrichment takes place by evaporation. The central region with electrical conductivities higher than about 4000 µS/cm is covered with a thin crust of salt. In some areas of the central part of the basin, highly mineralized groundwater with electrical conductivities of about 2000 µS/cm is used for irrigation which will lead to an increasing salt content in both soil and groundwater. There are also settlements where drinking water drawn from depths of between 25 and 60 m has electrical conductivities of nearly 3000µS/cm, caused by high concentration of sodium, sulphate and chloride. Prolonged use of this water could affect human health.

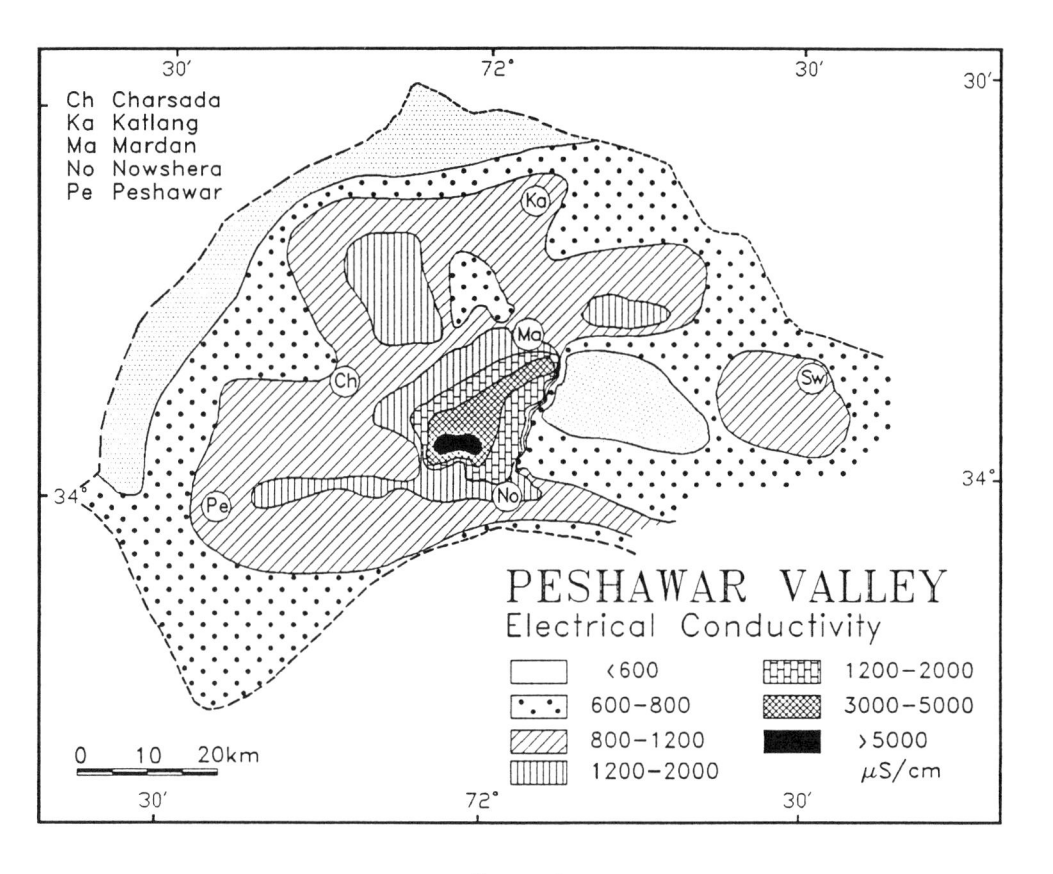

Figure 3.

Groundwater composition - Calcium and magnesium: In most samples the calcium (magnesium) concentrations range from 30 to 100 (15 to 50) mg/l without any regional trends being evident. Only in some of the highly mineralized groundwater samples from the central part of Peshawar Valley do we find higher contents ranging up to 260 (240) mg/l. **Sodium and potassium:** On the other hand, sodium (potassium) is distributed non-homogeneously, but with concentrations increasing from less than 50 (6) mg/l near the boundaries of the basin towards the center with values up to 850 (22) mg/l. **Hydrogencarbonate and sulphate:** The concentration of hydrogencarbonate ions in most of the groundwater ranges from 300 to 600 mg/l. This wide range is clearly caused by lithological heterogeneities in the aquifer. Also, the highly mineralized groundwater in the center of Peshawar

Valley has a low hydrogencarbonate content. The sulphate concentration increases from the margins towards the center. The chloride concentration increases from values less than 20 mg/l at the margins of the basin up to 1240 mg/l in the center. Additionally at some sites, increased contents have been found which are caused by anthropogenic pollution. Except for three human-polluted dug wells, where nitrate concentrations of up to 200 mg/l were registered, the nitrate contents are less than 50 mg/l, in most of the cases even less than 20 mg/l.

By way of summary, it can be stated that the concentrations of calcium, magnesium, potassium, hydrogencarbonate and nitrate in the Peshawar Valley are more or less uniform, whereas sodium, sulphate and chloride are especially responsible for the different grades of mineralization and the abundance of different types of groundwaters encountered in the Peshawar Valley. The low values of nitrate and chloride over the greater part of the area indicate that there is no or only negligible fertilizer-induced groundwater pollution so far.

Groundwater classification - The analytical data plotted in the PIPER-diagram show that three hydrochemical types (I to III) of groundwater can be distinguished (Fig. 4). Hydrochemical type I (to which the PIPER fields e and g belong) comprises "alkaline earth freshwater with higher concentrations of

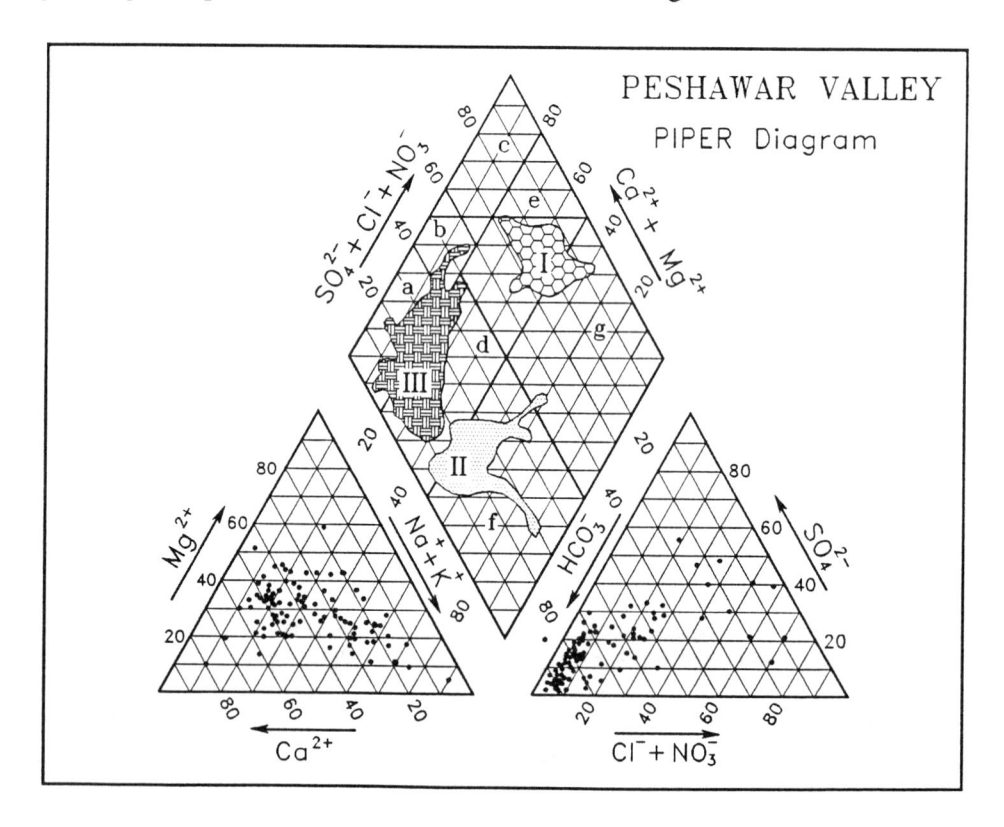

Figure 4.

alkalies prevailing sulfatic" (field e) and "alkaline freshwater prevailing sulfatic-chloridic" (field g) is found in the center of the Peshawar Valley. It has the highest mineralization (more than 2000 µS/cm). Hydrochemical type II belongs mostly to the PIPER field f and comprises "alkaline freshwater prevailing hydrogencarbonatic". Groundwater of this type with electrical conductivities ranging between 800 and 2000 µS/cm also occurs in the center. Groundwater type III is mainly restricted to the PIPER field d, but partly occurs in fields a and b as well. It comprises "alkaline earth freshwater with increased alkalies, prevailing hydrocarbonatic" (field d), "normal alkaline earth fresh water prevailing hydrogencarbonatic" (field a), and "hydrogencarbonatic-sulfatic" (field b). This groundwater type is distributed all over the Peshawar Valley, except for the central part.

Conclusions and Recommendations - From the hydrochemical point of view, the surface water in the Peshawar Valley is usable because of its low mineralization. Also the quality of groundwater, except in its center, is good. The groundwater in the central part contains the increased amounts of sulfate, chloride and sodium and should therefore not be used as drinking water as is done nowadays. It is desirable that it can be solved as soon as possible, either by drilling deeper wells or by installing pipes to existing wells in the vicinity that do deliver water of good quality. In some regions characterized by a shallow groundwater table, the people use groundwater with a very high salt content for irrigation. Since the salt content is increased still further by high evaporation rates, irrigation will lead to great salification problems with the soil if maintained. Also, the groundwater will become enriched by dissolved ions. Hence, it would be desirable to reduce the scale of irrigation with this highly mineralized water.

REFERENCES

American Public Health Assoc.(Ed.) (1979). *Standard Methods for the Examination of Water and Wastewater.* 16 th Ed. Washington, DC, USA.

Bundschuh, J. (1988). *Introduction to Quantitative Water Analysis: A Practical Guide for Hydrogeologists.* Institut of Geology and Palaeontology. Tübingen, Germany.

FAO (Ed.) (1986). *Codex Alimentarius, Methods of Analysis for Natural Mineral Waters.* Food and Agriculture Organization of the United Nations, Rome, Italy.

Fresenius, W., Quentin, K.E. and Schneider, W. (Eds.) (1988): *Water Analysis. A Practical Guide to Physico-Chemical, Chemical and Microbiological Water Examination and Quality Assurance.* Springer Verlag. Berlin, Heidelberg.

Hoell, K. (1968). Wasser, 7th edition. Walter de Gruyter, Berlin, New York (in German).

Rafiq, M.Irshad Ahmad & Tazeem Tahirkheli (1983). *A Geological Map of the Surrounding of the Peshawar Plain.* Geol. Bulletin, University of Peshawar. Vol. 6 1983.

HYDROLOGY AND WATER MANAGEMENT IN THE CONTEXT OF THE CHIHUAHUA STATE PROGRAM OF SCIENCE AND TECHNOLOGY

Adolfo Chavez
Facultad de Ingenieria,
Universidad Autónoma de Chihuahua
Apartado Postal 1528-C,
Chihuahua, Chih. 31160, Mexico

Alberto Ramirez
Subcomité Especial de Ciencia y Tecnologia,
Gobierno del Estado de Chihuahua
Edificio Heroes de 1a Revolucion, 4° Piso
Chihuahua, Chih. 31000, Mexico

ABSTRACT

In view of aridity conditions that prevail in most of the state of Chihuahua and northern Mexico, the limitted availability of water is a factor for social welfare and economic growth, so that the rational development of water resources and the appropriate water management are of the uppermost importance for these regions. The acknowledgment of this situation has prompted the Chihuahua state government to include research on hydrology and water resources management as a priority in the context of the Chihuahua State Program of science and technology. In formulation of this program the diagnosis of the state research institutions was done, a number of strategies were devised to promote the scientific and technological development, and a higher level of cooperation among the research institutions, the productive sector and the government agencies is encouraged.

INTRODUCTION

The government of Chihuahua, Mexico, has recently established the so-called State Program of Science and Technology (PECT), in an effort to promote scientific research and technological development in the state, increase the tranfer of scientific and technological knowledge, and encourage a high link and cooperation among the state research institutions, and between these institutions on one side and the productive sector and government agencies on the other.

It is recognized in this program that research in the area of hydrology and water resources management is a high priority for the state, in view of social and economic benefits that it entails.

We describe briefly in this paper the general situation of water resources in the state of Chihuahua, the characteristics of the state institutions where research in hydrology and water resources management is carried out, and strategies that have been devised to accomplish the objectives of the PECT.

WATER RESOURCES IN CHIHUAHUA

The state of Chihuahua, in northern Mexico, extends over an arid to semiarid region known as the Chihuahuan desert, where the low availability of water has always been a limiting factor for social welfare and economic growth. Productive activities such as rainfed agriculture and cattle raising are often affected by droughts, and the high variability of rainfall, both in quantity and timing from year to year, makes difficult the planning and sustained development of these activities. In some important agricultural areas the high salinity of groundwater used for irrigation precludes better crops.

Urban areas suffer traditionally the water shortages during the summer months, in particular Chihuahua City, the state capital, and in a lesser degree Juarez City, at the border to the United States of America. The industrial development of these cities resulting from the expansion of the "maquila" factories in the last decades has induced high rates of population growth, which has made difficult and expensive to supply water at the same pace as it is demanded.

In the state of Chihuahua groundwater contributes the most to water supply for cities and for some agricultural areas, and the relatively high rates of pumping have caused the overdraft of a number of important aquifers. On the other hand, industrial wastes, urban effluents and the use of agrochemicals have posed risks for surface and ground water contamination, with still highly unquantified types and amounts of hazardous substances affecting the sources of water, and the vulnerability of different aquifers to pollution.

Inasmuch as the water resources of the state of Chihuahua are scarce and they will be even more restricted in the future, their optimal and appropriate management is of a high priority. The Mexican National Water Commission (CNA) is taking resolute steps in this direction, but the cooperation by consumers is mandatory to avoid abuse and misuse of water and protect it from contamination.

With this background, the need to intensify scientific research and technological development in the area of hydrology and water resources management is clear. The state research institutions can positively contribute to the solution of many problems related to exploration, development, evaluation, use, treatment, protection, planning and management of water resources.

WATER RESEARCH INSTITUTIONS

Research in hydrology and water resources management in the state of Chihuahua is mostly carried out at the Universidad Autonoma de Chihuahua (UACH), in Chihuahua City, the Universidad Autonoma de Ciudad Juarez (UACJ) and the Escuela Superior de Agricultura Hermanos Escobar (ESAHE), these latter located in Juarez City. At the Colegio de la Frontera Norte (COLEF), also in Juarez City, some research is done on socioeconomic aspects of water.

At the Universidad Autonoma de Chihuahua water resources research is performed at the Schools of Engineering and Animal Science. At the School of Engineering research was instituted in 1978 with some projects on groundwater hydrology. Now, it is associated with a master program on Arid Lands Water Resources, being the main lines of investigation of surface and ground water hydrology and water quality. At the School of Animal Science research is done on watershed management, linked to master and doctorate programs on range management.

The Universidad Autonoma de Ciudad Juarez offers a master program in groundwater hydrology and some research is carried out on that line. Lately, however, the study of water quality and environmental engineering is getting more prominence.

With regard to the Escuela Superior de Agricultura Hermanos Escobar research is done on water management for agriculture, and it is associated with a master program on water resources management.

This review of the works of state institutions indicates that research production goes from low to moderate, with most of it generated at the School of Engineering of UACH, where it is however not at its optimum. Although these institutions count with physical resources and some equipment, all of them require a greater financial support directed specifically to research. This support has been so far insufficient, uncertain and untimely.

STRATEGIES OF THE PECT

The main objective of the PECT is to promote scientific research and technological development in the state of Chihuahua. It aims in a first step to set up a State's System of Science and Technology, which will have among its functions to establish and revise periodically the orientation of different areas of research and development according to the state's needs. To accomplish this general objective some basic strategies have been lined out in the PECT. These are:

(a) to encourage an interdisciplinary and multi-institutional approach to research and development in order to optimize the use of existent resources and equipment, and to promote the formation of research groups capable to generate solutions to actual regional problems,

(b) to design and implement mechanisms to link the state research institutions with the potential users of research results, such as local industry, government agencies, non-profit organizations, etc.,

(c) to establish a fund to support scientific research and technological development in the state of Chihuahua. This fund will be constituted by contributions of the private sector and the state government. Additionally, the federal government will contribute a share equivalent to that provided by the state government, which will be earmarked to specific projects, and

(d) to create an information center specialized in science and technology, not only to provide the up-to-date bibliography for local researchers, but also to serve as a means of communication at the state level among all the different research groups and institutions.

CONCLUSIONS

The diagnosis of the socio-economic and ecological problems in the state of Chihuahua, as described by the PECT, furnishes the main subjects of research and development to be confronted in the near future. Nevertheless, for these scientific and technological activities to be part of the decision-making process, an appropriate coordination between research institutions on one side and private sector and government agencies on the other is required. Additionally, a greater financial support is needed in order to increase productivity in the state research institutions and to generate research outcomes more competitive at the international level.

Although research in the area of hydrology and water resources management shares many of the problems affecting the other areas, the increasing appreciation of its importance by the federal and the state governments and by the private sector has to be accomplished. Times are now favorable to consolidate this area, and the achievements to reach in the state of Chihuahua can be of a unique nature in Mexico.

PART B

1 KEYNOTE LECTURES

DEVELOPMENT OF THE INTERNATIONAL BOUNDARY AND WATER COMMISSION: INTERNATIONAL WASTEWATER TREATMENT PLANT

Narendra N. Gunaji, Commissioner
U.S. Section, IBWC
4171 N. Mesa, Suite C-310
El Paso, Texas 79902

This presentation deals with technical aspects of the international border sanitation problem in the Tijuana River Valley, San Diego, California, as stipulated in IBWC Minute No. 283 which was signed on July 2, 1990.

This Minute is the first phase to allow the Commission to design and construct international treatment and conveyance facilities as part of the international solution to the border sanitation problem in San Diego, California, United States and Tijuana, Baja California, Mexico.

In 1984-1985, the two governments discussed an international plant solution and the U.S. Congress authorized initial expenditures for U.S. participation. Mexico chose instead to proceed with a first stage treatment plant system to serve the existing population through 1989 and left open talks for future works. In view of Mexico's decision, the U.S. then proposed the "Return to Sender" project, which was developed for intercepting flows of various canyons entering the U.S. in the Tijuana River Valley from Tijuana, Baja California, and returning these flows to Mexico through a pumping plant into Tijuana's conveyance system and on to Mexico's first stage treatment plant located 5.6 miles south of the border at San Antonio de los Buenos. As a result of the two governments' interest at the highest levels for an international plant solution, this "Return to Sender" project was later modified and included as a part of the international project stipulated in Minute No. 283. The agreement calls for the treatment of these flows in the United States, disposal of treated effluent Into the Pacific Ocean, and return of treated sludge to Mexico.

This new plan involves the construction, operation and maintenance of international treatment facilities in the U.S. in lieu of the construction of sewage treatment facilities at Rio Alamar for the City of Tijuana, Baja California. Also, it includes the design, construction, operation and maintenance of a conveyance system to convey treated sewage from the international treatment facility to the Pacific Ocean.

The first phase is the design and construction of the land outfall. The design of a portion of this phase was completed in August 1990 and construction is expected to occur between April 1991 and April 1993. The land outfall, or as it is titled, "South Bay Land Outfall" (SBLO), is a 12-foot diameter pipe approximately 12,300 feet in length in the Tijuana River Valley in the U.S.

The second phase is the design and construction of the international treatment facility. This treatment facility will be designed for an initial capacity of 25 million gallons per day (MGD) with the capability to enlarge to 100 MGD. This treatment facility will include a sewage collection and conveyance system in Mexico to capture sewage flows, to convey these flows to the proposed treatment facility in the U.S. and to return treated sludge to Mexico. This treatment facility will also include the interception of flows in the U.S. from various canyons along the border and conveyance of those renegade flows to the proposed treatment facility. Advertisement for the design of the treatment facilities was made on January 7, 1991. The U.S. Section is in the process of evaluating the applications submitted by various engineering firms to design the treatment plant with the intention to award the contract for the design of the facilities by June 1991 and to complete the design by December 1992. The estimated completion of construction is mid-1995.

The third phase is the design and construction of the land outfall extension, also known as the "South Bay Land Outfall Extension" (SBLOE). The proposed SBLOE will be designed to convey an average flow of 181 MGD with a peak flow of 343 MGD. The SBLOE will connect the proposed SBLO to the proposed ocean outfall. Advertisement for the design of the land outfall extension was made on January 7, 1991, and the engineering firms responding to this advertisement are being evaluated to determine the best qualified firm for the design of the land outfall extension. The City of San Diego will participate in the selection of the best qualified firm since the design of the SBLOE will be a joint project and the City of San Diego will be funding part of the design. The award of the design for the SBLOE is expected by June 1991, with the design completed by December 1991.

The fourth phase is the design and construction of the ocean outfall, also known as the "South Bay Ocean Outfall" (SBOO). The proposed SBOO will be designed as part of the SBLOE. As with the Land Outfall Extension, the City of San Diego will participate in the selection of the best qualified firm since the design of the SBOO is a joint project with the City of San Diego. Award of the design of the SBOO is expected by June 1991, with the design completed by December 1992.

The estimated construction cost for the entire project is over 300 million dollars. The estimated construction cost of the international sewage treatment plant is about 100 million dollars. The construction cost of the first phase of the 12-foot diameter discharge pipe is $19.7 million. The estimated cost of the land outfall extension for approximately 6,800 linear feet and the ocean outfall is estimated at about $150 million. Mexico's direct participation in the financing of the international project applies to only the international sewage treatment plant. The cost of the discharge line and ocean outfall will be funded in the U.S. by federal and City of San Diego funds.

The International Boundary and Water Commission is aware that the Tijuana River flows presently carry sizeable amounts of sewage and would continue until the international plant is on line. It has under consideration, interim works in Mexico to divert these flows out of the river and temporarily convey them through existing lines to treatment facilities in both countries.

This overall project, when completed and implemented in either late 1994 or early 1995, will be a permanent solution to the problem of renegade flows through the various canyons entering the U.S. and through the Tijuana River. This project would not be possible without Mexico's interest in improving the sanitary conditions along the border and, as an international project, is another example of the cooperation that has existed between the U.S. and Mexico through the IBWC in solving technical problems along the border.

DEVELOPMENT OF IBWC INTERNATIONAL WASTE WATER TREATMENT PLANT

Arturo Herrera Solis
Av. Universidad Num. 2180
Ciudad Juarez, Chih., Mexico

The City of San Diego (San Diego) -- City of Tijuana (Tijuana) border sewage disposal problem has existed since the early 1930's. The problem stems from the rapid growth in population of the City of Tijuana, in conjunction with a much slower growth of sewerage facilities. The following brief history of the United States/Mexican International Border (Border) area sewage disposal problems has been summarized from References 1 and 2.

The Tijuana septic system, operated in the 1930's, was frequently overloaded causing the discharge of untreated sewage to the Tijuana (also referenced Tia Juana) River Basin. Contamination of crops and wells in the San Ysidro area were reported.

Recognition of the significance of the sewage problem by U.S. and Mexican public health officials resulted in the construction of the Lower Tia Juana Valley Sanitation Project (San Ysidro Sewer) in 1938. The San Ysidro Sewer conveyed sewage discharge from the Tijuana septic system, along the Tijuana River, to an ocean outfall located 3/4-mile north of the Border.

The San Ysidro Sewer performed adequately for 10 years. In 1948 the Tijuana population had increased to over 50,000, creating a sewage flow of 2.5 million gallons per day (MGD). The California State Legislature, through the International Boundary and Water Commission (IBWC), requested that Mexican officials initiate construction of adequate sewage facilities for Tijuana.

By 1953, the sewage discharge from Tijuana had increased to 3.5 MGD and, to improve the Tijuana sewage disposal system, both Governments initiated a chlorination program for the disinfection of the San Ysidro Sewer ocean discharge. By 1957, the chlorination program, could not adequately disinfect the discharge. Mexican officials consequently developed the long-term solution to the problem. Meanwhile, California's beaches adjacent to the Border were quarantined by the San Diego County Public Health Department. Construction of various sewage facilities in Mexico were initiated, including two pumping stations, a pressure line, a conveyance channel and a treatment facility, the last one was not completed due to lack of funds.

In 1959, the IBWC was informed by San Diego that emergency capacity was available in the Metro system for sewage from Tijuana. Arrangements were made in 1965 for the construction of an Emergency Metro Connection. The contract between San Diego and the Mexican government allowed

Tijuana the use the excess capacity in the Metro system for more than 20 years.

Discharge to the San Ysidro Sewer was discontinued and the quarantine of the nearby beaches was lifted. In the late 1960's, most of the Tijuana sewage was discharged to a partially completed Mexican canal that routed the sewage 5.6 miles south of the Border to the ocean. The emergency bypass system only carried an estimated eight percent (8%) of the Tijuana sewage flow. Occasional breakdown of the Mexican facilities caused sewage to discharge to the Tijuana River Basin.

Increased availability of potable water to Tijuana through 1975 caused increased sewage flows. Approximately 20 MGD of sewage was now generated in Tijuana and the emergency bypass connection was carrying up to 70 percent of the Tijuana sewage flow.

By 1985 the Mexican Government prepared plans for execution of the Integrated Project for Potable Water and Sanitary Sewerage of Tijuana. These plans include, among other fundamental features for the first stage treatment and disposal of Tijuana wastewaters features such as: the new pumping plant No. 1, a new pressure conveyance line with a maximum capacity of 62 million gallons per day, (MGD) (2700 liters per second, 1ps), considerably greater than the previous one, a totally concrete lined gravity wastewater conveyance canal and accessory structures to finally dispose of these wastewaters in a secondary treatment plant with technology adequate for Mexican conditions.

The Integrated Project designed to provide service to a projected population of 1,200,000 inhabitants and planned in such a manner so as to function in two stages, a first stage concentrating all the wastewater into the new pumping plant No. 1. When the concentrated discharge reaches the design capacity of the plant, the system will be separated into two large basins. The Western Basin will continue to drain towards Pumping Plant No. 1 and the Eastern Basin will drain to a site tentatively located on the right bank of the Alamar Arroyo, approximately 500 meters upstream of its confluence with the Tijuana River.

The wastewater collection system is formed in two large stages, stage number one, or transitional, and number two, or final.

DESCRIPTION OF TRANSITIONAL OPERATION (STAGE NO. 1)

The first stage is planned in such a manner that the system will operate by concentrating all the the wastewater from the Tijuana River Basin in pumping plant No. 1.

The Integrated Project proposes expansion of the system, rehabilitating and expanding the subsystems; that is, all the existing collectors and subcollectors will be rehabilitated and new collectors and subcollectors will be constructed. In order to integrate the Eastern Basin of the Tijuana River, it will be necessary to construct, in the future, the additional Second Stage works to handle flows greater than the capacity of the Stage 1 works.

Along the route of the conveyance canal's path, the contribution from the area named "Playas de Tijuana" will be incorporated into it.

In summary, the first stage resolves the Tijuana wastewater discharge problems up to the year 1989 under the following outline:

a) Concentration of the Tijuana River Basin's wastewaters at pumping station No. 1.

b) Conveyance of these waters by a 42 inch (107 cm) pressure line and discharge to the conveyance canal.

c) Pumping and conveyance from the canyon areas, for disposition into the conveyance canal.

d) Pumping and conveyance from the Playas de Tijuana area to the conveyance canal.

e) Canal for disposal of wastewaters to 5.6 miles (9.0 km) south of the boundary.

f) Secondary treatment by means of a plant located at mile 7.8 (12 + 500 km) of the disposal system.

DESCRIPTION OF THE TREATMENT SYSTEM PROPOSED FOR THE 1985 FIRST STAGE

Considering the treatment objectives, it will be required to produce biologically stable and odorless water that meets the following parameters:

Reduction of BOD 5	Minimum 87% (winter)
Reduction of Suspended Solids	Minimum 85%
Reduction of Bacteria with disinfection	99.9%
Dissolved Oxygen	Minimum 2 mg/l

TYPE OF PLANT

Given the efficiencies required in the treatment and considering the values of the characteristics of the water to be treated, a system of AERATED FACULTATIVE LAGOONS has been chosen, taking into consideration the following criteria:

a)-Simple operation

b)-Reliable efficiency

c)-Minimum handling of sludge

d)-Elimination of sanitary nuisances

e)-Advance technology

f)-Minimizing imports of equipment

g)-Availability of lands

h)-Investment costs

i)-Costs of operation, maintenance, and replacements

j)-Time and construction

k)-Cost of treatment

The availability of lands, in adequate dimensions, soil quality, and proximity to the conveyance canal, determines the selection of the aerated lagoons to be located at the height corresponding to the elevation 361 feet (110 meters) above the sea level.

The plant now a days is in normal operation, giving service to the first stage sewage system design for the city of Tijuana.

In July, 1990, IBWC Minute No. 283 recommended to the both Governments the construction of international treatment facilities in US in lieu of the construction of second stage sewage treatment facilities at Rio Alamar for the city of Tijuana, Baja California.

2 WATER QUANTITY MANAGEMENT IN NORTH AMERICA

RUNOFF PREDICTION MODEL FOR TEPETATE RECLAMATION

Héctor Manuel Arias Rojo
Profesor Investigador Adjunto.
Centro de Edafologia, Colegio de Postgraduados
Montecillo, Méx., México 56230

ABSTRACT

A runoff prediction model was validated in badlands locally named "tepetate" in order to apply WEPP, the new generation erosion prediction technology, for its reclamation. Six runoff producing events were used to test the hydrologic component IRS in two 25 x 2 m-runoff plots in the Texcoco River watershed with natural rainfall. Hydrograph comparison, between observed and simulated data, using the Chi-squared tests showed that short duration rains did not fit to observed hydrographs, while long duration rains fitted the field data.

INTRODUCTION

Most of Central and Northern Mexico have tepetate, a hardened layer underlaying the shallow soils of semiarid and arid zones located in volcanic areas. Once erosion starts, tepetate shows up reducing the land productivity, since this material is extremely poor in nutrients, hard, and difficult to manage. However, those lands have been reclaimed for agricultural purposes since pre-hispanic times, and lately with heavy machinery. In Central Mexico, yields higher than the average have been obtained with reclaimed lands. Thus, a research project have started (1) to characterize tepetate, and classify it if possible, (2) to determine the optimal management practices in the reclamation process, and (3) to determine the origin of the cementing agent of tepetate (Quantin and col., 1989).

One of the factors that limit the reclamation of those lands is its high erosion susceptibility, once the lands are reclaimed. Since they are potentially productive, a research program started in order to select the best management practices that optimize the reclamation procedure. The optimization will be performed using mathematical models, since it allows the quantification of different management practices. A very recent mathematical model that accounts for erosion is WEPP (Water Erosion Prediction Project) a USDA research project that will substitute the USLE, a semi-empirical mathematical model (Lopez and col., 1989). A very important part of WEPP is the runoff component.

Runoff prediction plays a major role in erosion, since the removal and transport capacity of runoff is significantly higher than rainfall. There are several mathematical models to predict runoff. However, due to the system complexity, most researchers have used hydrologic models, where the system complexity is solved in a few system parameters. The use of hydraulic routing to predict runoff have been limited because the basic equations are not linear, and therefore, numerical methods have to be used. Numerical solutions are very involved, and they are very limited for practical purposes. WEPP uses IRS (Infiltration and Runoff Simulation) a semi-analytical approach to solve the equations. IRS is a computer model that solves the equation in a very simple and efficient way using the method of characteristics.

The objective of this paper is to present results found in field experiments comparing observed with predicted data obtained using IRS. The experimental data were collected during the summer of 1981, the original purpose of data collection was the calibration of a mathematical model that used the finite difference methods to solve the kinematic equations; however, the model had very limited application.

IRS is based on fundamental equations, such as: 1) the law of mass conservation, 2) the law of momentum conservation, and 3) the law of energy conservation (Hernández, Lane and Stone, 1989).

The law of mass conservation for overland flow can be represented as:

$$\frac{\partial h}{\partial t} + \frac{\partial q}{\partial x} = \sigma \tag{1}$$

where h is runoff depth, q is runoff rate per unit width, σ is rainfall excess, and x and t are space and time coordinates.

The rainfall excess is the result of lateral inputs and outputs, and it is defined as:

$$\sigma = r - i$$

where r is rainfall rate, and i is infiltration rate. Rainfall rate is obtained using recording rain gauges, and infiltration rate is calculated using infiltration models. The Green and Ampt model, as modified by Mein and Larson (Rawls, Stone and Brakensiek, 1989), is used according to the following equation:

$$i = K\left(1 + \frac{MS}{F}\right)$$

where i is infiltration rate, K is saturated hydraulic conductivity, M is soil water deficit, S is average suction at the wetting front, and F is the cumulative infiltration.

The law of momentum conservation is simplified by assuming that the only significant components are gravity and friction, as follows:

$$S = S_f$$

where S is the terrain slope, and S_f is the friction slope.

When the law of energy conservation is applied, a relationship between runoff depth h and runoff rate q is obtained through the Darcy-Weissbach equation, as follows:

$$q = \alpha h^n \tag{2}$$

where q and h were already defined, the exponent is a constant (3/2), and the coefficient is defined as:

$$\alpha = (8gS/f)^{1/2}$$

where f is the Darcy-Weissbach friction coefficient, g is the gravity acceleration, and S was already defined.

The computer model solves the kinematic wave equations using the method of characteristics (MOC) for unit step functions when rainfall and infiltration are discretized in time.

MATERIALS AND METHODS

The experimental site is located in the Texcoco River watershed, about 45 km from Mexico City. The average annual precipitation is 543.5 mm, average temperature is 16°C, and evaporation is about 1 700 mm (Figure 1).

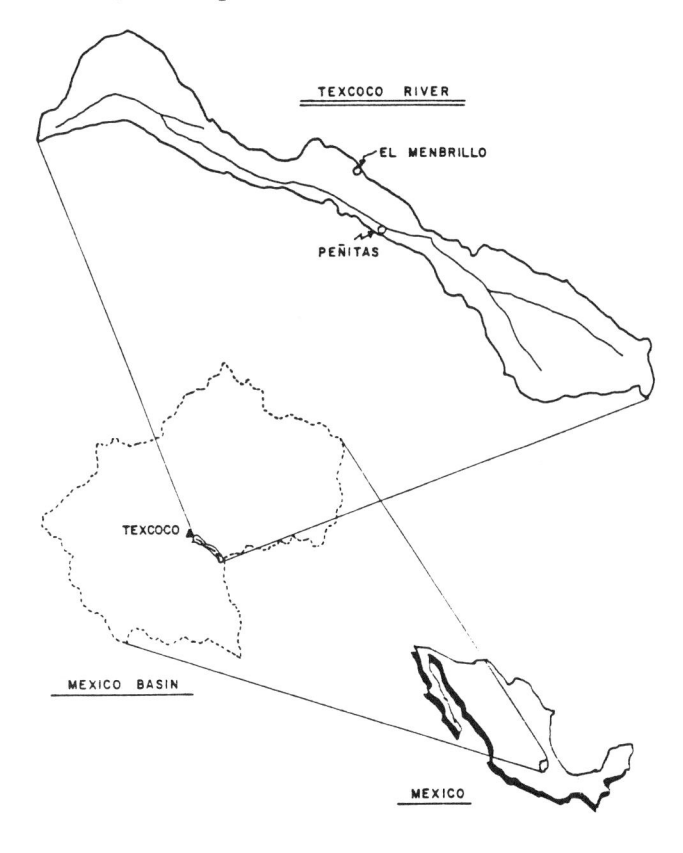

Figure 1. Map showing the location of experimental site.

Soils are locally named "tepetates", classified as litosols, according to FAO classification (Figueroa, 1975).

Two 25x2 m runoff plots were established in 1974 using 0.30 m asbestos sheets inserted 0.10-0.15 m into the soil on a 12% slope. A total collecting tank was installed to catch runoff water. In 1981, a water level recorder was installed to measure runoff rate in the two plots.

Rainfall data were collected using daily recording rain gauges 5 to 10 m far from the runoff plots. Soil moisture information was provided by samples collected every other day, and later analyzed by the gravimetric method. Saturated hydraulic conductivity was measured using constant head permeameters.

Three runoff events were selected for each plot to show possible limitations of the model. A short, mean and long duration runoff-producing events were selected to test the model performance for each plot. The short duration was about 1 to 2 h rainfall, the mean duration was from 2 to 6 h, and the long duration event was greater than 6 h rainfall. The main physical characteristics of the events are shown in Table 1.

TABLE 1. Main characteristics of the runoff-producing rains.

Plot	Date	duration (h)	Rainfall amount (mm)	peak (mm/h)	runoff amount (mm)	peak (mm/h)
El membrillo	18-6-81	16.67	22.9	24.0	11.4	23.4
	2-7-81	1.67	30.3	120.0	22.9	90.8
	4-7-81	1.92	57.5	300.0	24.3	77.3
Las peñitas	15-6-81	23.50	38.1	153.0	18.4	101.1
	3-7-81	3.43	12.9	102.0	8.1	87.2
	4-7-81	3.00	30.8	75.0	19.0	63.0

Field data were used to run the simulation program on a personal computer. The criteria used to analyze the model performance were differences between the observed and simulated data using the chi-square test at a 5 % probability.

RESULTS AND DISCUSSION

Although only three events per plot were used to run the simulation, the simulated data fitted well the field information. Table 2 shows the results of the chi-square test for both runoff plots. Although there were more degrees of freedom, the short duration events were not statistically significant; while the long duration events showed a better fit. It may be that the infiltration equations do not respond for high intensity rains, since it was the case for both events that did not fit well. If this is true, care must be taken when simulating thunderstorms.

TABLE 2. Results of the runoff simulation as compared with field data.

Plot	Date	duration (h)	DF	calc chi-square	tab chi-square	
El membrillo	18-6-81	16.67	41	29.94	55.80	*
	2-7-81	1.67	19	31.47	30.10	N.S.
	4-7-81	1.92	13	34.40	22.40	N.S.
Las peñitas	15-6-81	23.50	6	10.07	12.59	*
	3-7-81	3.43	10	15.65	18.31	*
	4-7-81	3.00	10	14.56	18.31	*

Figure 2 shows one of the long duration runoff producing event, where a good match between the observed and the simulated data was observed.

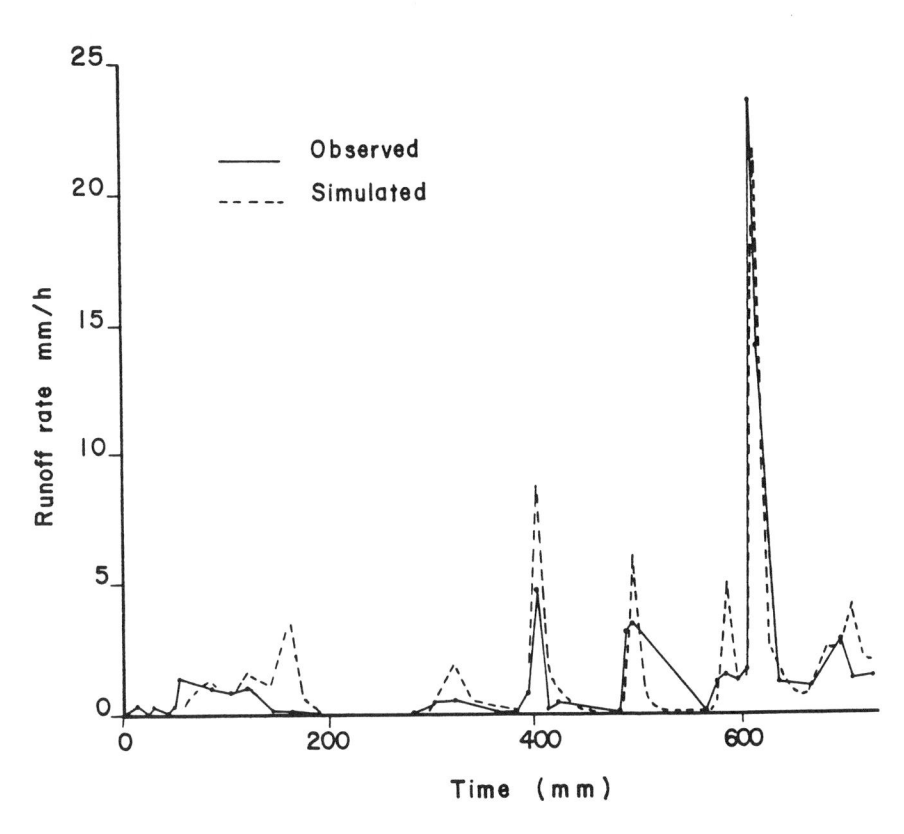

Figure 2. Hydrograph comparison for a 16.7 h runoff event. Site: El Membrillo. Date: 18/6/81.

CONCLUSIONS

The chi-square test to check the fitting of the hydrograph showed that short duration runoff-producing events did not work very well. In general, the runoff prediction model IRS, works fine for "tepetate". However, more research has to be done on short duration rains.

REFERENCES

Figueroa Sandoval, Benjamín. 1975. *Pérdida de suelo y su relación con el uso del suelo en la cuenca del Rio Texcoco.* Tesis M.C. Colegio de Postgraduados. Chapingo, Mex.

Hernández, M., L.J. Lane and J.J. Stone. 1989. *Surface runoff. USDA-WEPP: Hillslope Profile Model Documentation.* NSERL Report 2. USDA-ARS. NSERL.W. Lafayette, IN.

Lopez, V.L., M.A. Nearing, G.R. Foster, S.C. Finknerand J.E. Gilley. 1989. *The Water Erosion Prediction Project: Erosion Processes*. Proceedings of National Water Conference. IR and WR Divs/ASCE.Newark, DE. pp 503-510.

Quantin P., H.M. Arias R., C. Zebrowski, K. Oleschko,C.A. Ortiz S., J.D. Etchevers B., and D. Gabriels.1989. *Reincorporación de tepetates para producciónagr°cola. I. Descripción del proyecto en el Vallede México. Memoria del XXII Congreso Nacional dela Ciencia del Suelo*. Sociedad Mexicana de la Ciencia del Suelo. Chapingo, Mex. p 2.

Rawls, W.J., J.J. Stone and D.L. Brakensiek. 1989. *Infiltration. USDA-WEPP: Hillslope Profile Model Documentation*. NSERL Report 2. USDA-ARS NSERL.W. Lafayette, IN.

COMMENTS ON NORMS FOR DESIGN FLOODS OF MEXICAN DAMS

D. F. Campos-Aranda
Faculty of Engineering
Universidad Autonoma de San Luis Potosi
78290 San Luis Potosi, S.L.P., Mexico

ABSTRACT

For reference the next themes are described briefly: failures of dams, capacity of spillways, hydrological evaluations for dam safety and the problem of existing dams. The design criteria for floods from several countries are discussed with respect to educational aspects, including the diversity of methods to estimate floods, the revision of some typical norms and the concept of general minimum standards. Then the design criteria for floods in training of specialists are analyzed. At the end, several comments and criticisms of actual Mexican norms for design floods are formulated, in context of previous discussion.

INTRODUCTION

Failures of Dams

Large dams present important risks because of the possible loss of human lives and severe damage to property, that will result from their failures. Even small dams represent in many cases a high hazard which must be considered. This is essential to ensure the safety of these structures in design and in construction stages, and throughout the years of their use by the appropriate maintenance, observation and inspection. Laginha (1984) stated that dams must not fail even during the most critical conditions. However the absolute safety can not be guaranteed for any structure anywhere. Although it is impossible to guarantee a perfect behavior when designing a new dam, the engineer must ensure that it will not fail unless very improbable causes coincide.

Laginha and Cavilhas (1984) studied a total of 15,000 large dams, that is, dams above 15 m height. The number of failures of these dams was found to be about 1 percent, and one half of these failures was attributed to deficient design of the appurtenant works (spillways and outlets), including improper flood estimates, and deficient construction and operation of these structures or their foundations. Laginha and Coutinho (1989) presented the preliminary results of research on dam failures, in total 142 cases were analyzed from 24 countries, on events spanning three centuries. About 35 percent were attributed to flood overtopping and related problems.

Bouvard (1988) cited a slightly higher figure. The U.S. Bureau of Reclamation indicated in 1983 that 41 percent of dam failures could be attributed to inadequate spillway capacity and an additional seven percent to errors of operations. Thus, nearly one in two dam failures is likely to result from flood overtopping.

The above figures show the primary importance of hydrological calculations the safety of dams. Therefore, experts are focusing efforts on developing methods to prevent such disasters, on great diversity of available methods to determine the exceptional floods and spillway capacities. According to Lafitte (1989), the first falls within the competence of hydrologist, and the latter within that of the dam designer.

The Capacity of Spillways: Basic Ideas

Early, Snyder (1964) pointed out that discharge capacity of spillway for a given case will be governed by the selected inflow flood, the surcharge storage capacity of the reservoir available, and the magnitude of reservoir releases that can be made through outlet facilities other than the spillway. The selected combination of spillway dimensions and storage surcharge is based on appropriate economic analysis of various alternative combinations. Also, Snyder (1964) cited the following basic factors governing spillway capacity requirements: security to downstream interests, overall project economy, operational requirements and policies and standards of constructing agencies.

Taken into the consideration that design standards of capacity spillway must acceptably resolve the conflicting claims of safety and economy, it is logical that in several cases the result is an expensive spillway, built to a total protection of a dam against overtopping, that is, for the probable maximum flood. Then the ability of a flood to pass through a reservoir without damaging or destroying the dam, particularly if this is an earth/rock-fill embankment, depends not only on the hydraulic capacity of spillways but also on certain other features of the dam, as the effect of wind waves, or even overtopping which in certain cases can be without catastrophic results (Institution of Civil Engineers, 1978).

Hydrological Evaluations Associated with Dam Safety

For the protection standards it is necessary to specify a design flood, in combination with wind effects, which the dam must be capable of withstanding. The passage of this flood through the reservoir should not be the cause of fundamental structural damage to the dam. This flood is termed **dam design flood** (Institution of Civil Engineers, 1978). Recently the engineers prefer a clear distinction between the dam design flood and the **spillway design flood**, as can be seen in the standards of several countries.

Ray K. Linsley pointed out, that there is a number of other aspects which have to be included in the hydrological evaluations of dam safety (WP and DC, 1978). These are:

- diversion capacity during construction;

- discharge capacity for filling control or emergency releases; and

- emergency procedures.

The Institution of Civil Engineers (1978) stated that where an arbitrary criterion is appropriate it should be acceptable to design for the flood with the return period equal to the duration of risk (years of construction) by ten. This is a simplification, for practical purposes of analysis, done by Cochrane

(1967). Lewandowski (1977) suggested to analyze several con-siderations before the selection of the construction flood.

On the subject of filling control and for embankment dams, Linsley (WP and DC, 1978) stated the following requirements:

- to discharge one-quarter of the reservoir contents in 24 hours starting at full pool; and
- with pool at mid elevation to hold the pool level constant for 48 hours during the occurrence of the 10-year flood.

Since it is impossible to guarantee the zero risk, some measures for action in the event of a failure are needed, for example, the elaboration of maps to show the total area which would be inundated as a result of any possible modes of failure of the dam.

Safety of Existing Dams

According to Narayana et al (1984) it appears reasonable to accept that the hydrologic and hydraulic analyses of existing dams should not be as rigorous as for the new structures, since the cost associated with safety in a new dam is always a small fraction of the cost required to modify the existing structure. It is also likely that the experience gained while operating a dam could help to eliminate the need for more safety.

For L. Duscha of the U.S. Army Corps of Engineers (WP and DC, 1983) an unsafe dam was taken to be one where:

- the dam could not pass half the probable maximum flood without overtopping;
- there was reasonable probability that overtopping could cause failure; or
- failure would significantly increase the potential for loss of human life downstream.

DESIGN CRITERIA FOR FLOODS AND EDUCATION

Hydrological Estimation of Floods

It is remarkable that a great diversity of methods are in use around the world to estimate exceptional floods. This diversity results from varying climates and available data. Lafitte (1989) considered the diversification of hydrological methods as a great advantage, understanding them, and in doing so, stimulating imagination, remains a source of progress. However, more attention should be given to the need to have enough hydrological data of good quality, to reach the best estimations of floods.

To determine the floods in a watershed, no methods should be discarded without further analysis. As far as possible, all available data should be used: historical reports, empirical formulae, envelope curves, probabilistic analysis of floods and deterministic approaches and models.

Therefore, it is necessary to teach in hydrologic courses the diversity of actual methods for the estimation of exceptional floods, as a way to guarantee better projects, independently of design criteria for floods.

Revision of Existing Norms

The design criteria for floods recently issued (Mead and Hunt, 1981; Loukola et al., 1985;Cantwell and Murley, 1986; Xuemin, 1989) agree in the concept how to classify the dams with regard to potential hazard and with respect to its size (storage capacity and height).

In general the recent norms have as the objective a range of design floods in each category of dam, allowing the engineer to exercise judgment in assessing the circumstances of each case. Others are specific to the reservoir flood, because this is vital to dam safety; for example, the norms proposed by the Institution of Civil Engineers (1978), given in Table 1. On the other hand, there are norms which give the return period for design flood of spillway. This is for the normal operating conditions, as well as for the extraordinary operating conditions (safety of dam), as provisions for extremely unfavorable conditions which may occur only very rarely. Examples are the Norwegian standards (Bouvard, 1988), and the Chinese norms (Xuemin, 1989), given in Table 2.

The analysis of several norms in hydrologic courses point out to semblances and differences with respect to classification of dams, accepted risks and the combination of circumstances that may arise in rare events such as the initial reservoir level, the concurrent wind speed and constant inflow. All this will be useful to the student to begin to build a good engineering judgment.

Towards Minimum General Norms

The International Commission on Large Dams (ICOLD), the organization which proposed some minimum general norms, should specify the reservoir safety and the design flood of spillways. In general it is accepted that the passage of flood should cause no fundamental structural damage to the dam, because it is normally uneconomical to provide a waterway below the dam that is sufficiently large to contain the dam design flood outflow within its banks. Damage associated with rare overbank flows below or alongside spillway stilling basins may will be tolerated without risk to the integrity or security of the dam. Also, there are cases where it is not essential whether the spillway channel should be hydraulically designed to carry all the dam flood outflow (Institution of Civil Engineers, 1978).

These minima norms should include the specification of concurrent wind speed, procedures to obtain wave surcharge, freeboard, dam construction flood, capacity of controlled outlets, criteria for design of gated spillways, and others associated hydrological estimations. Moreover, it should include the differences for the analyses of existing dams.

The norms cited will be the minimum requirements of safety of dams defined by ICOLD. Each country will be able to increase them in function of its own circumstances economic, technical, moral, social and political.

DESIGN CRITERIA FOR FLOODS AND TRAINING

Application and Elaboration of Alternatives

The application of design criteria of floods to each designed dam will be the culmination of hydrologic knowledge, because the integration of different solutions helps make the use of engineering judgment, hydraulic designs, cost analyses and so on. This is very important in the aspects of training at student

Table 1
RESERVOIR FLOOD AND WAVE STANDARS BY DAM CATEGORY
(Institution of Civil Engineers, 1978)

| Category | Initial reservoir condition | Dam design flood inflow ||| Concurrent wind speed and minimum wave surcharge allowance |
		General standard	Minimum standard if rare overtopping is tolerable	Alternative standard if economic study is warranted	
A. Reservoirs where a breach will endanger lives in a community	Spilling long term average daily inflow	Probable Maximum Flood (PMF)	0.5 PMF or 10 000 year flood (take larger)	Not applicable	Winter: maximum hourly wind once in 10 years. Summer: average annual maximum hourly wind. Wave surcharge allowance not less than 0.6 m.
B. Reservoirs where a breach (i) may endanger lives not in a community (ii) will result in extensive damage	Just full (i.e., no spill)	0.5 PMF or 10 000 year flood (take larger)	0.3 PMF or 1000 year flood (take larger)	Flood with probability that minimizes spillway plus damage costs. Inflow not to be less than minimum standard but may exceed general standard	
C. Reservoirs where a breach will pose negligible risk to life and cause limited damage	Just full (i.e., no spill)	0.3 PMF or 1000 year flood (take larger)	0.2 PMF or 150 year flood (take larger)		Average annual maximum hourly wind. Wave surcharge allowance not less than 0.4 m
D. Special cases where no loss of life can be foreseen as a result of a breach and very limited additional flood damage will be caused	Spilling long term average daily inflow	0.2 PMF or 150 year flood	Not applicable	Not applicable	Average annual maximum hourly wind. Wave surcharge allowance not less than 0.3 m.

TABLE 2
DESIGN CRITERIA FOR FLOODS IN CHINESE DAMS
(Xuemín, 1989)

Classification of hydro projects				
Category	Reservoir Capacity ($10^8 m^3$)	Power installation (MW)	Irrigation area (10^4ha)	Object of flood protection
A	>10	>750	>100	Major cities
B	10-1	750-250	33.33 to 100	Fairly large cities
C	1-0.1	250-25	3.33 to 33.33	Medium-sized cities
D	0.1-0.01	25-0.5	0.33 to 3.33	Ordinary cities
E	0.01-0.001	0.5	0.33	—

Classification of hydraulic structures			
Category	Permanent structures		Temporary structures
	Main structures	Auxiliary structures	
A	Class 1	Class 3	Class 4
B	Class 2	Class 3	Class 4
C	Class 3	Class 4	Class 5
D	Class 4	Class 5	Class 5
E	Class 5	Class 5	

Criterion for design flood					
Class	1	2	3	4	5
Return period of flood	2000-500	500-100	100-50	50-30	30-20

Criterion for check flood condition					
Class	1	2	3	4	5	
Embankment dams	10,000	20,000	1,000	500	300	Return period
Concrete dams, etc.	5,000	1,000	500	300	200	

or postgraduate levels, and as the continuation of hydrologic education for engineers of governmental agencies.

In these cases, the computer programs for estimations of floods with several techniques available, are very important to reduce the time of the analysis, and to make analyses of sensitivity, according to variations of hydrological and hydraulic parameters.

Actual Mexican Norms of Design Floods

The Mexican standards for design floods were defined mainly on the basis of the norms of U.S. Army Corps of Engineers (Mead and Hunt, 1981), making simplifications to the hazard category of dams and ignoring the interval of return period, that is, adopted the more critical conditions.

Therefore, the revision of Mexican design criteria (Tables 3 and 4) may be urgent, because these norms are considered too rigid and severe

TABLE 3
RETURN PERIODS FOR DESIGN FLOODS IN LARGE MEXICAN DAMS
Technical Advisory of SARH, 1984

Size of Dam	Height of the dam (m) *	Hazard category	
		Low	High
Small	10 to 18	500	1,000
Medium	18 to 30	1,000	10,000
Large	more than 30	10,000	10,000

* From river bed level to top of dam.

TABLE 4
RETURN PERIODS FOR DESIGN FLOODS IN LARGE MEXICAN DAMS
Technical Advisory of SARH, 1986

Height of the dam (m) *	Capacity up to 10 Mm^3		Capacity up to 10.1 and 30 Mm^3		Capacity greater that 30 Mm^3***	
Risk	Low	High	Low	High	Low	High
Less than 15	500**	1,000	500**	1,000	1,000	10,000
15 to 40	500**	1,000	1,000	10,000	10,000	10,000
Greater than 40	1,000	10,000	1,000	10,000	10,000	10,000

*   Maximum height of dam from foundation to the top.
**   Can accept the regional envelope of maximum floods.
***   In dams with capacity greater than 300Mm^3 is necessary special.

(Campos, 1990). Rigid, in the sense of not defining an interval for design flood, which can help to judge each case from the viewpoint of security, economy, hydraulic design, and so on. The severe norms occur for small dams, (with capacity less than 10 Mm^3), according to the revised standards of other countries. On the other hand, norms, in fact, are incomplete according to the above discussion, with regard to the concurrent conditions of wind speed and the other factors.

It is also urgent to define the norms for existing dams, because with the actual norms (Tables 3 and 4), in many cases it will be necessary to build a new spillway, which is expensive and complicated. The analysis of each case, applying engineering judgment, will lead to acceptable solutions, which are important for the total safety of the dam.

REFERENCES

Bouvard, M. (1988). *Design flood and operational flood control.* GR.Q. 63. 16th Congress of ICOLD. U.S.A.

Campos-Aranda, D.F. (1990). *Propuesta de normas para la elaboracion de estudios hidrologicos.* Ingenieria Hidraulica en Mexico. pp.47.

Cantwell, B. and Murley, K. (1986). *Australian guidelines on design floods for dams.* Water Power and Dam Construction, 38 (12), 16-19.

Cochrane, J.N. (1967). *An engineering calculation for risk in the provision for the passage of floods during the construction of dams.* 9th Congress of ICOLD, 5 (C3), 325-341.

Institution of Civil Engineers. (1978). *Floods and reservoir safety: an engineering guide,* London, England, pp.58.

Lafitte, R. (1989). *Dam safety in relation to floods.* Water Power and Dam Construction, 41 (4), 12-13.

Laginha S., J. (1984) *Preface.* Proc. International Conference on safety of Dams. Coimbra, Portugal.

Laginha S., J. and Cavilhas, J.L.A. (1984). *Failures of dams due to overtopping.* Proc. International Conference on Safety of Dams. Coimbra, Portugal.

Laginha S.J. and Coutinho R., J.M. (1989). *Statistical of dam failures: a preliminary report.* Water Power and Dam Construction, 41 (4), 30-34.

Lewandowsky, E.R. (1977). *Diversion during construction.* Chapter XI in Design of Small Dams. U.S. Bureau of Reclamation. U.S.A.

Loukola, E., Kuusisto, E. and Reiter, P. (1985). *The Finnish approach to dam safety.* Water Power and Dam Construction, 37 (11), 22-24.

Mead and Hunt, Inc. (1981). *Inspection and evaluation of safety of non-federal dams.* Seminar Training sponsored by U.S. Army Corps of Eng., Huntsville Div., U.S.A.

Narayana, G.S., Singh, M. and Pandya, A.B. (1984). *Problems in dam safety encountered in India: case histories.* Proc. International Conference on Safety of Dams. Coimbra, Portugal.

Snyder, F.F. (1964). *Hydrology of spillway design: large structures-adequate data.* J. Hydr. Div., 90 (HY3), 239-259.

Water Power and Dam Construction. (1978). *New perspectives on the safety of dams. Part two.* 30 (11), 52-58. Water Power and Dam Construction. (1983). New perspectives on the safety of dams. 35 (10),47-52.

Xuemin, C. (1989). *Design criteria for flood discharge at China's hydroschemes.* Water Power and Dam Construction, 41 (4), 14-17.

THERMOELECTRIC WATER NEEDS FOR POWER PLANTS

Gustavo A. Paz Soldán C.
Comisión Federal de Electricidad
Asociación Mexicana de Hidráulica
México, D.F.

ABSTRACT

The generation of electric power in Mexico is mainly produced by thermoelectric power plants. The water supply is very important in this generation. This paper described the role of water supply to thermoelectric power generation in Mexico, and the program for construction of new power plants with water sources and requirements. The hydraulic design and main studies which are made in Mexico for the construction of thermoelectric power plants are also described.

INTRODUCTION

For many years the generation of electricity power in Mexico has been mainly done by thermoelectric power plants. The installed capacity of these plants is greater than of the hydroelectric power plants.

The ratio, in which 70 % of electricity is generated by thermoelectric power plants, will increase in the next ten years as shown in Table I. The time schedule of installment of different types of electric power plants, which will be operational before the year 2,000, is also presented. Thermoelectric generation uses heat to create steam which moves turbogenerators. The fuel use determines the type of thermoelectric power plant.

WATER FOR THERMOELECTRIC POWER PLANTS

Water is needed for thermoelectric power generation; first, because water is converted in to steam, which uses the caloric energy transferred from the fuel, and then moves the steam turbine; second, it is needed to condense the steam to complete the thermodynamic cycle. Where the pressure of steam in the turbine exhaust is less than the atmospheric pressure, the total head is increased and the generation of power is also increased. This condensation is achieved by the cooling water system, in which the water flows across thousands of small pipes that are integrated into the mechanical equipment named the condenser, where the steam transfers its heat to the cooling water that will be discharged with a temperature greater than that at the inlet.

Water is needed for cooling of auxiliary equipments and, or to resupply the main stream cycle, as well as for other services in the power plant, and for the construction of the plant.

TABLE I - Program for new thermoelectric power plants

YEAR 2000   THERMOELECTRIC POWER PLANTS, MW/(# units)

	Geoth.	Nucl.	C.C./Tg.	Conv.	Coal	Dual	Hydro	TOTAL
1990	25	675	140	860	-	-	-	1700
	(5)	(1)	(2)	(3)				(11)
1991	25	-	145	395	-	-	350	915
	(5)		(3)	(4)			(4)	(16)
1992	-	-	-	-	700	350	-	1050
					(2)	(1)		(3)
1993	40	-	30	1020	350	700	100	2240
	(2)		(1)	(4)	(1)	(2)	(1)	(11)
1994	40	675	-	160	350	700	648	2573
	(2)	(1)		(1)	(1)	(2)	(7)	(14)
1995	40	-	-	-	-	700	780	1520
	(2)					(2)	(3)	(7)
1996	40	-	-	738	-	1050	207	2035
	(2)			(3)		(3)	(1)	(9)
1997	40	-	-	350	-	2150	414	2954
	(2)			(1)		(5)	(2)	(10)
1998	40	-	-	-	-	1800	140	1980
	(2)					(4)	(2)	(8)
1999	40	-	-	-	700	1450	300	2490
	(2)				(2)	(3)	(2)	(9)
TOTAL	330	1350	315	3523	2100	8900	2939	19456
	(24)	(2)	(6)	(16)	(6)	(22)	(22)	(98)

Water resources development in Mexico has an economic priority. In the selection of locations of a new thermoelectric power plants, the availability of water is a crucial factor.

Two types of cooling water systems are used: the once-throw system and the closed-cycle system. The first type is used when there is a water source with a large quantity of water, from which it is taken, and after passing the condenser it is discharged in the same or a different water source. However, if there is not a sufficient water source near the location of a thermoelectric power plant, it is needed to utilize the closed-cycle system, in which water is recycled in a cooling tower or pond, in order to transfer the heat to the atmosphere. In the latter type of system, the water resupply is required in order to replace the loss due to evaporation, infiltration and washing. This minimal replacement flow is estimated at 1.0 l/s for each MW installed. This water supply for thermoelectric power plants in Mexico is taken mainly from groundwater. Actually, this industrial use is restricted. For this reason the new thermoelectric power plants must be located near a large water source, like oceans, in order to use the once-throw cooling water system. The characteristics of the location must be adequate for locating the water inlet and outlet structures, in order to avoid the unfavorable maritime conditions, such as a strong littoral transportation of sand or a recirculation of already heated water.

The importance of water for electric power production is shown in the schedule for construction of the new electric power (POSE) [1], in which the different electric power plants that will operate plants before the year 2,000 are presented. Almost all of the new thermoelectric power plants must employ the once-throw cooling water system, as shown in Table II, which is obtained from POSE [1]. The table shows different types of thermoelectric power plants, their capacity, starting operational dates for each unit, the type of water cooling system, with its water source, and the estimated flow for cooling in the once-throw system or the replacement flow for closed-cycle system.

TABLE II - Thermoelectric power plants which are planned to operate before the year 2,000

PLANT	TYPE	POWER (MW)	DATES	COOLING WATER SYSTEM	Q_{cool} (m^3/s)	Q_{rep} (l/s)
VALLADOLID	C.C.	2(70)	U1:05/89	CLOSED		40
		1(80)	U2:07/90	(GW)		40
LAG. VERDE	NUC.	675	U1:09/90	OPEN	40.5	
			U2:10/93	(G.M.)	40.5	
A.LOPEZ M.	CONV.	350	U1:09/90	OPEN	15.7	
			U2:10/90	(G.M.)	15.7	
			U3:07/92		15.7	
			U4:10/93		15.7	
LERDO	CONV.	160	U1:09/90	CLOSED		160
			U2:02/91	(GW)		160
ROSARITO II	CONV.	160	U1:10/90	OPEN	7.2	
			U2:07/91	(P.O.)	7.2	
SAN CARLOS	DIES.	32.5	U1:02/91	CLOSED		
			U2:08/91	(air)		
VALLADOLID	CONV.	37.5	U1:03/91	CLOSED		37.5
			U2:09/91	(GW)		37.5
CARBON II	COAL	350	U1:04/92	CLOSED	350	
			U2:10/92	(GW)	350	
			U3:11/93	(B.R.)	350	
			U4:05/94		350	
PETACALCO	DUAL	350	U1:09/92	OPEN	15.7	
			U2:04/93	(Ba.R.)	15.7	
			U3:07/93		15.7	
			U4:01/94		15.7	
PETACAL. II	DUAL	350	U1:07/94	OPEN	15.7	
			U2:01/95	(Ba.R.)	15.7	

TABLE II - Continued

TOPOLOB. II	CONV.	160	U1:07/93	OPEN	7.2
			U2:01/94	(G.C.)	7.2
MERIDA II	CONV.	160	U3:10/93	CLOSED	160
			U4:01/94	(GW)	160
ENSENADA	DUAL	350	U1:04/95	OPEN	15.7
			U2:04/97	(P.O.)	15.7
SABINAS	COAL	350	U1:01/99	CLOSED	350
			U2:07/99	(GW)	350
ALTAMIRA	DUAL	350	U1:06/96	OPEN	15.7
			U2:12/96	(G.M.)	15.7
		550	U3:04/97		24.7
			U4:10/97		24.7
LIBERTAD II	DUAL	350	U1:04/97	OPEN	15.7
			U2:04/99	(G.C.)	15.7
P.PRIETA II	CONV.	37.5	U4:05/96	OPEN	1.7
				(G.C.)	
COLMI	DUAL	550	U1:01/98	OPEN	24.7
			U2:07/98	(P.O.)	24.7
			U3:02/99		24.7
			U4:08/99		24.7
MATAMOROS	DUAL	350	U1:05/98	OPEN	15.7
			U2:11/98	(G.M.)	15.7
MINATITLAN	CONV.	350	U1:01/96	OPEN	15.7
			U2:07/96	(G.M.)	15.7
SAMALAY. II	DUAL	350	U1:02/96	CLOSED	350
			U2:02/97	(GW)	350
MAZATLAN II	CONV.	350	U4:02/97	OPEN	15.7
				(P.O.)	

GW: GROUNDWATER G.M.: GULF OF MEXICO
O.P.: PACIFIC OCEAN G.C.: GULF OF CALIFORNIA
B.R.: BRAVO RIVER Ba.R: BALSAS RIVER

HYDRAULICS OF THERMOELECTRIC POWER PLANTS

The discipline of hydraulics studies the physical behavior of water, which are applied in the thermoelectric power generation in order to guarantee the correct and continuous operation of plants. The thermoelectric power plant design is one of engineering activities in which almost all hydraulic specialities participate [2], from the location selection stage on. Several studies are needed to locate and design the inlet and outlet structures, as well as the other structures such as the marine piers, or the structures for fuel discharge.

Maritime, fluvial, open channel, hydrology, geohydrology, hydraulic models, field measurements and hydraulic transients are the main specialities in which the numerical methods are necessary in many problems that can be solved with the help of software. For any technical and economical evaluation, the influence of water in the selection of location for a new thermoelectric power plant has been a determining factor. It is important, before deciding the final location, to carry a good hydraulic study on the feasibility of water supply.

The thermoelectric power plants that burn nationally produced coal must be located near the deposits of fuels. The power plants have been planned to satisfy demand in electric power of all the regions of the country. They cover different electrical systems which are integrated into the nationally interconnected system, but also there are independent electric power systems.

When a region that requires installment of a new electrical power plant is identified, several locations are looked at with the corresponding technical and economical studies, considering all factors such as: water, electricity transmission, fuel supply, highways, railroads, land characteristics, etc. For these feasibility studies only the available information is used. After this first evaluation, a deeper analysis is made for at least three best locations, for which the field surveys and special studies need to be made. Actually, the most significant aspects in the selection of a new location are water and fuel supply. The latter turns out to be the most important factor for the thermoelectric plants that will burn imported coal, because they need the maritime piers to discharge the fuel, and these structures require some complex and long studies.

The final selection of the location for a thermoelectric power plant, which that will use sea water for its cooling water system, requires the determination of the locations of inlet and outlet structures, with a sufficient quantity of water and a sure operational water level in the pump suction all the time [3]. Also, it is needed to correctly select the design temperature, in order that the probability of decreasing production of the plant due to insufficient cooling is minimal. Other important aspects in the inlet and outlet design are to avoid recirculation of warm water from the outlet to the inlet. Also, the ambiental impacts should be minimized. All this requires several field and office studies, and often the construction of hydraulic models to obtain the best solutions.

Different types of inlet structures are available. Their selection depends mainly on the characteristics of the location. Direct inlet, open channel and just one submarine pipe have mostly been used in Mexico.

Due to the fact that availability of locations with the ideal conditions for inlet and outlet structures is limited, and the environmental impact restrictions are getting harder and harder to satisfy, so that all these factors require a special design. It is necessary to review carefully the submarine inlet and outlet structures.

CONCLUSIONS

The growth of electric power capacity will likely continue at the same pace of Mexico's development in the near future. For 30 years the electricity generated in Mexico has mainly been made by the thermoelectric power plants. This tendency will increase in the future, because of the planned potential until the year 2,000, that 85% will be produced by various types of thermoelectric power plants.

Water is essential in thermoelectric power generation. During the last years it has been decisive in the selection of location of new power plants.

Hydraulics is a very important discipline in the thermoelectric power plant design. Nearly all its specialities are applied.

In order to install the planned capacities for the coming years, and to continue with a good engineering quality of design and construction, it is needed to build large structures, like the maritime fuel dischargers and the submarine water inlets and outlets.

REFERENCES

Comisión Federal de Electricidad, 'Programa de Obras del Sector Eléctrico, (POSE)', México, Agosto, 1990.

Comisión Federal de Electricidad, 'Resumen de Capacidad Instalada', Subdirección de Producción, México, D.F., 1989.

Paz Soldán C., G.A., 'Determinación de los Niveles de Diseño para Centrales Termoeléctricas', 90. Congreso Nacional de Hidráulica, Querétaro, México, 1986.

Paz Soldán C., G.A., 'El Agua en la Generación de Electricidad', XV Congreso Nacional de Ingenier°a Civil, México, D.F., Diciembre, 1989.

Paz Soldán C., G.A., 'La Hidráulica en Centrales Termoeléctricas', 80. Congreso Nacional de Hidráulica, Toluca, México, 1984.

CHARACTERIZATION OF WATERSHEDS BY INTEGRATION OF REMOTE SENSING AND CARTOGRAPHIC DIGITAL DATA

Jose Luis Oropeza Mota
Profesor-Investigador, Colegio de Postgraduados, Montecillo, Edo. de México. CP 56230.

ABSTRACT

The different modeling techniques used in hydrology require information concerning various features of watersheds: type of soil, physical and hydraulic soil properties, slope, land use, type of vegetation cover. All these properties, components of conceptual hydrologic models, present spatial variability over the watersheds. Processing these data in digitized form makes models easier to use and enables one to check its sensitivity to any spatial or temporal modification of different features of the watershed. We present here the spatial characterization of small watersheds in Belgium by an integration of cartography and remote sensing data. The hydrologic model tested is the SWRRB (Simulator for Water Resources in Rural Basins). Results obtained with this model are quite satisfactory for small watersheds.

INTRODUCTION

A large number of watersheds are frequently damaged as a result of heavy rainfalls. At present, there are still very few means of protection against the often disastrous consequences. Among these, modeling techniques are starting to be developed in areas possessing a network for obtaining sufficient hydrologic data in order to predict the variation of flow volumes and peak flow following the exceptional climatologic phenomena.

As a result of impact of human interventions in the environment, the regime of many small streams is modified. The causes of these modifications can be of quite different nature. It is within the framework of rural land development that the engineer is called upon to undertake varied tasks, such as civil engineering construction work (dams, roads, canalizations), modification of land use (afforestation and/or deforestation, cultivation of grasslands, development of a natural site,...), and the land conservation.

These modifications taken as a whole, lead to an increase in extremes: rise in floods (higher peak flow rate, greater flow volume) and/or more severe low waters (smaller summer flows, drying up more frequently). The land developer must assess these flow-rate variations and the volume differences by comparing the present situation with that before any land development has occurred. Hydrologic simulation models are a very useful tool in this assessment.

In this study, we describe the spatial characterization of the basin and sub-basins of the Lesse at Resteigne (Fig. 1) by the integration of numerical data from satellite imagery and cartographic documents. The hydrologic model tested is the SWRRB, Simulator for Water Resources in Rural Basins, (Williams, et al., 1985).

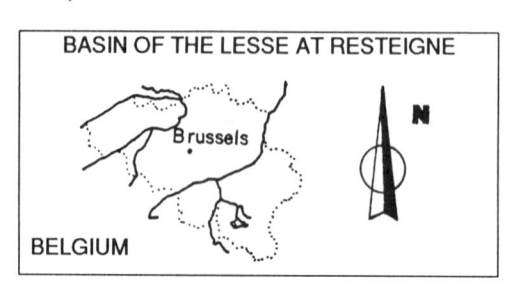

Figure 1. Map location of the drainage basin.

SWRRB MODEL.

The SWRRB model was developed to simulate hydrologic and related processes in rural basins. The three major components of SWRRB are: weather, hydrology and sedimentation. In this study, we are interested in the evaluation of the peak runoff rate.

Peak runoff rate predictions are based on a modification of the Rational Formula (Williams et al., 1984).

$$Q = \frac{a R A}{360 \, Tc} \quad (1)$$

in which Q = peak runoff rate in $m^3 \cdot s^{-1}$; a = a dimensionless parameter that expresses the fraction of the total rainfall that runs off during the watershed time of concentration, Tc in h; and A = watershed area in ha. The time of concentration can be estimated by adding the surface and channel flow times. R is the surface runoff predicted for daily rainfall using the SCS curve number equation:

$$R = \frac{(P - 0.2 \, S)^2}{P + 0.8 \, S} \quad (2)$$

in which P = daily rainfall and S = a retention parameter. The retention parameter, S, was related to soil water content by the equation:

$$S = S_1 \left(1 - \frac{RD}{RD + \exp(w_1 - w_2 (RD))}\right) \quad (3)$$

in which RD = soil water content in root zone; S value of S corresponding to the 1 (dry) moisture condition curve number (CN_1). W_1 and W_2 = shape parameters. They are obtained from simultaneous solution of Eq. 3 assuming that $S = S_1$ at the wilting point; and $S = S_3$ at field capacity; S_3 = value of S corresponding to the 3 (wet) moisture condition curve number (CN_3).

INTEGRATION OF SATELLITE AND CARTOGRAPHIC NUMERICAL DATA

With the launching of the first meteorological satellite, observation of the earth underwent a genuine revolution. A new step has been reached with the satellites LANDSAT and SPOT that possess the excellent spatial resolution.

Satellite imagery after geometric rectification, makes a series of radiometric values correspond to each spot known by geographic data. This spatial dimension of remote sensing facilitates the integration of satellite information with other numerical cartographic data.

In this context, a Geographic Information System can be very useful in the general optic of creating a numerical data bank prior to any characterization of watersheds. It should be regarded as a tool suitable for analyzing information within a spatial context. The whole of these numerical cartographic data can be used for matching and superposition, with or without previous processing, in order to obtain useful information for the land developer.

Remote sensing data can be perfectly integrated with this notion of G.I.S. in the optic of creating a computer environment for managing and manipulating spatial data necessary for operating a hydrologic simulation software.

We have tested the SWRRB model by using four numerical cartographic data bases:

- the Digital Terrain Model
- the digitized hydrographic network
- the thematic land-use map
- the map of hydrological soil classes.

The Digital Terrain Model is the numerical representation of altitudes in a x,y grid based on the digitalization of contour lines. This digitalization can be obtained via a scanner or from a digitalization table.

The digitized hydrographic network results from the digitalization of a hydrographic map at 1:50,000. The ensuing data base is in vectorial mode according to a linear structure based on sequences of couples of coordinates (x,y). To these coordinates is added a code so as to define beginning and end of the line and a value that characterizes it.

The thematic land-use map was drawn up on the basis of supervised classification of two satellite images (Landsat TM of 19/4/85 and 10/9/85). Many authors have demonstrated how the use of radiometric multi-date data reduces the number of errors of omission and confusion of a classified image (Wastenson, et al., 1981). The supervised classification on the basis of these multi-date and multi-spectral data results in a classified image indicating the main features of land-use.

The U.S. Soil Conservation Service (1972) suggests independently of rainfall characteristics, CN values in function of the hydrological soil class, vegetation cover and conservation management. American soils are all grouped into one of the four hydrological classes A, B, C, D, according to their runoff potential which in turn is closely related to their infiltration rate.

For Belgian soils, we have referred to the numerical basis of the European hydrological classes (A. Gustard, 1983). The soils are grouped into five classes, soils with lowest runoff potential (class 1) to impermeable soils (class 5). For calculating the CN values in this case, we estimated that the American and European classification possess a similar linear progression starting from a minimum of potential runoff (class A and class 1) to a maximum represented by classes D and 5. Calculation of linear interpolation is made for European classes 2, 3 and 4.

For four digitized cartographic bases, constituted accordingly, we are able for every basin outlet, to establish the different parameters required by the SWRRB model and to generate peak flow rates. Gumbel theory is then applied to obtain maximum annual flow rates and their return periods.

DIAGRAM OF METHODOLOGY USED

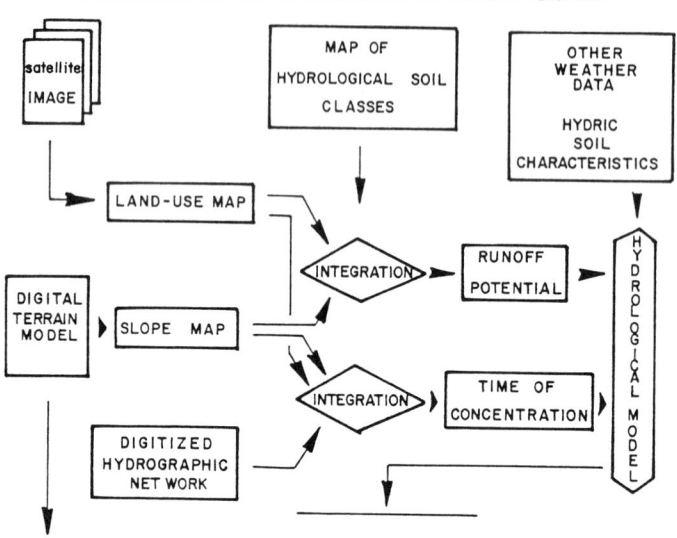

RESULTS

In Fig. 2 we have related the calculated times of concentration and the mean lag times of floods observed. Delwasche et al. (1982) has noted that the lag times are relatively constant on average per watershed for different periods of rainfall considered.

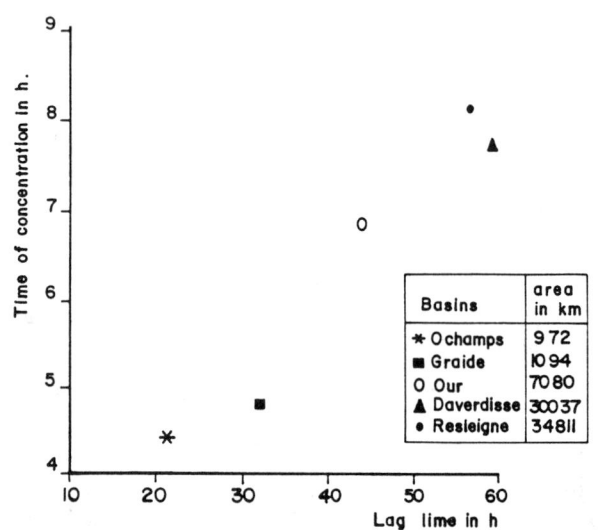

Basins	area in km
* Ochamps	972
■ Graide	1094
O Our	7080
▲ Daverdisse	30037
● Resleigne	34811

Figure 2. Relation between the calculated time of concentration and the mean lag times observed.

Despite their low values, the concentration times calculated on the basis of physical characteristics of the watersheds are highly correlated to the lag times observed during the floods.

Maximum annual flow rate observed and simulated by the model, after application of Gumbel theory, are presented in Figure 3.

Let it be noted that for small-sized basins (Graide, Ochamps and Our), the flow rates observed and simulated are of similar magnitude. For larger basins (Daverdisse and Resteigne), the model greatly underestimates these flow rates.

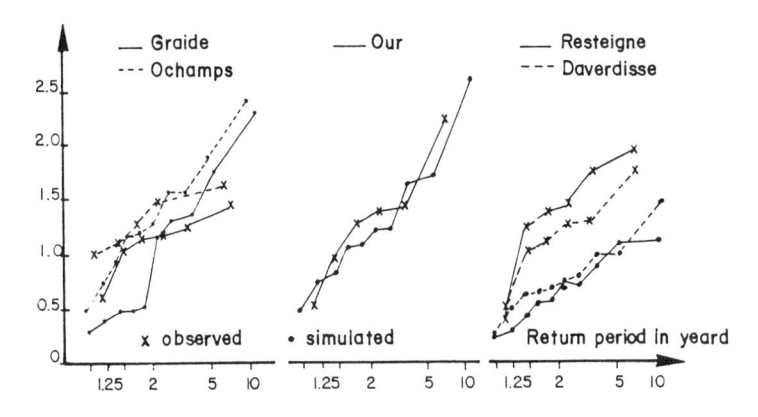

Figure 3. Comparison between annual maxima flow rates observed and simulated.

The model has also been tested to see how changing land use affects the maximum annual flow rate. To illustrate this, the Our basin was chosen with different land uses.

Figure 4 shows the maximum simulated flow rate over the period 1975-1985 in ordinates, and in abscissa the mean annual runoff volume for this

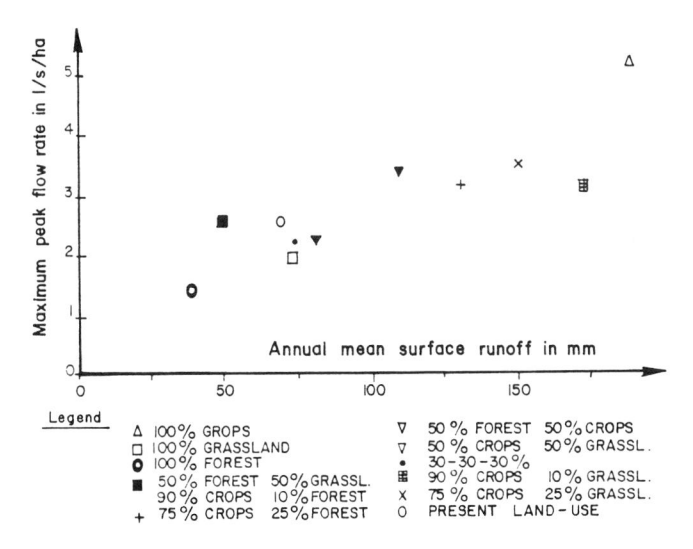

Figure 4. Incidence of simulated land-use modifications basin of Our 1975-1985.

same period. It should be noted that situation "entirely forested" and "entirely cultivated" are two extreme opposed situations. Any deforestation in the basin contributes to an increase in floods and runoff volumes, while reforestation of the basin reduces this phenomenon.

CONCLUSIONS

We have attempted in this study to point out the importance of creating a data bank in the form of a Geographic Information System prior to using a hydrological model.

G.I.S. type data have the distinct advantage of enabling algorithms, developed for processing numerical images obtained by earth observation satellites, to be applied to the majority of spatial parameters. This data bank, by its easy access and processing, will almost certainly become an essential tool for land developer in the context of simulation and impact studies.

Remote sensing provides the opportunity of establishing a numerical map of land occupation and fits in perfectly with the notion of G.I.S. in the widest sense of characterization of rural watersheds.

Results obtained with the SWRRB model are satisfactory for small watersheds, especially as the model was not adapted or adjusted for the flows studied.

REFERENCES

Delwasche, J. et Dautrebande, S. (1982). *Prevision des Crues de Projet : le Bassin Versant de la Lesse FAGEM-Genie Rural*, Volume I, 202 p.

Gustard, A. (1983). *Regional Variability of Soil Characteristics for Flood and Low Flow Estimation*, Agricultural Water Management 6, 255-268 p.

USDA, Soil Conservation Service (1972). *National Engineering Handbook*, Hydrology Section 4, chap. 4-10.

Wastenson & al. (1981). *Computer Analysis of Multitemporel Landsat Data for Mapping of Land Use, Forest, Clearcuts and Mires Methodologicals Studies*. Annales Geographiques 63A, 325-337 p.

Williams, J.R., Jones, C.A. & Dyke P.T. (1984). *A modeling Approach to Determining the Relationship Between Erosion and Soil Productivity*, Transaction ASAE 27 (1), 129-144 p.

Williams, J.R., Nicks, A.D. & Arnold, J.G. (1985). *Simulator For Water Resources in Rural Basins*, Journal of Hydraulic Engineering Ill (6), 970-986 p.

FACTIBILITY OF A DEEP KARSTIC LIMESTONE AQUIFER UNDER THE CITY OF CHIHUAHUA: A PROGRESS REPORT

Ignacio Alfonso Reyes Cortes
Departamento de Geologia
Facultad de Ingenieria
Universidad Autonoma de Chihuahua
Chihuahua, Chihuahua, Mexico

ABSTRACT

The City of Chihuahua area has undergone several tectonic events. The area was partially compressed during the Late Cretaceous - Early Tertiary and stressed afterwards, without producing major disruptions in the area. The volcanic period was followed by a second faulting event, but with scarce volcanism above the city area. As a topographic high, the area was deeply eroded up to the Santa Rosa batholith level. The third faulting event of Pliocene Pleistocene age formed the Chihuahua Graben. The graben was filled out by alluvium. The karstified limestones continuity is postulated to pass throughout and below the Chihuahua area, from the Haciendita to the Sierra de Sacramento. The inferred continuity of the karstic limestone aquifer below the city area makes it a future potential deep aquifer.

INTRODUCTION

The study area is located at the central part of the state of Chihuahua, in the Chihuahua City area. The access to this zone is well developed, nevertheless the Sacramento River and the Chuviscar River are evident obstacles in the sierra de Sacramento accesibility. Both rivers represent the sewage system of the municipality. The most important water infrastructure is represented by the three aqueducts that conduct water toward the city of Chihuahua from three different sites: The Ojos del Chuviscar, Tabalaopa, and El Sauz. (See Fig. 1.)

The weather of the area according to E. Garcia (1973) corresponds to the dry steppe with a summer rain regime and an annual average temperature of 20° C. The climate has extreme variations from -10° C during the winter months, up to 40° C during June and July in the summer. The rain period is restricted to fall from May to September time, and it is represented by intensive but short thunderstorms. The vegetation is dominantly xerophyte type and the relative abundance of small thorn varieties are scarcely distributed throughout

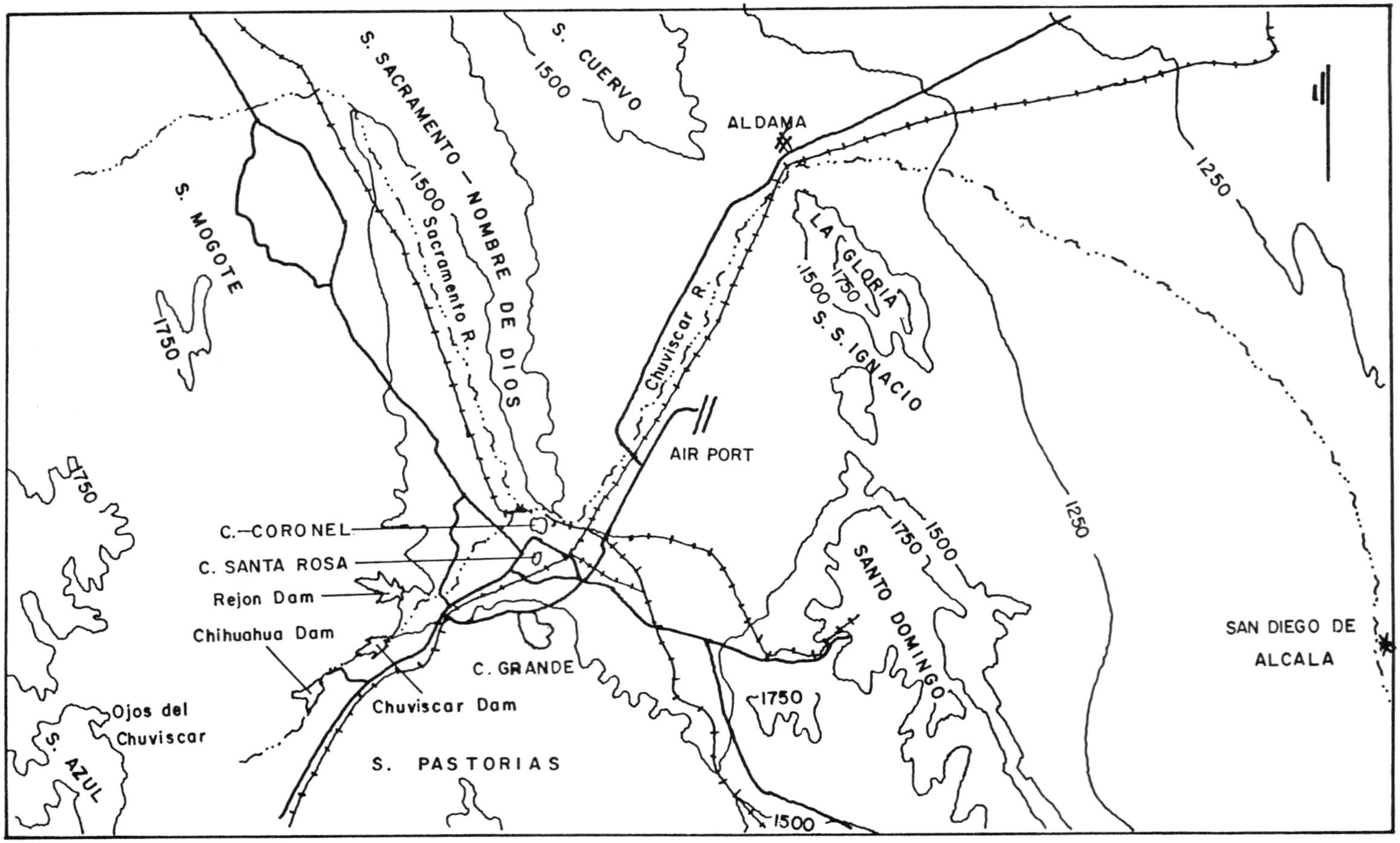

Figure 1. Localization

the entire area. The major species are developed along the river margins. The major fauna is restricted to minor species like lizards, mice, snakes, and coyotes.

The geologic literature of the area and the whole state is scarce and regional, such as the Burrows (1909-1910) work about the geology of the north part of Mexico; The Ramirez and Acevedo (1957) investigations on the geology of the northern part of Chihuahua, and the Mauger (1983) mapping of the Calera - El Nido block. More recently several thesis were performed within the surrounding area of the city of Chihuahua.

PHYSIOGRAPHY

The area is characterized by an arid to semi-arid zone. The elongated and narrowed mountain blocks emerge bordering wide and flat basins oriented north-south to northwest-southeast. In the east side of the Chihuahua state, most of the sierras are formed by marine sedimentary rocks of Cretaceous age; meanwhile the west side is constituted by tertiary volcanic rocks. This lithologic contrast gives as a result a quite different morphology to each part. It permits to make the physiographic division. Several authors divide the state of Chihuahua into two provinces. Ordonez (1946), Alvarez Jr., (1956), Raisz (1959) and Hawley (1969) recognize the Sierra Madre Occidental and the Basin and Range physiographic provinces. Each one of the authors describes the contrasting provinces not only by their lithology, but by the heights, the wideness of the basins, the size of the sierras, the climate, and the vegetation.

The Sierra Madre Occidental is constituted by a volcanic pile of ignimbrites of the more than 2,800 meters above sea level in average. In fact it is formed by a high volcanic plateau, its borders develop characteristic features, such as very high and steep cliffs toward the west and narrow basins in steps limited by wide sierras toward east. This last part is a transition to the east physiographic province.

The Basin and Range is characterized by an accommodation of the internal drainage basins of central north part of Mexico. This physiographic province covers the east part of the state of Chihuahua. It is constituted by isolated narrow sierras split by wide basins. The west part of this province is the transitional zone toward the Sierra Madre Occidental Province. The transitional zone between both provinces is featured by the development of internal drainage basins. The grabens have been filled by large amounts of alluvial material forming playa lakes at the central part of the basins.

The study area lies exactly at the border of both provinces in the transitional zone. Here the physiographic features of the basin and range are present, but all the sierras surrounding the area are topped by volanic rocks. The wide internal drainage basins are called "bolsones." They were formed by grabens filled with continental clastic sediments such as breccias, sand, and clay of Tertiary to Quaternary age. Their thicknesses vary from tens to thousands of meters. The average elevation above sea level of these basins are from 1,200 to 1,400 m and the surrounding isolated sierras rise from 600 up to 1,000 m above the basin level. The sierras are narrow blocks with lengths up to 150 km long. They were formed by block faulting and tilted or rotated blocks, which produced steep slopes at one side and gentle slopes at the other side. Steep slopes form most of the unaccessible cliffs. The wideness of the sierras rarely is over 15 km and their general orientations are north-northwest.

The city of Chihuahua area is represented by a typical elongated graben of 1,500 meters above sea level, bordered by two horts or sierras with a high of 1,700 meters above the sea level. The topographic expression of limits are the Sierra de Sacramento, east limit of the graben, which is a cliff zone formed by a narrow block tilted toward east. Meanwhile, the Calera - El Nido Block, west limit of the graben, is a less cliffed zone formed by almost lying flat block without any disruption.

HYDROGRAPHY

The main streams are the Sacramento and Chuviscar Rivers; the former is located toward the east margin of the Chihuahua Graben. It runs from north to south. The Sacramento River has its head at the Sierra de Majalca, 40 km northwest of Chihuahua. It runs eastwards in the northern part and changes its orientation toward south, when it approaches the Sierra de Sacramento up to reaching the Chuviscar River.

The Chiviscar River has its head at the sierras de La Calera and Azul, about 50 km southwest of Chihuahua. It runs east-northeast and changes abruptly its orientation toward south, when the Sacramento River joins it to increase its flow. The faulted west border of the Sierra de Sacramento controls the drainage orientation at this part.

The streams and creeks generally have a "V" shape, because they have dominantly erosive runoffs in character. The scarce runoffs are related to the summer thunderstorms. In this period, the direction of the stream beds are constantly modified. Another feature is that most of the streams practically disappear at the slope change from the sierra talus. The developing of streams are restricted to the surrounding portions of the topographically high sierras, and the limits of the graben.

GEOLOGY

Tectonically, the geologic history of the Chihuahua area is too complex and it should be reviewed in future investigations; the same should be done for the entire state. According to Campa and Coney (1983), north and northeast part of the state of Chihuahua corresponds to the Northamerican Craton; meanwhile, the rest of the state was accreated or at least it was mobile during the Paleozoic to Mesozoic time.

The pre-cambrian basement is outcropping in a couple of restricted areas: At the Sierra del Cuervo and Sierra de Carrizalillo; both sites are located toward the east of the city of Chihuahua. The paleozoic rocks have a wider distribution but equally restricted to small areas. The paleozooic rocks only outcrop over the Northamerican Craton part. At the end of the Paleozooic Era, in the area the Permo-triasic Orogeny took place. It corresponds to the Lautasia and Gondwana collision. Pangaea was formed during this time.

The thick sequence of clastic material, piled up at the Sierra del Cuervo during Late Permian, was produced by this Permo-triassic Orogeny. The orogenic activity generated an intensive erosional stage that almost flattens the tectonic belt formed along the suture between the colliding continental blocks. A distensive or rifting period was developed during the Triassic to middle Jurasic time. This structure was a kind of block faulting and tilting, which produced a basin and range event.

The distensive tectonism started at the upper Jurasic time in the eastern part of the state of Chihuahua. That was the beginning of the Chihuahua Through development. A constant accumulation of limestones, evaporites, and shale in the Chihuahua Through took place during the whole Cretacous period.

A new orogeny was produced at the end of Cretacous and early Tertiary. The continental blocks started to move again, but this time the collision between the East Pacific Plate against the Northamerican Plate produced the Chihuahua Tectonic Belt at the eastern part of the state of Chihuahua. The tectonic belt is sensibly oriented north-northwest to south-southeast. During the last part of the orogenic event and after the compressive period, a large and intensive volcanic event took place.

The volcanic activity accumulated more than 2,000 m thick of volcanic rocks, which now are forming the Sierra Madre Occidental. The later faulting and tilting block tectonism occurred during the late Miocene. This tectonic period generated the actual Basin and Range Province. Most of the grabens formed in this way were filled up with alluvial and clastic materials. This fill gives the present morphology, although the Rio Grande Rift tectonism has been acting since 10 Ma ago. The city of Chihuahua area lies just at the west side of the Chihuahua Through, in the transition zone of the Basin and Range Province and the Sierra Madre Occidental, and at the west border of the paleozooic basin.

LITHOSTRATIGRAPHY

The rock type distribution over the study area is the result of the undergone major tectonic events during the geologic evolution. The older rocks of the area are mesozooic in age. The limestone outcrops are located mainly at both sides of the graben; in fact, they constitute the basal outcropping part of the horsts.

Limestones outcrop along the west lower slope of the Sierra de Sacramento. Most of these rocks are covered by talus and alluvial material, which restricts the outcrops. Also they outcrop at the stratigraphic window of the Haciendita area, inmediately west of the city of Chihuahua.

The limestone has light grey color of fine grain with scarce diseminate nodules of various sizes and shapes. The limestone presents a massive character in general, but sometimes has thick beds up to 2.0 m. The limestone weathering through the fractures has developed several collapse breccia bodies, most of times are cemented by calcite, but sometimes it has a clayly matrix.

The argillaceous matrix probably came from the overlying weathered volcanic rocks. Limestones are from micrites or mudstone to wakestone according to the Dunham classification. They have abundant oolites, milliolids, such as quinqueloculine and numoloculine hemi, and some equinoderm and molusca shell fragments. There are several thin coquine horizons with abundant oyster shell fragments.

The limestone is part of the Aurora Group and it is equivaent to the Finlay Formation of the middle Albian of early Cretacous. Richardson (1904) calls Finlay Limestone to a massive limestone with abundant fossils, chert, and thin sandy horizons. It outcrops at the north part of the Finlay mountain, Texas.

The Finlay Formation has outcrops throughout the whole state, from the city of Juarez up to the city of Jimenez. This limestone was precipitated on a continental shelf environment of a post-reef facies, in warm and shallow waters. The measured thickness of limestone within the study area reaches more than 150 m, but this thickness is just a part of the formation.

A particular feature of the limestone is the karstic character. The karstic process is so well developed at the Haciendita area, that now it is outcropping only the remnants of the collapsed material and small spread remains of the walls. Meanwhile at the Sierra de Sacramento, part of the caverns were filled up by tuffs --they can be either ash flows or air falls introduced by percolating water flows.

This type of percolation structure can be seen at the Chihuahua quarry (Cementera de Chihuahua). It forms distorted dike type bodies, that were confused as a real dikes at the beginning of the quarry operations. In a general way, the Finlay Formation is overlaid by a calcareous to volcanic conglomerate. It represents the basal conglomerate of the upper volcanic sequence. In fact, this conglomerate has a red color and it is partially cemented by calcite. This conglomerate can be interpreted as the cretaceous-tertiary unconformity horizon.

The conglomerate is constituted by limestone (Finlay Formation), volcanic (andesite, basalt, and ignimbrite), and plutonic (granodiorite and monzonite) rock fragments. None of the plutonic rocks outcropping around the area corresponds to those types of fragments. The conglomerate thickness is very variable from 0.5 up to more than 50 m measured at the central part of the Sierra de Sacramento. The depositional environment corresponds to a continental deposit oftalus and alluvial type of restricted transport. The conglomerate accumulation was at the lower parts of the irregular topography.

It is postulated that before the deposit of the conglomerate, the area underwent an intrusive event. It practically uplift and tilt the limestone. Once the intrusive period took place, the weathering process worked intensively up to allow outcrop the upper parts of these intrusive bodies. The Cerro de Santa Rosa is part of one of these intrusives and it has a monzonitic composition. The Santa Rosa intrusive outcrops in a wide area within the city limits. The age of the Santa Rosa weathered batholith is still unknown, but by now the authors are divided in opinion. The intrusion can be pre-volcanic or post-volcanic event.

The volcanic sequence is overlying the conglomerate. The whole ignimbrite pile was emplaced after the conglomerate. This volcanic emplacement relatively flatten the irregular topography. That is, the lower topographic areas accumulated larger thicknesses of volcanic rocks than higher areas. Twelve volcanic units have been recognized in the area, from ash flow tuffs up to air fall tuffs and all the intermediate rock types, as well as some restricted andesitic and basaltic lava flows related to dikes and sills. But they will not be discussed in this paper.

An important feature of the volcanic rocks is their different degree of fracturation and weathering. This feature controls the permeability of the units. Most of them have low permeabilities, except of the upper thin crust of the outcrops.

The southern part of the city of Chihuahua is overlying an outcrop of the monzonitic batholith of an unknown age. There are several rhyolitic domes that tilt partially the overlying sequences such as those in the Sierra de Sacramento, Cerro Coronel, Cerro Grande, and some others in the Haciendita area.

There is well-defined relationship between rhyolitic domes and the pyroclastic sequence, but among the monzonitic batholith of the Cerro de Santa Rosa and the surrounding rocks, there are some controversial opinions. In fact, there are two positions: One, that the batholith has an upper Cretaceous age (Reyes and Carreon, in progress), and the other that it has a middle Tertiary age (De Santiago and Grijalva, 1989).

The monzonitic batholith is a porphyritic intrusive. It is consituted by oligoclase (20%); orthoclase (70%); and minor amounts of biotite, hematite, epidote, and unrecognized opaque minerals, which correspond to the last 10%.

The intrusive has deep weathering and relatively high amounts of chloritization, hematization, and argillitazation.

TECTONICS AND STRUCTURES

The major structural features in the study area define the typical characteristics of the faulting and block tilting of the post-orogenic tension (Eocene), the Basin and Range (Miocene), and Rio Grande Rifting (Plio-Pleistocene). Each new tectonic event masks the older one. The lack of the recognized caldera structures in the area suggests a potential relationship between the volcanic units within the area with the external structures such as San Marcos Caldera toward the north and the Pastorias Caldera southward.

The faults and fractures can be clustered into three different groups or systems according to their orientation and age. The older fault system has a N 45° W orientation that corresponds to the post orogenic tension. It was developed during the Eocene time. Most of the grabens formed were filled up with the cretaceous sedimentary material (limestone fragments), and scarce andesite and basaltic material. There are several grabens of that type toward the eastern part of the state of Chihuahua. Even more, the Sierra de Santo Domingo shows that type of calcareous conglomerate filling.

The second fault system has an orientation of N 30° W. It corresponds to the Basin and Range stage during the Miocene time. It is interpreted as a change in the plate interaction between the East Pacific and North American plates. The miocenic system is affecting most of the volcanic sequence at the central part of the state. It is less evident in the sedimentary sequence toward the eastern part.

The basins formed in this way were replenished by alluvial and volcaniclastic material. At this time, more of the internal drainage basins of the north of Mexico were formed. The western limit fault of the Sierra de Sacramento looks to be of that type, because its orientation and relative age correspond to it.

The last and younger fault system has an orientation of north-south direction. It is related to the Rio Grande Rift. Their relative age may be Pliocene-Pleistocene. Old grabens have been truncated and masked by the younger fault systems, resulting from that much more complex and combined orientations.

The new formed basins and tilted blocks accumulated large amounts of alluvial and lacustrine sediments. A special feature of this faulting stages that have not been totally recognized are the lava flows related to them. Only the last faulting event is assumed to be related to volcanic activity in very small and scarce dimension. The east side limit of the Calera - El Nido block is related to the north-south fault system. All these three fault systems have fracture systems in parallel and perpendicular orientations. The fracture systems develop a good hydrologic environments to hold or transmit ground water through volcanic rocks.

THE CHIHUAHUA GRABEN

The distribution of the karstic limestone in the Chihuahua area remarks a characteristic feature of a basin with a N 30° W elongation from the Basin and Range Province. But it was modified by the north-south tectonism of the Rio Grande Rift. Limestone outcrops at both sides of the Chihuahua graben.

The limestone is the basal outcropping rock in the Sierra de Sacramento toward east side, where the Cementera de Chihuahua (cement quarry) is located. The whole sierra block is tilted eastward producing a cliffed slope toward the city of Chihuahua area. Meanwhile, to the other side of the Sierra de Sacramento, it has a gentle slope in which volcanic rocks dip 20° to 30° toward the Nogal Mocho basin.

The Haciendita area borders the west side of the city area. This limit is formed by andesitic to basaltic lava flows and pyroclastiocs of the same composition. They are dipping eastward, toward the Chihuahua City area. The volcanic sequence tilting affects only the eastern part of the Haciendita area; even more this tilting looks like a step faulting.

The limestone outcropping shows less tectonic disruption, but outcrops are very restricted, because most of them are covered by alluvial material, volcanic rocks and some remnants of eroded collapse breccias of the same karstic limestone. Right below the Chihuahua City area, it is partially outcropping the monzonitic batholith of the Cerro de Santa Rose.

The weathering degree of the Santa Rosa intrusive represents an impermeable barrier for the ground water. This barrier splits the aquifer below the urban area in to northern part, mainly the city of Chihuahua and the southern part occupied by the southern part of the Chihuahua City, Villa Juarez, and Avalos.

The alluvial material forms a thick filling bed of more than 300 m along the Sacramento River. In this part several wells of that depth were drilled. These deep wells cut mostly filling material of alluvial character. None of the holes drilled cut out any volcanics or limestone, so the total depth of the basin is still unknown. The authors believe that at a depth of 500 m the limestone can be cut, because of the presence of the batholith in the the southern part of the city and the limestone outcrops toward the east and west of the city of Chihuahua.

The tectonic evolution can be interpreted as:

a) Deposition of the cretaceous limestone units over the Aldama Plataform, which is bordered by a reef, which actually is outcropping at the Sierra del Cuervo.
b) The orogenic tectonism during Late Cretaceous and Early Tertiary practically did not affect limestone in this area, because they were protected by the Aldama Plataform. Limestone underwent light and broad folds, even more by the end of this orogenic event, large intrusions took place, such as that of Cerro de Santa Rosa. The intrusions can be related to the next step.
c) After the orogenic event, the surrounding area underwent another faulting event. But now it was oriented N 45° W. The city of Chihuahua area was unaffected; nevertheless the Sierra de Sacramento - Sierra del Cuervo Block, and Pastorias Block were sunk. The limestone dissolving event started at this time. It generated large cavities that were filled out partially by volcanics of the next step, as is shown at the Sierra de Sacramento.
d) The area was covered by a volcanic sequence, but the thickness in the city area was very thin, because the area was forming a horst. Meanwhile it was much more thick in Sacramento-Cuervo Block because this block corresponds to an old graben. Even the basal conglomerate in the Sierra de the Sacramento gives a hint about this fact.
e) A second faulting event occurred by the Miocene age with an orientation of N 30° W. The second event affected partially the city of Chihuahua

area, but just toward the north of the area. It is interpreted that the Encinillas Basin was formed during this event. In the same way were formed El Nogal Mocho, El Cuervo Basin, San Diego de Alcala Basin, and the east part of the Pastorias.

The city of Chihuahua area was still as a topographic high area. In fact, it was being affected by intensive erosion, so practically most of the volcanic rocks were eroded away from that part, exposing most of the limestone and intrusions.

f) The formation of grabens around the city of Chihuahua area encourage the weathering and erosion at the same time ground water kept dissolving large parts of the limestone producing large cavities, which were collapsed in order to form breccia bodies. Most of the dissolved cavities in the limestone of the Haciendita area were filled up with clayly and sandy material from the weathered volcanics surrounding the area.

g) A third faulting event occurred in the Plio-Pleistocene age, but in this case the orientation was practically north-south. The city of Chihuahua area finally was sunk, but just part of the area, because the batholith of the Cerro de Santa Rosa remained as a horst. It limited the sunk zone. The new formed graben is bordered by the Sierra Nombre de Dios, Cerro de Santa Rosa, Sierra de Sacramento and the Haciendita area toward north, south, east, and west respectively.

h) This graben was replenished with alluvial material mainly from the Haciendita area. Most of the remaining volcanic sequence was eroded away. This erosion uncovered the limestone at the cavities level; that is why instead of having outcrops of limestone, there is outcropping loose clayly sand and collapse breccias. This material was filling the cavities when erosion occurred.

i) The lack of the volcanic sequence in the city of Chihuahua area and the relative age of the formation of the Chihuahua graben permits to interpret the hydraulic continuity of limestone thoughout the area as shown in Figure 2.

CONCLUSION AND RECOMMENDATION

As a conclusion and recommendation of this progress report, it can be said that:

a) There are two aquifers in the city of Chihuahua area, the freatic aquifer in the alluvial material and the probably confined or partially confined aquifer in the karstic limestone below the former.

b) The karstic limestone aquifer is inferred to have hydraulic continuity from west, in the Calera - El Nido Block, to the east, in El Cuervo - Santo Domingo Block.

c) The potentiality as a deep aquifer of the karstic limestone should be corroborated by deep drilling holes either in the Haciendita or Sierra de Sacramento outcrops.

d) The lack of volcanic rocks in the north central part of the city of Chihuahua area make the possibility of having a continuous limestone aquifer below the city.

e) It is necessary to perform indirect geophysical studies in order to define burden structures by the alluvial material, such as the Cerro de Santa Rosa batholith, Jesus Maria horst, and the limit faults of the tilted blocks.

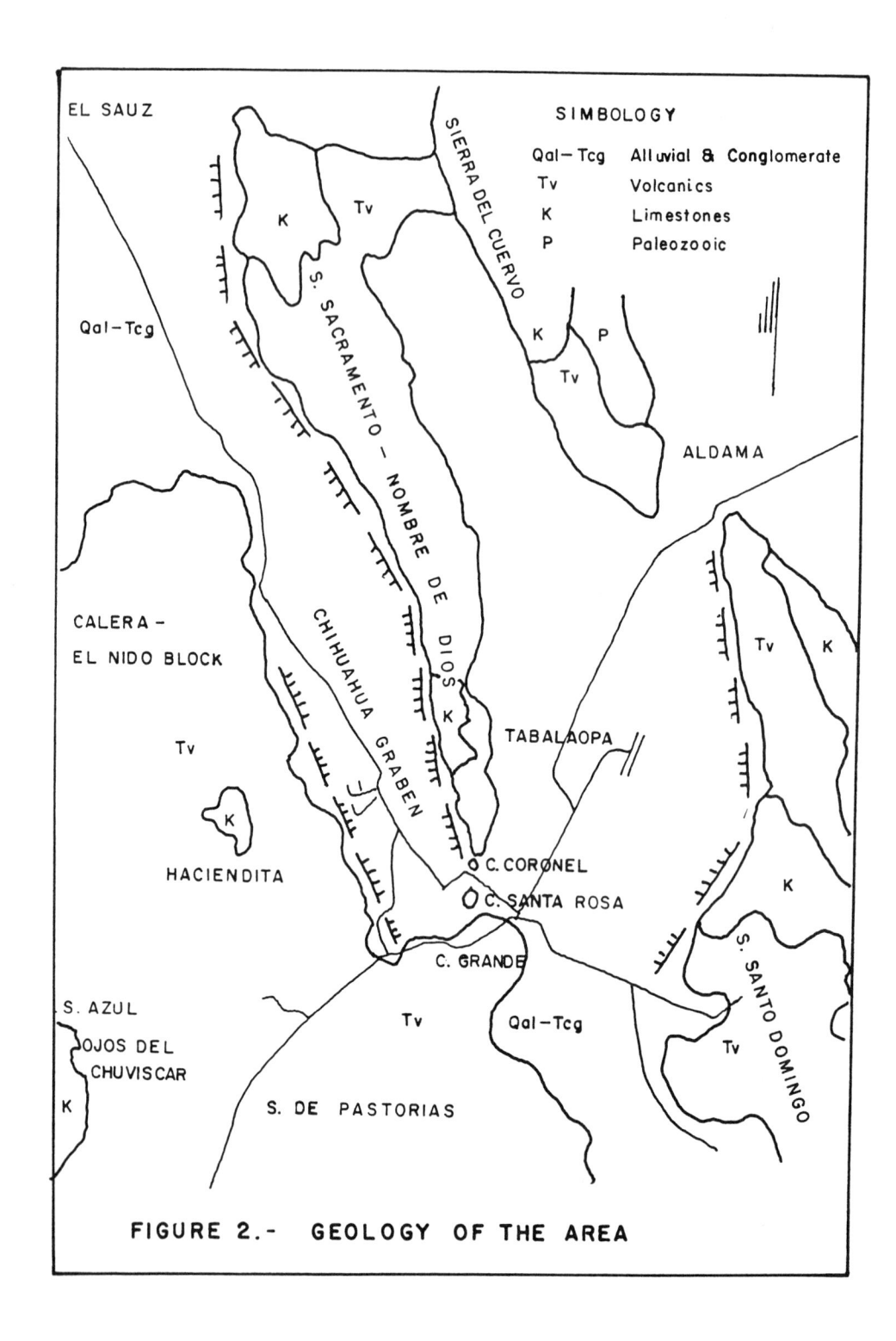

Figure 2. Geology of the area.

REFERENCES

Alvarez, M. Jr., 1961, Provincias Fisiograficas de la Republica Mexicana: Soc. Gel. Mex., Bol., No. 2, Tomo XXIV, p. 28.

Burrows, R. H., 1909, Geology of Northern Mexico, Mining and sc. press, v. 99, No. 9, p. 290-29.

Burrows, R. H., 1910, Geology of Northern Mexico, Soc. Geol. Mex., Bol., v. 7, pt.1, p. 85-103.

Campa, M.F. and Coney, P., 1983, Tectonostratigraphic Terranes and Mineral Resource Distributions in Mexico, Canadian Journal of Earth Sciences, v. 20, p. 1040-1051.

Carreon Murguia, Pedro I. 1987, Geologia del area de Penas Azules-Jesus Maria, Chihuahua, Mexico, Tesis Facultad de Ingenieria, UACH, unpublished.

De Santiago-Renteria, P. y Grijalva-Alfaro, R., 1989, Geologia del area sur de la Sierra de Sacramento - Cerro Grande, Municipio de Chihuahua, Chihuahua, Mexico: Tesis Profesional, Facultad de Ingenieria, UACH, unpublished.

Facultad de Ingenieria, UACH, 1988, Estudio geologico de semidetalle, prospecto Villa Ahumada, Chihuahua.

Garcia, E., 1973, Calsificacion de Climas segun Keoppen modificada para la Republica Mexicana. Isotermas e isoyetas medias anuales, escala 1:250,000, Hoja 13G1, INEGI.

Hawley, J.W., 1969, Notes in the Geomorphology and Late Cenozoic Geology of the Northern Chihuahua: New Mexico Geol. Soc., p. 130-141.

Instituto Mexicano del Petroleo. subdireccion de tecnologia de exploracion, 1981, Estudio tectonico-estructural a partir de imagenes de satelite del Estado de Chihuahua y norte de Durango. Proyecto c-1124.

INEGI, SPP, 1982, Carta hidrologica, aguas superficiales escala 1:50,000.

Lopez Ramos, Ernesto, 1983, Geologia de Mexico, tomo II editorial Trillas.

Mauger R.L. 1983, A geological study of the Providencia El Nido area, northeastern flank of the Sierra El Nido-Central Chihuahua, Mexico., Geology and Mineral Resources of North Central Chihuahua, Guide book field conference, El Paso Geological Society.

Ordonez, E., 1946, Principal Physiographic Provinces of Mexico: AAPG, Bull., v. 20, No. 10, p. 1277-1307.

Raisz, E., 1959, Landforms of Mexico: Geography Branch Office of Naval Res., Cambridge, Mass., 2nd. ed: Map scale 1:300,000.

Ramirez, J. y Acevedo, F., 1957, Notas sobre la Geologia de Chihuahua. Bol., Asoc. Mex. Geol. Pet., v. 9, p. 583-770.

Reyes-Cortes, I. A. y Carreon-Murguia, P. I., In Progress, Geologia de la Hoja de Chihuahua, Facultad de Ingenieria, U.A.CH., Chihuahua, Chihuahua, Mexico.

GROUNDWATER STUDIES AT THE FEDERAL ELECTRIC POWER COMMISSION OF MEXICO

Sergio A. Flores and José A. Maza
Gerencia de Ingenieria Civil
Comisión Federal de Electricidad

ABSTRACT

The Federal Electric Power Commission of Mexico is the agency responsible for the design, construction, and operation of the power plants, such as thermoelectric, hydroelectric, geothermoelectric and nuclear power plants. Power plants demand large quantity of water during their operational time, being in many cases groundwater as the only feasible alternative. Water is used for cooling and other uses, including water supply for construction and operation camps. This paper shows the importance of hydrogeologic studies in power generation industry. It describes the procedure used in different study stages: site identification, intermediate-level assessment, feasibility, control, and supervision related to groundwater development and management, as well as water utilization problems. On the other hand, power plants in operation are briefly described, including features such as water demand in terms of quantity and quality, well fields, and groundwater exploitation policies. Finally and as a case study, hydrogeologic characteristics of the aquifer that supplies water to the San Luis Power Plant are discussed, as well as the operation of well fields and groundwater protection measures that have been implemented.

The study of surface and ground waters and the other natural resources, such as oil and minerals, are in the realm of earth sciences. Water resources are of paramount importance for any country. Their rational developments are a source of welfare and prosperity, whereas its abuse or misuse may cause deterioration in water quantity and quality.

In Mexico, the ever-increasing population demands more and more water for municipal, agriculture and industrial uses. The ongoing exploitation has led to depletion of many important aquifers. Moreover, contamination of water bodies has turned out water supply into one of the most severe problems that the country faces and one of the main restrictions for its development. Also, conflict water use interests put an additional stress on scarcity of water resources.

The use of groundwater at the Comisión Federal de Electricidad (CFE) is mainly applied for thermoelectric power generation processes, and for the general utilities as water supply for field camps, electric power substations, and relocating human settlements, mainly for the construction of hydroelectric power plants.

The economic development of Mexico requires an increase of electric power generation, mainly of 8.3 % annually, which is now supplied by thermoelectric, hydroelectric, geothermal and nuclear power plants. The thermoelectric power plants contribute 63 % of the total generation in the country through 34 plants distributed in nine geographical regions, with an effective capacity of about 14,000 MW.

The use of groundwater for human consumption and agriculture is a priority in Mexico. For this reason the industrial use must be carefully planned. With this in mind, the CFE created in 1985 the Hydrogeology Department, which has among its main objectives the assessment of groundwater resources for power generation, to establish the rules for development, and to carry out technical supervision of groundwater studies. To accomplish these objectives the following procedures have been implemented:

1. *Identification.* This is the first stage in the study of groundwater prospecting, whose goal is to identify the water-bearing properties of geologic formations, and their potentials for water supply and quality of water. In this stage the following activities are undertaken:
   1.1 Collection of existent data related to the study area at a regional level, including geology, geophysics, surface and groundwater hydrology, hydrogeochemistry and socioeconomics. This information is provided by governmental agencies, research institutes and private companies.
   1.2 Data analysis to identify areas with potential for the groundwater development.
   1.3 Field verification at promising areas.
   1.4 Evaluation of field data to discard the non-promising locations and to propose those feasible for further investigation.
2. *Intermediate-level assessment.* This second stage of groundwater prospecting is directed to evaluation of selected locations in the field, applying the geologic and geophysical techniques, hydrologic analyses, inventory of water wells and springs, and drilling of exploration boreholes. This stage is covered in approximately a year, and a preliminary water balance is obtained.
3. *Higher-level assessment.* In this third stage the feasibility for groundwater development is studied in greater details. Hydrogeologic maps are produced illustrating lithology, structure and stratigraphy of the site, as well as subsurface connections. Also, water level and water quality maps are generated. Additional information provided by test holes and results of pumping tests is obtained. At this stage, the aquifer is well characterized, a conceptual model of its behavior is developed, and economic feasibility of the aquifer determined.
4. *Hydrogeologic monitoring and control.* In this last stage of study the groundwater management schemes are designed and the hydraulic response of aquifer is periodically observed. This includes:
   4.1 Measurement of water levels at the production and observation wells.
   4.2 Measurement of the discharge at pumping wells.
   4.3 Assessment of the chemical and bacteriological characteristics of groundwater.

4.4 Diagnosis of the mechanical functioning of the pumping equipment.
4.5 Well monitoring by down-hole camera, cleanliness and rehabilitation of wells.
4.6 Construction of mathematical models of the aquifer, and development of a management model for optimal groundwater exploitation.

The aquifer of the Thermoelectric Power Plant (TPP) of San Luis Potosi was modeled in 1990, using flow prediction and management models. Before these modelings, the hydraulics characteristics are determined and the aquifer type was verified by pumping tests.

The flow model was capable of predicting variations in head of the aquifer of the TPP and evaluating rates of water flow under differing patterns of recharge and withdrawal.

The prediction model was developed to solve mathematical equations for determining quantitative aspects of groundwater flow such as direction and rate of flow, changes in water level, and interference effects of wells, as well as the drawdowns in the aquifer area, between 1989 and 1994.

The use of management model in the TPP was of a great help in order to obtain the most appropriate decisions of pumping rates, to predict the outcome of decision on water level, to define rules and constraints on maximum pumping rates, minimum drawdowns, using objective function which evaluates a decision yield. The demand of 450 l/sec was considered during the five years of operation of a TPP.

The total pumpage will be 14,191,200 m^3/year (450 l/sec) in 1989. The predicted drop in water levels will be between 8-20m, depending on the well location. Considering the available data, very good agreement was found between observed and simulated water levels during the calibration period and the sensitivity analysis, with reliable results of the prediction period.

The map and the examples of some aspects of hydrologic data obtained at the three of the TPP which have been operated in different parts of Mexico are shown as as Figs. 1, 2, 3 and 4, and Tables 2 and 3.

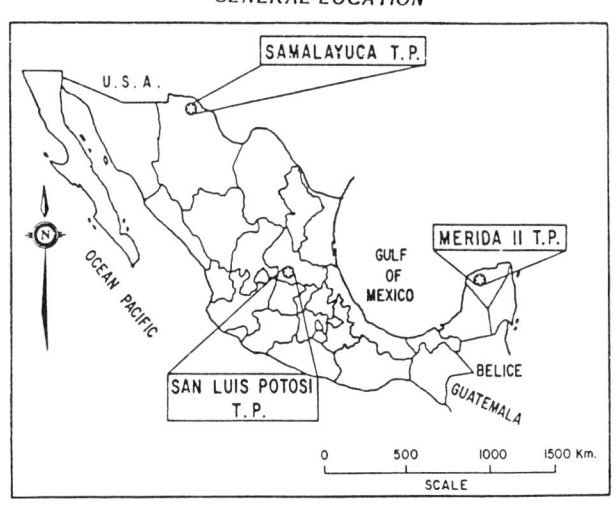

Figure 1. General location of the three thermal power plants (T.P.P.), used as examples.

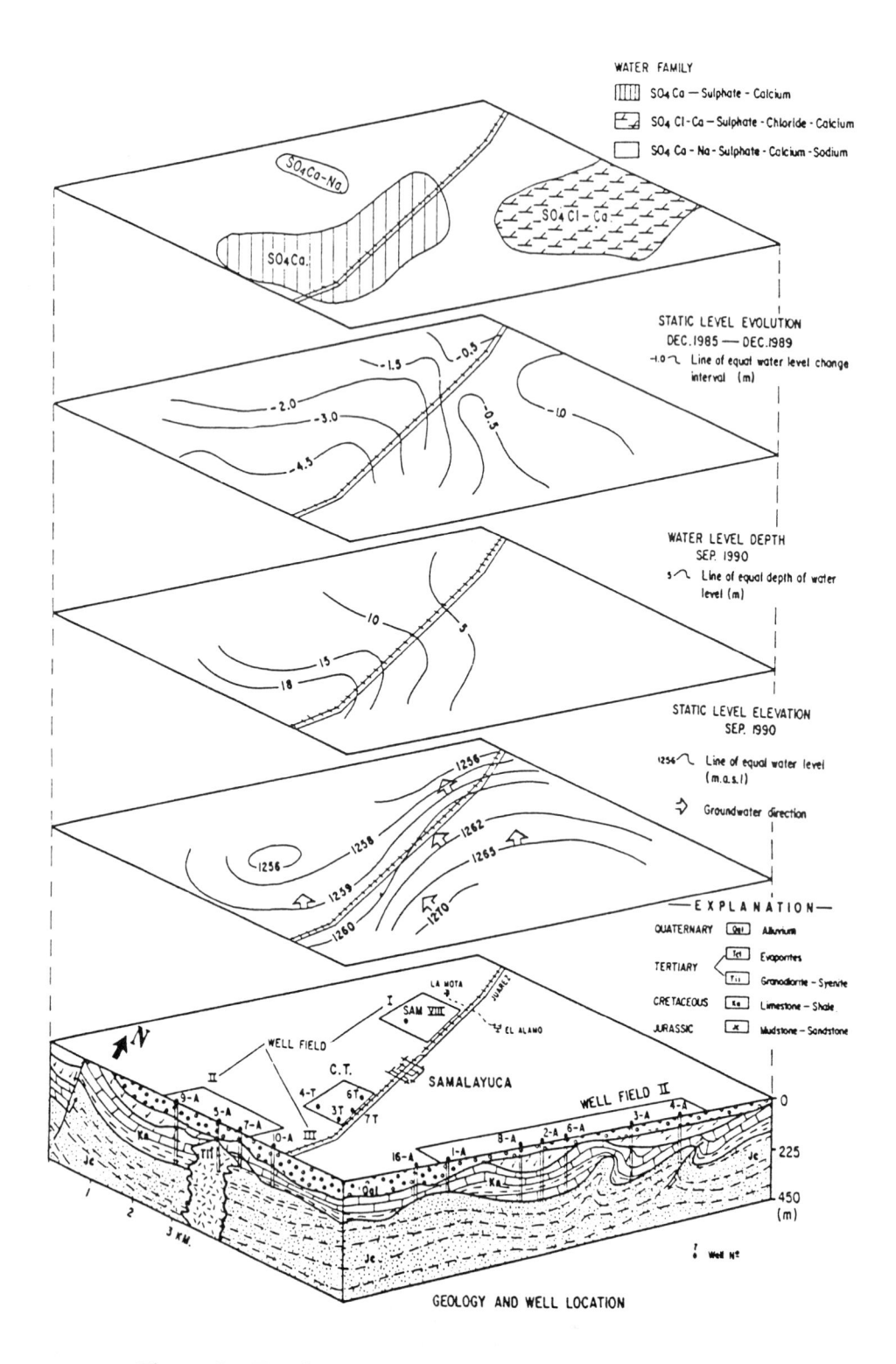

Figure 2. The Samalayuca Thermoelectric Power Plant.

TABLE 1
The Samalayuca Thermoelectric Power Plant

The power plant is located in the Samalayuca Valley, Chihuahua, Mexico. Commercial operation began in 1986. It has two electric power generation units with capacity of 316 MW. Both units required 210 l/sec of groundwater during 1990.

Hydrologic Region	Mean Annual Precipitation	Evaporation	Climatic Conditions	Aquifer type	Lithology	Hydrologic Properties	Water Type
No 34	243 mm.	2000 mm	Mean annual Temperature	1.- Semi-Confined	Limestone and sandstone	$T = 200-450$ m^2/d	SO_4-Ca
Cuenca cerrada del Norte			17 °C		Igneous		
			Dry Temperature	2.-Semi-Unconfined	Alluvial Material	$S = 2.9*10^{-4}$ to $9.4*10^{-4}$	SO_4 Ca-Na SO_4 Cl-Ca
Water level Depth	Water flow Direction	Mean annual Volume	Water level Evolution	Study Stage	Fields Wells	Well Depth	
2-40 m	SE-NW	$6.645*10^6$ m^3/year	1985-1989 0 to 3.5 m	Hydrogeology monitoring and control	8 wells	65 to 300 m	

TABLE 2
The San Luis Thermoelectric Power Plant

The power plant is located in the Villa de Reyes, San Luis Potosi, Mexico. Commercial operation began in 1986, it is formed by two electric energy generation units, and has a capacity of 514 MW. Both units required 376 l/seg of groundwater during 1990.

Hydrologic Region	Mean Annual Precipitation	Evaporation	Climatic Conditions	Aquifer type	Lithology	Hydrologic Properties	Water Type
No 26	408.8 mm.	1714.83 mm	Mean annual Temperature	1.- Un-confine	Alluvium	$T = 15*10^{-3}$ to $2.5*10^{-3}$ m^2/seg	STD 600 ppm
Panuco			17.5°C		Igneous		
			Semi Dry	2.-Semi-Confined	Rocks Ryolite	$S = 0.06$	$CaCO_3$-Na
Water level Depth	Water flow Direction	Mean annual volume	Water level Evolution	Study Stage	Fields Wells	Well Depth	
50 m	SW-NE	$10.872*10^6$ m^3/year	1989-1990 1.5 to 3.0 m	Hydrogeology monitoring and control	17 wells	350 to 500 m	

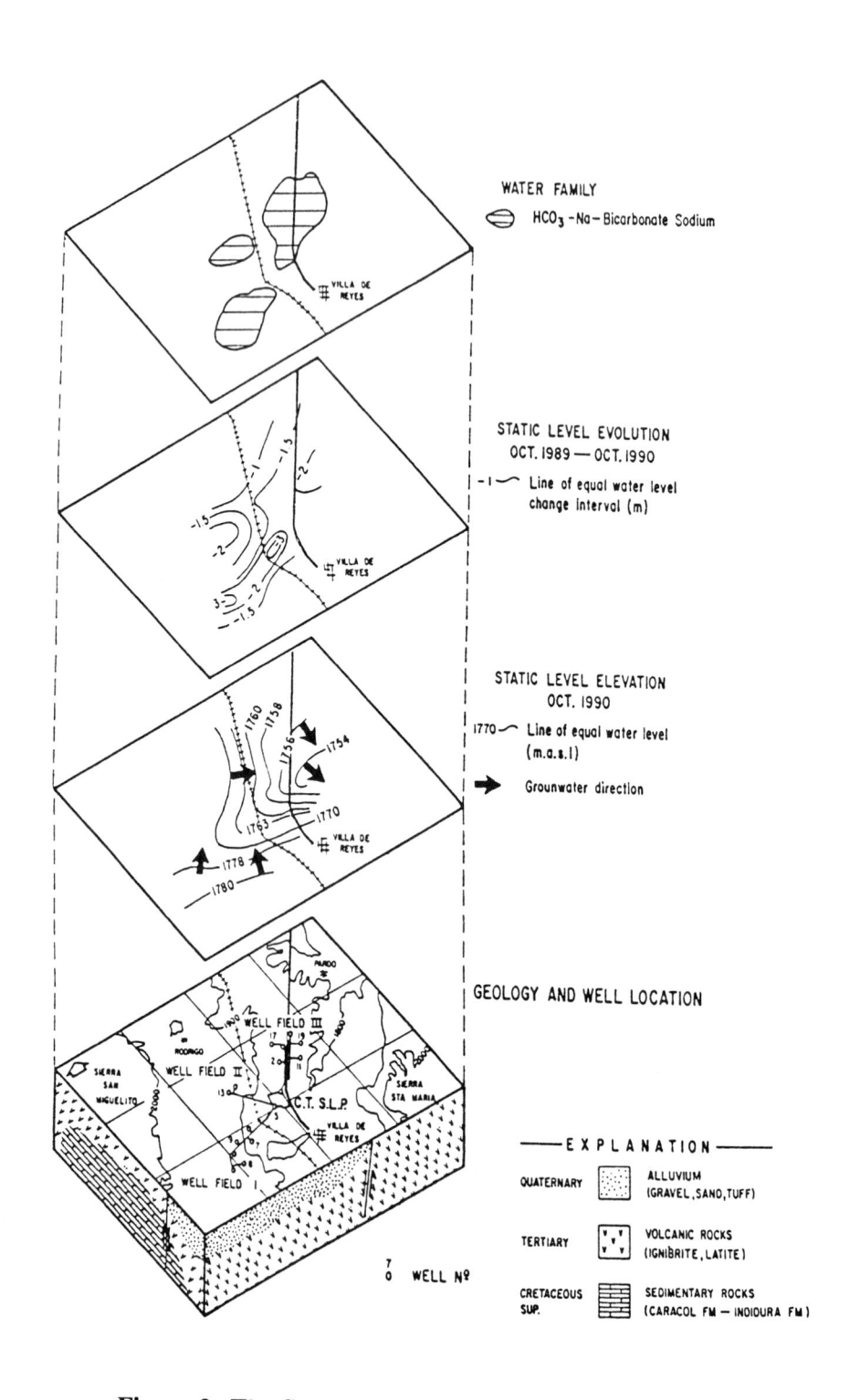

Figure 3. The San Luis Thermoelectric Power Plant.

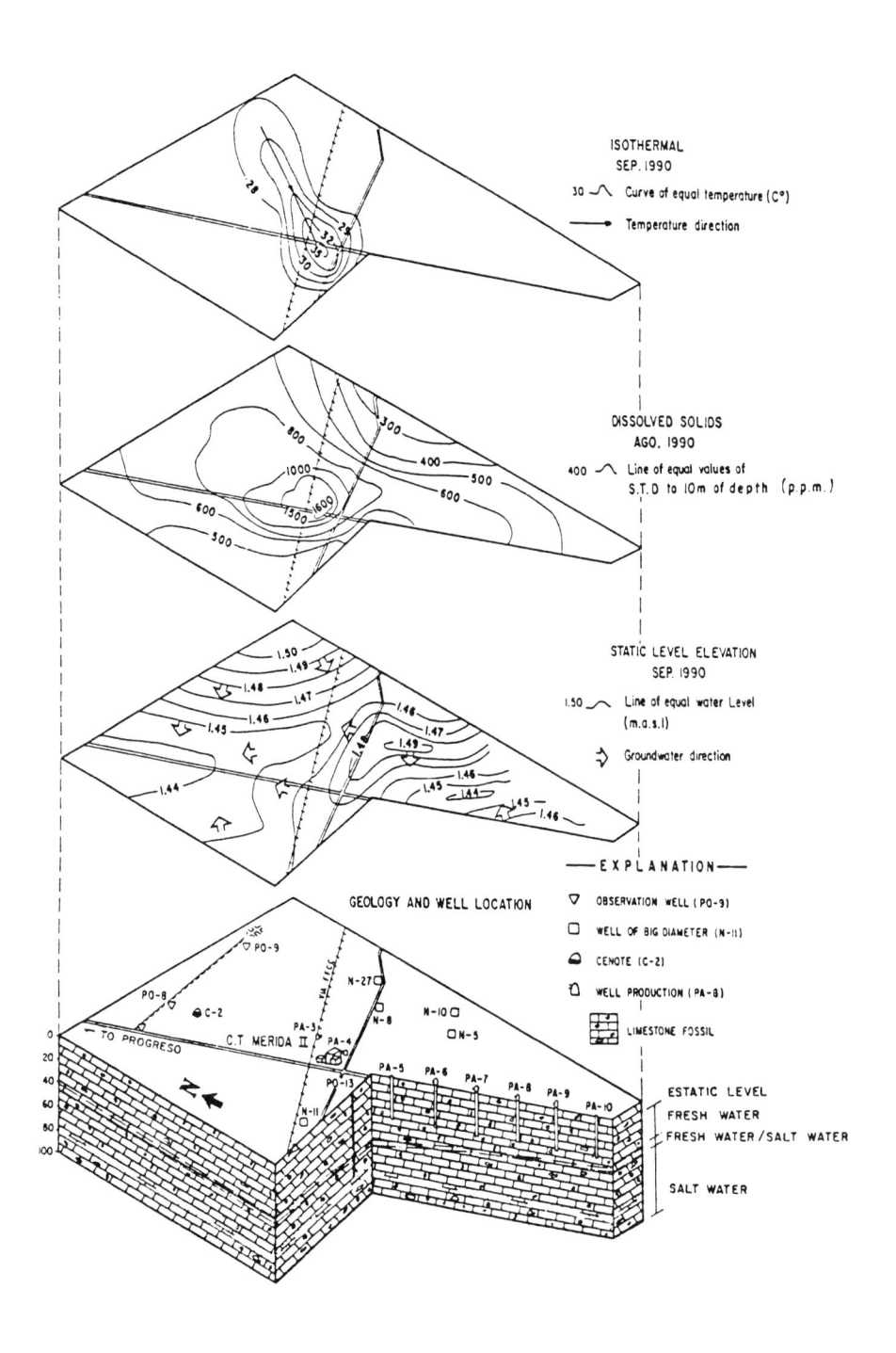

Figure 4. The Merida II Thermoelectric Power Plant.

TABLE 3
The Merida II Thermoelectric Power Plant

The power plant is located in Mérida, Yucatán, Mexico. Commercial operation began in 1981; it is formed by two electric energy generation units, and has a capacity of 171 MW. Both units required 130l/sec of groundwater during 1990.

Hydrologic Region	Mean Annual Precipitation	Evaporation	Climatic Conditions	Aquifer type	Lithology	Hydrologic Properties	Water Type
No 32	1050.0 mm.	2000.0 mm	Mean annual Temperature	1.- Unconfined	Limestone	Specific Capacity	HCO$_3$-Ca
Yucatán Norte			28.0 °C		Silt		
			Rainfall and Tropical	2.- Confined	Clay	4.5 l/seg/m	Cl-Na
Water level Depth	Water flow Direction	Mean annual volume	Water level evolution	Study Stage	Fields Wells	Well Depth	
9.5 m	SE-NW	4.04*10^6 m^3/year	1989-1990 0.01 to 0.05 m	Hydrogeology monitoring and control	10 wells	40 m	

GROUNDWATER ADMINISTRATION IN MEXICO

Ruben Chavez Guillen
Groundwater Administration
National Water Commission
Nuevo Leon 210-2. Mexico, D.F.

and

Pedro Martiniez Leyva
School of Engineering
University of Chihuahua
University Campus, Chihuahua, Chihuahua.

ABSTRACT

The large scale groundwater development in Mexico, which occurred in the last decades, has exceeded the established legal and institutional framework, or has been inadequate for the national needs, leading this to a non-regulated exploitation of the main aquifers of Mexico. This paper covers the problems and the corrective solutions and actions that are being carried out by the National Water Commission.

I. ACTUAL SITUATION

The Mexican United States area covers about two million square kilometers. About fifty percent are mountains and the other fifty percent plain lands at which the main aquifer systems are located and developed in order to satisfy the water needs.

The main groundwater systems are: cretaceous limestones aquifers in the east; tertiary limestone of the Peninsula of Yucatan that is one of the biggest and specific karst geohydrologic systems in Mexico. In the central part of the country vast aquifers in igneous rocks (rhyolite) outcrop in extended areas and form the fillings of tectonic grabens.

Aquifers are located in trans-Mexican volcanic bend, formed by the lava and pyroclastic spills, lacustrine and alluvial deposits that filled deep tectonic graben. The latter aquifers occur in alluvial deposits of big valleys and coastal plains.

In accordance with recent studies, the estimated natural recharge to all the known aquifers is about 40,000 millions m^3/year, with a similar distribution to precipitation: very scant in arid zones and abundant in humid areas. To this figure the induced recharge in the agricultural irrigated areas must be added, representing a volume of 15,000 millions m^3/year. Of the total recharge of

55,000 millions m^3/year, the groundwater extraction is estimated to be 28,000 millions m^3/year. A high percentage of it is used for agricultural purpose, namely two thirds of the total in arid zones, where the groundwater is the only water source.

It is obvious that the total country's groundwater balance is positive, because the groundwater withdrawal is about 70 percent of natural recharge. This global balance cannot be taken as real and does not present the critical situation that prevails in the extended regions of the territory. Most of the exploitation is located in arid regions where the natural replenishment is poor, the water balance negative and the underground storage is decreasing, while in humid regions which have the less developed groundwater, a large portion of this renewable volume is not used or needed.

In most of irrigated areas with water supply by pumping wells, the agricultural activities have been considerably affected by overdrawing of aquifers and the drop in water table or artesian pressure. In many areas, the results are a decline or cessation of water yield from production wells, an increase in operational costs, making the supply less profitable. The demographic growth has made the public supply more and more difficult to satisfy with the available water resources. New requirements are being covered by the reserve of aquifers, resulting in over exploitation.

The industrial activity has been also affected. The water supply for industry is hardly satisfied. In spite of this, the demand will grow so the legal and official actions towards the control and/or management of groundwater resources have become very important and must be reinforced in Mexico.

II. WATER RESOURCES ADMINISTRATION

HISTORICAL ASPECTS

From ancient times, that is, before the Spanish conquest up to the middle of the past century, groundwater was used through shallow wells or springs. The latter was the case in several important population centers. During the colonial period, that is, under the Spanish administration, water resources in general were subject to regulations, rules, real or royal commands, based on delineated property, at the same time on selected units for measuring water supply. For instance, Antonio de Mendoza, Viceroy of the New Spain, issued in 1536 a decree about the land and water measures, in order to fix the units for measuring the quantity of water.

In the "General Regulationes" on water measurements in 1761, they declared that water belongs to the real property and the Viceroy can determine the rules for its use and to build the necessary constructions for its use. They also declared that there is freedom for anyone who wants to get water for domestic purposes but nobody can divert water for irrigation purposes without the Viceroy's consent.

After independence, when the Republic was created, water rights were treated in several legal commands. For instance, in the Civil Code of 1870 the rivers, lakes and lagoons belong to common property. The Water Law of 1910 says that the "Executive Section" or "Executive Power" of the Republic will define which water belongs to Federal Jurisdiction. The Law also defines the benefit from divided waters. The law also defines what waters have to be considered as belonging to Central Federal Government. It points out that the President of the Republic can give the water use as a grant to companies or particulars. It is necessary to mention that all these laws or regulations consider water from rivers, lakes or lagoons but they don't mention groundwater. In the Constitution of 1917, groundwater is considered, in the fifth paragraph of the article 27, which says, "water from the subsurface can be freely drawn off and used by the land owner, but when the public interest demands it or other wells or springs are affected, the Federal Executive can regulate the withdrawal and utility and fix groundwater control areas." As one can see, groundwater was considered but there weren't regulations or limits for withdrawal. At that time groundwater was considered an unlimited resource, a perennial resource with no reason for limitations.

ACTUAL ADMINISTRATION

In accordance with Mexican legislation, the National Water Commission, created at the beginning of 1989, is the supreme authority concerning the regulation, administration and management of water resources in Mexico. In the last version, the Federal Water Law establishes that groundwater belongs to the nation and can be granted as a concession. This concession can be revoked in case when other people are affected or in case of violations of the concession terms, such as a higher extracted volume, change of the original pumping system or by not using the pumping well for the last two years.

In Mexico there are regions under control for groundwater exploitation. In several states of the Mexican Republic, these regions cover almost the total area, and in some cases the total. In these regions no one can drill a well without the respective license. The terrain outside of these the region is called "land of free exploitation" where the user or owner can extract water from the subsurface for any use and in quantities that are needed. The user must notify the authority, that is the National Water Commission. In areas under control, or the "restricted areas", several zones have been defined, according to geohydrologic conditions, such as the under exploited, over exploited and equilibrium areas.

To grant a new concession or to change its characteristics will depend on geohydrologic conditions. For instance, in the over exploited area new withdrawals will be authorized only for domestic, livestock and municipal use in some case. Volume increase is not permitted. In the case of re-application for concession, the new well may be authorized with a reduction of its original volume. New wells can be permitted only if the new user has acquired the concession rights from the other users. In the equilibrium areas, increase in the exploitation rates and the drilling of new wells for industrial, public and livestock use may be permitted under certain circumstances. If under exploitation conditions exist, the new developments are permitted as well as additional pumping volumes. It is possible to drill a new well for any purpose however with certain limits, such as depth and yield. The concession or licences for new wells, replacement, change in use, change of owner or equipment, usually require a cost to the user that is devoted to cover the administrative expenses. Regarding the water use fees, the Federal Rights Law defines the availability of groundwater zones, establishing for each one the cost of water per cubic meter, according to use, with higher fees for restricted groundwater areas (Region I). The rural irrigation and livestock uses are exempted.

III. GROUNDWATER DEVELOPMENT PROBLEMS

An adequate administration of water resources for a specific region requires the knowledge of their availability in order to define a management program with an appropriate administrative and legal framework and sufficient human and financial resources. In many cases, the groundwater administration has not been adequate, because of tremendous growth in use of this resource. That has caused an uncontrolled exploitation in many aquifers.

Geohydrologic studies were carried out after the over exploitation was detected in regional aquifers, with inefficient management programs, because of vested interests. As a consequence these studies were not carried out easily. On the other hand, the legal framework and its application was deficient in stopping the drilling of clandestine wells, as well as in the change in use, equipment and increase of extracted water volumes. The fines for these activities were insignificant or not applied. The financial resources devoted to this information and management were also insufficient. As a result most aquifers in Mexico have been overdrawn.

IV. CORRECTIVE ACTIONS

The creation of the National Water Commission in 1989 was intended to overcome the deficient groundwater administration and an overall management, taking the necessary actions in order to control this resource. However, the challenge is enormous if one considers that it mean to control the use of water resources of the whole country.

Some corrective actions to be implemented are:

- To declare all the national territory as a groundwater control zone.
- To update the Federal Water Law, emphasizing sanctions.
- To establish a regulatory system in the over exploited aquifers according to the users' needs, but reducing the groundwater withdrawal and increasing the average replenishment. This action is being applied at present to the aquifers of the Baja California (San Quintin, La Paz, Santo Domingo), Sonora (Caborca and Hermosillo), Coahuila (La Laguna) and Durango States.
- To establish reserve zones, mainly for water supply to big cities (by now, several decrees are being prepared in order to declare some aquifers, or part of them, as reserves for future demands).
- To apply fully the Federal Water Law. In order to implement this law, inspection visits are being carried out in every state in order to detect the irregular developments and acts.
- To promote a new national inventory for water wells through governmental contracts or the social service brigades. This new inventory of wells will be carried out in the future.

VALLE DE SAN QUINTIN

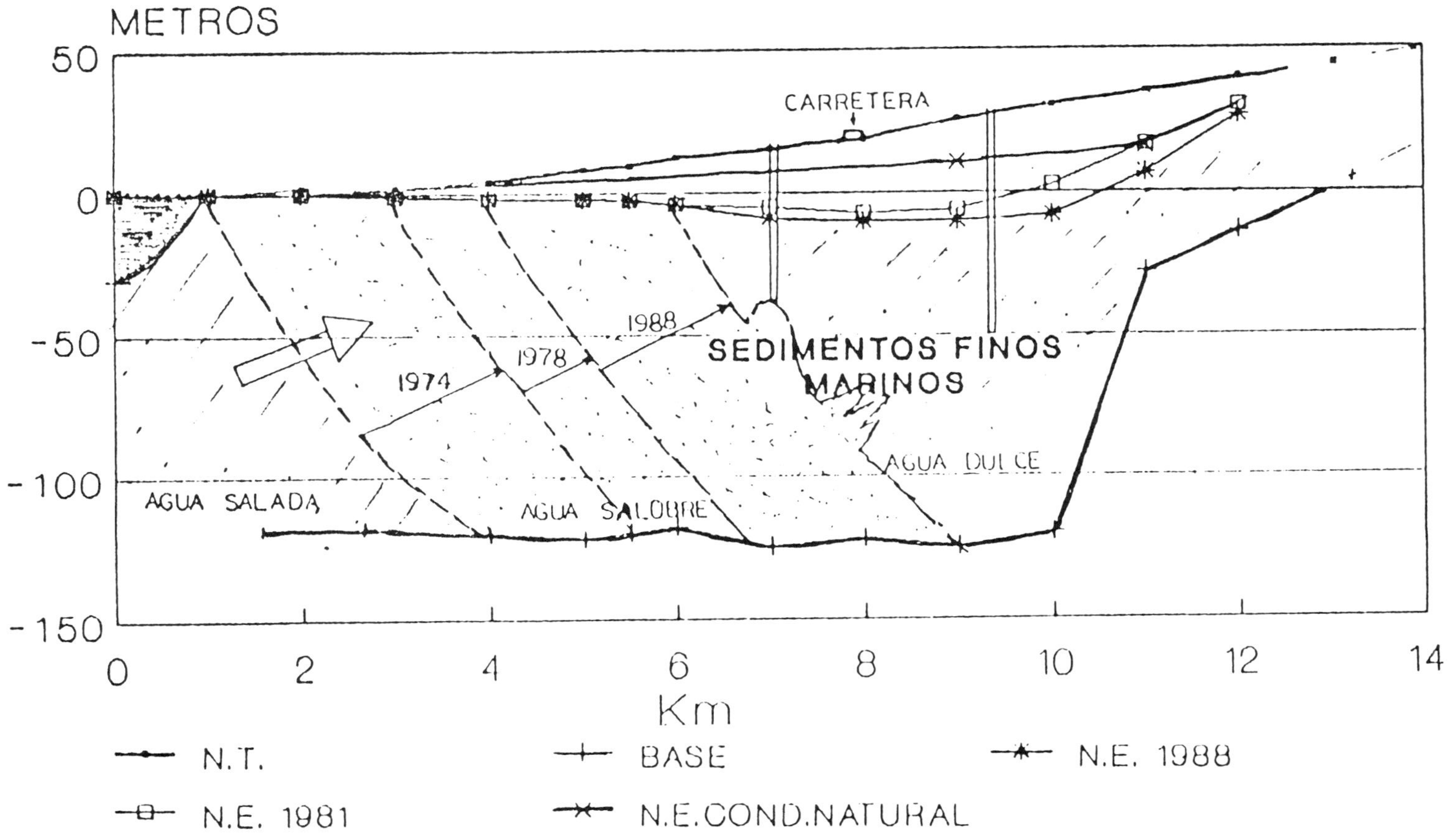

CRITERIO GENERAL DE MANEJO DE LOS ACUIFEROS

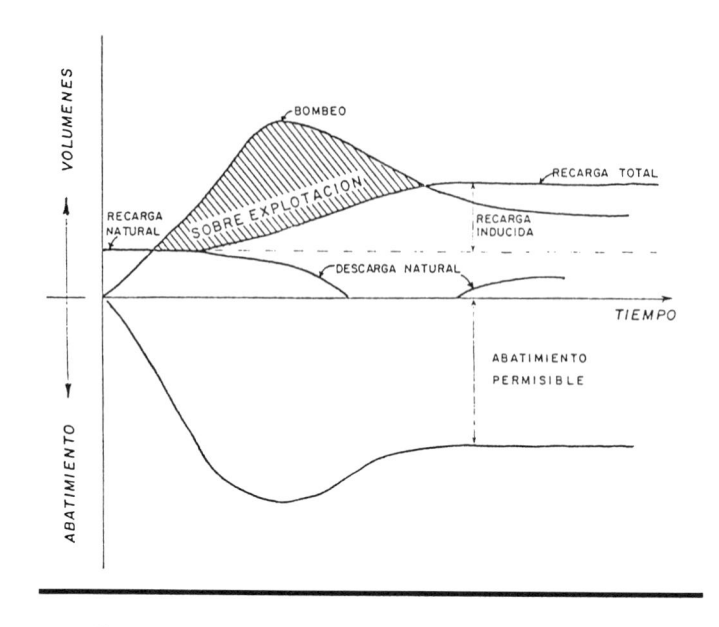

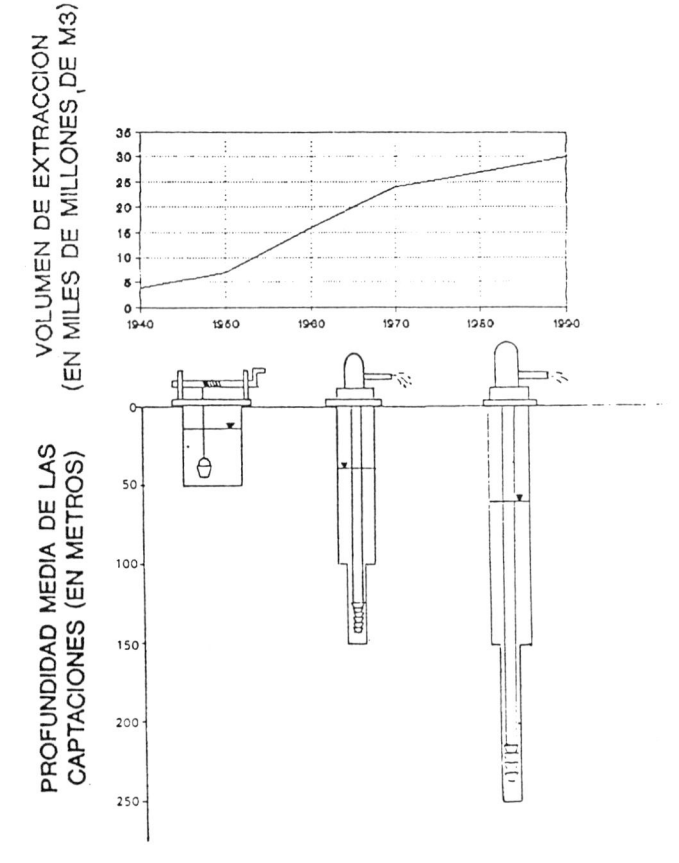

RENOVACION Y EXPLOTACION DEL AGUA SUBTERRANEA

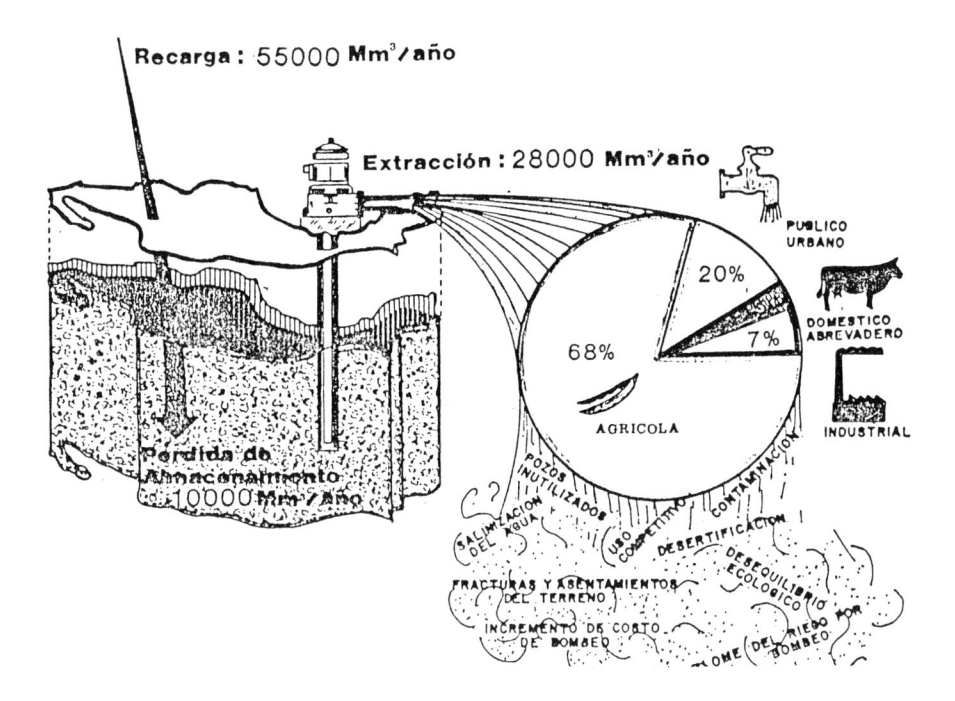

BALANCE HIDROLOGICO DE MEXICO

(cantidades en billones de M3/año)

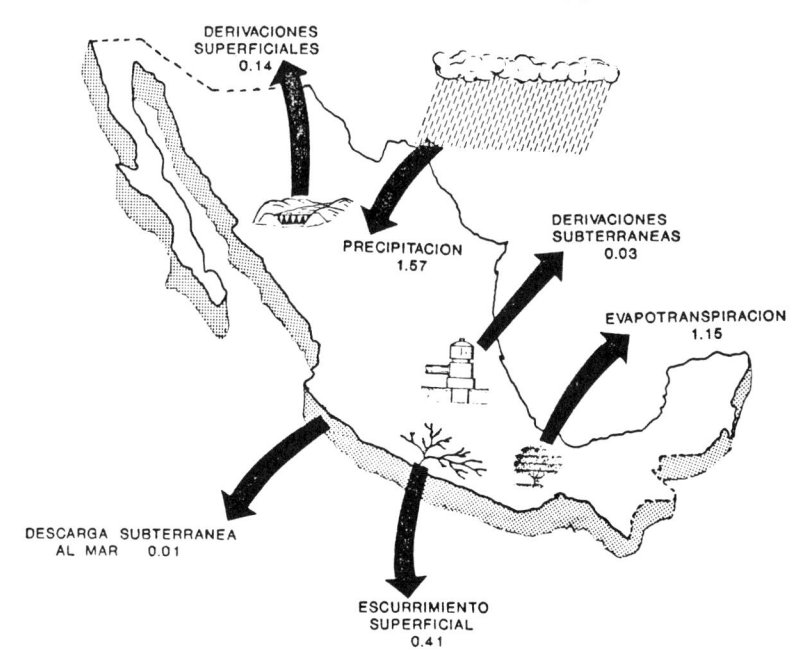

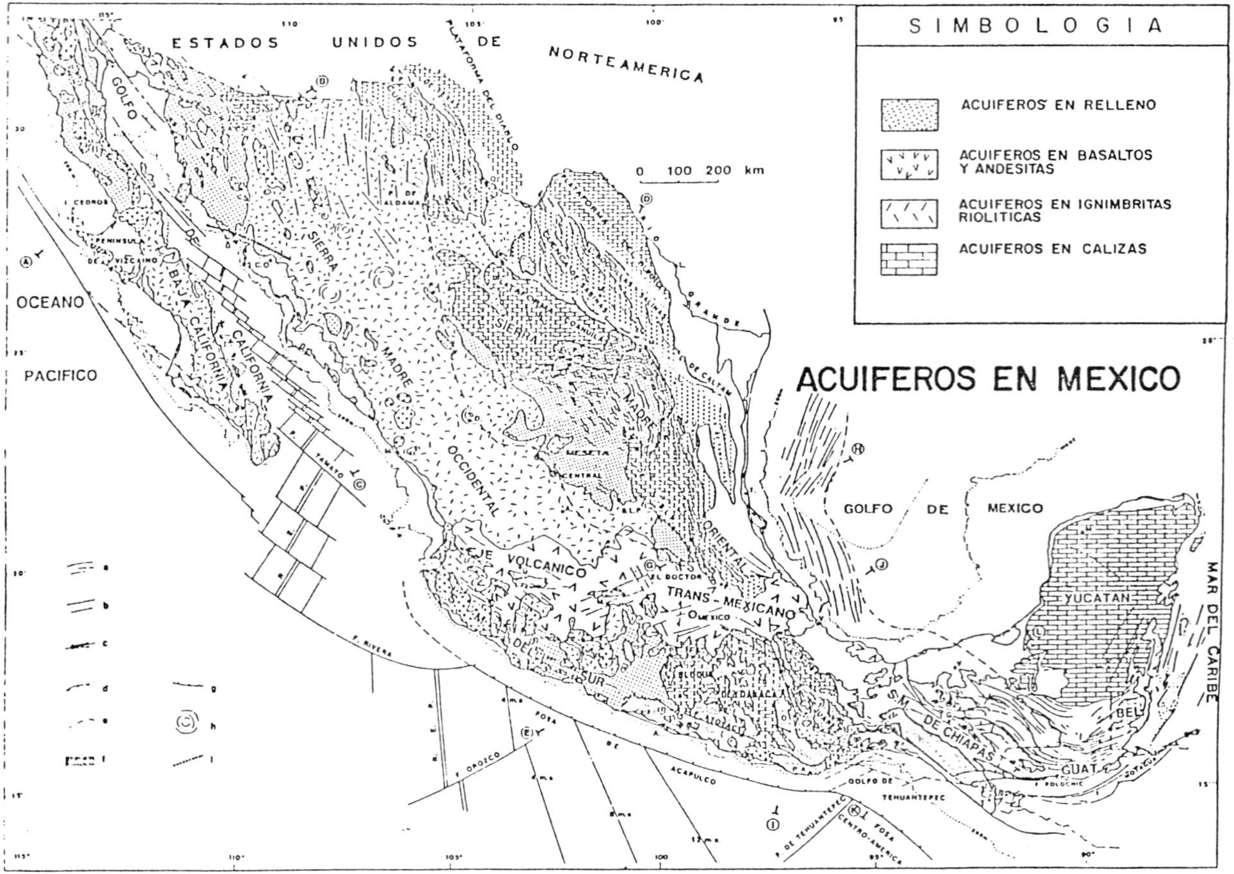

ACUIFEROS EN MEXICO
SIMBOLOGIA
ACUIFEROS EN RELLENO
ACUIFEROS EN BASALTOS Y ANDESITAS
ACUIFEROS EN IGNIMBRITAS RIOLITICAS
ACUIFEROS EN CALIZAS
0 100 200 km
ESTADOS UNIDOS DE NORTEAMERICA
OCEANO PACIFICO
GOLFO DE MEXICO
MAR DEL CARIBE
GOLFO DE CALIFORNIA
BAJA CALIFORNIA
SIERRA MADRE OCCIDENTAL
SIERRA MADRE ORIENTAL
MESETA CENTRAL
EJE VOLCANICO TRANS-MEXICANO
S.M. DEL SUR
S.M. DE CHIAPAS
YUCATAN
BEL
GUAT
PLATAFORMA DEL DIABLO
RIO GRANDE
ACAPULCO
GOLFO DE TEHUANTEPEC
FOSA CENTRO-AMERICA

GROUNDWATER STUDIES IN SEMI-ARID AREAS OF MEXICO, A CHANGE IN PERSPECTIVE

J. Joel Carrillo R.
Instituto de Geofisica, UNAM
04510, Coyoacan, D.F.

ABSTRACT

The determination of components of hydrologic cycle has been usually defined for humid and temperate areas. Through the years the results have been assumed as applicable for the semi-arid conditions also. However, although in principle they might be equivalent, the hydrologic regimes differ immensely. Vegetation water needs and intakes, as well as water (ground+surface) availability and climatic conditions are all different. Methods devised for a humid area with steadier rainfall, evenly distributed vegetation and full soil cover, should not be applied to semi-arid areas where the opposite conditions prevail. Although the application in a semi-arid area of methodologies developed to portray the behaviour of hydrologic cycle in a humid area, they may raise important questions in particular hydrogeologic conditions. The use of a thorough analysis to define local, intermediate and regional groundwater flow gives valuable concepts for understanding of hydrogeology of semi-arid areas. Therefore, interdisciplinary studies are required in order to have an appropriate management of water resources through the feasible engineering work supported by scientific methods. Increasing needs to fulfill water demand and to avoid contamination hazards require the proper assessment of groundwater resources of semi-arid areas of Mexico.

INTRODUCTION

The study of water processes along the hydrologic cycle has been taken through the years as the model approach for description of both the surface and groundwater movements and their interactions. Attempts have been made since historical times to describe, define and measure the various Earth's systems including the hydrologic cycle (Fig. 1) as a dynamic and broad system with well defined limits. In this discussion the interest will be focused on groundwater input and output by the limited techniques of evaluation in a semi-arid region.

The inflow to the natural catchment area is precipitation and occasionally snow-melt. In regard to outflow, runoff and evapotranspiration (transpiration by plants plus evaporation from open water reservoirs and soil) represent the main components, Fig. 2 (Freeze and Cherry, 1979).

Although groundwater may be considered as a separate entity, as water below the water table, its connecting link to precipitation is the system

HYDROLOGIC CYCLE

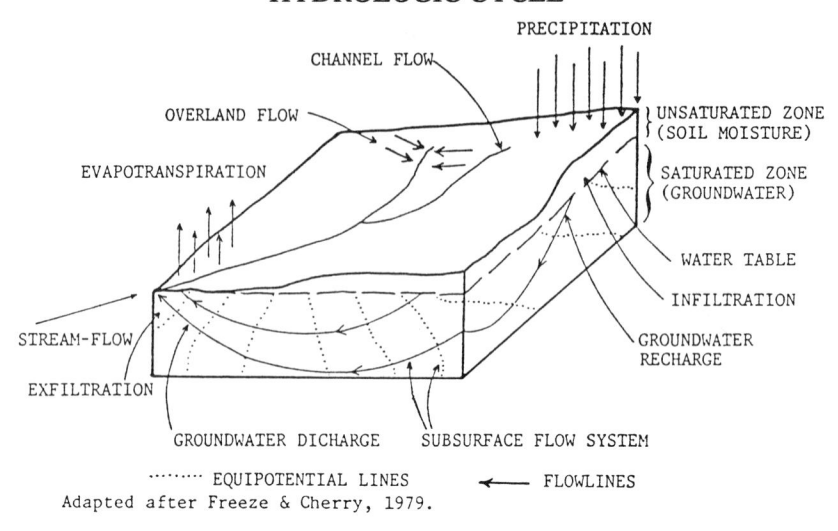

Figure 1. The hydrologic cycle.

that could be simplified as infiltration-groundwater recharge. Groundwater discharge takes place beneath the water table directly into a stream, as the base stream flow.

As noted in Figs. 1 and 2, the cycle is a simplified scheme, lacking particular cases where important recharge from beneath is taking place,

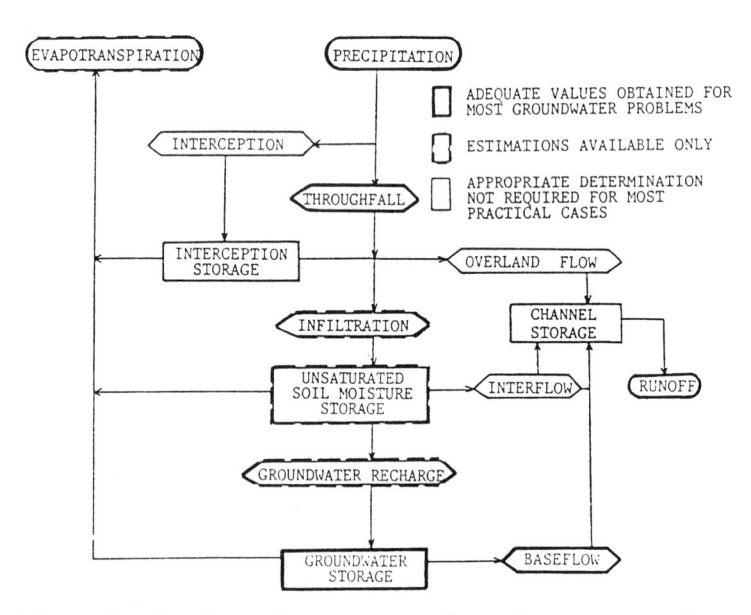

Figure 2. A schematic representation of the hydrologic cycle.

often also in terms of the thermal input to groundwater. This case is exemplified in Fig. 3. Various systems in Fig. 2 could be treated by hydraulic methods. Adequate evaluations of precipitation, runoff, groundwater storage (and movement) and base flow are usually available. Although the exact determination of interception, interception storage, overland flow, inter-flow and channel storage, are not required for most practical cases, their appropriate definitions and uses could help in particular cases. By eliminating these components from the system of Fig. 2, evapotranspiration and infiltration-groundwater recharge are left as only components, which can be defined and estimated in approximate ways.

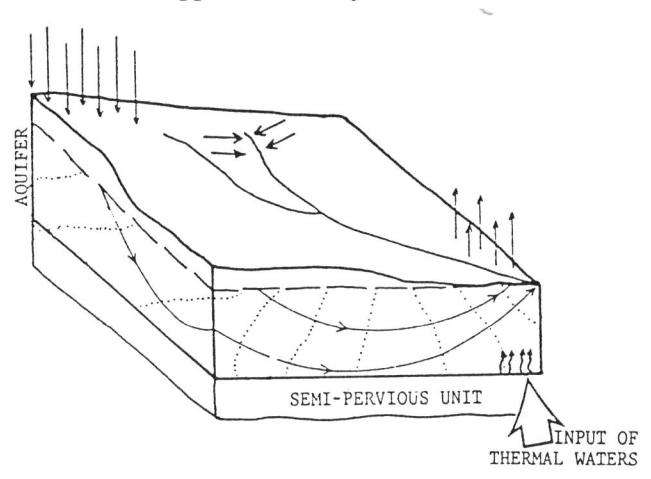

Figure 3. The hydrologic cycle with the thermal component.

Questions have been raised by particular findings and experience on missleading results obtained from indiscriminate application of methods of estimation of groundwater recharge and evapotranspiration.

EVAPOTRANSPIRATION AND GROUNDWATER RECHARGE

Evapotranspiration is the amount of water used by vegetation cover to fulfill its water requirement for growth and also the water lost from the soil and open water bodies directly into the atmosphere. This figure includes the real amount of water used, contrary to the potential evapotranspiration which is the water lost for the same processes by assuming always a full supply of evapotranspiration potential. The measurement of this variable is the most difficult in the hydrologic cycle. Related formulae result from the empirical approaches that are often far from representing the real and steady conditions over the area of interest. The use of those methods is frequent in arid and semi-arid areas where prevailing conditions are far from those of the humid and temperate areas for which they were devised. Lysimetres usually require costly and time consuming efforts. In some areas the last resort is to compute the evapotranspiration by water balance equations in which errors in measurement and estimation of other variables definitely affect the accuracy of the final results.

The transfer of methods from humid areas to arid areas is a questionable approach. In the former, the shallow rooted vegetation covers most of the ground leaving small areas for direct evaporation. In semi-arid areas vegetation covers only small patches and the root system is rather deep, whereas most of the soil is bare of vegetative cover. Also precipitation is more evenly distributed in time and space in humid areas. The semi-arid areas, where a scenario of 90% of the rain falling on 10% of the rainy season is common, also has the spatial distribution of rainfall highly non-uniform.

Recharge at present is a very controversial issue. The concept has different meanings for different people. For ecologists it takes place over the mountain slopes, vegetation uses it and the excess seeps to replenish the phreatic bodies. The agronomist think of it as water that moves beneath the root zone of crops, therefore represents a loss in water yield which should be minimized. The sanitary engineer needs an area where minimum recharge takes place. The hydrogeologist is eager to understand and define it in qualitative and quantitative terms.

The native vegetation in semi-arid areas often develops the root system that takes an important amount of precipitation through evapotranspiration. As a result, recharge is low but constant. Therefore, with clearing of vegetation, evapotranspiration diminishes and consequently there is an increase in the quantity of water ready for the aquifer recharge. (Allison, 1987; Shorma, 1987, Allison et al., 1988; Cook et al, 1988; Barnett, 1988, and Trewehells, 1988).

Physical measurements of related hydrologic variables are often difficult because water flows are slow in porous media. Although comparatively faster in fractured rocks, water follows the preferential and tortuous paths that are difficult to trace. So, only the estimates can be made through chemical and isotopic methods in unsaturated and saturated zones and through physical methods that required to know the wet front position and the assumption of a constant input (Allison, op.cit.). Estimates by numerical modelling require climatologic data, with their limitations in time and space.

Difference in precipitation regime and in the process of recharge implies a different approach for recharge estimation in humid and arid/semi-arid areas. Under the former conditions recharge is more constant and areal methods are suited. However, in the latter case the recharge is concentrated to small areas and is a rather intermittent process.

The challenge is to make a meaningfull simple scheme of hydrologic cycle, especially when the physical modeling is used. Then the scheme may already be complicated by the lack of data on various minor hydrologic phenomena.

GROUNDWATER FLOW SYSTEM

The understanding of behaviour of surface water and groundwater regimes is a prerequisite to studies involving engineering, ecology, agriculture, etc. A statement of a groundwater problem solution without the proper definition of the flow system governing the area fails to provide the adequate questions that need to be solved.

Assuming a steady state, groundwater flow paths must be determined in both horizontal and vertical planes, with recharge and discharge areas resulting. There are three groundwater flow systems to be defined within the topography and geological framework: local, intermediate and regional (Toth, 1963). A hilly topography such as in Fig. 4 produces various local systems. In each topography, water enters and leaves in the same valley. In some cases part of recharge water may discharge in another valley, located at a lower topographic level, implying an intermediate system. The regional system is the deepest one and will develop from the regional groundwater divide to the lowest discharge area. The flows in a natural environment will not overlap their flow patterns (mixture will not occur).

CHANGE IN PERSPECTIVE

In a broad sense the evolution of groundwater problems have been progressively shifted from the point solution by means of wells at the time when the available resource is not overwhelmed by demand. Then, hardly any attention was paid to the aquifer that provided the water. At the later times and occasionally, the recharge becomes as the leading variable. The following steps are either the well-fields and/or the use of deeper single wells that required better engineering capabilities. A focus on water management started to obtain proper attention when the aquifer properties are assessed and known, with the wide use of the hydrological balance equations giving an entirely new dimension to the resource.

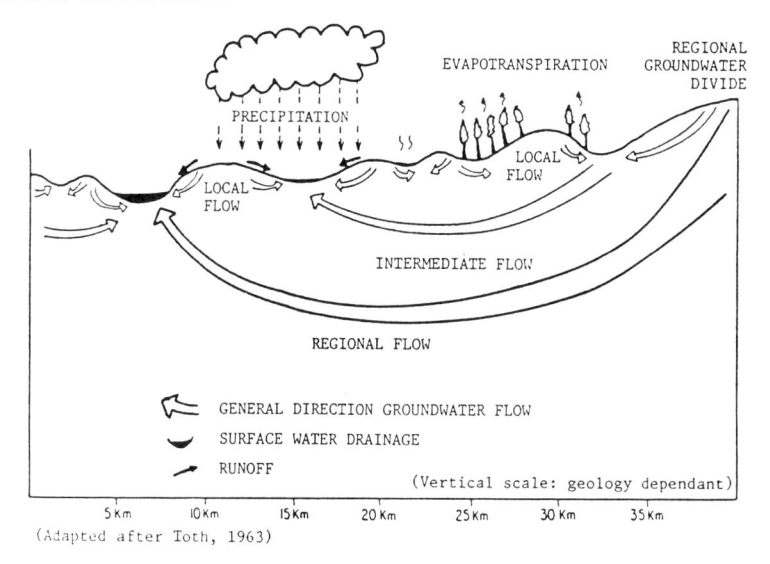

Figure 4. Relationship between the topography, the groundwater movement and the surface water drainage.

Although Hubbert as early as 1940 produced the comprehensive paper on the theory of groundwater motion, several conclusions indicated that progress was made. The fundamental misconception prevailed on the definition of the potential functions governing the groundwater flow. The analogy of ideas presented in this discussion are more relevant when considered in light of the Hubert's potential theory. It did not receive the acceptance when it was first read at the Geological Society. Now, it is the basis for the applications of groundwater flow systems.

The continuous increase in groundwater demands, with quality constrains, made it necessary to have a full understanding of the aquifer behaviour. That means to define the aquifer system involved and to have knowledge on local, sub-regional and regional groundwater systems. Applications of results of these investigations to the appropriate management of water resources and the feasible engineering works, supported by a scientific research, are needed for development of groundwater resources in the semi-arid areas of México.

CONCLUSIONS

Evapotranspiration and groundwater recharge are the two important components of the hydrologic cycle, which should not be considered as readily available, but needing the best estimates. The concern for groundwater has passed through various periods of approaches and uses.

Starting with the single well approach, and followed by the well-field/deeper wells approach, the concern evolved to the consideration of the entire aquifer. The water balance equation became in fashion when groundwater problems became acute. At present, special attention is being paid to the flow system definition and the groundwater flow controlling variables.

The undiscriminate application of methods of groundwater solutions in semi-arid areas, by using the hydrologic cycle components that were devised for specific climatic conditions (humid and temperable), may lead the groundwater solutions away from the reality.

Questions related to groundwater problems should be identified and dealt with by an interdisciplinary method. Then, the planned solutions will be more in agreement with the prototype conditions.

REFERENCES

Allison, G.B., 1987, *A Review of Some of the Physical, Chemical and Isotopic Techniques Available for Estimating Groundwater Recharge, in Estimation of Groundwater Recharge*, Simmers, editor, D. Reiple Publ. Co.

Allison, G.B., Walker, G.R., Hughes, M.W. and Cook, P.G., 1988, *Recharge, Salinity and Land use change in the Mallee Region. The Murray Basin, in Geology, Groundwater and Salinity Management,* Australia, Geoscience Council, Camberra.

Barnett, S.R., 1988, *Scenario Modelling of Aquifers in the Mallee Region, in Geology, Groundwater and Salinity Management,* Australia, Geoscience Council, Camberra.

Cook, P.G., Jolly, I.D. and Walker, C.D., 1988, *Recharge Studies in the Western Murray Basin, in Geology, Groundwater and Salinity Management,* Australia, Geoscience Council, Camberra.

Freeze, R.A. and Cherry, J.A., 1979, *Groundwater*, Prentice Hall Inc., London.

Hubbert, M.K., 1940, *The Theory of Groundwater Motion*, Journal of Geology, Vol XLVIII, No. 8, part 1, pp 785-944.

Sharma, M.L., 1987, *Recharge Estimation from the Depth-Distribution of Environmental chloride in the unsaturated zone, in Western Australian examples, in Estimation of Groundwater Recharge*, Simmers, Editor, D. Reiple Pub. Co.

Toth, J., 1963, *A Theoretical Analysis of Groundwater Flow in Small Drainage Basins*, J. Geophysical Res. 68 (16), pp 4795-4812.

Trewehells, W., 1988, *Irrigation Recharge, in Geology, Groundwater and Salinity Management,* Australia, Geoscience Council, Camberra.

3 WATER QUALITY MANAGEMENT IN NORTH AMERICA

WATER, GROWTH AND THE FUTURE OF A BOOMING U.S./MEXICO BORDER COMMUNITY

Hector R. Fuentes, Ph.D., P.E.
Department of Civil Engineering
University of Texas at El Paso
El Paso, Texas 79968-0516[1]

ABSTRACT

The U.S./Mexico border region defines a geographical area where population and economic rates of growth are causing great pressure on the environment and its limited resources. The pressure is worrisome because of its deteriorating effects on quality of life and future growth. The objective of this paper is to describe the situation in reference to the water resources management in El Paso (Texas) and Cd. Juarez (Chihuahua) urban area. The climate is characterized by a 10:1 ratio of evaporation to precipitation. A complex allocation of surface waters and overpumping of ground waters, the main water supply, combines with the lack of a comprehensive environmental management plan to produce a dismal future, limited by the availability of water resources and environmental quality. Conclusively, the United States and Mexico need to make effective and efficient steps to address the short and long-term environmental problems and issues for the region, with special focus on water resources.

INTRODUCTION

The United States (U.S.)/Mexico border is both a political separation of territories and a geographic region common and different to two nations. Although the physical boundary is well defined, what is known as the border region extends over areas on both sides of the boundary. Those areas are intertwined historically, socially, politically and environmentally. The length of the border is about 3,100 kilometers, which include 10 states, six in Mexico and four in the U.S. There are 38 border municipalities on the Mexican side and 23 border counties on the American side.

Certain facts are characteristic of communities along the U.S./Mexico border. First, population has increased at very high rates, mostly caused by the demand of labor offered by industrial development. Second, growth has created a pressing demand for all kinds of resources, such as urban infrastructure and the environment. And third, there is a critical lack of binational actions and programs to ensure growth within an adequate framework of environmental protection and resource management.

In order to illustrate the drama of the environmental reality developing along the U.S./Mexico border, this paper uses basic information for the binational community defined by Cd. Juares (Mexico) and El Paso (U.S.). Although the paper focuses on water resources, it should be understood that the drama affects and is affected by all areas of environmental protection (i.e., soil, air and waste). Certainly, water resources becomes more precious in an arid environment composed mainly of desert and sandy terrain.

The binational community of Cd. Juarez and El Paso is located midway along the international border between the U.S. and Mexico. This is a region within the northern portion of the Chihuahuan desert, where Western Texas meets Southern New Mexico and the northernmost boundary of the Mexican state of Chihuahua (Fig. 1). The climate is typical of arid deserts with average annual rainfall of about 9 inches, most of which occurs from July through September during thunderstorms. Average high temperatures range from 95°F in June to 55°F in January, resulting in average annual evaporation rates of about 93 inches. In fact, the area has abundant solar energy with an average of 293 days of sunshine.

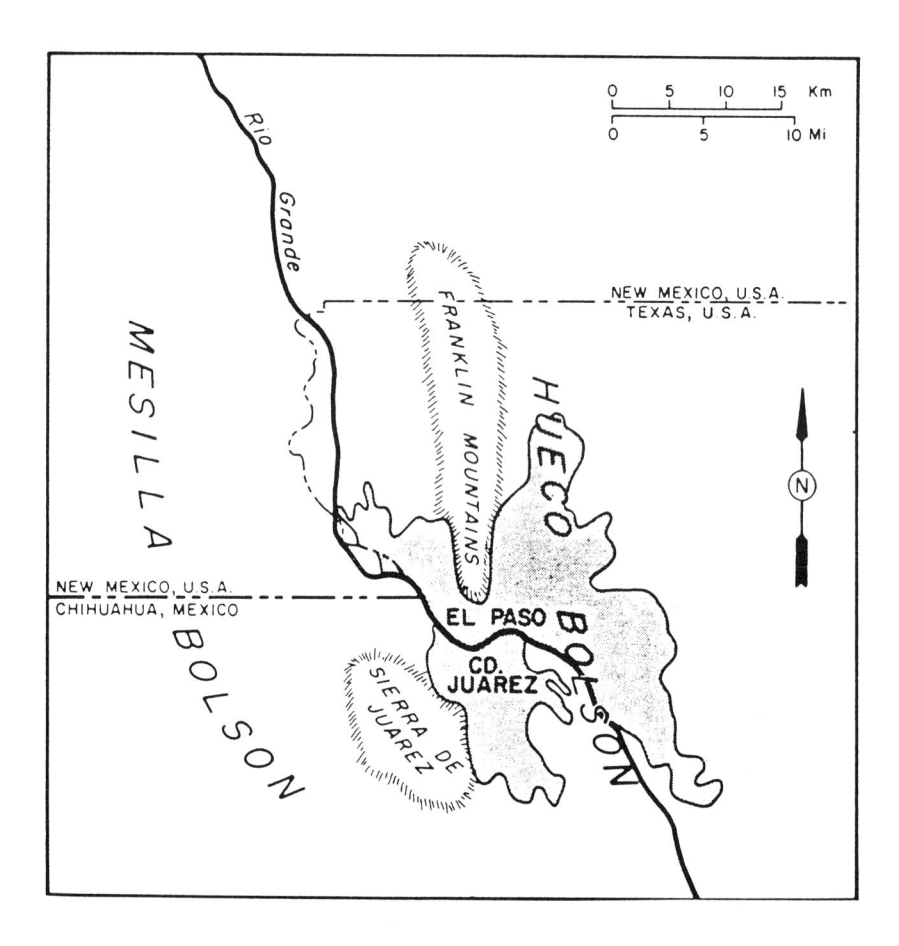

Figure 1. Location of El Paso and Cd. Juarez (Sepulveda and Hutton, 1984).

WATER RESOURCES

The community's water resources depend on two main sources (Lloyd and Marston, 1985; Sepulveda and Utton, 1984): the Rio Grande River (called Bravo River in Mexico) and various regional aquifers. The main regional aquifers are the Hueco Bolson, Rio Grande alluvium and the Mesilla Bolson. The region is unique in that the region's water supply is shared by West Texas, New Mexico and Mexico (i.e., the state of Chihuahua).

U.S. and Mexico share the water from the Rio Grande. A 1906 treaty guarantees Mexico an annual delivery in perpetuity of 60,000 acre-feet in a full allotment year. Both countries use the river water mostly for irrigation. Although about 20% of the present water supply in El Paso is from the river, any possible increases from the river depend on a complicated system of allotments defined by treaties and agreements with primary rights controlled by the farmers.

Almost all of Cd. Juarez and El Paso's municipal and commercial water supply is obtained from the Hueco Bolson and Mesilla Bolson wells (Department of Planning, Research and Development, 1988a). The largest percentage is supplied from the Hueco Bolson (e.g., 65% of the total consumption in El Paso). Groundwater in the Rio Grande alluvium complements agricultural irrigation needs. Primary sources for aquifer recharge amount to seepage of river waters, infiltration from irrigation and natural precipitation.

PATTERNS OF GROWTH

Tables 1 and 2 illustrate the booming characteristics of the community based on population growth and economic indicators. These factors combine to create dramatic changes in population and demand for and on resources. Table 1 indicates that the population has increased gradually over the last decades in both cities. A range of reported values for 1990 has been included since the 1990 census has been contested in Cd. Juarez.

TABLE 1
POPULATION FOR EL PASO AND CD. JUAREZ[2]

Year	Cd. Juarez People	% change	El Paso People	% change
1950	131,308	111	130,485	112
1960	276,995	53	276,687	16
1970	424,135	56	322,261	32
1980	663,094	20-94	425,259	21
1990	797,769[3] -1,286,734		515,342[4]	

The increase of industrial activity in both cities is illustrated in Table 2. The trend is mostly associated with the expansion of the "maquiladora" program, which is particularly large in Cd. Juarez. This program, which began as an exclusive assembling of parts into a variety of components and products mostly for the American market, has most recently become industrialized. Industrialization has produced greater needs for water and larger usage of raw materials with additional generation of contamination than what was initially intended within the "maquiladora" program.

TABLE 2
ECONOMIC GROWTH IN THE EL PASO/CD. JUAREZ AREA

Year	Cd. Juarez Maquiladoras[6]/Business Establishments[7]		El Paso[5] Services/Retail Sales	
1971	-	-	1,484	1,508
1980	-	-	2,141	2,317
1982	129	1,343	-	-
1985	195	1,816	2,875	2,677
1987	265	3,186	-	-
1990	289[8]	-	4,702	3,420[9]

Thus, the area has grown and is expected to continue growing as new economic initiatives, particularly enhanced by the coming North American free trade agreement, are implemented in the border region. These economic initiatives add to other well-known factors, such as the migration of Mexican nationals looking for economic opportunities or that of retired Americans in search of warm climates.

AGGRAVATING REALITIES

The combination of growth and an increased demand for a limited resource, both occurring in the midst of a lack of a binational approach to a reasonable management of limited water resources, defines an uncertain future for water availability and quality. For instance, the El Paso Water Utilities (EPWU) estimates the Hueco Bolson is being depleted by El Paso and Cd. Juarez at the rate of one foot to four feet (e.g., drop in piezometric lines) per year (Department of Planning, Research and Development, 1988a) (Figure 2). It appears that the present and future of these transboundary water resources, especially groundwater (the main supply in the border) will be defined by a "tug of war between users and abusers from both countries."

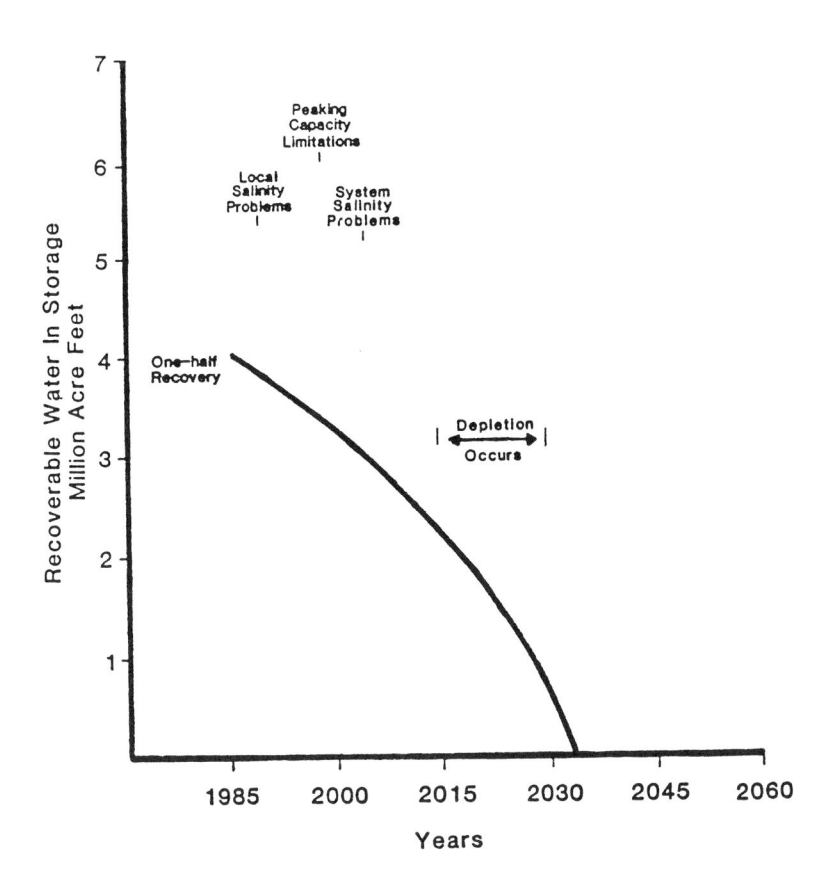

Figure 2. Prediction for the Depletion of the Hueco Bolson (Wilson Lee & Associates, 1986).

First, short-term natural increase of supplies, either surface or ground waters, are constrained by contrastingly high evaporation rates, low precipitation rates and limited storage and recharge capacity during wet periods. The long-term ratio of evaporation to precipitation is a disadvantageous 10:1. A poorly addressed question is the impact of greenhouse effects on the arid border. The question, quite neglected at the moment, requires special attention in any long-term planning initiative.

Second, patterns of growth do not show any indication of slowing down; furthermore, they are expected to increase as a new economic order brings free trade agreements between the industrialized countries of North America and Latin America. Undoubtedly, environmental impacts will happen more rapidly and intensively on the U.S/Mexico border communities than in other areas of the interior of Latin America. On the border, advantages such as immediate transportation of goods across the international boundary, low wages, poor enforcement of limited environmental regulations, and Mexican needs for currency and employment opportunities, among others, are a great motivation for population and industrial booming. Increasing population additions, industrial development and any improvements in materialistic quality of life will add great pressure to the already insufficient regional infrastructure and deteriorated environmental quality.

Of high concern is the potential impact of water quality of depleting water resources. This impact is strongly related to the adequate management of sophisticated materials and wastes by industry, households and municipalities. The materials are associated with all of the advanced industrial technology activities. Presently, the border constitutes an ideal place for improper and illegal disposal of all kinds of wastes in all kinds of media (air, soil and water). In addition, the region is not prepared to effectively and efficiently handle accidental contamination caused by unregulated or careless handling of materials used in industry. Examples include the present lack of a wastewater treatment system in the city of Cd. Juarez and the recent release of thousands of gallons from diesel storage tanks at the ASARCO smelter, meters from international river waters.

A third important reality is the lack of a binational plan with specific and effective programs in place for environmental protection. Besides the complex array of American and Mexican agencies with responsibilities for various aspects and levels of environmental management, the only binational agency responsible for enforcing water treaties is the International Boundary and Water Commission (IBWC). This agency lacks the authority to manage ground waters as well as all boundary rivers and streams.

Furthermore, while the IBWC was empowered in the U.S./Mexico water treaty of 1944 with limited responsibilities for the management of some aspects of surface water quality (e.g., salinity), the treaty failed to clearly define water quality criteria. This failure led to the Salinity Crisis on the Colorado River, which began in 1961 and was signed in 1973 (Minute 242 of the IBWC). Certainly, the issue of salinity is one of many comprehensive quality issues related to a large number of newly regulated contaminants, such as heavy metals, pesticides and solvents. It is important to note herein that the construction of a major desalting plant and related works for Wellton-Mohawk drainage waters at Yuma, Arizona, which was a major item in Minute 242, is only expected to begin operation in 1992 (19 years later!). In addition, the ten minutes produced by the IWBC on border sanitation agreements (IBWC, 1988) focus exclusively on basic sanitary problems, whose content is quite far from the complex environmental issues connected with advanced industrial development.

Nevertheless, both countries have recently shown encouraging signs in improving the situation. International awareness on environmental problems has resulted in heightened activism by local, regional, national and international environmental groups from both countries. In fact, it is difficult not to notice the intense attention given by the media to the issue of irresponsible management of wastes by border industry (Alm and Tomaso, 1989; Thompson, 1989; among many others). Most recently, the IBWC announced its participation in the development of a master border environmental plan under the direction of Regions VI and IX of the U.S. Environmental Protection Agency (EPA) and the Mexican Secretariat of Urban Development and Ecology

(SEDUE) (Conrad, 1991). At the federal level, the U.S. EPA and the Mexican SEDUE have intensified their cooperative efforts to implement binational agreements on issues, such as transboundary movement of hazardous wastes and substances and air pollution (EP/PAHO/90/006, 1990).

The Texas Water Commission, a state environmental agency has intensified its water quality monitoring of the Rio Grande and initiated random inspections of international transportation of hazardous materials and wastes (Texas Water Commission, 1989). EPWU, responsible for the water supply for the city of El Paso, is conducting a study on water resources management for the city, and is investigating ideas for water conservation (Archuleta, 1991).

Present water consumption rates at El Paso averages 201 gallons per capita per day (gpcpd) (EPWU, 1990) with less than 3% of the population lacking complete plumbing (Eaton et al., 1987); EPWU is targeting a reduction to 160 gpcpd by the year 2,000. In contrast, Cd. Juarez with a larger population than El Paso (Table 2) has a water consumption rate of about 80 gpcpd (Magdaleno, 1987; Nino, 1991) with less than 70% of housing units having private water taps inside the house (Sepulveda et al., 1984; Eaton et al., 1987; Nino, 1991). Interestingly, the percentage of Cd. Juarez housing units served with private plumbing varies in accordance with income level, length of residence and location within the city. A consequence of lack of plumbing and proper drainage and water treatment facilities in Cd. Juarez is certainly reflected in high rates of diseases (e.g., enteric infections, such as amoebiasis, gastroenteritis and typhoid fever) (PAHO, 1988). In addition, El Paso County areas outside the city have shown rates of Shigella Dysentery and Hepatitis that are over three times greater than the U.S. average (i.e., 30 reported cases per 100,000 people between 1978 and 1984) (Department of Planning, Research and Development, 1988a). Table 3 presents some information on diseases for various border states.

TABLE 3

ENTERIC DISEASES IN U.S./MEXICO BORDER STATES[10]

Disease	Chihuahua 1987	Sonora 1987	New Mexico 1986	Texas 1986
Amoebiasis	16,490 (743)	11,359 (641)	26 (0.2)	394 (2.4)
Typhoid Fever	116 (5.2)	190 (10.7)	1 (<0.01)	28 (0.2)

( ) = rate per 100,000 inhabitants

The current mayors of the cities of El Paso and Cd. Juares have shown a traditionally rare interest in addressing issues of common environmental concern in both communities. They have created the Mayor's Environmental Roundtable where representatives of the private and non-private sectors from the cities of El Paso (Texas), Las Cruces (New Mexico) and Cd. Juarez (Chihuahua) have begun to address environmental problems that affect the region, including water. Interestingly, the cities of El Paso and Cd. Juarez have established environmental committees by ordinance in the last two years. The committees are called the Ecology Committee in Cd. Juarez and the Citizens Environmental Advisory Committee in El Paso.

On the sixth of last March, the city of El Paso and New Mexico ended an 11-year, multimillion-dollar battle over El Paso's attempt to tap southern New Mexico ground water. The city of El Paso spent over $7.8 million in administrative cost during the fruitless dispute. This outcome represents a major lesson and a cornerstone in the development of approaches to manage the limited water resources of the border region. The problems first began when El Paso, having depleted much of its easily accessible supply from the Hueco Bolson, sought to drill 266 wells in New Mexico to pump about 246,000 acre-feet annually. Although El Paso won no rights to New Mexican waters, a cooperative effort will be made between the parties through a joint commission to find ways to solve the area's water problems. In the author's opinion, the commission will be more effectively responsive to the needs for water resource allocation in the region if Mexico is invited to participate than if discussions proceed without acknowledging the role of Mexico.

Although these are hopeful signs for environmental protection, the reality is that environmental priorities and economic resources in both cities are different and are expected to prevent an effective implementation of programs. Most importantly, all these initiatives do not respond to a comprehensive and adequate plan for border environmental protection. On the other hand, initiatives are overwhelmed by numerous problems created by the past and present lack of environmental actions. This drama can only be seriously magnified and aggravated by the implementation of a free trade program (Azar, 1991), that does not incorporate an immediate and timely implementation of border environmental protection. The high price of environmental damage will be paid by the border communities on behalf of any potential benefits for the two countries.

If environmental actions are to follow the historic pattern of the resolution of U.S./Mexican water conflicts, it must be expected that even if binational discussions begin immediately, results will not become effective until decades from now. Table 4 illustrates the long lag periods among important environmental agreements between Mexico and the U.S. In regards to Table 4, it must be noted that signing of agreements have not necessarily meant immediate actions. Certainly, if decades will pass before a well-structured environmental border plan is enforced, border communities will have suffered the unavoidable consequences of the misuse and abuse of their environment, as it has been the experience in communities all over the world.

TABLE 4
ENVIRONMENTAL DECISIONS ON THE U.S./MEXICO BORDER[11][12]

Decision	Objective
(1894)-1906 Treaty	Guarantees Mexico 60,000 acre-feet from the Elephant Butte Dam Reservoir.
(1906)-1944 Treaty	Conditional allocation from Mexico of 1,500,000 acre-feet/year from the Colorado River; binational apportionment of Rio Grande Waters below Fort Quitman.
(1961)-1973 Salinity Agreement	Construction of a major desalting plant; extension of the Wellton-Mohawk drain to the Gulf of California; lining or construction of a new Coachella Canal in California; and improved Wellton-Mohawk irrigation efficiency.
(1962)-1982[13][14]	Agreement between Reagan and de La Madrid to cooperate on border environmental issues, including import and export of hazardous materials and wastes and air pollution.
(1962)-1990[15] (IBWC Minute 283)	Conceptual plan for the international solution to the border sanitation problem in San Diego, California, and Tijuana, Mexico.

PRESENT AND FUTURE PRIORITIES

There are too many specific priorities that agendas in and for the border are already too late to define as high priority. However, there are two generic issues that in the author's view must be resolved first:

1) Recognition that the region is formed by interconnected ecosystems, that cannot be handled unilaterally by each country, if the region wants to reach a reasonable optimization of its resources, with minimum environmental quality, in the near future; and

2) Establishment of binational regulatory and economic programs to ensure a comprehensive and timely environmental resource management as growth takes place.

ROLE OF EDUCATION

Certainly, the complexities of managing transboundary resources go beyond those associated with managing resources within local, state and national political boundaries. This is particularly difficult along a political boundary between an economic power, such as the U.S., and Mexico, a struggling developing country.

In the search for solutions, both countries will need human resources capable in addressing all issues that will be involved in characterizing environmental problems and needs. They will also have to find political and regulatory pathways to explore solutions, and to develop and implement administrative and technological goals of any agreed solutions.

Conclusively, educational systems of both countries along the border region cope with the unique challenge of training the future leaders and professionals that will find and implement solutions. The problem is multi-disciplinary in nature; contributions are expected from almost every academic discipline (e.g., humanities, engineering, science and law).

Hayton and Utton (1989) documented "the Bellagio Draft", a summary of the results of a conference convened at the Rockefeller Conference Center, Bellagio, Italy, in spring 1987. Participants represented professionals from many parts of the world where transfrontier groundwater have been of concern. The draft provides an example of a treaty to manage international aquifers by mutual agreement. It covers contamination, depletion, drought and transboundary transfers as well as withdrawal and recharge issues.

If this draft, or a similar one, became an alternative agreement between Mexico and the U.S. to manage its shared groundwater, environmental data and analysis will be required to characterize hydrological and contamination scenarios, among other kinds of needed information. Environmental professionals, such as hydrologists and engineers, will then have the responsibility to provide adequate information to politicians, regulators and diplomats from each country. A satisfactory agreement should depend on well-founded information.

At the present time, the region, particularly on the Mexican side, does not have sufficient and adequate educational programs to address water resources and quality management issues. An enormous environmental market in the U.S. has taken the educational systems by surprise with no meaningful remedy in the near future, which has aggravated the situation. Professionals educated in universities of the American Southwest are attracted by opportunities in the most industrialized corridors of the U.S., where environmental problems are paramount.

SUMMARY AND CONCLUSIONS

This paper has attempted to describe the environmental crisis of the cities of El Paso (Texas) and Cd. Juarez (Chihuahua), a U.S./Mexico border community. This large metropolitan border area has been subjected to rapid rates of population economic growth. The cities have not been able to keep up with the demand for public services and the consequences of environmental impacts, including those related to water availability and quality. Adequate binational programs are not in place to ensure the solution of long-neglected environmental problems, as well as those foreseen to appear in the coming years.

Border communities, such as El Paso and Cd. Juarez, appear destined to cope with an uncontrolled deterioration of their quality of life. Additionally, the communities may be leading themselves into a limited growth condition, which is stemming from the lack of adequate management of the limited natural border resources, such as water.

Conclusively, border cities cannot afford to postpone the development and implementation of effective and efficient environmental management programs that would balance growth, resources and quality of life. Recognizing that the historical record of actions taken by the the two countries in regards to the management of their international surface waters shows lag times of decades between the time a problem is acknowledged and the time when measures are taken, the future of the region looks unpredictable and hopeless at the moment.

Thus, a need exists for the two countries to cooperate in establishing the proper mechanisms for a binational environment management program. The program must have the teeth to ensure an optimal utilization of preciously limited water resources and overall assurance of environmental quality.

ACKNOWLEDGEMENTS

The author expresses his appreciation to Mr. V. M. Zepeda of Woodward-Clyde Consultants and Dr. C. T. Turner of the University of Texas at El Paso for their suggestions and editing comments. He also thanks Mr. H. King, Bureau of Business and Economic Research, and Mr. S. Barrio, Institute for Manufacturing and Materials Management of the University of Texas at El Paso, for providing economic data on the border area.

REFERENCES

Alm, R. and B. Tomasco, "Rivers of Waste," *The Dallas Morning*, Dallas, Texas (January 30, 1989).

Amcham's Maquiladora Newsletter, American Chamber of Commerce of Mexico, A.C., V. XVII, No. 1, Mexico, D.F., Mexico (January, 1990).

Archuleta, E.G., Presentation at the Mayor's Environmental Roundtable, El Paso, Texas (February 20, 1991).

Azar, S.S., "Presentation to the Finance Committee Regarding the U.S./Mexico Free Trade Agreement," Office of the Mayor, El Paso, Texas, Washington, D.C. (February 20, 1991).

Bureau of Business and Economic Research, "Statistical Abstract of El Paso, Texas," The University of Texas at El Paso (1989).

Department of Planning, Research and Development, "Technical Report II, Environment," City of El Paso, El Paso, Texas (1988a).

Department of Planning, Research and Development, "Technical Report V,

Economic Development," City of El Paso, El Paso, Texas (1988b).

Eaton, D.J. and J.M. Andersen, *The State of the Rio Grande/Rio Bravo*, The University of Arizona Press, Tucson, Arizona (1987).

El Paso Water Utilities (EPWU), Information Provided to the Water Conservation Committee, El Paso, Texas (1990).

EP/PAHO/90/006, *The Maquiladora Industry: Environment and Development*, Fourth International Symposium on Health, Panamerican Health Organization, El Paso, Texas (August, 1990).

Hayton, R.D. and A.E. Hutton, *Transboundary Groundwaters: The Bellagio Draft Treaty*, International Transboundary Resources Center, University of New Mexico, Albuquerque, NM (Summer, 1989).

IBWC (International Boundary and Water Commission), "Minutes of the Commission," Chapter 250, Vol. V, Section 200, United States Section Manual (September 22, 1988).

INEGI, (Instituto Nacional de Estadistica, Geografia e Informatica), "Anuario Estadistico de Chihuahua," Secretaria de Programacion y Presupuesto, Mexico, D.F. (February, 1986).

INEGI, (Instituto Nacional de Estadistica, Geografia e Informatica), "Resultados Preliminares, XI Censo General de Poblacion y Vivienda, 1990," Aguas Calientes, Aguas Calientes, Mexico (August, 1990).

INEGI, (Instituto Nacional de Estadistica, Geografia e Informatica), "Crecimiento de Maquiladoras en Cd. Juarez," *In*: El Paso Times, El Paso, Texas (January 20, 1991).

Keys, C., Announcement at the Mayor's Environmental Roundtable, El Paso, Texas (February 20, 1991).

Kneese, A.K., "Environmental Stress and Political Conflicts: Salinity in the Colorado River," *Transboundary Resources Report*, V. 4, No. 2 (Summer, 1990).

Lloyd, W.J. and R.A. Marston, "Municipal and Industrial Water Supply in Ciudad Juarez, Mexico," *Water Resources Bulletin*, V. 21, No. 5 (October, 1985).

Magdaleno, R., "El Agua: Uso y Reuso," A Rough Draft, Universidad Autonoma de Cd. Juarez, Cd. Juarez, Chihuahua, Mexico (1988).

Mumme, S.P., *The United States-Mexico Groundwater Dispute: Domestic Influence on Foreign Policy*, Ph.D. Thesis, The University of Arizona (1982).

PAHO (Pan American Health Organization), "United States - Mexico Border Health Statistics," Field Office, El Paso, Texas (1987).

Presidencia Municipal de Cd. Juarez, "Ciudad Juarez en Cifras, 1988, Estadisticas Socioeconomicas," Ciudad Juarez, Chihuahua (1988).

Sepulveda, C. and A.E. Utton (eds.), *The U.S.-Mexico Border Region: Anticipating Resource Needs and Issues to the Year 2000*, Texas Western Press and the Center for Inter-American and Border Studies, The University of Texas at El Paso, El Paso, Texas (1984).

Texas Department of Commerce, "Data Base 1970-1990, Computer Tape," Bureau of Census, *In*: Data Bases of the Institute for Manufacturing and Materials Management (March, 1991).

Texas Water Commission, "Maquiladoras: Problems with Hazardous Wastes Along the Border?," The Texas Water Front, Austin, Texas (December, 1989).

Thompson, C., "Waste Problems Brew South of the Border," Waste Tech News, Denver, Colorado (April 10, 1989).

Visit with Mr. R. Nino, Junta Municipal de Aguas, Cd. Juarez, Chihuahua, Mexico (February 7, 1991).

U.S. Bureau of the Census, "1990 Census of Population, First Batch of Texas Demographic Data," *In*: El Paso Times, El Paso Texas (February 6, 1991).

Wilson Lee & Associates, "Water Resource Analysis for El Paso Public Service Board," El Paso, Texas (1986).

---

[1] H. R. Fuentes is also a Senior Consultant with Woodward-Clyde Consultants, 4105 Rio Bravo, El Paso, Texas 79902.

[2] Bureau of Business and Economic Research (1989).

[3] INEGI, 1991.

[4] U.S. Bureau of the Census (1991).

[5] Department of Planning, Research and Development, 1998b.

[6] INEGI, 1986 AND 1991.

[7] Eaton and Andersen, 1987.

[8] Amcham's Maquiladora Newsletter, 1991.

[9] Estimates from Data of the Texas Department of Commerce, 1991.

[10] PAHO, 1987.

[11] Mumme, 1982.

[12] IBWC, 1988.

[13] PAHO, 1990.

[14] 1962, an approximate year when the first "maquiladoras" began operation on the U.S./Mexico border, is used as a reference year.

[15] PAHO, 1990.

UNIVERSITY OF GUELPH RESPONSE TO EMERGING SOCIO-ENVIRONMENTAL ISSUES

Dr. H.R. Whiteley, P. Eng
Dr. R.L. Corsi
Dr. W. James, P. Eng
Dr. D. Joy, P. Eng
School of Engineering
Guelph Ontario Canada
N1G 2W1

ABSTRACT

The University of Guelph is responding through curriculum change to the increasing influence of environmental concerns on the design, operation and management aspects of engineering. In Canada, as in the rest of the world, expansion of environmental concerns will be a dominant feature of the XXIst Century. This is especially true in the field of water resources where traditional engineering approaches to management of water resources must be incorporated within a much-expanded definition of environmental engineering. The new environmental engineering will be based on ecosystem awareness and will incorporate the ethical imperative of a sustainable environment. New areas of emphasis will be reduction of resource demands and substitution of material or process to remove sources of pollution. In this paper we outline the approach being followed in the School of Engineering at the University of Guelph in our new program in Environmental Engineering, with its emphasis on biological, information-handling and societal aspects of this field.

INTRODUCTION

There is now wide recognition of environmental concerns as a core feature of water resources engineering and, indeed, of all types of engineering. The environmental concerns are based on documented threats to human health and to all life forms in the natural environment that depend on uncontaminated water, soil and air. The spatial and temporal scales involved are a small as metres and seconds for toxic spills and as large as the globe and millennia for global warming and ozone depletion.

As an institution established to provide education for engineers, the School of Engineering at the University of Guelph has been coming to grips with the implications of environmentalism for our undergraduate and graduate programs and for our research. In this paper, we will discuss the trends in environmental management that are most prominent in Canada at this time, with special emphasis on water resources and related soil and air topics. We will then outline how the School of Engineering has responded to these trends through new programme initiatives.

ENVIRONMENTAL TRENDS IN CANADA

The policy priorities and goals of the governments and of the people of Canada have been greatly influenced by the concepts of sustainable development and a sustainable environment presented by the Brundtland Commission in its 1987 report "Our Common Future" (The World Commission on Environment and Development, 1987). The main conclusions of the Commission were endorsed by a coalition of environmental ministers, business people and environmentalists in 1987 in a report to a joint Federal/Provincial Council of Resource and Environmental Ministers (Canada Task Force on Environment and Economy, 1987). In this report, the Task Force urged a fundamental restructuring of both the philosophy and the practice of resource use in Canada by all levels of government.

The federal government of Canada has responded to the challenges of moving to a sustainable environment in a number of ways. In 1987, a Federal Water Policy was presented (Environment Canada, 1987) which set as a goal the preservation of the fresh water resource of Canada through efficient and equitable use that is consistent with social, economic and environmental needs of present and future generations and the natural world.

In 1990, a Green Plan for a Healthy Environment was released (Environment Canada, 1990) that committed the federal government to a wide-ranging set of environmental initiatives. As examples of its contents, the Green Plan commits the government to enact a Drinking Water Safety Act, to set up a Great Lakes Pollution Prevention Centre and to enforce a National Regulatory Action Plan for the control of toxic substances. The goals set for Canada in the plan include promoting the wise and efficient use of water through reduced demands and protecting water through virtual elimination of discharges of persistent toxic substances into the environment.

The commitment to environmental action is shared by other levels of government in Canada at the provincial and municipal level. The Province of Ontario has set up a Roundtable on the Environment with representation from government, business and citizens. The Roundtable will consider a wide range of issues of environmental policy. The recommendations of the Roundtable will build on a large existing base of provincial activity.

Already, the province has initiated a Municipal Industrial Strategy for Abatement (MISA) that has created a large data base of measurements of concentrations and amount of emissions from industrial and municipal sites. This sampling is an ongoing responsibility and the MISA programme is now moving to establish emission limits that must be met on a site-by-site basis using standards set for each type of industry or municipality (Environment Ontario, 1989).

A somewhat similar programme for rural areas is the Soil and Water Environmental Enhancement Programme (SWEEP). This programme conducts research and valuations of remedial actions to reduce the movement of pollutants from rural non-point sources. It particularly focuses on reductions in nutrients and toxic chemicals moving with eroded soil and through subsurface drainage to streams or groundwater.

In treatment of solid waste material, the Ontario Ministry of the Environment has just announced a Waste Reduction Action Plan (Ontario Ministry of the Environment, 1991). This plan emphasizes reduction of unusable by-products by changes in the types of raw materials used in production or in the method of production chosen. It also calls for less use of disposal sites as a destination for by-product material through imaginative diversion to productive use. By 2000, the province's goal is to reduce the current annual mass of waste routed to disposal by fifty percent.

The City of Guelph, home community to the University of Guelph, is in the process of adopting a municipal Green Plan. It is expected that the plan will include targets for reduced use of toxic chemicals and of pesticides by local government, business and households. Reduced reliance on solid waste disposal, improvements in water and air quality and reduced energy use per capita are other likely target areas.

The City of Guelph already is noted for experimentation in wet/dry source separation and composting for solid waste. In addition, it has extensive stormwater management requirements for new development using detention ponds and recharge of groundwater through infiltration of storm runoff. Many individuals and groups within the city are undertaking environmental programmes ranging from fine paper recycling through tree planting and river remediation to environmental audits of industrial plants encouraged by the Chamber of Commerce Environmental Committee.

THE NEW ENVIRONMENTAL PARADIGM

The motivation for this breadth of environmental activity is easy to identify. Like most human residents of planet Earth, Canadians are acutely aware of a wide variety of environmental threats. In a report on sustainable use for water in the 21st century (Science Council of Canada, 1988), some of the most pressing environmental problems related to water are listed.

One example is the Great Lakes and the St. Lawrence River system which is heavily contaminated. This contamination creates concern for human health and for the survival of birds, fish, marine mammals, and other life forms that live adjacent to or in the waters involved. Acid rain and snow is another concern. It has drastically altered the ecology of over 14,000 lakes in Canada, reduces tree growth and creates accelerated corrosion. Diversion of water for hydroelectric production is a third concern. Diversions have caused increased shoreline erosion in receiving lakes, increased turbidity and eutrophication and have led to high mercury contents in fish in these affected lakes.

There are three main requirements for a new environmental paradigm that can be identified in these example problems. One is the need to make environmental decisions on a sufficiently broad scale in space and time to include all major environmental effects of any proposed or existing actions. The second is to allow for the complex interactions between living things and their environment. The third is to predict the cumulative effects that occur with repetitive incremental change.

In the case of the Great Lakes, the need for an appropriate scale of environmental planning and for allowance for all interactions has been met by the adoption of an ecosystem approach to the entire Great Lakes region. This approach is the agreed base for development of environmental policy as set out in the 1978 Water Quality agreement between the United States and Canada (National Research Council, 1985). One important outcome of this ecosystem approach has been the adoption of a goal of "zero discharge" into the Great Lakes of bio-accumulating toxic substances.

The need for assessment of cumulative effects is just now becoming apparent. Environmental assessment based on individual project approval often fails to detect the final results that will occur from repeated acceptance of individually-small incremental change. A recent report (Environmental Assessment Advisory Committee, 1989) has this summary comment on the situation in Ontario. "The existing land-use planning and approval process in Ontario is inadequate to the task of maintaining social and ecological quality in the face of development pressures."

The philosophical underpinnings of the new environmental paradigm in as far as they influence the teaching of engineering have been explored in a recent publication of the Universities Council on Water Resources (Fredrich, 1990; Priscoli, 1990). Priscoli sets the direction of change for environmental engineering in the following words:

"We must move from seeing ourselves as a set of solutions seeking application, to seeing ourselves as problem-solving capacities. We must move from defining ourselves purely as engineer constructors or designers to engineer managers and stewards. We must move from defining ourselves as manipulating things to managing systems, people, and life. We must come to see our milieu not as machines, but as growing, interdependent biological entities.

"We must move from a domination idea to a nurturing idea. We must move from being observers of events around us to an understanding that we are, inevitably, participants in those events. We must view our actions in the long as well as the short term and we must decide on actions in terms of how we think the world should be."

Applying these directions of movement directly to the teaching of environmental engineering, Fredrich (1990) distinguishes the necessary knowledge as being made up of philosophy, policy, process, and problem-solving. He finds that engineering education has neglected instruction in the philosophy that defines our understanding of what is fundamental in environmental issues.

Examining the coverage of policy, he finds that many environmental engineering programmes pay superficial attention to the laws and regulations governing environmental matters but are weak in presenting the conditions in society that lead to the enactment of the specific forms of legislation.

Similarly process, according to Fredrich, is not covered well. Little coverage is provided for techniques of planning, public involvement, assessment of social and environmental impact or economic feasibility. He observes that "Even as basic a process as planning, which underlies every civil engineering project of any size, is given such cursory treatment in civil engineering curricula that there is today no well-known textbook in civil engineering planning."

The remaining area, problem-solving, is the traditional strength of engineering. Environmental engineering, especially in its earlier phase as sanitary engineering has provided concentrated expertise in the design and analysis of treatment systems for wastewater and for unwanted solid and gaseous by-products.

The challenge faced by educators of environmental engineers is to broaden the coverage of topics to give weight to the philosophy, policy and process aspects of environmental engineering while maintaining satisfactory strength in problem solving. In the next section, we discuss how this challenge has been dealt with at the University of Guelph.

ENVIRONMENTAL ENGINEERING AT THE UNIVERSITY OF GUELPH

The School of Engineering at the University of Guelph has only recently instituted a specific programme in Environmental Engineering although it has been active in aspects of environmental engineering for many decades. The School has offered distinctive programmes of Biological, Water Resources and Agricultural Engineering since the 1960's and has not taught traditional programmes such as Civil, Mechanical or Chemical Engineering.

The six engineering programmes now taught by the School of Engineering have grown from the School's historical roots in agricultural engineering. The programmes offered include Food Engineering and Engineering systems and Computing in addition to the four already mentioned. Agricultural engineering has endowed the School with a tradition of integrative coupling, within its teaching and research, of biological, natural resource, and human enterprise themes, all based on a common core of fundamental engineering science analysis and engineering design techniques. This tradition is retained in all the new programmes.

The evolution in the School of Engineering parallels a similar growth in the University of Guelph from roots in agriculture and veterinary medicine. The University has developed particular strengths in areas particularly well suited to enhancement of environmental engineering. These include all facets of biological science, biochemistry, soil science, agrometeorology, rural planning, and resource economics. The Environmental Engineering programme makes extensive use of these strengths of both the School and the University.

Undergraduate Engineering Curriculum

The undergraduate programme in Environmental Engineering is organized around a series of programme segments as shown in Table 1 The core segment is common for all six engineering programmes at Guelph. It includes physical science, mathematics, systems analysis and a strong emphasis on the techniques of engineering design with one design course in each year, beginning with the first semester.

The discipline core segment for Environmental Engineering covers the arrival, flux, and storage of material in the three media of soil, water and air. There is good coverage of the interactions between pathways as mediated by the properties of the medium, including biological activity.

Special attention is paid to the need for data handling and analysis of spatial variability as provided by Geographic Information Systems. The basic forms of treatment for solid, aqueous and airborne byproducts are presented within the context of overall environmental systems. The final design project in environmental engineering requires students to integrate their analytic and subject-specific knowledge to create and evaluate alternate responses to complex environmental issues.

The philosophy, policy and process aspects of the new environmental paradigm that were mentioned earlier are included in the Environmental Engineering programme in a number of ways. The environmental science courses and the complementary studies courses are all taught outside of

TABLE 1: ENVIRONMENTAL ENGINEERING PROGRAM AT THE UNIVERSITY OF GUELPH

Core: General Math, Science, Engineering, Sociology = 25 courses

Core: Environmental Engineering
- 05-334 Geographic Info. Systems in Environmental Mngmnt.
- 05-336 Waste Management and Utilization
- 05-356 Basic Environmental Systems
- 05-365 Hydrology
- 05-425 Water Conveyance
- 05-426 Wastewater Treatment Operations & Design
- 05- Water Quality
- 05- Air Quality
- 05- Solid Waste Management

= 9 courses

05-413 Environmental Engineering Design Project = 1 course

Environmental Science Courses
- 65-100 General Microbiology
- 2 courses from sequences in biological or earth sciences

= 3 courses

Complementary Studies
4 courses from Humanities & Social Science or Environmental Policy and Economics or Humanities & Admin. Studies

= 4 courses

Free Electives
1 Free Elective = 1 course

engineering by a variety of disciplines. In these courses, students discover some of the contributions in approach and philosophy that come from perspectives of different disciplines. Some of the courses selected by the students, such as resource economics or environmental impact assessment, give specific instruction in policy formation and process.

The response of students to the Environmental Engineering programme has been most encouraging. The first students entered in 1989 and the programme has already become the largest engineering programme at Guelph. By the time that the first class graduates in 1993, there will likely be over 200 students enrolled in this programme. Encouragement of women to study engineering is a high priority in Canada. The offering of environmental engineering has helped Guelph to achieve the highest percentage of females entering engineering studies in Canada (over 30%).

Graduate Education and Research

The graduate education and research programmes in environmental engineering at Guelph are expanding rapidly in parallel with undergraduate numbers. The areas of emphasis include topics in water quality, management of solid byproducts and air quality. Specific topics of study in water quality are 1) nitrate contamination of groundwater, 2) transport of bacteria through porous media, 3) quality of stormwater for specific site types in residential and commercial land use, 4) pesticide transport in surface and groundwater, 5) reduction of erosion and sediment transport, 6) retrofitting of detention basins for water quality management, and 7) studies of reducing combined sewer overflows.

Research in management of solid byproducts includes composting of municipal solid waste and application procedures for animal manures. Aspects of air quality under examination include 1) fate and control of toxic organic contaminants in wastewater, 2) effects of transient mass loadings on the fate of VOC's during activated sludge treatment, and 3) VOC emissions from municipal wastewater.

As part of the expansion in facilities to accommodate environmental engineering, new environmental engineering laboratories are being developed. There will be separate laboratories for trace contaminant analysis, aqueous solution analysis, and solids analysis. The School is already well equipped for computer-based analysis with separate clusters of computers for modeling of spatially-distributed processes and analysis of temporal sequences. The School also conducts field experimentation in support of the development, validation and calibration of predictive models.

CONCLUSIONS

There is rapid change and expansion in the field of environmental engineering. This is a necessary response to societal recognition of the importance and complexity of the environmental problems facing the world. Environmental engineers should respond to this challenge by the adoption of a new paradigm for environmental engineering that is built upon an ecosystem approach and has as its goal a sustainable environment.

In this paper, we have outlined some of the ways that education in environmental engineering at the University of Guelph is evolving in response to our perceptions of the needs of the 21st Century. We acknowledge the need for continuous change in presentation as we struggle to keep pace with expanding knowledge and with expanding recognition of the need for comprehensiveness in approach to environmental management.

One area that requires constant attention is the appropriate balance between instruction in specific techniques and the encouragement of a breadth of understanding in practitioners of the philosophy, policy and process aspects of environmental engineering. We will continue to strive to find new ways to work toward a satisfactory balance and encourage others to report on their approaches to this important task.

REFERENCES

Canada Task Force on Environment and Economy (1987). *"Report of the National Task Force on Environment and Economy,"* Canadian Council of Resource and Environmental Ministers, Ottawa.

Environment Canada (1987). *"Federal Water Policy,"* Inlands Waters Directorate, Environment Canada, Ottawa.

Environment Canada (1990). "Canada's Green Plan in Brief," Minister of Supplies and Services, Canada, Ottawa.

Environment Ontario (1989). *"Kraft Mill Pollution Reduction Strategy Implemented,"* Ontario Ministry of the Environment, Toronto. MISA Update 2(1):1-2.

Environment Ontario (1991). *"Ontario's Waste Reduction Action Plan: Backgrounder,"* Ontario Ministry of the Environment, Toronto.

Environmental Assessment Advisory Committee (1989). *"The Adequacy of the Existing Environmental Planning and Approvals Process for the Ganaraska Watershed,"* Report 38 of the EAAC, Ministry of the Environment, Toronto.

Fredrich, A.J. (1990). *"Educating Environmental Engineers for the 21st Century,"* Universities Council on Water Resources, Carlsondale, Illinois, Spring 1990 Issue 82:31-34.

National Research Council and Royal Society of Canada (1985). *"The Great Lakes Water Quality Agreement: An Evolving Instrument for Ecosystem Management,"* National Academy Press, Washington D.C.

Science Council of Canada (1988). *"Water 2020 Sustainable Use for Water in the 21st Century,"* Science Council of Canada, Ottawa.

World Commission on Environment and Development (1987). *"Our Common Future,"* Oxford University Press, New York.

PROGRESS OF THE GREAT LAKES CLEANUP

William A. Steggles
Environmental Consultant
7 Kingscourt Drive
Toronto, Ontario, CANADA M8X-2P5

ABSTRACT

After the 1972 Great Lakes water Quality Agreement, Canada and the U.S. made considerable gains in pollution control, but recent results are mixed and efforts are faltering. The International Joint Commission (IJC) in 1990 reported a lack of committed resources with toxic substances affecting the health of children. IJC urged a binational strategy to control toxic inflows to the lakes. Progress of plans for restoring Areas of Concern are encouraging, although there are serious problems with spills and exotic species. Native people's respect for the environment and public demands for continued confidence in and support for the Agreement are noted.

INTRODUCTION

Under the Agreement on Great Lakes Water Quality between Canada and the United States, efforts were begun in 1972 to correct serious pollution problems which were choking lakes Erie and Ontario, some of whose oil-covered rivers caught fire.

Renewed in 1978 and 1987, the Agreement to restore and maintain the integrity of the shared waters of the entire Great Lakes Basin Ecosystem, pledged Canada and the United States to eliminate persistent toxic substances and progressively restore 42 "hot spots" or Areas of Concern where water quality continued to be polluted by point and non-point discharges and contaminated sediments. The 1987 amendment to the Agreement extended the point and non- point control efforts to also include pollution programs for contaminated groundwater and atmospheric deposition.

Tremendous technological efforts and very large expenditures have achieved control of many municipal and industrial pollution sources and runoff from urban and agricultural lands. Loadings of Phosphorus and corresponding over-enrichment of the lakes, together with concentrations of persistent DDT, PCB, Mirex and Mercury declined in the 1970's. Contaminants in water, fish and birds levelled off in the 1980's, but continue to be unacceptably high.

The International Joint Commission (IJC) which monitors and reports progress under the Agreement has stressed that the threats posed by persistent toxic substances to the ecosystem, particularly human health, require urgent and focussed attention to avoid inter-generational effects. In its Fifth Biennial Report on Great Lakes water Quality (1990), the Commission pointed out that "society continues to mortgage the future (of the lakes) by poisoning, suffocating and otherwise threatening them because of insufficient knowledge, other priorities and shortsightedness."

Decisions and actions by nongovernmental organizations and individuals must also be seen as an important part of the quest to achieve the goals of the Agreement. Increased public participation in environmental issues through citizen action groups, professional organizations and corporations, has shown strong and sophisticated awareness of the ecological consequences of individual decisions and behavior. This holds great promise for broadened community support for needed environmental measures, while institutional responses often lag behind demonstrations of public support.

THE GREAT LAKES AGREE - A COOPERATIVE OPPORTUNITY

The lakes are crucial for the almost 40 million people living in the drainage area of the two countries, and the people are directly dependent on them. Almost 30 million people use the lakes as their source of drinking water.

Improving commercial and sports fishing valued in excess of one billion dollars is an important component of an economy whose future prospects are limited by habitat loss and the quality of the lakes. The region is a net exporter of food grown on the lands of the watershed. Recreation and tourism comprise another major component of the economy.

The heart of U.S. and Canadian manufacturing is found in the Great Lakes region where two-thirds of the steel production of both countries is located. Heavy dependence is placed on the lakes and their connecting waterways for hydro-electric power generation, forest products, and other extensive industrial needs which demand high quality water. Shipping of commercial cargo through the Upper Great Lakes and the downstream St. Lawrence Seaway has been a mainstay of domestic and international trade. However, in recent times, shipping has declined because of interlake canal restrictions, recession, shifting world markets and labour disputes.

Clearly, the quality of life of tens of millions of resident Canadians, Americans and visitors to the region, and the health of the economy of the Great Lakes region is dependent upon the health of the Great Lakes Basin Ecosystem.

In implementing the initial pollution abatement measures called for by the 1972 Agreement, governments faced many difficult fiscal problems in their obligation to commit specific resources to the Agreement. These were not helped by the impoundment of Clean Water Act funds by the U.S. Administration late in 1972. The governments of Canada and the Province of Ontario, had by prior agreement secured the Canadian share of funding of sewage works construction in the northern part of the basin. Gradually, it became possible through progressive bites at the problem to dedicate billions of dollars to the undertaking.

Considering the competition for capital funding, the Agreement became one of the greatest success stories in environmental protection. As an instrument of international, intergovernmental cooperation, it drew upon the resources of eleven jurisdictions to demonstrate how institutional and technical limitations could be overcome. The accord between the United States of America and Canada embraced the environmental protection agencies of the States of Minnesota, Wisconsin, Michigan, Indiana, Illinois, Ohio, Pennsylvania and New York and the Canadian Province of Ontario.

Today, the Agreement provides the potential for new advances and the Great Lakes community has the opportunity to continue demonstrating a coordinated response to a serious binational environmental problem. However, recognizing that environmental concerns are widespread and real, continued public confidence in and support for the Agreement depends upon the responsiveness and resources directed to it by governments, industry and the community.

As restoration efforts unfold, improved management of the air, water and lands of the Basin should provide new opportunities and challenges for informed and strong communities to meet needs for water supply, food and industrial production as well as shipping, fishing, recreation and tourism. This will become a reality if sufficient resources are directed to address problems with innovative and adequate technical solutions to protect the ecosystem.

EARLY PROGRESS GIVES WAY TO FALTERING NEW PROGRAMS

In spite of the early advances in municipal and industrial pollution control, and the resulting declines in nutrient pollution and several toxic contaminants, recent progress under the Agreement has been mixed.

In March 1990, on the 18th Anniversary of the 1972 Agreement, the IJC reported that many other programs have faltered:

"Research funds increasingly have been insufficient...the number of personnel in research and enforcement has been inadequate. Many of the Commission's recommendations... unanswered. Attempts to regulate have only partially stemmed the inflow of pollutants... far from achieving virtual elimination of persistent toxic substances

Several thousand toxic chemicals continue in commercial use, with others added every year, without thorough testing or sufficient understanding of potential effects on human health and the... ecosystem. Early decreases .... toxins have level led out above acceptable targets and no clear strategy has been established to achieve further reductions".

The Commission also noted that "the environment has become a priority social and political issue - locally, nationally and globally with many competing issues when it comes to providing financial and human resources. In its view, sufficient resources congruent with each nation's pledge to implement the Agreement are [now] lacking."

The Commission's Water Quality Board stressed that basic programs begun under the earlier Agreements must be maintained and strengthened in order to hold onto the gains made thus far. The Board cited: pretreatment of industrial wastes; control of overflows and by-passes; programs for control of contaminated sediments, and changed industrial processes to avoid production of damaging contaminants.

In admonishing society for its failures under the Agreement, including ill-advised activities and ignorant attitudes towards the lakes, as well as commitments to other priorities and shortsightedness, the Commission stated:

> "What our generation has failed to realize is that, what we are doing to the Great Lakes, we are doing to ourselves and to our children".

GOVERNMENT ROLES UNDER THE AGREEMENT

In 1972, the governments agreed to implement remedial programs and other measures to achieve the water quality objectives of the Agreement. To develop candid assessments of the nature and extent of Great Lakes pollution, the governments agreed to empower the IJC to study and report to them and the public the progress being made in implementing the Agreement, and to make recommendations.

The Commission is advised by its Water Quality Board. It is comprised of an equal number of members from Canada and the United States, including representatives from the governments of the federal, provincial and each of the eight Great Lakes States. The Science Advisory Board, consists of research managers and scientific authorities in the environmental field. It provides advice on research to the Commission and to the Water Quality Board.

Central to the authority of the Commission is its power to independently collate, analyze and report surveillance and related information gathered under the aegis of the Agreement. The Commission's recommendations, if accepted, could have the effect of making the Agreement more responsive to new problems as they become apparent. This role was reaffirmed in the 1978 and 1987 revisions of the Agreement.

DIFFERENCES IN APPROACH TO THE AGREEMENT BY JURISDICTIONS

In the United States, the federal jurisdiction, expressed in the Federal water Pollution Control Act recognizes the primary responsibility of the states to prevent, reduce and eliminate pollution. It calls for state assumption of many responsibilities contained in the federal law, including such matters as permits, surveillance, enforcement, and area wide planning.

Congress established a Great Lakes National Program Office to place a high priority on achieving the goals of the Agreement. In addition, the Governors of the Great Lakes States signed an Agreement on Toxic Substances Control to strengthen their coordination of pollution control measures affecting the lakes.

In Canada, the federal and provincial governments entered into the Canada-Ontario Agreement on Great Lakes Water Quality which included agreed objectives for water quality and measures to meet them. The first agreement was made in 1971 and amended as necessary, to maintain its consistency with the Canada-United States Agreement and its amendments.

In 1987, to show their willingness to increase intergovernmental coordination at the state and provincial level, the Great Lakes States and Provinces signed a Memorandum of Understanding on Control of Toxic Substances in the Great Lakes. This international accord complements the State's Toxic Substances Control Agreement and the Great Lakes Water Quality Agreement.

NEED FOR A COORDINATED INTERNATIONAL STRATEGY FOR CONTROL OF PERSISTENT TOXIC SUBSTANCES

While the measures taken by government show some progress in coordinating toxic substance control programs, they have not satisfied the IJC. In 1990, the Commission called for a binational, multi-agency, multi-jurisdictional effort at a level not yet conceived or realized. Currently, adequate resources have not been made available to the agencies responsible for fish and wildlife and public health and welfare. The Commission believes this deficiency must be corrected.

Co-ordination of all levels of government is believed to be possible within the umbrella of the Canada-United States Water Quality Agreement provided these programs are adequately funded and include those responsible for economic, regional development and fiscal matters.

The object of this approach would be the taking of every available action to stop the inflow of persistent toxic substances into the Great Lakes environment.

The IJC also recommended that:

1. Local governments be fully informed and involved with the implementation of the Agreement.

2. Advisories for fish consumption and fish stocking programs for fish which may pose a threat to the health of animals and humans be reviewed and strengthened.

3. Use be made of comprehensive public information and education programs.

4. The Great Lakes ecosystem be included as a priority topic in existing school curricula.

5. The Great Lakes Areas of Concern be used as focal points in the development of educational programs and materials.

The Threat to Human Health

New knowledge about subtle disease and dysfunction occurring from exposure to toxins has brought into question the completeness of current impact assessments which largely rely on cancer risk analysis when controls for various chemicals are being developed. Serious impacts on wildlife, which are neither carcinogenic nor mutagenic are affecting a large number of Great Lakes fish, birds, reptiles and small mammals. These effects include population declines, reproductive problems, eggshell thinning, severe metabolic changes, gross deformities, behavioral and hormonal changes, and immunosuppression.

Other studies of the infants of mothers whose lifetime consumption of Lake Michigan fish laced with chemicals, particularly certain PCBs, found serious adverse affects on: the length of gestational period, birth weight, skull circumference and cognitive, motor and behavioral development.

The Commission concluded that there is a threat to the health of children resulting from the exposure of the community to persistent toxic substances, even at very low ambient levels. It urged governments to take a very restrictive approach to prevent further introduction of persistent toxic substances into the basin, to assist people to avoid contact with these substances, and to remediate areas already contaminated.

Adequate Legislation and Regulation

Direct translation of the objectives of the agreement into domestic laws and regulations and tightening of regulations affecting existing pollution sources combined with strict enforcement was also recommended by the IJC•

Reverse Onus for Required Test Results

The governments were urged by the IJC to strengthen the principle of reverse onus in policies and programs concerned with the introduction of new chemicals, through appropriate legislation that includes mandatory pretesting by companies prior to approval for production and use. This would prevent new, harmful chemicals from entering the market place.

RESTORATION OF AREAS OF CONCERN THROUGH REMEDIAL ACTION PLANS

The 1987 amendment to the Agreement required among other things the preparation of Remedial Action Plans (RAPs) for the 42 Areas of Concern that had been identified by the IJC. Here, the objective is to restore beneficial uses to the Areas of Concern.

Public involvement with RAPs embracing all local stakeholders, including pertinent governments has demonstrated the influence that the public can wield.

In its appraisal, IJCs Water Quality Board concluded that the RAP Program has succeeded in:

- enhancing communication and institutional co-operation,
- greater public awareness and stimulation of industry and community interest,
- emphasizing control of contaminants at source,
- developing greater emphasis on remediation of contaminated sediment, and
- increasing the financial and human resources focussed on Areas of Concern.

Major challenges recognized in the RAP program include:
- identifying responsibility and stressing accountability for remediation,
- developing political and business support,
- commencing remediation, despite incomplete information, and
- developing long-term funding and public support.

Public expectations are high in anticipation of the remedial actions to be taken through the RAP program. However, it is taking longer than expected to develop the plans because problems and solutions are complex. Their development in co-operation with the public takes time and resources are limited.

It is noteworthy, that in keeping with ecosystem principles, the remedial actions are evolving and providing good examples of integrated resource management. It is to be hoped that the momentum and success of current efforts will motivate further progress.

POTENTIAL FOR CATASTROPHE FROM SPILLS

IJC considered the readiness of shipping and shore-based industrial operations to prevent spills of toxic and other hazardous substances, and urged the governments to strengthen their provisions for pollution prevention and preparedness for emergencies. Increased requirements for pilotage of vessels and improved communication and tracking for those carrying hazardous substances were advocated.

The Commission also concluded that unplanned and illicit releases are a significant source of contamination of the lakes and noted that they are caused generally by human and technical factors. Factors such as boredom, communication problems, lack of training and inappropriate cargo handling, as well as equipment failure can be dealt with and can usually be prevented.

EXOTIC SPECIES

The potential of foreign species to cause serious disruption to the biotic community and the Great Lakes economy is great. Examples of such biological contamination include the sea lamprey (an eel which decimated lake trout in the 19505), the ruffe (perchlike fish whose larvae feeds on valuable whitefish), and the zebra mussel. Introduced in 1987, the latter is pervasive and disruptive, with serious potential for damage to biota and the regional economy.

Stronger measures are needed to protect against further introductions of such species.

CONCLUSION

In presenting its report to governments, the IJC noted that increasing levels of concern for the Great Lakes environment were being expressed by the public. The Commission also observed that public insistence on governmental response to Agreement objectives was strikingly expressed at the Commission's Fifth Biennial Meeting held in Hamilton, Ontario in October 1989.

A very noteworthy criticism and concern was offered at the meeting by representatives of Native Peoples and is repeated here as reported by the IJC. They pointed out that their people have for centuries been dependent on, but lived in harmony with, their environmental surroundings.... that they have been in truth a harmonious part of the ecosystem. Since they still rely on the integrity of the ecosystem to a greater degree than the non- Indian population, they are more directly and adversely affected by disruptions of that system. They asked for greater appreciation of this and greater opportunity for effective input and acceptance of their view that prevention at source, not cleanup after the event, is the only practical and effective approach to the problem of maintaining the integrity of the ecosystem."

INTERACTION OF POULTRY WASTE AND LIMESTONE TERRAIN ON WATER QUALITY: PROFESSIONAL AND PUBLIC INFORMATION DISSEMINATION

K.F. Steele
Arkansas Water Resources Research Center
University of Arkansas, Fayetteville, AR 72701

T.C. Daniel
Department of Agronomy
University of Arkansas, Fayetteville, AR 72701

D.R. Edwards
Department of Biological and Agricultural Engineering
University of Arkansas, Fayetteville, AR 72701

ABSTRACT

Large amounts of animal waste applied to pastureland in northwestern Arkansas generate concern about contamination of both surface and ground water. Although analysis of surface and ground water has not indicated large scale contamination, efforts have been initiated to protect the water supplies and to maximize the use of the waste as a resource. These efforts have included the cooperation of university researchers, the poultry industry, federal, state and local governmental agencies and farmers.

INTRODUCTION

Poultry production in Arkansas has recently been increasing by about 33 million birds per year. In 1989, the State led the U.S.A. in production, producing 960 million birds. Approximately one-third of the production is generated in a four-county area (5 million ha) in northwestern Arkansas (Arkansas Agricultural Statistics Service, 1990). Poultry wastes are applied to pastureland to meet the fertilizer need of the forage being produced. Beaver Lake Reservoir is located in this region and is the major water supply for approximately one-half of the population. Because of the large volume of poultry waste that is land-applied, concern exists regarding the effect this practice has on the quality of surface water. Ground water is also very susceptible to contamination due to the unconfined and fractured nature of the limestone and dolomitic aquifers. Watershed projects are underway in the region to demonstrate the effectiveness of implementing best management practices (BMPs) on water quality. Implementation of BMPs may not only protect water quality but also allow maximum utilization of the fertilizer contained in the poultry manure.

BACKGROUND

On a national basis, little information exists regarding the effect of land application of poultry wastes on water quality. A limited number of small-scale, research investigations have demonstrated a direct cause-and-effect relationship between degradation in water quality and land application of wastes. A small number of other projects have been broader in scale, attempting to compare the effect of different land uses on water quality. Fortunately, several of these projects have been conducted in northwestern Arkansas, including investigations of ground water (Steele and McCalister, 1991; Steele et al., 1990; and Adamski and Steele, 1988) and surface water (Edwards, 1989) quality as a function of land use. Nitrate and bacteria have been the focus of many of these studies. Throughout this paper nitrate + nitrite as nitrogen will be simply referred to as "nitrate".

Ground Water

Most of the domestic ground water supply in northwestern Arkansas is obtained from karstified limestone and dolomitic rocks which are exposed at the soil surface. These rocks contain fractures, solution enlarged fractures and bedding planes, caves and some sinkholes. Such geologic characteristics make the aquifer particularly susceptible to contamination from surface sources, including poultry wastes.

Researchers isolated broad sections of the landscape according to land use and monitored the quality of the ground water by sampling natural springs and wells. Watersheds receiving regular applications of poultry manure were selected and identified as the "treated area." Other watersheds in more pristine environments and not receiving wastes were selected and identified as the "control or untreated area." Table 1 demonstrates a slight but definite effect of land use on water quality. The nitrate content of the ground water in the control/untreated area was consistently lower than the treated area, exhibiting a mean concentration of 0.25 mg/L nitrate. The treated areas showed an increase in nitrate concentration in the springs and wells sampled. Mean concentrations of nitrate in the springs, shallow and deep wells were, 2.80, 2.82, and 1.51, respectively. While the nitrate concentration in the ground water of the treated area did increase, the levels were well below the 10 mg/L standard established by the U.S. Environmental Protection Agency (1985). Bacteria levels in the ground water were also elevated in the treated area (Figure 1) (Steele et al., 1990). The average concentrations of fecal streptococcus and fecal coliform in the treated area springs were 39 and 86 colonies/100 ml, respectively; whereas the concentrations in untreated area springs were 3 and <1 colonies/100 ml, respectively. Seasonal variation of nitrate in the ground water was shown to be minimal; with the shallow aquifers more susceptible to contamination than the deeper aquifers. (See Table 1.)

Storms can cause changes in nitrate concentrations of the ground water. Maximum nitrate and bacteria concentrations usually coincide with or follow

TABLE 1
MEAN NITRATE + NITRITE CONCENTRATIONS (MG/L AS N) OF WELLS AND SPRINGS FROM "UNTREATED" AND "TREATED" AREAS

(Boone-St. Joe Formations = shallow and Everton Formation = deep). Data from Steele and McCalister, 1991 and Steele et al. (1990).

SEASON	UNTREATED Springs Shallow	TREATED Wells Shallow	TREATED Wells Deep
Winter	0.16 2.73	3.04	1.45
Spring	0.02 3.23	2.90	1.59
Fall	0.40 2.58	2.44	1.51

the peak of the discharge hydrograph (Figure 1) (Leidy and Morris, 1990 and Steele et al., 1986). Whether the nitrate concentration increases or decreases depends on the amount of nitrate in the recharge water. One spring in the treated area obtained a maximum nitrate concentration (18 mg/L) almost an order of magnitude higher than poststorm background values (2.3 mg/L) (Steele et al., 1986).

Other springs exhibit erratic nitrate concentrations not only between storms, but also within storms. Variation in nitrate concentrations during a rain is probably due to variability in micro-environmental conditions, such as amount of nitrate available for leaching and/or amount of recharge (Steele et al., 1986). Low nitrate values (less than 1 mg/L) for wells (14 out of 57 samples) and springs (8 out of 56) in the treated area indicate spatial variability of amount and source of nitrate. Despite average nitrate concentrations in the treated area of about 2.4 to 3.2 mg/L, storm data suggest some sites may temporarily exceed drinking water limits of 10 mg/L (U.S. Environmental Protection Agency, 1985) following rain induced runoff events. This situation is most likely to occur during the spring when poultry litter application coincides with runoff and recharge of the aquifer, and nitrate uptake by vegetation is minimal.

Surface Water

Northwestern Arkansas contains several significant lakes which are designated for multiple uses (e.g., drinking water supply, recreation, flood control, etc.). Beaver Lake, as earlier noted, provides drinking water to approximately 100,000 people in northwestern Arkansas. The lake has also stimulated real estate development due to its recreational and aesthetic characteristics. Poultry waste, similar to other animal wastes if mismanaged, can lead to impairment of surface waters from the perspectives of human and animal health, aesthetics, and aquatic wildlife.

Depending on the source and history of the waste, poultry waste will contain significant carbon and microorganisms, lesser amounts of nutrients, and still smaller amounts of metals and other constituents. Carbon and

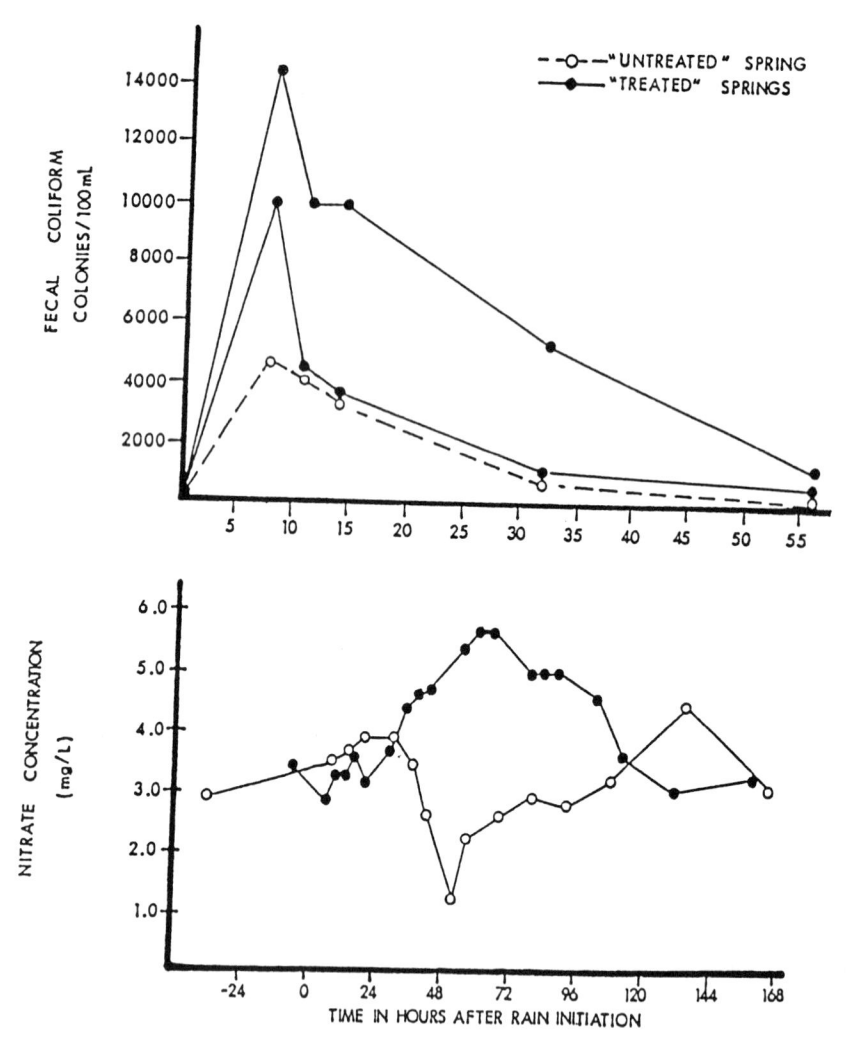

Figure 1. Plot of fecal coliform and nitrate as nitrogen concentrations in spring water versus time following initiation of rain.

ammoniacal nitrogen species can adversely impact aquatic wildlife through dissolved oxygen depletion and ammonia toxicity, respectively. Other waste constituents, such as copper, chloride, arsenic, iron, and zinc may also be detrimental to aquatic fauna depending on the concentration of the elements and the sensitivity of the fauna. Nitrogen and phosphorus are linked to eutrophication and associated nuisances (insects, odors, color, and others). Poultry waste has also been shown to contain pathogens, such as *Salmonella typhimurium, Mycobacterium avium, and Listeria monocytogens,* which are communicable to humans.

Very limited field-scale research has been conducted to quantify effects of land-applied poultry waste on runoff water quality. Only one such study (Edwards, 1989) has been reported for northwestern Arkansas. In this research, a small (approximately 1.6 ha) watershed was instrumented to measure and sample runoff. Runoff samples were analyzed for sediment, ammonium, nitrate, soluble phosphorus, and potassium. Runoff samples were collected from a storm occurring on May 21, 1989 prior to manure application. On June 1 (1989), 2.2 Mg/ha of poultry manure was applied to the watershed. The manure contained 2.21% nitrogen, 2.13% phosphorus, and 2.19% potassium. Additional runoff events were sampled on June 3, June 11, and June 13. Table 2 shows amounts and concentrations of nutrients transported off the watershed during the storms. The mass of nutrients transported off the field increased following poultry manure application on June 1 (Table 2). While mass transport differences may be attributed to differences in rainfall duration and intensity, it may be seen that nutrient concentrations are significantly higher following application of the manure. Both nutrient mass transport and runoff concentration are seen to decrease with increasing number of runoff events. For the June 3 (1989) storm, variation of nutrient concentration within-storm may be seen in Figure 2 which shows ammonium, nitrate, phosphorus and potassium concentrations, respectively. The peak of the nitrate concentration corresponded approximately with the first peak of the storm hydrograph; ammonium, phosphorus, and potassium peak concentrations coincided with the secondary peak of the storm hydrograph.

TABLE 2
NUTRIENT LOSSES FROM WATERSHED TREATED WITH POULTRY MANURE

Date	Ammonium Nitrogen M* g/ha	Ammonium Nitrogen C** mg/L	Nitrate Nitrogen M g/ha	Nitrate Nitrogen C mg/L	Soluble Phosphorus M g/ha	Soluble Phosphorus C mg/L	Potassium M g/ha	Potassium C mg/L
May 21	1.9	0.08	8.5	0.36	10.0	0.42	126.1	5.30
June 3	135.7	1.15	53.0	0.44	980.5	8.28	5466.6	46.17
June 11	7.8	0.31	5.0	0.19	38.9	1.53	262.0	10.28
June 13	1.1	0.28	0.8	0.21	7.4	1.86	34.3	8.67

* Mass
** Average Concentration in Runoff

It is presently unknown if the nutrient concentrations in runoff from areas receiving poultry waste are excessive. Although the nutrient losses represent a loss of fertilizer, the associated water quality impacts usually occur some distance downstream of the area of application. Thus, there is a need for further research to connect edge-of-field pollutant losses to downstream water quality impacts. This is a challenging task, but one that must be overcome before it is possible to make management recommendations which are "best" in the environmental sense.

INFORMATION DISSEMINATION

The normal process of dealing with such issues has been for the isolated researcher to conduct the investigations and make the data available for information dissemination. The data would then be used in formulating policy

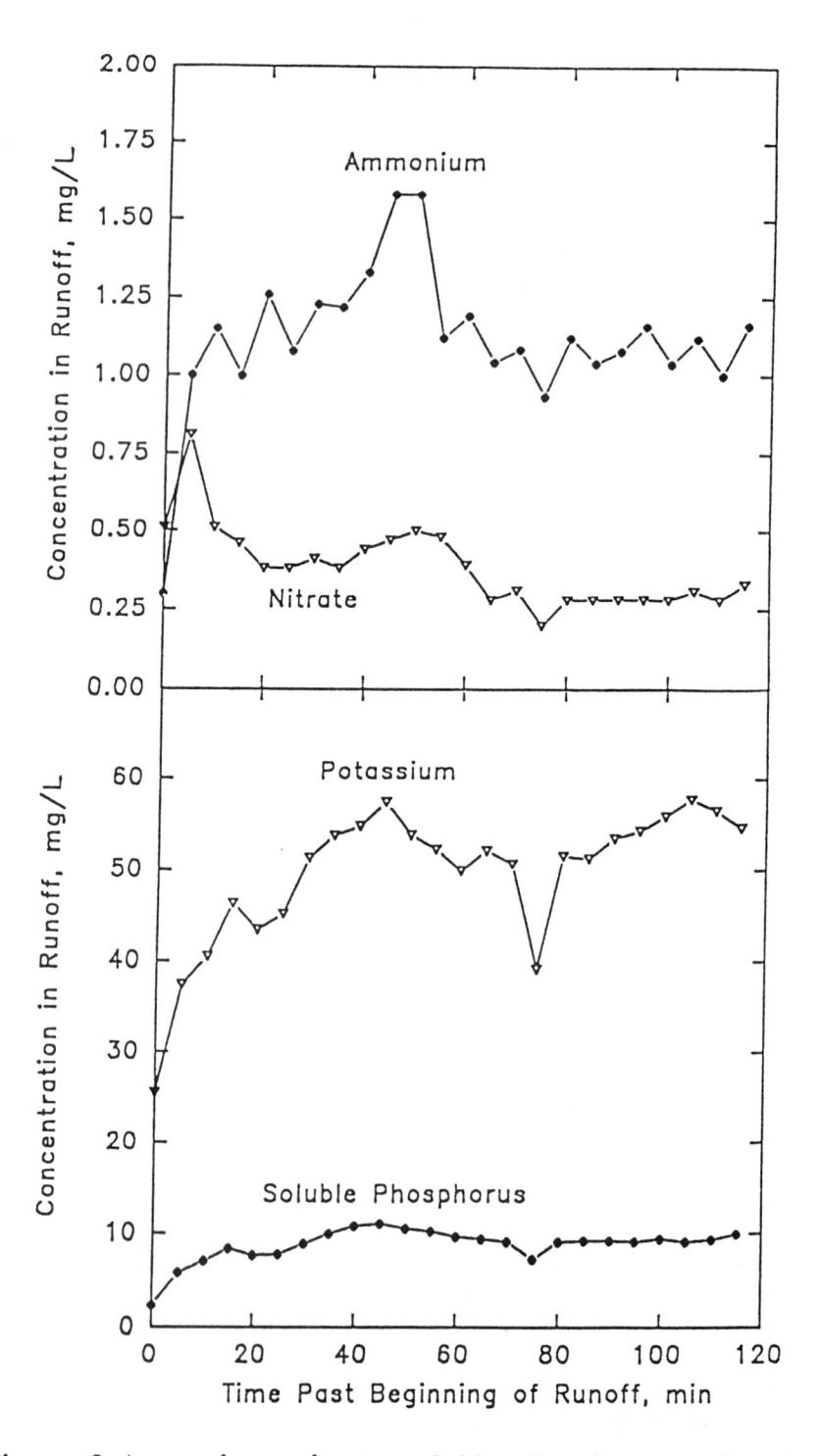

Figure 2. Ammonium, nitrate, soluble phosphorus and potassium concentrations, June 3, 1989 storm.

regarding how to adequately address the issue. After establishment of policy, the appropriate agency would be provided the regulatory power and logistic support to see that the program was implemented. For several reasons, this process does not work when dealing with the nonpoint issue. Several steps have been used and are being used to provide solutions to the water quality problems associated with disposal of poultry litter in northwestern Arkansas. The approaches used in this situation may be applied in other nonpoint source water pollution problems.

The first step in the process is to establish the necessary framework to quantify and describe the problem if it is shown to exist. Research and monitoring programs cannot operate independently in accomplishing this first step. Design of the research and monitoring program requires input from the poultry industry, appropriate state and federal agencies, individual growers, and the researchers. This process does several important things; first, it fosters much needed communication between the various groups and provides a forum for ongoing data exchange. This process has operated on an ad hoc basis in Arkansas. Individual and group meetings have been called from time to time to review proposed field research and monitoring programs. Meetings and field days have been used to update the parties on preliminary data. Communication between the appropriate groups will continue throughout the process of problem identification.

Research on what can be done about the problem needs to be conducted in parallel with problem identification. While not an entirely separate issue, measures should be taken to begin thinking about applied and implementable measures that can be used to circumvent water quality problems shown to exist. The interdisciplinary and interagency ad hoc forum is an ideal mechanism for accomplishing this ongoing process.

The results of the first two efforts need to be communicated on a broader scale to the water resource professionals. This step is being carried out in Arkansas in an informal but successful manner. The University researchers have a close relationship with the Cooperative Extension Service, U.S. Soil Conservation Service, U.S. Corps of Engineers, U.S. Geological Survey, as well as the Arkansas Department of Pollution Control and Ecology, Arkansas Soil and Water Conservation Commission, and Arkansas Department of Health. The Governor's State Ground Water Task Force and Arkansas Soil and Water Conservation Commission Ground Water Vulnerability Committee and the Department of Health Nitrate Committee are several groups that have interest in ground water quality and will continue to work together to address this and similar issues.

Ultimately, the information must be disseminated to the end user or grower. The USDA Cooperative Extension Service, which has an office in every county, provides the critical link between the farmers and state and federal agencies, industry and university researchers. It is this agency that is ultimately responsible for information dissemination to the farmers by a variety of ways including written material such as brochures, public meetings and, perhaps most importantly, through personal contact with individual farmers.

CONCLUSIONS

Additional controlled research is needed to adequately quantify and describe contamination resulting from land application of poultry waste.

While the major focus has been on nitrate and bacteria, future research should include additional parameters such as metals (Cu, Hi, and As), phosphorus, and pesticides. Concomitant applied research is also needed to develop and identify BMPs that minimize the impact on water quality while utilizing the manure as a nutrient source for forage production.

The cooperation of researchers; federal, state and local governments; and farmers to protect surface and ground water in northwestern Arkansas has been very encouraging. Federal and state agencies and university researchers have worked together to assess potential water contamination. Although present water quality in northwestern Arkansas is not severely contaminated, there is indication of some pollution and the potential for additional contamination. Because of this, university and state/federal agencies are working toward developing and evaluating best management practices for animal waste disposal. Local agents are the key to the implementation of selected BMPs by local farmers.

REFERENCES

Adamski, J.C. and Steele, K.F. (1988). *Agricultural Land Use Effects on Ground Water Quality in the Ozark Region.* IN Agricultural Impacts on Ground Water Conference. Nat. Water Well Assoc., Dublin, Ohio, 593-614.

Arkansas Agricultural Statistics Service (1990). *Arkansas Agricultural Statistics 1989.* Arkansas Agricultural Experiment Station, Fayetteville, Arkansas, p. 56.

Edwards, D.R. (1989). *Impacts of Land-applied Poultry Waste on Surface Water Quality.* Abstracts of the Third Arkansas State Water Conference. October 4, Little Rock, AR.

Leidy, V.A. and Morris, E.E. (1991). *Hydrogeology and Quality of Ground Water in the Boone Formation and Cotter Dolomite in Karst Terrain of Northwestern Boone County, Arkansas.* U.S. Geological Survey, Water Investigation Report, 90-4066, 57 p.

Steele, K.F. and McCalister, W.K. (1991). *Potential Nitrate Pollution of Ground Water in Limestone Terrain by Poultry Litter, Ozark Region, U.S.A.* IN Nitrate Contamination: Exposure, Consequence and Control, Springer-Verlag, New York, (in press).

Steele, K.F. and McCalister, W.K. and Adamski, J.C. (1990). *Nitrate and Bacteria Contamination of Limestone Aquifers in Poultry/Cattle Producing Areas of Northwestern Arkansas, U.S.A.* Environmental Contamination, 528-531.

Steele, K.F., Widmann, R.K., Wickliff, D.S. and Parr, D.L. (1986). *The Effect of Rainstorm Events on Spring Water Chemistry in Limestone Terrain.* Proceedings of the Southern Regional Ground Water Conference, 1985, National Water Well Association, Worthington, OH, 50-66.

U.S. Environmental Protection Agency (1985). *National Primary Drinking Water Regulations: Synthetic Organic Chemicals, Inorganic Chemicals and Microorganisms; Proposed Rule.* Fed. Register 50, 46934-47022.

WATER QUALITY ISSUES: UNITED STATES NEW MANAGEMENT AND POLICY DIRECTIONS

Jonathan W. Bulkley
School of Natural Resources
Department of Civil Engineering
University of Michigan
Ann Arbor, Michigan 48109-1115

ABSTRACT

Water quality management and policy in the United States evolved from a primary responsibility of local and state government to a major federal government function. Massive federal funding to assist state and local units of government to plan, build, and implement enhanced water quality control facilities has terminated. Costs of future improvements will be apportioned among the direct users and those that benefit. Future improvements in water quality will require recognition of the need to change basic social activities in the way we live, produce and consume, transport, farm, and plan. Risk reduction will become a major means to assess future regulations, management, and policies for water quality improvement.

INTRODUCTION

Regulation of water quality in the United States evolved as a public health issue with primary responsibility resting with state and local units of government. Direct involvement of the federal government began in 1899 with Amendments to the Rivers and Harbors Act which gave the U.S. Army Corps of Engineers the power to regulate the discharge of materials into the navigable waters of the United States. This initial focus was not to maintain water quality but more to maintain navigation. In fact, liquid waste discharges from municipal sewers were exempted from this regulation.

Increasing degradation of surface water quality led to federal legislation which was vetoed on a financial technicality by President Roosevelt just before the outbreak of World War II. In 1948, federal legislation addressing water pollution was enacted into law. This legislation became permanent in 1956, and it has served as the key foundation for federal government participation in formulating and implementing national water quality policies since 1956.

Policy Foundations

The involvement of the United States federal government in water quality management and policy developed, in part, as a consequence of the failure of effective policies to be developed and implemented by the state (s) and local units of government. During the 1960's, in spite of a base of federal involvement, surface water quality in the United States continued to deteriorate. Rivers caught fire; wildfowl were killed by oil spills; bathing beaches were closed because of threats to public health; Lake Erie was declared to be dead.

The National Water Commission (1968-73) - The National Water Commission examined future water issues in the United States. Its final report issued in 1973 articulated seven (7) key themes all of which bear a close relation to new management and policy directions for water quality. These themes include the following:

(1) The future demand for water is a policy decision for society as a whole.
(2) Restoration and enhancement of water quality has become an important value for society.
(3) Water resource planning and land use planning must be closely coordinated. Otherwise, land use activities may overwhelm the quality of adjacent surface waters.
(4) Sound economic principles need to be applied for all water project evaluation.
(5) Conservation of water is needed to assure more efficient use of a valuable natural resource.
(6) Laws and institutions associated with water planning, control, and implementation need to be examined and modified in view of current and anticipated future problems.
(7) The level of government closest to the water problem should be the governmental unit designated to resolve the issue.

PL 92-500: Water Pollution Control Act Amendments of 1972 - Congressional passage of these amendments by Congress over the veto of President Nixon represents a major policy shift in the United States for the improvement of surface water quality. Pl 92-500 set a rigorous time table for all point source dischargers to meet for the continued disposal of either municipal wastewater or industrial wastewater to surface receiving waters. Technology based standards of secondary treatment were established as a floor for all municipal dischargers. Categorical standards were subsequently established by U.S. EPA for all industrial point source dischargers. Municipalities were required to establish rigorous and enforceable industrial pretreatment standards applicable to those industrial locations discharging into a municipal system.

If the technology based standards would not allow the receiving waters to meet the water quality standards established for the segment of the receiving waters downstream from the treatment plant, then treatment technology higher than secondary is required to be implemented. All point source dischargers must have a NPDES (National Pollution Discharge Elimination System) permit in order to discharge treated wastewaters to receiving waters. The permits are issued for a maximum of five years. The permits become the instruments for requiring more stringent performance by point source dischargers in order to achieve specified water quality goals and objectives. The 1972 Amendments further established a goal of zero discharge of pollutants to the receiving waters by 1985. The "zero discharge" goal remains a goal. It is not a policy but rather a goal which one strives to attain but may never fully achieve. As a goal, zero discharge sets a tone and provides direction. It means that we shall remove as many and as much pollutants as possible prior to discharge to receiving waters. This goal is in sharp contrast to the prior policy of maximizing the use of the assimilative capacity of the receiving waters.

Toxic discharges in toxic amounts were to be eliminated. The enforcement of the provisions of the Water Pollution Control Act (now the Clean Water Act) is through the U.S. District Courts. Citizen suits are permitted. Finally, the 1972 Amendments both authorized and appropriated $18 Billion for the federal share of construction of facilities for municipalities to adequately collect and treat wastewater. These Amendments dramatically altered water quality policy and management in the United States. The new policy became to limit as much as possible the discharge of pollutants to receiving waters. Significant federal funds were made available to assist communities in building the needed treatment facilities. Rigorous enforcement through the federal Courts with stiff fines and penalties including incarceration helped compel performance to comply with the provisions of the Act.

Subsequent amendments to the Clean Water Act have occurred through the years. The most recent changes occurred in 1987. The basic policy thrust of the Clean Water Act has not been changed as a consequence of these Amendments. In fact, the provisions of the PL 92-500 passed in 1972, established a National Water Quality Commission in the mid-1970's to review the experience with the new water quality policies and thus have an opportunity for major mid-course corrections. The Commission affirmed and recommended continuation of the new policy directions established in 1972. One major change which took place in 1987 is the elimination of the federal grant program to provide funds to assist municipalities to build the facilities needed to be in compliance with the provisions of the Act. To date, more than $40 billion has been provided by the U.S. Congress as a federal share to assist in the construction of needed water pollution control facilities. In the future, the federal financial grant support is eliminated in favor of state-based revolving loan funds. The seed moneys to establish these loan funds in each state came from the federal government.

New Directions: Water Quality Policy

In a country as diverse as the United States, difficulties and conflicts arise as one attempts to provide uniform policy implementation in every location. Not only are the basic legal systems different as they apply to water in the humid East or the arid and semi-arid West, but there are different agencies, traditions, demands placed upon the increasingly valuable water resources of the nation. Two major studies which have direct bearing on future water quality policy and management have recently been undertaken. One study, Water Quality 2000, is on-going through 1992. The second study by the Science Advisory Board of the United States Environmental Protection Agency completed its task in September, 1990. Let us consider a number of key points which have been documented in reports distributed from these two important activities.

Water Quality 2000

Since 1988, more than eighty (80) public, private, and non-profit organizations have been working together to identify current water quality problems in the United States including the sources of impairment to water quality and to identify the root causes leading to deterioration of water quality. This problem identification phase (Phase II of a planned four (4) phase effort) has just been concluded. The next phase (Phase III) will be to develop solutions designed to address the problems identified in Phase II. Phase IV, the final phase of Water Quality 2000, will begin the process of implementation of the solutions identified in Phase III. It is important to recognize that the Water Quality 2000 effort is undertaken roughly 16-18 years after the passage of PL 92-500. While very significant progress has been made in improving surface water quality as a consequence of PL 92-500, much remains to be done. The findings, to date, of Water Quality 2000 suggest the need for new directions for water quality policy and management not only in the United States but in other countries as well.

The goal of the Water Quality 2000 Project is to provide "A Society Living in Harmony with Healthy Natural Systems." It is important to recognize that this goal is significantly expanded beyond the traditional protection of public health objective. The concern with healthy natural systems implies that society needs to be very aware and concerned regarding pollutants discharged to the environment as a consequence of development and enhanced living standards.

Problem Identification - In the Problem Identification Phase, water Quality 2000 had ten (10) separate work groups engaged in the specification of water quality problems. An analysis of the findings from each of these work groups led to the following identification of major sources of impairment to water quality (Water Quality 2000, 1990) :

(1) Agriculture-Agricultural runoff is the source of impairment of 55% of surveyed river miles found to be impaired and 58% of surveyed lake acres. Agricultural activities may contaminate groundwater, contribute to wetland losses, and serve as a source of acutely toxic chemicals reaching surface and ground waters.

(2) Community Wastewater-Wastewater treatment plants built and/or upgraded as a consequence of PL 92-500 serve a vital function in removal of certain pollutants from wastewater streams. Rigorous industrial pretreatment standards are needed to assure that such facilities do not serve as a pass-through source of persistent toxins. Issues associated with combined sewer overflows especially in older

urban areas require new approaches for resolution and mitigation.
(3) Industry-While more than 90% of the industrial point source dischargers are in compliance with federal discharge limits, it is estimated that nationwide industrial point source dischargers still contribute more than 180,000 tons/year of toxic pollutants to receiving waters.
(4) Land Alteration-Various land uses including logging, mining, grazing, road building, and urban development all contribute to additional runoff of water, soil, and chemicals to receiving waters.
(5) Stocking and Harvesting-Aquatic ecosystems have been stressed by over harvesting of fish and shellfish and by the introduction of non-native exotic species.
(6) Transportation-Major sources of pollution include spills and other discharges of oil and other substances from ships, surface vehicles, and pipelines. Wetlands and other aquatic resources are destroyed as a consequence of dredging navigation channels and building transportation works.
(7) Urban runoff-contaminated runoff continues as a major source of water pollutants. Regulations to control such runoff have just been issued by U.S. EPA.
(8) Water projects-dams and other physical works may result in the loss of physical habitat and water required by aquatic species.
(9) Atmospheric deposition-toxics and other contaminants reach receiving waters from the atmosphere through dry-fall and precipitation.

Root causes - In considering these existing water quality problems, Water Quality 2000 identified a number of root causes which contribute to these water quality problems. These root causes include the following:
(1) How we live;
(2) How we produce and consume;
(3) How we farm;
(4) How we transport people and goods;
(5) How we plan; and
(6) How we have acted in the past. It is very important to be mindful of these root causes of water quality problems. It is clear that without addressing these root causes no amount of after-the-fact action-such as PL 92-500 even with its vast expenditure can fully correct the quality problems.

Impediments to solutions - Water Quality 2000 has identified a number of existing impediments to finding and implementing effective solutions to existing and future water quality problems. Accordingly, as one considers new directions for water quality policy and management an awareness of perceived impediments is most important. The identified impediments include the following:
(1) Narrowly focused water policies the U.S. focused upon narrow technical solutions with a strong engineering component. What has been missed is a more holistic approach that would include watershed-based planning, cross-media transport, water quality and

water quantity, pollution prevention, and environmental outcomes.

(2) Institutional conflicts in the U.S., there is an system of government that involves federal, state, local units. In some locations, there is a regional unit between the local and the state. Conflicts arise over the allocation of authority and responsibility among these several governmental units. Federal requirements for pollution control without federal funding to assist implementation are particularly difficult at the present time. Not only are the units of government in conflict with one another but the private sector is a key player as well.

(3) Legislative and regulatory overlaps the complexity of the technical problems coupled with the historic approach of dealing with one problem at a time has resulted in programs that are inconsistent. Differences exist within the same agency between planning and implementation. Legislation designed to promote the agricultural sector may be very harmful to water quality.

(4) Insufficient funding the cost of environmental clean-up continues to increase and yet the federal contribution continues to decline. For example, to maintain the present level of drinking water quality and water quality programs, EPA has estimated that the cost will increase from $31.3 billion/year in 1987 to $42.3 billion/year in the year 2000. Putting into place new programs currently authorized but not implemented would add and additional $4.0 billion/year by the year 2000. It is anticipated that state and local sources will need to generate the vast majority of these needed funds.

(5) Lack of trained personnel it is estimated that the need for environmental engineers will grow more rapidly than for any other field of engineering through the year 2000. It is necessary to expand the skills base not only of environmental engineers but resource managers, lawyers, economists, planners, and public policy specialists in those areas which serve as a foundation for an effective clean water program.

(6) Needed research and development research and development activities are needed that focus on the complexity of water quality problems and help to improve the understanding of complex ecosystems.

(7) Inadequate communication to the public it is recognized that the public is usually well-informed during an environmental crisis. However, there has not been an effective communication of the links that exist between the way our society lives and the adverse impact on environmental quality.

U.S. EPA Reducing Risk: Setting Priorities and Strategies for Environmental Protection

The Science Advisory Board of U.S. EPA recently released a major report undertaken by the Board for the Administrator (U.S. EPA, 1990). This report has the potential to have a profound impact on the establishment and implementation of environmental policy including water policy in the United States. It addresses a number of the issues raised in the Water Quality 2000 effort. Let us consider the recommendations which have been made by the Science Advisory Board.

The recommendations include the following:
(1) U.S. EPA should target environmental protection where it achieves the greatest risk reduction;
(2) U.S. EPA should act to reduce ecological risk as well as human health risk;
(3) U.S. EPA should reflect risk-based priorities in both strategic planning and in budget priorities;
(4) There should be greater use of all available tools to reduce risk- including market incentives, information, as well as end-of-pipe treatment;
(5) There should be very strong emphasis on pollution prevention and waste reduction in all aspects of society;
(6) Actions need to be taken to integrate environmental considerations into broader aspects of public policy;
(7) Actions need to be taken to improve public understanding of environmental risks and to train a professional work force to reduce these risks;
(8) Improved analytical methods are needed to value natural resources and to account for long term environmental effects in economic analyses;
(9) Improved data is needed as well as improved analytical methodologies to support the assessment, comparison and reduction of different environment risks.

These recommendations are of particular importance since they specify that risk reduction is going to become the driving force behind future environmental protection strategy. This is a most appropriate finding. The costs of environmental degradation and subsequent environmental clean-up are simply huge. There are not sufficient funds in either the public or private sector to accomplish every last degree of either protection and/or clean-up. A policy has been announced which will provide guidance for future actions- namely risk reduction both human and ecosystem risk reduction.

Observations

Restoration and protection of water quality has a high value for society. It is a public trust responsibility to provide quality water not only for the present population but for all future generations as well.

The causes of water quality deterioration in the United States are complex. It has become clear that our lifestyle which includes high energy use, urban sprawl, lack of land use planning, agricultural practices, production and consumption all contribute as root causes to water quality deterioration.

Water Quality 2000 has identified a number of problems and conditions which hinder improving water quality. One must be mindful of these impairments in planning actions to improve water quality in the future. The narrow focus of past water policies is certainly a major factor which hinder improvements. It is well to note that in England and Wales the government addressed comprehensive water management in the late 1960's and early 1970's and the outcome of their work was the creation of the regional water authority concept where nearly 1600 separate water entities were replaced by ten (10) regional water authorities providing comprehensive water planning, water services, and implementation of all of these water functions based upon a watershed focus.

A policy framework is very important as a means to articulate goals and objectives, specify requirements, provide for monitoring, and enforcement. Absent an adequate policy framework, improvements to water quality is not probable.

Improvements to water quality is expensive. Since 1970, it is estimated that all levels of government in the United States have invested $239 billion for capital works. This amounts to roughly $1,000/person. In addition, operation and maintenance expenses over the past 20 years have been about $50/person/year. To meet provisions of the Clean Water Act especially for combined sewer overflows, it is estimated that an additional $90-180 billion will be needed for capital works alone.

It is clear that one needs to target investments in the future. The risk reduction strategies announced by the U.S. EPA provide one means to begin this important process.

REFERENCES

U.S. Environmental Protection Agency, *Reducing Risk: Setting Priorities and Strategies for Environmental Protection.* Science Advisory Board, SAB-EC-90-021, Washington, D.C., September, 1990.

Water Quality 2000, *Phase II Report Problem Identification.* Water Quality 2000, 601 Wythe Street, Alexandria, VA. 22314-1994, September 1990.

THE GREEN BAY, WISCONSIN REMEDIAL ACTION PLAN PROGRESS AND PROBLEMS

Harold J. Day
Department of Natural and Applied Science
University of Wisconsin-Green Bay
Green Bay, Wisconsin 54311-7001, USA

ABSTRACT

Water quality problems in the coastal communities of the developed world are discussed. A particular site, Green Bay, Wisconsin, located on the shore of Lake Michigan in North America, is chosen for a more detailed review. Following a site description and a summary of recent efforts to abate pollution, comments are made on the major problems remaining and on the efforts to resolve them.

INTRODUCTION

Water quality problems continue to challenge communities throughout the world although those in the developed are usually quite different from those in the developing world. The primary problems in the developing world are those that threaten human health, caused either by bacteria, e.g. cholera or by parasites, e.g. Guinea worm. Inadequate amounts of potable water coupled with extreme poverty in both rural and urban settings are the dominant reasons for these problems. In contrast, the primary problems in coastal communities of the developed world are those that threaten the adjacent aquatic ecosystem. These communities in the USA also suffer from the general problem of inadequate water resources planning and management (Viessman 1990a, 1990b). Features of the degraded aquatic ecosystem frequently include excess nutrients, soil particles and toxic chemicals.

The excess nutrients stimulate the growth of algae which upsets the delicate and complex web of life that begins with microscopic phytoplankton and ends with the fish and fish eating birds. The usual result is an increase in suspended solids in the water column and a decline in the sport and commercial fishery.

The soil particles enter the lakes and streams as part of the surface runoff from the land. Nutrients, either from commercial or animal fertilizer and toxic chemicals, usually from pesticides and herbicides, are chemically bonded to the soil and enter the water with the particles. This set of actions, often called non-point source pollution, is the dominant cause of degraded surface water in many areas of the developed world today.

The toxic chemicals, often chlorinated hydrocarbons such as PCB's, have entered the surface water from a variety of manufacturing and agricultural practices in the past. Many of these chemicals were discharged by industries to receiving waters in very low concentrations. For years most people thought that these small quantities were harmless additions to the natural surroundings. Recently, the knowledge of food chain multiplication has shown that these long term low concentration releases have been very damaging to life in the receiving waters. Fish are frequently found with tumors and with abnormally high body burdens of the same chemicals released in such dilute amounts. A multiplier effect, sometimes 100,000 times or more, has been measured (Harris,1990). Fish advisories have been issued in many areas to warn people against excessive consumption for fear of increased cancer risk. The bottom sediments in these rivers, lakes and bays contain a reserve of toxins which is taken into the food chain. These contaminated sediments, sometimes called in place pollutants, IPP, are considered a major source of pollution in many coastal communities of the developed world.

The Great Lakes of North America are no exception. Within the past decade, attention has been shifting from overloaded sewage treatment plants, often called point sources, to non-point source pollution and to contaminated sediments. The International Joint Commission, IJC, has identified 42 problem areas, known as Areas Of Concern, AOC, which have complex pollution problems. The AOC are shown in Figure 1. The IJC has recommended that plans for pollution abatement, called Remedial Action Plans, RAP, be prepared for each AOC. The Green Bay, Wisconsin AOC was the first in the USA to complete this planning report (Wisc. Dept. of Nat'l Res., 1988). Since completion in early 1988, implementation efforts have been

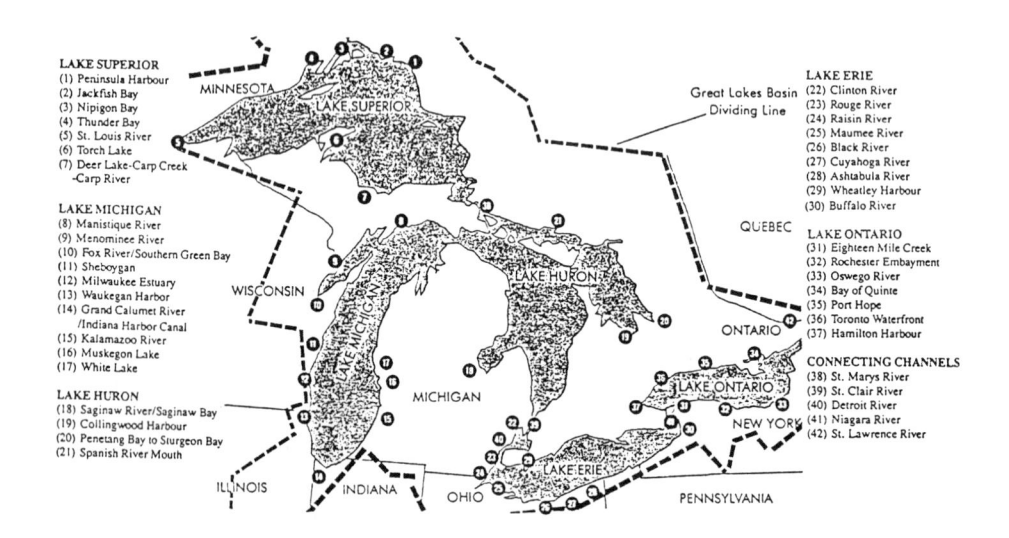

Figure 1. The Great Lakes Areas of concern from: the Great Lakes Reporter.7 (6),7, Nov/Dec 1990, Center for the Great Lakes, Chicago, Ill.

underway. Some progress has been achieved but significant problems still exist. This paper has been written as a brief report on both the progress and the problems. The Green Bay experience may serve as an aid to others committed to pollution abatement in their own communities.

DESCRIPTION OF THE AREA

Green Bay, Wisconsin is located at the mouth of the Fox River which empties into the largest fresh water estuary in the world, also named Green Bay. The Fox River drains an area of approximately 6000 square miles. While the majority of the land is used for either agriculture or forestry, the segment downstream of Lake Winnebago contains a large number of paper mills along with the associated urbanized area. Approximately 500,000 people live in the watershed between Lake Winnebago and Green Bay, a distance of 40 miles and an area of about 500 square miles. The bay itself is 135 miles long, oriented in a general northeast to southwest direction, and is located in the middle of the western shore of Lake Michigan. See Figure 2.

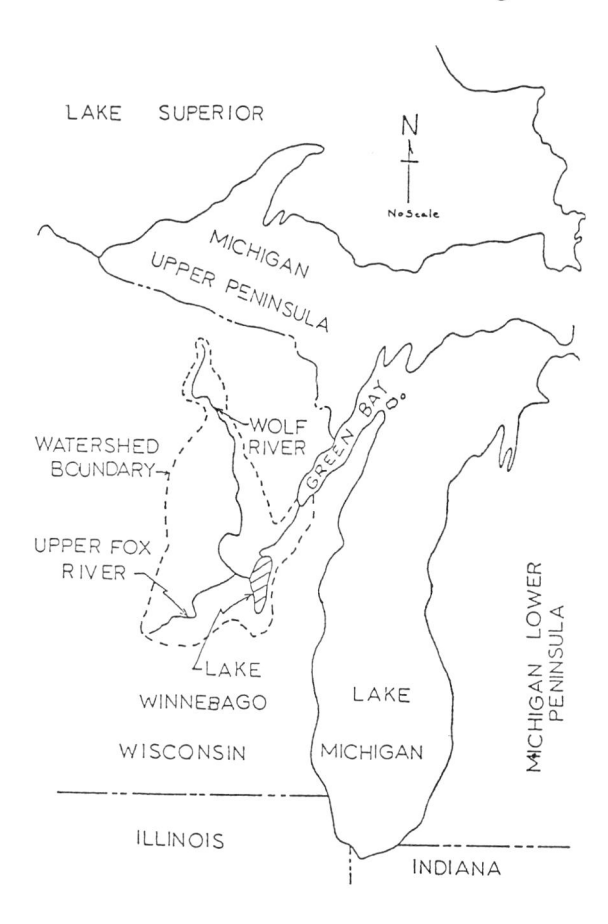

Figure 2. Location Map for the Fox River and the Green Bay.

The Green Bay AOC includes the immediate area of the river and the bay in and around the metropolitan area at the river's mouth. The bay is quite shallow for the first five miles or so, less than 8 feet deep, and has been a polluted water body for the last fifty or more years. Following a major investment in municipal and industrial wastewater treatment plant improvements during the late 70's and early 80's, a sum exceeding $400 million for the forty mile downstream reach, the point source pollution was brought under control. Most people believed it was only a matter of time before fishing and swimming would be resumed. Then, in the mid 80's, as fishing did improve, the problems of contaminated sediments became apparent. Further, the rural and urban non point source pollution, primarily in runoff containing soil particles from plowed fields and urban construction sites, became more apparent also.

The citizens of Green Bay knew there was more to do whenever the river and lower bay color changed from blue to brown, whenever the contaminated fish advisories were publicized and whenever the algae blooms appeared. The recommendation by the IJC to develop a RAP was no surprise in Green Bay. A citizen committee worked with the Wisconsin Department of Natural Resources, WDNR to prepare the RAP.

HIGHLIGHTS OF THE REMEDIAL ACTION PLAN

The Green Bay RAP was prepared over a two year period by the staff of the WDNR with the assistance of approximately 100 citizens representing a wide range of local community interests. The Citizens Advisory Committee, with a membership of 25, provided policy guidance in the plan preparation. This group met monthly to review progress and make suggestions. The primary end products of the Committee were presented in the form of three separate lists:

- The Desired Future State of the Bay and River
- Primary Goals for Restoring the Bay and River by the Year 2000
- Key Actions for a Clean Bay and River

The last list is presented in Table 1 as a sample of the results achieved.

TABLE 1. KEY ACTIONS FOR A CLEAN BAY AND RIVER TO RESTORE, PROTECT AND ENHANCE THE ECOSYSTEM

High Priority

1. Reduce Phosphorus Inputs to the River and Bay from Non-point and Point Sources.

2. Reduce Sediment and Suspended Solids Inputs.

TABLE 1. Continued

3. Eliminate Toxicity of Industrial, Municipal and other Point Source Discharges.

4. Reduce Availability of Toxic Chemicals from Contaminated Sediments.

5. Continue Control of Oxygen-Demanding Wastes from Industrial and Municipal Discharges.

Moderate Priority

6. Protect Wetlands, and Manage Habitat and Wildlife.

7. Reduce/Control Populations of Problem Fish.

8. Increase Populations of Predator Fish.

Lower Priority

9. Reduce Sediment Re-suspension.

10. Reduce Bacteria Inputs from Point and Non-point Sources.

11. Virtually Eliminate Toxicity Caused by Non-point and Atmospheric Sources.

TO IMPROVE PEOPLE'S USE OF THE ECOSYSTEM

High Priority

12. Create a Coordinating Council and Institutional Structure for Plan Implementation.

13. Increase Public Awareness of, Participation in, and Support for River and Bay Restoration Efforts.

Moderate Priority

14. Enhance Public and Private Shoreline Uses

MONITORING AND RESEARCH

15. Monitor to Evaluate the Effectiveness of Remedial Actions, Track Trends and Identify Problems.

16. Conduct Research to Better Understand the Ecosystem, Its Problems and How to Remedy Them.

The RAP document is over 300 pages in length, not including the four technical appendices which make the entire document in excess of 1000 pages. There are 120 separate recommendations, grouped according to high, medium and low priority, made to achieve the Key Actions listed in Table 1. Each recommendation has a cost estimate and an implementation schedule associated with it. The cost estimates are provided as a pair of values, low and high. The sum of these estimates for all of the recommendations was $68 million (low) and $640 million (high). The high level of uncertainty associated with the cost to abate the contaminated sediment problem was the primary reason for such a wide range of costs. A list of involved public agencies, federal, state, regional and local is included. Recommendations for an interim and a permanent institutional structure, including a staff, to coordinate the implementation effort are also made.

The Green Bay RAP was reviewed by the International Joint Commission and the Great Lakes Fishery Commission. The statement in the Water Quality Programs Committee Coordinated Review which best summarizes their opinion is :

"OVERALL RATING

The Lower Green Bay Remedial Action Plan is a very good attempt to combine significant public involvement and an ecosystem approach in developing a working document. It is well done as far as it goes, but lacks quantification and currently does not charge specific agencies with specific tasks." (IJC, 1988)

PROGRESS IN RAP IMPLEMENTATION

Over two years have passed since the implementation effort began. A major effort has been exerted during this time to implement the plan. Annual progress reports have been published (UWGB,1989;1990). The reports contain highlights of accomplishments in the categories: non-point source pollution, toxic and point source pollution, fish and wildlife activities, shoreline use and recreation, public education and participation, monitoring and research activities and structure. Comments follow on some particularly significant activities during 1990 in three of the categories: non-point source pollution, toxic and point source pollution and structure.

Non-point Source Pollution

A major effort to reduce soil erosion and runoff from rural and urban areas in the East River drainage basin is underway. The drainage basin contains an area of 120 square miles, about 1/4 of the land downstream of Lake Winnebago. The East River enters the Fox River less than a mile from its mouth so any improvements will impact directly on Green Bay. One of the priority watershed projects in the state, farmers receive up to a 70% subsidy on approved land management practices such as fencing off of stream banks, grassed waterways and animal manure control facilities. The project is expected to last for another 8 years, during which up to $10 million will be invested.

The US Department of Agriculture, in cooperation with the University of Wisconsin-Extension, has just begun a project in a part of the same area to demonstrate improved management of pesticides and nutrients used on cropland. This project is intended to help farmers increase profitability by matching the desired crop yield with the soil in a particular field and with a specific loading of fertilizer and pesticide. If successful, the project could lead the way to reducing the amount of nutrients and toxic chemicals entering the stream while at the same time maintaining a strong farm economy.

Toxic and Point Source Pollution

Two major capital investments have been made to address this important problem. The first is a massive research project designed to learn more about the pathways and fate of toxic chemicals in the river and bay. Called the Mass Balance Study, it is an effort to track four toxins - cadmium, lead, dieldrin and PCB, from upstream sources, primarily contaminated sediments, to downstream sinks (sediments, fish, water column and atmosphere). The project is a cooperative effort including the US Environmental Protection Agency, the Wisconsin Department of Natural Resources, the University of Wisconsin and others. At least $12 million will be invested in this study before it is completed in 1991. The results will be used in planning future abatement efforts in Green Bay and elsewhere in the Great Lakes.

The second is a pair of major expansion projects at two large municipal waste water treatment plants in the watershed downstream of Lake Winnebago. These plants, one in the city of Green Bay and the other in the city of Appleton about 30 miles upstream, are being expanded to treat the ammonia present in the waste water influent to each plant. The total capital cost is in excess of $100 million. When both are completed in 1993, ammonia toxicity from point sources in the lower basin will be virtually eliminated during the warm summer season.

Structure

Efforts to find an effective institutional structure for improved coordination between participating agencies and for improved communication with the public have been making progress. The WDNR staff has been holding meetings with all agencies and citizen groups involved over the past year and one half. A preferred structure has been identified and presented to WDNR administration for their review and approval. A decision is expected early in 1991.

PROBLEMS WITH THE RAP

While the progress has been significant, there are major problems remaining which, if not resolved soon, will make it very difficult for a successful long term abatement effort. In general, most of the implementation activities to date have taken place for reasons other than the RAP, i.e., they would have occurred anyway. Long term success depends upon a change in thinking by all of society, but in particular by elected officials and by agency administrators, about the management of complex natural resource problems. Most of us think about one problem at a time, e.g. municipal waste water or agricultural runoff. Our tendency is to try to solve each problem at the lowest possible level of government, e.g. each municipality owns and operates its own sewage treatment plant and each township has primary authority for the land zoning that often is at the base of soil erosion. We will need to think about more than one problem at a time and do so over a larger land area to have improved success. The RAP process has shown us that the watershed is usually the most important land area to work with. It has also shown us that we need to consider solving a number of problems at the same time.

A better understanding of this new framework for managing water resources (and most other natural resources) may be provided by considering three specific problems with the implementation of the Green Bay RAP at this time. They are cost effectiveness, limited mandate and institutional arrangements.

Cost Effectiveness

The Green Bay RAP contains cost estimates for abatement to the year 2010 but there is no attempt to predict future needs for the resources by the community. There is also no attempt to predict the relative cost effectiveness of different sets of abatement activities needed to meet the future needs. Such analyses would be very useful in helping to set priorities for the investment of the limited funds available. Some suggestions for the framework of this type of analysis have been made (Bower,1982).

Limited Mandate

Most citizens of northeastern Wisconsin support the effort to abate pollution and are willing to help pay for it. A recent study of local public support shows some interesting detail (Smith, et al., 1990). The study shows that only one of every five citizens in metropolitan Green Bay have knowledge of the RAP. In spite of this ignorance, people are willing to pay up to $35 per person more per year toward the cleanup effort. This limited mandate could evidently be strengthened through improved information transfer. A stronger mandate will be needed in the years ahead, particularly since the cleanup effort will probably require substantial new funds as well as a new perspective for effective action.

Institutional Arrangements

The primary federal, state, regional and local agencies have had very limited success in identifying their role as one party in the multi agency effort to identify effective abatement activities. The WDNR has tried very hard to lead in the effort but inter agency competition for limited funds has often hindered the development of a coordinated effort. Some mission oriented agencies, such as the US Environmental Protection Agency and the US Army Corps of Engineers have not participated in any of the local meetings, primarily due to limited travel funds and the need to meet their own priorities. Agency assignments for specific tasks with specific budget allocations are not likely in the near future unless some politically based intervention occurs.

CONCLUSIONS

Pollution abatement efforts in coastal communities of the developed nations, such as Green Bay, Wisconsin, have been very successful in the past decade. Now, the challenge to continue the trend in improvement is becoming more difficult to meet. A change in citizen perception of the nature of the problem will be needed. Improved inter institutional cooperation will be needed. A change in the procedures for planning and analysis of the problems will be needed. Elected officials will need more information to decide how to allocate the increasingly limited funds available for such purposes. The Green Bay RAP experience to date has helped to identify important features of the problem for the future; only time will tell whether it will be much help in finding new and better solutions. Each of us, working in our own communities during the years ahead, will determine that.

REFERENCES

Bower, B.T., Ehler, C.N. and Basta, D.J. (1982). *Coastal and Ocean Resources Management: A Framework For Analysis.* Report No. ABC-CW-D82/005, Int'l Federation of Inst. for Advanced Study-IFIAS, Solna, Sweden, 59 pgs.

Harris, H.J., (1990).*State Of The Bay.* Occasional report, Inst. For Land and Water Studies, UWGB, Gr. Bay, WI., 20 pgs.

International Joint Commission. (1988). Letter dated May 11, 1988 from Water Quality Programs Committee to Wisc. Dept. of Nat'l Res., Windsor, Ont., 6 pgs.

Smith, L.J., Baba,R.B., Johnsen, P.K. and Knaap, G.J. (1990) *Public Perceptions And Attitudes Toward Water Quality Rehabilitation Of The Lower Green Bay Watershed.* Draft Report, Cent. For Pub. Aff., UWGB Gr. Bay, WI., 35 pgs.

Univ. Of WI-Gr.Bay, (1989).*Lower Green Bay Remedial Action Action Plan-First Annual Progress Report.* Gr. Bay, WI., 50 pgs.

Univ. Of WI-Gr.Bay, (1990).*Remedial Action Plan For Green Bay And The Fox River-1990 Progress Report.* Gr. Bay, WI., 51 pgs

Viessman, W. Jr. (1990a).*Water Management:Challenge and Opportunity. J. Water Resour. Plng. and Mgmt.*, ASCE, 116 (2), 155-169.

Viessman, W. Jr. (1990b). *A Framework For Reshaping Water Management.Environment,* 32 (4), 10-15, 33-35.

Wisc. Dept. of Nat'l Res. (1988). *Lower Green Bay Remedial Action Plan.* PUBL-WR-175-87 REV 88, WDNR, Madison WI, 319 pgs.

DELINEATION OF MUNICIPAL WATER SUPPLY AQUIFER PROTECTION AREAS: INSIGHT FROM SOME MIDWESTERN EXPERIENCES

Robert J. Montgomery
Warzyn Inc.
Madison, Wisconsin 53705

ABSTRACT

This paper presents a summary of regulatory and technical approaches to the protection of municipal well water supplies through designation of wellhead protection areas, and presents several issues concerning delineation of protection areas in municipal well field systems. Topics presented relate to well field operation and protection of existing wells, as opposed to contamination source area clean-up or waste handling standards. Analyses of wellfield contamination in several Midwestern cities illustrate the value of using analysis approaches which can realistically model hydrogeologic boundaries, transient effects, and contingency plans for wellfield operation. The case studies suggest that a review of wellfield development history, operation and potential contaminant source areas within existing developed areas could be a useful supplement to delineation of wellhead protection areas.

INTRODUCTION

Development of planning and regulatory approaches for protection of public well water supplies has become an issue in overall environmental regulation in the United States. Over 50% of the U.S. population draws upon groundwater for its potable water supply, via approximately 48,000 community well water supply systems and over 12 million individual water wells (U.S. EPA, 1984). This dependance on groundwater supplies is particularly high in the Midwest. For example, in Wisconsin, over 90% of the state's communities are served by public well water supply systems. These groundwater supplies are being increasingly affected by contamination from agricultural, residential and industrial activities. Many sources of groundwater contamination are becoming controlled through a variety of federal and state toxic and hazardous waste programs. However, a more comprehensive approach to the protection of aquifers supplying public water systems is being developed. This class of regulatory programs, known as wellhead protection programs, specifically addresses analysis and planning for safeguarding the recharge areas of public groundwater supply systems.

APPROACHES TO WELLHEAD PROTECTION

Wellhead protection program guidelines have been developed by many regulatory agencies, prompted in part by the 1986 amendments to the Safe Drinking Water Act. These amendments provide direction for establishing a nationwide program to protect groundwater resources used for public water supplies from a wide range of potential threats. Previous federal programs (such as RCRA, Superfund, and TSCA) have focussed on sources of groundwater contamination. The wellhead protection approach provides technical and administrative means for delineating and regulating the recharge areas for public water supply wells, with the objective of preventing activities that may cause pollution of the public water supply. The federal policy in the area of protecting public water supply systems emphasizes the lead regulatory role of the states, and of local municipalities with land use regulatory powers. The Safe Drinking Water Act amendments called for the creation of state-lead wellhead protection programs, and authorized funding to assist in state program development.

Unfortunately, this federal funding assistance for development of state wellhead protection programs has not yet materialized. However, many states and local communities are developing wellhead programs on their own initiative. For example, in Wisconsin, the State Geological and Natural History Survey has developed an extensive set of technical and administrative guidance documents (Born, et al., 1987, Yanggen and Amrlhein, 1991, and Yanggen and Webendorfer, 1991). The state of Illinois has developed a draft state wellhead protection program which calls for wellhead protection areas and regulates activities within those areas (draft regulations, Illinois Admin. Code 615 and 616). Several local communities have adopted wellhead protection ordinances and are attempting to regulate land use to limit aquifer contamination potential (Robinson, et al., 1985).

CURRENT GUIDANCE IN WELLHEAD PROTECTION AREA DELINEATION

Technical guidance for delineation of wellhead protection areas describes development of wellhead protection area delineation criteria and techniques (U.S. EPA, 1987 and Born, et al., 1988). Delineation criteria can include distance, drawdown, travel time, flow system boundaries and the capacity of the aquifer to assimilate contaminants. Each of these criteria is an approach to identification of the actual aquifer area which could produce contamination at the well of concern.

Wellhead protection criteria based on distance from the well result in a circular protection area, which typically will not accurately depict the zone of contribution to the well, except under unusually isolated and homogeneous conditions. Distance criteria used in well protection area delineation typically range from several hundred to several thousand feet in diameter. Drawdown criteria attempt to identify the area of well pumpage influence by its effect on the water table. The wellhead protection areas resulting from drawdown criteria will be a better indication of the zone of capture than an arbitrary diameter, but will not identify the maximum extent of contributing area, and will not be accurate in areas of strong regional gradients. Drawdown criteria typically range from 0.1 to several feet. Travel time criteria are based on the assumption that contaminant transport to a well field can be approximated as being advective only, due to the relatively high flow velocities and hydraulic gradients present near pumping wells. Time of travel criteria produce "envelopes" of area, defined by advective travel time. These criteria vary enormously, from as low as 10 days to 50 years.

Flow boundary criteria explicitly set wellhead protection limits at locations assumed to be unaffected by pumpage, such as major rivers or groundwater divides. Assimilative capacity criteria are the most sophisticated, and are intended to take into account retardation and degradation processes which reduce contaminant migration from source areas to the well. These criteria are necessarily very site specific, and depend upon anticipated contaminant characteristics and detailed data on soil and rock chemical composition. Development of assimilative capacity criteria has been attempted at a few locations, where the contaminant threat can be identified, and where degradation mechanisms can be approximated.

Technical approaches to delineating wellhead protection areas vary in complexity, and vary according to the delineation criteria selected. The delineation techniques include the following:

- Geologic/hydrologic mapping, identifying hydrogeologic boundaries

- Calculated radius, based on water balance or algebraic approximations to drawdown or time of travel criteria

- Analytical flow models incorporating analytical solutions or combinations of analytical solutions using superposition, to evaluate drawdown or time of travel criteria

- Numerical flow models, utilizing discretized data on aquifer properties, for evaluation of drawdown or time of travel criteria

- Numerical flow and contaminant/fate modelling, which could be used to identify wellhead protection areas considering the complexities of flow, and contaminant dispersion, retardation and decay.

The techniques identified above are mainly applicable to evaluation of wellhead protection areas for unconfined aquifers. Evaluation of contributing areas for confined aquifers (or even semi-confined aquifers) is more complicated, and may include regional hydrogeologic evaluation of recharge areas located far from the public water supply well. In addition, since evaluation of karst or highly fractured bedrock aquifers is very difficult for any purpose, application of wellhead protection area concepts in these areas will also be difficult.

Selection of the evaluation technique will mainly be driven the availability of funding, staff and data, and the level of detail desired in the well protection area delineations. However, delineation of wellhead protection areas by any of the analytical or numerical methods according to currently described procedures include several additional key assumptions:

1. Wellhead protection areas for individual wells are considered independently.

2. Protection area analyses are conducted for steady state conditions.

3. Previously existing aquifer conditions are not taken explicitly into account.

Implications and possible consequences of these assumptions are illustrated in the examples described below.

CONTAMINATION EXPERIENCE AT SEVERAL MIDWESTERN WELL FIELDS

The four examples of well field contamination described below are located in areas which are similar in hydrogeologic characteristics. All these sites are located in the upper Midwest, and involve municipal well fields primarily developed in unconsolidated glacial deposits. Each well field has these additional similarities:

- Multiple wells in the system, installed within an urban environment over several decades of growth

- Unconfined aquifer conditions, with aquifer materials consisting of sands and gravels, sometimes with more complex interbedded silts and clays

- Historical contamination of several of the municipal wells by a volatile organic compounds (VOCs)

- Substantial variations in both long and short term pumpage at individual wells within the system.

In addition, three of the areas are bisected by substantial rivers, which would probably be defined as hydrogeologic boundaries in analysis techniques described in wellhead protection programs

Rockford, Illinois

Rockford is located in northern Illinois, on the banks of the Rock River. The Rockford well field consists of about 40 wells distributed throughout the City on both sides of the Rock River. Wells draw water from an unconfined sand and gravel aquifer with hydraulic connection to the Rock River and other streams. Rockford is a significant manufacturing center, and has recently been experiencing increasing wellhead VOC contamination from a number of source areas with long operational history.

The City of Rockford initiated a study in 1989 with the objective of evaluating development of a new municipal well field in an area south of the City. The sand and gravel aquifer in this area is highly variable in thickness, due to several deep bedrock valleys. Since substantial data was available from municipal and private water well logs, a finite-difference numerical groundwater flow model was used to evaluate the existing and proposed well field. In addition, an advective particle-tracking model was used to develop time of travel wellhead protection areas for the proposed well field.

Based upon the numerical groundwater flow model and advective time of travel analyses, the City could determine the well field capture area, and evaluate the potential for contaminant influx from known or suspected source areas. The advantages of using a comprehensive numerical groundwater flow model were important, due to the substantial variations in aquifer thickness through the study area, and due to the groundwater/surface water interaction with the Rock River. Use of simpler analytical models or regional assumptions on aquifer characteristics would not have been able to produce the results needed in the Rockford situation.

Wausau, Wisconsin

Wausau is located in central Wisconsin, adjacent to the Wisconsin River. The City operates seven groundwater production wells for its water supply system, all of which draw from an unconfined sand and gravel aquifer, in hydraulic connection with the Wisconsin River, and resting upon low permeability crystalline bedrock. Several waste disposal and spill sites, of long history of operation, are located in the well field area.

VOC contamination of certain of the City public water supply wells was severe enough to cause the Wausau well field to be listed as an EPA Superfund site. Site contaminant distribution included source areas and contaminated wells on both sides of the Wisconsin River, with contamination apparently migrating in several directions from the source areas. To assist in interpretation of the contaminant distribution, a finite difference groundwater flow model was constructed for the unconfined aquifer. Important aspects in development of the model included calibration in transient mode for water table fluctuations influenced by river stage changes, and calibration using transient historical operation data for the water supply wells. Interpretation of flow fields was through the use of particle tracking and contaminant transport models, as well as by inspection of the potentiometric surfaces resulting from the groundwater flow model analysis.

Use of the groundwater flow model was particularly useful in interpreting contaminant distribution at the Wausau well field in that the model simulated flow from contaminant source areas beneath the Wisconsin River to water supply production wells on the opposite side. The existence of flow beneath this apparently major hydrogeologic boundary was not at first considered in analysis of the contaminant distribution, and provided a key explanation for the occurrence of contamination in the City wells. In addition, the transient hydraulic analysis coupled with advective transport rate calculations indicated that variable pumpage schedules for each city well was sufficient to cause contamination to be drawn in two different directions from source areas. This result would not have been obtained through the use of steady state analyses such as are typically utilized for wellhead protection analyses.

Southern Michigan Municipality

An additional example is taken from southern Michigan, in an upland area several miles away from major streams. The community has a long history of manufacturing, and is served by six public water supply production wells distributed throughout the urban area. In addition, industry draws a major supply from groundwater sources. The hydrogeology of the area is complex, with several sand and gravel aquifers separated by discontinuous clay confining layers. The openings in these confining layers allow vertical flow in places to a lower aquifer. VOC contamination detected at several of the municipal water supply wells was significant.

The analysis approach for the well field required a model capable of simulating a multi-layered system over a substantial period of time progressive well installation and pumpage. A multilayer finite difference groundwater model was selected for use in the analysis, and was coupled to an advective particle tracking model for evaluation of capture zones. The field investigation indicated that the contaminant distribution at the site was actually located transversely with respect to several of the influence areas from city water supply wells, and could not have been produced by the current well field pumping program. A long term (40 year) transient groundwater flow analysis was able to simulate the conditions that led to the currently observed extent of contamination within the aquifer, and was also used to evaluate the migration of this in-place contamination to existing and proposed extraction wells.

A significant aspect of the this well field analysis with respect to planning of wellhead protection areas is that the long term transient analysis was able to simulate the observed existence of contamination in areas that steady state wellhead area analysis would fail to predict. Contamination distributions which are the results of earlier historic pumping distributions could be a substantial factor in potential contamination of many municipal well fields that have long periods of operation. In addition, the multi-layer groundwater flow model was able to simulate the lateral movement of contamination from one aquifer layer to the next, which occurred in a substantially different direction than gradients in the lower aquifer.

Battle Creek, Michigan

Battle Creek, Michigan is in east-central Michigan, and is located along the banks of the Battle Creek River, a relatively small stream. The well field for Battle Creek included 30 wells, located on both sides of the river. The aquifer at Battle Creek is a sandstone, with a thin mantle of sand and gravel, located above an impervious shale formation. VOC contamination of this well field water supply caused the listing of the site as a Superfund project.

The operation of the city well field during the incidents of contamination was important in evaluating the eventual extent of VOC contaminant migration. Initially, contamination was observed entering the well field from the south and southeast. In response, the southern-most wells were pumped to discharge into the Battle Creek River, isolating water supply wells to the north from contamination. Later, when these southern wells were shut down. contamination moved quickly to the north, as wells which became contaminated were shut down and wells further north were pumped more intensely.

Modelling analysis of the Battle Creek aquifer and well field also conducted with a finite difference groundwater model, assisted in the interpretation of contaminant migration when analyzed in transient mode. The significance of the experience at Battle Creek with respect to well protection analysis is in the application of transient hydraulic analysis to development of contingency plans for well field operation if contamination is observed. Analysis of multiple-well systems in transient mode would considerably extend the utility of wellhead protection programs.

CONCLUSIONS

The four situations described above suggest several extensions of current wellhead protection area approaches which could improve water supply protection for municipal well fields. These issues include:

1. Since many of the contamination problems currently affecting municipal well fields are the result of activities which occurred decades ago, a wellhead protection program which only controls present and future land use activities may only be partially successful. A useful supplement to wellhead protection programs could be a detailed historical review of the development of the well field, and also of the commercial and industrial activity in the surrounding community which may have produced contaminant threats. This review could suggest potential problems areas, and would be the basis for developing contingency plans for well field operation if contamination is detected.

2. Transient hydraulic analysis is important in evaluating how potential source areas can migrate into different parts of a well field. Historical development of the well field and pumping schedules over the last 20 to 40 years may have produced wellhead influence areas far different than what would be expected from current condition steady-state analyses.

3. The accurate evaluation of groundwater flow beneath or beyond apparently secure groundwater boundaries (such as large rivers) is important in municipal well field evaluations, where strong hydraulic gradients and high pumping rates can overwhelm local groundwater system controls.

4. Considering the relative costs of well construction, remedial water supply treatment and groundwater hydraulic analyses, the use of well-developed groundwater flow and contaminant transport models in defining wellhead protection areas for multiple well systems may be well worth the effort.

REFERENCES

Born, Stephen M., Douglas A. Yanggen and Alexander Zaporozec, *A Guide to Groundwater Quality Planning and Management for Local Governments,* Wisconsin Geological and Natural History Survey Special Report 9, 1987.

Born, Stephen M., Douglas A. Yanggen, Allan R. Czecholinski, Raymond J. Tierney, and Ronald G. Hennings, *Wellhead Protection Districts in Wisconsin: An Analysis and Test Applications,* Wisconsin Geologic and Natural History Survey Special Report 10, 1988.

Robinson, Patricia A., Douglas A. Yanggen, Stephen A. Born, *An Annotated Bibliography of Local Groundwater Management Publications,* University of Wisconsin-Extensions, November 1985.

U.S. EPA, *Ground-Water Protection Strategy,* August 1984.

U.S. EPA, *Guidelines for Delineation of Wellhead Protection Areas*, EPA-440/6-87-0/0, June 22, 1987.

Yanggen, Douglas A., Bruce Webendorfer, *Groundwater Protection Through Local Land-Use Controls,* Wisconsin Geological and Natural History Survey Special Report 11, 1991.

Yanggen, Douglas A., Leslie L. Amrhein, *Groundwater Quality Regulation: Existing Governmental Authority and Recommended Roles,* Wisconsin Geological and Natural History Survey Special Report 12, 1991.

SYMPOSIUM AND SEMINAR
LIST OF PARTICIPANTS

RICARDO ALMEIDA
CENID-RASPA
APDO. POSTAL 23 SUC. A
TORREON, COAHUILA MEXICO

HECTOR ARIAS-ROJO
5 DE DICIEMBRE # 25
TEXCOCO, EDO. DE MEXICO, MEXICO

PETER BLACK
COL. OF ENVIRON. SCI. AND FOREST.
STATE UNIVERSITY OF NEW YORK
SYRACUSE, N.Y. 13210 U.S.A.

BLAIR T. BOWER
3718 25TH ST. NORTH
ARLINGTON, VIRGINIA 22207 U.S.A.

MITJA BRILLY
FAC. ARCH. CIVIL ENGR. AND SURV.
UNIVERSITY OF LJUBLJANA
HAJDRIHOVA 28
61000 LJUBLJANA, YUGOSLAVIA

JOCHEN BUNDSCHUH
INST. F. GEOLOGIE U PALANTOLOGIE
SIGWARTSTR. 10
D-7400 TUBINGEN, GERMANY

JONATHAN WILLIAM BULKLEY
2506 B DANA BLDG.
SCHOOL OF NAT. RESOURCES
UNIVERSITY OF MICHIGAN
ANN ARBOR, MICHIGAN 48109, U.S.A

NATHAN BURAS
DEPT. OF HYDROLOGY & WATER
RESOURCES
THE UNIVERSITY OF ARIZONA
TUCSON, ARIZONA 85721, USA

MARTHA CALDERON-FERNANDEZ
FAC. DE ING. -UACH
P.O. BOX # 1528-C
CHIHUAHUA, CHIH., MEXICO

PEDRO CARREON-MURGUIA
CALLE 28 # 3612
CHIHUAHUA,. CHIH., MEXICO

ENRIQUE CAZARES RIVERA
1518 STANDLEY DR
LAS CRUCES, NEW MEXICO 88003, USA

RAFAEL CHAVEZ AGUIRRE
ARKANSAS # 2050
CHIHUAHUA, CHIH., MEXICO

RUBEN CHAVEZ GUILLEN
COMISION NACIONAL DEL AGUA
NUEVO LEON # 210 PISO 2
06170 MEXICO, D.F., MEXICO

ADOLFO CHAVEZ RODRIGUEZ
P.O. BOX # 1528-C
FAC. DE ING. -UACH
31160 CHIHUAHUA, CHIH., MEXICO

HAROLD J. DAY
2377 WEBSTER AVE.
GREEN BAY, WISCONSIN 54301 U.S.A.

ELVIDIO V. DINIZ
2905 LAS CRUCES ST. NE
ALBUQUERQUE, NEW MEXICO 87110
U.S.A.

CINDY DYBALIA
OFFICE OF POLICY ANALYSIS-EPA
MAIL CODE PM 221
401 M STREET SW
WASHINGTON, D.C. 20460, U.S.A.

F. EL-NAGAR
SNC INC, P O BOX 281
MANSOURA, EGYPT

SOCORRO ESPINO-VALDES
MADRID # 1802
CHIHUAHUA, CHIH., MEXICO

RAFAEL FIGUEROA
FAC. DE AGRIC. Y ZOOTECNIA
UNIV. JUAREZ DEL EDO. DE DURANGO,
APARTADO 142
35000 GOMEZ PALACIO, DGO.MEXICO

SERGIO FLORES-CASTRO
CALLE 5 # 33-404
COL. SAN PEDRO DE LOS PINOS
03801 MEXICO, D.F., MEXICO

HECTOR FUENTES
DEPT. OF CIVIL ENGINEERING
UNIVERSITY OF TEXAS AT EL PASO
EL PASO TEXAS 79968-0516 U.S.A.

HECTOR GARDUNO VELASCO
I.M.T.A.
PASEO CUAUHNAHUAC 8532
62550 JIUTEPEC, MORELOS, MEXICO

W.H. GILBRICH
DIV. OF WATER SCIENCES-UNESCO
7, PLACE DE FONTENOY
75700 PARIS, FRANCE

WOLFGANG GRABBS
BERGSTRASSE 41
D-5584 BULLAY-MOSEL, GERMANY

NEILS. GRIGG
COLO. WATER. RESOUR. RES. INST.
COLORADO STATE UNIVERSITY
FORT COLLINS, COLORADO 80523
U.S.A.

NARENDRA GUNAJI
INT. BOUNDARY AND WATER COMM.
4171 N. MESA, SUITE C-316
EL PASO, TEXAS. 79912, U.S.A.

CARLOS GUTIERREZ-OJEDA
MORELOS # 175
MEXICO, D.F. MEXICO

JAMES HANNAHAM
D.C. WATER RESOURCES RES.CENTER
3727 CAMDEN ST., S.E.
WASHINGTON, D.C. 20020, U.S.A.

JAN HENDRICKX
DEPT. OF GEOSCIENCE
NEW MEXICO TECH.
SOCORRO, NEW MEXICO, U.S.A.

ATEF HAMDY
DIRECTOR FOR RESEARCH-IAM BARI
VIA CEGLIE 23
70010 VALENZANO (BA), ITALIA

CARLOS HERNANDEZ
CENID-RASPA
APDO. POSTAL # 41
CD. LERDO, DURANGO, MEXICO

ISMAEL HERRERA REVILLA
INSTITUTO DE GEOFISICA
APDO. POSTAL 22-582
14000 MEXICO, D.F.

JOSE ARTURO HERRERA SOLIS
C.I.L.A.
APDO. POSTAL 1612-D
CIUDAD JUAREZ, CHIH., MEXICO

RICARDO JACQUES
COLLEGE OF ENGINEERING
NEW MEXICO STATE UNIVERSITY
P.O. BOX # 30001
LAS CRUCES, NEW MEXICO 88003, USA

FAUZY MOHAMED KAMEL
13 GIZA ST.
GIZA CAIRO, EGYPT

N. KHANDAN
CAGE DEPT
NEW MEXICO STATE UNIVERSITY
LAS CRUCES, NEW MEXICO, USA

WALTER LYON
20 CLIFTON RD
CAMP HILL, PENNSYLVANIA, USA

BENERITO S. MARTINEZ
449 DARTMOUTH APT. A
LAS CRUCES, NEW MEXICO, USA

PEDRO MARTINEZ-LEYVA
REP. DE CUBA # 812
CHIHUAHUA, CHIH., MEXICO

POLICARPO MARTINEZ-OJINAGA
MEXALIT, S.A.
AV. DE LAS INDUSTRIAS # 6920
CHIHUAHUA, CHIH., MEXICO

J. MCDONNELL
WATERSHED SCIENCE UNIT
COLLEGE OF NAT. RESOURCES
UTAH STATE UNIVERSITY
LOGAN, UTAH 84322-5200 USA

MIGUEL MEDINA-GARCIA
P.O. BOX # 202
CIVAC, MORELOS 62500, MEXICO

MARTHA MERCADER MARTINEZ
COORD DE DESARROLLO
PROFESIONAL, INST. MEX.
TECNOLOGIA DEL AGUA
PASEO CUAUHNAHUAC 8532
62550 JIUTEPEC, MORELOS, MEXICO

ROBERT MONTGOMERY
WARZYN INC.
P.O. BOX 5385
MADISON, WISCONSIN 53705, U.S.A.

M.C. LEOPOLDO MORENO DIAZ
CENID-RASPA
APDO. POSTAL #23 SUC A
TORREON, COAH, MEXICO

GUSTAVO A. MORENO-MARTINEZ
HACIENDA DEL TORREON # 2216
FRACC. CERRO GRANDE
CHIHUAHUA, CHIH., MEXICO

DUNCAN MOSS
DEPT OF GEOLOGICAL SCIENCES
UNIVERSITY OF TEXAS AT EL PASO
EL PASO, TEXAS 79968, USA

J.E. NASH
DEPT. OF ENGR. HYDROLOGY
UNIVERSITY COLLEGE
GALWAY, IRELAND

RONALD M. NORTH
INSTITUTE OF NATURAL RESOURCES
UNIVERSITY OF GEORGIA
ATHENS, GEORGIA 30602, USA

J.R. NUCKOLS
INST. OF RURAL ENVIRON. HEALTH
COLORADO STATE UNIVERSITY
FORT COLLINS, COLORADO 80523
U.S.A.

JUAN JOSE D. OLVERA SUAREZ
CALLE 12 # 12B
COL. SAN FRANCISCO
CAMPECHE, CAMPECHE, MEXICO

JOSE LUIS OROPEZA-MOTA
COLEGIO DE POSTGRADUADOS
MONTECILLO, EDO. DE MEXICO,
MEXICO

ABUNDIO OSUNA-VIZCARRA
P.O. BOX #1528-C
FAC. DE ING.-UACH
31160 CHIHUAHUA, CHIH., MEXICO

OSCAR PALACIOS VELEZ
CENTRO DE HIDROCIENCIAS
COLEGIO DE POSGRADUADOS
56230 MONTECILLO, EDO. DE MEXICO

EMILO PEREZ-ACUNA
P O BOX # 1528
FAC. DE ING.-UACH
CHIHUAHUA, CHIH. MEXICO

BRIAN K. RAWLINGS
DEPT. OF HYDROLOGY
UNIV. OF ZULULAND
PRIVATE BAG X1001, KWADLANGEZWA
3886 SOUTH AFRICA

JOSE A. RAYNAL
SIDNEY #4116
COL. RES. CAMPESTRE
31238 CHIHUAHUA, CHIH, MEXICO

IGNACIO REYES-CORTES
TEHUEQUE #6722
CHIHUAHUA, CHIH., MEXICO

ARMANDO REYES ROMAN
UNIVERSIDAD 2180
ZONA CHAMIZAL
CD. JUAREZ, CHIH, MEXICO

JOHN C. RODDA
HYDROLOGY AND WATER RES. DEPT.,
WORLD METEOROLOGICAL ORGANIZ.,
41 GIUSEPPE-MOTTA
CH-1211 GENEVE 2, SWITZERLAND

CARLOS E. RODRIGUEZ-TERRAZAS
P.O. BOX # 1528-C
CHIHUAHUA, CHIH., MEXICO

ALBERTO DE LA ROSA-AMBRIZ
CEDRO # 9
CHIHUAHUA, CHIH., MEXICO

JORGE A. SALAS PLATA MENDOZA
COORD. DE DESARROLLO
PROFESIONAL, INST. MEX.
TECNOLOGIA DEL AGUA
PASEO CUAUHNAHUAC 8532
62550 JIUTEPEC, MORELOS, MEXICO

ALFONSO SANCHEZ-MUNOZ
PRIV. CIPRES # 211
CHIHUAHUA, CHIH, MEXICO

IVONNE SANTIAGO
1906 COLE VILLAGE
LAS CRUCES, NEW MEXICO 88003, USA

ROCIO SAUCEDO-MARTINEZ
MANUEL GONZALEZ-COSSIO
CHIHUAHUA, CHIH., MEXICO

MAMDOUH SHAHIN
INST FOR HYDRAULIC AND ENVIRON.
ENGINEERING
OUDE DELFT 95
THE NETHERLANDS (HOLLAND)

DENNIS L SODEN
DEPARTMENT OF POLITICAL SCIENCE
UNIVERSITY OF NEVADA
LAS VEGAS, NEVADA 89154 U.S.A.

MANFRED SPREAFICO
SERVICE HYDROLOGIQUE ET
GEOLOGIQUE NATIONAL
CH-3003 BERNE, SWITZERLAND

KENNETH STEELE
WATER RESOURCES RES. CENTER
UNIVERSITY OF ARKANSAS
FAYETTEVILLE, ARKANSAS 72701
U.S.A.

WILLIAM STEGGLES
7 KINGSCOURT DRIVE
TORONTO, ONTARIO M8X 2P5
CANADA

GLENN STOUT
WATER RESOURCES CENTER
2535 HYDROSYSTEMS LAB.
208 NORTH ROMINE ST.
URBANA, ILLINOIS 61801, USA

MARIO VELAZQUEZ-LLORENTE
BULEVAR ATLIXCO # 58-1
COL. LA PAZ
PUEBLA, PUEBLA, MEXICO

RICARDO VALDEZ CEPEDA
URUZA-UNIV. AUT. DE CHAPINGO
APDO. POSTAL 8
BERMEJILLO, DURANGO, MEXICO

FRANCISCO VICKE-ANDREWS
MEXALIT, S.A.
AV. DE LAS INDUSTRIAS # 6920
CHIHUAHUA, CHIH., MEXICO

MIGUEL VILLASUSO
FAC. DE ING. -UADY
APDO. POSTAL 1423-B ,
97000 MERIDA, YUCATAN, MEXICO

HUGH WHITELEY
SCHOOL OF ENGINEERING
UNIVERSITY OF GUELPH
GUELPH, ONTARIO, CANADA N1H4R5

VUJICA YEVJEVICH
8837 S. BLUE MOUNTAIN PLACE
HIGHLANDS RANCH, COLORADO 80126
U.S.A.